I CHOSE FREEDOM

I
CHOSE
FREEDOM

*The Personal and Political Life of a
Soviet Official*

by

VICTOR KRAVCHENKO

GARDEN CITY PUBLISHING CO., INC.
Garden City, New York

CONTENTS

I CHOSE FREEDOM

CHAPTER I

FLIGHT IN THE NIGHT

EVERY MINUTE of the taxi ride between my rented room and Union Station that Saturday night seemed loaded with danger and with destiny. The very streets and darkened buildings seemed frowning and hostile. In my seven months in the capital I had traveled that route dozens of times, light-heartedly, scarcely noticing my surroundings. But this time everything was different—*this time I was running away.*

The American family with whom I lived in Washington had been friendly and generous to the stranger under their roof. When I fell ill they had watched over me with an easy unaffected solicitude. What had begun as a mere financial arrangement had grown into a warm human relationship to which the barrier of language added a fillip of excitement. I sensed that in being kind to one homesick Russian these good Americans were expressing their gratitude to all Russians—to the brave allies who were then rolling back the tide of German conquest on a thousand-mile front. They gave me full personal credit for every Soviet victory.

My rent was paid for a week ahead. Yet I left the house that night without a word of final farewell. I merely said that if my trip should keep me out of town beyond Tuesday, they had my permission to let the room. I wanted my hosts to be honestly ignorant of my whereabouts and of my intention not to return, should there be any inquiries from the Soviet Purchasing Commission.

For several days, at the Commission offices, I had simulated headaches and general indisposition. Casually I had remarked that morning to a few colleagues that I had better "remain home for a rest"; that I might not come in on Monday. I was playing hard for an extra day of grace before my absence would be discovered.

After collecting my March salary I insisted on straightening out my expense vouchers for the last trip to Lancaster, Pennsylvania, and the trip to Chicago before that. It appeared that about thirty dollars were still due to me. The idea was to erase the slightest excuse for any charges of financial irregularity to explain my flight. I also made sure that all my papers were in perfect order, so that others could take up the work where I had left off.

Later, when the news of my getaway was on the front pages of the Washington and New York papers, some of the men and women at the Commission must have recalled a peculiar warmth in my talks with them that Saturday, a special pressure in my handclasp when I said "So long." They must have realized that I was bidding them a final and wordless farewell. Never again, not even here in free America, would any of them dare to meet me. In the months of working together some of these people had come close to me; without saying much we had understood one another. Had I been able to part with them openly, emotionally, Russianly, some of the weight that pressed on my spirits would assuredly have been lifted.

It was a chill, starless night. The railroad station seemed to swarm with threats. What if I ran into some colleague and he sounded the alarm? Certainly the two suitcases and the unauthorized journey would instantly arouse his suspicions. What if Comrade Serov or General Rudenko already had discovered my plans? As if in answer to these fears, I suddenly caught sight of a Red Army uniform. I went cold with dread. Pulling my hat lower over my eyes, drawing my head more deeply into the raised collar of my overcoat, I slunk along the wall, keeping my back turned to my countryman.

Because Soviet officials always travel in Pullman style, I took a seat in a plebeian coach. That reduced the risk of meeting anyone who knew me. In the dimmed-out, crowded, somnolent car I was alone with my thoughts.

For a long time I had known that this decisive hour was inevitable. For months I had planned the flight. I had looked forward to it as a release from the maze of hypocrisies, resentments and confusions of spirit in which I had wandered for so many years. It was to be my expiation for horrors about which, as a member of the ruling class in my country, I felt a sense of guilt.

But now that it was actually happening, there was in it no exhilaration, no lift of new freedom. There was a painful void in which fears and self-reproach echoed so loud that even the sleepy soldiers and sailors in the smoke-filled car must hear them.

I am cutting my life at its roots, I thought to myself. Irrevocably. Perhaps forever. This night I am turning myself into a man without country, without family, without friends. Never again shall I see the faces or press the hands or hear the voices of relatives and friends who are bone of my bone and flesh of my flesh. It is as if they were dead and therefore something precious within me is dead. Forever and ever there will be this emptiness in my life, this dreadful void and aching deadness.

So far as the land of my birth is concerned, I shall be an official outcast and pariah. Automatically the political regime into which I poured a lifetime of toil and faith will pronounce a sentence of death upon me. Always its secret agents will haunt my life. They will trace my steps and keep vigil under my windows and, if ordered by their masters, will strike me down. And these Americans among whom I hope to anchor my new life— how can they ever understand what it means for a Russian Communist to break with the Soviet dictatorship? They are so blessedly innocent, these Americans.

In my home land, those who worked with me and befriended me, let alone those who loved me, will be forever tainted and suspect. To survive they will have to live down my memory. To save themselves, they must deny me and disown me, as in my time I pretended to deny and disown others who incurred the vengeance of the Soviet state.

Did I have a moral right to endanger these innocent hostages in Russia in order to indulge my own conscience and pay my own debt to truth as I saw it? That was the cruelest problem of all. What would my pious grandfather, Fyodor Panteleyevich, that upright servant of God and Tsar, have thought of my action if he were still alive? What will my father, that fanatical Russian revolutionist, say if he has survived two years under the brutal German occupation?

There was consolation, at least, in that train of thought. Grandfather never understood why his son Andrei, my father, opposed the Tsar and the tradition of the ages. But because Andrei believed deeply and was willing to go to prison for his strange new faith, grandfather always ended his reproofs with a blessing. As for my father, though he loved his wife and his children, he had not scrupled to expose us to hunger and tears to serve his cause. *He* would understand and approve; of that I had no doubt.

There was bitter consolation also in the thought that my brother Constantine, who had always been close to me, was dead—killed in defending our fatherland against the Nazi invaders as an officer on the Caucasian front. Would official vengeance be visited on a lonely and helpless old woman, just liberated from a German concentration camp, because she is my mother? Or on the woman who for three years was my wife, though she knew nothing of my political doubts and my escape?

These thoughts were still pounding in my mind, a painful tom-tom that has grown fainter but has never ceased, when the train pulled into New York at three that Sunday morning. On the platform I saw the Russian officer again, carrying a suitcase and quite oblivious to my existence. But I hung back to put more distance between us.

I registered under an Italian name at a dingy uptown hotel—the kind of hotel where you pay in advance for your room. It was a room made to order for suicide; narrow, musty, depressing. I locked the door. In the half-light of the one electric bulb I began to write out a statement, parts of which were to appear in the American press two days later.

Had anyone observed my furtive behavior in these tense days, my sleepless nights, my stealthy escape from Washington, my concealment in New York, he might suppose I had committed some fearful crime and was evading the police. But I had neither robbed nor killed. I had merely decided to give up my job as an economic emissary of my government!

No American, assuredly, could comprehend that for the subject of a totalitarian regime there is no "crime" more terrifying in its implications and its consequences. It was the supreme act of apostasy towards an earthly god. Not only did it make the culprit officially an outcast, living on borrowed time, he could not even exchange letters with his loved ones in his native land. The mark of Cain was on his forehead. For a Soviet citizen to meet him or to show him kindness would be political suicide, perhaps physical suicide.

Mine was not a step any Soviet Russian, especially a Communist of long standing and fairly advanced in the ranks of the bureaucracy, took frivolously, on sudden impulse. It was an act that had its beginnings somewhere far down, in the substratum of his mind; that grew slowly and could not be smothered. The reasons for the kind of thing I had done are never on the surface. They must be sought for deep inside, at the core of a man's whole existence.

On Monday, April 3, 1944, I talked to several reporters. Late that night the news was displayed on the first page of the New York *Times*. The timing was important. It may, indeed, have saved my life. Had my Soviet guardians learned about my flight before it became public knowledge, the Washington Embassy would unquestionably have denounced me to the State Department, as a German agent perhaps, and demanded my instant apprehension for deportation to the U.S.S.R. But with the American people apprised of the facts and watching the drama, the Soviet Embassy was checkmated, at least for the moment.

"Soviet Official Here Resigns," the *Times* headline announced. The dispatch itself began:

Accusing the Soviet Government of a "double-faced" foreign policy with respect to its professed desire for collaboration with the United States and Great Britain and denouncing the Stalin regime for failure to grant political and civil liberties to the Russian people, Victor A. Kravchenko, an official of the Soviet Purchasing Commission in Washington, announced his resignation yesterday and placed himself "under the protection of American public opinion."

Mr. Kravchenko, whose passport bears the title "Representative of the Soviet Government" . . . is a captain in the Red Army, and before coming to the United States last August he was director of a group of large industrial plants in Moscow. Prior to that he served as chief of the munitions section attached to the Soviet of People's Commissars of the Russian Socialist Federated Soviet Republic, the largest of the affiliated Soviet republics. He has been a member of the Russian Communist Party since 1929 and has held many important economic posts under the Soviet regime.

Mr. Kravchenko declined for patriotic reasons to discuss matters bearing upon the military conduct of the war by Soviet Russia or to reveal any details bearing upon economic questions, particularly as they affect the functioning of lend-lease as handled by the Soviet Purchasing Commission and in Russia.

Then followed parts of the long statement on which I had toiled all Sunday. It was written with my heart's blood, but little of its color showed through the cold printer's ink. The citizens of a free country have nothing in their personal experience to make my feelings and my behavior credible. The utterly tragic must seem to them merely eccentric.

In the statement I tried to explain to the American people, to my comrades at home and my friends in the Washington Commission, why I had taken the dread step. But the more I wrote and crossed out and rewrote, the more hopeless the task seemed. There were no words, in any language, to sum up a whole life.

My decision to break with the Soviet regime—amounting to a personal declaration of war against that and all police-states—was not accidental. It was implicit in all I had been and thought and experienced. In that sense it was not so much a decision, not so much an act of volition, as the logical and inescapable climax of a process.

To explain it I must reach back to the zeal for justice which pervaded my childhood on the banks of the Dnieper; to the passion for freedom that throbbed in a boy's heart as revolution and civil wars swept the Ukrainian cities and steppes; to the enthusiasms of a Communist Youth, then of a full-fledged Communist Party member; to the doubts and frustrations and the desperate attempts, year after year, to bolster a battered and crumbling faith with stout illusions.

To explain it I must rehearse my whole life and the life of Russia as it touched mine.

CHAPTER II

A RUSSIAN CHILDHOOD

To the three sons of Andrei Fyodorovich Kravchenko—of whom I was the second, younger than Constantine and older than Eugene— the revolution of 1905 had a deeper reality than mere personal experience. It glowed with the color of romance and even the defeat was high-pitched and radiant. It held, as if in a museum case, perfect samples of heroism, horror, idealism and sacrifice by which such values must be measured in later life.

True, it was a rather circumscribed revolution, limited not only to the city of Yekaterinoslav but to the meetings and battles and man-hunts in which my father was involved. Great names destined to a place in history first streaked across the skies of Russia in 1905. But mere history could never compete with our inner knowledge that the real leader and hero of the uprising was our intense and handsome father, lean and strong, his dark hair curling and his blue eyes flashing.

And indeed there were a few grains of truth in our fond fantasy. The revolt had been ushered in by a general strike, and the strike of the railwaymen had been the beginning, and remained the heart, of the larger strike. My father, who was employed in the railroad workshops of Yekaterinoslav, was on the strike committee, remained in the thick of the hopeless struggle and paid heavily for his enthusiasm in the aftermath of failure.

We heard the details so often in our young years that they seemed woven into our own lives. Not only the things that happened but why they happened. I did not have to be taught hatred for autocracy and love of freedom, justice, equality. I accepted them as simply, as naturally, as my playmates accepted reverence for uniforms and authority.

The revolutionary events of 1905, recounted by my father and his friends, deepened by my own contact with similar events in later years, are so deeply imprinted on my mind that even now I can feel the thundering hoofs of Cossack horsemen trampling the workmen and women of our city. No other childhood sounds are as distinct in my memory as the awful swish of sabers and *nagaikas*. I am behind the barricades of overturned carts, piled-up furniture, cobble-stones, railroad ties; comrades fall, groaning, all around me; then waves of Cossack fury spill over us. I am in the mesh of streets and alleys of the workers' district, pursued by Circassian horsemen and gendarmes far into the wintry night. Then all is still as death. Corpses sprawl grotesquely and pools of red spread slowly on the snow like inkspots on rough paper on my school desk. . . .

Had my father been caught that October night, he would have been hanged as a rebel along with some of the other members of the strike committee. Before he escaped he could not resist the temptation of a last look at his wife and Constantine and *babushka*, my mother's mother, who always lived with us. In the middle of the night he made his way through side-streets, pressing into the deeper shadows from house to house, until he reached No. 8 Kanatnai Street off Pushkin Prospekt which was our home.

His heart sank. All the lights in the house were burning and he could hear sounds of activity inside. There seemed to be no doubt of it: the police were searching the place. Yet he could not retreat, whatever the risk, without one last glimpse of the home and the family he might never see again. He crawled to the window, lifted himself cautiously and peeped inside.

Then he realized he was mistaken. Grandmother opened the door to his gentle knock and signaled him to be quiet. He started to go into the bedroom but she stopped him. "Tanya is sleeping," she said. Then, smiling, "Yes, another boy." She went into the bedroom herself and soon returned with a little bundle which she placed in my father's arms.

That was the night of my birth—a night of death behind barricades, rifle shots, bloody sabers and cries of anguish in the web of shabby streets.

Suddenly I began to yell so lustily that my mother awoke. "Listen to him—The Rebel!" my father said softly. Always thereafter, in moments of affection, he would call me The Rebel; sometimes, when I was a grown man and busy with the affairs of a triumphant revolution, he would utter the nickname with an ironic inflection that bit deeper than he suspected.

I nestled between them in those first hours of my life, as my father tenderly bid his wife farewell. Nobody can convince me by mere logic that I didn't hear his words of endearment, that I didn't see him cover her hands with kisses, that I didn't see with my father's eyes the pale loveliness of a young mother's face against the snow-white heap of cushions.

2

In the first nine years of my life, father was a glamorous stranger. His intervals of freedom were never long enough to make him familiar and ordinary as other fathers were to their children on our street. Most exciting were his visits during escapes. I looked forward to them as if they were part of the cycle of existence, like colored Easter eggs and Christmas trees.

I built up an image of him from random hints and pieces. From affectionate words by mother and *babushka*; from sudden alarms for his safety; from scraps of whispered talk by his revolutionary comrades. Often hunted men hid in our house; students in uniform with ascetic faces; shabby, bearded men from that mysterious and monstrous world called Siberia. These flitting visitors and their stories of prison breaks, bribed officials, passwords and disguises also became part of my romantic image of father.

Constantine, who was about eighteen months older than I, brought me every crumb of information.

"We must remember, Vitya," he would say importantly, "that papa is not a robber or murderer. He's a 'political.' "

"Yes, Kotya," I would agree without understanding.

One Christmas night—my third Christmas on earth—remains fixed in my memory to the last detail. A page in an album to which I turn often with a delicious kind of sorrow.

Babushka wakes us out of a deep holiday sleep. I can see our new toys scattered on the bare bedroom floor.

"Come, little doves, and say good-bye to your poor father," she says, sobbing.

In our long nightgowns, sleepy-eyed and bewildered, each of us gripping one of grandmother's hands, we are led into the parlor. I blink at the lights and the crowd. One is a friend of the family, others are strangers in uniforms.

The candles are still burning on the Christmas tree, but now mama is crying soundlessly as she packs a suitcase. *Babushka* leads us to the holy lamp in the icon corner where we kneel with her while she murmurs a prayer and touches her forehead to the floor. A man whom I know to be father lifts me up, presses me tight and kisses me many times. But this night he is strange—his face seems to me naked, with the familiar beard and mustache removed. He takes Kotya into his arms and kisses him. Then grandmother leads us out of the room.

At the door—and somehow that remains with me more sharply than any other item in the picture—an enormous bearded gendarme, with a lot of braid on his uniform, is crying shamelessly; big tears roll into his billowing mustaches.

Later I knew that father, who had been in hiding, had decided to visit his family on Christmas Eve. The police, aware from experience that fugitives sometimes risked arrest to be with their loved ones on important feast days, swooped down on our house. While they searched the premises, they gave the rebel an hour to pack his things before leading him away.

I turn often also to another page in that private album of my childhood:

A tall, good-looking student arrives one evening while we are at the supper table. Mother draws a glass of tea from the gleaming samovar for him and I can tell by the way her hand trembles and the glass rattles that the young man's words are important.

Everything is ready for the jail-break that night, he says. If there are no complications, Andrei Fyodorovich should be home before midnight. But he will remain only a few minutes. Mother must prepare certain things for his journey. A hiding place in Yekaterinoslav is waiting for him as well as excellent identification papers.

Alas, we were bundled off to bed before we could find out how the thrilling story would end.

The following day mother and *babushka* wept repeatedly, consoled one another and only wept some more. The tall student, his face drawn and filled with grief, came several times with news.

The plot for a mass escape from the Yekaterinoslav penitentiary had failed miserably. Evidently there had been a provocateur somewhere. Several guards and many prisoners were killed in the fighting. Though a few knives and revolvers had been smuggled in during the long weeks of planning, the mutineers were easily overpowered. The massacre and beating of political prisoners that night became celebrated in Russian revolutionary history.

Father, it appeared, had been flogged within an inch of his life. He carried the scars, proudly, through all his years. He was in the prison hospital and if he remained alive would probably be tried with several other ringleaders. It might be *katorga*—hard labor in Siberia—or even hanging this time. . . .

Some months later the student arrives once more. This time a slender and very beautiful girl is with him. In great agitation mother bundles us into our overcoats. "If you're quiet and do as you're told, you'll see papa," she says.

Outside our door there are two carriages. The student and the girl get into one, the rest of us into the other. Theirs goes first and ours follows at a discreet distance, down the broad Pushkin Prospekt. Soon we are in sight of the gloomy old prison in the heart of the city. In front of one of its towers the advance carriage stops for a minute—that is the signal—then drives on. When our carriage reaches the same spot the coachman steps down and fusses with the harness.

Mother's eyes burn with excitement. "There, there, it's your father," she whispers, pointing to a window in the tower. I try hard to see but can only make out a shadowy figure behind one of the barred windows, waving a handkerchief. The man's head is shaved and glistens as he nods to us. Tears stream down my mother's cheeks and Kotya cries "Papa! papa!" Then the coachman climbs back and whips his horse to a trot. Mother looks back and waves as long as the tower is in view.

The student and the girl are waiting for us at an agreed spot in the park. He kisses mother's hand, he takes us in his strong arms, and he stuffs our pockets with candy. The beautiful girl, too, is very tender with us. All in all it is a memorable day, sad, important and tense. Often when I am alone and afraid I think of that day and somehow feel reassured.

It was a miracle that father was not hanged or sent to Siberia, *babushka* often said, glancing at the icon lamp and crossing herself. Prisoners awaiting the death sentence were kept in that particular tower and they were not permitted to receive visitors. But somehow his punishment had been reduced to an ordinary prison term.

I was too young to wonder how the Kravchenko brood managed to live with its breadwinner behind bars. By that time Eugene had been born. Father's comrades in the cause helped a little. A few men from the railway workshops brought presents. Sometimes chickens, ducks, fruit and vegetables came from Alexandrovsk, where my paternal grandparents lived. I saw nothing strange in the fact that mother was always sewing clothes for other people, even when our own clothes needed repairing.

One night—I was going on six at the time—I could not sleep. I tiptoed guiltily to the door, opened it cautiously and looked out. I saw my mother, her head bent over her sewing, in the circle of light of a kerosene lamp. When I think of her today, across the years, I sometimes see my mother as I saw her that night, framed in light, her face sad and her hair gleaming.

"Why don't you go to bed, *mamochka*?" I asked.

"I'm not tired," she smiled. "But why aren't you asleep? Never mind; come over here, son. I want to talk to you."

She bit off the thread, laid the work aside and took me on her lap.

"You're a good boy and a clever one," she said. "I'm sure you will understand . . . if not now then later, when you grow up. It's not easy to feed so many mouths, no matter how late I work. And there are packages to be sent to your father.

"It will be a little easier, Vitya, when you go to live with Grandpa Fyodor Panteleyevich in Alexandrovsk. He and your other *babushka* and Aunt Shura love you dearly. You will go to school and we will come to see you often. Aunt Shura will be here to fetch you tomorrow. Now go to sleep."

She put me off her lap brusquely, but I knew she was crying.

3

Alexandrovsk—renamed Zaparozhe after the revolution—was a clean, peaceful provincial town. Its life flowed serenely and, it seemed, eternally between the wide and placid Dnieper and the thickly forested outskirts. Although there were some brick and tile works, a few scattered metal plants and some other industrial beginnings, the life of the town was still closely connected with the Ukrainian soil. Most of its households had truck gardens and many cultivated orchards. Nearly every yard, like the one which now became the center of my new life, was cluttered with chickens, ducks, geese, pigs.

For a lively boy of six, after urban Yekaterinoslav, the place was endlessly exciting. The seed shops breathed spicy odors any one of which, for the rest of my life, would touch off nostalgia. I watched the sparks fly at blacksmiths' shops, or observed the labors of men and women around steaming brick kilns.

On market days the main street filled up with peasant carts, the men in padded coats or sheepskins, the women in voluminous skirts like our tea-cosy doll at home. Barefoot peasant children looked shyly at us city lads. On the edge of Alexandrovsk were the big vegetable farms of the Bulgarians and beyond that, in the groves, the Gypsies deployed their gaudy wagons, pitched their tents and lit campfires in the long nights.

Although there were a few families of beggars at one extreme and a few wealthy families like the Shtchekatihins in their red-tiled mansion at the other, people were neither very rich nor very poor in Alexandrovsk. The town boasted two cinema theaters; older peasants, viewing the cavorting figures on the screen for the first time, crossed themselves by way of precaution against such deviltry. Several times, in the five years I lived there, a theatrical troupe from Kiev or Odessa arrived for a week of performances. But tumblers and acrobats, jugglers, and foreign-looking men with performing bears frequently drew crowds in the park.

The Kravchenkos—grandfather Fyodor Panteleyevich, grandmother Natalia Maximovna and Shura, the daughter of their old age—lived simply but amply on a modest pension, supplemented by the rent from two of their three small houses. They also earned a few rubles monthly on their water supply. For the privilege of drawing water in our back yard, neighbors dropped a small coin now and then through the slit in an iron box.

Grandfather held the key to the box, but Aunt Shura, through lifelong practice, was expert in extracting kopeks to meet unbudgeted expenses beyond the spartan notions of her father. Her little nephew from Yekaterinoslav soon shared her secret and felt guilty for her sake, but not guilty enough to refuse a share of the booty. Helping her in the weekly floor scrubbing rated three kopeks—enough for a cinema show and a candy stick—and keeping out of the way when her suitor called added to my weekly income.

Our garden and the compact orchard provided fresh and dried vegetables, fruits and melons for the whole year, not to mention a fascinating array of jams in which *babushka* took a justified pride. The season of jam-making is indelible in my memory—the copper basins overflowing with juicy fruits, the redolence of simmering sugar, the wonderful evenings of pitting cherries until one's hands were dyed a deep red.

Fyodor Panteleyevich was about eighty at the time I came to live with him. He was a man of medium height, sturdy, broad-shouldered and self-important, with an immaculate white beard and a respectable paunch. He had fought in the Russo-Turkish war in 1878 under General Skobeliev and after many years of service had retired as a noncommissioned officer. Natalia Maximovna, about twelve years younger than her husband, was a neat, gentle old lady, with a twinkle in her clear eyes and a sense of humor that left grandfather baffled. She treated all of us, her husband included, as if we were children to be humored and placated.

In the long winter evenings, with logs crackling in the huge whitewashed oven, with the flames through the open door making strange patterns on the floor, Fyodor Panteleyevich liked to tell tales of the Turks and Kurds, of battles and surprise attacks. Especially if some old cronies were present, he could tell of feats of daring which the Little Father himself, in far-off St. Petersburg, had deigned to notice. The feats grew more remarkable with every telling.

"How wonderful," *babushka* would say disparagingly, "to ride horses, twirl mustaches and shoot a lot of Turks. As if that took any brains!"

On Sundays and holidays, Fyodor Panteleyevich would put on his dress uniform, a resplendent affair in blue, with glittering brass buttons and white piping down the edges of the capacious cavalry breeches stuck into high boots. He would polish those boots until they shone like mirrors, arrange the medals and crosses on his chest and spread his beard above them like a banner. Thus arrayed, he would take my tiny hand into his big calloused palm and start out for church. There was no prouder boy in all of Alexandrovsk, and it seemed to me only proper that humbler townsmen should lift their hats deferentially and ask after *babushka's* health.

Grandfather was no less proud of his grandson, though his spartan code forbade any sentimentalities. "Andrei's boy," he would say, with studied casualness. It was no secret that grandfather's first-born, Andrei, was an *arrestant*, a jailbird, but neighbors never mentioned it in his hearing. Just one of those misfortunes that the Lord might visit on any of his pious servants. Fyodor Panteleyevich loved Andrei and even admired him, but he simply could not square my father's good head and "good blood" with his blasphemies against the Tsar. He blamed it, in a vague fashion, on book learning and the sad decline of the martial spirit in Russia.

"All my life I have been a good soldier," he liked to proclaim, "and that's how I will end my days. I work and worship God and have no complaints. But what does Andrei want? I'll be damned if I know!"

Grandmother and Shura, knowing that such talk hurt me, would try to silence him. Andrei is an educated man, he understands the world, not only Turks and Kurds, they would declare.

"Maybe so, maybe so," Fyodor Panteleyvich conceded gloomily, adding for my sake: "Andrei sits in prison, that's true, but not for stealing or killing. Only for politics. That makes it different."

When I received letters from mother, which Aunt Shura read aloud before I learned to read, there was always a bit of news about father. At such times Fyodor Panteleyevich sometimes forgot himself and uttered bitter words about his headstrong son. On one such occasion I became so enraged that I screamed and in blind fury bit grandfather's hand. Instead of whipping me as I expected, he tried to soothe me, took me tenderly in his arms and said he was pleased that I defended my father. "That's my blood in your veins," he said. "We Kravchenkos are loyal."

Now and then I spent a week-end with a friend of my father's, a metal worker whom I called Uncle Mitya. It was almost like being home with father, plus the excitement of three pretty and mischievous little girls in the household. All three were to grow up into attractive women who would be as close to me as blood relations in later life.

Uncle Mitya talked about liberty and justice and a better world in birth, just like father, and often he read to us slowly from dog-eared books by Herzen and Gorki and Tolstoy. There was piety in his voice, like grandpa reading from Scriptures. But what I liked best were the mornings when Uncle Mitya roused me before dawn to go hunting. After a strenuous day in the woods, I would return with his gun over my shoulder and a bagful of hares and wild fowl, as proud as if I had shot them myself.

Grandfather preferred fishing. The Dnieper was his second home. As our rowboat floated on the smooth surface of the river and we waited for bites, he would tell me again my favorite stories in which Turks died by the thousand and Russians, especially Ukrainians and Cossacks, always dashed off with booty and honors. Without his wife's restraining humor to curb his imagination, his tales were more thrilling.

When the sun climbed higher we would tie up the boat in a clump of trees on the bank, take off our clothes and swim about, splashing and kicking up the water in sheer exuberance, scarcely remembering that three-quarters of a century separated us. Tired but tingling with vitality and so hungry that it hurt, we would return home lugging the day's catch, and Grandma Natalia Maximovna would fry some fish in the yard. There was usually enough not only for ourselves but for favorite friends, and for one of those fish chowders, next day, which only grandmother could cook.

We Kravchenkos at Alexandrovsk lived under a semi-military regime tempered by *babushka's* civilian softness. For her husband work was not merely a necessity but a duty, like going to mass and keeping the lamp lit under the icons and giving bread to beggars. We went to bed early and rose with the sun for work in the garden, in the orchard and with the animals. Even on schooldays I was expected to do my stint, as a matter of discipline, before breakfast; lessons, no matter how hard I labored at them, did not rate as real work in grandfather's code. He taught me to wash and bathe in the open air in all weather, in ice-cold water, "like a man and a soldier." He taught me to accept pain without whimpering and hardened me early to heat and cold alike.

The only time grandfather punished me was when, at the age of seven or eight, I went to a barber on my own to have my curls cut. Shura's kopeks made that premature assertion of manhood possible. When I reached home, in a cloud of strong smelling pomade, grandfather took one look and exploded. The punishment fitted the crime. He brought out a large pair of lamb-shears and, in full view of neighbors and playmates, proceeded to undo the barber's work, after which he applied soap and water to the ragged landscape of my scalp to wash out the sissy smells.

In the public school I made friendships many of which, amazingly, lasted into maturity. School hours were long and always there were tasks to be done at home. Corporal punishment for slackness and inattention was a matter of course and regarded as an essential ingredient in a boy's education.

Luckily I was quick in learning. Only religious instruction, conducted by old Father Maxim, mumbling through his beard, gave me trouble. We were expected to recite long meaningless prayers in Old Slavonic by heart and if we failed, which nearly all of us did, a ritual of retribution was in order. It was then that Father Maxim's favorite pupil, the pock-marked Kuzya, prepared a rod; the culprits kneeled in a row and Kuzya methodically applied the rod to the line-up of posteriors while the priest counted. No doubt it was good for our souls even if it did not improve our Old Slavonic. After school, of course, we regularly waylaid Kuzya and gave him better than we received—that, too, was part of the ritual.

Another target of our boyish cruelties was young Shtchekatihin, son and heir of the richest man in town. Unlike the rest of us, who walked long distances to the schoolhouse, Nick arrived in a handsome carriage

under escort, and he wore velvet jackets, starched collars and shoes with
shiny buttons. Moreover, he liked to jingle coins in his pocket. Clearly
such crimes could not go unpunished. Sometimes he managed to buy us
off with coins and candy, but often, I must confess, we accepted the bribe
and then beat him up for good measure.

Despite the rigorous regime in school, we played hooky and indulged in
childish mischief. There was the time—I remember it more clearly than
real tragedies in later years—when a classmate and I decided to raid a
vegetable farm on the town's outskirts. We had stuffed our pockets with
young cucumbers and tasted the luscious new melons when the big Bul-
garian was upon us. He didn't beat us—instead he delivered a lecture on
the evil of theft, and ordered us to remove our trousers. Then he gave us
each a handful of cucumbers and sent us trouserless on our way.

We waited hours for nightfall. In the dark, by roundabout paths to
avoid meeting anyone, we made our ignominious way home. The shame of
it lingered for a long time and the laughter that the episode evoked in town
stung more painfully than any rod or leather strap.

I shudder now to think how miserable we made life for the more pompous teachers. But the starved looking, bespectacled Averichev who was
our Russian language teacher was exempt from our petty persecutions. He
was almost the prototype of the Russian intelligentsia—intense, poetic, full
of words and a little helpless. His eyes were deep and fanatic and he made
the lessons in Russian literature exciting even for the younger boys. Years
later, during a business visit to Zaparozhe, I learned that this Averichev
had been killed during the revolution.

Little boys of respectable families were forbidden to mix with the
Gypsies, but I went often notwithstanding. Having made friends with a
Gypsy lad named Saideman, I became almost a member of the clan. Once,
when we were skating on the frozen Dnieper, the ice suddenly gave way
under me. Saideman plunged into the icy water and pulled me out. This
cemented our friendship.

Many times I managed, on one pretext or another, to leave the house
and race to the Gypsy camp. I would sit by their fires and listen to their
folk songs and watch in fascination the strange ways of these friendly and
always cheerful people. In return for a kopek or two, the Gypsy women
would tell my fortune. Invariably they assured me that I would grow up
to be rich, handsome and famous; my life would be a stretch of heaven
studded with precious stones in which rivers of honey flowed, and I would
share it with a beauteous damsel, sometimes blonde, sometimes brunette.

An important wedding was to take place in the Gypsy camp, and great
preparations were being made for weeks ahead. Saideman insisted that I
attend and, of all things in the world, that was what I wanted most to do.
But how would I get out of the house on that particular night? In despair
I took grandfather into my confidence. At first he was angry but when I
told him how Saideman had saved my life, martial gallantry got the better
of race superiority. Not only could I go, but he would escort me.

Grandfather donned his uniform for the occasion, combed his beard
wider than ever, and brought a few little gifts with him, with the result

that he became an honored guest at the ceremony. My stock with the Gypsies soared sky-high. Young and old had brought out their most colorful finery and jingliest jewelry for the wedding; violins and guitars made gay and soulful music deep into the night. All in all it was an experience that set off fireworks in a boy's mind and heart and made him sorry, forever after, for people who didn't have the feel of Gypsy life.

4

I was going on nine when the first World War started. Life was suddenly brimful of excitement and emotion. Soldiers, speeches, tears, glory. I felt as if existence had been turned into a continuous feast day. Our teachers forgot the lessons and declaimed patriotism instead; all of them, that is, except Averichev. Father Maxim led us in impassioned prayers for victory. Women wept and wrung their hands as sons and husbands marched off.

Babushka, too, wept in sympathy. But grandfather seemed a new man, more erect, more soldierly in giving orders to his family. He now wore his blue-and-white uniform almost daily, and a week without a war demonstration seemed to him a week wasted. "Akh! if only General Skobeliev were alive, he'd teach the Germans a lesson. Why, even the Turks couldn't stand up to him!"

One day in August, 1914, when grandfather and I had returned from a fishing excursion, there was a knock at the door. *Babushka* went to open it and we heard her cry out in excitement, tears in her voice. "Andrusha! Look who's here, children, Andrusha himself!"

It was, indeed, my father. He was neatly dressed and when he took off his black hat I saw that his hair was brushed straight back in the new style. His beard was trimmed, like a doctor's rather than a workingman's, and was a few shades lighter than his hair. He seemed to me shorter, less radiant than my memory of him, but also more approachable, more like a father, and I was pleased. After kissing his parents and his sister, he came to me. First he held me off at arm's length and appraised me sternly. Apparently I passed the test, for he lifted me and hugged me and bade all the world to note how strong and good-looking his son was growing up. The others looked on in evident pleasure, as if I were their own handiwork.

The Tsar had declared an amnesty for some types of political prisoners which, happily, released my father, and here he was to see his parents and his son. Fyodor Panteleyevich was flattered and flustered by the visit. His happiness was genuine. But by the time we sat down to supper his old resentments against the son who made trouble were well to the fore.

Grandfather drank a glass of cold water, crossed himself, then began to eat. That was the signal for all of us to reach our spoons into our plates of fish chowder. For a little while grandfather restrained himself and listened to the exchange of family news. But finally he spoke his mind:

"Well, tell me, Andrei, what's all the nonsense about? Why do you sit in prisons like a criminal? What do you want? Have you no sense of duty to your wife and children?"

Father listened patiently. His face clouded, but his eyes kindled. His words went deep into my memory and even more the earnestness that was under his words.

"I'll tell you what I want, papa," he said. "I hope you'll understand, because I value your good opinion. I want people to be free and happy. I want all men to live like human beings. I want to put an end to political despotism and economic slavery. Believe me, I am sad that my loved ones must suffer. But because of the sacrifices of one generation, many generations to come will be happier and more civilized.

"You should understand me, papa, because you are a believing man and light candles to your favorite saints and martyrs. Did they let their wives and children influence them in preferring good above evil, virtue above vice? Our beloved Russia is a dark land, where people are exploited and so many are ignorant. But it can and will be a bright land in which there will be neither masters nor slaves."

Although he was talking to his father, I sensed that his words were directed to me. They made me tingle, like the voice of the priest at high mass.

"As for my children," father concluded, now looking into my eyes, "for the blood we've shed I want that not only they, but all children, shall be happy."

Grandfather thought for a long minute. "There's nothing wrong in what you say," he replied, "but much in it that leaves me perplexed. I have always served the Tsar, like my father before me and his father before him. But you're different, Andrei. You see things from a different angle, from the underside, so to speak. May God forgive you, son, if you're wrong. But since you honestly believe in your cause, you must act on your beliefs, and I will do the best I can to help your children as long as I live."

For a long time, before I fell asleep that night, my father's words made patterns in my mind.

Next morning we went to a patriotic demonstration. The people paraded, bands played, priests in flowing robes blessed the crowds, and street vendors sold ice cream, sweet-flavored water and meat patties. But soon father led me to a park bench, where we ate ice cream and talked.

"And so, my son, we meet again," he said. "Do you remember when you came with mama and Constantine to prison and I waved to you from the death tower?"

He told me about life in the prison which, as he described it, seemed somehow splendid, the suffering transfigured by comradeship and dedication to a great cause.

"I want you to remember these things all your life. Never forget who you are. Always remain true to the fight for freedom. There is no life without liberty. Whatever happens to me, you must go on studying, working, fighting with all means for what is ideal. We are either swine or we are men, and if we are men we cannot submit to be slaves. If my comrades and I fall, our children will take up our work."

That night he left for Yekaterinoslav, after buying me presents and promising that I would be allowed to go home for Christmas.

In the following months time seemed to drag, I was so eager to see my parents and brothers again. Mother wrote cheerful letters. Now that papa was working again, she no longer took in sewing, she wrote, and everything was so pleasant that I would scarcely recognize our home.

As the holidays approached, the excitement of the looming visit mounted. Grandmother toiled over her jams and cakes. The big sow that had been fattened especially for this occasion was slaughtered and for weeks everyone was busy boiling pork, smoking hams, grinding meats and vegetables and stuffing them into fat sausages. Finally the great day arrived, and a sledful of bundled-up Kravchenkos, wooden suitcases and miscellaneous bundles drove to the railroad station. Aunt Shura and I boarded the train; the others waved from the platform in tearful emotion as if we were departing for America.

At the Yekaterinoslav end, my whole family was waiting. Kisses, tears, exclamations. By the time we reached our house, the ice of strangeness was broken between my brothers and me, so that we all talked at once and about everything. Mother never took her eyes off me. "How well you look, Vitya! A real little man! So healthy and blooming!" she kept repeating.

The Christmas dinner that evening, too, has turned into a page in my private album of childhood scenes. The Christmas tree touched the ceiling and sparkled like a green and gold church steeple. The table was loaded with food and drink. The children joined in the toasts, drinking sweet wine from tiny colored glasses.

My maternal *babushka,* as the eldest, offered the first toast.

"Thank God we are all alive and healthy and together," she said. "I wish you all, my dear children, what you would most wish for yourselves!"

Then father rose, handsome and serious as always, raised his glass and said: "I propose that we drink to all those who tonight sit behind prison walls. May their faith and mine in a better life come true!"

Babushka whispered, "Andrei, not in front of the children!" but she drank with the others.

For hours, around the Christmas tree, we sang Russian and Ukrainian folk songs, as well as revolutionary songs like *You Fell as Victims* and the *Marseillaise.* A gramophone with an immense horn was one of the proofs of the family's new prosperity, and the children danced to squeaky songs. Between the wine and the excitement, Eugene dozed off while papa was reciting a poem about sacrifice and glory and even as I was laughing at his seven-year-old frailty from my nine-year apex, I too fell asleep.

I returned to Alexandrovsk and lived there another eighteen months, until the end of the school year in 1916 which wound up my elementary course.

Graduation was truly memorable for me, though the ceremony and the speeches were stuffy and dull. The great day began with my first authorized haircut. My curly mop of dark hair stirred the artist in the barber. I emerged with a coiffure—its elegance punctuated with a dashing cowlick over my left eye—that advertised my new manhood. Then grandfather presented me formally with a student's uniform with long pants. A cherished dream come true! It was good to be going on eleven and the center of attention.

Fyodor Panteleyevich in his own uniform, all the medals gleaming, drew more eyes at the graduation that afternoon than papa Shtchekatihin himself. Grandma was arrayed in her one black silk gown and moved in an aura of lavender and camphor. Aunt Shura was there, of course, as well as Uncle Mitya.

Another thrill awaited me at home that evening. Father's younger brother, my Uncle Peter, unexpectedly arrived from the front on leave. He was a complete contrast to my father—carefree, life-loving, full of jokes and pranks. Between Peter and his father there were none of the tensions which marred the relations between Fyodor Panteleyevich and his son Andrei. I felt vaguely, with a slight twinge of jealousy, that Peter was the favorite here.

Told about the fine marks I had received in my final examinations, Uncle Peter implored me, laughing yet half in earnest, to model myself after him rather than my crusading father.

"Damn it, let others save the world, Vitya," he roared. "It's enough of a job saving yourself. You only live once and might as well enjoy it, I say."

The night before I was to leave for home I was permitted to go to the Gypsy encampment to say good-bye to my many friends. I carried a few presents: a packet of tobacco for Saideman's father, a pipe for Saideman himself and bright ribbons for his sisters. That, too, was like parting from my own family.

Next morning I returned to my native city and a few months later entered the *gymnasium* or higher school. Our family was united for the first time. Eugene was attending the elementary school and Constantine was in his second year at the *gymnasium*. With father earning from eighty to a hundred and twenty rubles a month, a very handsome income for a workingman, and his two sons well on the road to an education, life seemed at last normal and orderly.

Mother was happier, and more beautiful, than I had ever seen her before. But father, by nature somewhat on the morose side, was uneasy under the calm surface. He was more conscious than the rest of us of the storm clouds in the Russian skies.

CHAPTER III

GLORY AND HUNGER

THE WINTER of 1916 rolled ominously toward the collapse of Tsarism. Like clammy fog, the feeling of approaching disaster soaked through the routines of our existence.

The war was going very badly and grumbling became more open, more insistent. It was no secret that soldiers were deserting the fronts in droves, that discipline was cracking. Even in Yekaterinoslav dark rumors rumbled everywhere, about a sinister monk named Rasputin, about graft in high places, food riots, pro-Germans around the Tsarina. Our teachers made scarcely any effort to curb the revolutionary talk of the older boys, and father's friends talked in low, tense voices about the stirring of "the masses."

After a long day in the factory, father rarely had time to wash, eat and relax. There were meetings, discussions, reports by emissaries from Petrograd or Kiev. More often than ever, our home now served as a way station for fugitives from Siberia and the exile regions of the Far North. Again and again we children were shut out of the parlor where grim-faced factory workers and local intellectuals argued for hours behind the locked doors.

One afternoon my parents, having gone to meet their friend Paramonov, just escaped from prison, returned greatly disturbed. Mother was crying and father's teeth were clenched. As one of the sailors on the Cruiser *Potemkin* whose insurrection touched off the uprisings of 1905, this Paramonov was a heroic figure in our eyes. He was my younger brother's godfather. In the following days I pieced together the story, which has remained in my mind as a symbol of sacrifice.

A bench on a secluded path in the city park had been agreed upon as the rendezvous and a few of his comrades met the sailor there. They had been together only a few minutes when several strangers strolled by, self-consciously casual. Suspecting that they were police officers in plain clothes, Paramonov said farewell hastily and cut through the bushes, hoping to scale a fence and get away. Soon his friends heard pistol shots. The fugitive was killed.

Despite the demands on his time, father managed to spend many evenings and an occasional Sunday with his three sons. Together we read out of books by Herzen, Tolstoy and others; father would take some passage as text to enlarge on his views of Russian emancipation and human freedom. His ardent and perhaps unreal idealism stirred me deeply. It was on a plane of religious sentiment.

At this time, too, I developed a strong friendship with a schoolmate

19

named Spiridonov, the son of a *gymnasium* teacher, and spent much time at his home. Here, for the first time, I came to know an intellectual household, where literature, music and the theater seemed as real and vastly more important than bread and work. The elder Spiridonov steered our avid reading into broader channels, not only among the Russian classics but among the works of Shakespeare, Goethe, Anatole France, Knut Hamsun, Hugo, Flaubert, Zola, Dickens.

Looking back, I am amazed by the extent and variety of my reading during that springtime of mental discovery. Somehow the beauty and the pathos of books, along with the exalted hopes of my father, became part of the revolution as it swept over an eleven-year-old boy. It seemed as if in a few weeks the distance between literature and reality, between words and deeds, was being bridged.

The storm clouds burst in the last week of February, 1917 (early March in the Western calendar). Even those who had been most certain of its advent were surprised and bewildered. Revolution, which had been an intimate and half-illicit word, was suddenly in the open, a wonderful and terrifying reality. What had seemed a simple solution of all problems had exploded into a million new problems, some of them ridiculously petty, like finding food and clothes.

The seams of accustomed life came apart. Schools, factories, public institutions lost their old meanings. The people of our city crowded into the snow-covered streets. It was as if homes and offices and workshops had been turned inside out, dumping their human contents into the squares and parks. Demonstrations, banners, cheering, flaring angers, occasional shooting—and above it all, enveloping it, almost smothering it all, there was talk, talk, talk. Words pent up for centuries broke through in passionate oratory; foolish and inspired, high-pitched and vengeful oratory.

Slogans filled the air and seemed to have a proliferating life of their own. *Down with the war! War to a victorious end! Land and freedom! The factories to the workers! On to the Constituent Assembly! All power to the Soviets!* New words and new names burst and sputtered in our minds like fireworks. Bolsheviks, Mensheviks, Kadets, Social Revolutionaries, Anarchists. . . . Kerensky, Miliukov, Lenin, Trotsky. . . . Red Guards, Whites, Partisans. . . .

Platforms grew on the main squares. Speakers followed one another in a loud procession. Men and women who had never spoken above a timid whisper now felt the urge to scream, preach, scold and declaim. Educated men with well-tended beards made way for soldiers and workmen. "Right! Right!" the crowds thundered or *"Doloi! Von!*—Down with him! Out with him!"

Once, on a day of demonstrations under a forest of homemade banners, my father spoke from a platform. Everyone seemed to know his name.

"Friends and brothers! Workers, peasants, intellectuals and soldiers!" he began.

It was the first time I had heard him speak in public and I could scarcely contain my excitement. His voice was resonant and he seemed transfigured, so that I had to reassure myself that it was, indeed, my own father. Words and ideas that had been intimately our own, almost a family secret, were miraculously public, so that everyone became part of the family. He told about prison and exile, about the heroic life of Comrade Paramonov, about the beautiful future. He pleaded for order and self-control and warned against those who would drown the revolution in blood. He spoke with marvelous simplicity and sincerity, as if these were his three sons multiplied to hundreds.

When he stepped from the platform and a band played the *Marseillaise*, I rushed toward him, elbowed a way through his admiring friends, and shouted "Hurrah, papa!" Father laughed with a full voice.

"You see, Vityenka," he said, "now people will be free. It was worth fighting for this!"

I knew then, or perhaps I only understood later, that he was justifying himself, explaining the years of penury and worry he had visited on his family.

The honeymoon of the revolution, however, soon trailed off into dissensions, accusations, suffering. Enthusiasm gave way to anger and bitterness. Stones, fists, revolver shots were increasingly mixed with the words and arguments. At the same time food became scarcer; wood, coal and kerosene seemed to disappear; some factories worked only intermittently, others closed down altogether. "There's your revolution! You asked for it!" people, especially the well-dressed people, now muttered.

My father grew more depressed, more silent, with every passing day. He became more irritable than I had ever seen him in the years of danger and sacrifice. When I pressed him for an explanation of the many parties and programs he seemed embarrassed.

"It's too complex," he would say. "You're not old enough to understand. This is a struggle for power. No matter what any party stands for, it will be bad if *one* party wins. That will only mean new masters for the old—rule by force, not by the free will of the people. It is not for this that the revolutionists gave their lives."

Another time, after we had listened to Mensheviks, Bolsheviks, Kadets and others in the Mining Institute, now the headquarters of the Yekaterinoslav Soviet, he shook his head sadly and said:

"I have been fighting to overthrow Tsarism. For freedom, for plenty, not for violence and vengeance. We should have free elections and many parties. If one party dominates, it's the end."

"But what are you, papa? A Menshevik, Bolshevik, a Social Revolutionary or what?"

"None of these, Vitya. Always remember this: that no slogan, no matter how attractive, is any indication of the real policy of any political party once it comes to power."

Father went to the Rumanian front, one of a group of worker-agitators. He was still there in November when the Bolsheviks in Petrograd, headed by Lenin and Trotsky, seized control of the government and the revolution. He returned with news that the war was over, that the soldiers were simply throwing away their guns and going home. But we knew this already. Kotya and I, and our friends from the *gymnasium*, spent hours at the railroad station. Every train from the south and the west was jammed with soldiers. They crowded the roofs of cars, hung on to windows, clung to the rods under cars and overflowed onto the locomotives. They sang songs, swore, quarreled, shouted slogans. We youngsters could make little sense out of the chaos and our elders seemed as confused as we were.

The only certainties, closing in on us like the shrinking walls in a horror novel, were *golod* and *kholod*, hunger and cold. Money lost its value and the shelves in shops grew emptier and dustier. A thousand simple things that had been taken for granted—street cleaners, telephone service, the water supply, transport—suddenly became difficult, precious, sometimes unattainable. Typhus spread and the funerals every day made an almost continuous procession.

As long as I remembered, *babushka* had saved crusts and remnants of bread. These she had toasted at intervals and presented to her favorite monastery and orphanages. Now we were grateful for her frugal habit. Now we treasured every crust for ourselves. The gay, warm lamplight seemed a thing of the past; a "smoker"—a wick dipped in a saucer of oil—provided the only light on long winter nights.

By the flickering dimness of a "smoker" I used to read aloud to *babushka*. She loved Nekrasov, Tolstoy and Turgeniev. Now and then she would repeat a luscious phrase after me, missing the sentences that followed.

One night, while I was reading a sketch by Turgeniev, I felt her hand reaching out for mine. I continued reading. When her grip relaxed, I assumed she had fallen asleep and I was about to tiptoe out of the room so as not to awaken her. But this time, when I looked up, I saw that her eyes were open and that she was strangely quiet. A smile was frozen on her lips.

"*Babushka! Babushka!*" I shrieked and others came running.

The death of my maternal grandmother, too, remains with me as part of the pattern of revolution. She had been a vigorous woman until caught between the upper and nether stones of *golod* and *kholod*. Spiridonov and I searched the city for hours until we found a few fresh flowers for her coffin. To carry her to her rest without flowers seemed to us indecent.

Up north, in part of Russia proper, the Soviet regime was consolidated in a few months. In the rest of the country, and especially in our Ukraine, civil war, brutal, bloody, senseless in its confusion and often obscene, lasted for several years. Control of Yekaterinoslav passed from one group to another almost every month, sometimes several times in a single week. We ceased trying to remember who represented authority. Reds, Whites, Greens, Petliurists, the forces of Hetman Skoropadsky, of Batko Makhno, of Grigoriev. For a few months the Germans were in occupation. Then they withdrew and the tides of competing armies, most of them in rags and all of them disdainful of their own lives and the lives of others, washed back and forth over the emaciated body of our city.

Pictures remain in my mind, like pages torn out of a book:

Two soldiers in Tsarist uniforms on horseback dashing along Pushkin Prospekt near our house, pursued by two Chinese riders, one flourishing a sword, the other a rifle. The horseman with the rifle pulls up sharp, aims his gun and shoots. One of the White soldiers topples over and his horse stops. The other soldier pauses for a moment to look and the pause enables the second Chinese to reach him. He slashes wildly with an unearthly shout, and a shapeless mass of bloody flesh falls to the cobblestones. Two corpses remain grotesquely peaceful in the sudden silence.

In the course of a walk during which we argue heatedly about a book we've been reading together, Kotya and I come to the Goryainov station at the other end of town. The previous night had been crowded with the sounds of shooting, though no one knew who was firing on whom. Now the station is littered with corpses. A train filled with German troops is on the tracks. Many Germans, warmly dressed, laughing, pick their way among the bodies. Near one heap of corpses, several soldiers are eating sandwiches and drinking coffee, each resting a foot on the bodies for comfort.

Late one night I hear noises outside our house. I rush out curiously. The snow glitters in the moonlight and somewhere a dog is barking. Suddenly a huge man runs past me, shouting obscenities as if drunk, and a few seconds later many other men rush by, flourishing knives, sticks, rifles. I remain for a while, listening to shots in the distance, and screams that rend the night. The following morning everyone talks about the chase and how the bandit leader called Byeloshapka—Whitecap—had been pursued on foot through the town, cornered in a side street and shot by Red Guards.

There was scarcely a day without its gruesome stories of pogroms in the Jewish quarters, bandit raids on banks, train hold-ups. Every new government called its predecessors "bandits" and soon was in turn being denounced as "bandits." For a week, maybe longer, everyone was excited about the Makhno or Anarchist government which was now entrenched in Yekaterinoslav; then the Reds were back again and it was as if Makhno had never been.

It is not easy to recapture that period as it impinged on a boy's mind. The memory has been edited by later knowledge and understanding. But the amazing fact, in retrospect, is that under the turbulence of civil war, disorder and dangers, the processes of ordinary living somehow went on. We worked, studied, ate, slept, read and laughed. We made new friendships and even planned for the future. The turbulence became a familiar and natural thing, almost a way of life; it was a new element within which the routines of everyday existence were conducted.

Life, the will to survive and the habit of survival, were stronger than all the violences.

2

The telegram from Alexandrovsk was signed by Aunt Shura. Was Uncle Peter, by any chance, with us? Father immediately wired that he was not. A few days later we received a letter: Peter had been found: dead, murdered. If we could come to the funeral it might help the old folks weather the tragedy.

Father started out without delay, although he had small hope of getting to Alexandrovsk before the funeral. After a consultation with my mother, he decided to take Kotya and me along—the sight of their sturdy little grandsons might be good for the bereaved parents.

Peter had taken no part in the revolutionary turmoils. The whole business bored him. It seemed to him an annoying interruption of a life which might be pleasant enough, for all its brevity, if only folks stopped fussing with it, reforming it. After his return from the front he discarded his uniform and obtained the post of director of a small Alexandrovsk bank. We wondered, as we boarded the train, how he had met his death.

The train was crowded to suffocation. Millions of people at this time, or so it seemed, were traveling—running from one fire into another, searching for safety in the midst of a national conflagration, keeping a few steps ahead of vengeance or rushing blindly to meet it head-on. Passengers and bundles jammed every inch of space. People sat on the upper sleeping shelves, their muddy boots and rag-bound feet dangling among the faces below. The air was heavy and fetid.

At the Slavgorod station I went to the lavatory to fetch some water. When I returned, a man with a drawn Mauser stood at the entrance to our car. Frightened, I cried out "Papa!" "The devil take your papa! Get in there and shut up or I'll shoot your brains out!" the man snarled.

The train began to move as I made my way to father's side. All the passengers had their hands raised over their heads. Children whimpered in fright. At both ends of the car armed men were stationed and several others were gathering up money and valuables, systematically, compartment after compartment. Now they reached ours.

"What have you got? Hand it over!" one of the bandits growled at my father.

"What have I got?" he answered calmly, smiling, "a watch, a few rubles and my two boys."

When the robbery was completed, the train slowed down again and the brigands jumped off. There were shots from some of the cars. I saw one of the robbers stop in his tracks, as if surprised, then topple over slowly. Another wa shot dead by a passenger before he had time to get off. His body was still on the train when we reached our destination. Clearly the holdup had been staged by men who were new to the trade.

I hardly recognized Alexandrovsk. Its enchantment had run out in these two years; its ancient neatness seemed mussed up, scrawled over by mischievous history. The station was deserted. Street lamps were smashed. Even the snows seemed grimy. When father asked someone "who was in power," the stranger shrugged in disgust and muttered, "The devil knows!"

The house in which I had spent the happiest years of my childhood seemed to have shrunk and grown pathetically old overnight. We had arrived too late for the funeral; Shura's letter had not reached us in time. She was sewing something in a corner, her eyes red, her cheeks streaked with weeping. Grandma Natalia Maximovna embraced us and tried to smile as of old, but the twinkle in her eyes was gone forever. She restrained herself only for a few moments, then broke into singsong lamentations, gazing at the icon lamp and crossing herself continually.

"Your good Uncle Petya is no more, Vitya! My little son Petya is gone, gone! They killed him, dear God, and our Petya is no more!"

Fyodor Panteleyevich sat at the table and took no notice of us. I could scarcely believed that this was my strong, dignified grandfather. It was as if something had melted inside his frame, leaving him limp, and incredibly old. After a while he looked at us, nodded a greeting and rose slowly.

"Well, Andrei," he said bitterly, "what you've waited for has come. There's your precious revolution! People kill each other, shoot, rob, torture our folk with hunger and cold! It's murder, crime, not revolution."

His voice rose in grief and anger. "The sons-of-bitches, why did they kill Peter? Why?" he shouted, seizing my father by his shoulders and shaking him. "The Germans didn't kill us like our own Russian brothers are doing. Thank you, thank you, Andrei, for your dear revolution."

Father remained silent, his head bowed. He saw the futility of words and explanations. For the first time his family saw Fyodor Panteleyevich weep. Tears clotted his white beard. Slowly he walked to the icon corner —the martial erectness was gone—and sank to his knees.

"Help, O Lord, Thy straying lambs. Let not brother kill brother and son kill father. Restore Thy people to their senses, Holy Virgin, and let them not perish."

He arose, quieted, and wiped the tears from his cheeks.

"Well, Andrei, may God forgive you, even as your father forgives you," and turning to his wife: "Natasha, feed the children and put them to sleep."

Then Shura, sobbing, told us about her brother's end. One evening he failed to return from the bank. Supposing that he might have decided, for some reason, to visit us in Yekaterinoslav, Shura sent that telegram. Four days after his disappearance, a peasant found Peter's body near the tracks far outside town. A handkerchief was stuffed in his mouth; his hands were tied behind his back; there were several bullet holes in his head. The keys to the bank which he normally carried with him were gone.

"His heart was silent but his watch was still ticking . . . the five-day watch of which Petya was so proud," Shura broke anew into wailing.

Apparently would-be bank robbers, having seized the keys, had decided to kill Peter to destroy a witness; possibly they were people whom he recognized. Then, it may be, they lost courage and abandoned the robbery project.

We returned home with heavy hearts. Grandfather never recovered from the blow of his younger son's murder. A few months later he died and his wife followed him soon after.

3

The Ilyin estate, near Korbino, on the Dnieper was one of the richest and most attractive in its region. It embraced thousands of acres of fertile wheat and grazing land, forests, fruit orchards, spacious stables and dairy houses. Wide gravel roads marched elegantly between shade trees to the great mansion where the landlords once lived in splendor. The river at this point sheds some of its stately languor and pushes its way roughly below steep and craggy cliffs; nature had outdone herself to give this corner of the country variety and an almost theatrical beauty.

After the revolution most of the land was parceled out among the peasants who had worked it. But the core of the estate—some five hundred acres of plow land, the orchards, a big fish pond, the Ilyin mansion and other structures—was turned into an agricultural cooperative or "commune" for city workers early in 1919. The settlers, about a hundred families from Yekaterinoslav, called it *Nabat,* the Tocsin.

The Kravchenkos were among these families and for nearly four years, until I was more than seventeen, the commune was our new home. My father, in fact, was one of the initiators of the project and drew many of the mechanics from his factory into it. The Regional Soviet approved the idea, allocated the land, and provided some supplies and livestock to supplement what was still on the old estate.

In the city, production had been almost entirely stalled, for lack of raw materials, and food shortages were reaching a level of near-hunger. Escape to the soil offered a hope of survival. The gnawing of spiritual hungers, too, entered into the undertaking. Within the limits of one cooperative farm some of these men yearned to put into practice a few, at least, of the dreams that had filled their years of revolutionary ardor. The Tocsin, they hoped, would sound an alarm and a reminder of ideals of brotherhood which seemed forgotten in the tumult of fratricidal struggle, in this time when Communists, through their Cheka, were making wholesale arrests and shooting people on the slightest pretext.

My father had been repeatedly invited to join the Communist Party. He refused. He had no stomach for dictatorship and terror, he said brusquely, even under a red flag. He saw workers and intellectuals who had held aloof from the struggle under the Tsar entering the Party now that it seemed headed for permanent power; some of them invented romantic revolutionary biographies for themselves. This only hardened his resolve to remain a "freelance" in the fight for a better world.

The city workers brought to their farm tasks an enthusiasm that had in it an element of desperation. They wanted to make good so that their families would eat, of course, but also to justify their past sacrifices for their cause. The local peasants on and near the Ilyn estate mocked the city slickers turned farmers. "Now we'll see how 'communists' farm our land," they would say with a broad wink.

Their jibes were good-natured, disguising a simple friendliness. Many of them went out of their way to advise us and to help us at every turn. Far from resenting the experiment, the local peasantry took it under a kind of unofficial good-neighbor patronage. Frequently they pitched in when work was heaviest and helped to make that first year a success. Although the famous Erastovka Agricultural School was not near the commune, some of its expert agronomists, too, came to our aid.

For the young people, life on the commune was full of excitement. I relished the work, the country life, the sense of doing things together with comrades. Our parents worried about the neglect of our education and tried to make up for it with improvised schooling, but not one of us shared their alarms on this subject. Swimming, fishing, boating, games, the exploration of the neighborhood filled the intervals of an existence that was mostly hard work. A love of horses that I seem to have been born with now found exuberant expression. Grachev, the stableman, had in me an eager helper. The life of the peasants, too, drew me. I made friends among them and spent many an evening in their houses, with boys and girls of my own age.

The civil war, of course, was never far away. Again and again it disturbed our lives and on several occasions threatened to blot out the commune. Constantine and I were proud to be old enough now to take part in the armed self-defense units formed by father and other leaders and even my little brother Eugene learned to shoot. Now the Reds, now the Whites, then again some unidentified freebooting gang, invaded our lands, demanding food, blankets or even horses. A show of strength, plus a readiness to share what supplies we could spare, saved the commune from major maraudings.

One incident remains indelibly stamped on my mind. I was grazing some horses that morning on a rise in the land, which gave me as clear a view as if it were all taking place on a cinema screen. About three hundred cavalrymen, mostly Cossacks and other Whites, suddenly galloped from the main road across our wheat fields, in the direction of the river. Behind them, in hot pursuit, came a far greater number of Reds. Hopelessly cornered, the Whites dashed straight over the cliff into the river, where they tried to swim across. But the pursuers, their machine guns planted on the edge of the cliff, mowed them down almost to the last man.

Less than a month later the incident was repeated, almost in every detail, except that now the Reds were driven over the cliff and picked off, one by one, as they sought to reach the opposite shore. We became so accustomed to finding bodies washed up on or near the commune that we no longer mentioned such incidents.

Toward twilight on an autumn day, after our first harvest, Grachev and I were in one of the stables when a long peasant wagon drawn by two horses came into view. Four men and a woman were in it. Riders and horses alike were crusted with dust and running sweat. A machine gun was mounted toward the back of the vehicle. The woman, who was about thirty and good-looking, wore the insignia of a nurse; one of the men was in civilian clothes, two others in the uniforms of the Cheka, the new and already dreaded Soviet secret police; the fourth, a large, gross looking fellow, wore a sailor's uniform.

The civilian introduced himself as Lihomanov—the same Lihomanov who later, as president of the Yekaterinoslav Provincial Committee, was to become a power in our region. He said that a detachment of Whites was on their trail and that they must have fresh horses to get away. No, there was no time to consult anyone but if we wanted our horses back we could come along as far as Kamenskoye.

We agreed to these arrangements and soon the seven of us were in the wagon, lashing our animals and eating up road. We drove so fast that I could barely make out the debris on the road as sprawling corpses. Liho-manov told us that these were mostly Red Guards, that there had been a big battle here in the last few days.

"We'll get even with the bastards!" the sailor shrieked every now and then. "We'll cut their gizzards out, the sons-of-bitches!"

There were no untoward incidents until we had passed through the town of Auly and I even began to wonder whether the danger we were escaping was not largely imaginary. Beyond Auly we turned into a road that skirted the river. We had been riding ten or fifteen minutes when we heard the drumbeats of galloping horsemen far behind us and realized that about a dozen men were after us. We could make out shouts and knew, without hearing the words, that we were being ordered to halt. Our sailor, with a lusty oath, sprang to the machine gun and began to spit fire. We saw some of the pursuers topple from their horses. The survivors seemingly decided to call off the hunt.

We reached Kamenskoye that night and put up in a small house where Lihomanov evidently was known. "You'll sleep in the same room with the nurse," he told me. "You're only a kid." Grachev and the sailor, who were to take turns in guarding the wagon and the horses, were assigned to a room next to ours. I stepped out to give the nurse a chance to go to bed, then undressed in turn in the dark and was soon fast asleep.

It must have been some hours later that I was aroused by noise and excited voices. As I shook off sleep I heard the nurse crying in choked hysterical tones, "Let me alone, you beast, or I'll wake the whole house! Get away, I tell you!" Enough moonlight seeped into the room to enable me to see that our sailor, half dressed, his features distorted by passion, was attempting to force himself on the woman. She was struggling with all her might, her hair disordered, her breasts exposed where he had ripped her blouse.

When the sailor saw me sit up in bed, he released her and ran out, cursing and slamming the door. "Dirty bourgeois!" I heard him mutter. The nurse was weeping.

"Such people, such terrible people!" she sobbed. "And that's the material with which we must make a revolution."

Nearly as upset as she was, I offered to call Lihomanov and the others.

"No, we'd better not worry Lihomanov," she said. "He has enough to worry about without this. He's one of the real ones, a true idealist."

Neither of us fell asleep again. We were still talking—more exactly, she was talking, I was listening—when dawn came. She was the daughter of a high Tsarist official, she told me, adding:

"When the revolution occurred, I met it with my whole heart. All my life I have loved the plain people and wanted to help them. It was for them that I broke with my family and took courses in the medical school in Kharkov. Now I'm in the Cheka. I don't like many of the things they are doing, but my work is healing, not shooting.

"We mustn't lose faith or renounce the struggles of thousands of honest men, men like Lihomanov, because of dark and bestial creatures like the man who attacked me tonight. For one such dirty episode there are a hundred heroic ones."

Her attacker was not even a real sailor, she told me in confidence. He had picked up the uniform somewhere and wore it because it gave him a certain revolutionary prestige.

As Grachev and I rode back to the commune that morning I told him what had happened during the night. He was a simple workman and understood little of what was going on in our country. But what he said that morning I had reason to recall in subsequent years.

"Yes, Vitya, that nurse was right. There's good and there's bad, in revolution as in everything. The question is: who will come out on top when the revolution settles down, the honest people or the beasts, the Lihomanovs or the fake sailors."

Now that we were taking our time, we could observe the corpses we had passed the previous evening. At some points there were mounds of freshly turned soil, where local peasants had already buried some of the bodies. Many of the corpses were naked and only a few had their boots on —the dead were being stripped to clothe the living.

4

At the end of the commune's second harvest, in the autumn of 1920, both Constantine and I were enrolled in the Erastovka Agricultural School at Komissarovka.

The institution had been founded and generously endowed a generation earlier by Erastus Brodsky, a big landowner of the district. He carved it out of his own estate, erecting handsome buildings on a hill overlooking a lovely lake. The architecture in some of the halls was adapted from traditional Ukrainian mansions; there were murals by celebrated painters, fine mosaics on folk themes, and of course the latest in imported farm machinery.

The school had suffered greatly at the hands of vandals. Several of its structures and dormitories were wrecked beyond use; furniture and even wall and ceiling beams had been carried off as fuel; the machinery was in pitiful disrepair. Most of the famous Erastovka livestock—medals won at continental shows in Vienna and Prague were still on display—had been scattered.

But many of the old teachers remained at their posts and new ones had joined the school, so that about six hundred students from all parts of Russia were again studying and practising modern farming here despite the pervasive food shortages and the lack of materials. Products raised on the school grounds helped to keep them alive and common hardships seemed to bring teachers and pupils closer together. The school was under Soviet control but there was little of politics in the studies. It was taken for granted that in preparing ourselves to make the Russian soil yield more and better food for the Russian people we were doing all that "the revolution" expected from us.

My brother and I and a third student named Fyodor, from Tuapse, lived together in the cottage of a local peasant. The winter passed quickly and with the spring classroom lessons were replaced by practical work on the school acres. Later I came to appreciate that I learned far more than I then suspected; the smattering of scientific farming was to stand me in good stead in the period of collectivization.

It was becoming harder every day to obtain food. Money had lost all value and what trade still went on was on a primitive barter level. We could look for little help from the commune, where the idyllic vision of a cooperative enterprise was petering out in bickering and bitterness. More and more of the settlers were deserting. The bread reserves were running so low that the strictest rationing had to be enforced. Poverty, it appeared, was a most inappropriate godmother to a new world, even on the tiny scale of the Tocsin.

But boys in their early teens were not to be intimidated by trouble. We were used to doing with little and to foraging for the next meal. That spring trainloads of Red Army troops were passing through Komissarovka towards the front, where war with the Poles was under way. Our problem was simply to separate the soldiers from some of their food supplies, and this the three roommates of Erastovka solved in the grand style.

On free days, and sometimes on schooldays when we could steal a few hours, we set up in business at the railroad station as a "Student Mobile Barber Shop." That was the inscription on a large placard in Kotya's most artistic hand lettering. Under it was the sales message: "Shaves and haircuts. . . . Good and conscientious service. . . . Pay in kind." Finally came the signature, with a touch of unsubtle humor: "Useless Labor Artel." Fyodor, who had picked up the art somewhere in his travels, did the shaving. The Kravchenko brothers did the haircutting. "Don't worry," Fyodor instructed us, "it's like mowing a hayfield—long easy strokes, then even up the stubble."

The soldiers crowded around the youthful amateur barbers, poked fun at them—and paid for the butchery with the generosity of simple people. Often we brought back enough bread, pork, vegetables and other produce to entertain our friends. Some Sundays the open-air Student Mobile Barber Shop raised its standard in the town bazaar and did a thriving business. The peasants paid in eggs, potatoes, occasionally even a chicken.

Too soon, however, this bonanza ran dry. No one had any more food to exchange for barbering. The great drought of 1921 was in the making, and the peasants, recognizing the signs, grew frugal and morose. There being nothing to eat in the school, we returned to the commune, to find that the early enthusiasm had burned out in cinders of quiet despair. Only a few of the original settlers remained and these, for the most part, had taken employment in nearby plants.

I was now sixteen. At Korbino, a few miles from the Tocsin, there was a small iron foundry. There I found a job as apprentice to a locksmith. It was the first time I had done hard physical labor on a paid basis. It gave me a feeling of being "really grown-up" at last to return home in my oil-stained clothes, dirty and aching with fatigue.

Civil strife was almost over and the Soviets were in undisputed control.

Party agitators sometimes came to the plant and harangued us at lunch-time meetings or after work. The older workers for the most part ignored them, but the younger men and women listened intently. For us it offered hope in a time of general distress and pessimism. There was also a factory club, decorated with lithographs of Lenin, Trotsky, Marx and Engels and slogans in crude white letters on strips of red bunting.

I listened eagerly to lecturers from the centers and even worked up the courage to ask questions. The promised future was more magnetic against the background of immediate hardships. I was caught between the skepticism at home and my own thirst for a faith. I understood my father's objections to the harsh Communist methods, but as time went on it seemed to my young mind that he was too rigid in his virtue; that his idealism was somehow "old-fashioned."

"Why don't you come to the club and hear the lectures?" I would ask him. I was eager to draw him with me into the new life.

"What can they tell me?" he would reply sadly. "I've forgotten more than they know. No, thank you, the egg doesn't teach the hen."

In the summer of 1921 the famine was in full tide, and with it the brother of famine—epidemic typhus. They were to take many millions of lives before running their gruesome course. After the long years of war and civil strife, we faced hunger in its most elementary and cruel forms. The drought was centered in the Volga regions but its skeleton fingers reached out grimly beyond the Dnieper. The area of most intense famine coincided in a general way with the area of most intense civil war; it was as if the soil were revolting against its long diet of blood.

There are no words to describe the suffering and horror. Men eyed every living thing—horses, dogs, cats, house pets—with greedy despair. The cattle that were not slaughtered died of starvation and were consumed despite official warnings against pestilence. Trees were stripped of their bark which was brewed for "tea" or "soup." Untanned leather was chewed for sustenance. Fields were picked bare of every last stalk of straw and blade of grass. Stories of peasants eating their own dead became more frequent; and unhappily they were often true—I knew of such cases in Romankovo, Auly, Pankovka and other neighboring villages.

Death—bloated, cadaverous, ugly death—was the commonplace fact in our lives. All of us were too deeply concerned with our own survival to notice or, at bottom, to care about the others. Good people who normally could not bear to see others suffer now buried their food to prolong their own lives by a few weeks or months, without a thought of neighbors who swelled and died of hunger all around them.

I was strong and healthy and needed little to keep me alive. With another lad in the commune, Senya, I went by train up north to the province of Poltava in search of food. We took along everything that might be converted into edibles: old clothes, silver spoons, oddments of jewelry, brushes and other household articles. Money now meant nothing, but goods might be bartered if one were fortunate.

In a few days we reached Priluki and decided to try our luck there. Hundreds of others had come on the same mission and the competition was fierce. We stood all day in the market places, our poor stock spread on the ground and begged peasants to examine these treasures. In the evening we went to the villages, from house to house. The fact that we were both young helped; so did the fact that I was able to talk to the peasants in their own Ukrainian language.

Every day we disposed of a few things and saw our sacks fill up with groats, flour, peas, beans. Nights we had no trouble finding shelter in peasant homes, especially if we made our approach through girls of our own age. In return for rings and cheap brooches, the girls managed to dig up salt, sugar, sunflower-seed oil, salt pork and other luxuries.

Senya and I were happier than any financiers who had concluded a ten-million-dollar deal. We were bringing back months of life to our families.

The train was crowded with men, women and children, all returning to the famine regions with their precious sacks and bundles. We dared not close our eyes for fear that we might be robbed. Late at night, at the station of Znamenka, soldiers and conductors ordered us all to get out. We were herded into a waiting room already packed with unfortunate people. No one had any idea why the train had been emptied. Everyone waited, with a bovine patience born of long suffering and dulled senses, for another train; when it arrived, only the stronger and more agile would succeed in boarding it. Senya and I remained behind.

Oil wicks provided the only light in the filthy station room. The crowd was so thick that people stepped over each other to get to the toilets. Here and there children cried; infants sucked at empty breasts. In one corner a couple lay in a passionate embrace, oblivious to the rough jokes of those around them.

But the center of attention, for those who still had a flicker of curiosity, was a young woman who was groaning like a stricken animal. Other women cleared a space around her, men brought pails of water, people forgot their own fight against hunger in the excitement of a new life being born. The thin wail of a new infant announced that the miracle was completed and people sank back into their own troubles.

In the morning I saw the mother on the filthy station floor, her face white and bloodless against the dirty sack under her head. The new-born child, swathed in rags, was at her breast. My throat swelled with pity. Leaving Senya to watch our belongings, I rushed into the village. I had three silver Tsarist rubles in my pocket and in half an hour of foraging succeeded in exchanging them for a small bottle of hot milk and a small wooden dishful of porridge. When I brought these gifts as well as a clean towel of my own to the young woman, she stared in unbelieving gratitude.

"Thank you, young man," she said in Ukrainian. Her eyes were beautiful in a tortured face. "What's your name?"

"Victor Andreyevich," I said.

"May God guard you and bring you joy," she said weakly, smiling for the first time. "I shall call my daughter Victorina, so she may remember your good deed all her life."

I was returning to Senya on the other side of the room when a young ruffian, who had watched the scene, shouted obscenely, "And look, comrades, the baby's papa is here!"

He was a head taller than I, broad-boned and tough looking. But fury knows no arithmetic. I struck out at him and, to my own amazement, sent him sprawling. Observing that the crowd was volubly on my side, he picked himself up quietly, wiped the blood from under his nose and retired to his own bundles.

No conquering hero was ever received more warmly than young Victor staggering under a sack of food. In the following months I made several other journeys, by train and on horseback. *Babushka's* gold cross was the last family treasure to go; we had held on to it as long as there was any hope of keeping alive without bartering it. Later help came from America, through the Quakers, Hoover's American Relief Administration and other groups, but it went mostly to the Volga area. As to the Ukraine, a new harvest was in the offing and life slowly resumed its normal course.

I returned to my locksmith's bench at the Korbino plant.

CHAPTER IV

YOUTH IN THE RED

THE NEW crops came up tall and fat in the summer of 1922 and with it a welling of hope and a zest for living. The dead, millions of them, were buried and by a kind of unspoken agreement no one referred to the catastrophe. The nightmare was consigned to the night.

Our orchard on the Tocsin was heavy with fruit, the berries grew big and juicy, the pond swarmed with fish, breezes from the Dnieper rumpled the golden hair of our wheat fields. Ukrainian girls again sang haunting melodies in chorus as they harvested the grain. It was good to be nearly seventeen, to sprout a mustache and to be suddenly abashed in the presence of girls whom one had ignored only yesterday.

My decision to become a miner was somehow related to this season of burgeoning new life. I was impatient to dig into the entrails of mother earth, to build, to expand. No doubt the words of the lecturer at the Korbino club were commonplace enough: prescribed formulas from the Communist Party instructions to *agit-prop* workers. But to me they were so many trumpet blasts challenging to action.

"Comrades," the speaker said that night in early autumn, "our country needs coal, metal, oil. Those are the sinews of the future. All of you to whom the revolution is dear must go into the factories and the mines. Our Soviet Republic needs strong working hands. Thousands of men are needed, for instance, in the collieries of the Donetz Basin."

Senya and I looked at one another and knew without speaking that the same resolution was in both our minds.

When I announced at home that I was going off to the Donetz coal mines, father looked sad. Mother wept softly and reminded me that I was only a boy and that I would have plenty of time to work later. But they did not attempt to stop me. For days mother prepared my clothes and packed them tenderly.

We were sent to a mine in the Alchevsk district, near Algoverovka. One of the oldest coal areas in the Donetz Basin, it was now being greatly enlarged. We spent the first night in a long, gloomy barracks where several hundred men slept on the bare boards of upper and lower bunks. The stench of crowded bodies and stale food and bad tobacco was almost unbearable. Several grimy miners were playing with greasy cards and cursing lustily in the half-light of "smokers."

But the two boys from the Dnieper, weary from the long ride in an overcrowded train, slept sweetly. We awoke in the morning to find that our suitcases had been stolen. We possessed nothing but the soiled clothes in which we had traveled and slept. A walk through the miners' settlement scarcely raised our spirits. It was a long, dingy lane flanked by time-worn shacks and raw-new barracks. A pall of coal dust enveloped everything. The romance of "building socialism" with our own hands ebbed rapidly, and it took many weeks to restore some of the zest with which we had started.

Senya was assigned to one of the pits, deep in an oak forest. But my fate was an anticlimax. Because of a lack of literate men, the trade-union functionary insisted that I work in one of the administration offices. The vision of myself swinging a pick, a miner's lamp on my forehead, resolved into the reality in which I swung pens and an abacus.

In the first months we lived in one of the huge, filthy barracks where the newcomers were concentrated. Later we obtained a room in one of the small dwellings occupied by the old or permanent miners. Once I had become accustomed to the coal dust and primitive living conditions, the new existence took on color and even excitement. I found myself in the midst of what was almost a cross-section and sampling of the races and the social groups composing the Soviet empire.

Russians and Ukrainians, of course, were in the majority, but there were also Tartars, Armenians, Chinese; hill people from the Caucasus, Kazaks from the Asiatic steppe. A few had come, like Senya and myself, to immerse themselves in the tasks of industrialization, in a mood of patriotic earnestness. The mass of recruits came because, by their village standards, the wages were good. Thousands of them remained only long enough to save the price of a cow, a horse or the building of a new house; the fantastically high turnover of labor was the biggest single headache of the administration.

There was not much love lost among the different races. They tended not merely to live by themselves but to work by themselves; the Orientals in the deepest and toughest pits, the Russians and Ukrainians on the lighter jobs. But the chasms that divided class from class were even wider than those that separated race from race. The remnants of "former" people—sons of merchants, landlords and priests, ex-officers and ex-officials of the old regime, former students—felt themselves outsiders, barely tolerated and openly despised.

Life in the barracks was crude and often ugly. Men drank vodka from the bottle and worked it off in quarrels and fist fights. Some of them gambled and argued at the top of their voices on absurd subjects. I saw miners lose not only their wages but their last pair of boots and their one blanket in card games. The workers' clubs, the literacy classes and the library drew off a minority of the serious-minded workers.

I found it interesting to watch the rapid transformation of peasant lads, awkward and wide-eyed, arriving for their first contact with the big world outside their villages. In bast shoes, baggy homespun trousers, long peasant blouses, they gaped at the "proletariat" and at the outlandish peoples from distant parts of Russia.

But how quickly they became different, if not better, men! Many of them would return from town in store clothes, shaved and perfumed, with new shoes that had an elegant squeak; they would have themselves photographed in their new finery for the amazement of the folks back home; they would swagger through the settlement in rowdy groups, to the tune of accordions, in high spirits. But there were others who were attracted, just as naturally, to the club and classes and were soon deploring the "backwardness" and lack of "culture" of their friends, and arguing politics as if they had been born to it.

My own life, of course, centered around the club. My passion for reading, interrupted by civil war and famine, was now fully revived. Besides the books available in the library, we borrowed from one another. Nearly every evening and on free days I took courses in chemistry, mathematics, physics or listened to technical discourses on coal mining. Senya and I made friends with boys and girls as eager as we were to learn, and my advantages of early training gave me a certain influence among the more serious young workers and workers' children.

The newspapers were shrill with the call to a better life for the country. Poor and backward Russia was at last on the highroad to progress—it only remained for everyone to dig more coal, raise more grain, acquire more culture. I read the invocations as if they were addressed personally to me. Occasionally one of the great new leaders—Petrovsky, Rakovsky or even Lunacharsky—passed through our district. Listening to them, I felt myself part of something new, big, exciting. In the Moscow Kremlin sat men whom we called simply Comrade—Lenin, Trotsky, Dzherzhinsky— but I knew them to be of the stature of gods.

Looking back to my private history as a Communist, I am inclined to date my conversion to the arrival of Comrade Lazarev, who gave a series of lectures on the problems of socialism. He was a man of about thirty, on the staff of the University of Sverdlovsk, tall, slim, neatly dressed. He talked simply in his own words, not in quotations from Marx or Lenin. What impressed me especially was that he wore a necktie, thereby bringing powerful reinforcement to those of us who argued that one could be a good Soviet citizen yet indulge in such bourgeois accessories.

One day I was in the library, engrossed in a book, when someone behind me said:

"What are you reading? I'm curious."

I turned around. It was Comrade Lazarev.

"*The Disquisitions of Father Jerome Cougniard* by Anatole France," I replied, smiling in embarrassment.

"So? Anatole France," he said. "Why not the Russian classics, or some contemporary Soviet writer?"

"I find a lot in Anatole France that I don't find in the Soviet writers," I said. "He's subtle and very honest. I do read Russian classics, but the new authors—they write only politically and seem to avoid the real life around us."

"Very interesting, let's discuss it some night. Come to my room and we'll get acquainted."

I met him again a few days later at a *subbotnik:* a work session, when hundreds of volunteers pitched in to do some urgent job without pay. On this occasion it was the removal of a mountainous heap of coal to clear a road. Comrade Lazarev was in work clothes, covered with soot and plying a shovel with great diligence. He greeted me like an old friend and I was pleased.

That evening he saw me again in the library. And what was I reading now, he wanted to know. *What to Do?* by Chernishevsky, I told him.

"An important work," he nodded approvingly.

"Yes, and his question, what to do, is one that bothers me now," I said.

"It's a question that has already been answered for millions by Lenin, and before him by Marx. Have you read Lenin and Marx?"

"A little of Lenin, here and there," I replied, "but not Marx. I've read the Party literature, of course, but I'm not sure that it quite answers the question what to do."

"Come over to my room, we'll have a glass of tea and some refreshments and we'll talk without disturbing anyone," Comrade Lazarev smiled.

It was a spotlessly clean, bright room. The divan was covered with a gay rug; books neatly ranged on the desk between book-ends; a few flowers in a colored pitcher. On one wall hung several family pictures, one of them of Lazarev himself as a boy, in *gymnasium* uniform, a dog at his feet; another of a pretty sister, also in student garb. On another wall were framed photographs of Lenin and Marx and between them—this was the touch that warmed me and won me over, though I did not know exactly why—the familiar picture of Leo Tolstoy in old age, in the long peasant tunic, his thumbs stuck into the woven belt.

This isn't an obscene sailor attacking a nurse at night, I thought to myself. *I could follow this kind of Communist.*

"Since I have to live here for several months," Lazarev explained, "I've tried to make the place homelike."

We talked for hours that night, about books, the Party, the future of Russia. My place was with the Communist minority who must show the way, Lazarev said, and I ought to join the Comsomols and later the Party. Of course, he conceded, the Party wasn't perfect and perhaps its program wasn't perfect, but men are more important than programs.

"If bright, idealistic young people like you stand aloof, what chance will there be?" he said. "Why not come closer to us and work for the common cause? You can help others by serving as an example of devotion to the country. Just look around you in the barracks—gambling, dirt, drunkenness, greed where there ought to be cleanliness, books, spiritual light. You must understand that there's a terrific task ahead of us, Augean stables to be cleaned. We must outroot the stale, filthy, unsocial past that's still everywhere, and for that we need good men. The heart of the question Vitya, is not only formal socialism but decency, education and a brighter life for the masses."

I had been "pressured" by Communists before this. But now, for the first time, I was hearing echoes of the spirit that had suffused my childhood. I argued with Comrade Lazarev; I said I would think it over, but in fact I agreed with him and had already made up my mind.

When Comrade Lazarev departed for Moscow some weeks later, I was in the large group—ordinary miners and office workers as well as the top officials of the administration—gathered at the station to see him off.

"There you are, Vitya," he singled me out. "I heard by accident that you've joined the Comsomols. Good for you! Congratulations! But why didn't you tell me? I would have recommended you."

"I know, and I'm grateful, but I wanted to do it on my own . . . without patronage."

"Maybe you're right," he smiled, "and here's a little present I saved for you especially."

It was a book. Marx or Lenin, I supposed. On the way home I looked at the title: *Three Plays of Shakespeare.* Lazarev, a fervid Communist and an effective leader, combined the humanism of Tolstoy, the love of beauty epitomized by Shakespeare, with his Lenin-Marxist faith. Would the amalgam survive? Would the Lazarevs triumph?

2

Now life had for me an urgency, a purpose, a new and thrilling dimension of dedication to a cause. I was one of the *élite,* chosen by History to lead my country and the whole world out of darkness into the socialist light. This sounds pretentious, I know, yet that is how we talked and felt. There might be cynicism and self-seeking among some of the grown-up Communists, but not in our circle of ardent novitiates.

My privileges, as one of the elect, were to work harder, to disdain money and foreswear personal ambitions. I must never forget that I am a Comsomol first, a person second. The fact that I had joined up in a mining region, in an area of "industrial upsurge," seemed to me to add a sort of mystic significance to the event. I suppose that a young nobleman admitted to court life under the Tsar had that same feeling of "belonging."

There was no longer much margin of time for petty amusements. Life was filled with duties—lectures, theatricals for the miners, Party "theses" to be studied and discussed. We were aware always that from our midst must come the Lenins and Bukharins of tomorrow. We were perfecting ourselves for the vocation of leadership; we were the acolytes of a sort of materialist religion.

Having discovered that I could write and speak on my feet with some natural eloquence, I was soon an "activist." I served on all kinds of committees, did missionary work among the non-Party infidels, played a role in the frequent celebrations. There were endless occasions to celebrate, over and above the regular revolutionary holidays. The installation of new machinery, the opening of new pits, the completion of production schedules were marked by demonstrations, music, speeches. Elsewhere in the world coal may be just coal—with us it was "fuel for the locomotives of revolution."

Through the intercession of Comrade Lazarev I had been transferred to work in the pits. I no longer needed to envy Senya on that score. The two of us and several other young miners formed an "artel," a cooperative group doing jobs and being paid as a unit. The artel system was at this time encouraged as a means of raising output. Members of efficient artels usually earned more than individual miners. This, however, was the least of our concerns. We bid for the most difficult and dangerous assignments, eager to prove our zeal by deeds. We even had a slogan which we solemnly communicated to the officials: "If it's necessary, it can be done."

The members of our artel lived together in a clean and comfortable house stocked with good books. We took turns at scrubbing the floors and other household chores. The Soviet leaders and classic Russian writers deployed on our walls looked down approvingly, I was sure, on this example of "culture" in the midst of backwardness. Among them was Sergo Ordzhonikidze, one of the men close to Lenin and later to become Commissar of Heavy Industry. I liked his rough-hewn Georgian face, with its huge eagle beak and shaggy drooping mustaches. Perhaps I had a vague premonition that this man would one day be the patron, and in a sense the inspiration, of my busiest years as a Communist.

On occasion, of course, we allowed ourselves an evening of light-hearted sociability. Friends and comrades liked to gather in our house—it was so "civilized" and the talk so "elevated." One of our crowd played the guitar superbly; we would sing and dance and dispute far into the night. A number of the more attractive girls in the community would join us on these occasions. If we had too good a time we all felt a bit guilty and did Comsomol penance by more intensive work, study and political discussion in the days that followed.

In the late fall the boastful slogan of our artel was put to a critical test. One of the mines had been flooded. It was propped with wooden beams for fear of a collapse, but work went on without interruption. It was this mine that we offered to operate, in order to set an example to the regular miners there, mostly Tartars and Chinese.

I was in the pit, working intently though I was almost knee-deep in icy water. Suddenly the whole world seemed to shudder, creak and groan. I heard someone shriek in terror—probably it was my own voice in my ears. Part of our shaft had caved in. When I opened my eyes again I was in a large whitewashed room, in one of a row of hospital beds. A doctor in a white gown was feeling my pulse and a handsome middle-aged nurse stood by with pad and pencil in hand. She smiled in greeting when she saw I had regained consciousness.

"You'll be all right, Comrade Kravchenko, don't worry," she said, and the doctor nodded in confirmation.

They told me I had been in the water inside the caved-in mine for two or three hours. The Chinese worker next to me had been killed. Little hope had been held out for me—if I had not been finished off by the collapsing walls, I must have been drowned in the ice water. But here I was, with bruised legs and a high fever, but otherwise in good shape. The fever later developed into pneumonia.

The two months in the hospital of Algoverovka, curiously, remain with me as one of the pleasantest interludes of my youth. The story of my artel and its climax in the cave-in was embroidered, in the telling, into a saga of socialist heroism in which I was one of the heroes. Important trade-union and Party officials came to my bedside; the boys and girls of my Comsomol unit visited me regularly and never failed to bring little gifts. I was still in the hospital on my eighteenth birthday. Members of the artel and its friends arrived in a body in a heart-warming show of fellowship.

The handsome nurse treated me as if I were her own son. Indeed, in the cosy languor of convalescence I had the sense of having been adopted by all of Russia—its workers, its Comsomols, its officialdom—as the favorite son of a vast and wonderful family.

The doctors forbade me to return to the mines, at least for a year, and no pleading on my part could upset their injunction, conveyed to the administration. I had no wish to go back to an office job and therefore prepared to return to the Tocsin commune and Yekaterinoslav.

In the midst of these preparations came the news that Lenin had died, on January 24, 1924. The shock and the sorrow were real and deep in this corner of the Donetz valley. The reaction had little to do with politics. To the plain people in the collieries—even to the gamblers and brawlers in the barracks, the swaggerers with shoes that creaked, let alone to the Communist Youths—he had become a symbol of hope. We needed to believe that the sufferings of these bloody years were an investment in a bright future. Each of us had a feeling of personal loss.

I marched three miles, with thousands of others, to the memorial meeting outside the mine office, called "Paris Commune." It was a bitterly cold, snowy afternoon; the winds cut like sharp knives. The rostrum in the open air was draped in red and black bunting, though a pall of snow soon covered everything. One after another the orators shouted above the howling wind, declaiming formulas of official sorrow.

"Comrade miners!" a pompous delegate from Kharkov shrieked, "Lenin is dead, but the work of Lenin goes forward. The leader of proletarian revolution . . . leader of the working class of the world . . . best disciple of Marx and Engels. . . ."

The formal words left me depressed. Why don't they talk simply, from the heart rather than from *Pravda* and *Izvestia* editorials? Trudging home through the snowstorm I was pleased to discover that Senya and others had the same let-down feeling. The orators had failed to express how we felt about Lenin, because what we felt had less relation to the dead leader than to our own living hopes.

Several days later we read in the local newspapers Joseph Stalin's oath at Lenin's bier on Red Square in Moscow. It was a short, almost liturgical promise to follow in the path indicated by the dead leader and it moved me as the oratory at our memorial gathering had not done. Stalin was a member of the all-powerful Political Bureau, Secretary General of the Party, and had been an important figure in the new regime from the beginning. Yet this was the first time that I had become acutely aware of his existence. Strange, I thought, that his portrait was not even on our walls.

From that day forward the name Stalin grew so big, so inescapable, that it was difficult to recall a time when it had not overshadowed our lives.

3

I had been in the mining district only over a year. Yet it was hard to wrench myself loose from its life. Had anyone told me, on that melancholy morning of my arrival, that I would come to cherish that bleak place, its crude humanity, its grueling work, I would have thought him mad. Despite myself, I had begun to feel like a mine worker—I saw his faults and frustrations from the inside sympathetically, and no longer from the outside critically.

There was a deep pathos in the desolation, the drabness, the dangers of existence in the collieries that brought them close to me. It is not true that we love only what is cheerful and beautiful. The tragic and the ugly, too, can grip the imagination and senses. We love that which stirs our hearts. We are bound to people and places by the emotions they arouse in us, even by the unpleasant emotions. I have never forgotten my sojourn in the coal fields. I have always felt close to the diggers of coal, the denizens of the black underworld.

In my compartment, on the train out of the Donetz Basin, there were six passengers. In the way of all Russians, we were soon in an argument. Though I was the youngest in the group, I felt responsible for the trend of the talk. As a Comsomol, I must never lose a chance to preach the happy life to come, to explain away immediate troubles.

"You keep on talking about life getting better, comrade," the intellectual complained, "but all the same, there's no bread, no kerosene, no shoes. My wife and I, we freeze and shiver and half the time go without eating. It's not life, it's an ordeal. . . ."

He was a lanky, middle-aged man, with thin features and he wore thick spectacles in gold rims. He had on an unseasonable spring overcoat, a woman's woolen shawl around his neck; white socks showed through cracks in his shoes.

"But excuse me, what do you do?" another passenger asked him.

"I'm a composer," the intellectual replied, aggressively, "I write notes, music."

"Oh, you write notes," the other sneered. "Who needs your notes? Who wants some rosy-sunshine waltz in a time like this? Go to the factory, do some real work and you'll have less reason to complain."

"So everyone must work in factories!" the composer exclaimed with great heat. "Don't the new builders of socialism need music? Shall we all turn into machines without souls?"

"You're right, we don't need any damned notes and melodies. We need to produce more goods."

"Souls have been liquidated," a third man interjected sourly.

"In that case there's no use talking to you," the composer now shouted. "You're vulgar and I won't waste breath on you."

At that point my Comsomol conscience intervened to save the situation.

"Allow me to talk to all of you," I said gravely. "You argue with too much warmth and not enough understanding, if you'll permit me to say so.

It's quite true that we still lack a great many things, but we are exerting ourselves to make up those lacks. In time we will have everything—and that includes music.

"Maybe this citizen is no Tchaikowsky, but if he writes good music, he, too, is helping to build socialism. I've just come from the coal mines and I know how much we need coal. But believe me, we need music no less than coal. We must keep our spirits warm as well as our bodies."

They were obviously impressed with my words. I didn't have to tell them that I was one of the elect; there was authority in my voice. A dozen subjects were thrashed out before the train reached Dniepropetrovsk—as Yekaterinoslav was now called—and on all of them I was the final arbiter. Perhaps those who disagreed with me preferred discretion to valor—why argue with a Comsomol?

I reached the commune toward evening. My dog, Reker, met me down the road and went wild with excitement. I looked through the window of our cottage and saw my mother, reading in the light of a kerosene lamp. She had grown a little older, a little thinner, a little grayer. I opened the door softly and in a disguised voice said:

"Does Citizeness Kravchenko live here?"

"Vitya darling, dear one!" she cried and burst into joyful tears.

In the course of the evening I caught up with the local news. The commune was dead. Only three or four families still worked on the land. A few others still lived here but had industrial jobs in nearby towns. My father and brothers were back in Dniepropetrovsk, earning good wages. By spring they hoped to find an apartment of two or three rooms so that the family could be reunited.

The commune grounds were neglected and gloomy. Everywhere ceilings gaped and doors were off their hinges. Wooden beams had been torn out of walls and roofs and carried off as fuel. The peasants of the neighborhood said: "You see, communists can't work the land. They can only make arrests and collect taxes." A few of them, learning that I had returned, came to call. They treated me with the deference due to a grown-up who had been out in the world and plied me with questions about the intentions of "the new power" in relation to the peasants and their land.

At the Korbino plant, too, I was surrounded by workers and subjected to questions. I improvised the kind of answers which, it seemed to me, a faithful Comsomol ought to provide. A few days later I gave a talk at the factory club on the life of the Donetz miners. Without concealing the difficulties and shortcomings, I must have made existence there sound sufficiently attractive. Four of the younger Korbino workers announced their intention of going to work in the mines and I gave them the names and addresses of the appropriate trade-union officials.

After cutting a huge pile of wood and repairing the barn door—we still had one cow—I left the commune for the city. Father and my younger brother Eugene were working at the Petrovsky-Lenin metallurgical factory, and I was soon working there also, in the mechanical laboratory. Constantine had a job in another plant in Dniepropetrovsk (the Soviet name for Yekaterinoslav still sounded strange). I remained there for about three years, until I was called to join the Red Army in my twenty-first year, in accordance with the military-service regulations.

Our metallurgical plant consisted of a number of structures covering several acres on the fringes of Dniepropetrovsk. It employed some 24,000 men and women and was one of the largest industrial enterprises in southern Russia. Before the revolution its workers had figured in strikes and insurrections, so that an aura of historical importance attached to the plant. Here Comrade Petrovsky, president of the Soviet Republic of Ukraine, had worked as a young man; other important Communist leaders had their proletarian roots here.

The Communist Party organization, including our Comsomol sections, numbered about two thousand, and propaganda activities were always in full blast. Petrovsky, Rakovsky, Kaganovich and other top-shelf leaders often came to address the factory meetings. I became more and more active in Comsomol work, enrolled in technical courses that occupied most of my evenings, and took a prominent part in the political and literary debates staged in the various plant clubs.

The passing years had not reconciled my father to the Communists. He was willing to acknowledge that many of them were honest and earnest, but the reality of revolution still had too little resemblance to the dream of his youth. He never interfered with my Comsomol activities and at bottom was pleased that I was carving a place for myself in the new environment. But he could not refrain from bitter comment, now and then, on the contrast between the ample life of the officials and top engineers and the misery of the plain workers.

"We talk about unity, son," he would say, "and equality. But look how Comrade N . . . lives, with his big apartment and motor cars and good clothes; then look at the barracks where the new workers from the village are packed like sardines. A clean room and decent food in the administration restaurant, but anything is good enough for the workers' restaurant. . . ."

"Give us time, Papa," I would plead. "So many problems to be solved at once."

"I know about the problems. But I also know that the distance between the upper and lower classes is growing bigger, not smaller. Power is a dangerous thing, Vitya."

From the mechanical laboratory I was soon promoted to the pipe-rolling mill and in less than a year I became a control foreman, in a wage category that swelled the family exchequer. With four of us earning money, we lived well despite high prices. NEP, the New Economic Policy, under which private trade was again legal, had brought with it hundreds of new shops, restaurants, cafes. With money you could now obtain almost anything.

My contacts in the factory were increasingly on the upper levels of shop superintendents, management officials, Party and trade-union functionaries. Despite myself and despite my father's injunctions not to lose touch with the masses, I tended to see Soviet life more and more from the vantage point of "the leadership." Neither Gene nor Kotya had de-

veloped much political enthusiasm. They worked well and hard, attended
no more demonstrations and conferences than they absolutely had to,
and like most of the rank-and-file workers accepted the official propaganda
with handfuls of the salt of skepticism.

"You've got the makings of a real Communist bureaucrat, big brother,"
Gene would gibe me, "if only you don't let our dad's romantic humanitarian streak lead you astray."

The spring of 1927 probably was no different in kind than the springs
that preceded and followed. But for me it will be forever touched with
flame, its colors higher, its shadows more tender. Her name was Anna,
she was seventeen, blue-eyed and golden-haired. We met at a party at
the home of a shop superintendent, and from the moment we shook hands
the party and the other guests faded out.

Anna's father was the chief engineer on an important railroad. Although he came from a working-class family, and in his student days had
joined secret socialist circles, he was pretty far from the new Soviet society.
Her mother had carried over the mannerisms and the disdain for "common
folk" of her pre-revolutionary background. Even in the fervor of this my
first authentic love affair, the consciousness that Anna was not "my kind"
was always under the surface of my emotions. She pretended to be interested in my Comsomol activities, but I knew well enough that they
bored her. As for her mother, she made no attempt to disguise contempt
for Communists, for Soviet slogans and for my own humble status as a
factory foreman.

"If your Comsomol were at least an engineer," I overheard her saying
peevishly one night to Anna.

Anna herself was torn between the influence of her Soviet school and
the "bourgeois" surroundings at home. We managed to spend a month
together at a Rest Home belonging to my factory, on the shores of the
Dnieper. She countered my attempts to propagandize her with kisses and
embraces, which I found unanswerable arguments.

But both of us realized, without putting it into words, that marriage
was out of the question—that we were "ideologically" incompatible. Only
one who has lived in a time and a place surcharged with politics can
understand this. After our return to Dniepropetrovsk Anna and I drifted
apart. When I left for military service, late in 1927, we both knew in
our hearts that it was the end. I was to meet her again fourteen years
later—in an air-raid shelter in Moscow.

4

The fifteen hundred miles of frontier where the immense sun-baked
empire of Soviet Central Asia meets Persia, Afghanistan and Kashmir in
India had long been the scene of a struggle with the *basmatchi*. Repeatedly
they were "wiped out" in the military dispatches, only to show up again,
sinister as ever, in new raids and new atrocities.

For years the press had been filled with blood-curdling tales of *basmatchi* terror and venality. They were depicted as ferocious bandits fighting for loot under the prod of Moslem priests; as hirelings of the deposed Emirs and tools of British imperialism. The cruelty of these enemies seemed bottomless. They tortured Soviet prisoners. A favorite procedure was to bury captives up to their necks, leaving them to die by degrees from heat and thirst; to be devoured alive by insects and vultures.

There were some contradictions in this journalistic picture. Banditry and loot could not quite explain the persistence and daring with which small *basmatchi* groups pitted themselves against organized and well-armed Red Army forces. Robbery did not entirely jibe with the religious implications of *mullah* influences and the political implications of the British and Emir involvements.

Later, when I had a more mature grasp of the problem, I realized that the Soviet version was in large part a figment of propaganda. The *basmatchi* were, in effect, local guerilla patriots fighting against what they looked upon as suppression of their national independence by foreign invaders. They were risking their lives to head off what seemed to them a pollution of their ancient ways of life and their faith. In principle, if not in detail, they were not unlike the Indian patriots fighting against the British on the other side of the border.

The Tsarist overlords had exacted tribute from Central Asia but left the local princes and *mullahs* in control. They did not offend the established order. The new overlords, in the name of strange gods called Lenin and Marx, had driven out the Emirs and were ridiculing the Moslem religion; they were importing "infidel" machines and ideas to waken the nomad populations from a millennial slumber; they were corrupting the youth with Western ideas and even prevailing on the women to burn their veils and abandon their harems.

It was against these threats that the *basmatchi,* entrenched in the frontier hills of Persia, in the towns of the Afghan plains and in Turkmenistan proper, were struggling with heroic zeal. There is no doubt, moreover, that at least in these earlier years they had the sympathy of the mass of Central Asians. It was no accident that troops from Russia proper, rather than local contingents, had to be used in the intermittent war.

But the Soviet version had elements of truth in it, too. The accounts of *basmatchi* fury and cruelty, for instance, were not overdrawn. I was to hear many horrifying details from eye witnesses and rare survivors. It was also a fact that loot and profitable contraband trade were mixed up with the political and religious fervor of the guerillas, so that in some cases it was hard to judge where patriotism ended and business began.

In any case, the whole thing was remote from young workmen and peasants in southern Ukraine. We knew of it, if at all, as an exotic blood-and-thunder drama in a far-off and only half-credible world. Now, over-night, we were part of that drama, keyed up by the looming adventure and a little uneasy, under the brash surface, in the thought of its dangers.

The twenty-four of us in the freight car, all fresh recruits from the Dniepropetrovsk district, were being carried to the *basmatchi* country. We sang, told stories and were honestly proud to have been selected for the picked cavalry divisions stationed in the Soviet Republic of the Turkmens. But at night, in the dark car, we recalled harrowing episodes of *basmatchi* barbarism of which we had heard or read.

In a homesick mood we also talked of the girls we had left behind. As it happened, Kostya, a first cousin of my Anna, was also in this batch of recruits. That, and the prospect of a long separation, stirred the embers of my love.

The thrill of a few days in Baku, the city of "black gold," drove everything else from our minds. The great oil center was a curious amalgam of modern industrialism and Eastern ways. It had a motley population of Russians and Mongols, most of them in Western clothes but a good many in the multicolored flowing robes of the Near East, the tight-waisted knee-length jackets and peaked fur hats of the Kazakstan steppes. In the narrow, odoriferous Moslem streets I saw for the first time women in *paranjas*: head-to-toe shrouds, with a wedge of horsehair veil over the face, that turned them into shapeless and ageless walking sacks.

Baku would be forever associated in my mind, too, with my first glimpse of a great sea; the sight of water stretching beyond the curve of the planet is always a memorable one to inland folk. The smell of oil pervaded the whole city and seemed to have soaked into the faces and hands of all inhabitants.

In Baku we were joined by hundreds of recruits from other parts of the country. The small freighter *Kollontai* carried us across the Caspian to the port of Krasnovodsk. Before boarding a freight train for Askhabad, we loitered on the water front. Chardjui melons were stacked on the wharf in yellow mounds, like cannon balls. Big swarthy Turkmens, many of them bearded, all of them stripped to the waist, colored kerchiefs bound turban fashion on their heads, were tossing the melons to comrades on a ship, rhythmically, singing a plangent tune.

Askhabad—later to be called Stalinabad—was Eastern enough to satisfy a youthful appetite for the picturesque. Unpaved narrow streets wound between blank windowless walls; flowed into noisy, tangled squares, some of them roofed over. The bazaars echoed to the hammering of cobblers, coppersmiths, and other artisans working cross-legged in the open air. The shapeless moving pillars of Moslem womanhood were everywhere. Now and then one of them flipped open an edge of her horsehair veil in a coquettish gesture to the gawking Russians.

Our train had been met with music and a demonstration. Workers from the local cotton mills stood by expressionless as officials made grandiloquent speeches hailing the brave comrades come to guard the frontiers against the *basmatchi* rascals. At the time I had no reason to doubt their words, but later I wondered why frontier guards could not be recruited from their own people; still later I understood that the Red Army, for all the pretensions of comradeship, was an army of occupation in an alien territory.

From Askhabad we drove in trucks to the huge camp on the Persian border which was to be my home for the next seven or eight months. We were housed in the same long bleak barracks where the Tsar's soldiers had been stationed before us. The country we had come through was for the most part desert—yellow arid stretches alternating with sagebrush—but the immediate frontier region was more varied in landscape, with lots of lush green. Here we were in the foothills of the mountain chain guarding the northern rim of Persia.

Our military training began with a steam bath, the disinfection of all our clothes, a haircut that left our scalps as smooth as our faces, and a political lecture. As between *basmatchi* and Red soldiers, we were given to understand, it was kill or be killed. We would be called on to patrol dangerous stretches, alone or in pairs, day and night and had need for alertness, good horsemanship and good marksmanship. Even the least ambitious among us trained with sufficient energy in the following weeks.

Almost from the start I joined the editorial staff of the camp paper, *Red Frontier Guard*. We Comsomols were in a minority among the troops and took our responsibility very seriously. There was a large measure of democracy in the military set-up, combined with strict discipline. We did not hesitate to criticize conditions and officers, often by name, in the camp paper.

There was a Commander Galushka whose gruff ways did not go too well with the rank and file. Precisely because I wanted to be free to criticize him in my capacity as editor, I obeyed him without a murmur. I wished to make it clear that I obeyed him as an officer even though I felt it necessary to dress him down in print.

For a while he pretended to disregard little articles in which I took him to task for shouting at soldiers, using obscene language and acting the tyrant. But soon he capitulated.

"Comrade Kravchenko, I should like to talk to you," he said one day.

As we walked from the barracks to the stables, he wanted to know why in hell I was persecuting him. Was it right for a Comsomol to undermine the authority of a Red Commander?

"Comrade Galushka," I explained, in the self-importance of my twenty-two years, "my purpose is to increase your authority rather than to diminish it. If you continue to treat your men like so much dirt, they will despise you and will obey only sullenly. If you treat them like human beings and Soviet comrades, they will obey you gladly and with a good spirit. In time of action that may make the difference between success and failure in the field."

We entered into an agreement—the officer and the private. He promised to mend his manners and I promised to lay off him in the *Red Frontier Guard*. The strange part of the story is that Commander Galushka not only kept his word but to his own surprise soon became one of the most popular officers in the outfit. When Galushka led, his men were eager to follow. On risky expeditions we were impressed with his personal courage under fire.

After training was completed we were sent on night hunts for smugglers and *basmatchi*. There was never any dearth of "hot tips" from paid informers on both sides of the frontiers. In Persian and Afghan cafes men picked up scraps of information about goods to be received or delivered, raids on Soviet villages being planned. Through intermediaries the scraps reached the Red Army command.

Several times the expeditions, after much searching, failed to make contact with the quarry. Sometimes a few shots were exchanged. But at least once in my own experience, a curious battle was fought in which both sides suffered casualties—curious because it was fought in a pitch-black, rainy night against an unseen foe.

A bearded Turkmen in a towering black fur hat led our forces that night to the area where, according to his information, a caravan of smugglers could be intercepted. For nearly an hour we rode slowly through the chilly rain, pausing now and then to pick up sounds. Finally the trail was found. Red rockets were sent up to illumine the landscape briefly and Tarasov, head of the G.P.U. detachment in command of this expedition, ordered us to deploy and attack.

I had been shooting blindly at noises for some time when suddenly, so close to me that I could see his eyes in the dark, I was almost on top of a Turkmen. He was aiming his rifle at me but I succeeded in shooting first. He fell, but apparently was only wounded, for he made another attempt to shoot. I jumped from my horse and wrenched the rifle from his hands.

"Stand up!" I ordered.

Before me stood an old man, with a broad beard, his hands raised over his head. Blood trickled down one cheek. He was saying something in his native tongue and weeping; no doubt he was pleading for his life. I removed his dagger from its scabbard and turned the man over to an officer.

Before the sun rose, the engagement was ended. No doubt many of the smugglers escaped. But a large number of them, along with a number of heavily loaded camels, were brought into camp. And before that sun set again every one of the captured Turkmens had been shot by a firing squad on orders of the commanders.

Soon thereafter I was assigned to an outpost some miles away, along with Kostya and others. The men stationed there were overjoyed at our arrival, which meant that they would be relieved. One of them was a countryman from Kiev. His only regret was having to leave his horse, a handsome, high-spirited animal whom he called Lord Curzon, for reasons that were never quite clear to me. Having exacted solemn promises that I would be kind to Lord Curzon, he turned him over to me. "Treat him right, and Curzon will be a brother to you," he assured me. "He has more sense than most people."

Our post was near the outlet from a narrow pass through the hills. I had reason in the following weeks to be grateful to my countryman for making me heir to Lord Curzon. The horse was sensitive not only to my slightest touch but, it seemed, to my very thoughts. It was comforting to feel him under me when I was on guard duty alone at night far from my comrades. Every noise, the fall of a pebble, a rustling sound in the trees, the howl of a hungry jackal, put both Curzon and his rider on the alert.

Any soldier who captured a smuggler was entitled to one-third of the value of contraband goods seized. No such good fortune came my way, but many a man in the frontier patrols returned to his home village, on completion of his service, a rich man, as such things were reckoned in the Soviet land.

I shall never forget the thin, dark Jewish youngster Zyama. By what trick of bureaucratic logic Zyama was put into the cavalry and sent to the Persian border neither he nor anyone else knew. He began his cavalry career with only one handicap—a deadly fear of horses. Some of the men made sport of the poor fellow, but most of us were sorry for him. We tried to teach him how to mount a horse, how to hold the reins; sometimes we thought he would faint or die of sheer terror. But amazingly, having overcome his fear, Zyama in short order became a splendid horseman with a taste for daredevil stunts. He followed the scent of contraband night after night and once, with a sure instinct, he managed to capture a heavily laden smuggler, thus winning a neat fortune in prizes.

Lord Curzon, whose sure-footedness had saved me many times, was also responsible for the wind-up of my military career. I was on patrol late that night with another soldier in a wooded area far from the post. In the distance we heard noises. I shouted an order to the unseen to halt and the two of us dashed forward. Curzon stumbled and pitched me forward over his head.

That's all I knew until afterwards. My companion, some distance away, called to me but got no answer. He found my horse, but no trace of me. After a fruitless search he returned to camp. A few hours later a searching party found me in a puddle of water, terribly bruised and unconscious.

For many weeks I lay in a military hospital near Askhabad, racked with pain. Although I felt as if no single bone in my body was whole or in its proper place, it developed that my injuries were all external. The kindness of two elderly nurses endeared them to me and to all the other patients. It was no secret that they were aristocrats exiled from Petrograd; one of them, Lydia Pavlovna, admitted to me that she had been born a princess.

When I was well enough to travel, I was sent to Kiev and remained in a hospital there for about a month; after two additional months in a Kiev sanitarium, I was demobilized, and returned to my job as foreman in the Petrovsky-Lenin factory at Dniepropetrovsk. This was in the summer of 1928, and I was going on twenty-three.

CHAPTER V

BREAK WITH THE PAST

THE MINOR actors in a great historical drama rarely are conscious of its greatness. They are too deep inside the action to see its large contours. I was among these actors at the beginning of 1929—one of the young enthusiasts, thrilled by the lofty ideas and plans of this period. It was a time when my country began to move into a new and in some ways more profound revolution; a time when Stalin and his close associates were engaged in a sharp struggle with opponents in the Politburo and to some extent in the whole Party. They were intent upon rooting out remnants of capitalist economy and capitalist mentality, in order to lead Russia into industrialization and into collectivization of farming.

It became, therefore, a period when everything wavering, hesitant, non-conformist that still clung to the revolution began to be sloughed off. The Party Line—that is to say, duty towards a specific set of objectives—became more important than any personal interests. The modern machine, as symbol and substance of industrialization, loomed large in our lives, intensifying every day of existence. The machine became a jealous god to be appeased. It acquired an almost mystic power in the everyday life of the country. The distress of "humanitarians" seemed merely a leftover from a strange past.

Millions of people—some voluntarily, some by force—were drawn into the process, wrenched from their accustomed existence and driven along new paths. They were for the most part underfed, insufficiently clothed, without the solace of illusions. I knew the individual events of this process, of course; the bad as well as the good. But I looked on them with the eyes of a twenty-three-year-old youngster, brought up politically by the Comsomol and the Red Army, who believed that a better future was on its way for Russia. I was among the more alert and socially conscious of the workers in our plant, thrilled by the creative drive of my everyday tasks.

There were many defects, extensive suffering. But there was also the lift of terrific excitement, and inflamed hopes. There was the deep hope in the future of the country, so that it was no accident that I chose precisely this period to join the Party. I belonged to the minority that was stirred by the ideas behind the great effort. We were caught up in a fervor of work at times touched with delirium. Others might suffer the new revolution in sullen discontent, just as they had suffered the great famine. They might accept it as a sort of natural calamity. But to people like myself, possessed by the idea and the faith, today's pain seemed only a necessary payment for the glorious future awaiting the country and its people. Industrialization at any cost, to lift the nation out of backwardness, seemed to us the noblest conceivable aim.

That is why I must resist the temptation to judge the events of those years in the light of my feelings today. My life was brimful of work, strain and privation; the nagging of the "outmoded liberals," who only criticized while themselves remaining outside the effort, seemed to me merely annoying.

I was deeply absorbed in my work as technical foreman in the rolling mills, in new friendships among officials and influential Communists, in my pressing duties as one of the editors of the factory paper. I had a great relish for work. It never occurred to me that after an intense day in the hot, noisy workshop or laboratory I might be too tired for meetings, technical courses, social-work projects, writing chores. Fatigue seemed a bourgeois prejudice.

The press and radio were shrill with the slogans of the new period. *Overtake and Outdistance the Capitalist Countries! Forward to Industrialization of Our Country! Liquidation of the Kulaks as a Class!* It was like living permanently in a boiler factory; you ate and slept and worked amidst the prodigious thunder of battle. Workers' meetings, study and more study, scolding speeches against foreign and internal enemies, inundated our lives.

To question decisions announced in lightning words from the heavens of the Kremlin seemed about as reasonable as arguing with an earthquake. We accepted them often at their face value. Of course, they were explained and justified to us in the course of our continuous political education. What we were told did not necessarily coincide with what was in the minds of the Kremlin leaders—but that is belated wisdom.

The shadows of the G.P.U., the state political police, did not touch me; besides, it seemed to me quite natural that at such a critical, strained moment in the life of the country everyone should be carefully checked and controlled. Only old men with long memories, like my father, were offended, but their squeamishness seemed as out of place as pacifism on a battlefield.

Early in 1929 one of the foremost Old Bolsheviks, Christian Rakovsky, came to our factory and addressed a mass meeting. It was almost the last time that an enemy of Stalin would be permitted to talk to the people. A few days later my father brought up this meeting in conversation. He had been morose—now I understood why.

"Rakovsky criticized the Party leadership," he said. "I'm not sure that I agreed with him or that many of the workers did. But we gathered that there was a struggle for authority and that Stalin was winning. Some in the audience seemed sympathetic to Rakovsky; they asked questions and applauded. Then Rakovsky left. The very next morning, son, the workers who had shown a friendly attitude towards him were summoned by the G.P.U. . . ."

Some weeks later I ran into Kozlov, Secretary of the *Raikom* (Regional Committee) of the Party. He greeted me warmly. I was about to apply formally for admission to the Party, as he knew, and he regarded me as a valuable recruit. I had become increasingly active in factory and city affairs. My name and portrait were appearing more frequently in the industrial, trade-union and local city publications.

"Ekh, Comrade Kravchenko, you sure have an eccentric father," Kozlov laughed.

"What's happened?" I asked, a little worried.

"Nothing much. A few of us from the *Raikom* went into the mechanical department. There are still some rotten echoes of Rakovsky's visit and we wanted to talk to a few of the workers. Just to get the feel of the situation. Well, we questioned one here, one there, and finally came to your old man.

" 'How are things?' I asked him in the kindliest way. What do you suppose he answered? He looked me up and down and said, 'Don't interfere with my work. This is a factory, not a club. If you want to know what the workers think, ask your G.P.U. They should know.'

"What a father you have, Victor Andreyevich! Senya Volgin was with me; you know, from the Comsomol Committee. So he also made a try at winning over your father. 'You're an old and respected proletarian, Citizen Kravchenko,' he says. 'You fought against the Tsar. We know all that. That's why we want your opinion.' Then your old man lost his temper. 'Listen, youngster,' he says, 'politically you're a spring chicken. There's nothing *serious* I could possibly discuss with *you*.' "

Then Kozlov magnanimously brushed the whole episode aside—just the vagaries of a soured and aging man out of tune with the brave new world—and said:

"Well, when are you making your application for membership?"

"Soon, I think," I replied.

"Good! I will be at the meeting to give you a hand. We need you, Kravchenko. We've got a lot of tough work ahead. We can't count on the old generation, not even the best of them."

From time to time leading Communists had thus been urging me to enter the Party. I was working with them anyhow, they pointed out; I was supporting their great fight for a new life; why should I stand aside organizationally? I agreed with them. In my heart, in my hopes, I was already committed to their side. I would enter the Party honestly, without misgivings, without doubts. I would be one of the unsentimental army of builders of a new industrialized world and ultimately a new socialist world!

2

Within the limits of the Party Line, we enjoyed considerable freedom of speech in the factory paper. Only two of us on the editorial board, a certain Bleskov and myself, were not yet Party members. The paper was issued at first weekly, later daily. Its circulation was around 35,000. It was read, of course, by practically everyone employed in the Petrovsky-Lenin plant. Even more important, it was read by economic and Party officials in our whole province and even in Moscow.

The contents of the paper, it is true, passed a censorship. Nothing that might throw a shadow of doubt on industrialization, on the policy of the Party, could see type. No one would ever think of writing such things, unless he were out of his mind. Attacks on the factory administration, trade-union functionaries and Party officials, exposés of specific faults in production or management, were allowed and this created the illusion that the paper expressed public opinion.

Samokritika, self-criticism, was one of the important slogans of the time. Everyone was stimulated to "tell all" about defects, errors, methods for improving things—in the general press, in factory and farm papers, on the bulletin-board sheets known as wallpapers. Self-criticism was a device to raise the quality of work, but sometimes it was also a whip brandished by big bureaucrats over the heads of little bureaucrats.

Factories at that time were still administered by a "triangle" consisting of representatives of the management, the Party and the trade union. Among this multitude of officials, who watched each other's activities, self-criticism sometimes became an underhanded method of struggle for place and for power.

I threw myself into the job of self-criticism with a crusading zeal that alarmed some of the leaders in our factory. I struck out honestly and vigorously at shortcomings, regardless whom it hurt. Afterwards I began to understand why some important people in the plant suddenly wished to befriend me. No doubt they considered it good insurance to win over a young man who had a sharp pen which he was sticking into complacent posteriors.

My articles appeared not only in the factory paper but in Kharkov and Dniepropetrovsk publications for which I acted as correspondent in the great plant. The city organs of the Party commented on my work and held me up as an example of "activist youth."

What did I write about? Unconscionable waste and spoilage of goods. Mechanics who showed no proper respect for their tools and machines. The high cost of unit production in our plant, as compared to similar plants in Sweden or America. The unpardonable attitude of Comrade So-and-So towards the workers. Bad quality in the current output. How a certain process could be "rationalized" to save thousands of man-hours.

More disturbing to the even tenor of factory life, however, were my broadsides against the insufferable housing conditions of those of the workers who lived in barracks. Wages were ostensibly higher, I pointed out, but they did not keep pace with the new prices of products in the factory dining rooms and stores. And when would those new apartments about which there was so much talk be finished? Why were certain officials living in excellent conditions while the elementary needs of so many factory hands were being neglected?

I won myself a good many powerful enemies in these journalistic outbursts. Their hatreds in some instances pursued me for years. But I also made close friends. In particular I found strong support for my repeated complaints that there were too many officials in the factory in proportion to its output. In some technical journals I had dug up statistics to show that Swedish metallurgical plants had only one administrative official where we had two or three. They stepped over each other, I wrote, slowing up work and raising costs of production.

The period of self-criticism was the last expression of power from below in the Soviet Union. It was a species of public opinion. It succeeded in curbing the local shifts of officialdom, even if it had no influence on over-all policies and decisions at the center of authority in Moscow.

For reasons that I could scarcely explain to myself—reasons that had their roots in the underground of my mind, where memories of childhood ideals lived a life of their own—I felt embarrassed when I announced to my father that I intended to join the Party.

"I knew you would join up sooner or later," he said. "I've watched you becoming more and more involved in political activities. You write, you study politics. But I won't say that I'm overjoyed. You know your-self how much injustice there is around us—how the distance between the rulers and the masses is growing. . . . I'd like to know how you look on things, what's in your mind."

"I'm pleased you ask, papa. I want to speak frankly. I'm grateful to you and I owe you a lot. I respect your honesty and honor your revolutionary past. But please try to understand me. I am almost twenty-four. I've grown up and worked with modern people in an environment devoted to the new ideas and to vast plans for the future of our country. I did not come to the Party in one jump. My faith in it has been built slowly, brick by brick. In time I came to *feel* like a Party man.

"I know that there are plenty of shortcomings, careerism, swinishness and hardship in practical everyday life. I don't like those things any more than you do. But I look on them as phases which will pass. The job of turning a primitive country into a modern industrialized socialist state is gigantic. It can't be done without mistakes and even injustices. But I don't want to stand aside and criticize. I want to work honestly inside the Party, fighting against evil and sustaining what is good.

"I thought long before I took the step. Whether the Party is on the right road, only experience and time can show. But I believe in its pur-poses and want to give all I have to make them come true. After all, you're not against industrialization. You're not against displacing the worn-out horses by tractors. You're not against letting the peasants voluntarily join collectivized farms."

He looked at me severely, not angrily.

"Of course I'm not against these things, Vitya. And I know how you feel. In fact, I recognize myself in you. That was how I behaved in my day. I followed my conscience, sparing neither myself, my wife, nor my children. Better some faith than none. You remember Luk in Gorki's *Lower Depths*: 'If you believe, there's a God; if you don't there isn't.' You have found a faith. I wish you luck and success—from the bottom of my heart.

"But remain close to the people, Vitya. Judge your usefulness not by the posts you will get but by how these people will live, whether they will be better off, happier *and freer*. If you really come close to them,

understand them, help them, I shall be forever grateful to you. Don't live
by slogans—judge politicians by their actions, not their fine words. They
are great masters of theory in the Kremlin. Let's see how it will work
out in practice. May you never have cause to lose your faith!"

He paused, then continued.

"Who knows," he conceded, "maybe you, our children, will succeed
in bringing true freedom and a better life for the masses."

"I'm sure we shall, papa."

The conversation remained fresh in my memory in the years that
followed, as I labored in the Party and for the Party. It was as if my
father were watching and judging—looking at the facts and deeds behind
the slogans.

In the middle of 1929 I was admitted to the Party. It seemed to me
the greatest event in my life. It made me one of the *élite* of the new
Russia. I was no longer an individual with a free choice of friends, interests, views. I was dedicated forever to an idea and a cause. I was a
soldier in a highly disciplined army in which obedience to the center was
the first and almost sole virtue. To meet the wrong people, to listen to
the wrong words, thereafter would be inadmissible.

One day, after I had joined the Party, the manager of my shop and
I were summoned to the factory director's office. The quality of our
materials being supplied to the Druzhkovsky plant in the Donbass was
deteriorating, he told us. We must go there immediately, investigate
exactly what was wrong with our materials for their purposes, and report
back to him.

After a week's trip, I returned with a full report. I thought I had
put my finger on our difficulties and made a series of suggestions for
eliminating them. The director was pleased. He would recommend that I
be given a substantial cash reward for my good service. Was that satisfactory?

"I don't need money," I said. "But I do need an apartment. One
of my brothers and my father work in this plant, as you know. But for
several years we have been without a real family life because of the housing trouble. At the moment we are not even living together, and my mother
has to remain in the country."

"I'll see what can be done," the director promised. A few days later
the Kravchenkos were living together in a comfortable and quite modern
apartment belonging to the factory. My mother was able at last to abandon our house on the former Tocsin commune.

3

The socalled Shakhty affair, in 1928, filled the press at home and was
even reported in the press abroad. A group of leading engineers in the
coal industry were put on trial in Moscow, in the presence of foreign and
Soviet correspondents, with newsreel cameras grinding and radio micro-
phones carrying the proceedings to the whole country.

"Here," the Kremlin was saying in effect to the population, "is why we have so many serious shortcomings. Agents of capitalism, remnants of the old regime, are deliberately causing accidents, undermining output."

It was the first of the melodramatic exhibition trials, later to become standard, in which men calmly confessed to crimes against the State. In the Shakhty trial some of the accused still denied the charges and fought for their lives. Such eccentricity would be avoided in future trials.

Two years later there was another, much bigger and more melodramatic trial against engineers. It was the demonstration trial of the alleged leaders of an alleged Industrial Party dedicated to overthrowing the Soviets, restoring capitalism and taking all power into their own hands. Though the picture was full of absurdities, I believed it, as the majority of the country did. At that time Party men of the new generation accepted uncritically the assumption that many of the engineers and technicians educated before the revolution would as a matter of course be partisans of the old order—potentially if not actually enemies of the industrialization effort.

To replace the engineering forces inherited from the past, it was obviously necessary to create and train a new crop, without memory of that past, thoroughly loyal to the Soviet ideas and the plans of the Party. They had to be drawn chiefly from the young workers and employes as well as responsible workers belonging to the Party, or at least close to it in their thinking. Therefore a decision was reached in high places for the creation of Party and trade-union "thousands" to study in old and new universities and technical institutes. It was a plan that originated in the all-powerful Politburo itself.

In 1930 a group of representing the Central Control Commission of the Party arrived to investigate the activities and personnel at our plant. I was summoned to the director's office. Behind the vast mahogany desk and its forest of telephones, in the director's chair, now sat a stranger whom I recognized from pictures as Arkady Rosengoltz, one of the most important Moscow leaders and a prominent member of the Central Committee.

"How do you do, Comrade Kravchenko," he smiled and shook hands. "I called you because I have been informed of your work. You are interested in rationalization of production. That's fine. You speak out boldly in our press. That is also to the good. Is there anything you need?"

"No, thank you, Comrade Rosengoltz."

"Well, tell me about yourself."

I gave him a brief sketch of my life. My childhood in a revolutionary family. The work on the commune. The period in the coal mines and how I joined the Comsomols. My service in the Red Army. My job in this plant and how I entered the Party. How many times I would have to tell that story! This unreeling of one's private biography is almost a ritual in Soviet society, to be performed verbally and in questonnaires on the slightest provocation.

Rosengoltz listened, studying me carefully. Then apparently he reached a decision.

"You're a young man, not yet twenty-five," he said. "The Party needs industrial engineers. Would you like to study? We'll send you to a technical institute for a few years. You will repay the Party by giving it your best efforts. The Party needs its own technical intelligentsia, to carry on the task of industrialization in loyal conformity with its policy."

"Thank you, I'd be happy to do all I can for our country."

The following day Sergo Ordzhonikidze himself came to the plant. Unexpectedly he strode into our department, followed by a retinue of plant and Regional officials. Only the presence of Stalin himself could have excited me more. Ordzhonikidze, intimate of Stalin, Commissar of Workers and Peasants Inspection, head of the Central Control Commission of the Party. The first thing I thought was: "Just like the photograph on the wall of our artel in the Donetz Basin!"

He was wearing the same tall gray caracul hat, the same blue tunic with its gray collar. His baggy trousers were tucked into soft knee-high boots. His eagle nose curved even more grandly than in the picture, the mustaches swept from under the cliff even more expansively. I felt as if I had known him all my life. Something about his homeliness and his smile abolished the distance that separates a god descended from the Kremlin Olympus from mere humans below.

The director introduced me.

"Yes, I've heard about you," Ordzhonikidze boomed, extending his hand. "How's work going here?"

"Good," I said, then added, "though it could be better."

"Interesting! And what can we do to make it better?"

"That's hard to say in a few words," I replied.

"Don't be ashamed, talk out," Ordzhonikidze laughed.

"Well, it's like this, Comrade Commissar," I said. "There's too much apparatus, too many people checking on each other. I've looked into the record of pre-revolutionary years in this very plant and I find that our administrative staff have gone up almost 35 per cent. That seems to me wrong. People are in each other's way. Everybody is responsible for results, which means that nobody is responsible. We work badly and spend too much. Why is it that capitalists made profits in this plant, and we show only losses? After all, the workers work as well as in the past, so the trouble must be in ourselves."

Even in the heat of my outburst I noticed that the factory officials were becoming more and more uneasy. The director coughed. The Party and trade-union representatives fidgeted. Work ceased in the department and from somewhere a voice exclaimed:

"Right, Victor Andreyevich, right!"

"Yes," I went on, carried away by my own words, "often there's more noise than results. Discipline is weak because so many people are enforcing it. What we need, Comrade Ordzhonikidze, is a single direction and a single responsibility, without interference from so many places."

"Interesting!" he said again. "And on the whole you're right. The *Vozhd* (Leader) too is thinking along these lines. You must go and study, Comrade Kravchenko."

He shook hands and walked off, followed by the half-frightened retinue. But after a few steps he turned back to me and said:

"If you're ever in trouble or need something urgently, write me! I'll help!"

In difficult years to come I would accept that invitation. Already I felt as if Ordzhonikidze had "adopted" me. I had a patron in the seats of the almighty. Until he died early in 1937 I had a feeling of sanctuary. In my worst moments, the knowledge that I could turn to Stalin's fellow-Georgian of the hawk face for help gave me a boldness that others could not muster.

My "lecture" to an exalted friend of Stalin was the talk of the factory for weeks. Workers slapped me on the back, pleased by my candor.

But the next day I was called to the Party Committee office. The Party Secretary, Constantine Okorokov, was there, as well as the director, Comrade Ivanchenko.

"What's come over you, Kravchenko?" the Secretary shouted as I entered. "Have you gone crazy? Do you know that Sergo kicked up a terrible scandal and almost threw inkwells at us? He was so mild and happy until you got him started. Then he bawled us out as lazy and inefficient bastards."

I held my ground. I had only spoken the truth, I said. Hadn't Lenin himself declared that the industrial process calls for a single and responsible leadership? With Lenin and Ordzhonikidze on my side, even the Party Secretary was powerless in his fury. Ivanchenko, who in his heart agreed with me and was annoyed by the prying and interference of the Party and trade-union officials, could not repress a smile of satisfaction.

Besides, I was only finishing up some work in my shop, after which I would be once more a student. I suspected that a few of the plant administration people were pleased to see me go.

My parents and brothers were joyful at the turn of events. Mother, in particular, had never reconciled herself to my remaining a foreman like her husband. In her heart she worried because the revolution had interrupted my education. Now, though belatedly, I was to prepare myself for a career as engineer and she was thrilled by the idea. Even my father seemed thoroughly happy. He listened with approval to my description of Comrade Ordzhonikidze.

"My son will be an engineer," I heard him say to cronies one evening around the family samovar. There was pride in his tone.

I devoted several months to cramming for the entrance examination. Special pre-Institute courses were made available to the fortunate young men selected for the "thousands," those chosen to be the new Soviet intelligentsia. Then, early in 1931, I matriculated in the Technological Institute in Kharkov.

CHAPTER VI

A STUDENT IN KHARKOV

HERE I WAS, a student again at the age of twenty-five, and a ward of the state. A monthly stipend, paid out of the Petrovsky-Lenin plant budget, gave me enough to sustain life, with a margin for clothes and amusement. But *Golod* and *kholod,* hunger and cold, the twins with whom I had become so familiar in the civil war period, were again my companions. They were no longer as ruthless and insistent as in the past; now and then they gave me a bright respite; yet they were always gnawing and nagging, like a chronic toothache.

The Technological Institute in Kharkov was housed in massive old structures set on the edge of a fine park on Kaplunovsky Street. In normal times, no doubt, it had been a typical university campus. I could readily imagine young men in trim uniforms, drawn mostly from well-to-do families, mixing work with the frivolities of student life; the spirit of youth must have pulsed within the atmosphere of study. But now it was noisy, overcrowded, as intense as a great foundry in full blast. The urgency, the slogans, the bustle of the Five Year Plan were as much in evidence here as on a construction job.

Probably never before or since has such a bizarre assortment of men and women, boys and girls, been herded into a single educational institution. Most of the students were over twenty-three and a good many were in their thirties. Men with background and culture shared classes with young workers to whom study was a sort of miracle and also a species of torture. From factories, blast furnaces, mines and offices, from state farms and army camps we had been mobilized for this mass production of a brand-new technical intelligentsia. Along with local students who lived with their families, there were solemn-faced Central Asians who had never before seen a western city. There were war veterans, former partisans— guerilla fighters—from Siberia, as well as Communist functionaries wise in the ways of the new politics.

Probably, too, no more serious-minded body of students ever tackled a tough curriculum. We went about it like men hacking a path through dangerous jungles, like men conquering a hostile army. The process had nothing in common with the scholarly repose of ordinary schools in ordinary times.

Along with thousands of other students from various Kharkov institutes, I lived in the vast beehive of a dormitory on Pushkin Avenue called *Gigant,* Giant. Here we were packed four, five or more in a room, numb with cold in winter and grilled by the summer heat.

Often, in that winter of 1930-31, the Gigant was so cold that the water in our washbasin was frozen. We picked up stray pieces of wood, fence slats, broken furniture, old newspapers to feed the tiny iron stove in our room, with its crazy, many-jointed chimney stuck out of a window. Thus we lived, studied, argued and dreamed of our country's industrialized future while fighting frost and hunger here and now.

The women lived in their own wing, although we mixed freely in the social halls and dining rooms and had no inhibitions about studying together in one another's rooms. Naturally, many liaisons were formed among the students. Of puritanism there was no trace in the Gigant. But in general moral standards were remarkably high. The temper of the students was too grim, their everyday hardships were too big, their mutual respect too real, for light-hearted affairs.

I shared a room with four others—Alexei Karnaukhov, George Vigura, Vanya Avdashchenko and Pavel Pakholkin—all of us belonging to the mobilized "thousands," all of us Party people.

Alexei, in fact, was a man of some consequence, being a member of the Central Committee of the Comsomol organization. Compactly built, with straw-blond hair and earnest brown eyes, he was as pleasant in character as in looks. He was honest, outspoken and of a critical mind rare among Communist officials. He neither put on airs because of his position nor avoided frank discussion of school and public affairs.

Alexei and I became close friends instantly. We loved our Party. We believed in it. And for that very reason we did not hesitate to talk about it candidly. Why was there such a horrible chasm between slogans and accomplishments, between official claims and obvious facts? This problem we explored in tender concern for the Party, not in anger. Together we found it easier to rationalize the unfolding terror, to discover noble motives for seemingly ignoble behavior, and in general to fortify our common faith in a distressing period.

George Vigura was a Communist of quite different mold. To him the very idea of discussing Party instructions and decisions seemed blasphemous. What was there to discuss? Wasn't everything perfectly clear? George had no opinions—only quotations from Stalin, *Izvestia, Pravda* and other authority. Subjects on which there was no formal pronouncement simply didn't exist for him. He was quite sure that Alexei and I, with all that infidel probing and worrying and loose talk, would end badly.

Pakholkin, as rigidly faithful to the Party as George, was a colorless, plodding, long-suffering fellow. He was deferential to all his room-mates and gave me the uneasy feeling that he was grateful for being allowed to live. He stood equally in awe of Vigura's unquestioning Party piety and my own daring questions. I'm afraid that we took advantage of poor Pakholkin, loading more chores on his meek shoulders than rightly belonged there.

But the real problem child of our room was Vanya Avdashchenko. Vanya was the oldest of us, probably over thirty. He was big, lusty, good-natured and incredibly lazy. A partisan fighter in the civil war years, he lived in the fading glories of those exploits. They exempted him, he seemed to believe, from the need for serious exertion forever after.

He was not stupid, our Vanya, and might have absorbed his lessons if he could have brought himself to make the effort. We lectured him on the subject and exacted solemn promises that he would apply himself to the job for which he had been drawn into the "thousands." Our efforts came to nothing. Stretched out on his cot, he would pretend to be memorizing chemical formulas when, in fact, he was reading a cheap novel.

His deficiencies as a student, however, were more than balanced by Vanya's talent for political contacts. He knew everybody and everybody knew him. As a matter of course he was put on important committees where, just as naturally, he did exactly nothing, and therefore made no tangible mistakes. He had friends in the Gigant kitchens, in the best cooperative groceries and other places where extra rations might be rustled. We shared the dividends of his political genius even while chiding him for his laziness.

Before the term was over, Vanya was expelled from the Institute. However, I was not at all astonished to learn, when I ran into him in Moscow many years later, that he had become the head of an important trust. In his climb up the bureaucratic ladder our Vanya was not impeded by excess baggage of knowledge, understanding or sensibility.

Political education rated even higher in our curriculum than technical subjects. What the government was after was not simply engineers but Soviet-minded engineers. Our Leninism Faculty, with the Red Professor Fillipov at its head, made us toe the mark. Those who could not digest Marx's *Das Kapital,* the dialectics of Engels, the works of Lenin and above all, the dissertations of Stalin, were thrown out of the Institute more quickly than those who merely had trouble with calculus or blueprints.

We five room-mates were in the Airplane Construction Institute, though only Vigura had any practical experience in building planes. There was a symbolic quality to the very subject of aviation, as the most modern item in Russia's scheme for modernization, that did our hearts good.

In the morning we did calisthenics in our narrow room to take the edge off the frost. Then we would eat in the Gigant dining room. The standard breakfast was a small bowl of porridge, a piece of black bread and tea without sugar or lemon. Hiking to the Institute, chilled to the bone and still hungry, however, we were by no means a sorrowful lot. We were full of talk and plans—about the Institute, the Gigant, the Party and ourselves.

Despite the differences in our views, and clashes of personality, a certain group loyalty did develop among us. When any one of the five had an important date with a girl, the others contributed ties, a clean blouse, that good pair of pants, even a few rubles to equip him for the occasion.

The Institute, like every other Soviet institution, had its own newspaper. I was soon serving as an assistant editor. Grumbling against the Gigant administration was widespread and found many echoes in our columns. The short rations, the bad cooking, the lack of laundering facilities, the dirt and disorganization came in for plenty of criticism.

It all came to a head in a student mass meeting, organized by our Party and Comsomol cells. There were many speeches and suggestions. By prearrangement with the steering committee, I proposed that the students themselves assume some of the responsibilities of administration. Alexei thereupon suggested that I be designated, there and then, to take the job in hand. At this point an attractive girl whom I had not before noticed asked for the floor.

"I arise to support the election of Comrade Kravchenko," she said. "I have known him for eight years and I can testify that he is a devoted comrade."

She was a decidedly pretty girl, on the plump side, neatly dressed, and she spoke out boldly, with an air of self-reliance. Through the rest of the proceedings I wondered who she was and how she knew me. I was chosen head of the "Gigant commune." After the meeting I overtook the girl in the lobby.

"How are you, Victor Andreyevich?" she laughed, a bit mischievously. "I'm sure you don't remember me, but it's enough that I remember you."

"Well, take me into the secret," I countered.

"I'm Pasha. Does that help?"

"Pasha? No, I'm afraid not."

"Well, here's one more clue: I pushed a coal wagon in the mine pits at Algoverovka. . . ."

And suddenly I remembered. "My God! Can this be the same Pasha!" I exclaimed. We both laughed and I hugged her in real joy.

"Alyosha!" I shouted as Alexei came to join us. "Meet Pasha. Last time I saw her she was black as coal, in peasant rags. . . .

"And illiterate," she helped me.

"Yes, and look at her now! A student and as cultured as you please, besides those good looks hidden under the coal dust," I continued. "Now that's a triumph for the revolution!"

And in fact the metamorphosis was extraordinary. In this girl it was almost impossible to detect a trace of the backward, sullen young peasant, with rags around her feet and long braids down her back, whom I had known in the mines. I recalled that she had been like a trapped wild creature, resentful of our attempts to civilize her.

Somewhere in the depths of my consciousness I chalked up the evolution of Pasha on the credit side of the revolution, to help balance accounts.

The acquaintance of Alexei and Pasha prospered. I felt myself the patron and guardian of their friendship.

With the help of the Kharkov city Soviet and the local Party organs we succeeded in improving living conditions in the dormitory. Our food rations were raised. The fuel allotment was increased. Several community laundries were equipped in the basement. Volunteer clean-up squads swept the corridors more often and—greatest achievement of all—a combination barber shop and beauty parlor was installed in the building. As director of this effort, my stock with the student body went up high.

But with all the improvements, existence remained on a spartan level. Besides our own difficulties, most of us were uncomfortably aware of the rapid deterioration of conditions in the city generally, and even more so in the countryside. Despite the hush-hush attitude, despite the actual danger of open discussion, everyone knew some, if not all, the facts.

Rumors of incredible cruelty in the villages in connection with the liquidation of the kulaks were passed from mouth to mouth. We saw long trains of cattle cars filled with peasants passing through Kharkov, presumably on their way to the tundras of the North, as part of their "liquidation." Communist officials were being murdered in villages and recalcitrant peasants were being executed en masse. Rumors also circulated about the slaughter of livestock by peasants in their "scorched earth" resistance to forced collectivization. A Moscow decree making the unauthorized killing of livestock a capital crime confirmed the worst of these reports.

The railroad stations of the city were jammed with ragged, hungry peasants fleeing their homes. *Bezprizorni,* homeless children, who had been so much in evidence in the civil war and famine years were again everywhere. Beggars, mostly country people but also some city people, again appeared on the streets.

The press told glorious tales of accomplishment. The Turkestan-Siberian railway completed. New industrial *combinats* opened in the Urals, in Siberia, everywhere. Collectivization 100 per cent completed in one province after another. Open letters of "thanks to Stalin" for new factories, new housing projects. Delegations from foreign lands—from as far away as America and Australia—came to stare at the marvels of the *Piatiletka* and in interviews hailed the Soviet triumphs in almost hysterical enthusiasm. How these visitors overlooked the other side of the picture was a mystery we Russians never solved.

Which was the reality, which the illusion? The hunger and terror in the villages, the homeless children—or the statistics of achievement? Or were both, perhaps, part of the same complex truth? Such questions were neither asked nor answered publicly. But in private we talked of them, Alexei and I, and millions of others.

2

Another dimension of confusion was added to our life in the Institute soon after I entered by an order that all instruction and examinations be conducted in the Ukrainian language, not in Russian. The order applied to all schools and institutions. It was Moscow's supreme concession to the nationalist yearnings of the largest non-Russian Soviet Republic.

In theory we Ukrainians in the student body should have been pleased. In practice we were as distressed by the innovation as the non-Ukrainian minority. Even those who, like myself, had spoken Ukrainian from childhood, were not accustomed to its use as a medium of study. Several of our best professors were utterly demoralized by the linguistic switch-over. Worst of all, our local tongue simply had not caught up with modern knowledge; its vocabulary was unsuited to the purposes of electrotechnics, chemistry, aerodynamics, physics and most other sciences.

Poor Vanya, lost in the forest of education in any language, was reduced to pitiful helplessness by the storm of Ukrainization. Hundreds of other students were in no better case. George Vigura, of course, translated all his holy texts from the Party authorities into Ukrainian and remained perfectly adjusted. The rest of us suffered the new burden, referred to Russian textbooks on the sly and in private made fun of the *opera bouffe* nationalism.

What should have been a free right was converted, in its application, into an oppressive duty. The use of our own language was not merely allowed, it was made obligatory. Hundreds of men and women who côuld not master it were dismissed from government posts. It became almost counter-revolutionary to speak anything but Ukrainian in public. Children from Russianized homes were tortured and set back in their studies by what was for them a foreign language.

Ultimately, of course, all these excesses would be denounced. The Ukrainian patriotism which they engendered, as distinct from Soviet patriotism, would be punished by exile or death. The old Bolshevik Skripnik, Commissar of Education for Ukraine, would be made the scapegoat of the reversal and driven—for this and other ideological "crimes"—to a demonstrative suicide.

But while it lasted the tragi-comedy allowed for no criticism. One evening the five room-mates of the Gigant returned home from an address by Comrade Skripnik on the blessing of Ukrainization. We were all impressed by the man's honesty and intelligence, even where we were in doubt about the wisdom of the language policy.

"Maybe he's right," Vanya said. "But, damn it, I simply can't learn anything in Ukrainian. It's tough enough in Russian."

"You have no right to talk like that," Vigura shook his head sadly. "The Party considers it necessary and our job is to follow its orders."

"Such a formal approach makes no sense," Alexei declared. "You don't do the Party any good, George, by refusing to think. This extreme Ukrainization program is hurting our cause, not helping it. After all we can see the results more clearly than the Politburo in the Kremlin can."

"Alexei is right!" I said. "The whole business is stupid. People should use any language they please."

"Now you're attacking the Kremlin!" Vigura shouted. "The question has been settled and I refuse to discuss it further."

When we continued to analyze the situation and expressed hopes that it would be changed, Vigura angrily left the room. The next day Alexei and I were summoned by the secretary of the Party Committee. He began by talking about other things but soon edged over to the Ukrainization program. He gathered that we were critical, he said, and were spreading doubts.

Obviously Vigura had reported us. That evening, when he returned from dinner, the four of us were waiting for him. Vanya took the lead.

"George," he said, "you can help us settle an argument. You know the Bible, don't you?"

"I do."

"Then tell us how many sons did Noah have and what were their names."

"Three sons." the literal-minded Vigura answered. "Shem, Ham and Japhet."

"No, you're wrong!" Vanya said, with heavy irony. "There were three all right, but their names were Shem, Ham—and Judas! I hope you understand."

Vigura turned red. For once his self-righteous piety was shaken. "I always do my duty," he stammered and left the room. It took many weeks to clear the air of this incident. After Skripnik's suicide, when the Party itself took a view closer to that of Alexei and myself, Vigura saw nothing inconsistent in his own behavior. Every period has "its own truth," he said.

The right to use its own language is, in the final analysis, the only "autonomy" which non-Russian constituent Soviet Republics or Regions possess. To write or think in that language anything that is not strictly in accord with the Party Line is treason. Linguistic freedom, which should be the beginning of national self-reliance, in practice is its end. "Nationalist in form, socialist in content" is the slogan that covers what is in effect a completely centralized police control.

"There's our whole national autonomy!" a cynical friend once whispered in my ear. He was pointing to a public toilet where the words "Men" and "Women" were inscribed in two languages—Ukrainian and Russian.

The myth that the various Soviet Republics enjoy some measure of independence, and even the right to secede, has for some reason taken root abroad. No one in the Soviet Union, of course, believes this. Any cultural emphasis among a minority people which in the slightest contradicts the Communist dogmas is suppressed without mercy. Hundreds of Ukrainians have been executed, tens of thousands have been imprisoned and exiled, for "nationalist deviations" and alleged separatist sentiment.

3

My stay in Kharkov was cut short without warning by a decision on which I was not even consulted. Suddenly I was transferred from the aviation quota to the metallurgy quota and ordered to enter a Metallurgical Institute, first in Leningrad, then in my native city. But brief as it was, the Kharkov sojourn bulks large in my memory, it was so crowded with Party work, editorial activities, the tasks of administering the Gigant.

And in that memory, well in the foreground, are two women. Both of them were beautiful and both of them, by a coincidence, unhappily married.

Dr. Samarin, our professor of chemistry, was a hunchback. His long arms were grotesquely out of proportion to his stunted stature and his head was shaped like a melon. But his eyes were so tender and wise, his mind so keen, his sympathy for people so real, that the students quickly forgot his deformities. I looked forward to his lectures with relish.

One day I invited him to dine with us at the Gigant. I led him through the rooms and social halls and he was delighted with the order and cleanliness. After dinner he said, "Vitya, you must return this visit soon. Come to my house. My wife plays the piano beautifully, and I know you like music."

The Samarins occupied a tastefully furnished apartment, in which a grand piano took most of the living room space. There were pictures of Russian classic writers on the wall. A bronze bust of Beethoven stood on a pedestal in one corner.

I saw Clavdia that first night not only through my own eyes and senses but through those of her husband. His love for this slender brunette was almost a tangible thing in the room. It was as if her beauty canceled out his deformities and made him whole. Because I was so strongly drawn by her charm and by an indefinable sadness that enveloped her, a feeling akin to guilt spoiled my joy in the music and the conversation. I invented an excuse for leaving early.

A few days later, as I was walking through a soft snowfall, I found myself face to face with Clavdia.

"You ran away the other night," she said at once, without greeting. "By way of punishment, you must come to visit me tonight. That's a promise. I'll expect you."

I was quite sure in my mind that I would not go there. Yet several hours later I was ringing her doorbell. The table in the dining room was set for two.

"But where is Dr. Samarin?" I asked, suddenly embarrassed and feeling myself trapped—not by Clavdia but by my own emotions.

"Oh, he's visiting his brother, who lives in the country not far from here. He won't be back for a few days."

Our conversation at supper was strained, despite the aid of a bottle of Caucasian wine. After supper I suggested a walk through the park—snow in the moonlight.

"No, my dear prisoner," she laughed, "if you must have lunar effects, here's the *Moonlight Sonata*," and she played it on the piano.

Then she played and sang Gypsy songs, many of which I remembered from my childhood in Alexandrovsk. I told her about the Gypsy camps and my friendship with Saideman. All the time I sat, tensely, in the big armchair where her husband had sat the other night. It seemed to me a citadel of self-defense. Suddenly, almost in the middle of a sentence, I announced that I must leave.

She looked at me with a sad smile.

"Running away again," she said. "But this time I won't let you."

"I'm sorry . . . but lessons . . . I promised Alyosha I'd join him. . . ."

"You're lying, Vitya dear, and I know it. Come, let's talk it over frankly. Why shouldn't I have the right to spend an evening with someone —well, someone more like myself?"

Her voice was by now full of suppressed tears. I sat down again. She told me some of the story of her life and as she talked the strain between us disappeared. She seemed to me just an unhappy girl pouring out her heart.

Clavdia was nine years old when the revolution came. She was the child of a wealthy family, and had been brought up by private tutors and governesses. In the first months of the upheaval, both her parents were arrested and some time later were killed in a general slaughter of "bourgeois" hostages. Clavdia went to live with an old aunt, in a dark garret room of what had been their own family mansion. Theirs was the bitter, half-illicit existence of "former" people, the declassed and outlawed. Young Clavdia had neither the right to school nor the right to work. They sustained themselves by selling hidden remnants of their old possessions.

"I know that young Communists like you have never looked at the picture from our side," she said. "You can have no idea what it means to be despised, outlawed, to feel yourself unwanted. Especially when you're young. Poverty is hard enough for anybody. It's worse for those who have known comfort and plenty."

When she was about seventeen, Clavdia fell in love with a poet twice her age and went to live with him. The few months with him, she said, were the nearest she had come to real happiness. But suddenly he disappeared and to this day she had no idea what had happened to him. He had been opposed to the new regime and, she supposed, was in some concentration camp if he was still alive.

"I was pretty and many young men courted me. But they were all boys of my own kind, children of the past. I was so tired and had suffered so much that I yearned for security. My Prince Charming, if he ever arrived, would have to carry a Party card. . . . Then one day I met Dr. Samarin. I was repelled physically, but I was flattered that a Communist, a young man who had a name, who *belonged*, was interested in me. He loved me timidly and tenderly and at a distance. I was at once alarmed and fascinated by his animal-like devotion.

"Above all, I was grateful for his goodness. My aunt and I agreed that he had a beautiful soul, even if he was a hunchback and a Communist. I'm afraid that to my poor aunt both items seemed deformities of the same order. For more than a year he visited us, brought us food and clothes, and gave me lessons, without a single word about his feelings for me. He even managed somehow to obtain a piano for me.

"Then one day, while I was playing his favorite pieces from Tchaikowski, I said to him: 'I know you love me. I don't love you. But I admire you and I need your protection and companionship. Why don't we get married?' He sat there like a man who had been struck by lightning—happy, unbelieving and also ashamed. I suppose he knew the truth, even if he pushed it out of his mind—the truth that a has-been, an outlaw, a child of the past, was accepting a physical monster out of despair.

"So there you see, Vitya, how little you clever Communists really know about life," she concluded. "You don't know how many thousands of Russian women who were pushed aside and avoided because of their origins have sought sanctuary by marrying the new aristocrats, the Communists and proletarians. Some of them have also found happiness. I'm not one of these, alas. I can't forget or forgive those who've destroyed the people and the things I cared for most.

"People like me are lonely. That's the worst of it, I think. The loneliness. We pretend to belong. We live a secret life in our thoughts. I've tried to be active. Once I offered to teach music in the schools. The authorities seemed interested—until I filled out the questionnaire and revealed that I was a 'former person.' "

It was past midnight before I left.

"Let's part friends, Vitya," she said at the door. "Don't think ill of me. I'm miserable and see nothing ahead of me but endless loneliness. Please drop in to see us—when Dr. Samarin is home. He's a good teacher and I know how much you admire him."

I had too much respect for Samarin, as a professor and as a man, to intrude again on his family life.

4

I used to call occasionally at the home of Comrade F., a Ukrainian official who occupied an important place in the Commissariat of Workers-Peasant Inspection. He was an old Party member, in his late fifties, well educated and had known most of the great revolutionary figures personally. He referred to Lenin, Trotsky, Lunacharsky, Zinoviev and the others by their first names. His wife, a gray-haired and benign-looking woman, always reminded me of Krupskaya, Lenin's widow.

When the three of us were alone, Comrade F. could not resist political talk. We might start with the theatre, a new book, my studies, but soon he would be discussing the agrarian troubles, the terror against his old comrades, the tempo of industrialization. Ideas which elsewhere would have shocked me, somehow seemed natural and credible coming from him. Reports which I had dismissed as "counter-revolutionary rumors" he would mention casually as commonplace facts. Because of his work in the Commissariat he was in a position to know and speak of atrocities in the village, of peasant resistance, of mass arrests as if these were matters of general knowledge.

In any case, Comrade F. unwittingly was responsible for my meeting Julia. He presented me with a pass for two in a loge in the Opera Theatre for a performance of *Chio Chio San*. I took Alexei Karnaukhov with me. In an adjoining loge sat two well-dressed and extremely handsome women. One of them I recognized immediately as a patient in the Kiev sanatorium where I had convalesced after my mishap on the Persian frontier.

"That's Julia Mikhailovna, the wife of R—," I whispered to my companion.

"R—!" he exclaimed.

There was ample reason for his exclamation. R— was one of the most important officials in the Ukrainian government, a man of immense power and reputed to be close to Stalin himself. I recalled that he had sent his wife flowers by airplane from Kharkov regularly while she was in Kiev.

Julia evidently recognized me and gestured an invitation to join her between acts. "How beautiful she is!" I thought. "Why had I not noticed it three years ago in Kiev? What a young dolt I was!" For the rest of the act we exchanged glances, and she smiled at me with a candid pleasure over the encounter that made me blush. I made no effort to conceal my admiration.

The opera was a deadly bore. It had been doctored to make it ideologically suitable and was full of the bombast of revolutionary cliches. But for the rest of my life any of its arias would be enough to revive the memory of my love for Julia. She was a woman of medium height, a little older than I, something fruit-like in her luscious beauty. Her golden hair was plaited in thick braids which were twined on her head in a coronet, making a frame of burnished gold for her lovely features.

When the curtain came down we went to her loge. I introduced Alexei and she introduced her friend, Mary. We talked the commonplaces of a new and as yet awkward acquaintance, but the meeting was pervaded by an excitement; there was about it a peculiar tension, which had no relation to what was being said.

We remained in their loge for the second act. Before it was over Julia whispered: "Why stay to the bitter end? Let's go home and have a bite of supper." We agreed readily.

Outside the theatre, Julia dismissed the big motor car that was waiting for her. It would be more fun, she said, to drive home in sleighs. We selected two of the cleanest looking from the line-up; Alexei and Mary took one, Julia and I the other.

That ride has remained etched on my mind in amazing detail and clarity. The cold, clear, tinsely night wrapped in shining snow. The showers of snow-dust kicked up by the galloping horses as we slid along noiselessly. The clouds of exhaled breath. The feel of Julia's hand in mine under the fur rug on our knees.

I told her about the Institute, about my career in the factory and in the Party. I told her about Alexei and my other room-mates. And in the midst of the aimless talk, I interrupted myself to exclaim: "How wonderful everything is tonight!" Our lips met in a long kiss.

Soon we turned into a side street and stopped in front of a small, two-story house set back behind a high fence—the kind of private dwelling which might have belonged to a rich merchant in the old days. A militiaman stood guard at its gate. Mary and Alexei, sensing that we wanted to be alone, insisted on going to a restaurant. Julia, using a latchkey, opened the door and invited me in.

When she turned on the lights I found myself in the most elegant home I had ever seen. Oriental rugs on the floors, tapestries and paintings on the walls, crystal chandeliers, soft divans and gleaming mahogany tables. Everything was rich and colorful, yet there was tasteful restraint in its arrangement.

I stood in the midst of the grandeur, dazzled and frankly bewildered. Julia laughed. "It's real, darling, it's not a movie set," she said as she threw off her sealskin wrap.

"But I didn't imagine that anything like this still existed, outside museums," I said.

"Never mind, Vitya, there are lots of things you don't imagine in our country. Come into the kitchen and help me fix a snack. I'm starved.

The servants are out tonight—and he's in Moscow for some conference or other."

The kitchen only deepened my sense of the unreality of the whole scene. There was an atmosphere of overflowing abundance. Fine china and arrays of crystal glassware, some of it bearing Tsarist coats-of-arms, filled the cupboards; a big-bellied silver samovar gleamed on a side-table. When she opened the huge icebox I glimpsed the kind of plenty that took my mind to grandmother's ice cellar in Alexandrovsk. It all seemed another world, far from the penury and privations which had become the accustomed setting of our Soviet existence.

When I returned to my room at the Gigant in the morning I had barely time enough to wash and shave before running to the Institute. And throughout the day the lecturers had a sleepy, inattentive and rather moonstruck student in me. My thoughts were with Julia. So there was such a thing as "love at first sight" after all, I said to myself in amazement. But why must it be a married woman—a woman married, moreover, to one of the leaders of my Party and my country!

I resolved solemnly not to see Julia again, at the same time wondering how I could survive the few days before the meeting we had agreed upon.

"Comrade Kravchenko," I said to myself sternly in the aerodynamics class, "you're behaving like a character in a cheap French novel. Snap out of it! What's all the melodrama about?"

I took Alexei into my confidence that night. He realized that I was in no mood for ribbing and we talked seriously. From Mary he had learned that Julia had long been unhappy. She was not in love with her famous husband. Worse than that, she objected to his ruthlessness, his luxurious way of life, his indifference to the sufferings of the masses.

"I know it sounds like something out of Ibsen's *Doll's House*," Mary had told him, "but Julia feels herself caught and imprisoned. She says being the wife of R— is like being the wife of a grandduke and she thinks it makes a mockery of the sufferings of the Russian people."

I met Julia frequently in the following weeks. One night I asked her about her husband.

"Not tonight, darling," she pleaded, bursting into tears. "We'll have lots of time to talk. I don't want to spoil our first evenings together."

We were walking arm in arm in the spacious walled-in garden behind her house. The paths had been cleared of snow and strewn with fresh sand.

"No, the sooner we talk it out the better," I insisted. "R— is not only your husband. He's one of the leaders of my Party."

"I'm not a member of the Party," she said, "but from the beginning I have felt close to it, or at least close to the revolution. My father was a scholar and a great liberal. We've forgotten the word liberal, Vitya. We dismiss it with a laugh. But with every year I hold it in higher regard—at least in the sense that my father used it. To him it meant love of the common people, justice for everybody and above all respect for every man and woman. He placed a high value on life. We may have forgotten about it, but I think that's what the revolution was about."

"Strange," I said, "your father was a scholar and mine is a simple factory worker. One called himself a liberal, the other a revolutionist. But when you tell me what your father believed, I can almost hear my own father talking. . . ."

"It's not strange at all. My husband today preaches socialism to the toilers and appeals to them to bring it about in the future. Meanwhile he lives now, not in the future. So far as he's concerned, I'm afraid, the socialism of today is good enough. Why should he have all this comfort"— she made a sweeping gesture that included the garden, the luxurious home, her fur coat—"while millions are undernourished and the prison camps are growing bigger and uglier? You may not believe me, but I am opposed to all this gluttony of the leaders. Do you happen to know what's going on in the villages now?"

"I'm afraid I know, Julia, more than I care to admit to myself."

"Don't be surprised that I talk like this. My feelings are no secret to R—. I have often told him how it all looks to me, but he only laughs, and calls me a sentimental little fool. It harms no one, he says; the leaders work hard and deserve a good life. But he's wrong. Of that I'm sure. Leaders who lack nothing themselves soon forget what it means to suffer. Their talk of sacrifice turns into sheer hypocrisy.

"Darling, I feel that we're living under masks, in the midst of a great deception. Sometimes I think that the exploitation and barbarism of the past was more honest. At least it didn't pretend to be idealistic. Nobody passed it off as socialism. Honest young Communists like you are really lucky. You still have faith and you don't know about the filthy intrigues and the deadly duels for power among the top leadership.

"Do you know what disgusting battles are waged for the possession of some country home in the Silver Woods outside Moscow? Or a winter home that once belonged to a merchant prince in the Caucasus? There are too many lies and pretenses. I'm so close to them where I happen to be situated that sometimes they seem to choke me. It's like being caught in a swamp, where you sink deeper the more you struggle to get out."

Extravagant as it all sounded to me, I could not doubt her sincerity.

"If you were deeply in love with your husband, you wouldn't be so aware of this," I ventured. "I hope you won't misunderstand me, but your political dissatisfaction may be only an echo of your personal dissatisfactions."

Julia thought for a long while.

"No, I think that isn't so," she finally said. "Even in the first years of my marriage I resented the way R— and his important friends lived, the way they talked, their contempt for the very people whose toil they exploited. From the first I felt that I was a serf on a powerful man's estate."

"All right, then why don't you leave your husband, get a job and live for your ideals? I love you and I think you love me. What's to stop us?"

"No, Vitya, it's not as simple as that. I know a lot that you don't. It's not easy for a woman in my situation. I can't simply part from my husband and sink into the anonymous crowd. I've been too close to the men in power and they won't have it that way. I beg you not to ask me to explain more than that. If you love me you won't refuse me. It's my only request of you."

The whole world of unlimited power and unlimited intrigue to which she referred was mysterious and incomprehensible to me. No doubt a simple Russian falling in love with a member of the Imperial family must have felt a little as I did.

After her husband's return from Moscow, I met Julia frequently at her friend Mary's house. It was obvious to me that her husband was aware that she was living a life of her own but closed his eyes to the fact. We talked about some day living together openly as man and wife, but neither of us really believed it. The name of R— was in the newspapers frequently. Now he was making a speech, now he was signing some decree. His name was also cropping up constantly in conversation. "R— said this, R— did that. . . ." His prominence, his power, his ubiquity seemed so many walls separating me from Julia, even in those moments when she was in my arms.

Then events took a sudden turn. I was summoned to the Central Committee of the Party. The Assistant Chief of the Personnel Division, a Comrade Shulkin, received me.

"Comrade Kravchenko," he informed me, "there is a Party resolution instructing us to bring the preparation of engineers more closely in line with their previous experience. You were working in a metallurgical factory before entering the Institute, weren't you?"

"Yes, the Petrovsky-Lenin plant."

"Well, there you are. What's the sense of training you for airplane construction when you have such a good start in metals?"

"But I prefer aviation," I said weakly.

"Maybe, but you'll admit that that's merely a personal preference." Then, turning to a secretary, he added, "Will you see to it that Comrade Kravchenko is transferred to the Metallurgy Institute in Dniepropetrovsk?"

For hours I wandered through Sumskaya park, oblivious to the slush of late spring. How could the Party know that it was not airships versus metallurgy, but Julia versus a life without her? Not until much later did it occur to me that perhaps the Party, or at least some people in the Party, did know. All the same, the Party decision seemed to me essentially just.

I telephoned Julia and broke the news to her. We met several times more before my departure. They were stormy, tearful meetings. I urged her to come with me, whatever the consequences. At times it seemed to me that she was weakening and might actually follow me. But whatever the pressures on her they were too strong to break.

"Don't ask me, don't be cruel, Vitya. I can't do it, though living without you will be a living death. Don't ask me. It hurts too much as it is."

On the night before my departure I walked for hours through the Kharkov streets with my friend Alexei. He promised that he would keep me informed about Julia. I was determined that she should join me, if not soon, then after I was through with the Institute and could afford to marry.

Julia, Mary, my room-mates and other friends saw me off at the railroad station next morning. Tears were rolling down Julia's cheeks and everyone pretended not to notice. It did not remotely occur to me that I would never see her again.

I wrote to her repeatedly from Dniepropetrovsk but received no replies. Alexei, at my insistence, went to the R— residence. He rang the bell and the door was opened by a maid. When he asked for Madame R—, the maid began to sob. "Julia has left, she's no longer here," she cried, but could give no other information. Mary said that Julia had parted from her husband soon after I returned to Dniepropetrovsk and left town. Either she did not know any more or she was under rigid instructions not to disclose any more.

The painful wound of the separation healed slowly. But the dull ache of the mystery and the uncertainty remained with me always. Once, in the passing years, I heard a vague report that Julia Mikhailovna, under a new name, was teaching school in a far-off province, but I was powerless to check the truth of it. By that time, moreover, it might have been cruel to dig up the past from under the debris of time.

CHAPTER VII

TRIUMPH OF THE MACHINE

MY PARENTS and brothers were overjoyed to see me back in Dniepropetrovsk. Not wishing to spoil their happiness, I acted up to it. This took considerable effort, for the ache of separation from Julia saturated my life. Work seemed the only antidote. I threw myself fiercely into study, Party chores, factory projects, leaving no margins of time for moping or self-pity. To add a little to my student stipend, I also taught several classes in political economy in the Tekhnikum.

"You're working yourself to death, Vityenka," my mother constantly complained. She suspected, I have no doubt, that my zeal was not entirely normal.

Living at home, I avoided the hardships of residence in the dormitory buildings which were, if anything, more disordered and uncomfortable than the Gigant in Kharkov. My relations with the factory, as its official ward, were now real and close. I resumed old friendships among engineers and administrators and made new friendships deep down in the ranks of foremen and labor. The Petrovsky-Lenin combine by this time employed some 35,000 men. It played a big role in the drama of the Five Year Plan.

The new plant director, N. Golubenko, turned out to be honest and intelligent. Aware of my long connection with his factory and my special interest in rationalizing and modernizing production processes, he invited me often to sit in on business conferences and entrusted me occasionally with special studies on new plant problems.

Living under the same roof with my father and mixing with other simple factory laborers, I could no longer escape the tormenting knowledge of the tragedy in the farming areas. We Communists, among ourselves, steered around the subject; or we dealt with it in the high-flown euphemisms of Party lingo. We spoke of the "peasant front" and "kulak menace," "village socialism" and "class resistance." In order to live with ourselves we had to smear the reality out of recognition with verbal camouflage.

But ordinary workers were under no such compulsions. Many of them were ex-peasants, nearly all of them still had relatives on the land. They could not take a detached "scientific" view of the collectivization. They talked freely of violence, cruelty, hunger and death—not as generalizations but as intimate episodes affecting Ivan or Stepan in a specific village. Now and then I heard them tell tales of cannibalism in our own province which I dismissed as exaggerations, but which struck terror to my heart all the same.

In the Institute, too, the awareness of horror just outside the door could not be exorcised. Warnings were issued against the purveyors of "anti-Party rumors" spread by "Right deviationists, Trotskyites and kulak agents." But the rumors persisted. Indeed, they thrived on threats and suppressions. They gave furtive, muted overtones to the life of the two thousand students. Active members were frequently sent to the villages on special missions. Though they returned under instructions not to discuss their experiences, their silence and evasiveness were eloquent enough. Besides, many of them did tell, under pledge of secrecy, things that horrified me utterly.

"You look as if you've seen ghosts," I said to a classmate whom I had come to know at Party nuclei meetings. He had just come back from the Poltava area.

"I have," he said and dropped his eyes.

I did not pursue the matter further. I sensed that he was aching to open his heart to someone and I ran away, in moral panic, from what it might do to me.

Now and then "rumormongers" among the students were arrested. Surveillance of the political morals of the student body absorbed even more energy than the technical studies themselves.

There was at the Institute, as in every Soviet industrial undertaking or government bureau, a Special Department connected with the G.P.U. It was headed by a Comrade Lebed. No one could enter its office, except in a state of terror when summoned for questioning. Few of us knew what went on behind the grated little window in the steel door. At the same time few of us were so naive that we did not realize that every student had his own *dossier* in the Special Department, where his every word and act, where the very accent of his behavior were recorded.

The files on "Personal Cases" contained information about the student's or teacher's private life, his relatives, his political past. It contained, above all, the reports and denunciations by secret agents deployed through every class and dormitory and by volunteer informers currying favor with officialdom or moved by grudges and rancor.

To protect the informers and strengthen the network of everyday espionage, not even the Institute director or the secretary of its Party Committee was given access to the *dossiers*. The Special Department had its secret agents in every branch of the Institute and even in the Party nuclei. But the Party Committee had its own informers in the nuclei, whose identity was not known to the Special Department. Thus there were spies upon the spies in an intricate pattern that spread a tangible pall of fear.

But that was not all. Besides the Special Department, the G.P.U. had agents in the Institute who reported directly to its regional headquarters, as a double-check on Lebed and his staff. The City Committee of the Party deployed agents through the nuclei, and the Regional Committee received secret reports from its special people in the City Committee. This interlocking pyramid of surveillance extended to the very top, to the Central Committee of the Party in Moscow and finally to the Politburo headed by Stalin.

Multiple webs of espionage by the Party and of the Party, by the
G.P.U. and of the G.P.U., pooling information at some points, competing
at other points, covered Soviet life from top to bottom and back again.
We lived in a world swarming with invisible eyes and ears. The average
man, to be sure, was not aware of the extent and intricacy of the system;
even in this brief sketch I am drawing on discoveries that I made later,
in the course of years. He was aware only that "walls had ears" and that
candor was the shortest road to ruin.

Illicit knowledge spread notwithstanding. That is sufficient indication
of the emotional tensions of the period. It is an indication, too, of the
peculiarly Russian hunger for talk, for sympathy, for baring one's soul.
With solemn promises of secrecy we risked discussion of plaguing doubts,
tortured by the fear that every word would somehow find its way into our
personal case history. How often, in the purge years that lay ahead, I would
be confronted with casual remarks made in privacy to trusted friends! How
often I would be asked why I had not reported remarks made in my hearing by others! Failure to denounce "anti-Party" or "anti-Soviet" sentiments was construed as agreement and complicity.

The Special Department was not squeamish in its pursuit of "enemies."
Some of us knew, for instance, the strategy it devised to keep a close
check on the aged and erudite Academician, Professor Dinnik, who taught
us construction mechanics. More important than his teaching was his
laboratory work on vital industrial construction plans involving vast expenditures. A non-Party man, a pre-revolutionary intellectual, a specialist
seemingly disinterested in politics, he was naturally an object of intense
suspicion. But how could his activity be checked, when it was so highly
technical that sabotage might be hard to detect?

The answer was found through the professor's wife, who also served as
his chief laboratory assistant. She was a tall, angular blonde, not unhandsome, in her middle thirties and therefore about thirty years younger than
her husband. Since she obviously respected his work and learning, she was
not considered sufficiently reliable to serve as an agent for the G.P.U.
Instead an irresistible lover was deliberately planted in her life. The engineer and Party stalwart Pavlenko, virile, broad-shouldered, with a bulldog
face, swept the young wife off her feet. Professor Dinnik was one of the
few people in the Institute who did not know that his wife had a lover; and
his wife was one of the few people who did not suspect that her lover
was merely doing a chore for the Special Department. His sacrifice
proved useless—not a trace of sabotage was ever discovered in the professor's laboratory.

Though rarely referred to, except in sinister hints and in symbolic
"political anecdotes"—that is to say, jokes with political significance—the
complex spying was as real and as all-pervading as the air we breathed.
It enclosed and penetrated the factory no less than the Institute, the local
newspapers to which I contributed no less than the Party organizations in
which I was increasingly active, being at the time a member of the Political
Bureau of our Party Committee at the Institute.

Floods of personal data and denunciation, some of it self-righteous, some of it vengeful and cynical. Tons of *dossiers*. Millions of spies. All of it sorted and studied, filed and cross-indexed. Copies to the Prosecutor, to the disciplinary officials of the Party, to the secret tribunals of the G.P.U. when immediate action was warranted. Deadly ammunition against back-sliders or doubters for future use. Tens of thousands of filing cabinets, each of them an arsenal of intimacies, indiscretions, lies, flatteries, errors.

Within our ruling Party this whole thoroughly secret process of surveillance and exposure in which old-fashioned privacy was forever liquidated had a name. It was called "Party democracy."

2

In June, 1931 Comrade Stalin made a speech at a conference of economic functionaries which churned Soviet industry to its depths and changed the color of life for all industrial workers and officials. The speech included his famous "six points" for raising efficiency, the most important of which were strict cost accounting, more centralized direction of enterprises, more rigid responsibility for failure and waste, and a far-reaching differentiation in incomes.

"Rationalization of industry," Stalin complained, "has long gone out of style. Our enterprises have long ceased to count, to calculate, to make up actual balance sheets of income and expenditures. . . . Nobody seems accountable for anything. . . . Leaders hold their tongues. Why? From all evidence because they are afraid of the truth."

I was pleased by some parts of this swing in official thought. They seemed to me almost a personal victory, because I had long written and argued for just that kind of rationalization. But other parts disturbed me. To people like my father they seemed confirmation of their most pessimistic forecasts.

Equality of income, which had been a Soviet ideal, was suddenly turned into a crime. *Uravnilovka*, equalization, was denounced as unworthy of a socialist society. The "Party maximum," under which Party members had been kept to an income not far above the average, was now removed, releasing torrents of greed and self-seeking in officialdom. Piecework was introduced throughout Soviet economy, even in types of work where such a system of payment was palpably silly if not impossible. With that strange Soviet genius for extremes, the evil of too many bosses was now replaced by the evil of the single and arbitrary boss, in which the last pretense of "workers' control" from below was thrown overboard.

Of course, it was one thing to order reforms, quite another to enforce them. Stalin was right in his charge that the leaders feared the truth. They feared it because truth was an almost counter-revolutionary and always dangerous luxury. An honest error of judgment or an unwise technical experiment might be punished by exile or prison as sabotage. To discipline a subordinate for mistakes might prove inhuman, since the police-minded authorities were likely to charge him with wilful treason. The flight from responsibility tied the gigantic economic effort into crazy knots. As Golubenko said to me at the time:

"They want us to rationalize and modernize and cut costs. That's all very fine, Comrade Kravchenko. But as soon as we do something bold or unusual we are risking our lives, aren't we? The safest way is to do nothing."

In late fall of that year I was called to the Regional Party Committee, along with the director of our Institute, Comrade Tsiplyakov, and another student, Beretzkoi. The secretary closed the office door and announced that he wished us to undertake an investigation at Nikopol, a town a few dozen miles away.

"Despite the 'six points' of Comrade Stalin," he said, "work is going badly. Lots of noise and meetings but the plans are way behind schedule. Discipline is lax and discontent is rife. Nikopol is a case in point. As you know, we're building a big metallurgical *combinat* over there. It will cost us several hundred million rubles. But for some reason the construction job isn't moving and the labor turnover is fantastic.

"We want you three to go there. Stay as long as you have to—a week, two weeks. Then report on what's wrong and what can be done. Your report will be studied here and if found worth while will be placed before Comrade Ordzhonikidze."

Arriving at Nikopol, we found that the construction had been undertaken about three years before, in an empty steppe six miles from town and several miles from the railroad. This added to the discomforts of the workers. Nobody seemed to know why the inconvenient site had been selected. Had the construction been placed closer to the city, the problem of housing would have been eased to some extent.

The director of the plant, Peter Brachko, was new to the post. He was under no constraints, therefore, in revealing the multitude of mistakes and stupidities under which the work was bogging down.

"I found the place so deep in confusion and filth," he sighed, "that digging out is in itself a major enterprise. Besides, there is no balance in the various parts of the undertaking. You know well enough, comrades, that every metallurgical plant depends on other plants. To build one without reference to the others is foolish. It may look fine in the total statistics, but it won't look so fine when actual production gets going."

Scattered over the immense area occupied by the planned array of factories, foundries, administration buildings and housing projects we were appalled to find expensive imported machinery, mostly German, rusting in the open air. Everywhere we saw abandoned structures, some half finished, others not far beyond the foundation stage.

"But this is awful, Comrade Brachko," I said as we picked our way in the muddy wilderness of brick and metal.

"I know, but what can I do? No sooner do we get well started on one building, than an order comes through from the center that everything must stop and all effort must be thrown into some other place. Plans have changed! Meanwhile the workers fall way below the quotas theoretically set for them. Sickness and absenteeism are fearful. The workers are bored, they live under harsh conditions and, between ourselves, they haven't enough to eat for this kind of work."

Then he added, with a touch of satisfaction, "Of course, I'm new here. This is all an inheritance from the preceding administration."

Poor Brachko! How was he to guess that in a few years he would pay with his freedom for the mess in Nikopol? For that matter, how was I to guess that one day I would myself be designated to take a leading part in directing this very metallurgical "giant"? In blessed ignorance of our various destinies we strode through the incredible confusion.

The visiting commission questioned engineers, foremen, individual workers. It became clear to us that work was proceeding spasmodically, that money and effort were being squandered. The main reasons for this, it seemed to me, fell into two groups.

The first was major interference and pin-pricking from outside. The undertaking, immense though it was, fitted into an over-all scheme so huge as to be almost beyond the grasp of the human mind. A small variation in the central plan, even when justified, often meant an upheaval in its distant segments. Far-off officials could not always foresee the shattering effects of their casual orders on this or that undertaking. Local officials could only obey and hope for the best. The interference, moreover, was also of a police character, with endless arrests, interrogations and threats generating an atmosphere of fear and uncertainty.

The second group of causes can all be summed up as disregard of the human factor in the process of production. Although tens of millions of rubles were being thrown away recklessly in unused machines and abandoned construction, wages were kept pitifully low when measured in what the ruble could buy just then. Workers' homes existed in blueprints, but the flesh-and-blood workers were packed into hastily constructed wooden barracks, with leaking roofs, moist walls and floors, lacking even the most primitive hygienic comforts. The emphasis was on output, in utter contempt of the men who did the work.

During our second evening in Nikopol, I decided to visit the barracks, with the construction chief, the local Party secretary and the housing officer. Trudging through ankle-deep mud, we came to the rows of bleak dwellings. Though there was electric power in the administration buildings, it had not been extended to the workers' quarters. Kerosene lamps, reinforced here and there by a wick in a saucer of oil, shed a funereal half-light over scenes of filth.

One of the barracks seemed almost totally dark from the outside. I knocked, and an elderly bearded man opened the door.

"Good evening, comrade, may we come in?"

"Who are you?"

"I'm the Party secretary and here"—indicating me—"is a commission from the center."

"That's fine!" the worker said, in crude irony. "Welcome to our palace! Will you have some rats, or do you prefer bedbugs? Never mind the odor."

The barrack was nearly dark. On a few cots, younger men were reading by the light of "smokers." Others were playing cards on an upper bunk. Most of the fifty or sixty men ignored us. Others crowded around us, eager to complain and curse. A rat scampered under our feet.

"Call this stuff bedding?" one of the workers said. "Are these pillows? No, it's all dirty rags!"

"How often are the sheets changed?" I asked.

"Every month if you're lucky, otherwise two months, three months, never."

"There's no relief from vermin and mice," another man shouted. "Come here, let me show you."

He lifted one end of an iron cot and banged it several times on the floor. The bedbugs, disturbed in their nests, blackened the floor. Involuntarily I stepped back in alarm.

"Why shouldn't there be vermin?" another worker took up the story. "We work in shifts. One gang goes out and the other comes in before the beds are cold. And the floors aren't washed more than once a month. This isn't life, it's torture. When it rains it's a Noah's ark and when it's cold it's the North Pole."

"Why do you keep quiet? Why don't you complain?" I asked.

"Complain!" he sneered. "A lot of good it does. Commissions come, just like yours, and then we hear no more. We want to work; we understand it's important. But we're made of flesh, not stone. Besides, over in another barrack the men did decide to do something about the terrible conditions. They decided not to go to work until things were improved. Well, you should know what happened."

"What happened?"

There was a general silence.

"Don't be afraid, tell me. I'm from Dniepropetrovsk and really don't know."

"Why, the ringleaders were called out," one man volunteered.

"Called out where?"

"Not to church or the beer saloon, you may be sure—to the G.P.U. of course. And what's more, they never came back."

"They needed a vacation in Siberia, maybe," the bearded worker interjected with a bitter laugh.

I reported to my colleagues of the commission. They had also inspected houses and the finished factory buildings. None of us had any optimistic findings to contribute. I tossed in bed all night. The dirt and the suffering and the bitterness weighed on me. The stupor of those who had seemed too tired and indifferent to complain oppressed me even more than the irony and hatred of the men who had talked up. And somehow the episode of the ringleaders who had been "called out" made the whole picture more dismal, more hopeless.

The following day a meeting of all the responsible leaders of the Nikopol plant was called in the City Committee of the Party. I spared no words in describing what I had seen. Director Brachko declared that if some order were not brought out of the chaos in the barracks within five days, the plant officials would be held to an accounting by "the highest instances" of the Soviet power. Comrade Tsiplyakov announced that the commission was not going home. It would remain here to check up at the end of the five days.

Those were weird days. Hundreds of men scrubbed, washed and repaired. By dint of desperate telephoning to Kharkov and in one case even to Moscow, crates of new sheets and pillow cases arrived. Work was begun on drawing electric lines into the barracks. The very officials who had permitted the horrors to accumulate now seemed eager and even pleased to improve conditions.

"It isn't that we approve the evils," one of them told me, "but that we haven't the power to remedy them. It's easier to let things drift than to act. No one wants to take the responsibility on himself. Take this clean-up —it's possible only because you men represent the Regional Committee. There's no money in the budget for clean sheets or essential repairs, and who would dare to monkey with the budget? It's a vicious circle."

The night before our departure I had supper with one of the chief engineers. He was an elderly man, non-Party.

"I'm not one of you," he said, "but just an old Russian intellectual. I don't interfere in your internal affairs. But I'm an engineer and I don't want my work to go to waste. I love my country and I want it to prosper. Please believe me.

"Everything we propose to the center is criticized. It's studied not from an engineering but from a 'political' standpoint. And whatever the decision, we must obey, even if it makes no sense. When the center makes mistakes, we suffer but keep our mouths shut. In fact, we must thank our stars if we're not blamed for their blunders."

"What about the local Party people? Don't they help?"

"Ekh, my dear Comrade Kravchenko, there are plenty of offices for watching us, but not many for helping. The plant committee of the Party investigates, the city committee investigates, the G.P.U. investigates, now you're here to investigate. They investigate us and each other. You'd think that once intelligent people have been entrusted with millions of rubles, they'd be allowed enough leeway to spend it properly. As it is, we use up more time worrying about what this one or that one will think than in actual engineering and construction. I'm an old man, so I dare to speak up."

I left Nikopol with a heavy heart. The amazing part of it, looking back at the visit, is that somehow, miraculously, a large part of the big metallurgical combine was built. More slowly, more expensively than planned, at an almost incalculable cost in life and suffering, but it was built.

We made a detailed report to the Party, which in turn made recommendations to Moscow. My own account omitted nothing unpleasant, not even the bedbugs and the G.P.U. arrests of complaining workers. Whether the last item ever reached Moscow I could not know.

The experience strengthened a plan that had been taking shape in my mind for months. I would go to Moscow and attempt to see Comrade Ordzhonikidze. I would talk to him, as man to man, about the shortcomings and evils I saw all around me. Since the plan fitted in with the needs of the Petrovsky-Lenin factory, I received director Golubenko's consent and he agreed to pay the expenses of the trip.

3

Directly from the station, I headed for the Commissariat of Heavy Industry.

This was my third visit to Moscow. On the previous visits, however, I had not been so conscious of the contrast between the capital and the rest of the country. It was a contrast due in part to improvement in the appearance of the capital, but even more so to the rapid deterioration of the provincial cities.

After Dniepropetrovsk, or even Kharkov, Moscow seemed a haven of plenty. The lines outside shops were not so long, the shelves inside shops not so bare. There was an almost audible rhythm of activity, a note of optimism. The streets were cleanly swept and the main avenues newly asphalted. The new modernistic buildings impressed an outsider tremendously. The *droshky* took me through Theatre Square, bounded by theatres, hotels, the big opera house, many fine shops. The people crowding the sidewalks seemed better dressed and, what pleased me most, they were not wandering aimlessly; about their very gait there was a briskness almost alien to Russia as a whole.

Having identified myself and obtained a *propusk*, a pass, I presented myself to Commissar Ordzhonikidze's secretary, Comrade Semushkin. Fortunately I had met him before and he smoothed my way. I showed him my letters from Golubenko and others and he undertook to tell the Commissar of my arrival.

I counted sixteen people in the waiting room. They were all well fed, well dressed; a few of them, it was evident, were wearing foreign clothes. Nearly all of them carried briefcases. As a whole their appearance bespoke comfort and self-importance. Obviously these were heads of big trusts, administrators of great industrial projects—from the uppermost layer of the economic leadership. As the youngest man in the room, my clothes distinctly on the threadbare side, I felt a little like an intruder, a poor relation. The others looked me over a bit distrustfully, as if to say, "What's this specimen doing in our important company?"

From behind the big doors leading into the Commissar's office we suddenly heard noises and shouting. I recognized the Georgian accents of Ordzhonikidze. We all watched the doors with interest and some alarm. If the Commissar was in a bad temper, it boded ill for all our various purposes. Then the door opened violently. A fat, perspiring and obviously frightened man came out precipitately, dragging an open suitcase. From the suitcase a batch of tableware spilled to the floor: spoons, knives, forks. The poor fellow, impeded by his weight, stooped to gather the things, threw them nervously into his suitcase, locked it with trembling fingers and rushed out without looking at any of us.

A minute or two later Ordzhonikidze emerged, smiling and friendly, with scarcely a trace of the violent scene in his demeanor. We all stood up as a sign of respect.

"I sure gave that scoundrel a tongue-lashing," he explained to the room in general, laughing, "and he deserved it. Samples of tableware for mass production he'd brought me! Why, those things weren't fit for savages —as crude and ugly as a lot of spades. We'll just have to get over the idea, comrades, that anything is good enough for the Soviet people. We want quality as well as quantity. Well, now let me see what brought you all here."

With Semushkin at his elbow, the Commissar went from one caller to the other. Having heard the man's mission, he either turned him over to an assistant or asked him to return at a specific time. In the years since I had met him, Ordzhonikidze had grown stouter. There was more gray in his bushy hair and sweeping mustache. But the humorous and unaffected quality of his oversized features still inspired confidence.

When he reached me, I handed him my letters. He glanced through one of them quickly, then looked up with a twinkle in his eyes.

"How are you, old friend?" he said. "Yes, I remember you very well, Comrade Kravchenko. I hope you're making progress in your studies, and I'll be pleased to confer with you. Let's say tonight at ten. Comrade Semushkin, take care of this comrade. See that he's comfortable."

When the Commissar had retired to his office, Semushkin came over and pressed my arm by way of congratulation. Evidently Ordzhonikidze was friendly towards me and his secretary acted up to the hint. The others now looked at me with a certain envy—such a young man and already the almighty smile upon him. . . .

I was driven to the Metropole Hotel in a big Lincoln. Upon presentation of a note from the Commissariat, I was immediately assigned a large room on an upper floor. I felt the inner lift of my propinquity to power, the tingle of reflected influence.

Towards evening I went to the hotel restaurant, a huge room, high-ceilinged and decorated with enormous potted tropical plants. It was crowded and a big jazz band was playing syncopated music. There was a kind of fish-pond in the center of the room, and crowded on its polished shores, so thick-packed that it seemed one undulating mass, were couples dancing to the jazz rhythms.

It took me some minutes to adjust myself to the novelty of this scene. Could this really be part of our Soviet Union? Had I blundered by accident into a cinema set? From behind one of the potted palm trees I watched the diners and dancers. Here and there I saw men in Russian blouses, but the rest were in European clothes, wearing neckties. Some of the women were in low-cut gowns such as I had never seen outside of book covers. There were many foreigners; one group was in dinner jackets and stiff white shirts. Through an archway at one end of the restaurant I caught a glimpse of a bar, several attractive girls serving drinks to foreign-looking men on high stools.

The thought of the barracks in Nikopol intruded on my inspection of the place. "Welcome to our palace, comrades. What will you have, rats or bedbugs?" But I pushed the thought aside. This was Moscow. Soon I would be "conferring" with one of the half dozen most powerful leaders in our land.

Long before the appointed hour I was in the reception room at the Commissariat again. A little before ten, Semushkin approached me.

"You may have to wait a while. Comrade Bukharin is with the Commissar."

Comrade Bukharin! My heart skipped a beat. It was almost like meeting Lenin. Among the great names in the Revolution, Bukharin's ranked only behind Lenin and Trotsky. In preparation for joining the Comsomols I had studied his *ABC of Communism*. In the last few years, it is true, Nikolai Bukharin had been damned as a "Right deviationist" and had been deprived of his official posts. His books were banned. But there was still magic about the name and the consciousness that he was right there, on the other side of the door, thrilled me despite myself.

In a little while Semushkin motioned me to come in. "Bukharin is still in there," he whispered. "The Commissar asked him to remain and meet you."

Soon I was shaking hands with Ordzhonikidze and with Bukharin. The Commissar sat behind a vast desk littered with papers, books, half a dozen telephones and an array of push buttons. Bukharin and I sat facing him on the other side. It was an enormous room, on the walls of which hung big portraits of Marx, Lenin and Stalin. Another photograph of Stalin stood on the desk, with a personal inscription, "To Sergo," scrawled at the bottom.

"All right, Comrade Kravchenko," the Commissar said, obviously trying to put me at ease, "tell us briefly and clearly what you know about the Nikopol project."

"First, Comrade Commissar, I should like to talk about the Dniepropetrovsk plant. I have my own views of its work which I should like to lay before you."

"Go ahead."

Having formulated the problem in advance in my mind, I was able to present it clearly. Certain departments of the plant needed modernization and expansion. In the eagerness to build new factories, I argued, some of the old ones are being neglected. In actual figures I tried to show that by investing a few million rubles to improve the existing plant we would get more production than by investing ten times as much in new plants.

Bukharin smiled broadly and shook his head in agreement. As was generally known, he was opposed to the "extreme tempo" in new construction. Before he had been silenced he had denounced some aspects of the Five Year Plan as "sheer adventurism."

"In general I agree with you, Comrade Kravchenko," said Ordzhonikidze, "although the specific problems of the Petrovsky-Lenin *combinat* will have to be studied." He made some notes on a pad. "Tell Director Golubenko that his requests will receive careful analysis. Now go on——"

I then proceeded to describe my impression at Nikopol. At first I stuck to the formal, technical phrases I had shaped up in my mind in advance. But as I talked, the memory of the barracks, of the discontents and the dirt, overwhelmed my discretion. A note of indignation crept into my voice as I detailed the waste, the confusion and especially the intolerable living conditions of the ordinary workers.

"Comrade Commissar, by putting some millions into better living conditions for the workers, I'm sure we would save enormous sums on the project. The neglect of the human element reduces the whole plan in a place like Nikopol to a tragedy of waste."

"Bravo!" Bukharin interjected and Ordzhonikidze tried unsuccessfully to suppress a smile.

"The central problem," I went on, carried away by my own eloquence, "is the wage system, for everyone from the top engineers to the lowest workers. And second is the problem of consumption goods, so that the money earned can buy the things the workers need—food, clothes, household goods. When I first met you, Comrade Commissar, I complained about interference in the administration of an enterprise. Single direction and responsibility are all to the good. But now we've gone to the other extreme and the workers have nothing to say. They're even called out by the G.P.U. if they venture to protest against terrible conditions. But I suppose I'm talking too much. Forgive me but I feel this deeply."

"No, no, go on, comrade," Ordzhonikidze exclaimed. "It's refreshing to hear someone talk with his whole mouth and not with a part of it. Everything you say is true. Don't think that we don't know it. I assure you that Comrade Stalin is very much concerned with the wage problem, for instance. But it is easier to diagnose the disease than to cure it."

The conference lasted nearly an hour. At one point the Commissar asked me whether I had ever been abroad.

"No, I haven't," I replied, "but I have read technical journals from Sweden, Germany and America. We have a lot to learn."

"When you finish your Institute, maybe we'll send you to America and to Germany. Now let's forget business for a moment. Have you been to our theatres here? And the museums?"

"Not yet, but I hope to take in as much as possible."

"Well, I am granting you five days of vacation in Moscow. Wait in the reception room for Semushkin. And now good-bye until we meet again."

I was a little dazed when I left them. It was the closest I had ever been to Power and the feel of it was heady. The people sitting around the reception room regarded me with unconcealed curiosity. Anyone who had monopolized an hour of the Commissar's time must be "important." Semushkin soon joined me.

"Well, comrade, I congratulate you. Your stock has certainly gone up!" he said. "Here are tickets for the Bolshoi Theatre and for the Moscow Art Theatre. Your expenses in the hotel will be taken care of. And here's a thousand rubles for pocket money. A gift from Comrade Ordzhonikidze. Have a good time and if you need anything, just ring me."

Again I was conveyed to the hotel in a big motorcar. A Gypsy chorus of some twenty people was singing familiar folk songs when I went into the Metropole restaurant for supper. Somehow the strangeness of the scene had worn off. The fact that I had just been closeted with Ordzhonikidze and Bukharin made me feel at home here, almost like one of the elect. How easy it was to yield to the fleshpots of power and luxury! How long would the sufferings of some anonymous verminous workers in places like Nikopol weigh on my conscience if I, too, were to live in Moscow, with plenty of money in my pockets, an automobile at my disposal and jazz bands to drown out self-reproof?

In the next five days I took in a ballet performance, several operas, a Moscow Art show, an evening at the Vakhtangov Theatre. I spent long hours at the Tretyakov Art Gallery, the Museum of the Revolution, the Lenin Library and other "must" institutions. What a wealth of beauty and knowledge there was in the world!

Recalling that Comrade Lazarev, the lecturer who had drawn me close to the Party and its ideals so many years ago in the Donetz coal mines, was in Moscow, I decided to look him up. He remembered me and was most cordial in his reception. He was living in a small apartment in one of the new housing units on the other side of the Moscow River. For reasons that I would have found it hard to put into words, I was pleased to see that the picture of Tolstoy was still on his wall. . . .

He introduced me to his wife, an attractive young woman and, like himself, an active Party worker. Over steaming glasses of tea, I gave them a brief account of my life since our meeting in the mining region. The account, of course, was climaxed by a detailed and enthusiastic account of my meeting with Ordzhonikidze and Bukharin. Lazarev listened to me in silence. I sensed that my ecstasy irritated him.

"A thousand rubles, theatre tickets, Lincolns, the Metropole," he said, a little sadly. "Yes, that's how the granddukes of the old regime treated their favorite retainers. Only the names have changed."

"You're not being quite fair, Comrade Lazarev," I retorted with some heat. "What impressed me is that the Commissar was willing to listen. I'm sure he understands the plight of our common people and sympathizes with them. And if he does, I must assume that Stalin does too. That's why I feel encouraged."

Lazarev now occupied an important post in the Moscow University. He served on powerful committees of the Party. Yet, as we talked that afternoon, our roles seemed strangely reversed. His bubbling hope and ardor had ebbed. Now it was I who apologized for the Party.

"Have you been to the villages recently?" he asked me suddenly.

"No, but I know a good deal about what's happening."

"Knowing is one thing, seeing is another. You see, I've just returned from the Ukraine, near Odessa. My job was to put through the collectiviza-tion in one region. I'm afraid, my friend, that I cannot talk about it as calmly as you talk about the Commissar's generosity. . . ."

Lazarev had gone to Odessa, he told me, as one of a committee of trusted Party people from Moscow after many of the local leaders had been dismissed for failure to accomplish the tasks set for the area. Peasant resistance there was especially embittered, often suicidal, and the "firm measures" for dealing with it seemed beyond the capacity of the Odessa officials. The situation was considered so serious that Molotov himself came down, in behalf of the Politburo, to stiffen the government's ruthlessness.

"Comrade Molotov called the activists together," Lazarev said, "and he talked plainly, sharply. The job must be done, no matter how many lives it cost, he told us. As long as there were millions of small landowners in the country, he said, the revolution was in danger. There would always be the chance that in case of war they might side with the enemy in order to defend their property. There was no room for softness or regrets. We did not misunderstand him. After such a warning, Victor Andreyevich, there could be no limit to horror."

Lazarev covered his face with both hands, as if to shut out the gruesome memory.

Before leaving the capital I visited several other acquaintances. There were some among them who mouthed the Party slogans and the press editorials. They were the contented ones, living in a paradise of propaganda, in an insulated Moscow world little related to the country as a whole. And there were the others, like Lazarev, outwardly conforming to the artificial optimism of the capital, but inwardly bleeding and disturbed. They spoiled the high-pitched mood induced by my visit to the Commissar and gave new direction to my thoughts.

There was no ecstasy in my recital of my experiences, at home and in my report to Golubenko. Through some dim feeling of guilt, too vague to identify, I said nothing about the thousand rubles, the motorcars and the theatre tickets.

Nikopol, Moscow and other interruptions of my studies had to be compensated by extra hours of cramming. Luckily I found technical studies easy to absorb and quickly caught up with the classes.

4

A few months after my return from Moscow, little Katya came into the life of my family. One evening, returning home from classes, I was about to go into the bathroom to wash up for supper. My mother stopped me. The little girl was in there taking a bath, she whispered.

"What little girl?"

"Shsh . . . I'll tell you later. Terrible things are going on in the villages."

I went into my room and mother soon followed. In a few words she told me the story. My cousin Natasha, a Party member who was directing a factory college, was on the train returning from some business trip. A dirt-crusted, ragged little girl of ten or eleven, one of the new crop of "wild children," came into the car, begging for bread in a tremulous, hardly audible voice. The sight was familiar enough, yet something about the child's pitiful eyes and shriveled features touched Natasha to the quick. She brought the waif to our house.

"I suppose it was the temperature," Natasha had apologized to mother. "I couldn't bear the thought of the barefoot, half-naked bit of humanity out in the cold on a night like this."

Mother at once decided to let the child remain. One more mouth won't matter, there are so many of us, she smiled. I took her into my arms and hugged her.

"You're a real mother," I said. "I'm happy you've decided that way."

We went into the dining room. Little Katya was sitting on the floor near the radiator pipes. She was pale and frightened, all hunched in a ball, as if to make herself small and invisible. She was lost in the folds of one of mother's dresses. Her wet black hair was parted in the middle and braided. The little face was oval, gray with exhaustion and prematurely old, but the features were good, even handsome. She sat there deadly still, only her large blue eyes darting in every direction.

"Why are you on the floor, Katya? Come, sit on this chair. This is my son, Victor Andreyevich. Shake hands with him."

The child did what she was told.

"Hello, Katya," I said, squatting to face her. "Why are you so silent? Don't be afraid. We all love you. Has anyone hurt you?"

"No," she said in a faint whisper.

At the supper table Katya was shy and quiet. She held her spoon clumsily. But then hunger won over her embarrassment and she began to wolf the food. We tried to talk indifferently about many things, but the pathos of this child had us all depressed. My father said scarcely a word.

After supper, when mother went to wash the dishes, Katya said, "Auntie, may I help you?" Carrying the dishes from the table to the kitchen, she seemed for the first time a normal little girl, a touch of masquerade in her dragging grown-up gown. Our neighbor, Olga Ivanovna, came in. She was an active employe of the Regional Party Committee. She not only approved our taking in the child but offered to share the cost of clothes for her. Suddenly we heard the girl weeping in the kitchen.

"Let her cry it out," mother said.

But the weeping grew louder until it became hysterical sobbing. In the primordial singsong wail of the peasant she kept repeating, in Ukrainian, "Where's my mama? Where's my papa? Oh, where's my big brother Valya?" We went into the kitchen. The girl sat hunched over in a chair, wringing her bony little hands, tears streaming down her sunken cheeks.

"Please quiet down, Katya darling," mother pleaded. "No one will do you any harm. You will live with us, we'll get you shoes and clothes, we'll teach you to read and write. Believe me, I'll be a good mother to you."

The child would not be comforted. She began to tell about herself.

"Don't, little dove, don't. You'll tell us some other time," mother urged.

"I can't," Katya sobbed. "I must tell now. I can't stand not talking. I've been a whole year without my folks. A whole year! We lived in Pokrovnaya. My father didn't want to join the *kolkhoz*. All kinds of people argued with him and took him away and beat him but still he wouldn't go in. They shouted he was a kulak agent."

"Was your father a kulak?" I asked. "Do you know what a 'kulak agent' means?"

"No, uncle, I don't know what these words mean. Our teacher

didn't teach them to us. We had a horse, a cow, a heifer, five sheep, some pigs and a barn. That was all. Every night the constable would come and take papa to the village Soviet. They asked him for grain and didn't believe that he had no more. But it was the truth, I swear it."—She crossed herself solemnly.—"For a whole week they wouldn't let father sleep and they beat him with sticks and revolvers till he was black and blue and swollen all over."

When the last *pood* of grain had been squeezed out of him, Katya recounted, her father slaughtered a pig. He left a little meat for his family and sold the rest in the city to buy bread. Then he slaughtered the calf. Again "they" began to drag him out every night. They told him that killing livestock without permission was a crime.

"Then one morning about a year ago," Katya went on, "strangers came to the house. One of them was from the G.P.U. and the chairman of our Soviet was with him too. Another man wrote in a book everything that was in the house, even the furniture and our clothes and pots and pans. Then wagons arrived and all our things were taken away and the remaining animals were driven to the *kolkhoz*.

"*Mamochka,* my dear little mother, she cried and prayed and fell on her knees and even father and big brother Valya cried and sister Shura. But it did no good. We were told to get dressed and take along some bread and salt pork, onions and potatoes, because we were going on a long journey."

The memory was too much for Katya. She again burst into wild sobbing. But she insisted on going on with the story:

"They put us all in the old church. There were many other parents and children from our village, all with bundles and all weeping. There we spent the whole night, in the dark, praying and crying, praying and crying. In the morning about thirty families were marched down the road surrounded by militiamen. People on the road made the sign of the cross when they saw us and also started crying.

"At the station there were many other people like us, from other villages. It seemed like thousands. We were all crushed into a stone barn but they wouldn't let my dog, Volchok, come in though he'd followed us all the way down the road. I heard him howling when I was inside in the dark.

"After a while we were let out and driven into cattle cars, long rows of them, but I didn't see Volchok anywhere and the guard kicked me when I asked. As soon as our car was filled up so that there was no room for more, even standing up, it was locked from the outside. We all shrieked and prayed to the Holy Virgin. Then the train started. No one knew where we were going. Some said Siberia but others said no, the Far North or even the hot deserts.

"Near Kharkov my sister Shura and I were allowed out to get some water. Mama gave us some money and a bottle and said to try and buy some milk for our baby brother who was very sick. We begged the guard so long that he let us go out which he said was against his rules. Not far away were some peasant huts so we ran there as fast as our feet would carry us.

"When we told these people who we were they began to cry. They gave us something to eat right away, then filled the bottle with milk and wouldn't take the money. Then we ran back to the station. But we were too late and the train had gone away without us."

Katya interrupted herself again to wail for her mother, father, brothers and sister. Now most of us in the kitchen were weeping with the child. The harder mother tried to soothe Katya, the louder she wept herself. My father looked grim and said nothing. I could see the muscles of his face working convulsively.

Katya and her sister, new recruits to the vast army of homeless children, wandered together from village to village. They learned to beg, to forage for food, to "ride the rails" on trains. They became expert in the special jargon of the wild waifs. Then they were separated in a city marketplace, while being chased by a militiaman, and Katya remained alone in the world—until Natasha led her to our home.

We learned to love Katya and she came to feel at home with us. But from time to time, at night, we could hear her smothered sobs and that ancient dirge-like complaint, "Where are you, little mother? Where are you, *papochka?*"

CHAPTER VIII

HORROR IN THE VILLAGE

To spare yourself mental agony, you veil unpleasant truths from view by half-closing your eyes—and your mind. You make panicky excuses and shrug off knowledge with words like exaggeration and hysteria. Then something happens that startles you into opening wide both your mind and eyes. For the first time you look without blinking.

It was thus with me in the weeks after little Katya entered our household. Unconsciously I had protected my faith against corroding facts. I had edged away from opportunities to go into the nearby collectivization areas. Then the ordeal of one innocent child shocked me into facing the ordeal of all peasant Russia. I was determined to accept the first chance to go deep into the collectivization regions.

The chance came sooner than I had hoped. Through the Party office at the Institute I was instructed to report at the Regional Committee. The purpose: mobilization of Party brigades for work in the villages.

About eighty of us were in the conference hall, mostly younger men. A few of them I knew from association in Party activities in the last few years. All of us were tense, some of us could not conceal our worry. We were being sent into the farm districts to help collect grain and speed up the final phase of the harvest. But we felt and behaved as if we were about to plunge into the thick of a bloody war.

Comrade Hatayevich, a member of the Central Committee of the Party, made a speech. It only increased our nervousness. We had half expected to hear a technical discourse on agriculture and village economy. Instead we listened to a fiery summons to go forth and do battle in a do-or-die spirit.

"Comrades," he said, "you are going into the country for a month or six weeks. The Dniepropetrovsk Region has fallen behind. The Party and Comrade Stalin ordered us to complete collectivization by spring, and here we are at the end of summer with the task unfinished. The local village authorities need an injection of Bolshevik iron. That's why we are sending you.

"You must assume your duties with a feeling of the strictest Party responsibility, without whimpering, without any rotten liberalism. Throw your bourgeois humanitarianism out of the window and act like Bolsheviks worthy of Comrade Stalin. Beat down the kulak agent wherever he raises his head. It's war—it's them or us! The last decayed remnant of capitalist farming must be wiped out at any cost!

"Secondly, comrades, it is absolutely necessary to fulfill the government's plan for grain delivery. The kulaks, and even some middle and 'poor' peasants, are not giving up their grain. They are sabotaging the Party policy. And the local authorities sometimes waver and show weakness. Your job is to get the grain at any price. Pump it out of them, wherever it's hidden, in ovens, under beds, in cellars or buried away in back yards.

"Through you, the Party brigades, the villages must learn the meaning of Bolshevik firmness. You must find the grain and you *will* find it. It's a challenge to the last shred of your initiative and to your Chekist spirit. *Don't be afraid of taking extreme measures.* The Party stands four-square behind you. Comrade Stalin expects it of you. It's a life-and-death struggle; better to do too much than not enough.

"Your third important task is to complete the threshing of the grain, to repair the tools, plows, tractors, reapers and other equipment.

"The class struggle in the village has taken the sharpest forms. This is no time for squeamishness or rotten sentimentality. Kulak agents are masking themselves and getting into the collective farms where they sabotage the work and kill the livestock. What's required from you is Bolshevik alertness, intransigence and courage. I am sure you will carry out the instructions of the Party and the directives of our beloved Leader."

The final words, conveying a threat, were drowned in obedient applause.

"Are there any questions? Is everything clear?"

There were no questions.

"Then wait right here. You will soon be called separately to see Comrade Brodsky."

I asked myself: Can this be all the "instructions" we will receive? Is it possible that a lot of students and industrial officials are expected to solve the tremendous economic and political problems of the agrarian villages just by applying more and more "Bolshevik firmness"? How can a group like this, youngsters and most of us ignorant of farm problems, be entrusted to decide the fate of hundreds of thousands of peasants?

As if he had eavesdropped on my thoughts, a young man sitting at my right said in a low voice:

"Comrade Kravchenko, I suppose we'll receive further instructions. I mean along *practical* lines."

"I don't know," I said. I recognized him as a student at the Institute, but that was all I knew about him. I had no intention of beginning the exercise of "Bolshevik firmness" by being inveigled into "dangerous" discussion with a stranger.

"You see, comrade," he continued, "I've never lived in a village. I know nothing about life in the country and I haven't the faintest idea how to go about those big tasks the Secretary outlined. Yet it's clear, isn't it, that we will pay with our Party cards and maybe with our heads if we fail?"

I was irritated. Either the fellow is incredibly naive, I thought, or he is trying to provoke me into unguarded speech.

"I'm sorry," I said, not bothering to hide my annoyance, "but you had your chance to ask questions."

"That's true. Only everyone applauded and I couldn't get up the nerve to say that *nothing* was clear to me. But I know you from the Institute, Comrade Kravchenko, and trust you. If only I could get assigned to the same brigade with you, I'd feel better."

I looked him straight in the eyes and suddenly felt ashamed of my misgivings. His distress seemed genuine. Though he was only a few years younger than I, he had a sheltered, small-boy look about him.

"It's all right with me if you can arrange it," I said, "though I suppose assignments have already been made."

"I'll try," he smiled, new courage in his voice. "My name is Tsvetkov, Sergei Alexeyevich Tsvetkov."

He went off. In a few minutes I was summoned to the office of Comrade Brodsky. A powerfully built man with a big mop of black hair was sitting behind a big desk.

"Comrade Kravchenko," he said at once, "do you know anything about the village?"

"I lived in an agrarian commune for some years during the civil war. Besides, in 1920–21 I had a few courses at an agricultural school."

"Excellent! So few of these brigadiers know the difference between wheat and stinkweed."

He pressed a bell and two other men were led into the office. One of them, smiling shyly in token of his success, was the student Tsvetkov. The other was a man of about forty whom I did not know.

"Shake hands all around," Comrade Brodsky said. "You three will work together. You're to go to the village of Podgorodnoye. You, Comrade Kravchenko, will be in charge of completing the threshing. You will also be responsible for putting all the tools and machinery in order. You, Comrade Tsvetkov, together with Comrade Arshinov, will wind up the collectivization and grain collection. And both of you will operate under Comrade Arshinov here. He's in charge of the brigade of three. He's not only an old Party worker but has had experience in the Prosecutor's office.

"That's all. Go across the hall and get your mandates and money."

Arshinov was a thickset man of short stature, his head and face smoothly shaven and mottled like old marble. There was no line of demarcation between his forehead and scalp. His face was flat and a little out of focus, as if seen through defective glass, and his eyes were mere slits in the flatness. The whole effect was decidedly unpleasant.

In the outer office Arshinov instructed us to bring along warm clothes, any food we could manage to buy, "and of course," he added, "a revolver." After we had agreed to meet at the station waiting room the following day, Arshinov went one way, Tsvetkov and I the other way.

Tsvetkov apparently was not one to keep impressions to himself.

"Victor Andreyevich," he said, "to tell you the truth I don't quite warm up to our chief. I hope I'm wrong but I have the feeling we'll have a hard time with him."

"Don't talk nonsense, Comrade Tsvetkov. Why must you start with a prejudice against a comrade who's a total stranger? He may turn out to be a decent fellow. Evidently the Party trusts him and the least we can do is to trust him too. The main thing is not to begin in a defeatist temper."

Even as I spoke I realized that I was reassuring myself rather than my companion.

"And why do we need revolvers?" he persisted. "I don't expect to take away grain by force. Why, Lenin said that the collective farm is a voluntary association and Stalin has said the same thing many times. Only the other day I read——"

"Look here, Tsvetkov. Don't be hurt if I speak frankly. But you do talk strangely. I have every right to think that you're an extraordinarily naive person—or that you've been planted on me."

"My God! What a terrible idea!" he exclaimed in a horrified voice that made me regret my candor. "I'm sure you'll realize you're mistaken about me. Even about the naive part of it. I do understand the seriousness of the tasks ahead of us. That's why I am amazed we were not given more explicit and practical information. I am a Russian and the son of a Russian. I have never been a *provocateur* and couldn't be one if my life were at stake. How awful that people must suspect one another of spying and provocation. . . ."

Then, as if an inspired thought had come to him, he added:

"Come over and meet my family. My home is only a few blocks from here."

His inspiration was a sensible one. The meeting with his parents, the atmosphere of his modest home, removed my last doubts as to his integrity, although it strengthened my impression of his weakness and inexperience. His father was an oldish man in spectacles, with a tiny pointed beard. His mother was a frail little lady, gray and kindly.

Both of them were like characters out of a pre-revolutionary book, curiously unspoiled by the violence of these crowded years. They seemed to live in a private world which external evils could not easily breach. It seemed to me almost incredible that the elder Tsvetkov should be a Party member of the pre-1917 vintage. It was also heart-warming that a Russian who was so thoroughly "good," in the old-fashioned and almost forgotten sense of the word, should have survived in the Party.

"But Seryozha," Mrs. Tsvetkov complained, "why didn't you tell me you were going to the village? I hear the most terrible things. . . ."

"No, no, my dear," her husband protested, "all this talk of the horrors of collectivization is overdrawn. Things can't be as bad as they're painted. I myself am an old Party member and I agree that collectivization is the one hope for solving our agrarian problem. A lot depends on the kind of men who carry out the orders. I hope that neither you, Sergei, nor Comrade Kravchenko will sink to committing outrages. The Party, I'm sure, doesn't want that."

Reaching home, I told my family about my mission to the peasant region. Still under the influence of Katya's story, everyone was both excited and worried by what awaited me. I was already in bed that night when I heard a knock at my door. My mother came in.

"Forgive me for intruding, Vitya," she said, sitting on the edge of my bed, "but I may not get a chance in the rush of your going off tomorrow. "I know that the peasant troubles have been weighing on your mind.

and you're not the only one. Please be calm and steel yourself for whatever you may find. Also remember that one district is no indication. I should hate to see your whole life as a Communist wrecked by one sad experience. And I know that you'll make the lot of the unfortunate peasants as easy as you can."

"Thanks, mother, and don't worry about me. I'll be all right. I know revolution is no picnic."

2

Conversation among the three members of the brigade, on the train headed for Podgorodnoye, was far from amiable. Arshinov's Mauser, dangling showily from a strap on his shoulder, set us on edge. Arshinov, for his part, made no effort to hide his contempt for the blond, good-looking young man Tsvetkov. We avoided mention of our common assignment.

"Victor Andreyevich, my old folks send you their regards," Tsvetkov said.

"Thank you, Seryozha. By the way, where does your father work?"

"In a railroad office. He's an engineer, you know. He's been there for a long time and he was in the Party even before 1917."

Arshinov seemed startled on hearing this. Evidently he had discounted Tsvetkov as the son of some white-collar intellectual without influence. As the son of an Old Bolshevik, the youngster might prove harder to handle.

"Your father a Party member!" Arshinov exclaimed with evident annoyance.

"Yes, of course, why do you ask?"

"Oh nothing. I just asked."

We reached our destination toward sundown. It was drizzling and the road to the village was muddy. The peasants we met regarded us with no special interest. Only Arshinov's pistol, slapping his fat thigh as he walked, drew attention.

"Look here, Comrade Arshinov," I whispered, "would you mind putting your Mauser under your coat? There's no sense in scaring people."

"That's my own business!"

"No, comrade, it isn't. We're in this together. It concerns us and what's more, it concerns the Party. I insist on your doing as I ask, or I just won't go into the village with you."

"Comrade Kravchenko is right," Tsvetkov said. "Why frighten the horses for nothing? I have a revolver, too, but I carry it under my coat."

Reluctantly Arshinov gave in, but he didn't talk to us for the rest of the walk to the village Soviet, which proved to be a large wooden house, ugly and in disrepair. Inside, a kerosene lamp glowed dimly under a paper chimney. The room was filled with smoke and the floor was strewn with cigarette tubes. About twenty peasants were squatting on the floor, silent and obviously in a bad mood.

"Where's the chairman of the Soviet?" Arshinov asked in a loud voice, intended to announce his authority.

"There, in his office," the peasants pointed.

"And what are you people doing here? Have you nothing better to do than sit on your haunches?"

"There's plenty to do," one of the peasants spoke up. "We've been called here. They're demanding bread of me but I'm begging bread myself."

Arshinov sneered at him. "I see I'll have my hands full in this stinkhole."

We followed him into the office. A thin-faced, tired young man with a beaten look was sitting behind a table, talking to an old peasant.

"We're the Party brigade, and we're here on business," Arshinov declaimed.

"Glad to see you, how do you do?" the chairman rose and shook hands. His face belied his words; he was by no means overjoyed by our arrival. "I'll get the plan right away and we'll get down to business."

"And what are all those people waiting for out there?" Arshinov asked.

"I asked them to come. It's hard with these peasants. They insist there's no grain and that's that. The harvest in these parts has been bad and everyone's alarmed about the coming winter. It's not easy to pull the grain out of them, comrades. And they won't join the collective. Kill them, but they won't join."

"We'll see about that," Arshinov said, making a grimace. "Well, since you've called them you'd better finish with them and we'll get going tomorrow morning."

The chairman summoned one of his assistants and gave him some whispered instructions. This man took the three of us into the village. A depressing quiet pervaded the main street, broken only by the occasional barking of a dog. Here and there we saw a flicker of light in a window, smoke rising from a chimney. When we came to a large house, distinctly better than its neighbors, our guide stopped.

"This is where you will be billeted, Comrade Arshinov," he said; "I hope you'll like it."

Then he led us farther down the street, to a substantial looking house with outbuildings, a small garden and a well with a draw bucket.

"You'll like it here," he said. "The Stupenkos have just joined the collective farm. Their house is clean and there are no small children. Elderly people and"—with a wink in Tsvetkov's direction—"a pretty daughter."

At the door we were met by a tall man of perhaps sixty, clean-shaven except for long drooping mustaches in the old-fashioned Ukrainian style. He greeted us with reserve and a natural dignity that pleased me, and led us to a small but neat and comfortable room.

"When you've washed up," he said, "come in and join us. You're welcome to whatever God has sent us, which is not much."

We found the entire family at table. The daughter of the house, about eighteen, was indeed pretty. The kindly old woman, a colored kerchief drawn tight under her chin, had the gnarled work-worn hands of the peasant wife. There was also a boy of eight. We introduced ourselves and joined them. A steaming Ukrainian *borshcht,* without meat, was poured into our bowls. The second course consisted of baked potatoes and dill pickles. The bread was cut into thin slices which everyone ate as carefully as if they were holy wafers.

Knowing peasant life and the fact that normally bread in generous chunks is the staple of their diet, it was clear to me that the family was in hard circumstances. Seryozha and I excused ourselves, went back to our room and returned with the food bundles we had brought along. The Stupenkos stared as we unpacked sausage, several kinds of fish and even cold chicken. We urged them to join us and the frosty atmosphere immediately thawed out.

"Thank you, thank you," the old woman kept repeating, "you surely bring joy to our humble home."

"I don't know when we've seen sausage and candy," her husband added. "We're better off than most of the folks here, but it's hard enough. What we have won't last until the new harvest. Oh, comrades, comrades, what a pass we've come to in our Ukraine! If one does have a piece of bread he eats it so that his neighbors won't see him."

"What's your little son's name?" I asked. I had watched the boy, who was unnaturally silent and melancholy. Even the candy, which he munched without enthusiasm, failed to stir his interest.

"Vasya," the boy answered my question, and suddenly left the room.

"He's no son of ours," the host explained. "He is—how shall I put it? —an orphan of collectivization?"

"What do you mean by that?"

"He's an orphan, that's all. But don't ask the boy anything. He's still stunned by the blow. Every evening he goes back to his house and wanders around the yard for hours. We try to tell him, 'What's the sense of tormenting yourself?' but he keeps going back."

"What happened? Tell us."

"I don't know whether I should. You're new people, and besides you're from the government."

"Come on, daddy, don't be afraid. We didn't come here to harm anybody. We love the peasants and want to help them."

"Well, I'll take a chance on you. Both of you look decent. Besides, I'm too old to be afraid. Only it would be a pity if anything happened to my daughter."

He told us the story:

"About ten houses away from here lived the Vorvans—man, wife and one child, the very Vasya you saw here. They were a happy family. They worked hard. They were good people. Not kulaks—only a couple of horses, a cow, a pig, a few chickens, like everybody else. No matter how much 'they' argued with him, he wouldn't join the collective.

"All his remaining grain was taken away. Again they argued and threatened. But he wouldn't budge. 'It's my land,' he kept saying, 'my animals, my house and I won't give them up to the government.' Then people came from the city—the people in charge of exiling honest folks from their homes. They made a record of his property and took everything away, down to the last pot and towel, while the implements and livestock were turned over to the collective.

"Vorvan was declared a kulak and a kulak agent and in the evening they came to arrest him. His wife and boy began to weep and yell and the man wouldn't go. So they beat him until he bled all over and dragged him out of the house, through the mire, all the way down the street to the village Soviet. His woman ran after them yelling, wailing and calling on people and on God to help her. We all ran out but no one could do anything against armed guards, though we knew Vorvan was no kulak and we all liked him.

"The unfortunate woman kept shouting, 'Who's going to take care of us, Piotr? Where are they taking you, the beasts, the infidels!' One of the G.P.U. men pushed her so hard she sprawled in the mud, while they dragged Vorvan off to the cattle cars. Where he is now, only God knows. We took the woman back to her house and tried to comfort her. Finally she fell asleep and we all left."

The two women at the table had begun to cry as he told the story. Our host took a deep pull on his home-made, evil-smelling cigaret and continued:

"In the morning a neighbor came to see the poor Vorvan woman but couldn't find her. She called her name and got no answer. So she went into the empty barn and there met a sight that caused her to shriek like mad and many peasants came running, myself among them. The woman was hanging from a rope tied to a rafter and she was quite dead. I'll never forget the scene if I live to be a hundred. All of this happened no more than a month ago.

"My old woman and I decided to take Vasya into our home, as we have no small children of our own. He's been silent or crying for a month now and every evening, as I said, he haunts the deserted house; then he comes home and goes to sleep on the oven without a word.

"After what happened to the Vorvans, my woman and I talked it over and decided to join the *kolkhoz* . . . voluntarily."

We sat there silent for a long time. The fate of the Vorvans, like the experience of little Katya, touched me in a way that statistics of deportations and deaths could not.

"Thank you, daddy, for your trust in us," Tsvetkov finally said. "You may be sure I will not betray it. Please believe me that not all Communists are the same. Some of us are as opposed to such things as you are, and the Party itself is opposed."

He seemed to be apologizing for himself, for me, for the Party.

"Yes, thank you for your hospitality and your trust in us," I supported my companion. "We will live with you for a month. We want to be as little burden as possible. Here's all our money. We insist on paying. Buy what you need and don't go out of the way for us."

"I've been instructed not to accept any money."

"Just ignore it. That's what the Regional Committee gave us the money for. I do hope you will help us. We want to do what's right and you know your village; we don't."

I could not fall asleep for a long time, but I lay still for fear of waking Tsvetkov. I was greatly pleased that he had turned out to be a decent human being, not a formal and pious Communist.

"Are you asleep, Victor?" I heard him say.

"No, Seryozha, I can't sleep. Things keep going round and round in my head."

"Do you know, I'm ashamed to look these good peasant people in the eyes. Somehow I feel personally to blame for what those scoundrels did. And to think that they did it in the name of our beloved Party!"

I had decided to avoid saying too much to Tsvetkov. He was clearly not a strong man. There was always the danger that under pressure he might break down and unwillingly repeat my words. The less he knew, the better both for him and for me.

"Better go to sleep," I urged. "We must be up early."

When we reached the Soviet in the morning, Arshinov was already there and in a sizzling temper. He was furious because he had been put into a home where there was not enough to eat and where his hosts, though correct, were not too friendly. All morning we went over records and the chairman brought us up to date on conditions. We divided the village into sections and decided which people, among the collectivized peasants, would be responsible for plan fulfillments in each segment.

Then the Soviet chairman, Arshinov and Seryozha went into the village to get acquainted with the local situation, while the president of the collective and I went to the collective farm.

In the large court of a former estate, now half in ruins, stood ricks of newly harvested grain. I was pleased that the grain had at least been carted from the fields. If everyone worked with a will, the threshing might be completed in ten or twelve days. But that was the only satisfactory item. Everything else was in an appalling state of neglect and confusion.

Large quantities of implements and machinery, which had once been cared for like so many jewels by their private owners, now lay scattered under the open skies, dirty, rusting and out of repair. Emaciated cows and horses, crusted with manure, wandered through the yard. Chickens, geese and ducks were digging in flocks in the unthreshed grain. We went into the stable; horses were standing knee-deep in dirt, "reading newspapers," as the peasant phrase has it when cattle stand without feed in the stalls. The cows in the barn were in no better condition.

I was shocked by the picture. It was a state of affairs so alien to the nature of our Ukrainian peasant.

"Get the members of the *kolkhoz* board together immediately," I ordered the president indignantly.

In half an hour the men and women theoretically in charge of the collective were in the yard. The look on their faces was not encouraging. It seemed to say: "Here's another meddler . . . what can we do but listen?"

"Well, how are you getting along, collective farmers?" I began, eager to be friendly.

"So-so. . . . Still alive, as you see," one of them said in a surly voice.

"No rich, no poor, nothing but paupers," another added.

I pretended that the irony was over my head.

"I've come from the Regional Committee of the Party to help you with the threshing, with the repair of machinery and in putting things in order generally. Tell me, collective farmers, who elected the president of this *kolkhoz?*"

"All of us," the board members answered.

"All right, then why do you get him into trouble? Don't you see that he will be held responsible for all this confusion? Just look around. As peasants, doesn't it make you ashamed? Dirty cattle. Unprotected grain ricks. Valuable tools rotting all around. It would be no trouble putting your president in jail for this, and the board members as well.

"But that's not what I'm here for. Jails don't raise bread. Whom are you harming by this awful neglect—me or yourself? I've lived in the country. Some of my folks were peasants. But I've never seen anything as shameful as these stables, these barns, this yard. I know how some of you feel. But why should the cows and horses be punished? I'm ashamed of you. I know that you're still good farmers and I want to appeal to your pride as farmers."

"Right! This comrade makes sense," someone exclaimed.

"Then let's get down to business. Comrade president, open the meeting. Elect people so that each one knows exactly what's expected of him. We'll write down names and dates and what each one must do."

We talked and planned for hours. Many of the peasants refused responsibility, but in the end each board member agreed to a specific duty —to organize the threshing, to clean up the animal houses, to inventory the implements and so on. The meeting ended on a friendly note.

At supper time, my host told me that he had seen some of the board members after the meeting. "They say you started things right. They're pleased with you, especially because you don't swear or holler and threaten."

"Tell me, daddy, did I do right in demanding that they put things in order at the collective farm immediately?"

"Absolutely right. The peasants themselves know that things are not going as they should. Only in their hearts they're bitter about having lost their land and cattle and machines. All the same, things have to be put in order. Life must go on."

After the meal, I saw Seryozha alone. He looked unhappy.

"Well, how are things with you?"

"Not so good, Victor Andreyevich. I'm doing things according to Arshinov's plans. But I don't get many results. I called delinquents on the grain collection one after another. It was always the same story. The peasant takes off his hat and sits down respectfully.

" 'You haven't delivered your grain so far,' I begin.

" 'Maybe I have, maybe I haven't.'

" 'You still owe the state twelve *poods*,' I say.

" 'Where will I get so much grain?' he shrugs his shoulders. 'I haven't got it.'

" 'How much can you deliver today?'

" 'Maybe two *poods*, maybe three.'

"So we argue back and forth. The government needs the grain, I insist, and the peasant says, 'The government needs it, and how about my wife and children? They don't need it, I suppose. You know yourself the harvest was bad. Who's going to feed us all year after you've robbed us of our grain?'

"I collected fifty-two *poods* today but that isn't a fraction of what Arshinov expected me to do. I can't do any better. These people are tired, sullen and frightened to death. Maybe some of them have more grain than they admit, but they won't give it up, they don't dare give it up, with the long winter coming on and so many mouths to feed."

"Don't worry too much, Seryozha," I tried to calm him. "Do the best you can. Worry doesn't help."

The following morning I went to the collective farm with my host. I was delighted to see that work was in full swing. Tools were being cleaned and oiled. Manure was being carted out of the barns and stables. Preparations were under way for threshing. Work went on for several days, until the place began to look almost normal. What is more, the collectivized farmers themselves were in better spirits. The women and girls were even singing Ukrainian work songs as of old. These simple people, at bottom, loved their work. The weather was good and they understood even better than I did the value of every rainless day.

More than a week passed. The repair jobs were slowed up by lack of nails, wire, iron, lumber and other essentials. But peasant ingenuity made up for these lacks. Our accounting system, however, could not be straightened out because we had no paper. It was therefore decided to send Seryozha to Dniepropetrovsk for a day to make purchases.

When I came home that night I found Seryozha with a string in hand, measuring little Vasya, making knots in the string. I pretended not to notice.

The next day, with Seryozha away, I called on Arshinov. He was aware that my work was proceeding well and seemed jealous of my success. He worked off his irritation in a tirade against Tsvetkov, whom he abused as a softie, yellow-livered and worst of all, a rotten liberal humanitarian.

"Yesterday I searched some houses," he said. "People whom our softie let off easy. In every case I found grain hidden away. I confiscated every bit of it without nonsense. Lying to the Soviet power, the dirty bastard kulaks! I'll teach them a lesson they'll never forget! I was at the District Committee today and they're behind me. On Tuesday things will happen."

"What will happen?"

"That's my business."

Threshing went on all day Sunday. I did not have to persuade the peasants. Even the most religious ones understood that time was short. Towards sundown Seryozha returned carrying a large suitcase and several bags. There were gifts for the whole family—books for the daughter, sewing thread for the mother, tobacco for old Stupenko. The grand climax of the happy occasion was when Seryozha pulled out of his fat suitcase a pair of long pants, a coat, shoes and underwear for Vasya.

The boy was immediately dressed in his new finery and roundly admired. A couple of neighbors came in to view the miracle of orphaned Vasya in elegant new attire. The boy himself smiled for the first time since we met him. "Thanks, Uncle Seryozha," he said. Tears came to his eyes when Seryozha the magnificent also presented him with a notebook, crayons and a box of hard colored candy.

It was past midnight when the family retired. When we were alone in our room, I asked Tsvetkov how he was getting along with Arshinov.

"He's a son of a bitch and a sadist, Victor Andreyevich. I hesitated to tell you about it but I can't keep quiet any longer. The beast drags the peasants from their homes in the dead of night, swears at them, threatens them with his Mauser. I've been told he even beats them up brutally."

"Why in hell didn't you tell me sooner? Get dressed, let's go!"

Through the wooden shutters I could see lights in the Soviet building. We found peasants squatting on the floor. There was an armed sentry at the door and a village constable with a revolver was sitting inside, smoking. As I entered I heard the cries of a peasant and the swearing of Arshinov behind the closed office door.

"Why are all these people here at this hour?" I asked the constable, my voice shrill with anger.

He jumped to his feet. "As usual," he said, "Comrade Arshinov is pumping grain and having a little talk with those who won't join the collective farm."

Suddenly Arshinov's voice rose to a hysterical pitch, a heavy object crashed to the floor, and we could hear the peasant groaning: "Why are you beating me? You have no right to beat me. . . ." Then Arshinov yelled, "Constable, throw this trash into the cooler. I'll teach you, you kulak rat!"

The constable rushed toward the adjoining room. I caught him by the arm. "Stay here," I said, "I'll go in myself."

I swung open the door. Arshinov was startled. He bit his lips, fidgeted in his chair and made a motion to remove his pistol from the table. The peasant sprawled on the floor was an old man, in ragged clothes, his face streaked with blood. I motioned him to leave.

I walked up to Arshinov. I could scarcely restrain myself from using my fists on him.

"Let the peasants go!" I shouted. "And immediately, do you hear?"

"I'm in charge here, Comrade Kravchenko. I'll thank you to take your nose out of my business."

"No, this is Party business. As a Communist I won't have you dishonor the Soviet power by acting like a sadist and barbarian. Comrade Tsvetkov," I called into the outer room, "please take down the name of the old man who's just been beaten up, also the constable's name."

Arshinov put up a bold front but was obviously disconcerted by my anger. "What in thunder are you up to?" he said. "What is this—provocation? Are you trying to discredit an emissary of the Regional Committee in the eyes of the masses?"

"Stop that hypocrisy! It's people like you who discredit the Party and the country. Constable! Let everyone go! Comrade peasants, if anyone is beaten up again make sure to tell me. It's against the law."

Tsvetkov came into the office. He was pale as a ghost. His hands trembled. I ordered him to go home and wait for me. Then I turned to Arshinov:

"Look here, Arshinov, do you realize what you're doing? Is this collectivization or is it banditry with the help of a Mauser? You have a right to demand grain and to search premises if necessary. But you have no right to use violence and to carry on nocturnal inquisitions. If you don't want to get into trouble with the Regional Committee, you will stop this sort of thing. Otherwise I shall expose you, whatever the cost. Do you understand?"

I turned and left. Seryozha was not yet home. I was worried about him. But in about half an hour he arrived.

"I've been at the hut of the peasant who was beaten up," he told me. "He has a sick wife, five children and not a crumb of bread in the house. His house reeks of poverty and despair. And that's what we call a kulak! The kids are in rags and tatters. They all look like ghosts. I saw the pot on the oven—a few potatoes in water. That was their supper tonight.

"Here, Victor"—he showed me a dirty scrap of paper—"the old man has given me a declaration of his willingness to enter the *kolkhoz*. I begged him to stop being bull-headed, to take pity on his family. Finally he agreed."

"Go to sleep, Seryozha. Don't worry. We'll think of something to do." And forestalling his questions, I added: "I'll tell you tomorrow about my talk with Arshinov. You keep on working with him as if nothing has happened. And, oh yes, I want to thank you for Vasya's suit."

I kissed him on both cheeks.

"Thank you, Victor. When I got home I told my folks the whole story. Father went out and somehow dug up the pair of shoes among his friends. Mother rummaged in the garret and found an old suit of mine, when I was a schoolboy. She worked all day, fitting it to Vasya's measurements."

"Yes, the Party has people like your father—and people like Arshinov," I said.

3

At the collective farm things were going well, better even than I had hoped. Threshing was in full swing, the cattle and horses were being cared for, the farm implements were almost in order.

The Board, at my suggestion, decided to give a dinner in honor of the completed threshing. Wednesday was to be the big day and on Tuesday everyone agreed to work until the following dawn to justify the celebration. Pigs were slaughtered. Long tables were improvised in the *kolkhoz* yard. The smell of cooking and the excitement of a party gave the village a kind of holiday air.

On Tuesday afternoon I went into the fields where the women were husking the corn and stacking it in wagons. I joined in the work—and the songs—for a few hours, enjoying the physical exertion. Though I had taken a bold attitude, I felt none too sure that I could curb Arshinov. The problem gnawed ceaselessly at my mind. Here in the fields I could forget. The women pretended to be amused by my amateur work in husking, but they were clearly flattered that "the government" had come down to their humble level.

Evening was falling when I drove into the village, with several companions. Immediately we realized that something was happening. Agitated groups stood around. Women were weeping. I hurried to the Soviet building.

"What's happening?" I asked the constable.

"Another round-up of kulaks," he replied. "Seems the dirty business will never end. The G.P.U. and District Committee people came this morning."

A large crowd was gathered outside the building. Policemen tried to scatter them, but they came back. Some were cursing. A number of women and children were weeping hysterically and calling the names of their husbands and fathers. It was all like a scene out of a nightmare.

Inside the Soviet building, Arshinov was talking to a G.P.U. official. Both of them were smiling, apparently exchanging pleasantries of some sort. In the back yard, guarded by G.P.U. soldiers with drawn revolvers, stood about twenty peasants, young and old, with bundles on their backs. A few of them were weeping. The others stood there sullen, resigned, hopeless.

So this was "liquidation of the kulaks as a class"! A lot of simple peasants being torn from their native soil, stripped of all their worldly goods, and shipped to some distant lumber camps or irrigation works. For some reason, on this occasion, most of the families were being left behind. Their outcries filled the air. As I came out of the Soviet house again, I saw two militiamen leading a middle-aged peasant. It was obvious that he had been manhandled—his face was black and blue and his gait was painful; his clothes were ripped in a way indicating a struggle.

As I stood there, distressed, ashamed, helpless, I heard a woman shouting in an unearthly voice. Everyone looked in the direction of her cry and a couple of G.P.U. men started running towards her. The woman, her hair streaming, held a flaming sheaf of grain in her hands. Before anyone could reach her, she had tossed the burning sheaf onto the thatched roof of the house, which burst into flame instantaneously.

"Infidels! murderers!" the distraught woman was shrieking. "We worked all our lives for our house. You won't have it. The flames will have it!" Her cries turned suddenly into crazy laughter.

Peasants rushed into the burning house and began to drag out furniture. There was something macabre, unreal, about the whole scene—the fire, the wailing, the demented woman, the peasants being dragged through

the mud and herded together for deportation. The most unearthly touch
of all, for me, was the sight of Arshinov and the G.P.U. officer looking on
calmly, as if this were all routine, as if the burning hut were a bonfire for
their amusement.

I stood in the midst of it, trembling, bewildered, scarcely in control of
my senses. I had an impulse to shoot—someone, anyone, to relieve the unbearable tension of my emotions. Never before or since have I been so
close to losing my mind. I reached under my coat for my revolver. Just
then a strong hand gripped my arm. It was my host, Stupenko. Perhaps
he had guessed my thoughts.

"You must not torment yourself, Victor Andreyevich," he said. "If you
do anything foolish, you'll only hurt yourself without helping us. Believe
me, I'm an old man and I know. Take a hold of yourself. You'll do more
good if you avoid trouble, since this is beyond your control. Come, let's
go home. You're as white as a sheet. As for me, I'm used to it. This is
nothing. The big round-ups last year were worse."

At home I paced my narrow room in mounting agitation and despair.
I had planned to protest against Arshinov to the District Committee of
the Party. But here were representatives of the Committee, along with
the G.P.U., indulging in the same kind of brutality. What hope was there
that I would get any more satisfaction from the Regional Committee?

The suspicion that the horrors were not accidental, but planned and
sanctioned by the highest authorities, had been sprouting in my mind.
This night it flowered into a certainty that left me, for the moment,
emptied of hope. The shame of it had been easier to bear as long as I
could blame Arshinov and other individuals.

I fell asleep, in sheer fatigue, without taking off my clothes. When I
opened my eyes, some hours later, I was alarmed by the fact that Seryozha
was not in his bed. I rushed into the yard, then into the garden.

"Who's there?" I heard Seryozha's voice and caught the gleam of a
revolver. He was sitting on a bench under the cherry tree.

I was near him in one leap and wrenched the revolver from his hand.
Seryozha buried his face in his palms. He shook with sobs.

"You're a fool," I said, "and a weakling. I'm not at all proud of you.
Whom will you help by shooting yourself? That's stupidity. It's not the
answer, Seryozha. We must keep alive and do what we can to lighten the
burden of our Russian people. If we destroy ourselves, only the Arshinovs
will remain."

He calmed down a little and looked into my eyes.

"Victor Andreyevich, I have seen everything and I understand everything. Politically, I am a head taller than I was. There's no point in fooling ourselves. The Party itself is guilty of inhumanity, violence, murder.
The fine phrases in our speeches are just camouflage for the awful realities.
Was this what my good-hearted father labored for all his life? Was this
what I myself believed in ever since I joined the Party?"

I induced him to go to bed. But neither of us fell asleep. We talked
about what we had seen. It fitted so well into what we had been hearing
that we could no longer doubt the truth of the "anti-Party rumors." We

were glad when the old man knocked on our door and said: "Time to get up, comrades."

The celebration dinner took place that day as planned, but the joy had been drained out of it. The memory of the "kulak" round-up weighed on all of us.

My relations with Arshinov remained strictly official. I drafted a long, detailed report on his behavior and sent it to the Regional Committee. After the mass arrests, the few remaining diehards "voluntarily" joined the collective. And every *pood* of grain in the village was handed over— again "voluntarily." These people had apparently decided to face starvation at home rather than banishment to the unknown. In many cases peasants pleaded for permission to sell their remaining livestock, even their furniture, to buy grain in the cities to meet the government's demands.

The local church had been turned into a granary and as it filled up, Arshinov was triumphant. He boasted of his "successes" and he lost no chance to needle Tsvetkov. "Watch how I do it and learn," he said. "The trouble is you don't know the meaning of Bolshevik firmness."

The day for our departure approached. Arshinov informed us that he would remain for five days longer for a final check-up. I had little doubt that he was staying behind to gather "evidence" against Tsvetkov and myself. I spent the last day on the collective farm, preparing the data for my final report.

"Now that the harvest is all gathered in, I suppose you can figure what you'll receive for your labor?" I said to the board members.

"Yes, we've figured and figured," the president said, shaking his head sadly. "It comes out about 1200 grams [about 2½ pounds] of grain for each day worked by each collective farmer. We worked only part of the year and this payment must last for the farmer and his family for a whole year. How to stretch 1200 grams to feed a family until the next harvest is something only God—and maybe your Party—can figure out."

"I suppose we'll all die of hunger," another added bitterly.

Probably he did not mean this literally. How was he to guess that nearly the whole population in this village of Podgorodnoye would be wiped out by famine in the year to come? How was he to guess that the authorities would take away even some of the grain to which they were entitled for their work?

We parted from the villagers as friends. They showed a real affection for both Tsvetkov and me. Our hosts, too, were genuinely sorry to see us go. During the farewell supper, old Stupenko brought a large bottle of cherry brandy into the dining room, dug up from the back yard and still covered with earth.

"I have been saving this, the Lord help me, for some important holiday," he announced. "I thought to myself, when I marry off my daughter or after I die, let people drink a glass of brandy and say a good word about me. But I've decided that your going away deserves the best I've got. So here, let's drink to your health and to the salvation of our poor tortured country."

After dinner we sang old Ukrainian songs and Stupenko's wife, emboldened by a sip of the strong brandy, told nostalgic tales of legendary heroes, in the very words she had heard from her grandmother.

Back in Dniepropetrovsk, the Regional Committee seemed satisfied with my work. But I could stir nobody into active interest in my report on Arshinov. "Well, he has his faults," I was told, "haven't we all? But I'll say this for him—he gets results!" I wrote a letter to the Moscow *Pravda* about a case of brutality which was discrediting the Party in the village. The letter remained unanswered and unpublished.

Because of the time I had spent in the village, I was seriously behind in my studies. To catch up, I worked harder than ever. The more deeply I buried myself in technical books, the less time I had for anguished thoughts and doubts. Work became a soporific of which I took long draughts.

4

In war, there is a palpable difference between those who have been in the front lines and the people at home. It is a difference that cannot be bridged by fuller information and a lively sympathy. It is a difference that resides in the nerves, not in the mind.

Those of the Communists who had been directly immersed in the horrors of collectivization were thereafter marked men. We carried the scars. We had seen ghosts. We could almost be identified by our taciturnity, by the way we shrank from discussion of the "peasant front." We might consider the subject among ourselves, as Seryozha and I did after our return, but to talk of it to the uninitiated seemed futile. With them we had no common vocabulary of experience.

I do not refer, of course, to the Arshinovs. Under any political system, they are the gendarmes and executioners. I refer to Communists whose feelings had not been wholly blunted by cynicism. Try as we would, the arithmetic of atrocities—a thousand victims today to insure the happiness of unborn thousands tomorrow—made no sense. We found it hard to justify the agrarian terror.

At the January, 1933, session of the Party's Central Committee, Stalin told our country that the collectivization of farming had been victoriously finished. "The collective farm regime has destroyed pauperism and poverty in the village," he said. "Tens of millions of poor peasants have risen to a state of security. . . . Under the old regime the peasants were working for the benefit of the landlords, kulaks and speculators . . . working and leading a life of hunger and making others rich. Under the new collective farm regime, the peasants are working for themselves and for their collective farms."

The session, according to the press account, broke into stormy applause. The delegates shouted, "Hurrah for the great and wise Father and Teacher, Comrade Stalin!"

Reading of the proceedings, I thought of Podgorodnoye and its terrorized population . . . of Arshinov beating the peasants . . . of the de-

mented woman setting her house on fire . . . of the ragged creatures
being herded into the back yard for banishment. Like everyone else in the
Ukraine, I was aware that a famine as catastrophic as the one I had lived
through more than a decade ago was already sweeping the land of total
collectivization and the "happy life."

No, we could not be soothed by Stalin's words. To restore our faith,
or at least to keep from sinking into despair, we had to avert our eyes
from the village and contemplate other parts of the picture. The industrial
achievements, for instance, and "the rising tide of revolution in capitalist
countries."

"You know, Victor Andreyevich," Seryozha said, "I've read Comrade
Stalin's speech at the January Plenum of the Central Committee many
times. What he said about the villages gives me the creeps. Now the
peasants are 'free' . . . 'poverty banished from the village' . . . After
what you and I have seen!"

"But the industrial side, Seryozha, that's another story. How many
new factories, mines, foundries, dams, power stations! It's wonderful to
feel that we're striding forward in seven-league boots. We will no longer be
a backward, colonial nation. Even in America qualified engineers are
selling shoelaces and apples on the streets, while here you and I are studying hard because our country needs more engineers. Over there—unem-
ployment; over here—not enough hands to do the work."

"All the same, Victor Andreyevich, I can't forget the horrors of Podgorodnoye. . . ."

"Neither can I, Seryozha."

Stalin's speech was being hammered home by Party lecturers at nuclei
and district meetings. The cost was high, they said, but look at the new
enterprises growing like toadstools. Magnitostroi. Dnieprostroi. The Stalingrad tractor plant. The Nikopol metallurgical *combinat*. Dozens of others.
While the outside capitalist world was bogged down in crisis after crisis, the
Soviet socialist world was marching forward. Our crises were those of
growth, not of dissolution.

The breakdown of world capitalism, the end of its "temporary stabiliza-
tion," was the great consolation in Russia's travail. Our shrinking food
supplies were being rigidly rationed. In the villages, famine held sway.
Prisons, isolators and concentration camps were filling up with "enemies
of the people." Thousands of our intelligentsia—engineers, officials, even
well-known Communists—had to be liquidated as saboteurs and "agents of
foreign governments." But the international working class was about to
revolt! As Stalin put it, "The successes of the Five Year Plan are mobiliz-
ing the revolutionary strength of the working class in all countries."

*Then, exactly twenty-three days after Stalin's speech, Hitler came to
power in Germany!* The bubble of our great consolation burst in our
faces.

All Soviet propaganda for years had earmarked Germany as the first
great capitalist country which would follow the Soviet example. Day and
night the morale of our Party masses had been sustained by the vision.
The German Social Democrats, those "lackeys of the bourgeoisie," were

bankrupt, whereas the Communist Party was rolling up millions of votes.

Little wonder, therefore, that we were stunned. For several days nobody knew what to think. Then the machinery of propaganda went into high gear. The official explanation, having been decided upon in the highest Moscow quarters, was pumped through the mass of the Party. Top officials addressed Regional meetings, smaller officials relayed the message to district meetings, journeymen agitators carried it to the smallest Party nuclei.

In substance we were told that the triumph of Fascism in Germany was really a disguised victory for the world revolution. It represented the last stand of capitalism, its death agony. The grimacing of the parliamentary harlequins of fake democracy was over. Even with the help of socialist and liberal lackeys, the capitalists could no longer control the discontented masses and had to resort to unadulterated terror through Fascism.

"German Fascism is the spearhead of world capitalism," a speaker at the Institute explained. "Capitalism finally has thrown off its mask. The workers of the world now face a clear choice between Fascism and Communism. Can we doubt which they will choose? The Soviet Union stands alone as the bulwark against Fascism, and the proletariat of all countries is with us. Mussolini in Italy, Hitler in Germany, comrades, are the precursors of our revolution. By revealing the true face of modern capitalism-fascism, they push the masses to an understanding of the truth. There is force in our slogan: *The worse the better!*"

And thus the defeat in Germany was twisted into a species of victory for the Five Year Plan. In intimate groups, in our own rooms, however, we were far from certain. After all, Social Democrats and liberals, even reactionary trade unionists, were being liquidated along with Communists in Germany. Wasn't there a flaw somewhere in the Party thesis? Had it really been necessary to waste all our strength fighting the socialists and democrats when together we might have held off the Nazis? Is it truly inevitable that the capitalist countries, especially England, will join Hitlerite Germany against Russia in the coming war?

To answer such questions we could draw only on the limited and contradictory information doled out by the government. Foreign newspapers and magazines were forbidden to us. The Party men, it is true, through special bulletins, were allowed to know more than the general population, but our mental fare was selected and "processed." Only an idiot could doubt that even our superior confidential news was strictly rationed and in large part synthetic.

The authorized version of the Hitler blow did not sit well with most Communists. Coming at a critical moment in Soviet life, it deepened the gloom that was spreading through the ranks of the faithful. The inner Party press talked ominously about "defeatist moods" which must be rooted out. The groundwork was being laid for a great "purge" of the Party, to winnow out the doubters, the squeamish ones, those surfeited with blood and suffering.

CHAPTER IX

HARVEST IN HELL

OR ACTIVE Communists, world events and events at home were not impersonal matters apart from their immediate lives. The boundary between private and public affairs hardly existed for us. Our day-to-day life was integrated with political developments. The triumph of Hitler, the figures on collectivization, the latest *Pravda* editorial were items in my personal biography.

It may sound incredible to an outsider, yet it is a fact that in my memory of that period such political facts loom larger and clearer than my brief marriage to Zina.

I met Zina a couple of months before my mission to the village. Hers was a soft, flower-like beauty with nothing of the lusty, passionate quality that had drawn me to Julia. She was fragile: thin, soft-voiced, sentimental; but the fragility covered a hard core of selfishness. Our Soviet girls, for the most part, lived outside themselves. They were plain, robust and as we put it in our Party lingo, socially conscious. But Zina's interests were all centered in herself.

For Zina nothing existed except in relation to her private emotions and preferences. She was a "bourgeois type," my friends warned me; and from the outset, indeed, my infatuation was touched with an uneasy sense of guilt. Even before we registered our marriage she was irritated by my crowded Party schedule. "And how about me? You never seem to have time for me," she would complain. She was no less irritated by my modest financial situation and by the fact that we had to live with my family. Her own relatives made no secret of their disappointment that she had not made a "good match."

The order that sent me to the collectivization area therefore came as a relief to both of us. It provided a welcome interruption, and the few weeks' separation was enough to wreck the marriage. When I returned from the village, sick at heart and disturbed in mind, Zina's lack of interest in my experience offended me. At first I did not notice that she was wearing new finery—a silk dress, even jewels.

Divorce at that time was still a simple, one-sided act. You registered the liquidation of your marriage and your spouse was notified of the fact by post-card. After I broke off the marriage I learned that during my absence Zina had made "interesting new friends." Her innate selfishness had led her in the right direction. Among these friends was a man with a good position and connections in the upper brackets of power and influence, who could afford to indulge her "bourgeois tastes." She married him soon after our divorce.

Zina's flower-like beauty had proved too much of a luxury for an impoverished student—even more of a luxury for an earnest Communist. For years I kept running into her at the theatre, at concerts. She was always well dressed, aloof from the mob, one of the successful in our new society. I could hardly credit the memory that I had once been married to her.

2

The first dividends of collectivization were death. Although not a word about the tragedy appeared in the newspapers, the famine that raged throughout southern Russia and Central Asia was a matter of common knowledge. We denounced as "anti-Soviet rumors" what we knew as towering fact.

Despite harsh police measures to keep the victims at home, Dniepropetrovsk was overrun with starving peasants. Many of them lay listless, too weak even to beg, around railroad stations. Their children were little more than skeletons with swollen bellies. In the past, friends and relatives in the country sent food packages to the urban districts. Now the process was reversed. But our own rations were so small and uncertain that few dared to part with their provisions.

Because the famine coincided with the triumphant finish of the first *Piatiletka* in four years, the press was hysterical with boasts of "our achievements." Yet the deafening propaganda could not quite drown out the groans of the dying. To some of us the shouting about the new "happy life" seemed ghoulish, more terrifying even than the famine itself.

Everything depended on the new harvest. Would the starving peasantry have the strength and the will to reap and to thresh in the midst of million-fold death? To make sure that the crops would be harvested, to prevent the desperate collective farmers from eating the green shoots, to save the *kolkhozes* from breaking down under mismanagement, to fight against enemies of collectivization, special Political Departments were set up in the villages, manned by trusted Communists—military men, officials, professionals, N.K.V.D. men, students. An army of more than a hundred thousand stalwarts, selected by the Central Committee of the Party, was thus deployed through the collectivized areas, charged with the duty of safeguarding the new harvest. I was among those mobilized.

Three hundred of us from various city organizations gathered at the Regional Committee headquarters. The secretary of the committee and one of the foremost Communists of the Ukraine, Comrade Hatayevich, made the principal speech. He did not conceal the difficulties we would face in the villages. Again and again he referred to the "purge" of the Party scheduled for later in the year. The hint was too clear to be missed. Upon our success or failure in the famine regions would depend our political survival.

"Your loyalty to the Party and to Comrade Stalin will be tested and measured by your work in the villages," he declared ominously. "There is no room for weakness. This is no job for the squeamish. You'll need strong stomachs and an iron will. The Party will accept no excuses for failure."

Armed with a mandate from the Regional Committee, I set out for the Piatikhatsky district in the company of a schoolmate who was also my friend, Yuri. The local officials of that district, we found, were unnerved by what they had lived through. We questioned them about the new crops, but they could talk only of the mass hunger, the typhus epidemics, the reports of cannibalism.

Yes, they agreed, we must prepare to reap and to thresh the new grain; but how to get started seemed beyond their paralyzed wills. The police stations and jails were jammed with peasants from surrounding villages, arrested for unauthorized reaping of grain—"sabotage" and "theft of state property" were the official charges.

We arrived at the large village of Petrovo towards evening. An unearthly silence prevailed. "All the dogs have been eaten, that's why it's so quiet," the peasant who led us to the Political Department said. "People don't do much walking, they haven't the strength," he added. Having met the chief of the Political Department, we were conducted to a peasant hut for the night.

A feeble "smoker" provided the only light in the house. Our hostess was a young peasant woman. All feeling, even sadness and fear, seemed to have been drained from her starved features. They were a mask of living death. In a corner, on a narrow bed, two children lay so quietly they seemed lifeless. Only their eyes were alive. I winced when they met mine.

"We're sorry to intrude," Yuri said. "We'll be no trouble to you and in the morning we'll leave." He spoke in an unnatural subdued voice, as if he were in a sick-room or a cemetery.

"You're welcome," the young woman said, "and I'm only sorry I cannot offer you anything. We haven't had a crust of bread in this house for many weeks. I still have a few potatoes but we daren't eat them too fast." She wept quietly. "Will there ever be an end or must my children and I die like the others?"

"Where is your husband?" I asked.

"I don't know. He was arrested and probably banished. My father and brother were also banished. We have surely been left here to die of hunger."

Yuri said he wanted to smoke and left the house precipitately. I knew that he was afraid of breaking down and crying before this stranger.

"Don't give way to despair, my dear," I said to the woman. "I know it's hard, but if you love your children you will not give up the struggle. Bring them to the table. My comrade and I have some food from the city, and you will all dine with us."

Yuri returned. We put all our provisions on the table and ate sparingly ourselves so that there would be more for the others. The children looked at the slab of bacon, the dried fish, the tea and sugar with startled eyes. They ate quickly, greedily, as if afraid that it would all vanish as miraculously as it had appeared. After she had put the children to sleep, our hostess began to talk.

"I will not tell you about the dead," she said. "I'm sure you know. The half-dead, the nearly-dead are even worse. There are hundreds of people in Petrovo bloated with hunger. I don't know how many die every day. Many are so weak that they no longer come out of their houses. A wagon goes around now and then to pick up the corpses. We've eaten everything we could lay our hands on—cats, dogs, field mice, birds. When it's light tomorrow you will see the trees have been stripped of their bark, for that too has been eaten. And the horse manure has been eaten."

I must have looked startled and unbelieving.

"Yes, the horse manure. We fight over it. Sometimes there are whole grains in it."

It was Yuri's first visit to the village. Afraid that the initial impact of the horror might unnerve him, I interrupted the woman's story and insisted that we all retire for the night. But neither Yuri nor I slept much. We were glad when morning came.

Arriving at the Political Department shortly after sunrise, we found only the agriculturist of the State Farm there. He turned out to be an old acquaintance, a student from the Erastovka Agricultural School, and embraced me warmly. I asked him about his associate, Yasha Gromov, who had worked with me in the factory some years ago.

"He'll be here soon. Will you stay in Petrovo or are you going on?"

"We're going a bit farther," I replied. "We just stopped here for the night and to get acquainted. But I want to ask a favor of you, Comrade Bashmakov. Can you spare some provisions?"

"You mean for yourself?"

"All right, let's say for myself. I'll pay you of course."

"Pay me! As if money were the problem. Come to my house—I'm not far from here—and I'll see what we can spare."

As we walked to his house he said:

"I know, of course, that you want the food for some poor wretches and I don't blame you. But Comrade Kravchenko, you won't be any good if you let pity get the whip-hand. You must learn to feed yourself even if others are dying of hunger. Otherwise there will be nobody to bring home the harvest. Whenever your feelings get the better of your judgment, just think to yourself: 'The only way to end the famine is to make sure of the new harvest.' Don't think I've found it easy to adjust myself. I'm not a beast."

All the same, he gave me some bacon, a bottle of oil, a bit of flour and a small bag of some cereal. I thanked him and took the parcel to the house where we had spent the night. The young woman was too overwhelmed to thank us. I escaped from her gratitude as if it were a cruel rebuke.

Then Yuri and I walked through the village. Again we were oppressed by the unnatural silence. Soon we came to an open space which, no doubt, was once the market place. Suddenly Yuri gripped my arm until it hurt: for sprawled on the ground were dead men, women and children, thinly covered with dingy straw. I counted seventeen. As we watched, a wagon drove up and two men loaded the corpses on the wagon like cordwood.

While Yuri went to the State Farm to arrange for transportation, I returned to the Political Department for a talk with Gromov. He was excitedly happy to see me—any visitor from the strange world beyond this famine zone seemed a welcome reminder that somewhere life was still normal. He took me to the State Farm. This was a type of enterprise owned and operated outright by the government, its farmers working for wages, as distinct from the *kolkhoz* or collective farms, run in common by the peasants.

"Yasha," I said, as we walked through the fields of half-ripe wheat and barley, "I was in the market-place this morning, and——"

"Yes, I know, Vitya. How many were there this morning? Only seventeen? Some days there are more. What can we do but collect the bodies and bury them? You see, the government pumped all the grain out of them last fall. What little they got for their work or managed to hide they've used up long ago. It's all sad and horrible. Come to my house and we'll talk. I've been alone with my thoughts too long."

Death by starvation is a monotonous subject. Monotonous and repetitious. There is something macabre about using commonplace words to describe infernal facts. What Yasha told me was, after all, only what the peasant woman had told me the night before; what I had seen with my own eyes in the village square. Already I was becoming accustomed to this climate of horror; I was developing an inner resistance against realities which only yesterday had left me limp.

We talked for a long time. Gromov described the men with whom I would have to work in the villages assigned to me and promised to help me in every way possible. He waved farewell to us as Yuri and I drove off in a *tachanka*, a two-wheeler, put at our disposal by the State Farm.

The sun was going down and the sky seemed bloodshot. The old man who was driving the wagon talked to his horses. "Ekh, my little falcons! Let's get on, my darlings!" I offered him a cigarette. His spirits apparently lifted by the good tobacco, he rummaged under his seat, drew out a reed flute and began to play sad Ukrainian folk melodies.

"You seem to be leading a gay life, daddy," Yuri said.

"Oh, yes, we live like grandees hereabouts, with one pair of pants for two men and everyone alive until he's dead. No poor, no rich, all beggars. Now take that hill, my little falcons! Show the city folks, my little ones!"

"And who are you, grandpa?" I asked.

"Everybody here knows me. When I had my own farm and plenty to eat, people called me Kuzma Ivanovich. Now that I'm a coachman they call me just Kuzka. There's nothing left but this pipe, so I play it.

"My old woman died of starvation last winter. My daughter got married and works in the mines. Two of my sons and their families have been sent to Siberia by the comrades . . . kulak agents. But seeing that I'm an old man and harmless, they gave me the job of coachman on the State Farm. For a long time they wouldn't take me, thinking I'd do damage to the farm. But why should I do damage to anything? I've got one foot in the grave anyway.

"I do anything they tell me and my only joy in life is these horses. I take good care of them. True, they belong to the government, but I pretend they belong to me. They're the only family I have left. I feed them and scrub them and talk to them. They understand me—every word. With my horses I'm still Kuzma Ivanovich, not simply Kuzka. Now all I want is to be buried next to my old woman when my turn comes. I have asked good people to remember that and they have promised. So you see, I have nothing to worry about."

He resumed his playing.

It was night by the time he stopped at the Political Department of the village which was our destination. The Political Department was located in a fine house at the end of a gravel road flanked by poplars. Inside, several officials had been expecting us. They met us in a friendly fashion. After mutual introductions, we went with them to the hut occupied by the Assistant Chief. The place was clean and the supper, though plain, was good and ample.

In the cheerful light of the kerosene lamp, around the well-stocked table, it was hard to imagine that in all the surrounding houses hunger and death were in full command. I studied these men with whom I would have to work and it was obvious that they were sizing me up in their turn.

The Chief of the Political Department, Somanov, was a military man, a lieutenant-colonel of artillery. He was short, stocky, about forty, with a calm and sympathetic face. I liked him immediately. His assistant, our host, was the manager of a metal factory in the Donetz Basin. He was well-dressed, noisy, a glib talker and brimming over with funny stories. The second assistant was a young G.P.U. officer, a dark, handsome chap who said little but listened attentively. The fourth member of the P.D. was a newspaper editor from a town in my province.

Each of us took the measure of the others. I managed to mention, casually, the names of my important friends and even insinuated a reference to my personal acquaintance with Commissar Ordzhonikidze. When I threw out the names of acquaintances in the G.P.U. of my home town, the young G.P.U. officer unconsciously straightened up to attention. Whatever lay ahead of me. I needed every ounce of political prestige I could muster to see me through it.

After supper we held a formal conference. Yuri and I were initiated into the plans and tipped off about the character of various local officials in the collectives for which we would be responsible. Fortunately the crops in this area seemed to be coming up well. Our task was to conserve it, oversee its harvesting and make sure that the government got its full share. September first was the deadline set for the harvesting. Although each of us had a special sector in his care, the common responsibility drew us close together.

The following morning Comrade Somanov asked me into his private office.

"You have had more experience in farming than most of the Authorized Representatives, which is a good thing," he told me. "I want to warn you. You will see a lot of suffering and you're entirely on your own. I won't presume to tell you how to handle the situation. Only this: don't go to pieces, or you'll be useless to yourself and to the job. Do what you think necessary and slap down interference. If you carry out the plan in your section, everything else will be forgiven. If not . . . well, we all know the consequences. I'll help you all I can. The presidents of the collective farms and the chairman of the village Soviet are expecting your arrival. Best of luck!"

Soon Yuri and I were again on the road. His villages were about eight miles from mine. When we reached Logina, which would be my head-quarters, I jumped off at the local Soviet building and Yuri drove on alone.

The Soviet headquarters was small but clean. I found a conference in progress. Having introduced myself and shown the mandate designating me Authorized Representative of the Political Department and the Regional Committee, I urged that they proceed with their meeting. The chairman of the Soviet, I learned, was named Belousov and he evidently stood in awe of the local Party secretary, Comrade Kobzar. The manager of the machine-tractor station, Karas, was also present.

"Comrade Kravchenko, you're in charge here now. Take over the conference," Kobzar said.

"No, no, go right ahead, and I'll just listen in if you don't mind. From now on, comrades, there should be no 'us' and no 'you.' We must work together. You know the problems here better than I do, and I shall depend on you. At the same time, I'm being held responsible and must make the final decisions. I should like to have my own first conference tomorrow, and I trust you'll all come prepared with the necessary data. I want every one of your *kolkhoz* presidents, especially, to bring his work plans. Meanwhile, go right on with whatever you were discussing."

They resumed their meeting. The presidents of the collectives each spoke in turn. They insisted that unless their farmers had something to eat they would not be strong enough to harvest the grain.

"My people are starving," one of them said. "Those who are bloated lie around in their houses. We must count them out as work-hands. Many more will be eliminated or will die before the harvest gets under way. What are we going to do about it?"

Belousov and Kobzar replied in generalities, quoted the Party directives and left me with the impression that they were confused, blundering and at bottom disinterested. I said to myself: "I'll have to depend on the peasants themselves, rather than on these officials, from the looks of it." It was clear to me that the Soviet and Party functionaries had become too accustomed to the famine and that their apathy must be overcome if the harvest was to be gathered.

"You come to my house and sleep," Belousov suggested, when the meeting ended. "You must be tired from the journey. I think I can scare up a drop or two to give you new strength."

"I would be pleased if you came with me," one of the collective presidents interjected. "My name is Chadai. My family is small and we can spare a separate room for you."

I decided at once to accept Chadai's invitation. The closer I came to the collectives, I felt, the better off I would be. I shook hands all around and left with Chadai—a simple, intelligent man of middle age, clean shaven and pleasant in appearance. Another *kolkhoz* president, Demchenko, accompanied us.

"Well, friends," I smiled when we reached the house, "let's go to the stables first. That's how I was taught. Before going to bed, my old grandfather in Alexandrovsk used to say, see that the horses and cattle are taken care of."

"So you're of peasant origin?"

"Not exactly, Comrade Demchenko, but I've lived a lot on the land."

By the light of a lantern I saw that the horses were in the stalls, but without hay. Besides, the stable was not too clean.

"The son of a bitch!" Chadai self-consciously exclaimed. "Neglected the stable again! I'll give him hell tomorrow."

"I don't know who's supposed to be on duty," I said. "But in my opinion you better give that hell to yourself. You're the president and if things go wrong, the fault is yours. That's what leadership means."

"I guess you're right," Chadai conceded meekly. "Yet it's not so simple. When people are hungry they won't work. They can't keep their minds on work."

"Yes," Demchenko agreed, "it's not at all simple. Well, good night to both of you, until tomorrow."

Inside the house, I met Chadai's wife and children. Although all of them were thin and haggard, it was evident that here conditions were not as bad as in most peasant homes.

"Comrade Chadai, tell me as man to man, not officially, how the people here are getting on," I said. "What are your plans for harvesting? What's the condition of the machinery? Don't hide things from me. On the contrary, be honest with me because after all we're both interested in the same thing."

"I don't know where to begin, Comrade Kravchenko. The crop is not bad. The machines are in order, though some parts are missing. Without those parts we're stuck."

"Make me a list of what's needed and I'll put it up to the Political Department at Petrovo."

"Thank you, that will be a great help. Another thing that's bad is the situation with the horses. We have no fodder. If only we could get some oats. . . . Of course, we could mow down some from the new crop, but that's strictly against orders."

"Orders or no orders, we'll do it if you think there's no other way," I said. "I'll take the full responsibility. That's one of our first tasks tomorrow. Without horses, what can we accomplish? And without oats we'll soon have no horses."

"I'm afraid Belousov and Kobzar won't stand for it," Chadai warned.

"Let me handle them."

"Finally and most important, Comrade Kravchenko, there's the situation of the people themselves. They're dying like flies. Or they're too weak and blown-up to move. Who's going to harvest the grain? I begged the Soviet to loan us some grain. Finally they sent me thirteen *poods*. But I'm not Moses or Jesus. I can't feed thousands of people with thirteen *poods*. I tell you, comrade, I saw blood and death when I was in the army but nothing as terrible as what's been going on right here in my village."

Then he looked me straight in the eyes. A brooding hopefulness broke through his sadness.

"Comrade Authorized Representative, if you want to harvest the crop you'll first have to save these people from starvation. Besides, I can no longer bear to look at the misery. I just can't stand it any more!"

"I can't promise you anything, Comrade Chadai—except to try. Tomorrow we'll get up early and go from house to house. I want to see for myself before I make up my mind to act."

3

What I saw that morning, making the rounds of houses with Chadai, was inexpressibly horrible. On a battlefield men die quickly, they fight back, they are sustained by fellowship and a sense of duty. Here I saw people dying in solitude by slow degrees, dying hideously, without the excuse of sacrifice for a cause. They had been trapped and left to starve, each in his home, by a political decision made in a far-off capital around conference and banquet tables. There was not even the consolation of inevitability to relieve the horror.

The most terrifying sights were the little children with skeleton limbs dangling from balloon-like abdomens. Starvation had wiped every trace of youth from their faces, turning them into tortured gargoyles; only in their eyes still lingered the reminder of childhood. Everywhere we found men and women lying prone, their faces and bellies bloated, their eyes utterly expressionless.

We knocked at a door and received no reply. We knocked again. Fearfully I pushed the door open and we entered through a narrow vestibule into the one-room hut. First my eyes went to an icon light above a broad bed, then to the body of a middle-aged woman stretched on the bed, her arms crossed on her breast over a clean embroidered Ukrainian blouse. At the foot of the bed stood an old woman and nearby were two children, a boy of about eleven and a girl of about ten. The children were weeping quietly and repeating in a plaintive peasant chant, "Mama, dear little mama." I looked around and my eyes rested on the swollen, inert body of a man lying on the shelf of the oven.

The nightmarishness of the scene was not in the corpse on the bed, but in the condition of the living witnesses. The old woman's legs were blown up to incredible size, the man and the children were clearly in the last stages of starvation. I retreated quickly, ashamed of my haste.

In the adjoining house we found a man of about forty sitting on a bench, repairing a shoe. His face was swollen. A tidy looking little boy, reduced to little more than a skeleton, was reading a book, and a gaunt woman was busy at the stove.

"What are you cooking, Natalka?" Chadai asked her.

"You know what I'm cooking," she answered, and in her voice there was a murderous fury.

Chadai pulled me by the sleeve and we went out.

"Why did she get so angry?" I asked.

"Because—well, I'm ashamed to tell you, Victor Andreyevich. . . . She's cooking horse manure and weeds."

My first impulse was to return to the house and stop her, but Chadai held me back. "Don't do it, I beg of you. You don't know how starving people feel. She might kill you in despair if you take away the contents of her pot."

After we had been in a dozen homes, I yielded to Chadai's urging that we stop the inspection. "It's the same everywhere. Now you know enough," he said.

My course seemed to me clear. The situation was too desperate for half-measures. Whatever the consequences to myself, I would ignore laws and orders. Unless I restored the strength of these peasants, everything would be lost. Returning to Chadai's home, I wrote a letter to Comrade Somanov, chief of our Political Department, and dispatched it by messenger. Toward evening the messenger returned with an answer:

"I am well aware of the conditions. I urge you to think the matter over again and to weigh all considerations. What you propose is a serious breach of our definite orders. If you see no other way out, however, you may do what you deem necessary. I shall try to find you some grain, but frankly I have very little hope of succeeding."

The answer satisfied me. At least he did not say No. What I proposed was to reap some oats to feed the horses and to mow a little barley at the sides of the fields for the population. Such premature reaping was being denounced, in the *Izvestia* spread before me, as "theft of state property" and "kulak sabotage." Peasants were being arrested and deported for such "crimes."

At the second collective farm conditions were essentially the same. Some of the peasants still had cows, but they were delivering all the milk to the State butter plant. Even the people who were still moving around were weak, listless and in deep despair.

I asked Chadai and Demchenko to summon the two village school-teachers, the woman doctor and a few of the more intelligent and enterprising women of the *kolkhozes*. At the same time I sent for Belousov, Kobzar and Karas. When they had all gathered, they sat around expectantly, wondering what kind of rabbit I would pull out of my Party hat. Some of them, Kobzar especially, could not hide their skepticism.

"I have asked you to come here, comrades, especially the women," I began, "because I need your advice. I'm glad that the Soviet chairman, the Party secretary and the manager of the machine-tractor station are here too. I've been going from house to house and I know the picture. I'm especially alarmed by the condition of the children. How can people be expected to work when their children are starving to death at home?

"This is my plan. Chadai tells me there are some empty houses in the village. I want you women to clean them up, whitewash them, make them fit for human beings. Let's begin with the children. They will live in these houses until the harvest is over. Round them up, give them haircuts, bathe them, inoculate them against typhus. I know, doctor, that you have the necessary medicines. Prepare some tables in the gardens of these houses and get large kettles for cooking food. Are you willing to help?"

"Certainly we're willing," one woman spoke up. "But what will you use for food?"

"That I'll tell you later. In the meantime I want to know whom you consider most reliable to take charge of the children on your behalf."

"Kononenko," several voices cried. "Ivan Petrovich . . . the teacher."

"Ivan Petrovich," I turned to the old man when he was pointed out to me, "since the people trust you, so will I. You're in full charge of the project with the children. Get others to assist and you can count on me to the full. If anyone tries to interfere, let me know."

"I'm perfectly willing," the teacher said, "and why shouldn't I be? These are my own people. If you'll only give us food, I'll guarantee the rest." There were tears in his voice.

"Thank you, Ivan Petrovich. Get started on the assumption that there will be food. Take my solemn word for it."

I dismissed everyone but the officials. Leading them into another room, I closed the door.

"Comrades, let's get down to business," I said. "Don't be shocked by what I'm about to tell you. I know the orders as well as you do, maybe better. All the same, I'm giving the collective farmers permission to reap oats and feed the horses. In the second place, I am giving immediate permission to reap the barley on the sides and in spots where it is already ripe.

"Start threshing it right away, and get it ready, enough to issue a kilogram of groats per family per day. And keep increasing the amount slowly so that by the time reaping starts people will be strong enough to work. Provide Ivan Petrovich with enough of the new cereal to take care of the children. You are also authorized to kill as many collectivized pigs as necessary to provide a little meat and fat to go with the barley groats for the children."

As I talked, an expression of doubt that quickly changed to horror spread over the faces of the local officials. Their eyes said more distinctly than words: *Has this man gone crazy? Does he want to get us all shot, including himself?*

"But Comrade Kravchenko," Kobzar began.

"There are no 'buts' about it. Do as I tell you. The responsibility is entirely my own."

"It's my duty to inform the Political Department—" Belousov exclaimed, rising excitedly.

"No, Comrade Belousov," the manager of the machine-tractor station came to my aid, "you're wrong. If the Authorized Representative of the Regional Committee orders it, then he knows what he's doing and the rest of us should shut up."

"I don't forbid you to inform anyone you please," I said. "That's within your rights. But if you don't carry out my instructions, I'll hold you accountable. As for you, Comrade Kobzar, you'll pay with your Party card if you don't see to it that my plans are carried out without delay. That's all, comrades."

As we filed out, I felt a hand grip mine in a pressure of gratitude. It was Chadai. Then Demchenko came to me.

"I'll help you if it costs my life," he whispered hoarsely. "Now that you've taken the plunge, how about getting after the cooperative store? Come along, I'll introduce you to Makarenko, the manager."

The store was dirty and neglected. Except for plaster busts of Stalin and piles of lithograph portraits of other leaders, the shelves were empty. Makarenko was a servile little man, sly and ingratiating. I told him briefly about my decision to feed the children of the villages and asked him to help.

"I know you have some foodstuffs hidden away. You must give them up. As soon as the harvest is in, you'll be paid off in grain and nobody will be hurt."

The little man was alarmed. He was torn between his orders from headquarters and his fear of offending me as the Party Representative.

"Yes, comrade, I have some salt, candy, about ten *poods* of groats, some smoked fish and a little soap. If the *kolkhozes* will sign a promise to pay in grain and hay, I'll agree. But first I must obtain permission of the district office. I'll give you my answer tomorrow. But I also want to give you a little advice. Why not tap the butter station?"

"What do you mean?"

"He means the place where we deliver all our milk," Demchenko explained. "It's processed into butter for export."

"For export!"

"Yes, Comrade Kravchenko—abroad. It's packed in paper with outlandish foreign words on it. You see, starvation is one thing and foreign exchange is another."

"All right, take me to the place," I said.

The butter plant was some distance outside the village. The manager was a Party man, affable and deeply unhappy. He took me through the establishment. In one of the rooms, butter was being sliced in bars and wrapped in paper which bore the imprint, in English, USSR BUTTER EXPORT.

"I know that the peasants are starving," the manager said. "The idea of this butter going to stuff well-fed foreigners cuts me like a knife. But what am I to do? I have my orders. I'm far behind my plan and no doubt will be punished. The peasants steal the milk; they're hungry. And the cows don't produce because there's not enough fodder."

"All the same," I said, "I must have your help. The children must be fed. Surely there are by-products of the butter making that we can use."

"That's easy for you to say. But like Makarenko, I not only have to fulfill plans from the center but I have to feed local officials. All of them, Kobzar, Belousov and their various assistants take my butter and milk."

"Well, from today all buttermilk must be turned over to the new children's project," I declared.

"That's all right with me, provided I obtain the approval of my superiors." Then he paused a moment, as if gathering his last reserves of courage. "No, I'll not do any asking. Tell your people to come for the buttermilk tomorrow. I, too, have children."

Anger lashed my mind as I drove back to the village. Butter being sent abroad in the midst of the famine! In London, Berlin, Paris I could see with my mind's eye people eating butter stamped with a Soviet trade-mark. "They must be rich to be able to send out butter," I could hear them saying. "Here, friends, is the proof of socialism in action." Driving through the fields, I did not hear the lovely Ukrainian songs so dear to my heart. These people had forgotten how to sing. I could hear only the groans of the dying, and the lip-smacking of fat foreigners enjoying our butter. . . .

As I reached our *kolkhoz* fields, I saw that oats and barley were being reaped. In the villages, several hundred children were gathered in the gardens for a great wash-up and clean-up. Old Ivan Petrovich generalled the work, about a score of men and women were assisting. Chadai's wife, my hostess, was among the women busy whitewashing the houses. My angry thoughts melted in affection for these simple people. I had seen them sullen under whips and guns. I was seeing them eager, selfless, in a common task that carried no threats.

When we were at supper that evening, a stableman came to see Chadai. A horse had just died. Chadai instructed him to skin the animal, take the carcass far outside the village, pour kerosene over it and cover it with quicklime. Otherwise hungry villagers would eat the diseased flesh, he explained to me. Later the teacher and the woman doctor arrived. They reported good progress. The new barley was being oven-dried and by tomorrow the children of the collectives would have their first good breakfast. A number of pigs had been slaughtered.

"We know about the buttermilk," Ivan Petrovich said, "but it's not enough. Some of the children are too far gone. We must have some milk."

I thought a moment. I was already so deeply involved in rule-breaking and "kulak sabotage" that I might as well go further.

"Chadai," I said, "I authorize you officially, in front of these witnesses, to deliver no more milk to the individual officials who've been getting it and to retain one-third of the whole output for the use of the children's home. You're to tell Demchenko that the same applies to his *kolkhoz.*"

In bed that night I thought of the new privileged class in the village—the Party and Soviet functionaries who were receiving milk and butter and supplies from the cooperative shop while everyone else around them starved. Slavishly they obeyed orders from the center, indifferent to the suffering of the common people. The corruption of character by privilege was fearsome to behold; these men who only a few years ago were themselves poor peasants had already lost the last trace of identification with their neighbors. They were a caste apart, living in an intimate clique, supporting each other, banded together against the community.

The following morning I was inspecting the harvesters, threshers and winnowing machines. The spare parts I had asked for had arrived and men were working on repairs. A *kolkhoz* board member was telling me about his troubles when one of the peasants came over and whispered something in his ear.

"Speak up, let the Authorized Representative hear you!" the board member said.

"Well, it's like this, Comrade Authorized Representative. Last night a horse died. The hide was taken off and the carcass was soaked in kerosene and quicklime. But this morning, when they got ready to bury it, there was no sign of the carcass. All of the diseased and spoiled meat has been carried off overnight. God, what we've come to, comrade!"

4

The time for starting the harvest was approaching. A new mood had spread through the village. Most families had one or more children in Ivan Petrovich's kindergarten and some barley was distributed to all members of the collectives. One morning I addressed a mass meeting of *kolkhoz* farmers. After the meeting I remained to chat with the people. Someone brought out a *balalaika* and one peasant played an accordion. I heard our Ukrainian songs again and my heart was warmed.

A young man came up to me. The message he was carrying seemed too much for his tongue, but at length he stammered it out.

"Comrade Authorized Representative! You're wanted at the Soviet! Somebody to see you. From . . . from . . . the G.P.U.!"

Those close enough to hear him stopped singing. The three dread letters fell like blows. The news that I was being called by the secret police spread through the whole gathering. Silence descended. As I knew from the *kolkhoz* presidents, it was generally expected in the village that I would be punished for feeding its people.

At the Soviet building I found the handsome young G.P.U. officer whom I had already met at the Political Department. Kobzar and Belousov were with him. I addressed Kobzar:

"Why weren't you at the collective meeting today? I asked you to be there."

"I'm sorry but I had other work," he mumbled. His manner was surly.

"I'd like to talk to you privately, Comrade Kravchenko," the G.P.U. officer said.

"All right. Come with me to my office at the *kolkhoz*."

He accompanied me. On the way and after we were seated in the office, we talked in general terms about the affairs of the village, the chances of a good harvest and the like.

"Comrade Skopin," I finally said, "let's get down to brass tacks. What really brought you here?"

"You see, we've received several statements and official declarations about your conduct here," he said. "They all amount to this: that you're breaking the law, ignoring Party orders and riding roughshod over local authorities."

"Whom do you mean when you say 'we' have received? Are you referring to the Chief of the Political Department? Are you here at his request?"

"That's beside the point."

"No, it's the main point. Have you been authorized to examine me?"

"I'm just here for a private friendly talk. It isn't an examination."

"Comrade Skopin, I am doing what I think right and I can't discuss my conduct with you. Only the head of the Political Department can question me. I am the Authorized Representative of the Regional Committee and am responsible to them for my conduct. Local authorities are obliged to help me. Instead of that, the local officials do nothing, stuff their guts with good food while the people die of hunger. I have lists of every official and what he has taken from the collective farms and the village store for his private use. I know well enough who's been writing denunciations of me. But I also know that they indulge in drunken orgies. I've learned a lot."

"To tell you the truth, Comrade Kravchenko, I'm here entirely on my own. The Chief knows nothing about it. I decided to have a little talk with you before putting the documents before him. I was told you took provisions from the butter plant and the cooperative stores, that you're diverting milk deliveries belonging to the State and reaping grain ahead of time. These are serious matters."

"Please make your report to the Political Department. Tell them I shall stand by all my acts. I shall be there tomorrow morning to report personally. Now, would you like to see the village, Comrade Skopin?"

"No, I haven't the time. Well, good-bye. I'm only doing my duty as I see it."

"Good-bye, comrade. I'll see you tomorrow."

Next day I reported to Comrade Somanov.

"You were perfectly right in refusing to talk to Skopin without my consent," he told me. "Those loafers in your villages write denunciations, just as insurance . . . in case you get into hot water. I know you've been working hard. I know the chances you're taking, and of course I, too, will be held responsible. If we carry out the harvest and deliveries to the State by the time set, everything is saved. If not, it's off with both our heads."

"I've been entirely frank with you, Comrade Somanov. I've kept you informed of my action. But I want to carry the load myself. Here's the note you sent me in which you more or less told me to do what I pleased. Take it back!"

He took it, put it in his pocket and shouted "Comrade Skopin!" The G.P.U. officer came in. "Please bring me the whole file of declarations and material referring to Comrade Kravchenko." Skopin brought in a thick folder, which Somanov in turn handed to me, and left. He waited while I read them. I made a note of the names of the G.P.U. informers who had been reporting on me and the officials who had denounced me. Somanov then promised to destroy the file, meanwhile putting it in his own safe.

"I'll be in Logina to see you tomorrow. Have the local officials on hand. I'll give them the kind of hell they deserve."

Returning to the village, I checked the names of the informers against the official list of citizens. I discovered that they were all carefully distributed through the whole district. One worked in the cooperative, another in the butter plant, a third in the *kolkhoz* administration, a fourth was a driver at the machine-tractor station. The G.P.U. had its eyes and ears carefully deployed so they would see and hear everything. Behind the backs of the formal authorities and the economic managers, I realized, there was a network of spies—spies of the secret police system and others of the Party, unknown to one another. Behind the ostensible government was a real government.

Later that day I ran into Ivan Petrovich. He was fairly glowing with the thrill of his work.

"It's wonderful to watch the kids restored to health," he said as we walked together, "to see their childhood return. We all are aware of the chances you're taking. To be perfectly candid, the whole village is worried about the G.P.U. call."

"No reason for worry," I smiled, "the gods are on my side. So far, at any rate. But I'm glad the peasants are conscious of the situation. Now it's their turn to repay me—and incidentally themselves. The harvest is about to begin. I want you to pass the word around, in case there are some loafers anywhere, that I don't want any thanks. I want work, hard work, day and night.

"Tell them this: 'Collective farmers, do you want to save Comrade Kravchenko's head? Then reap, thresh and deliver the grain according to plan.' I can't very well appeal for myself, but you can do it."

"You may be sure I'll do as you ask. You have friends here. Believe me, anyone who slacks on the job had better run off to hell, we'll make things so hot for him."

Somanov had already arrived when I reached the Soviet headquarters the next day. I could hear his booming voice even before I entered. Virtually all the local official family was gathered there, including even the store manager.

"Comrade Kravchenko is boss here," the Chief of the Political Department was laying down the law. "His instructions are law. Time is pressing and we have no energy to spare for your nonsense. Get down to work and help him. Go into the fields yourselves. It will be good for your health. And here's the Authorized Representative in person!"

He greeted me warmly, as if he had not seen me for years. It was a demonstration of friendliness to impress my enemies. We left the meeting together and walked to the *kolkhoz* administration house.

"Victor Andreyevich," he said, "I'm of peasant origin myself and the sufferings of my people hurt me deeply. Tears, blood, death, exile. And why? The land is fertile, the people are hard-working. Why must we let them starve and die and perish? The more I think of it the more confused I get. But I'll send you some more flour in a day or two. Also some more parts for the threshers.

"Only that's not what I really wanted to tell you. I wanted to tell you how much I appreciate what you've done, especially for the children." He stopped suddenly in his tracks. "Victor Andreyevich, you and I are Communists, but we also are human beings. I shall stand up for you as if it were myself."

Two days later everything was ready. At dawn I drove into the fields. The collective members, men and women, were there ahead of me. Already they were mowing the grain, binding it into sheafs. Soon the local officials arrived and offered to help—the lecture had evidently done its work. There was a feeling of eager activity. Just as the driver of an automobile can recognize by the hum of the engine that it will work well, I sensed by the mood of this first morning that all was well.

The preceding night, food supplies and water had been carted to the fields. Tents had been set up for the small children. These peasants, now as of yore, would live in the open, away from their homes, until the harvest was completed. With my permission, a bull and some pigs had been slaughtered. Though there were few among the hundreds of men and women who had eaten their fill, few who were not weakened or actually sick, they sang and joked and worked from sunup to sundown.

"It's all right," Ivan Petrovich whispered in my ear, "they're all anxious to save your head." We laughed.

The next day I spent at the collective farm of which Demchenko was president. Here, too, the harvest was well started and the spirit was excellent. In a few days, even while the reaping was under way, other brigades began the threshing. Grain began to flow to the elevators in heaping cartfuls.

One day, at the peak of the harvest, I rode out to Demchenko's fields. Observing that one of the harvesters was standing idle, I galloped over to see why. I found that its operator had lost consciousness from sheer fatigue. Several women were around him, trying to revive him. I ordered them to take the man into the village and myself mounted the harvester. Not since my days on the Tocsin commune had I managed the machine and it was exhilarating to be working, hour after hour.

Towards twilight, when I was relieved by another driver, I discovered a horrible loss. My wallet was gone. The loss of all the money I possessed in the world didn't bother me. But my mandate was gone and, more disturbing, my Party card. That evening and the following day we searched the fields but found no trace of the wallet. I reported the loss to the Political Department and to the Regional Committee. The accident would plague me for years.

Another instalment of unpleasantness came in the form of an order through the P.D.:

"In accordance with instructions of the Regional Executive Committee, the church in your village is to be put in order as a storehouse for government grain. This task must be carried out within 48 hours and its accomplishment reported."

The directive disturbed me, for I had no doubt what the emotions of the peasants would be. It was a stupid act; a monkey-wrench thrown into the machinery of a crucial harvest. But Kobzar, Belousov and the others undertook the job with a relish. Slowly, imperceptibly, they had become antagonists of the population, enjoying most of the things which other villagers disliked—precisely because they disliked them. The local Comsomols did the actual work of stripping the church of its hangings, icons and valuables.

The news spread like wildfire through the fields. Scores of peasants dropped their implements and rushed to the village. They cursed and pleaded and wept as they saw their sacred objects removed. The sacrilege was only part of what hurt them—in the whole business they sensed a direct insult to their dignity as human beings.

"They've taken everything from us," I heard one elderly peasant say. "They've left us nothing. Now they are removing our last comfort. Where shall we christen our children and bury our dead? Where shall we turn for comfort in our sorrows? The scoundrels! The infidels!"

I was helpless. It took all of my own and Ivan Petrovich's efforts and eloquence to restore the rhythm of labor. Just when we thought we had succeeded, a new incident upset everything again. It was on the following Sunday. The secretary of the local Comsomol, a stupid, pimply-faced youth named Chizh, suddenly appeared on the street, playing a *balalaika*, his girl friend by his side, and singing popular anti-religious songs. That was a familiar enough scene. What caused the trouble was their attire. Both Chizh and the girl were wearing bright-red silk shirts, caught at the waist with gold ropes and silk tassels. The villagers immediately recognized their church hangings. Quickly their indignation flared into a lynching mood. Only the fact that they outran the older peasants and took refuge in the cooperative shop saved the two Comsomols from harm at the hands of an infuriated mob.

When I heard of the episode, I sent for Chizh.

"Why did you steal the church hangings?" I shouted.

"I didn't steal. I took the things openly. Other comrades have done the same."

"Well, you and your comrades immediately restore everything you've taken. Do you hear me? If not, I'll turn you over to the police, along with any scoundrel who stands up for you. And another thing, as long as I'm in town we'll have no more of the anti-religious antics in public. That's an order!"

A few days later the *kolkhoz* killed a huge bull. The meat was salted and put away in an ice cellar for future use. In the evening Chadai informed me that part of the meat had been stolen. I summoned Comrade Karas from the machine-tractor station. He consented to help me. We waited until nearly midnight. Chadai and Karas carried hunting guns. I had my Browning revolver. We all had a few shrewd guesses about the likely thieves and were determined to check up without delay.

"Let's stop on the way and pick up Secretary Kobzar," I said. "He ought to know what's happening in his bailiwick."

His house was dark. Chadai knocked. Receiving no reply, he opened the door. Suddenly we heard voices. I walked in and turned on my flashlight. A woman cried out. I turned the light in the direction of her voice. A totally naked young girl was trying to pull a dress over her head. Shrieking with fright, she ran out of the house into the night.

I lit the lamp on the table. It disclosed a bottle of vodka, two tumblers, a big platter of fried meat. Kobzar, half naked, was sitting on the bed, disheveled and bewildered. In a wooden bowl, on a chair, I saw a big bull's heart.

"Where did you get this meat?" I asked.

"I bought it . . . at the cooperative shop . . . you can check up on me."

"You bet your life I will. Come on, comrades, let's leave him to finish his meal, including that bull's heart."

With Chadai leading, we then went up the hill toward a house on the outskirts of the village. This was reputed to be the scene of the "orgies" about which peasants talked so bitterly. Moving carefully, silently, we approached the house. Through a broken slat in the shutter of one window, I looked into a large room. A table was loaded with bottles, meats, bread and vegetables. Disposed in intimate groups were three men—the warehouse manager, the assistant manager of the cooperative store and the miller—and three women in various degrees of undress.

Karas posted himself at the front door, Chadai at the rear door. I rapped on the window.

"Who's there?" a frightened voice cried.

"The Authorized Representative. Open at once or I'll shoot."

The door was opened. The scene of amusement had changed into one of confusion and panic. The women were weeping. "I only came because I was hungry," one of them wailed. "They forced me to come here," another cried. I told the women to dress and leave, then I asked my two companions to search the house. They found a *pood* of meat, a lot of fats, groats, honey and several sacks of flour.

"While your neighbors are dying of hunger, you good-for-nothings steal the food from their mouths!" I shouted in a rage. "And you call yourself Communists! Take these provisions on your back! Now march to the Soviet house!"

I walked behind the three men until we reached the village Soviet. In the morning the militiamen arrived and the three thieves were taken to the district center, Piatikhatky, for trial. When the story got around town the peasants were indignant.

"You shouldn't have sent them off for trial," many of them told me. "We'd know what to do with them better than the court."

When the first of the new grain was being delivered to the granary near the railroad station, I made a discovery which left me tremulous with horror. Stacked in the brick structure were thousands of *poods* of the previous year's grain collections! These were the State reserves for the district ordered by the government, their very existence hidden from the starving population by officialdom. Hundreds of men, women and children had died of undernourishment in these villages, though grain was hoarded almost outside their doors!

The peasants who were with me when we found the "State reserves" stared with unbelieving eyes and cursed in anger. I didn't blame them, of course, but I exacted their pledges to say nothing about the matter, for fear that the news would undermine harvesting morale. Subsequently I came to know that in many other parts of the country the government hoarded huge reserves while peasants in those very regions died of hunger. Why this was done, only Stalin's Politburo could tell—and it didn't.

5

The harvest was virtually completed. In the twilight of a balmy day I was driving into the fields in a two-wheeler. From a distance I heard a harvest song, the voices of men and women beautifully blended. After all the death and the suffering, they were singing once more! The blessed simplicity and the bottomless goodness of these people of our Ukrainian earth!

Soon I noticed that the singers were marching toward me, as in a procession, with the teacher Ivan Petrovich leading. It was a heart-warming sight, the men in their best clothes, the women in embroidered holiday blouses, with wreaths of field flowers on their heads, real joy mirrored in their faces. I stopped the horse and alighted. The procession came close and stopped; there were perhaps two hundred peasant men and women.

"Victor Andreyevich," the teacher said in a loud voice so that all might hear, "we have done what we promised. The harvest is in—ten days before the scheduled time. You saw how we worked. Knowing what you do—that most of us were hungry and weak from a terrible winter and spring—this is real heroism."

"Thank you, Ivan Petrovich," I responded, "and thank you all, comrades."

The procession broke up. Accordions let loose and the younger people danced. Chadai and Demchenko joined me. In the year since the previous harvest, almost half the population of the village had died of hunger and the diseases that flourish on hunger. Now those who remained had started life again. The State would take most of the new grain, but the harvest was good and what remained would be almost sufficient to sustain life for another year.

An open-air feast was spread on Demchenko's fields and though I had urgent letters to write I could not refuse his invitation. Hundreds of peasants were crowded around tables. The scene was illuminated with lanterns and huge bonfires. After hours of handshaking, mutual congratulations and speeches, the dinner dissolved in music and dancing. Here, too, the hope of a new life seemed to have been revived.

In my room that night I wrote my final report to the Political Department, announcing completion of my assignment ten days before the deadline. I also reported the arrest of the thieves, and recommended the removal of Kobzar, Chizh and several other functionaries.

A few days later, while I was inspecting one of the fields, I suddenly heard the honk of an automobile. I was astounded to see several big, handsome cars coming down the road. Clearly these must be important visitors. Urging on my horse, I galloped towards the machines. They stopped and half a dozen men stepped out. One came towards me. I recognized Comrade Hatayevich. I dismounted and walked towards him.

We shook hands. Then, in a stern voice, he asked:

"Comrade Kravchenko, when did you finish harvesting?"

"Three days ago, which is ten days ahead of schedule for this district."

"So I hear. But I hear other things. For instance, who gave you permission to cut the oats and barley and to divert government milk supplies? Why did you forbid anti-religious work? Are you a disciplined Party member or are you some kind of anarchist?"

"Comrade Hatayevich," I answered calmly, "I could not do otherwise. Children were dying. Horses were dying. The collective farmers hadn't the strength to do any harvesting. The State has received its grain in good order and ahead of schedule. True, this has cost me several hundred *poods* of grain. But by investing these few hundreds I saved many thousands of *poods*. If that's a crime I'm ready to answer for it."

Hatayevich took my arm. He pressed it in a friendly way that belied his harsh tones. Apparently he was making a scene "for the record." He began to stroll out of earshot of his associates and guards.

"You're a future engineer, I'm told, and a good Party man. But I'm not sure that you understand what has been happening. A ruthless struggle is going on between the peasantry and our regime. It's a struggle to the death. This year was a test of our strength and their endurance. It took a famine to show them who is master here. It has cost millions of lives, but the collective farm system is here to stay. We've won the war.

"I'm afraid your heart is stronger than your mind, Comrade Kravchenko. If everyone were as soft as you, we might not have won this war. Mind you, I'm not scolding you. In fact, I see you've done a first-rate job here. Personally, and between ourselves, my heart also bleeds for the poor peasants. But I want you to remember my criticism—and if there's any question, don't forget that I did try to discipline you."

Even the mighty Hatayevich, it seemed, was worried about his record . . . and the coming "purge."

In a few minutes he was again surrounded by his assistants and armed guards. The motorcars drove towards the next village, in billowing clouds of dust. I rode back home, wondering who had denounced me to Hatayevich. I was certain that Somanov was not guilty of such a breach of friendship. It must have been Skopin. Outwardly under Somanov's orders, actually Skopin's only allegiance was to the G.P.U., the real power in our land. No doubt he had made copies of the denunciations. That my deductions were correct would become clear in the future, when my own turn to be "purged" came.

I was preparing to leave. The excitement of the successful harvesting had died down. Already the peasants were grumbling about the smallness of their share of the crop. After paying the State for the use of its machines, after making up the seed fund and delivering the fixed percentages of the total crop to the government, little enough remained. A bit over four and a half pounds of grain per work-day per person was the average. The amount was shockingly small, far from enough to feed a family, let alone enable it to buy clothes and other essentials for a year.

True, they received in addition some sunflower seeds, corn and vegetables. But what could they buy for the product of their labor? The cheapest kind of peasant shoes at that time cost 80 rubles, the simplest cotton dress, 100 rubles. At the official prices which the State paid for grain, the collective farmers were receiving so little for their work that a dress and a pair of shoes represented almost a year's work! Since the same regime was buying the grain and selling the shoes, and in both instances fixing the prices to suit its own convenience, it was in truth a system of multiple exploitation, with the secret police and the Party bureaucrats to enforce the economic heartlessness.

Some of the peasants might not be able to write, but all of them understood the injustice only too well. "Socialism," they sneered. "Robbery is a better name for it."

Several times in these months I had met Yuri. On one occasion I had interceded in his behalf with the Political Department. He was disheartened by his experience and depressed because his harvesting was lagging far behind mine. I felt very close to him. How was I to surmise that in years to come he would be among those who denounced me when I was in political trouble? I would have no doubt that he did it under irresistible pressures.

Nearly the whole village turned out to bid me farewell. Tears ran down the cheeks of kindly old Ivan Petrovich. Chadai and his family made me promise to write them. I waved to them all as the coachman whipped up his horses.

CHAPTER X

MY FIRST PURGE

ADJUSTING MYSELF to the commonplaces of normal life after returning from the famine regions was not easy. The Institute classes, factory conferences, nuclei meetings, even the routines of life at home seemed trivial in the light of my memories. I was "jumpy" and impatient. After a few futile attempts to get a coherent story out of me, my father gave up. Communists in time develop a sort of immunity to the political cant of newspapers, radio and meetings; but now it exasperated me to the point of physical pain.

I am inclined to believe, looking back, that inwardly, in the secret recesses of my being, I must have begun to break with the Party at this time. The village horrors left psychological lesions which never healed. For that very reason, however, my conscious mind reached out desperately for alibis, for compromises with conscience. How could it be otherwise, when to survive at all one had to come to terms with a reality from which there was no escape?

After all, one could not simply "leave" the Party. One could not even slacken his activities or betray symptoms of fading faith. Having joined the Party, a man was forever caught. He might be expelled, which would be a disaster for him, but he could not secede. Had I indicated my real emotions, it would have meant removal from the school, disgrace and persecution, possibly with concentration camp or worse as the inevitable end.

It was imperative to squelch those emotions, to drive them into the underground of my mind. I labored to repair my loyalties. With the purge in the offing, this urgency was even greater.

Hundreds of Purge Commissions were being selected. Soon they would begin their public sessions in factories, offices, institutions, schools. Every Communist in the land would run the gantlet of public confession and inquisition. More than ever we were aware of those invisible but ubiquitous eyes and ears; of the fat files where our private lives and thoughts were registered; of the personal enemies who might use the chance to expose our real or imaginary sins.

Will I come safely through the ordeal? This was the question uppermost in my mind, as in the mind of every Communist. It echoed through all our activities; it was implicit in all our talk. We ceased to plan for the future—there would be no future unless that hurdle were safely taken.

On every floor of the Metallurgical Institute a special box was installed to receive signed or anonymous "statements" about Communists. The

Special Department, behind its steel door, worked day and night, arranging, sorting, comparing. Purge time was open season for hunting out people against whom you harbored a grudge. It was a Roman holiday for the envious, the embittered and the sycophant.

A Purge Commission usually consisted of two or three members and a chairman: Party men of unblemished loyalty. It constituted a kind of court, acting at once as prosecutor and as judge. A certain Comrade Galembo, later high in the People's Commissariat of Iron Metallurgy, was chairman of the Commission at the Institute.

Those found wanting would be deprived of their Party cards. They would become *ex*-Party people, which is quite different from being *non*-Party people. The ex-Party citizen is one who has been rejected. Forever after he must be distrusted, barred from promotion, rounded up as a "potential enemy of the people" in time of crisis. Expulsion was the worst fate that could befall a Party member. It made him a political leper, to be shunned by former friends and disowned by meek relatives. To meet him would be to run the risk of political contamination.

There was ample reason, therefore, for the fear that pulsed through the Institute as the purge came near, towards the end of 1933. It was a fear touched with hysteria. The press published lists of who was to be purged and where. Anyone wishing to smear a purgee could send a denunciation to the Commission, adding to the materials already in Party files and G.P.U. *dossiers*. The all-too-human relish for tearing down more prominent or more successful neighbors was artfully inflamed.

The first condition for retaining membership, of course, was unwavering allegiance to the General Line of the Party; above all, spotless loyalty to Stalin. Even the hint of "deviation" thrice removed was fatal. But the purgee's most intimate life and his thoughts on all subjects were also fair targets for public attack. The proceedings combined the worst features of confession, third-degree interrogation and bear-baiting, with the Communist in the role of bear. For the victim it was a fearsome time of distress, for the audience it was too often a circus. Attendance throughout the weeks of purge was obligatory for all Party people, and the "non-Party masses" were encouraged to be present.

No Communist was ever informed in advance of the charges that would be brought against him. Uncertainty was the most upsetting element in the drama. You groped in the dark and prepared yourself for surprises. You reviewed your past, over and over again, wondering whence the danger might come.

Didn't you talk too much one night three years ago under the influence of good fellowship? Perhaps one of the good fellows reported your unguarded remarks. . . . One of your uncles had been an officer under the Tsars. True, you had never met him. But what if someone has dug up that ghost and you're accused of "hiding" him from the Party? A woman who was your lover was later arrested as a Right deviationist. What if this relationship with a class enemy were suddenly thrown up to you? Pavlov is likely to be expelled—how shall I disassociate myself from him before he drags me with him to ruin? Save your own skin—somehow, anyhow—for the stakes are life itself.

The purge at our Institute opened formally with a long-winded and painfully dull speech by Chairman Galembo. He told us that our beloved Party was honeycombed with "alien elements," with double-faced enemies, opportunists, masked deviationists and actual class foes. Our job was to ferret them out, to rip off their masks and expose their chicanery. The country had just carried through full collectivization and liquidation of the kulaks as a class. Triumphantly it has completed the first Five Year Plan and launched a second. Those who doubt that we are on the highroad to full socialism and the happy life are scoundrels and enemy agents. They must be rooted out for the health of the Party and its great Leader and Father, our Beloved Comrade Stalin!

Thundering applause, stretched for many self-conscious minutes, greeted every mention of the Leader's name.

Finally the purge got under way. Here was the procedure: The Commission members sat behind a red-draped table on a platform decorated with portraits of Politburo members and slogans; a bust of Stalin, banked with flowers, held the most prominent position. The Communist to be examined was called to the platform. He handed over his Party card to the chairman and began a recital of his life history. It was a political and spiritual strip act—an outline of his origins, his career, his interests, with confession of sins, near-sins and mistakes as the chief purpose. It was always better to bring up errors yourself, if you suspected that they were known to the Commission; "concealing" anything from the Party compounded the gravity of the crime concealed.

After the confessional, the purgee was questioned by members of the Commission and by people in the audience. He was reminded of omissions and tricked into contradictions. Comrades spoke up in his favor or against him. If the Commission seemed friendly to the victim, the process was normally brief and often purely routine. But once the audience sensed that the purgee was in disfavor, or actually "on the skids," it jumped on him and trampled him without pity; especially his frightened friends and associates hastened to join in the verbal lynching to protect themselves. The ordeal might last a half hour or an entire evening. The purgee might fight back, argue, plead, offer proofs of innocence, weep—or he might be crushed into confusion and wretched silence.

Those who passed the purge were handed their Party cards. Friends congratulated them, relieved for their own sakes. In some cases the Commission postponed decision to investigate further. The rejected were ignored and avoided. They stood alone. They could only look around in bewilderment on a shattered world and slink out of the hall, feeling themselves outlaws and pariahs. Suicide among expelled members was no rare thing.

Everywhere in the vast Soviet land, in the provinces and the big cities, similar purge gatherings were under way. Press and radio carried excerpts from these multitudinous exhibitions. All of it was ballyhooed as "Party democracy." Sitting in the Institute auditorium I was strangely aware of the immediate scene as just a tiny segment of a super-drama, with millions of men and women as the actors, one-sixth of the earth's land surface as the stage.

I waited uneasily, in mounting nervousness, for my turn on the stage.

2

"Comrade Sanin, please," chairman Galembo announces.

A blond man in his middle thirties steps briskly to the rostrum and hands over his card. He is thin, gangling, pleasant looking and wears glasses. We all know him and like him—a lecturer in mathematics, popular because he is a little ineffectual and not too strict. He tells his life story. The son of a peasant, he began his Communist career by joining the Comsomols. His professional life he started as a lathe hand in a factory; then he attended the Institute, did research work and finally became a teacher.

It sounds like an exemplary career. The crowd is bored. But suddenly his blameless biography is interrupted by a member of the Commission.

"Comrade Sanin," he says quietly, "did you ever sign a Trotskyist program document jointly with other students when you were taking your studies?"

There is a stir in the audience. People whisper and exchange glances.

"Yes, I did, but I renounced it long ago and everyone knows that I have."

"So you did sign it?" the Commission member persists. "You don't deny it."

"Of course not. I never made a secret of it. All my colleagues and the Party know that I made the mistake and confessed it subsequently."

"Maybe, Comrade Sanin. Still, I wonder if *everything* is known. I wonder if it's known that you still hold some of the views condemned by the Party and the Soviet people?"

The excitement in the hall rises perceptibly. The crowd smells blood. Sanin's comrades of a few minutes ago are beginning to worry. One after another they throw questions at him, with the obvious intention of "catching" him and saving their own necks. The closer their association with him, the more eager they seem to incriminate him, to display their own righteous disapproval of his heinous "crimes." They know his foibles, his weaknesses and play on them. Sanin gets mixed up, he does not always say what he really intended to say.

"Comrades of the Commission," he pleads, "I have condemned my own error long ago. I never seriously supported the Trotskyists. I never joined their organization. Only once in a weak moment I was induced to sign a document, which I quickly denounced. These people who are accusing me know all this well. I cannot understand why they're speaking the opposite of the truth. . . ."

But the chairman interrupts him. His voice is an audible sneer.

"Never mind, never mind," he says, "we know perfectly how you Trotskyists, you enemies of the Party, change color. We have data showing that you have not changed internally and it's not for nothing that your closest comrades are raising doubts." Turning to the audience he added, "Who wants to speak?"

There is little doubt that Sanin's fate is sealed. His friends rush to kick him now that he is down, to push him over the precipice into the abyss. They rise to say that Sanin is a deceiver, outwardly loyal to the Party but rotten with deviation inside. No one gives any specific information, condemning in ritual phrases. Suddenly the unexpected happens. The audience is electrified. An engineer, known and respected by the whole Institute, asks for the floor.

"I have been listening attentively to all the remarks here," he begins, "but I have heard nothing that's really to the point. Comrades, we are deciding the destiny of a Party member, whether he is to live or die politically. Where are the concrete charges? There aren't any!"

His defense only adds fuel to the fire. Passions are aroused. Encouraged by the Commission, which no doubt has made up its mind in advance, Sanin's associates continue to denounce him, to heap abuse on him. He is expelled from the Party.

Soon we are listening to the life story of a student, a dark fellow with lots of hair and Semitic features. He is young and his career is short. Quickly enough he is in the inquisitional stage of the process.

"Tell me, Comrade Shulman, what was the social status of your parents before the revolution?"

"My father was a tailor, my mother an ordinary housewife."

"Shulman is lying!" someone in the audience shouts.

There is a flurry of excitement. This will turn out to be an interesting session after all. Shulman is a morose, bookish fellow who has few friends.

"How can you prove that this Party member is deceiving the Commission and the Party?" Galembo addresses the man who shouted. Evidently the interruption is no surprise to the Commission.

"I can prove it all right. Shulman and I both came from the city of Cherkassy. I have just entered the Institute and this is the first time I have seen Shulman. But I know his family. I know that his father had a tailor shop—*and employed several workers*. He was an exploiter of labor. The shop was on Alexandrovsky Street. I know what I'm talking about. As the son of an exploiter Shulman should be driven from our beloved Party."

The purgee has blanched. He is cracking his fingers in nervousness. The turn of events is unexpected and he can hardly organize his words.

"Are you from Cherkassy?" the chairman asks sternly, after rapping for order.

"Yes, of course. . . . I said so before."

"Did your father have a tailor shop at the address mentioned?"

"Yes, of course. But he was not an exploiter. The other tailors were members of an artel. He was just head man. It was a kind of cooperative,

I swear it, comrades. Besides, I had nothing to do with it. Personally I worked in a factory, in another city."

"Wasn't he your father?"

"Sure, sure, he was my father."

"Then you hid from the Party the fact that you come from a family of exploiters?"

"I'm not hiding anything. It was an artel, a cooperative. I worked in a factory and my record as a Party man and as a student is good."

His manner is against him. The more excited he gets, the thicker his Jewish accent becomes. Laughter ripples through the hall. "Throw him out!" someone cries. "Out with him, he deceived the Party!" Shulman stumbles as he leaves the platform; he's blinded by tears. Everyone realizes that he will now be kicked out of the Institute, that his career is ended.

The next few purgees are fairly routine. They receive their cards from Galembo in short order. Then Comrade Tsarev is in the limelight. Although close to forty, he is a student. His forehead and cheeks are deeply furrowed. There is a brisk, military emphasis about his bearing, and his confession soon reveals that he has been in the Army for many years, has won citations during the civil war. Subsequently he became a factory official and two years ago matriculated at the Institute. He is married and has two children.

"Now tell us, Comrade Tsarev," the chairman asks, "what did you think of collectivization? What was your real attitude?"

"I worked in the villages, comrade, and helped to liquidate the kulaks as a class. I admit I found certain measures rather embarrassing and unpleasant but in principle I was in agreement."

"You don't seem to understand my question, Comrade Tsarev, or maybe you prefer not to understand it. You are not the only one who found this great undertaking unpleasant. I want to know your political reactions."

"I have never opposed the Party."

"Unfortunately that's not true." The Commission member gestures with a few mysterious sheets of paper in his hand. "We have data here to show that in the period of liquidation of kulaks you referred with approval to Bukharin's statement criticizing the policy of Comrade Stalin. Comrades Kasarik and Somov, please come forward and confirm your declarations to the Commission."

Many of us know the two students: the kind who study little and talk a lot. They step to the front of the auditorium and rehearse their depositions to the effect that while they were in the country with Tsarev he had spoken critically of the whole collectivization policy. They quote his supposed words in detail. Tsarev's attempts to interrupt come to nothing. It is obvious that his case is hopeless.

I break out in a cold sweat. Tsarev's behavior in the villages, his very words, seem reminiscent of my own.

"Now, Tsarev," the chairman turns to him, "do you still deny your disagreement with the Party?"

"I do. They exaggerate. Besides, criticism is not necessarily disagreement. I am only human. There was so much suffering around me."

Galembo shouts him down, fearful he may say too much.

"Loyal Party members trust their Central Committee, and our beloved Leader, Comrade Stalin." Applause from the audience. "There is no room in the Party for such as you, who have the impertinence to deny their errors." More applause. "Expelled."

"I will appeal to the Central Committee," Tsarev cries out. "My war record speaks for itself and my assignment in the villages was successful. I have shed my blood for the revolution. You have no right to ruin me!"

But the Commission members are not listening. Already they are drawing out the files of the next man. Tsarev has been one of the most popular men in the Institute, but now everyone shrinks from him as he leaves the platform. He can hardly credit what has happened—to him of all people!

The fellow now on the rostrum is Dukhovtsev. He has been working with his hands since he was eight years old, became a foreman and was selected among the "thousands" to become an engineer. He makes a first-rate impression. His answers to political questions and trick questions about Party history are flawless.

"Comrade Dukhovtsev, are you married?" Galembo inquires, almost casually.

"Yes, I am."

"When were you married and who is your wife?"

"I was married last year. My wife is the daughter of a bookkeeper and is now a nurse in a hospital."

"Tell me, did you register your marriage or not? In other words, how was your marriage consecrated?"

Dukhovtsev turns red. He fidgets in embarrassment. Suddenly he recognizes the import of this line of inquiry. The audience becomes tense, expectant. There is not a sound in the hall. Finally the purgee, in a low voice, admits the awful truth:

"I was married in church," he says dejectedly.

The tension is broken. The audience rocks with laughter.

"I know, comrades, that it sounds funny," Dukhovtsev raises his voice above the laughter. "It's ridiculous and I admit it. A church ceremony means nothing to me, believe me. But I was in love with my wife and her parents just wouldn't let her marry me unless I agreed to a church comedy. They're backward people. My wife doesn't follow superstitions any more than I do but she is an only daughter and didn't want to hurt her old people.

"I argued with her and begged her and warned her it would lead to no good. But she wouldn't budge, and on the other hand I couldn't live without her. So in the end we married secretly in a distant village church. On the way back I hid the veil and flowers in my brief-case."

The crowd cannot control its merriment. The chairman raps for order but to no avail. Dukhovtsev, now having lost control, shouts still louder: "We are not believers, I can assure you. My wife is working, I am studying, we have a child. I beg you, comrades, to forgive my mistake. I confess that I'm guilty for having hidden this crime from the Party."

Although several people come to his defense, he is expelled. Not only the church marriage itself, but especially the fact that he failed to report such a serious transgression to his superiors, are his real crimes.

Thus the purge continues, day after day. The sessions begin immediately after the lectures, which is to say about five in the afternoon, and continue far into the night. At the end of the first week, when the business has become a dreary grind, droning on with its accompaniment of tears, laughter and absurdity, we are suddenly aroused. A gifted teacher and research specialist, Comrade Peter Yolkin, is called. We know that his father is a former priest, which makes his position precarious. Of course, his father had renounced the church and even joined the Godless Society, to wipe the stain from his children's record.

Without that renunciation Peter would never have been accepted into the Party, despite his brilliance as a scientist. The man's devotion to his research has been utterly selfless. He has worked long hours, as consultant to several factories, in the laboratories, in classrooms. It is as if, by boundless zeal, he has sought to live down his "shameful" family background.

I happened to run into him in the corridor the morning before his scheduled purge.

"Well, Peter, how do you feel?" I asked.

"Not too good, Vitya. 'And will I fall, pierced by the arrow, or will it fly past me?' "

"Oho! If you're driven to quote from *Eugene Onegin* then you're really worried," I laughed.

Now, standing before an unusually large gathering, he is telling his personal story. Perhaps because of his ecclesiastical background, he shows a talent for confession. He has never hidden the shame of his life, he declares, and besides, his father broke with religion, publicly, through the newspapers. It has not been easy to eradicate the old and make room for the new; it has been a long and earnest labor to wipe out every last trace of childhood superstition. But he has done it, comrades, and now he gives all his thought to research. In that way, he feels, he can best serve the Party and Stalin.

"Tell me, Comrade Yolkin," chairman Galembo says, "have you known Sanin long?"

"Yes, for quite a while. We were classmates, graduated from the Institute at the same time and now we are both teaching here."

"Did you know that Sanin signed a Trotskyist document?"

"Yes, just as so many others here knew about it."

"I'm not asking about the others but about yourself."

"Yes, I knew about Sanin and I don't deny it," Yolkin concedes.

"In that case," Galembo raises his voice angrily, "why didn't you inform the Purge Commission that you knew about it?"

"I saw no reason for making such a declaration. The fact was so generally known that it didn't occur to me. Sanin himself had renounced his error publicly and the whole thing happened long ago."

"Look here, Yolkin, you don't deny you were on close terms with Sanin. You are an informed Party member. You ought to know how the enemies of the Party, both Left and Right, hide their true face. Did you show any signs of Bolshevik vigilance? Did you report the kind of things we know Sanin was saying?"

"He never said anything like that in my presence. I have nothing to add."

"All right, and did you know Ponomerev?" It is another member of the Commission taking the offensive now.

"Yes, I knew him. He also signed the Trotskyist platform."

"And did you inform the Purge Commission about him?"

"No, and for the same causes as in the Sanin case."

"In other words, you not only had Trotskyist friends but hid their dirty work from the Party."

"In the first place, these teachers are not personal friends but professional associates, neither more nor less than a lot of other staff members. In the second place, neither of them made any secret of his past."

"Apparently, Comrade Yolkin, you are not aware that the Party is struggling against deviationists. You take the whole struggle rather lightly, don't you? What if your friends are masked Trotskyists? It doesn't concern you. How can we trust you?"

"I don't see the nature of my guilt," Yolkin says in a firm voice.

"So much the worse for you," Galembo declares.

The interrogation is taking a bad turn for Peter. Several people, sensing the direction of the tide, arise to push the scientist's head under the water. One of them, suddenly overcome by his own dishonesty, stops in the middle of a sentence, stammers, then blurts out:

"But I'm talking nonsense. Comrade Yolkin is a wonderful comrade and great man."

The hall is suddenly silent, as if paralyzed by the shock of this bold act. It takes another five minutes of rhetoric for the members of the Commission to whip themselves into a proper state of anger. Yolkin is deprived of his card, to the surprise of nearly everyone.

I learned later that his family was crushed by the expulsion. To make things worse, his sister, a student at another Institute, was expelled merely because her brother was in disgrace. Thus their father's sacrifice of his religion came to nothing and two useful careers were wrecked. However, after months of appeals in which many prominent comrades, impressed by Yolkin's genius, interceded for him, he was restored to membership. Automatically his sister, too, was rehabilitated.

Now the meeting continues. Four or five comrades pass the purge without trouble. Then a young woman student whom we all know and admire for her intelligence and devotion is summoned to the rostrum. She is a brunette with flashing eyes and a ringing voice: one of those women who

are attractive without being in the least pretty. She declares that she is
the daughter of an artisan, a carpenter; that she went to work in a factory
in her early 'teens; that she studied in the evenings and was finally selected
to enter an Institute for engineering courses.

"Comrade Granik," the chairman asks, "are you married?"

"Yes."

"How long?"

"Five years."

"And who is your husband?"

"He is a former worker. I met him on the job. Later he was foreman in
an iron-smelting plant."

"Is he a Party member?"

"No, not now. But he used to be."

The audience suddenly smells blood again. Those who were leaving for
a smoke in the corridor return to their seats. Heads strain forward.

"Why did he leave the Party? Or was he perhaps expelled?"

"My husband was expelled," Granik says in a calm voice, "for taking
part in the Workers' Opposition movement."

"And did you divorce him then?"

"No."

"Where is this husband of yours now?"

"He was arrested. He's in a G.P.U. prison."

The crowd is now tense. This is real drama: the Party wife with a
deviationist husband is a stock situation in Soviet plays, where, with the
author's help, she always chooses the Party above love.

"Is this your husband's first arrest?"

"No, the second."

"And still you did not divorce him!"

"No."

"Have you visited him in prison?"

"Yes, I visit him every week."

"Why?"

"Why? I bring him food packages, laundry, cigarets."

"Isn't there anyone else who could do that?"

"Well, I suppose so—he has a mother and a sister."

"Then tell us why you visit him in prison. You are a Party member,
aren't you? Yet you have no qualms about helping a man who is an
enemy of the Party."

"He is my husband."

"Oh! He's your husband! Isn't the safety of the Party more important,
perhaps, than narrow personal considerations?"

"I do not agree with him politically. I try to argue with him and show
him he's wrong. Every time we meet we argue to the point of quarrel-
ing."

"Oh, you merely go to prison to agitate?"

Galembo's irony snaps the tension. Here and there people laugh. There
are exclamations of "Enough! Expel her!"

"Excuse me, Comrade Chairman," the girl raises her voice. "Is this a Party purge or is it a circus? I ask you to state your political charges against me and not to turn my personal life into a laughingstock for this audience."

"Very well then, why don't you answer to the point and tell us exactly why you make weekly visits to a class enemy and a Party deviationist."

"I told you. Not only is he my husband, but he's a human being. It would be disloyal and cowardly to divorce him when he's in trouble. I condemn his views. But we worked together, we studied together, we have lived together. We have definite emotions for one another. In fact—we're in love!"

Loud laughter greets this admission. An alleged Communist in love with a G.P.U. prisoner!

"In short," Galembo sums up, "as a Party member you do not even admit your error in associating with an enemy of the people. I think the issue is clear. Citizeness Granik does not deserve to remain in the ranks of the Party. She will no longer be allowed to trifle with the interests of our country."

There is applause. There are shouts of "Right! Out with her!" Yet a wave of sympathy sweeps the crowd as the girl, her head held high, her lips tremulous, walks off the platform, down the middle aisle and out of the hall. A student sitting near me whispers in my ear: "I'm not for Granik. But after all, this is a personal matter and shouldn't have been handled this way." I remain silent. How can I know whether my neighbor is honestly disturbed or has some ulterior motive, perhaps to provoke me to some dangerous comment?

3

When Seryozha Tsvetkov's name is called, my heart begins to pound. His testimony will certainly touch on his village experience. It may involve me. I know that he is emotional and fear for his safety and my own.

On the stage, with all eyes focussed on him, he seems too young and helpless. His youthfulness seems almost an affront in this grim setting. He is obviously nervous. Yet he tells his story connectedly. He keeps looking toward the far corner of the hall; I follow his eye and see his father smiling encouragement. Once Seryozha's eyes meet mine; I smile and also make a sign of encouragement. As he begins to tell of his work in the village, the chairman interrupts him.

"Comrade Tsvetkov, is your father a Party member?"

"Yes, and he has already passed the purge successfully."

"Tell us, how did you feel during the collectivization in the village?"

I can see that Seryozha had turned pale. He looks in my direction and says: "I carried out the task assigned to me by the Regional Committee but I admit that my reaction to certain occurrences in the village were negative."

"We have evidence," Galembo continues, "that you were not sufficiently firm and on many occasions showed wavering and inadequate decisiveness. What is your answer?"

I feel that Tsvetkov will sink unless he gets some support. It is absolutely necessary to give him a chance to collect his senses. Impulsively I rise and ask for permission to speak.

"What is your question?" the chairman says.

"I would urge that you announce the name of the person who made the hostile declaration about this comrade."

"He's from the Prosecutor's office."

"All the same, comrade, his name is important. I was in the village with Comrade Tsvetkov and I know the facts."

"Well," the chairman agrees, "his name is Arshinov."

"I thought so," I say with a note of triumph which gives Seryozha his cue. The interlude has helped him to calm down. The very mention of Arshinov's name seems to revive his anger and restore his self-confidence.

"Arshinov!" he says. "I can tell you that this man's declaration is incorrect and worthless. It's motivated by personal considerations. He is so afraid that I will tell what I know about him that he insures himself by denouncing me. This was my first time in the village. Naturally I had no experience and may have fumbled in the work. On the other hand, Arshinov used methods that were shameful—the kind of methods that have since been disowned and attacked by the Party. On my return I reported his behavior to the Regional Committee. It is not I who am guilty but this very Arshinov."

"But isn't it true that Arshinov made a superb record in grain deliveries, sometimes after you failed?"

"Yes, that was true on several occasions. But it does not follow that I should violate Party instructions and behave like he did!"

"Very well, who wishes to speak?"

I stood up and the chairman signalled me to go ahead.

"I worked with Comrade Tsvetkov and Comrade Arshinov in Podgorodnoye. I shall tell the details when my turn comes. But now I want to say that I found Comrade Tsvetkov an honest, cooperative, and conscientious Communist. He's a decent fellow generally even though he has not much experience. We should not make him the victim of this Arshinov's methods—if he were here I'd make mincemeat of him. If you allow me, I'll tell you something of Arshinov's 'achievements.' "

"Let's hear! Go ahead!" voices cry, but the chairman clearly is alarmed. He does not want a recital of village horrors.

"Comrades, we're checking the record of Tsvetkov, not Arshinov. The comrade on the floor can tell his story privately to the Commission."

I walk to the platform, and in a low tone recount some of Arshinov's brutalities. The Commission members make notes. Whether they go through the scene for the audience's sake or are actually ignorant of the facts I shall never know. I had reported the facts in detail, but it was always possible that Arshinov had friends powerful enough to keep my reports out of the hands of the Purge Commissions.

My championship of Seryozha encourages others. Three men and two women make speeches in his behalf. His card is handed back to him. From the stage he comes straight to where I am sitting. He presses my hand gratefully, tears in his eyes. Then he joins his father, who embraces him.

I am hoping to be called for my ordeal immediately after Tsvetkov. I might benefit from the favorable impression he seems to have made. But the name called is that of Comrade Grinchenko, lecturer on Marxism and Leninism in the Institute and therefore, in a sense, a minor "spiritual" and ideological preceptor of the Institute. If there is anyone on the Institute lists who is, *ipso facto*, above criticism it should be this tall, plain-looking lecturer. We think him rather on the dull side as a teacher, but entirely admirable as a human being.

Grinchenko lectures in Ukrainian, which is his natural tongue, despite the fact that the old language excesses had not merely been dropped but condemned as a "nationalist deviation." He is a fanatic Communist of whom the students say, "Grinchenko—why he goes to bed with Marx every night." Because we know little about his history, we listen to his confession with exceptional attention.

He is the son of a poor peasant family, he says, and until the revolution worked as stableboy on a wealthy estate. He was nineteen when the Tsar fell and he joined the Bolsheviks at once. He attained the rank of Company Commander in the Red Army and was wounded several times in battle. After the civil wars he attended a special Institute for Communist theory and here he is, lecturing on Leninism. It is, indeed, a blameless Soviet career.

"However, I must confess to the Commission and to the assembled comrades," he concludes, "my errors in the matter of the nationalist deviations. I followed the lead of Skripnik and others who distorted the General Line on the subject. That is part of my bitter past, which I regret and which is all forgotten."

"So everything is *forgotten*?" the chairman interjects in his most ominous manner. Again everyone is on the alert. "But do you still see certain people—let me say—" and he mentions three or four names.

"Yes, I might have run into them now and then. One can hardly help that. They were Ukrainian nationalists and I am not on good terms with them."

"Did you ever correspond with them?"

"No."

"After the Party generously forgave your sin, did you meet these men?"

"No. Though if I recall right I did once meet a common acquaintance of these people. We didn't talk politics."

"Do you know where these nationalists are now?"

"I have heard the report that some of them were arrested. I don't know which."

"Who brought you the report?"

"The mutual acquaintance whom I met by accident."

"You just said you didn't discuss politics with him. How does it happen he gave a report of the arrests?"

"Well, maybe I used the wrong word. Not a report—just a remark in passing."

"You are naive, Comrade Grinchenko, if you think you can pull the wool over our eyes. We know, for instance, that when you heard of their arrests you were indignant."

"I'm sorry but someone must have lied against me."

"On the contrary. We have confirmation from many sources that you are still a Ukrainian first, a Leninist second. We have depositions from two of your closest comrades—" and again he mentions names.

Grinchenko seems stunned. It is obvious to us that the men named are no longer among the free.

"I cannot understand why they should say such things about me," Grinchenko murmurs. "Yes, they were my best friends."

"And I suppose, Grinchenko," a Commission member adds, "that you did not speak against collectivization."

"No. Maybe I spoke against certain excesses, but never, never against the Party decisions."

"That's enough. Let's hear from the comrades in the auditorium."

One after another the lecturers on Marxism and Leninism now rise to strike at their colleague. They make speeches about the incompatibility of nationalism and Communism. They search in their minds, in a panic, for accusations against the man on the platform; and in fact they dig up half-remembered scraps of his conversation. They give no dates, so that even Grinchenko's nationalist enthusiasms at the time when they were obligatory, before the change of the General Line on the matter, serve as nails for his political coffin.

And so Grinchenko, too, the fanatic Leninist with the fine Ukrainian head, is among the rejected and disgraced. His career is ended.

I am still wondering what will happen to him when I hear my name called and hurry to the stage. I tell the story of my life—in the farm commune, the Donetz mines, the factory, on the Persian frontier, back in the factory, and finally in the Institute. I feel, as I talk, that it is an impressive biography. My "origins" are decently proletarian, my activities have been consistently Communist. As if in passing, I mention my inspection of Nikopol and my long visit to Ordzhonikidze. . . . Finally I plunge into a summary of my two assignments in the agrarian districts. Knowing that others have reported on me, I do not conceal the fact that I made some daring decisions but argue that the emergency required them.

"Under what circumstances did you lose your Party card? Are you aware that it is a serious breach of Party regulations?"

"I know and I am sorry, comrades. It was during the heat of the harvest. I replaced a collective farmer who had suddenly fainted and in the excitement lost my wallet. Here is a certification of the fact from the local Political Department."

The Commission inspects the document, adds it to my *dossier* and proceeds with the questioning.

"We have evidence that you were opposed to the energetic measures applied in the grain collection and that you discredited an Authorized Representative of the Party."

"On the contrary, comrades. It was he who discredited the Party. I assume you refer to Arshinov. I have already told you about his methods."

"All right, let's say it's Arshinov."

"In that case, comrade chairman, here's a copy of my report to the Regional Committee and to *Pravda* about him. You will see that he was a disgrace to the name of Communist. I did everything possible to guard the good name of the Party against his actions and that's why he seeks to undermine my standing. He used *physical methods.*"

"What kind of 'physical methods'?" someone in the audience asks.

"The Commission is fully aware of the facts now," the chairman says quickly. He is eager to change the subject. "You had better tell us something of your own methods—during the harvest at Logina."

This is my biggest hurdle. I had organized my version in my mind. For days now I have known exactly what I would say. But somehow the prepared sentences have melted into a ball. I can't untangle them. I confess to having reaped oats and barley in order to save the harvest, to having organized a collective kindergarten and used "firm methods" to feed the children, save people and save the situation.

"Comrade Hatayevich thanked me personally for the harvest, which was ten days ahead of schedule, and here's a formal testimonial to my good work from the Political Department." I hand over the paper. "What else can I say?"

The chairman is embarrassed. I have come well documented. If he has planned to push the case against me, he now wavers. I may still be saved. He takes another tack and I breathe more easily.

"What is your father's occupation?"

"He works in the Petrovsky-Lenin plant along with my younger brother, and my older brother is an accountant in a chemical factory."

"Is your father a Party member?"

"No."

"Your brothers?"

"No."

"Why was your father in prison before the revolution?"

"For revolutionary activities—in the 1905 insurrection and afterwards too."

"To what party did he belong?"

"He never belonged to any party."

"Are you sure?"

"Quite sure, Comrade Galembo."

"Well, does anyone care to say anything?"

Three comrades rise to attack me. Several others, among them Seryozha, praise me. But there are no fireworks. People stroll out to smoke and chat. A dull case. . . . I receive my card.

Before leaving the platform I ask the Commission members to tell me who denounced me on the Logina period. They consult the files. Evidently the man did not ask to have his identity shielded.

"It's a Party member, a Comrade Skopin," I'm told.

"Just as I thought," I smile. So the G.P.U. member of the Political Department had not forgiven my refusal to talk to him!

Friends surround me, pump my hand. Life is an open road ahead of us—we are still Party men in good standing.

Early in 1934 Comrade Lazar Kaganovich in Moscow announced that 182,500 members had been driven out of the Party. The final figures would be even larger, because in some districts the purge was not yet finished. Over 200,000 Party careers were thus ended. This, however, did not prove, as Kaganovich claimed, that the Party had been "cleansed," and that it was now truly "monolithic."

The proof to the contrary was in myself. Though I had passed the test, I was without doubt more skeptical, more deeply disturbed, than thousands of the men and women thrown on the political scrap heap. The same was true of tens of thousands of others. The leaders might tell themselves that the "last remnants of deviation and disagreement have been liquidated." The rank and file of the membership knew better.

CHAPTER XI

ELIENA'S SECRET

A GREAT MANY familiar faces, in the faculty and among the students, disappeared from the Institute after the purge. Those who remained, however, worked with freer minds and greater energy now that the fingers of fear were no longer at their throats. It was my last year of study. Already, as part of my curriculum, I was giving most of my time to practical engineering problems at the plant. After graduation I could look forward to a responsible post in the expanding metallurgical industry.

It was soon after the end of the purge that I met Eliena. Through the alchemy of love, the drama of her personal sufferings became an integral part of my own experience: it belongs in my private story. Indeed, few things that happened to me directly have left such strong marks on my attitude to the Soviet power as the things that happened to Eliena.

I have often marveled at the role of sheer accident in the fulfilment of man's destiny. On moving to Dniepropetrovsk, Eliena obtained an apartment in my neighborhood. She went to work mornings at about the same time that I went to the Institute. The result was that we sometimes took the same streetcar. I noticed her for the first time as we waited in a driving snowstorm, together with a dozen other huddled men and women, on the cement trolley platform.

That was accident. The second and third such meetings in the following weeks were also accidental. After that I began to look for the tall brunette and finally I began to wait for her. I let many cars pass and was illogically annoyed because she was late. When, out of the corner of my eye, I saw her lithe figure approaching, my heart skipped a beat or two. I suspected—quite correctly, it turned out—that she was quite conscious of my interest and not indifferent to it. Later we often laughed at this wordless courtship on a streetcar curb.

When I was finally introduced to her—again an accident—we felt as if we had known one another a long time. It was late in the evening. I was returning from a long session at the Regional Committee. The hall had been filled with smoke and the discussion had been boring. It was good to be out in the open, inhaling the crisp air and tingling under the bite of the frost. Suddenly, as I was striding along, I heard my name called. I had scarcely noticed the two women whom I had just passed.

I turned around and recognized a woman physician who had treated me when I was in the hospital after my service on the Persian border. And with her was the beautiful stranger.

"Victor Andreyevich," the physician greeted me heartily, "how have you been? I'm truly glad to see you. I've been reading your articles in the papers and I've heard about your fine progress through mutual friends. But excuse me, I want to introduce my young friend Eliena Petrovna."

She was rather startled by the eagerness with which Eliena and I shook hands and the embarrassment in our manner. She could hardly surmise that for nearly a month we had dreamed of just such a meeting to bridge the distance between us. Her astonishment was further deepened, no doubt, when we found an excuse for seeing her to a streetcar and walking off together. Living, as we did, in the same district, the excuse was easily fabricated.

The main ingredients of Eliena's unique beauty were grace and elegance. She had a pretty face. But it would not occur to a painter merely to put her face on a canvas. He would quite naturally wish to paint her whole figure. On this night of our first formal meeting she was wearing a black fur coat, tight-waisted and with a flaring skirt in the Caucasian style. A brimless hat of some white fur, set on her dark hair at a provocative angle, accentuated her slim height. A few snowflakes sparkled like jewels on her eyebrows.

We walked for nearly an hour, arm in arm, talking about ourselves, the world, and again ourselves. She, too, had just come from a stuffy meeting and found the intense cold and the crystalline air stimulating. It was her first visit to Dniepropetrovsk, she said, but she was working as an architect in a government planning bureau and would most likely be settled here for a long time. She had graduated from the Art Institute in Kharkov, where she had specialized in architecture, about four years ago.

"How happy I am to have met you," I said, at one point. "I have a feeling that the meeting will flourish into real friendship."

"So do I," she said, smiling, "but frankly, for your sake, I hope it doesn't. If you had any sense, Victor Andreyevich, you would make this first meeting the last."

Though she laughed, her remark disturbed me. I suspected at once that it was more serious than her demeanor indicated; that it hinted at some personal tragedy. There was no trace of joy in her smile, and in her eyes there lurked a curious melancholy that at once clashed with her beauty and enhanced its effect.

"I'll take my chances on you," I said.

"Remember that I warned you."

"All right, I'll remember. But in return you ought to tell me more about yourself. For instance——"

"Don't ask me," she interrupted. "Yes, I am married. My husband is a good man, but an unfortunate one. We live under the same roof and I care for him like a sister. But beyond that we are husband and wife in name only. I do not love him . . . in that way. . . . I'm glad I've met you. I have been lonely."

"Lonely? You? With a home, a career, your beauty. . . ."

"Oh, I know many people; perhaps too many. Yet I envy you because you have a real home, a mother. My father is dead and my mother lives in Kiev. In a way I'm glad—these days there are things one can't tell even to one's mother. I envy you also your illusions, since you're obviously a devoted Communist."

"One can be devoted even after shedding some illusions," I said. "But let's postpone politics. Tell me more about your husband. . . ."

"Please don't ask me that. If you really want to see me again, I make only one condition: that you act as if he did not exist. In the deeper sense he doesn't. But I must repeat my warning. You are full of hope and faith. I have neither. I'm one of the least of the camp followers, while you're at the head of the procession. You'll march better if you walk alone."

"I refuse to accept your warning. Whatever the price I intend to see you often." I adopted a light-hearted manner. "I shall never regret know-ing you even if all the plagues of hell befall me."

"Did you say 'plagues of hell'?" she smiled sadly. "I know nothing about the plagues of hell, but I know plenty about the plagues of our present lives. They are worse, much worse, because they befall people in life, not after death."

When I left her at her door, we agreed to meet again in the park the following Saturday evening. I bought tickets for a gala concert that night at which the celebrated artists of the Moscow Ballet, Victorina Krieger and Golubin, were to perform. Waiting for Saturday was a torment, yet I avoided meeting her on the streetcar platform. I was pleased by the approach of bedtime because it brought the day of our rendezvous nearer.

When we met, I was happy to sense in the pressure of her hand and the flush of her cheeks that Eliena, too, had been impatient for this reunion. We walked, talked, then went to the Opera Theatre. She seemed as thrilled as a child on a holiday.

"When I'm with you I forget all my troubles," she whispered in the midst of Golubin's performance of the Corsair.

Krieger, though no longer young, still danced divinely and was adored throughout Russia. This night she did scenes from her famous role in *Swan Lake* and drew stormy applause. Then a singer began the aria: "Give me, oh, give me my freedom. I shall know how to vindicate my shame. I shall save my honor and my fame. . . ." I felt Eliena pressing my hand until it hurt.

"Listen, Victor Andreyevich, these words have a deep meaning for me, and for so many many others," she said in a low, tense voice.

Then a stout woman sang Lisa's aria from *The Queen of Spades*. I felt that Eliena's joy in the concert was gone. She fidgeted and sighed. The singer came to the passage: "The little cloud came, brought the thunder along, and broke up happiness and hope. . . ." Eliena suddenly arose and drew me with her.

"Please let's go, Victor Andreyevich," she said; "please! I cannot listen to any more."

Out in the frosty air she calmed down. I did not ask any questions. Whatever the melancholy mystery shadowing her life, I had decided not to probe it.

"Let's go to some restaurant," I said. "Let's hear some gay music."

"All right—but only one condition: I pay for myself. You're a student, I'm working. There's no reason why you should pay."

We met at least once a week, usually oftener, in the following months. Winter turned to spring. I introduced Eliena to my mother—it was love at first sight between the two women. Thereafter she and mother met frequently even when I was not around.

"She's a sweet woman," my mother told me, "and she is very much in love with you. I know how you feel about her. But there's something in her life that weighs heavily on her spirits."

"I know, mother, and I have no clue to her unhappiness. I've discovered that probing only hurts her and I ask no more questions."

"You're right, Vitya. She's a good person and you should trust her. Whatever it is that troubles Eliena, it cannot be to her discredit. She is the sort who couldn't hurt anyone—except herself."

One night, after dining with my family, Eliena remained for the evening. We read together and listened to the radio. Both of us knew, without putting it into words, that she would not go home.

"This is our marriage night, Victor. I love you with all my heart and soul," Eliena said. "Please believe me that you are the first and only man in my life since I ceased to love my husband."

2

Months passed. Eliena came often to our house and became, to all intents and purposes, a member of the family. My parents, my brothers, all adored her. There was an aura of glamor around her that imparted its brightness to our whole household. Yet I was rarely without the gnawing awareness that an important part of her life was closed to me. Sometimes I felt that she lived in a permanent state of alarm, as if her existence were a house poised dangerously on the edge of an abyss.

Then came the day when my worry found a focus. Though I explained my suspicions as concern for her well-being, they were in large part the product of ordinary male jealousy.

After lectures, one afternoon, a few classmates and I went to a football game at the city Stadium. Between the halves we rushed to the refreshments buffet for beer. As usual, there was a long queue at the counter, and we took our places. As I stood there, looking aimlessly through the door into the adjoining restaurant, I caught sight of Eliena, elegantly dressed, in the company of two men who were unmistakably foreigners. The three of them were drinking wine, chatting gaily, and the men, it seemed to me, were looking at Eliena boldly, hungrily.

Though I sat through the rest of the game, I did not see it. What was Eliena doing in the company of foreigners? After the game I saw her depart with her escorts. They drove off in a big foreign motorcar. I was in a daze for the rest of the day and did not sleep that night.

Next day Eliena came to supper at my home, as previously agreed. I kept watching her throughout the meal, but she showed no sign of change. Could this contact with foreigners—a dangerous matter in our country—

be so routine that it left her unaffected? When we were alone, she mentioned casually that she had been at a football game the previous day.

"The head of my bureau asked me to go with a couple of visitors," she said. "They certainly were a bore."

I said nothing about having seen her there. When she left my room to go to the kitchen, I noticed that her handbag was open and caught a glimpse of papers in it. Still consumed with doubts and jealousy, I hurriedly glanced at the papers. One sheet was in German. Though I did not know the language I recognized that its contents were technical, with references to measurements and machines. The other sheet was in Russian. It began: "Enclosing the material on the attached report I wish to state. . . ." At this point I heard Eliena's footsteps and quickly replaced the papers.

I had no doubt that these papers were somehow related to the two foreigners and that the whole episode, in turn, held the key to the mystery of her life. When we parted late that night, I asked when we would meet again.

"Friday evening," she said.

"Unfortunately I am lecturing again this Friday. Let's make it Thursday."

"I'm sorry, darling, but Thursday I expect to be busy with some urgent business."

Made sensitive by my suspicions, I suddenly realized what had escaped me until then: that for several months Eliena had usually been too busy to see me on Thursday. I made up my mind to follow her that Thursday, if possible, to learn what I could.

It turned out to be a dark, rainy night, which made my amateur sleuthing easier. Having seen her board a streetcar, I jumped on the back platform. When she got off, near the center of town, I also alighted and followed her at a distance on the other side of the street. I saw her approach what looked like a large private dwelling. She rang the bell. A uniformed man opened the door, let her in, looked around cautiously, then closed the door.

From a doorway which gave me a clear view of the house, I watched it for nearly two hours. I saw people come and go. There was enough light from the windows of surrounding houses and from the door when it was opened to enable me to see their faces. Each time he opened the door, the uniformed man scanned the street, as if to make certain there were no observers. Most of the callers were women. A few of them I recognized. One was a woman famous throughout our city for her good looks and her charm as a hostess; she was the wife of a leading physician, a professor of gynecology. Another was a well-known singer in our local opera. There was a prominent engineer whom I saw often at technical conferences. Some of the callers, as they stood waiting for the door to open, I identified as women I had often seen at the theatre and at sports events—the Dniepropetrovsk equivalent of ladies of fashion.

Finally Eliena emerged, accompanied by two men in civilian raincoats. As one of them opened his coat to take out a cigaret from an inside pocket, I saw that he was in uniform. It was unmistakably a G.P.U. uniform. I knew all that I cared to know. Eliena, it was now clear to me, *belonged to the legion of spies operating in all crevices of our Soviet society!*

My mind was in a panicky turmoil. Tossing in bed that night I tried to organize my thoughts. Theoretically, as a Communist, I could hardly condemn the pervasive G.P.U. espionage. It was no news to me that thousands of persons seemingly engaged in other activities actually were devoted to spying. Yet the discovery that the woman I loved was apparently a G.P.U. agent shocked me deeply. Some atavistic instinct against spying sent chills down my spine.

Though we banished such knowledge to remote regions of our minds, some of us Communists knew well enough that hordes of innocent men and women were being herded into prisons and forced labor camps. We explained it to ourselves as "preventive" action—or we evaded the moral problem altogether by refusing to look at it with undimmed eyes. Could it be that Eliena, so close and dear to me, was responsible for bringing pain and death to innocents? The more I wrestled with the terrifying discovery, the more hopeless my situation seemed, torn as I was between love and a sense of horror.

In the morning I sent a note to Eliena. I told her that I had to leave town for about a week. For fear that she might come to look for me at home, or that I might run into her in our neighborhood, I moved to the home of a friend. The following Thursday night again found me observing the mysterious private house from my hiding place across the street. Again I saw Eliena and some others, mostly women, arriving. The pattern seemed clear to me. All of them, including the wives of well-known officials, were making reports on their week's work and presumably receiving instructions. A private house made the business easier and safer than calling at G.P.U. headquarters.

That night I returned home. I wrote Eliena that for reasons which I was unable to reveal, I could no longer see her. All contact between us, I said, was ended and I should be thankful if she accepted my decision in this matter and did not attempt to reopen a relationship which had become impossible.

I was so broken up by the decision that I could neither work nor think clearly. I stayed away from the Institute and paced the streets of the city for hours, in a futile attempt to escape a consuming pain. Under it all, mixed with my burning desire to see Eliena again, was the tormenting doubt whether I was treating her justly.

A few days later, when I returned from the Institute, my mother handed me a letter.

"Eliena left it for you," she said. "She seems to be in great distress. Her eyes were swollen with crying. I don't want to intrude on your personal affairs, Vitya, but I hope you know what you're doing. Wounds inflicted by persons we love are the most painful of all."

Eliena's letter was brief:

"Vitya darling: I beg of you to do me the last favor. Meet me tomorrow at six in the evening at the railroad station. I plead with you to do this last thing for me before we part forever."

I was waiting for her when she arrived. She was carrying a small suit-case. The suffering evident on her lovely face went to my heart like a knife.

"We're going to the Samara River," she informed me, "and we'll eat and talk in the open air. I have the railroad tickets already."

In the train we talked of trivialities: about my preparations for the final Institute examinations, about a building project on which she had been working. Arriving at a small station, we walked along a country road until we reached the shore of the river. For a time we both avoided serious conversation, as if deliberately postponing the very moment which had brought us here. The evening was close and there was a rumble of distant thunder.

"Let's have a swim before the clouds burst," I suggested.

We threw off our clothes and plunged into the river. After the refresh-ing swim, we dressed and she spread the food on a tablecloth. She had also brought along a bottle of Napareuli wine.

"Once, long ago, we drank to our meeting. Now let's drink to our part-ing," Eliena said. Her eyes were brimming with tears. "Remember that I told you then it would be better if we did not meet again. I am going to lose you. I shall be alone again."

Neither of us touched the food, but we drank the wine.

"Now Vitya, tell me what has suddenly happened? Why have you ceased to love me?"

"I love you as much as ever. That's why I'm here. I have come here counting on your honesty, Eliena. Can you tell me your secret? I will not continue to be led by the nose like some brainless boy."

"What do you want to know? Is it about my husband?"

"No, it's about you. I know why you go out with foreigners. I know about your Thursday evening meetings at the house on Y—— Street. What else do you want me to say?"

"O my God! My God!" she began to sob. "What shall I do? What shall I do?"

There was a flash of lightning. The first big drops of rain fell. We took shelter in an abandoned fishermen's hut nearby. In the deepening dark, sitting on a pile of fresh aromatic hay, Eliena told me her story.

"I love you too much to give you up," she said. "Darling, try to hear me with an open mind. I shall tell you what I have told no other living soul, not even my mother, certainly not my poor husband. After you've heard me to the end, you'll decide your course."

This, in her own words as I remember them, is the story of Eliena's life:

3

We lived in Kiev. My mother was a former schoolteacher. My father was a well-known professor of engineering. He worked in a local trust and earned good money. I was their only daughter and I had a happy childhood. I wanted for nothing. I was taught music, languages and grew up without a care in the world. What I liked best was drawing.

Our neighbors had a son, Sergei, who was attending the Technological Institute at Kharkov. He would come home for the summer. We were friends. Then, as I grew older, the friendship ripened into love. I was only a little over seventeen when he proposed to me. I accepted him and we moved to Kharkov. There I was able to follow my ambition by entering the Art Institute, from which I graduated in 1930.

You remember, of course, that it was the year when many engineers and specialists were being accused of wrecking. I happened to be visiting my folks in Kiev when the G.P.U. officers arrived to arrest my father. They made a search of the house, even cutting icons, sofas and mattresses open, but of course found nothing. The whole idea of my mild and scholarly father going in for sabotage was fantastic. It was so absurd that mother and I consoled ourselves he would soon be released.

Naturally, I remained in Kiev to help see her through the ordeal. Our happy life was ended. We had no inkling of what they had against papa and were not allowed to visit him. Every evening, week after week, then month after month, I would go to the prison gate to deliver food packages. For hours I would stand in queues, in rain or snow, with many hundreds of other miserable women. I also haunted the outer offices of the G.P.U. in the forlorn hope of helping my father.

Once, when I went to the G.P.U., I was asked to go into the office of the chief. I wondered why he had sent for me. I found a middle-aged man, courteous and impressive. He listened as I pleaded for my father. Then he said:

"Now *you* listen to *me*, Eliena Petrovna. You are a handsome woman, in fact you are beautiful. What's more, you have culture and carry yourself well. These are gifts that can be most useful to our country—not to mention yourself and your father. We can help you, provided you help us. I don't have to tell you much more, because I can see you're intelligent as well as personable. Now don't make a wry face and draw back. What I propose is not as filthy as life itself. I'm not asking you to go to bed with anyone. We have such women, too, and some of them are highly respected ladies in our city.

"You'll be more useful to us as a pure, unattainable woman. We'll see that you meet the right people, where you can hear a lot that our government needs to know. Naturally, we'll pay you well, and will protect not only you but those dear to you."

He offered me a cigaret, which I declined. Then he drew a box of bonbons from a drawer and motioned me to help myself. I looked at him incredulously.

"In other words," I finally said, "all you want me to do is to deliver a few human lives to you, maybe friends and acquaintances of my father, to help you concoct a few more sensational cases? If I do that, you'll release my father. Did I understand you right? Just that, with some bonbons thrown in for good measure?"

He laughed. "That's oversimplifying the picture."

"Well, I'm sorry I can't oblige."

"Don't be hasty in your decision, Eliena Petrovna. We have lots of time. Think it over and come back here. Meanwhile, if you give anyone a hint of this interview, we shall put the little bird in a cage for a long, long time. Please sign this paper."

It was a form in which the signer agreed not to tell anyone of the conversation and listing dire punishments for any breach of the undertaking.

Time passed in deep sorrow, Vitya. Having been given the chance to buy my father's liberty by becoming an agent, I almost felt guilty for his continued incarceration. Fortunately I knew that he would be the last person in the world to blame me if he had known. I was tired in mind and body. Then I was again invited to the G.P.U. chief's office. This time his courtesy was gone. There were no offers of candy or cigarets.

He busied himself with papers as I entered and pretended not to notice me. As I stood there awkwardly, I heard horrible shrieks somewhere down the corridor. Involuntarily I cried out in fright. He looked up.

"Oh, you're here again," he said. "Are you annoyed by the unpleasant noise out there? You're right, it's someone being encouraged to remember. . . . Yes, ours is a difficult task. It calls for nerves of steel. Well, will you accept my proposition?"

"No. I don't accept it—I can't accept it."

"Is that final?"

"Yes, it's final."

"In that case I'm awfully sorry for you—and your father. I still think you'll change your mind. Now good-day."

He again busied himself with those papers. I left.

That night, when my turn came to hand in a parcel for my father at the cage near the prison gate, the Chekist in charge repeated my father's name after me:

"Ladynin? No, I can't accept the parcel."

I stood there frozen with fear.

"What's happened?" I cried. "It's my father. Is he dead? Has he been sent away?"

"I don't know anything. Move on. Next!"

"But he's an old man. He's innocent. I must know what's happened to him."

"Get away or I'll have you removed by force. You're holding up the queue."

I went over to another window, marked "Information." I told the guard I wanted to find out about my father and gave him the name. He closed the window and I saw him telephoning. I strained to hear what he was saying, but I caught only one word—*hospital*. He opened the window again and announced: "No information. Sorry."

Scarcely able to move my feet, I turned to go home. In order not to alarm mother, I gave the parcel of food to a beggar. The following day I tried to find a doctor who served in the prison hospital, in the vague hope of some news about my father. I began with several doctors who were friends of our family. One sent me to another. After hours of this search, someone gave me the name of a physician who, he thought, was connected with the Kiev prison.

I went there. The doctor let me in, thinking I was a patient. But just as soon as his office door was closed, I sank to my knees before him and in tears told him what I was after. He was a kind man, but my story scared him out of his wits. He begged me to leave him. His work in the prison hospital was secret, he said, and he could tell me nothing.

"Please remember, my dear," he said, "that I have a wife and children. I can take no chances. I'm truly sorry but I can do nothing, nothing. Please leave and for the love of your own family, don't get mine into trouble."

But I refused to leave. I cried and talked until I wore him down. He agreed to locate my father, if he were indeed in the prison hospital. I was to call him in three days from a public telephone booth.

My mother continued to make food parcels which I regularly turned over to beggars. I waited for the appointed day. At last I had the doctor on the telephone.

"Get hold of yourself," he warned me. "I have unpleasant news. Your father is in the hospital. His condition, I fear, is hopeless. He has inflammation of the lungs. . . . Besides"—he hesitated—"he is rather badly bruised. Now good-bye. I'm very sorry."

Reluctantly I went to G.P.U. headquarters and sent in my name to the chief. I was admitted almost immediately. He met me at the door of his office, smiling expansively.

"Well, what's new? Have you finally decided?"

"No," I said. "Before I decide I must see my father."

"That will be hard to arrange. I don't want to upset you but your father is in the hospital—and he's not exactly in a presentable condition."

"Please, please let me visit him. After all, you're a human being——"

"There are no human beings here, Eliena Petrovna, only humble guardians of the revolution. There's no room for sentiment here. Our tools against enemies of the State are pain and death. The sooner you realize it the better. I'll let you see your father, but only because I need your help. Go to the prison. By the time you get there I'll have word through. And while on your way, think again of my offer. Don't be an idiot."

I was taken to a ward. My father, in preparation for my visit, had been moved to a separate room. He lay on an iron cot, as still as death. He had grown a gray beard in the months since I had last seen him. He was all skin and bones. There were ugly blue welts on his forehead and his hollowed cheeks. His fingers and arms were bandaged. I went to his bed. He was too exhausted to smile in greeting. When he began to talk I saw, with a shock of horror, that his front teeth had been knocked out.

"Don't cry, Yolochka," he said in a weak voice. That was his pet name for me since childhood.

I had been cautioned to talk only of family affairs and to avoid politics. But the Chekist guard was moved by the scene. He turned his back, as a hint that he was not listening. My father motioned me to bend down, and he whispered in my ear.

"You see what I look like, Yolochka. They've beaten me, day after day. Torture is their business. Hundreds in the cellars of this prison are being whipped with wet towels, kept awake for weeks, or kept in ice-cold rooms. They've beaten me without mercy to make me tell them the names of my 'fellow conspirators.'

"How could I tell them, when there wasn't any conspiracy? Nothing but their own inflamed imaginations. They see ghosts. Sometimes I wished I had something to confess. I remembered ordinary mistakes and confessed them as acts of sabotage. I invented examples of wrecking. But they only beat me more, because the falsehoods were too naive to stand up. But why tell you more? I had heard about the G.P.U. and its methods, but the worst I had foreseen was nothing compared with the actuality. These are not men but monsters. Oh, Yolochka, my child, what these people have come to. . . ."

"You'll get well, father, and I'll get you out of this hell. I promise. . . ."

"No, it's hopeless, my child. The doctors have been frank with me. The wounds of torture might have healed. But the 'cold treatment' gave me pneumonia. In my condition and at my age I cannot recuperate. I'll be dead in a few days. Try to forget this and go on working as if nothing has happened. Be good to mother and Sergei."

"Citizeness, the five minutes are up. You must leave."

A few days later my father died. I returned to my husband in Kharkov.

4

I interrupted Eliena's story.

"Never mind, darling, I don't want to know any more. I'm so sorry for you and so ashamed of myself. Forgive me for my stupid behavior."

"No, no, now that I've begun you must hear me to the bitter end," she said. "I want you to know and to understand. This is only the beginning of the horror." And she went on with the macabre account:

The year 1931 passed and most of 1932. My husband by this time had graduated and was working in a big plant. Like other technical men at this time, he was in constant dread of arrest. He had nothing on his conscience, yet there was this senseless and unending fear, as he saw one after another of his associates dragged off.

All the same, when he was actually arrested, I could not believe it. I knew all his friends, all his thoughts, all his actions. He was perfectly innocent of even a hostile thought. Again I was standing on the dismal queues, in rain, in snow, with thousands of other women, to deliver parcels to the prisoner.

I was dismissed from my job on some silly pretext. It was obvious that my superiors did not want the wife of an arrested engineer near them. Gradually I sold everything I possessed, piece by piece, to buy food for myself and my imprisoned husband. I gave music lessons. A few friends helped me with money, but always on the promise that I would not reveal they had seen me, or shown me kindness. As the wife of an "enemy of the State" I had myself become an outcast, an untouchable.

A few months after Sergei's arrest, his parcel was rejected at the prison gate. It was like an old horror film being run off again. I went to another window and asked to see the chief. After about two hours of waiting, I was conducted to the office of Comrade T., one of the assistants to the head of the Kharkov G.P.U. He was a tall, handsome, well-fed blond man. He radiated charm.

"Ah, I rather thought I might expect a visit," he said as he shook hands and gallantly helped me to a chair. "I relish visits from beautiful women. Besides, I've had a full report on you from our Kiev headquarters. What a pity that we meet under such—shall I say official—circumstances. All the same, I'm grateful for the opportunity."

"You mean you *made* the opportunity by refusing to accept a package for my husband," I said.

"Really, they wouldn't take the parcel? What blundering dolts! I'll see about it immediately."

He pushed a button and a trim officer came in. He gave instructions that parcels were to be received for my husband. The officer left.

"Please believe me, Eliena Petrovna, that I regret the suffering you have undergone. But after all, it's your own choice. The suggestion made in Kiev two years ago still stands, you know. We Chekists keep our word."

"Why do you hold my husband?" I replied. "You know as well as I do that he's innocent. If you ever had a mother or a sister, you'd take pity on me. I can't become your spy. It's not in my character. I'd rather die. But I'll do anything else to save my husband. I simply can't bear the thought of his sufferings."

I talked on and on, repeating myself, begging and accusing in turn. He listened patiently. When I had exhausted myself he came over, patted me on the shoulder in an almost paternal gesture.

"Life is cruel, Eliena Petrovna," he said, "therefore one must be practical. You should think of yourself first. Why are you being stubborn? Why don't you come with us?"

"I'll tell you why. The murder of my innocent father is one reason, and the murder of thousands of others like him are thousands of other reasons. Even for my husband I will not take the tears and blood of other wives and mothers on my conscience. That's why."

"I understand your squeamishness about tears and blood," he said. "But be sensible, if you can. We won't give you the kind of assignments that will mean blood and tears. We need you to work among foreigners. Our country is surrounded by capitalist hyenas howling for the blood of the revolution. I won't press you now. But any time you change your mind, I'm at your disposal. Your father is dead. That can't be undone. But you can still save your husband. It's not up to me but to you."

However, he promised that Sergei would receive my packages—until he was formally sentenced and exiled. A few weeks later I was informed that he had been sentenced to ten years of hard labor and sent to a concentration camp in the Urals.

For a long time I fought with the temptation to go to work for the G.P.U. I yearned for Sergei. I was weary of the struggle. In a time of so much falsehood and injustice, why should I behave like a Don Quixote? Many times I made up my mind to take the fatal step. But each time, at the last moment something inside me, something too deep-rooted for me to explain sensibly, said "No! You shall not!" The idea of spying, of pretending to be a friend while leading someone to the slaughter, revolted me. It made me physically ill.

For nearly a year I kept writing petitions to various government departments, pleading for a review of my husband's case. Nothing came of it, of course. Then something happened. I was visiting an exhibition of Ukrainian painting with a friend from art-school days. Suddenly, in the crowd, I saw Comrade T. He was accompanied by a strikingly beautiful woman. His manner towards her made it obvious that he was in her power, rather than the other way around. I watched them carefully. She was capricious and he was as attentive and obedient as a lovelorn schoolboy.

The ruthless Chekist official, who held the fate of tens of thousands in the palm of his hand, behaving like a mooncalf with a radiant woman! The paradox of the picture, I suppose, put an idea into my head. Fantastic though it seemed at first blush, I was determined to try it.

It was not too hard to find out the identity of Comrade T.'s friend. Then I traced her address. I watched for her at the entrance to the new apartment house where she lived. I followed her up the stairs. As she was fumbling with a key at the door of her apartment, I went up to her boldly and began to talk.

"For the love of God, Madam, I beg you to let me speak to you for just a few minutes," I said.

At first she was frightened. But then, looking me over, she apparently decided that I meant no harm.

"I don't understand. What is it you want? But come inside. We can't stand here in the corridor."

We went into her drawing room, which was furnished in excellent taste. A large grand piano stood in one corner. I must have looked tired and miserable after my hours of waiting in the streets.

"Take your coat off, child, and sit down," the woman said. "I'll make some coffee. You look more dead than alive."

I grasped her hand, and made her listen to my troubles. I told about my father's death, my mother's suffering, the banishment of my husband. I needed her help. Through her Chekist friend she could obtain for me the right to visit my husband. It was the one thing I could still do for him. My anguish was so deep that it infected the woman, and she began to cry herself.

She asked me many questions. Then she walked up and down the large carpeted room, thinking. In her distraction she even sat down at the piano and played some chords.

"Eliena Petrovna," she said at last, "I am sorry that I cannot make any promises, except the promise to try. You realize of course that under no circumstances must you ever mention this visit, not even on the telephone when speaking to me."

She kissed me with a tenderness that surprised me. I guessed that she was not as happy, and perhaps not as worldly, as she seemed. That evening I went to church and prayed for a long time. I am not a believer, Vitya, but in moments of crisis I go back to the habits of childhood. Anyhow, I prayed as devoutly as any believer. Then I telephoned T.'s mistress and learned that my prayers had been heeded. She asked me to come to see her at once.

When I arrived, I wept with joy and kissed her hands. She instructed me to write another formal petition for an interview with my husband and assured me that this time it would be granted. About herself she gave me no more than a hint.

"Life is life, Eliena Petrovna. There was a time when I did not live as comfortably as this, but I was far happier then. It will give me at least one moment of joy to know that I could bring a little relief from misery to you and your husband. It's refreshing to do a decent thing for a change. Please forget we ever met. You must never phone me again or recognize me if you see me."

And so, within a few weeks, I was on a train bound for the Urals. I carried big bundles. I had spent every kopek I had for provisions, warm underwear, boots, tobacco. I visualized our meeting, Sergei's joy, his bright face, a few moments of happiness. Beyond Sverdlovsk, I left the train at one of the small stations. An autumnal rain was falling and I seemed to have landed in a world of drabness and deep mud. The concentration camp was miles from the station, and I had a hard time inducing a peasant to drive me there. We rode for a long time. Around us were thick forests and wild cliffs. Finally we came to a kind of plateau, a huge open space surrounded by tall barbed-wire fences.

Beyond the fence I could see the long rows of barracks, with their tiny barred windows. I could see guards walking around, some of them with vicious-looking dogs at their heels. As I stood at the gate in the rain awaiting admission, a detachment of about three hundred prisoners, walking four abreast, returned from the forests to the camp. Never in my life had I seen human beings so degraded and ravaged. These were not men but the obscene shadows of men, repulsive-looking caricatures of human beings in rags and tatters. They were all bearded, with wasted bodies, dragging their feet through the mud in the last stages of deadly fatigue. Vitya, I simply haven't the words to make you feel the misery of the sight.

In the guardhouse I presented my documents. A Chekist came in, asked many questions, then had a woman agent search me. She searched not only my clothes but my body. Pencils and paper were taken away, even a small manicure scissors in my handbag was removed. Then they said I couldn't take in packages, allowing me to keep only the loose tobacco, cigarets and soap.

"This is no summer resort or rest cure, citizeness," the Chekist barked at me. "What we give them to eat and wear is enough. These are enemies of the State."

I sat down in the dirty little room to wait for Sergei. On the walls were fly-specked portraits of Stalin, Dzherzhinsky and Yagoda. There was also a crude strip of bunting with the words "Regeneration Through Labor" on it. I kept looking out of the window. Soon I saw a haggard old man approach, followed by a Chekist with drawn revolver. The man's ragged beard was gray, his hair was white; he was emaciated and horrible to look on. A dirty rag was bound around one of his eyes and in general he looked as if he had emerged from some purgatory. Moved to sympathy by the dismal creature, I turned to the official.

"Look here, comrade," I said, "do you see that old man over there? Please give him this package of cigarets."

It was the only thing I could do to show my sympathy.

The officer burst into laughter and slapped his thigh in high spirits. "I'll be damned! Are you kidding me or have you really failed to recognize your own husband?"

I was petrified with horror. The door opened and the old man walked in. When he came close I realized that it was, indeed, Sergei—but broken, aged, scarcely human. It was all incredible. I went to him and took him in my arms and whispered, "Seryozha, darling, poor Seryozha."

He looked at me in confusion, his tortured face aquiver with emotion. Suddenly he fell on his knees, began to sob and kiss my dress, my knees, my hands. I calmed him and made him sit beside me on the bench. I had been granted only ten minutes with him after the journey across half of Russia, and we had been warned to speak only of personal things. Almost before we had settled down to talk, we heard the announcement:

"Your time is up. One minute for good-bye."

"Eliena, dear," poor Sergei whispered, "save me if you possibly can. Life here is more terrible than anyone in the outside world can imagine, worse than I ever dreamed it could be. We're treated like animals, not like people. Prisoners die every day like flies. We're beaten and starved. Eliena, Eliena, save me. I won't survive another year in this hell."

"Shut your mouth, you scoundrel!" the Chekist yelled at him.

I promised Sergei to do what I could. With the agonized vision of the wreck who used to be my husband before me I returned to Kharkov. All hesitations were erased. I could not let him remain there just to save my own pride and moral purity. I went to Comrade T. and we struck the bargain—I would accept the G.P.U. bondage in return for Sergei's freedom.

"I assure you, on my personal word of honor, Eliena Petrovna, that you will never receive an assignment that might involve 'blood and tears' as you once put it. On the other hand, you will pay with your head if you ever reveal the slightest hint of your connection with us."

"Always bear in mind," I replied, "that I am not going to save my husband in order to send some other woman's husband or father or brother to a similar fate. You know perfectly well that Sergei is innocent and that most of the others in that hellish hole are innocent. I will let you kill me before I'll be a party to any such injustice.

"Also, I must retain the right to leave the service. I must have that in writing."

"I understand and you already have my word on it, though I can't give you anything in writing. You must trust me. You will have the privilege of withdrawing. Now let's seal the bargain. Fill out this application blank."

It was a questionnaire covering ten pages. Nothing about my life and views, about the life and views of my relatives and friends, was overlooked by the queries. I labored over it for a long time and finally signed it. The G.P.U. Assistant Chief Comrade T. looked it over, made some marginal notations and locked it up in his safe. Then he put on a civilian overcoat and cap and we left his headquarters together.

An automobile took us to within a few blocks of the Intourist Hotel. There we stepped out.

"I shall go ahead alone," he said, "and you follow me in exactly three minutes. Go to the fifth floor of the hotel." He mentioned the room number. "I'll be waiting for you. And don't look so shocked. Just now I'm a Chekist, not a man, so you needn't be alarmed."

A few minutes later we were together in the room. When a waiter knocked, bringing some food and wine, I hid in an adjoining room.

"Clever girl," my chief congratulated me when the waiter had left. "But here discretion is not so important. Everyone in the tourist hotels, from the manager to the scrubwomen, works for the G.P.U."

As we dined he gave me my first instructions and a sort of speed-up course in G.P.U. methods.

"I regret to say that for the time being you will not work with me," he explained. "But some day, upon your return to Kharkov, you and I together will do wonders."

"Where will I have to go first?"

"You will remain in Kharkov a few months. You have many things to learn. Then we have you lined up for Dniepropetrovsk. It's a nice town. Because of the big dam, plant construction and other work in progress, a lot of foreigners are concentrated there—engineers from America, German specialists and so on. There's lots of work to be done.

"What you should understand is that I have recommended you personally, which means that I'm responsible for you. If you pull any tricks, it will be blamed on me. You may think that I have you in my power, but it's the other way around, my dear. I am in your power. If you ever make honest mistakes, you'll be forgiven. But Allah help you if you attempt to deceive us or to work 'to the left' as the saying goes. Yes, I'm in your power, and that's why I thought it a good idea to have this heart-to-heart talk right away."

"I'm listening," I said.

"My first piece of advice, Eliena Petrovna, is to train your memory, especially your visual memory. Never write anything down. Grasp it with your mind and hold it. It's a knack that comes with practice. Papers and notations are dangerous. Memorize what you need—names, addresses, telephone numbers, facts. Memory is your main tool.

"Practice your foreign languages. Those are also valuable tools. And the same goes for your beauty. You're one of the most attractive women in our service and part of your job is to keep yourself attractive. Don't be stingy with clothes and cosmetics—that's justified expense account.

"You will meet other of our workers from time to time. Never confide in any of them. Never refer to the nature of your assignment, no matter how casually. If you have to work on some job with several other G.P.U. people, follow only the instructions that apply to you, even if they seem absurd. That's your only responsibility.

"Another important piece of advice, my dear. Never accept a drink unless it was poured in your presence and unless your host drinks it first. And never become friendly with any man in our service without explicit approval from your chief, and report every new acquaintance, however trivial and casual it may seem to you. You will have access to our special shops and coupons that will give you clothes and food beyond ordinary citizens. The guardians of the country's safety must want for nothing, and now you're one of us."

"Just one more question," I interrupted. "When will my husband be home?"

"Don't worry. We keep our word. He will have a good job in Dniepropetrovsk and you will work as an architect."

Sergei did return in about two months. He is a sensible man and a kind one. He knew that I felt for him only pity and that intimate love, in the old sense, was out of the question. That part of our relationship had been killed by the Soviet regime. He never asked me how I managed to get him out—perhaps his suspicions are even more horrible than the gruesome truth.

It was a fearful decision that I had to make. But Vitya, if you had seen the concentration camp, and the horrifying transformation of Sergei, you would understand why, after years of resistance, I finally had to yield. I am only one of an army of thousands who are thus forced to do the bidding of the G.P.U. We are kept apart. In the house where you saw me, no caller ever sees the others. Each one is led to a separate room and we never confront one another even by accident. Yet I've met some of these people in the course of assignments. They include the wives of high officials and of prominent men generally.

Sometimes they are caught in some indiscretion and blackmailed into accepting service. Sometimes G.P.U. agents deliberately lure some woman into an affair, then force her to work for them under threat of denouncing her to her husband. Often, I believe, women are accused of crimes they did not commit; they are framed so convincingly that no husband would believe them innocent. And so they, too, sometimes yield. There are hundreds, thousands, of dirty tricks for building up the army of spies, Vitya. Not many do it just for the money and the power. Usually it's under some sort of irresistible pressure. It's all so brutal and nauseating.

"So that's why you came to Dniepropetrovsk, Eliena?"

"Yes, Vitya. And that's how I met you, about a month after I moved from Kharkov. I reported our acquaintance—I had no way out. But nothing else, Vitya darling."

"Did your chiefs tell you anything about me?"

"Of course. But there was nothing compromising. It seems your record, so far as the G.P.U. is concerned, is clean. Are you still astonished and horrified that I am an agent?"

"To tell the truth, I am. It will take time to absorb the shock."

"And yet, Vitya, you are a Communist. As a Communist it is your duty to report everything that could be harmful to the Party, whether you like it or not. Is there, after all, such a great distance between these millions of willing informers and those who are forced to inform? Aren't we both caught in the same filthy net?"

"There's some truth in what you say, even if the comparison is—what shall I say?—primitive. Willingly or unwillingly, we in fact both defend the regime."

"Now, my dear, that I've taken the fatal step of telling you, my life is in your hands. As a good Communist you are obliged to betray me. Yet I know perfectly well that you won't. I'd go to the end of the world to escape the clutches of the G.P.U. but its reach is long. There is no escape but death. I think of suicide often as the only way out.

"Vitya, darling, do be careful. We live in a country where everyone around us wears a mask. Trust no one, no one, with your thoughts. I'm not talking of janitors and keyhole spies, but of the most respectable people in town. The only safety is in assuming that everyone, without exception, is reporting, reporting, reporting. . . . Oh, Vitya, I'm so tired and despairing. I shall love you tenderly even if you cast me off."

"Eliena, don't talk nonsense," I said with a rush of affection for the trapped girl. "I am miserable only because I cannot help you. It's infuriating for a man to be so powerless to help the woman he loves."

"Let's go swimming," Eliena proposed. "Just recalling what I've gone through makes me feel sticky."

The water was warm. We swam in the dark, in the rain, amidst the flashes of lightning and rumble of thunder. It was foolish and heedless but somehow it seemed to wash away the horror of her story. I carried her out of the water into the fishermen's shed, and I dried her as if she were a child. Then I tucked her to bed in the sweet-smelling hay. Exhausted by the emotions of this strange day, she was asleep almost instantly.

In the morning we took the train back to town.

"You know, Vitya," she whispered to me, "I feel ever so much better, cleaner, now that the awful secret is no longer between us. If only you continue to love me, I shall be happy as never before."

Some weeks later Eliena went to Kiev to visit her mother and I joined her there. One sunny day we went to the cemetery. I pulled the weeds off her father's grave and decorated it with cut flowers. I had brought along a can of paint and painted the gratings around the grave and the iron cross at its head. Eliena didn't cry. But as I worked she told me about her father and her happy childhood.

"If the G.P.U. knew that you had decorated the grave, they'd arrest you, Vitya," she said on the way back to town. "Even in death it is dangerous to be good to my poor innocent father. But your little human act has endeared you to me."

"In that case it's worth the risk," I said.

"And it doesn't disturb you as a good Communist?"

"No, not a bit. Maybe I'm not a good Communist in that sense."

We went to the Kiev park. An orchestra was playing in what was formerly called the Tsar's garden. The song, then popular, was a silly tune celebrating the "happy and joyous life" of Soviet citizens. Eliena and I looked into each other's eyes. We needed no words to share our thoughts.

CHAPTER XII
ENGINEER AT NIKOPOL

THE GRADUATING form at our Institute was preparing excitedly for its final examination. An individual engineering project approved by a government commission was a condition for receiving the diploma, and I toiled over mine anxiously. In addition we were spending a lot of time at various metallurgical plants, in a kind of interneship. What we needed most was some mental peace, a holiday from politics. But fate would not have this—precisely those last months became hectic with political drama.

At best there was little enough academic calm in the Institute. Outside assignments and purges seriously sapped our energies. Sometimes it seemed as if study were merely a sideline activity. Now even the marginal calm was shattered: a revolver shot in far-off Leningrad, on December 1, 1934, hit our lives in Dniepropetrovsk with the force of an earthquake.

The shot was fired in the vestibule of the former Smolny Institute, now Party headquarters in Leningrad, by a young Communist named Nicolayev. Sergei Kirov, a member of the Politburo and virtual dictator of North Russia, fell dead at Nicolayev's feet. The echoes of that shot would reverberate for many years. Hundreds of thousands of lives would be wrecked or snuffed out altogether before they subsided. I would myself pay with years of suffering for that act of terror by an unknown young man.

Stalin and Voroshilov rushed to Leningrad. According to stories circulated in Party circles, Stalin personally supervised the intensive cross-examination of Nicolayev. No outsider, of course, could know what he learned, but from his subsequent behavior it can be surmised that Stalin was alarmed to the point of panic.

Hundreds of suspects in Leningrad were rounded up and shot summarily, without trial. Hundreds of others, dragged from prison cells where they had been confined for years, were executed in a gesture of official vengeance against the Party's enemies. Local prisons were filled to suffocation. Freight trains hauled additional thousands of "politically alien elements" out of the city to distant exile places. Then the new terror spread to Moscow, Kiev, Kharkov and ultimately to the whole country.

The first accounts of Kirov's death said that the assassin had acted as a tool of dastardly foreigners—Esthonian, Polish, German and finally British. Then came a series of official reports vaguely linking Nicolayev with present and past followers of Trotsky, Zinoviev, Kamenev, and other dissident Old Bolsheviks. Almost hourly the circle of those supposedly implicated, directly or "morally," was widened until it embraced anyone and everyone who had ever raised a doubt about any Stalinist policy.

Propaganda machinery was thrown into high gear. Forgetting that only yesterday they had been boasting about the unexampled unity of their "monolithic" Party, the leaders and their press now shrieked hysterically that the Party contained traitors, deviators, double-faced deceivers and saboteurs. There were dark hints of plots and conspiracies in connivance with a capitalist world that was preparing to make war on the Socialist Fatherland. Those of us with the least sense of political weather knew that blood-letting on a Genghis Khan scale was about to begin. And we were right; the next few years were to bring the most horrifying official terror in all Russian history.

A rumor spread through Party circles that Nicolayev's act had not been political at all—that he had shot in a jealous rage because Kirov had seduced his pretty wife. Such illicit whispers and planned propaganda combined to wrap the assassination in mystery and conjecture which have not been resolved to this day. In time an official "closed letter" was issued by the Central Committee and read, under pledges of secrecy, at special meetings of the most active Party members throughout the country. This presented the murder of Kirov as an expression of a far-reaching struggle against the Party's policies and leaders by enemies of the revolution.

But whatever the immediate cause or the deeper motivations of Nicolayev's shot, to thinking Communists it seemed a symbol of the desperations under the policed surface of their country's life. Each of us knew the bitterness and despair in his own heart. Sometimes we dared to share our doubts in twos and threes. It took the murder of one of Stalin's closest associates to make us conscious that our private griefs were part of the great subterranean river of discontent flowing through the heart of a vast nation.

Outwardly everything was tranquil. Critics from the Left and the Right had been crushed and Stalin, Our Sun, shone benignly over a united Party. The peasants had been whipped into surly submission by firing squads and famine. No murmur of protest was any longer heard about the killing tempo of industrialization, the food shortage, the hardships, the many arrests. But inwardly many in the Party and the nation seethed with resentment. Under the stupor of indifference, under the crust of silent despair, there was the hot lava of primitive angers.

This should be made clear to the world in ordinary justice to the Russian people. They were impotent in their suffering; weakened by twenty years of war, revolution, undernourishment and systematic persecutions; dizzied by slogans and bewildered by lies; cut off completely from the outside world. Yet they never approved the brutality of their rulers. The bitterness was deepest in the Party itself, because it was mixed with a feeling of guilt and churned by galling helplessness as against the rulers and their might.

It was no accident that Nicolayev and those accused of direct complicity in his crime were all young people, products of the Soviet epoch, mostly students. Traditionally the higher schools of Russia have been the breeding ground of revolutionary idealism. Now such idealism was called *counter-revolutionary* but it was still in the same tradition.

Although not a word about it ever reached the press, it was common knowledge among Communists that thousands of students had been arrested and hundreds of them condemned to death after the Kirov affair. It was enough for a group of students to get together in someone's home for an evening of dancing and amusement to inflame the suspicions of the G.P.U.

The sudden disappearance of students at our Institute was not an uncommon occurrence. We asked no questions. We pretended not to notice. But our sympathies were always with the arrested students, never with the police. We decided in our secret minds to keep a better guard on our tongues, for to speak candidly was to speak in an "anti-Communist vein."

My personal disillusionment was already deeper than I dared to admit to myself, let alone to others. For that very reason I avoided involvement in political arguments. But being human, and Russian to boot, I found myself saying too much now and then among friends whom I trusted—and spent miserable weeks thereafter worrying whether one of them had informed on me.

The assassination in Leningrad sent a thrill of romantic hope through the student body. Could this act of terror be the expression of a truly popular movement? Was it possible that the G.P.U., for all its prowess, had failed to root out underground opposition? We were, after all, part of a nation reared on memories of secret revolutionary circles, political plots and bomb-throwing for freedom.

It also sent a chill of fear down our spines. New purges were inevitable. The first sign of the Politburo's intentions, in fact, came quickly in an announcement that all Party cards would be checked and renewed. Without calling it openly a *chistka* or purge, we would in effect be investigated once more, less than a year after the nationwide political house-cleaning.

My classmate M. was one of the few Communists with whom I sometimes allowed myself frank remarks about political affairs. We sensed a certain community of mood which made us bold when we were together. Soon after Kirov's death, M. invited me to meet a few friends at the home of Andrei S., a student whom I did not know too intimately. "We'll drink tea and chew the rag," he told me. I hesitated about going—there was a false note in the casualness of the invitation. But in the end curiosity and my disturbed state of mind drew me to the rendezvous.

Andrei was a tall, pale man of about thirty, with open features and deep-set blue eyes. He was well read and could wax eloquent even on such uninspiring subjects as processes of steel making. He was universally liked and respected.

In his small room that night I found M. and two other students, both of them from other Institutes. We sat around the glowing samovar by the dim light of a single bulb and talked at random, skirting around the subject that was on everyone's mind, as if taking one another's measure. I noted the curious fact that the men addressed each other by false names. That in itself gave the gathering a conspirative edge, at once frightening and somehow intriguing. Playing with fire is for many Russians a fascinating exercise.

I was a newcomer to this risky business of political talk, but the others seemed to be continuing a familiar game. After a while discretion was forgotten. As we warmed to a discussion of Kirov's assassination, voices became more intense and eyes blazed. Inflamed by our own words, we were soon talking of "the tyrant in the Kremlin" and commiserating with the "oppressed Russian people." Somehow it was as if I were reliving a childhood memory: my father and his revolutionary friends in a heated political discussion of Tsarist oppression in our parlor off Pushkin Prospekt. . . .

"Nicolayev's shot," Andrei said, "we hold to be the act of a *provocateur*." That "we" sounded ominous; I had not the remotest idea whom he had in mind. "Yes, the act of a *provocateur*! It was unnecessary and harmful. Stalin must find a point of vantage from which he can launch a pogrom of extermination against the dissenting sector of the Party—now he has it ready-made. The question is no longer Nicolayev. He and his friends are doomed. The point is that the Kremlin gang now has the perfect background for liquidating its critics and opponents to the last man.

"Remember my words, comrades. Many thousands, maybe millions, will pay for Nicolayev's shot. If until now we could dream of freedom and democracy in the Party, the dream is ended—ended, I tell you. The last hope is gone! Russia will soon be bleeding to death!"

He paced the room in rising excitement. His passion and his gloom infected us all. We felt like people caught in a sinking ship, with the swirling waters already close to our nostrils. Andrei paused, swayed as if he were drunk, and went on:

"Stalin and Voroshilov were present when Nicolayev was tortured. I happen to know, comrades. They wanted names, names and more names . . . fodder for their firing squads. But it doesn't matter what the Chekists squeezed out of Nicolayev. They will write the kind of confession that Stalin needs and then the blood-letting will go forward smoothly, theoretically justified."

The youngest member of our group was a small, anemic-looking student. He seemed strangely beautiful in his frailness as he arose suddenly and began reciting the *Credo* of the Decembrist poet Ryleyev:

> I know that death awaits
> The one who first arises
> 'Gainst the tyrant of the people.
> Already doom awaits me. . . .
> I'll die for my beloved land,
> I feel it and I know it. . . .

His pinched face seemed transfigured as he spoke the words. He seemed a character out of the great revolutionary scenes in Dostoievsky and Gorki come to life. Though it was inspiringly beautiful, I felt deeply sorry that I had allowed myself to be drawn into the meeting. It was all so alarmingly naive, impractical, senseless. The very purpose of the gathering remained incomprehensible to me. A forbidden mimeographed pamphlet by a leading Oppositionist—Slepkov—was read, in which the Kremlin dictator and his clique were sharply assailed; this was the only interesting information I learned at the strange session. How Andrei had obtained this dangerous document I could have no idea. In any case, the mere reading of such a pamphlet would have been enough to land me in Siberian exile had the G.P.U. become aware of it.

It was almost dawn when we broke up. Only when I was out in the pale morning, trudging through the snow, did I awake to the enormity of what I had done. I had been involved in a conspirative meeting of the sort for which thousands of other students throughout Russia were paying with their freedom and their lives. If the authorities got wind of it, I was through. All the same, at the Institute that morning I kept looking around for Andrei. I was drawn to him, not despite the danger but because of it. I was eager to know about the "we" who figured in his talk all night.

At one o'clock I was summoned to the Party office. I found others there, including my friend M. The Party Secretary looked solemn as he closed the door and faced us. I expected the worst.

"Comrades," he said, "I have sad news for you. I thought it better that you should know right away. One of our best comrades committed suicide this morning, in his room. Probably a love affair, or some other personal tragedy."

"Who is it?" I asked.

"Andrei S. He was a good student and good comrade. A pity. . . ."

As we filed out, M. found my hand and squeezed it. Tears were rolling down his cheeks. So poor Andrei's impassioned gloom had not been a pose: "The last hope is gone! Russia will soon be bleeding to death!" His words echoed in my mind for months. Fortunately for the rest of us that nocturnal session when we heard the *Credo* recited remained a secret throughout the purge years that followed.

Though no one knew precisely why Andrei had killed himself, the Institute buzzed with feverish conjecture. Everyone sensed that in some mysterious way his death was related to the assassination in Leningrad and to the panic of fear which already was sweeping through the whole Party and the whole Soviet bureaucracy.

The check-up of Party cards was not public, as the purge had been. Instead it had the character of a police investigation. We were called and questioned one by one. When my turn came, I entered the office in a state of alarm which made me clammy with perspiration. What if the meeting in Andrei's room a few hours before he shot himself had been discovered? The question was illogical—had the G.P.U. known about it I would have been arrested long ago. But great fear, like great love, knows no logic.

"Have a seat, Comrade Kravchenko," the man behind the desk said. "Let me have your Party card."

I knew him as one of the active Communists of Dniepropetrovsk. Two other men were present. One was a stranger to me, but I realized that the second, though he was in civilian clothes, was an official of the G.P.U. The others did the questioning, but it was obvious that this time the police official was the real judge. He had a file, presumably my personal *dossier*, in front of him, consulted it occasionally, and now and then handed some document to the man at the desk.

It was the familiar line of examination—the ritual recital of my biography, friends, blood relations and Party work. The very dullness of the repetition, however, was reassuring. In particular they wanted to know about my sponsors when I joined the Party. I gave the names.

"Are they still Party members?"

"Yes, as far as I know," I said.

"Was any of them ever in any kind of opposition movement?"

"If he was I am not aware of the fact."

"Comrade Kravchenko, isn't it strange that you alone in your family are a member of the Party? Why are your brothers and your father outside our ranks?"

"Why strange? In the final analysis there are more non-Party than Party people in our country."

"His father," the G.P.U. man interjected, "had been active politically before the revolution but apparently the Bolsheviks are not to his taste."

"I'm sorry, comrades," I said, "but it is not fair to make such assumptions just because people don't join the Party."

"Oh, I don't mean to attack your father. I was just pointing out the facts," the police official said with an ironic smile.

The examination continued for perhaps an hour. As it went on I regained my composure. Obviously my record was still clean. I was safe again. My Party card was restored to me at the end of the interview. But the proceedings left a bitter taste in my mouth. Theoretically we Communists were the rulers of the country, the "best of the best" among the builders of a new world. In practice we were helpless pawns in a game played by a police regime according to rules of its own making.

Thousands of Communists in our city were expelled from the Party. The same was true in every other city in the nation. And this time expulsion often meant immediate arrest.

2

My diploma project—the description and design of a new pipe-rolling machine of my own invention—was not only graded excellent but honored with a government patent. Though the machine was never produced, it put me, theoretically at least, in the category of technical innovators.

The written tests completed, I went through the final oral examination before a State Qualifying Board. A graduation banquet marked the end of my life as a student. We stuffed ourselves and drank and sang and piled up the cliches of Soviet patriotism. One after another the orators rubbed in the fact that we had been educated at public expense and must now begin to pay back a hundredfold in service to the Five Year Plans for the glory of the Party.

And so, at long last, I was a graduate engineer. Four years earlier the goal had seemed haloed with glory. Somehow the glory had departed. It had been dimmed by the village terror and the great famine, by the Party purge and the tides of cynicism all around me. The last sorry remnants of lustre had been erased for me by Eliena's story and Andrei's suicide and the mood of desperation and futility from which they stemmed.

To a proletarian family like mine a full-fledged engineer was cause for pride. I simulated a joy that I didn't feel. My mother no doubt saw through my pretense but played up to it in her turn. Father knew well enough that a Soviet engineer's path was pockmarked with political pitfalls; he was reserved and even worried. To my brothers Eugene and Constantine, who were indifferent to politics, my diploma meant simply a chance for improvement in my economic status.

Eliena's pride was lined with melancholy. Her affection and sympathy helped to quiet my own disturbed mind. She was expecting to be transferred to Kharkov, and now it seemed likely that I would be assigned to some distant metallurgical center. Neither of us was a free person. Our relationship, swinging wildly between ecstasy and sorrow, was fated to pass through a series of trials. Try as hard as I would to exorcise it, the knowledge that she was a secret police agent was ever a ghost at the banquet of our affections.

I sent a copy of my graduation project to Commissar Ordzhonikidze and received a warm response. I had kept up my contacts with him during the school years. Imperceptibly, indeed, the official connection had mellowed into a personal friendship.

Once, in 1933, I hatched the idea of a permanent Soviet Industrial Exposition, not unlike the expositions in Germany. I made the proposal in articles the newspapers featured, along with my picture and editorial praise of such "Bolshevik initiative." I then worked out an elaborate plan in support of the idea, complete with blueprints, and put it into Ordzhonikidze's hands. Nothing ever came of the proposal but my Kremlin patron was pleased and in his warm-hearted Caucasian fashion made me aware of his pleasure. I followed that with a similar proposal for an Agricultural Exposition which had a kindlier fate; some time later it was actually functioning, although my initiative was nowhere mentioned.

I might have applied directly to Ordzhonikidze, as the number one man in Soviet industry, for a post, but I preferred not to exploit his friendship. Instead I was placed at the disposal of Trubostal, the metallurgical trust charged with the manufacture of all steel pipe and certain other steel products for the whole country. It was headed by Jacob Ivanchenko, who had been for a time director of the Petrovsky-Lenin factory and therefore knew me well. At a conference in his Kharkov office it was decided that I be assigned to the new metallurgical *combinat* in Nikopol, which was scheduled to start operations in April.

I had not forgotten the filth, confusion and bitterness which I had seen at Nikopol as a Party investigator, and the memory was sufficiently depressing. It seemed incredible that the plant was about to begin production, despite all the waste and human suffering. Nikopol, I thought, was symbolic of the whole industrialization effort—prodigal in spending life and substance, barbarous in its inefficiency, yet somehow moving forward.

My mother and Eliena waved to me from the pier until the boat taking me to Nikopol turned the bend in the Dnieper. I was deeply conscious that a new phase in my life was beginning. I was now twenty-nine years old, an advanced age for the launching of an engineering career, but I was starting near the top—as one of the chiefs in a great industrial enterprise.

I was now, overnight, transformed into one of the *élite* of the Soviet society, one of the million or so top Party officials, industrial managers and police functionaries who were, taken together, the new aristocracy of Russia.

Nikopol is an ancient Dnieper town redolent of the river and surrounded by lush forest and wheat lands. It is in an area famous throughout the world as one of the richest sources of manganese, a metal essential in the production of steel. There are also important iron deposits nearby, making it a natural center for metallurgy. The streets and houses of Nikopol stirred nostalgic echoes of my childhood years with grandfather Fyodor Panteleyevich in neighboring Alexandrovsk, now known as Zaparozhe.

Unhappily the plant itself was far from town, in a dismal emptiness. Its five thousand workers were still for the most part packed into crude barracks, better than those that had shocked me during my first visit, but still more fit for animals than for human beings. The ordinary workers ate in a huge, unsanitary, evil-smelling cafeteria; a cleaner and better supplied restaurant served the top foremen and engineers; a third and quite modern restaurant was at the disposal of a handful of the most important officials who, in addition, were supplied with ample food in their homes from produce raised on the factory grounds. These steep class distinctions were so traditional in Russia that only foreigners thought them paradoxical in a "proletarian" country.

Personally I was installed in a commodious five-room house about a mile from the factory. It was one of eight such houses for the use of the uppermost officials. Mine was set among tall trees and had a pleasant, well-tended flower garden as well as a small orchard in the back. It was equipped with a bathtub, radio, and even a substantial icebox. There was a car in the garage and a couple of fine horses were at my disposal—factory property, of course, but as exclusively mine while I held the job as if I had owned them. A chauffeur and stableman, as well as a husky peasant woman who did the housework and cooking, came with the house; I paid the woman, the others were on the factory payroll.

My income ranged between 1500 and 1800 rubles a month, though often, with bonuses, it came to 2000 and more. What this meant under Soviet conditions may be judged from the fact that foremen and skilled workers under me rarely earned more than 400 rubles, while unskilled men and women earned only from 120 to 175. The proletarians in whose name the Soviet society was run, of course, enjoyed none of the privileges reserved for me, and for perhaps ten others in the entire *combinat*.

I worked intensely, always under terrific pressure. The day when I spent less than twelve hours at the plant seemed almost a holiday, and there were times when I remained on the job for forty-eight or even seventy-two hours, snatching a few hours of sleep on the couch in my office. Yet sometimes, alone in my fine house, with the buxom, ruddy-faced Pasha preparing a good meal for me in the kitchen, with a state gardener watering my garden, with the icebox full of fresh vegetables, melons, caviar and sour cream, I felt guilty.

I thought of the men in the barracks, of their children, of their bleak existence. How could I blame them if, as I guessed, they resented me, even hated me, as one of their *novi barii*, their new masters? How was I to convey to them that this contrast between their misery and my comfort was not of my choosing; that I, too, was just a helpless cog in an enormous machine; that my prosperity was a gift of the State and could be withdrawn arbitrarily, without so much as a warning?

I wanted sincerely to establish friendly, open relations with the workers. I understood them; their needs and hopes were close to me. But for an engineer in my position to mix with ordinary workers might offend their pride; it smacked of patronage. Besides, officialdom would frown on such fraternization as harmful to discipline. In theory we represented "the workers' power," but in practice we were a class apart. A deep gulf gaped between the world of slogans and the world of reality.

The same Comrade Brachko who had been in charge of the construction of the factory was now its director. Time had rubbed some of the brashness from his character and made him a much pleasanter associate. Only Brachko and the chief engineer, Vishnev, outranked me in the technical administration. At the political end the key people were Alexei Kozlov, head of the factory Party Committee, and Comrade Starostin, the trade-union chairman.

Kozlov was an elderly man, quite human, honestly concerned with the well-being of the workers. But Starostin was a careerist of the purest water, and stupid besides. He looked as gross and oily as he was in fact. Fortunately, as the trade-union official, he had more title than power. Since the trade-union functionaries could not open their mouths, let alone make decisions, without permission from the Party, they were generally men of no importance.

The whole institution of labor organizations under a dictatorship seemed a curious remnant of the distant past. It was not even a hoax, since no one was fooled by the rigmarole of meetings and decisions, least of all the workers. Only the union dues, paid out of their miserly wages, were real to the members. Starostin's influence was so negligible that any high official could ignore him, but Kozlov's every word was law.

We leaders were naturally thrown together a great deal. We became uncomfortably aware of one another's weaknesses and peculiarities. The Secretary of the Nikopol City Committee of the Party, Brodsky, a big burly man whom I had known in Dniepropetrovsk, also kept an eager eye on our plants. As for the head of the Nikopol secret police, Dorogan, he kept hundreds of eyes on us—through the Special Department, the Secret Department in my plant, legions of professional, volunteer and coerced informers in every shop, office and department.

Dorogan was a rude, quick-tempered man with the face of a bulldog; a man carved from granite by his Creator to be a police official under any regime. I remembered his kind in the years when my father was being hunted by Tsarist secret police.

The G.P.U. had recently been renamed. It was no longer a State Political Department (G.P.U. or O.G.P.U.) but a Commissariat of Internal

Affairs, abbreviated N.K.V.D. Originally Cheka, then G.P.U., now N.K.V.D., the changes in name had altered neither the methods nor the awesome reputation of this "naked sword of the revolution." People connected with the dread organization were still referred to as Chekists, derived from the original name, and for years after it became the N.K.V.D., Russians continued to talk of the G.P.U.

Our contacts with the local N.K.V.D. organization were less with the chief, Dorogan, than with his energetic assistant, Gershgorn, who was in charge of the Economic Division of the N.K.V.D. for the city of Nikopol and its environs. This Gershgorn holds a special niche in my private hall of infamy. An obese man, with shifty little eyes embedded in a fleshy, clean-shaven face, his shaved skull rising to a point like a mountain peak, he was by turns ingratiating and insulting, depending on whom he was addressing. If he had a spark of human decency in his make-up, I saw no evidences of it in the years of our unpleasant acquaintance.

My first month was devoted largely to assembling machinery and other preliminaries in the organization of production. There were two pipe-rolling sub-plants, each employing about fifteen hundred men and women, and after a while I was in full charge of one of these. By late June production was under way. I liked the responsibility, for all its risks, and left myself barely enough time for sleep in my anxiety to keep the work moving on a three-shift basis.

Now and then, as I walked through the plant and sensed that everything was humming smoothly, I felt inexpressibly happy. At such moments I knew in the marrow of my bones what one meant by "the joy of work." If only there were fewer spies, less suspicion, an end to the blight of fear which paralyzed men's minds and pressed so heavily on their spirits!

I knew quite well that my every step was watched and recorded, not only in the conduct of the plant but in my private life. I took it for granted that my private secretary, a middle-aged woman named Tuvina, sour and efficient, was reporting on me; likewise my chauffeur, my maid, at least one and perhaps more of my assistants. I pushed that knowledge to the back of my mind, but it was always there, like an itch, intruding on my work and thought.

Repeatedly I discovered that every word uttered in some routine production conference which I had called was known to Hantovich, the head of the Special Department, and through him, of course, to the shifty-eyed Gershgorn. There was nothing secret or remarkable about these conferences; I would gladly have filed minutes for all to see. It was the technique of espionage that made me feel sticky with distaste. Precisely because I never thought of myself as a potential "wrecker," this espionage seemed to me offensive to the point of being insulting.

No industrial process ever functions with absolute perfection. Machines break down, mistakes are made, tired men grow careless, production plans go awry. This is especially the case in a brand-new factory, using foreign-made machinery and staffed in large part by inexperienced men and workers fresh from the villages. Yet every untoward incident brought the N.K.V.D. men running on the double, sniffing excitedly for the scent of "sabotage" and "wrecking." There would be open interrogations in the offices of the Secret Department, often secret nocturnal questioning and browbeating at N.K.V.D. headquarters in town.

In case of an accident, however trivial, my orders were that I be summoned, even if it meant waking me in the middle of the night. But no matter how fast I rushed to the scene, the N.K.V.D. minions were always there ahead of me, grimly suspicious, ironically accusing.

Such was the atmosphere in which we worked from the start. The older engineers and administrative officials regarded it as the natural climate of Soviet industry and had private jokes about the ubiquitous "writers" on the premises. I never could become completely acclimated to it. And this condition was destined to become worse with every passing month, as the Great Purge growing out of Kirov's death gathered force. Within a year Nikopol seemed not so much an industrial establishment as a hunting ground for the police and their secret informers.

3

My mother arrived for a visit. She was impressed with the elegant house, its fine furniture, its multitude of modern comforts, and especially the fact I had five rooms all to myself. Her second son had certainly "made his way in the world"! The kitchen, with its roomy icebox and ample supplies, drew her like a magnet. When I invited some colleagues for supper and a party in her honor, she insisted on doing the cooking herself. Pasha looked on admiringly as her employer's mother made special dishes he had loved since childhood.

After the supper a few other guests dropped in, among them a foreman and several workers from the plant. Everyone treated the little woman with the gray hair and the trim figure most gallantly. At one point she whispered in my ear:

"You're popular with your people, Vitya. I can see by the way they behave. That's good, very good!"

The following morning, kissing mother good-bye, I asked her not to be too bored; I'd be home very late. Little did I suspect that she had plans of her own for the day. The first inkling of her activity came to me that afternoon. One of the engineers said he had seen my mother in the cafeteria, talking to the cooks and waitresses. Apparently someone had given her a pass, I thought, and feminine curiosity had led her straight to the kitchen.

That night I returned so late that mother was already in bed. The following day I was again tipped off that she was on the factory grounds—"prowling with notebook in hand," as my informant put it. I heard that she had been through the barracks, the cooperative stores, the children's creches. I had a most trying day in the office, without mental leisure to worry over my mother's "prowling."

When I reached home in the evening I found her sitting at my desk, steel-rimmed glasses low on her tiny nose, writing on a pad in very businesslike style. I asked no questions, waiting a bit uneasily for her to make the first move. After the meal, when Pasha had cleared off the table, mother announced:

"And now, Vitya, I want to talk to you—seriously."

"All right. What's worrying you, mother?"

In the manner of an executive reporting to his board, she informed me that she had made a thorough inspection of the factory: its housing, creches, clubs, bathing and hygienic facilities. Her voice was filled with reproach.

"I'm shocked by what I saw," she summed up. "Do you realize the kind of treatment your workers get here? Where you directors and officials are concerned, there's enough of everything, but when it's a question of ordinary workers, there's only dirt and neglect. The kitchen is foul. The menu is deadly monotonous. As for the barracks—tell me, do you really think them fit for Soviet workers?"

"Why take it out on me? I do all I can. The responsibility is hardly mine."

"You're one of the leaders here, Vitya, and you should feel responsible. Look how you live—doesn't the contrast ever bother your conscience?"

"I'm afraid you don't understand, mother. We officials are not bosses in the old sense. Orders come from the center and we're bound hand and foot. I've had the cafeteria whitewashed. I insist on having it scrubbed three times a day, after every shift. Beyond such little things I'm helpless. It's a matter of wage scales, housing projects, budgets, prices fixed for clothing and footwear—things decided in Moscow. I've got my hands full making pipe."

"At least you ought to know the facts! I've made notes and here they are. Did you know that the women have to ride or walk to town, four miles and more, to do their shopping? Why isn't there a market right here to which *kolkhoz* farmers can bring their produce? I see you have a lovely white bath all for yourself. But the workers, thousands of them, have only a vile hole that doesn't deserve the name of bath—and even that's not working. In a project like this, costing tens of millions, why not decent bathhouses, both for men and women? And here's another sample, Vitya: the creches. Not enough linen, not enough medicines, not enough anything."

"You're painting the picture blacker than it is," I said weakly. I had no doubt that my mother was right.

"I'm not blaming you, son, but maybe if you knew and if the other directors knew, something would be done about it."

By this time mother's businesslike manner had collapsed. It was a pose she could not maintain too long. Her eyes brimmed over with tears. She had been hurt by what she had seen—hurt even by the contrast of her son's comfort.

A few days after she had left for Dniepropetrovsk, Comrade Kozlov called a conference of technical, Party and trade-union officials. The Party office was overcrowded by the time I arrived. There was only one question on the agenda, Kozlov was saying, namely *the living conditions of our workers*. I was thrilled. Here, sooner than I had hoped, was the opportunity to lay before the administration the facts my mother had marshalled for me! What a lucky coincidence, I thought.

Many people spoke, in the generalities called for by the subject. Of course conditions were abominable, but what could one do? When my turn came, I was able to get down to cases. My mother's lecture fresh in mind, I proceeded in effect to repeat her findings.

I found myself echoing not only her facts but her anger, her sorrow, her reproaches. Evidently most of my listeners were as moved as I had been some nights earlier. There was so much we could do, I said, even with the means at our disposal if we were not so busy with "our own affairs." Let's begin to regard the everyday problems of the workers, too, as "our own affairs," I urged.

"Where does Kravchenko get so much information?" someone asked.

"Oh, it's that mother of his," Starostin, the union head, spoke up; there was a note of mockery in his voice. "Didn't you know? She's a self-appointed snooping brigade, inspecting and smelling everything like a *barina* on her estate. . . . The 'grand lady' thinks she owns Nikopol because her son's one of the bosses. We understand such nosiness. . . . Making political capital for her son!"

There was a general uproar. Everyone spoke at once. The blood rose to my head and I was tongue-tied with sheer rage. Kozlov pressed my arm to restrain me.

"Comrades, quiet!" he banged his desk. "Comrade Starostin talks like an idiot. Kravchenko's mother is no *barina* and he knows it. She's the wife of an old worker, a veteran of 1905 with a revolutionary prison record. You ought to be ashamed to attack her. Can it be that you're covering up your own laziness and indifference to the conditions of the workers?"

There was a roar of laughter. The trade-union chairman was so widely despised that a chance to ridicule him with the Party Secretary's blessings was too good to be missed.

"I happen to know that the old woman tried to see you, Comrade Starostin, but you wouldn't receive her," Kozlov continued. "No doubt you didn't care to be bothered about such nonsense as bedbugs in barracks and dirty diapers in the creches. But I did talk to her—she showed the kind of Soviet initiative that goes a long way."

So my mother had not only examined everything but had gone to the top people with her findings! That part of it she had not disclosed to me. And this conference was not a coincidence but a direct result of her "nosiness." The goodness and the courage of the woman! Despite the embarrassment to which she had exposed me, my heart overflowed with affection for her.

In the following months my mother's naive intercession bore some fruit. A *kolkhoz* market was fixed up near the plant. The children's homes were cleaned up and provided with more linen. Plans for a new bathhouse were announced. A few other minor improvements were made. The story of Mrs. Kravchenko's campaign in their behalf spread among the workers, and her son shared in the modest "glory."

4

In town one night I caught sight of my old-maidish secretary, Comrade Tuvina, coming out of the Nikopol N.K.V.D. building. I never doubted that she was reporting on me; spying on the boss is the main job of Soviet secretaries. But knowing it was one thing, stumbling on the proof was another. The very next day I instructed our Personnel Department to remove this woman from my office and to recommend someone else, preferably a man.

In a few days a man of about thirty-two came to me with a note from the Personnel chief. His appearance was remarkable. The first word that came to my mind as I looked up was "scarecrow." He seemed a skeleton hung with rags. His shoes were torn, his trousers patched, his jacket a crudely tailored thing made of sacking. Even under our Soviet conditions he was an extreme specimen of squalor. But his starved features were cleanly cut and even attractive, under reddish hair gray at the temples.

"I know what I look like, Comrade Kravchenko," he said, "but I beg you not to hold it against me. You see, I've just come from a prison camp, after finishing a four-year term. The Personnel Department knows this. If you give me a chance, I know you'll find my work satisfactory."

He spoke like an educated man. My initial revulsion turned to pity. The poor fellow had evidently passed through some fearful ordeal. I rang for tea and sandwiches. He tried to restrain himself, eating slowly and casually, but it was evident that he was famished. As we talked, my phone rang. It was Romanov, an important and likable official from another department. Though he was not a Party man, Romanov enjoyed the confidence of the administration, from Kozlov down.

"Victor Andreyevich," he said, "I would consider it a personal favor if you hired Citizen Groman, who's in your office now. Despite his misfortune, he's a reliable fellow."

"Have you known him long?"

"No, but I'm in a position to vouch for him."

"Thanks, it's kind of you to let me know."

While Groman waited in the reception room, I telephoned the N.K.V.D. and was connected with Gershgorn. It was my duty to inform him, since my secretary would handle important official documents. When I told him the story, he asked me to wait a minute. After a brief interval, he returned to the phone and assured me that he had no objection if I found the man otherwise acceptable.

When I told the dilapidated ex-prisoner that he could show up to work in a day or two, he smiled for the first time. He was embarrassingly grateful. I gave him enough money in advance and instructed the plant store to give him essential clothes. I also helped him, through my assistant, to find a livable room in one of the factory apartments.

Groman proved himself quickly to be both intelligent and efficient. He took many details off my shoulders. Better dressed, his bones slowly taking on flesh, his eyes coming alive, he seemed a man reborn. He came to my house often for work, and occasionally I drove him home after work. Our relations were on an easy human basis. I thanked Romanov for his recommendation of a first-rate secretary.

Many weeks passed. One morning Groman failed to appear for work. I assumed that he was ill. When he didn't show up next day, I became worried and decided to send someone to his house at the end of the work day to see what was wrong. He had no telephone. As I was going through some papers stacked in my desk, I came to a batch of sheets, hand-written and clipped together. I recognized Groman's handwriting. Instinctively I avoided touching the sheets as I read the opening words:

"Dear Victor Andreyevich, when you read these words I shall no longer be in Nikopol. I am trying to escape this land of horror. Even death will be better than life as a slave. . . ."

I broke out in cold sweat. Nervously I locked my door. Then I put on gloves and picked up the letter. It was an extraordinary document. Though I do not remember all the words, the substance remains engraved on my mind:

"Thank you from the bottom of a true Russian heart for all you have done for me. Your kindness has awakened in me feelings of humanity which I thought were dead beyond recall. That, in fact, is one of the reasons why I decided to run away. If God is with me, I shall cross the frontier. If I'm caught, I'll be shot, of course.

"I hate the Soviet regime and its police with a deadly hate. Though I have committed no crime—unless loving freedom is a crime—I have been through their torture chambers and prison isolators. When I was released, I realized that my freedom would be short-lived and that I could not even find work unless I put myself at the service of my torturers.

"The evening before you met me I had just arrived in Nikopol from concentration camp, as I had been ordered. I went to the N.K.V.D. and was taken to Gershgorn. That's how I came to you. All that happened—including the recommendation by Romanov—was part of an ugly comedy of which you were the victim.

"I did not mind working as a spy. Hating all Communists, it seemed to me a chance to revenge myself by getting a few of them into trouble, the deeper the better. I looked on you as my first victim. But very soon I came to respect you and loathed myself for what I had planned to do to you.

"I want you to know that after a while I became the main informer so far as you are concerned. Once a man has been through the purgatory of the N.K.V.D. he is trusted. Those devils know that fear will keep their human tools loyal. Every day the other agents who fill your plant and offices reported to me. About once a week I assembled their information into a comprehensive report about your work, your words, your friends, even the expression on your face, along with defects in the work of your plant.

"Though the spies did not know one another, I knew them all. The least I can do, in gratitude for your sympathy, is to reveal them to you."

A list followed. It included Romanov, the genial Romanov whom we all liked and trusted for his soft, paternal ways. It included several of my closest colleagues in the plant, foremen, plain workmen, clerks in the commissary. The network of informers was spread through every shop and office in the factory, covering all stages of the technological process.

"Beware of these people, Victor Andreyevich! They have no respect for truth. Their careers depend on uncovering plots, and their temptation is to invent plots to uncover. You should know that men who have been physically broken and psychologically demoralized by the Chekists will do anything, confess anything, accuse anybody. There are several such around you"—again he gave me names—"for I was not the only one.

"I assume you will suspect this letter to be a trap. I cannot blame you. I can only swear by God and my sainted mother that I am telling the truth, that I am trying to expiate the weeks of spying on a man who was kind to me and considerate of the human spark in me. Whether you will believe me I leave to your instincts.

"If you turn this letter over to Gershgorn, he will say I'm a liar and will immediately reshuffle the network of informers. But if you can bring yourself to trust me, destroy the letter, pretend to be indignant over my mysterious desertion, and they will never suspect that I have betrayed them.

"Whatever you decide, I beg by all that's sacred to you to give me at least one day's leeway before reporting my absence. The extra day may be the difference between life and death. I implore you on my knees, dear Victor Andreyevich.

"Thank you for all you have done for me. Thank you for having helped to revive the decent human being whom the torturers had nearly wiped out. If I remain alive I shall pray for you always."

Some inner feeling prompted me to trust the fugitive. Perhaps I had come to trust the kind of mind he had unveiled to me in our random talks during the past weeks. Despite this inner assurance, I felt as if I were gambling with my very life as I copied out the names he had given me. Then I burned the letter, carefully removing every trace of ash.

Toward the end of the day I sent a messenger to Groman's residence. He reported the following morning that the family with whom Groman lived said he had not been home for two days. I thereupon called the Personnel Department and in simulated anger asked why they couldn't find me a more dependable secretary. This was the third day he had absented himself, without so much as an explanation, I complained.

Within the hour, Gershgorn himself, accompanied by a uniformed man, arrived in great excitement. They asked me questions, ransacked Groman's desk, and departed. Whether the fugitive escaped I could not ever know. The chances of stealing across a Soviet frontier are very slight, yet hundreds have accomplished the feat.

The information about the spies around me was helpful. It enabled me to safeguard myself and sometimes to protect others. If I wanted something to reach the ears of the police without delay, I needed merely to mention it casually within earshot of the informer at the furnaces, the one in the tool department, the head of the finishing department, the engineer

Makarov, the foreman Yudavin, the trade-union official Ivanov, who was Starostin's assistant. Social contact with Romanov became a painful chore, yet I could not drop him without arousing suspicion.

Groman's successor was a young, pretty and hard-working Comsomol. No doubt she picked up the espionage threads where the unhappy Groman had dropped them.

My chauffeur's name had been on Groman's list, which hardly surprised me. He reported directly to the Informational Division of the N.K.V.D. rather than to Gershgorn's Economic Division. But my maid Pasha's name was not on list. In time, however, I learned that this was an oversight or that Groman simply did not know about her.

One day, when Pasha had been in my home for nearly a year, I returned from a visit to Moscow. She helped me unpack two suitcases. I had bought her a few presents—a garishly printed shawl, several pairs of cotton stockings, a pair of house slippers. She accepted these, it seemed to me, with strange reserve.

"Don't you like them, Pasha?" I asked.

"Oh yes, I do, and I am most thankful, Victor Andreyevich."

But that same evening, after serving my supper, Pasha came into the dining room carrying the gifts. She was crying noisily in peasant fashion. I looked up in questioning alarm.

"I can't accept these things, Victor Andreyevich," she sobbed. "Please, please take them back."

"All right, but tell me why. What's the mystery?"

"God forgive me," she crossed herself, "but I can't tell you. Only don't make me take these gifts."

After some urging and a pledge of secrecy, however, she did tell me. It added up to this: that she could not take gifts from a good man while acting as informer against him.

"Yes, ever since I came here I've been reporting once a week to the N.K.V.D.," she said. "I came from the village and got the job. But no sooner was I settled in your home than I was ordered to come to the N.K.V.D. and told what to do. I refused and cried and said that it was against my religion but the uniformed man only said: 'Pasha, don't be an idiot. You want your father to come back from his banishment, don't you? Well, if you serve us right and loyally, we'll see about it.'

"Once a week I go to a private house in Nikopol and tell all I know, especially who comes here and what they say. 'And did they curse the government?' they ask me, and always I cross myself and say, 'No, on the contrary.' They laugh when I make the sign of the cross, the infidels!"

I assured poor Pasha that she had my forgiveness. I would never mention what she had told me, provided she, too, held her tongue. I even convinced her that it was proper to accept my gifts, now that she had taken me into her confidence.

For the rest of my stay in that house Pasha continued to report on me. We never referred to her tearful confession. But several times she asked me questions intended, I was sure, to ascertain whether it was desirable that she report certain incidents. I made it clear that I had nothing to hide and that, in any case, what she overlooked would be communicated by others.

<h1 style="text-align:center">5</h1>

There were usually a few foreign engineers at Nikopol, Americans and Germans, to install imported machinery and raise its efficiency. To the Russians, high and low, they were at once objects of fascination and of fear. To associate with them—to make "contacts with class enemies"—was dangerous but the aura of danger itself gave foreigners a dimension of thrill. Well dressed, uninhibited in their speech and behavior, they seemed creatures from another planet. The utter fearlessness in which they worked and talked and even criticized to a certain extent—as if there were no N.K.V.D., no Gershgorn, no informers—seemed the most remarkable fact about them.

When Comrade Brachko suggested that I take two Americans into my home, I was frankly alarmed. The men in question hailed from a place called Youngstown. Their work would keep them in Nikopol for several months. The local hotel was squalid. As a bachelor with a large house to myself, I could not refuse to take them in. But I feared the complications of this enforced "contact with alien class elements."

Larry and Joe were tall, blond, good-natured men, bewildered by their drab surroundings and evidently homesick. In the months when they were my guests we became friendly despite language difficulties. Not once did either of them touch on political questions. To a Soviet citizen, for whom politics and life are almost the same thing, this indifference seemed not only incredible but unnatural. The minds of these Americans were focussed on their jobs. When shop talk gave out, they told stories, played cards and looked for "parties." Gregarious and utterly frank in their relations with other people, they could never understand why they were left so strictly alone, why they were so rarely invited, by the men with whom they worked in the plant.

Larry and Joe had been with me a number of weeks when Gershgorn phoned me early one morning.

"Your Americans are going hunting today," he informed me.

"So I see. What about it?"

"I want you to telephone me as soon as they leave. Tell your servant to take the day off and not to return before five."

After breakfast the Americans, in high spirits, set off for the hills. They slapped me on the back in their exuberant fashion and promised to bring me anything they might bag. I had no alternative but to ring the N.K.V.D. At about eleven, Gershgorn arrived, accompanied by another man. They entered my home as if it belonged to them and moved around it as if familiar with every detail of its geography. A disturbing thought crossed my mind: *Probably they've searched the place often enough in my absence!*

In the room occupied by my guests the agents made a painstaking search. They examined the insides of pockets, trouser belts, shirt cuffs, coat lapels, the soles of shoes, anything which might conceivably serve as a hiding place. All books, magazines, notebooks, letters were thoroughly scrutinized. Some things were photographed; every local name or phone number was carefully copied. Gershgorn seemed particularly intrigued by the American shaving sets. He squeezed and shook the razor handles, studied the brushes and felt the cream tubes, perhaps convinced that these were the most likely repositories of American secrets. Gershgorn's companion was not a local agent; apparently he knew English well.

By four o'clock the search was completed. The police agents had found nothing, for there was no joy of discovery in their faces.

"You understand, of course, Comrade Kravchenko, that not a word of this must ever be known," Gershgorn said. "If there's a leak, the N.K.V.D. will hold you directly responsible. Sign this pledge."

It was a form with which anyone who had dealings with the secret police was familiar: a "voluntary" pledge to keep your mouth shut. When the men left I wandered through the house, depressed, a stranger in my own home. I was ashamed to face the Americans when they returned, and found an excuse for staying away that evening.

Neither of them, I am sure, had the slightest suspicion that his belongings had been examined; or, for that matter, that every minute of his sojourn in Russia was watched and recorded. In an expansive moment, long after the two men had left Nikopol, Gershgorn permitted me a glimpse of their *dossier*. It contained, among other things, photographs showing the foreigners in compromising circumstances with some women in a Moscow hotel. Little did they dream, in that hotel room, that concealed cameramen were recording their transient romances. Gershgorn smacked his thick lips appreciatively as he showed one off-color picture after another.

"But why do you need these?" I asked. "The men are back in America by this time."

"Yes, they're back in America. But you can be damned sure they won't write any scurrilous attacks on our Socialist Fatherland the way some American bastards do after taking our good gold and eating our best food."

Another foreign engineer whose misadventures in Nikopol remain in my memory was named Lentz. He was a German, heavy-set, with a bull neck that fell in three distinct folds. He had been sent to install an imported set of machines. Though he was provided with two interpreters, I preferred to deal with him through one of my men in the plant, Yurev, who spoke some German.

One of Lentz's interpreters was a Dniepropetrovsk agent brought to Nikopol for the occasion. In her early thirties, lively and not unhandsome, she had no difficulty filling her assignment. It was soon an open secret that Alexandra was living with Lentz. She was sporting silk stockings, imported handbags and other telltale gifts. The N.K.V.D., however, must have decided that one woman was not enough and added young Natasha to the staff.

Natasha was the daughter of a priest who had been exiled years before and was therefore well known in town. Not quite twenty, she was pretty in a tender, childlike style. Through Yurev I knew that she had been forced into becoming Lentz's interpreter by threats against her father and promises to permit him to correspond with her.

One balmy Sunday the German, his two interpreters and a supposed friend of theirs, a "motorist," went for a boat ride on the Dnieper. They had lots of food, wine, and vodka in the motorboat, and, by way of romantic flavoring, a gramophone with both Russian and German records. After picnicking in a cool and charming spot on the river's edge, and listening to music, the "motorist" went for a stroll with the older woman. Lentz, now glowing gently with wine, women and German song, remained in the company of the toothsome Natasha.

As expected, he grew amorous. The girl, half provoking, half shy, resisted his advances. Engineer Lentz grew more insistent. Precisely at the point where he ripped the girl's blouse exposing her young breasts, the German thought he heard a noise in the nearby bushes. He dropped his prey and was in the bushes in one bound, just as the "motorist" was snapping another photograph of the scene.

Lentz, remarkably sobered, grabbed the camera, broke it in pieces and hurled it into the river. He cursed out the N.K.V.D. "motorist" and returned home. When he complained to the administration next day, threatening to report the episode to the German Embassy, he was assured that this was just a holiday prank without political significance. But Lentz was no fool.

"I'm a better photographer than your police," he boasted, now roaring with laughter. "Look at this batch."

And he exhibited pictures of himself and Alexandra in an array of erotic postures.

"If your government wanted pictures of me with pretty Natasha, I would have gladly obliged," he said. "You didn't have to invest in a motorboat and a picnic. You see, I'm something of a camera fan myself."

Lentz was soon asked to leave Russia. His agreement not to complain to the German Embassy, I suspect, was well paid for in German marks. Alexandra went back to Dniepropetrovsk, where she had ample scope for her talents among the numerous foreign technicians working in that city. Whether Natasha ever was paid off with the privilege of writing to her father I do not know. Yurev, when he was arrested a year later, was accused, among other things, of "associating with German Fascists." The accusation rested entirely on his occasional services as interpreter for Lentz.

CHAPTER XIII

FASTER, FASTER!

I

IN SEPTEMBER, 1935, a "miracle" occurred in the Donetz Basin coal region. A worker named Stakhanov mined 102 tons of coal in one shift—fourteen times the normal output per miner! Few events in all modern history have been greeted with such sustained, hysterical and histrionic acclaim. It was, to be sure, a quite mundane miracle and a bit shabby at the edges. To a practical engineer the elements of deceit in it were fairly transparent. It was obvious that special conditions and special tools and assistance had been provided to enable Stakhanov to achieve the record. It was a miracle made to order for the Kremlin in launching a new religion—the religion of speed-up.

What Stakhanov had done, all miners could do! What miners could do, all other industries could do! There you have a summary of the new religion. Doubters were damned and would not have to wait for the next life for their share of inferno. Technicians who raised practical objections were defeatists, enemies of Stakhanovism! Workers who could not toe the mark set by the Donetz miner were slackers!

Moscow screamed the new Stakhanovite slogans. Telegraphic orders began to pour into Nikopol from Kharkov and Moscow headquarters. Every order was a blunt threat. We must instantly create Stakhanovite brigades, as pace-setters for the slowpokes. Engineers or superintendents who raised objections would be treated as saboteurs.

Our plants had been operating less than six months. They worked on three shifts under many handicaps. Neither the amount nor the quality of the steel and other raw stuffs was adequate. The workers were mostly green, the staff mostly inexperienced. Because of undernourishment and bad living conditions, the physical vitality of the personnel was low. What we needed most was smoother integration of the productive process. This seemed the worst possible moment for overloading either the men or the machines. Rhythmic teamwork, rather than spurts of record-breaking, was the key to steady output. More than fifteen hundred workers engaged on a common task, in which every operation meshed into the next, couldn't speed up arbitrarily without throwing the whole effort into chaotic imbalance.

But orders were orders. Party leader Kozlov and Director Brachko summoned the engineers and department heads. Comrade Brodsky was on hand for the City Committee. Both Brodsky and Kozlov, as laymen, may have had some illusions about applying Stakhanovism in our plants. Brachko was a practical industrialist and saw its absurdity as clearly as

I did. Yet none of us had any alternative but to institute speed-up Stakhanovite brigades, at any cost in order and efficiency.

"Will Comrade Brachko permit a question?" one of the engineers asked.

"Go ahead, Lazar Petrovich."

"I am the head of a section employing 180 men. If some of them work faster than the rest, the whole section will be tied into knots. Will you please tell me, concretely, what I can do to develop Stakhanovism?"

Brachko, of course, couldn't tell him. He could only repeat the slogans being drummed out from Moscow and tangle himself in futile political verbiage. I felt sorry for him. He was as much a victim of long-range super-planning as the rest of us.

In the end, in my own sub-plant, I was obliged to resort to artificial speed-up which, in my heart, I considered a crime against the machines and the workers alike. On direct orders from the Party Committee, I regrouped my labor, putting the best workers, foremen and engineers into one shift. Then we selected the best tools and materials, setting them aside for the special shift. Having thus stacked the cards, we gave the signal for the specious game to start.

At eleven o'clock one evening, with reporters and photographers present, the "Stakhanovite" shift got under way. As expected, it "overfulfilled" the normal quota by 8 per cent. There were flaming headlines. Congratulations arrived from officials in the capitals. Everyone breathed more freely —we had diverted the lightning. As the responsible technical leader I was given a lot of the credit.

But this "victory" on the industrial front merely left me heartsick. It was, at bottom, fraudulent and must boomerang. The other two shifts, deprived of their best personnel and their best tools, lost more than the favored group had won. By contrast they seemed ineffective if not actually "lazy." They naturally resented being made the scapegoats. They cursed the lucky ones and the officials.

Throughout the Soviet land the speed-up drive turned into a furious campaign unfolded in the familiar atmosphere of fright and repressions. Thousands of administrators were dismissed, many of them were arrested, for sabotage of the new "socialist production" and for "failure to provide the proper Stakhanovite conditions." Every lag in output was blamed upon the engineers and technicians. The picture created in the public mind was that of workers eager to step up production but intentionally "held back" by scheming managers.

A wedge was thus driven between workers and technical staffs.

Even to the simplest-minded factory hand or miner it was apparent that the new records set by forced speed-up would soon be set up as "norms" for everybody.

When the drive was at its height, in November, a national convention of leading Stakhanovites was called in Moscow. It was addressed by Stalin, who loaded them with flattery, contrasting their zeal with the backwardness of other workers. In effect, from that time forward, the Stakhanovites became an *élite* of labor, earning a lot more than their fellows and enjoying all sorts of privileges—especially in the matter of food and clothes —not available to labor as a whole.

And thus the Kremlin drove a wedge also between various categories of workers. The ancient technique of dividing to rule was being applied to a whole nation under the banner of "building socialism."

It was not long before the worst misgivings of the workers came true. Peremptory orders arrived to revise the "norms" of production, on which wages were based, upward by 10 to 20 per cent. It was nothing more than a roundabout order to exact 10 to 20 per cent more work for the same wage. In my plant, of fifteen hundred men, perhaps two hundred qualified as Stakhanovites or speed-kings. For the others the revision of norm meant simply a serious cut in earning power. The general resentment was silent, sullen, unmistakable.

To add insult to injury, the new norms had to be presented and accepted by the workers "themselves," not only "voluntarily" but enthusiastically. The farce was played out in a series of meetings. First there was an all-factory gathering of Party, technical and trade-union leaders and "activists" from the rank and file. Theirs was the responsibility of educating the mass of workers to an "understanding" and acceptance of the new quotas.

Everything had been prepared and rehearsed in advance. Stalin's speech in praise of Stakhanovites was read. Starostin for the union, Kozlov for the Party, others for the technical personnel, explained with straight faces that the low norms then in force were an insult to the socialist zeal and productive genius of our Party and factory. Ambitious Communists seeking recognition and advancement used the opportunity to demonstrate their worship of Stalin in harangues echoing the press and radio.

In the end a resolution proposing steep increases in quotas was read and approved "unanimously."

Then separate meetings were called of the various sub-plants, where all workers were present. Technical and political leaders, assisted by "activists," proclaimed the rehearsed slogans and proposals. At the meeting of my sub-plant, the workers sat glumly, silently, scarcely interested. Automatically they applauded every mention of Stalin's name. The perspiring Party cheer leaders scattered through the hall could not pump up the desired temperature of enthusiasm. Most of the men and women had just finished eight hours of hard labor. They were tired, bored, eager only to have the comedy over with and go home. A report on the glorious achievements of Stakhanovites was read; newly proposed quotas were announced. Then some rank-and-file trade-union members, previously prepared for this role, took the floor and urged the adoption of the new quotas. Voting began. . . .

"Comrades, I propose that the resolution be adopted unanimously," the trade-union chairman shouted, as he had been instructed to do.

Who is in favor? A forest of listless hands. Who is opposed? Silence. Suddenly a woman's voice exclaimed:

"Comrade chairman, Kiryushkin here didn't vote."

For the first time the meeting came to life. A rebel in our midst! A lion among the rabbits! Some obscure Kiryushkin, whoever he might be, had dared not to raise his hand and his crime against socialism had instantly been uncovered! Rebellion at one end, vigilance at the other, the country saved in the nick of time. . . .

"Comrade Kiryushkin, aren't you voting?" the chairman asked, in a peeved voice.

A thin, meek-looking man stood up. His face, stained with oil, was calm and he spoke with dignity.

"Why should I vote?" he shrugged his shoulders in a pathetic way. "One way or the other the norms will be passed. It's my job to work and I work. What else do you want? I should show my hand? All right, here's my hand." He raised a calloused hand over his head. "My wife and children expect me to make some more money and this means that I'll make even less. . . ."

Some people laughed, but on the whole the audience was silent, touched by the man's words and manner.

"Comrades, Kiryushkin is compromising the meeting and throwing mud on the great Stakhanovite movement!" someone yelled. "He's not class-conscious."

"Class-conscious?" Kiryushkin, still on his feet, again shrugged his shoulders. "I don't know what you mean. Yes, I'm conscious that I make only 140 rubles a month and have three children and a wife to feed."

"Enough of this comedy! Let's accept the resolution!" the chairman interrupted. But the meek workman seemed overcome by his own daring. He was feeling his oats.

"What do you mean comedy?" he raised his voice unexpectedly. "Look at me: This one working suit is the only one I have. Soon it will fall off altogether. With my 140 rubles a month my family goes hungry. If this is a comedy, then what's a tragedy?"

He sat down. There was very little laughter.

It was my appointed job to explain to the meeting, from an engineering angle, that the new norm was both possible and fair. I had no alternative. As I talked I almost convinced myself, if not my audience, that a new and richer life awaited all of us once we all learned to work well and to produce efficiently. We had centuries of sloth and backwardness to make up in one short generation, I said. I was sorry for myself and for these harassed men and women who were my people. Right or wrong, we were the generation earmarked by history for sacrifice and suffering.

At the back of my mind, as I warmed to the subject, there was a persistent thought: *I must help Kiryushkin.* . . .

The mass meeting came to an end with desultory applause. The people dispersed. Next day the Nikopol papers and radio described the gathering in the hypocritical language of political hyperbole: "Amidst thunderous enthusiasm the proletarians of the Nikopol Metallurgical Combinat demanded yesterday that the outmoded norms be revised. Unanimously they acclaimed . . ." Not a line about Kiryushkin.

I sent word to Kiryushkin to come to my office at the end of the workday. When his shift ended, I heard a commotion in my reception room.

"Where are you going? Comrade Kravchenko is too busy!" my secretary was saying.

"Believe me, I have no wish to see him. He sent for me."

"What's your business with him?"

"What business can I have with the boss? He calls, I come."

I buzzed for my secretary and told her to let the comrade come in. Kiryushkin entered, hat in hand.

"Please sit down," I said.

"Thanks, I can stand."

"But why stand? Do sit down."

He took a seat on the other side of my desk. I asked him how work was going.

"As it goes with everyone," he replied. "I work as long as my strength holds out."

He had come to the factory two years ago, I learned, from the village, after his farm had been collectivized. Before that he had served in the Red Army. He had brought a few belongings with him but had sold them, being in need.

"My wife washes floors in the apartments of some of the officials, which helps, and she does some laundry too. But there are the three small children. It isn't easy. But why complain? Not many workers are any better off than I am."

He spoke slowly, weighing his words, and looked straight at me. There was neither arrogance nor fear in his behavior—just a bottomless, fatalistic sorrow.

"Yes, Victor Andreyevich, what is there to talk about? You—you're one of the bosses. You live well. You live in your world, I live in mine. You will never understand the lot of folk like me."

"Don't be too sure, Comrade Kiryushkin. Maybe I understand better than you suppose. But tell me, would you like to go to work on the cutting machine? You'll be making 220 rubles or more and you'll be entitled to special clothes—shoes, a suit."

"Willingly. One must live, you know."

I gave orders that he be transferred to the new job. He thanked me and left. I was pleased, deep inside, that he had remained dignified throughout, without a suggestion of fawning. I called Starostin and arranged that some money be advanced to him from the Mutual Assistance Fund. In addition, I ordered that a set of working clothes and shoes should be issued to him.

2

The social distance between a Kiryushkin and a Stakhanovite "aristocrat" was felt more acutely than the distance between the workers and management, if only because the Kiryushkins and the Stakhanovites were in continuous daily contact. Official policy seemed intent upon widening these gulfs and setting up other tensions of antagonism and suspicion wherever possible.

Engineers and administrators as a class were being denounced, day after day, for supposed "conservatism," for "holding back" the pace-setters. Party functionaries, to evade blame themselves, joined this game of specialist-baiting. Our authority kept falling. Sensing that they had the upper hand, some engineers, foremen and even lathe hands would make arbitrary decisions to increase their own piecework earnings, often with disastrous results for production as a whole.

Politics, flying the banners of efficiency, had the right of way. Communist and police officials often had the final word as against the engineer and manager, even on purely technical problems. We were in the midst of an era of anarchy and civil strife in industry. I was caught between instructions from Moscow and suspicion from below, between tougher tasks and declining discipline. Nervousness and strain became almost my normal condition.

One night I was awakened by the telephone. One of the machines had suddenly broken down, leaving half my sub-plant idle. "More headaches!" I murmured and began to dress. By the time I reached the factory, it was swarming with officials. The Nikopol N.K.V.D. chief himself, Dorogan, was there, along with Gershgorn and other assistants. Kozlov, Starostin, various engineers ran around in circles, while in my office police specialists questioned suspects and took notes.

What had happened was instantly clear to me. Several Stakhanovite enthusiasts and an engineer had decided arbitrarily to increase the rotating speed of a roller. As the pipe had not been imbued with Stalinist faith, a large segment of it burst on the main belt and one of the machines was put out of commission. The matter was serious enough; the machine, being of German manufacture, could not be repaired or replaced for a long time.

The police-minded swarm of officials, however, was less concerned with restoring operations than with finding culprits. The investigators buzzed through the plant. Private interrogations went on at N.K.V.D. headquarters to the tune of threats and curses. Several times I was called out and questioned; after a night of it I was hardly much good at the factory. Simple and obvious explanations made no appeal to Gershgorn's devious and incompetent mind. He shouted, fumed and demanded "evidence" against this or that person. Each time he mentioned a name, out came a *dossier*. . . . Not only officials but simple factory workers were under surveillance.

"Kravchenko, you're not cooperating with us," Gershgorn screamed. "You may pay for this, believe me! For your own sake you should help find the saboteurs."

In the midst of those days of excitement, the skilled mechanic Dubinsky came to see me, accompanied by his assistant, Shpachinsky. While others were exploding and investigating, these two veteran mechanics had been testing metals, making thermal experiments and sketching plans. They thought they might be able to build duplicates of the broken parts, but wished to be assured that, in case of failure, the loss of time and materials would not be held against them.

After studying their plans and figures, I decided that the experiment was worth a trial. To shield these men and to protect myself, I apprised Brachko, Kozlov and Brodsky of my decision. I also dictated a full report to Trubostal in Kharkov. Then I assigned the necessary men and materials and gave the signal for work to start.

Despite all my political precautions, I was deeply worried. I happened to know, from the trend of questions at the N.K.V.D., that this Dubinsky, of all people, was under a cloud of official suspicion. He was a quiet, dignified, very competent old man whom everyone admired. Self-educated and well read, he was typical of the pre-revolutionary intellectual—a type which just then was regarded as peculiarly prone to political heresy. Dubinsky had been a member of the Menshevik wing of the Social Democrats under the Tsar; eighteen years of devoted labor under the Soviets had not wiped out that terrible stain on his record.

All in all, he seemed a perfect object of persecution for the police-minded, the panicky, the climbers and witch-hunters. There was sharp irony in the fact that Dubinsky was the only one who had come forward with a practical idea for restoring production. Should his experiment fail, I feared that it would provide just the chance Gershgorn and his gang had been waiting for. They could then accuse the ex-Menshevik of intentional obstruction.

I remained in the plant, with Dubinsky and Shpachinsky, for nearly four days. The N.K.V.D. informers watched from the sidelines, ready to denounce us if things should go awry. Finally, with real emotion, we tested the machine with the newly made parts. It worked! Production was rolling again.

Nevertheless, the investigation continued for weeks longer. Having failed to find a scapegoat for the breakdown, the police remained surly and frustrated, as if cheated of their legitimate prey. My relations with them were scarcely sweetened by the episode. I had made little secret of my view that the whole thing was a minor accident unworthy of such police attention.

Neither were my relations with the trade-union and Party "activists" improved by time. There was rarely a week when their political zeal and my production common sense did not clash. From dozens of incidents I choose a few at random in my memory.

There was the morning when I found my sub-plant curiously disturbed. Tempers were short. The atmosphere seemed charged with electricity. I soon confronted the explanation. In one corner, within easy view of everyone in the shop, a lot of pipe had been stacked artistically, and over it was a huge placard reading:

"The workers and engineers of this section should know who impedes the Stakhanovite movement:"

There followed a long list of names. It appeared that a batch of defective pipe had been discovered and the group responsible was thus being publicly humiliated. I knew the men listed as average and loyal workers. The defects were probably due to impurities in the steel and could not be blamed off-hand on these men.

I ordered the "exhibit" and the placard removed. Starostin was furious.

He chided me for interfering with his work of "political education" of union members and hinted darkly at denunciations to the "proper instances."

Not long thereafter I noticed that the elderly gray-haired Makayev, a turner whose work I valued, was crying silently as he worked. When I asked him what was amiss, he pointed to the opposite wall. A caricature of this worker had been posted and under it was the inscription: *"Spoiler of Stakhanovism."*

"Victor Andreyevich, free me from this disgrace," he pleaded. "I admit that I may have made a mistake. The truth is that my wife is sick and I haven't slept a wink for several days. I'm only human and so perhaps I made a mistake. Isn't it enough that I'm being docked for the spoilage? Must I be exposed to ridicule in addition?"

I called the foreman.

"Who put up this placard?" I asked.

"The trade-union chairman of our section."

"Tear it down right away and send it to my office."

"But I can't, Comrade Kravchenko. I'd get into hot water."

"Tell him I ordered it and will take full responsibility."

The insulting placard was removed. In a few minutes a bevy of trade-union functionaries and Party zealots swooped down on me. They all talked at once. I was impeding "political education" and encouraging backwardness. I was "undermining the authority of the trade union and the Party." They would complain against me to Kharkov, even to Moscow.

"Very well, comrades," I said. "Complain to your heart's content. As far as I'm concerned, it's you who are doing the impeding by insulting my personnel and undermining work morale. I'm the chief here, and it's your duty to cooperate with me instead of going over my head. And some of you, incidentally, should be working now instead of arguing here."

Later that day Kozlov sent for me. The complaints on the "great" Makayev affair had reached him. I presented my view and was delighted to find that he agreed with me; he would support me should the silly business draw fire from higher up. The news that I was taking the side of the workers against the zealots created a sensation and raised my popularity among the workers but it offended any number of officials and influential Party people.

Many weeks of my time and energy were also sapped by the case of a broken German machine. When the main bearing snapped, replacement proved difficult and one of my shops was tied up for three or four days. Once more our section was overrun by police agents and grim-visaged "authorities."

My own analysis quickly showed me the true picture. The accident had occurred at night. The light in the shop was bad and someone had accidentally picked up the wrong piece of steel. The machine was set for steel of low carbon content. When steel containing 18 to 20 per cent chromium and 2 per cent nickel was put into the works, the bearing broke. The mystery was no deeper than that.

Dissatisfied with my explanation, still on the scent of the elusive sabotage dear to its heart, the Economic Division made its own analyses of the steel, questioned dozens of workers, called in specialists from out of town and obtained reports by a professor of metallurgy in the Dniepropetrovsk Institute. The very unanimity of the reports seemed "strange" to the police mind. What was the "political countenance" of the professor who agreed with Kravchenko? Were we perhaps acquainted? Again I spent long nights in argument, aware that any unguarded word, any slip of the tongue, might spell ruin for some worker or engineer, let alone myself. This time, as before, Gershgorn tried desperately to narrow down his accusations to Dubinsky. I defended the mechanic at every turn.

An emergency order for rustless pipe reached me over the signature of Ordzhonikidze. Our factory was not equipped for this particular order; we had no experience in this type of work and undertook it only after warning the authorities not to expect too much. To help us, a special brigade came down from Moscow, composed of men experienced with the special type of pipe and with the chemical industry for which it was being made. In the brigade was a metallurgical specialist named Timoshenko—a lean young man, spectacled, already graying and, it seemed to me, permanently scared. I was told that he was the son of a famous Professor Timoshenko, then living and teaching in the United States.

As was to be expected, work was slow in starting. Only 10 per cent of the first pipes produced were usable and there were days when the entire output was defective. Experts came from various trusts to give us advice. We held long conferences on temperature, processing speeds, types of steel, amalgams. Every one of us was eager to fulfill the order and distressed by delays; whatever our secret political attitudes, we felt that Stalins come and go, but Russia remains forever, and it was the industrial future of Russia that was at stake. But so far as the teeming informers were concerned, the difficulties spelled only one thing—possible sabotage.

Ultimately we solved the technical problems. The rustless pipe was manufactured and duly accepted by the Kemerovo Chemical Combinat. Handsome bonuses were distributed all around. But Gershgorn and his associates thought they had their teeth in something and would not let go. The something, of course, was young Timoshenko, along with some engineers sent by the trust in Kharkov. In a volcanic midnight session Gershgorn spurted lava over my weary head. Why was I "protecting" this son of a foul émigré? Didn't I know that Timoshenko was in touch with his father, who had "sold out to the capitalists"?

"All I can tell you is that the young man is able, worked hard and did his full duty," I insisted. "We had plenty of trouble, but I assure you none of it was his fault."

"You're playing with fire, Kravchenko! Remember, this concerns the chemical industry. It's a matter of national defense! Yet you don't lift a finger to help us root out the wreckers!"

Only when I threatened, in sheer despair, to telephone Ordzhonikidze and expose this police interference with my work did Gershgorn subside. The fact that I had a powerful patron was my one advantage in a situation where an engineer without influence would long since have found himself in some prison or forced-labor camp.

Early in 1936 Comrade Ordzhonikidze summoned me to Moscow. It seemed to me the act of my protecting angels. I had reached an impasse in my relations with the N.K.V.D. My refusal to incriminate innocent men or to connive in support of police obsessions was making my life at Nikopol intolerable. I had been getting up the courage to put the facts before the Commissar, and this was my chance.

After cordial greetings, Ordzhonikidze told me why he had sent for me. There was a most urgent need for special pipes for the Baku oil industry. The whole oil plan depended on the speed with which we could turn out a certain quantity of pipe.

"I'm turning to you, my friend," he said, "because I feel I can depend on you. You'll get all the instruments, the materials and the extra men you need. If you succeed, there's an automobile and a decoration for you as a reward and bonuses for all your associates."

"I shall, of course, do all I can and I'm pleased that you realize we lack certain instruments. But Grigory Constantinovich, I want you to know that I'm working under conditions of N.K.V.D. interference that make life impossible. I'm in despair."

"What do you mean?"

I plunged into a detailed account of the artistic sleuthing and the mania of persecution and denunciations which were turning my factory—and all the other enterprises in Nikopol—into a purgatory. I told of Dorogan's and Gershgorn's efforts to conjure fancy sabotage out of plain accidents, of the pressures to incriminate innocent people like Timoshenko and Dubinsky.

"I don't like to talk of these things," I concluded, "but I can no longer keep quiet. Is the Commissariat of Heavy Industry running metallurgy, or is it the N.K.V.D.? How can we try anything new, how can we follow orders that involve experiment, how can we make any progress, if every failure and every false start will be construed as wrecking? How is a man to work at all, when he's being constantly 'controlled' by police investigators, Party commissions, trade-union brigades, Stakhanovites and a hundred others?

"Why can't we end this spy scare and let people work in peace? The old generation of engineers and specialists is mostly dead or liquidated. We are Soviet people, most of us products of Party education. If we can't be trusted to labor honestly, what hope of progress is there for our country? I for one, Comrade Commissar, can no longer work under such conditions. Those rascals keep me spinning like a top. How's one to produce in a state of permanent vertigo?"

Ordzhonikidze looked grave. He bit his lips. He had aged rapidly in the past year or two. He no longer smiled as readily as before, no longer effervesced with the old confidence and the old energy. Whatever he felt, he was scarcely in a position to bare his heart to a minor industrial manager. After all, he was a member of the Politburo, one of the dozen or so men closest to Stalin.

"Calm down, my friend," he said quietly. "I don't hold it against you that you speak as you do. There are many things you can't see from where you sit. I shan't conceal the fact that you are only one of hundreds of leading engineers, Party members, who have made the same complaint right in this office. . . . As for your personal case, I promise that as long as I live and you continue to work honestly, no one will touch you. You have my word on that."

Even as I sat there he put through a call to Comrade Hatayevich, Secretary of the Dniepropetrovsk Regional Committee, whose domain embraced Nikopol. In my presence he sternly reprimanded Hatayevich and ordered that the Nikopol N.K.V.D. stop annoying Comrade Kravchenko, or he would know the reason why.

"Well, are you satisfied?" he smiled as he put down the receiver.

"Many thanks. But this hardly solves the larger problem. The awful system remains."

From that day until Ordzhonikidze's sudden death, I was never again called or cross-examined by the N.K.V.D. The informers around me— Makarov, Romanov, Yudavin, a hundred others—worked as diligently as ever. But I remained untouchable. Whatever doubts or resentments the secret police may have had against me were dammed for the time being by the orders of my Moscow patron. One day they would be suddenly released and would inundate my life in a terrifying flood.

Back in Nikopol, I called together the principal members of the factory and technical administrations and laid before them the task that Ordzhonikidze had entrusted to me. I assigned various men their duties. The materials and tools arrived as promised by the Commissar and work was quickly under way. In the following weeks I slept in my office more often than at home. The Baku pipes were produced ahead of schedule. Once more official congratulations poured into the factory from Kharkov and Moscow, my portrait was in the papers, Ivanchenko flew down from Kharkov and thanked me personally.

There had been a genuine thrill in meeting the challenge of a difficult industrial undertaking. The knowledge that I had licked a thousand obstacles gave me, and those around me, more joy than the official recognition and the generous cash bonuses.

While in Nikopol, Ivanchenko entertained me with a dinner. We had known each other now for many years. I trusted him. I had been in the factory now for more than a year. Through the Commissar's intercession my private lot was improved. Yet I writhed in the net of espionage. I gave Ivanchenko one example after another of how police interference and the sabotage panic were destroying initiative and tying up production.

"I know how you feel, Victor Andreyevich," he commented sadly. "Don't think it's any better on the higher levels. Here I am, the head of one of the biggest trusts, a member of the government, an old Communist, a man who helped storm the Winter Palace in the October Revolution. You'd think I'd be trusted. But no! These ants and termites have multiplied so fast that I'm terrified of them—I who was never afraid to risk my life in battle. They've made me so jittery with their investigations and suspicions that I don't know whether I'm coming or going. What's it all about? I suppose only The Boss knows. . . ."

3

The temporary easing of police pressure gave me a short-lived illusion of personal independence. That, in turn, predisposed me to a hopeful view of the newly announced Stalin Constitution. The fact that all power remained in the hands of a single party seemed of less moment than the explicit guarantees of civil rights and, above all, the limitations on the forms of seizure and arrest. If the new document was an indication of thinking in high places, then assuredly the worst of the terror was over.

To survive, man needs hope even as he needs air. Like millions of others, I reached out for the promise of more human rights for the ordinary Soviet citizen. We grasped at the straw of hope to save ourselves from sinking to the lower depths of despondency. Except for the minority of hard-bitten cynics, to whom the Constitution was just one more hoax, Communists especially wanted to believe.

An occasional revival of hope was almost a condition for remaining alive. We needed to succumb to extravagant faith, we needed to fool our minds and cheat our senses. Anxiously we fought off doubts, made excuses, excited one another with optimistic expectations which, when alone again, we did not really credit. The "most democratic Constitution in the world" evoked mirages in our political desert.

Could it be that the death of Kirov had alarmed our masters into loosening the screws? Europe seemed headed for war. The Italian theft of Ethiopia had been followed by civil strife in Spain. Hitler was brandishing his Nazi sword. Perhaps our masters had decided to unite the Russian masses behind them by a lordly grant of a few crumbs of freedom? It was thus that we kindled our hopes and beat down our doubts. It was not easy to keep faith glowing at a time when the winds of arbitrary terror were blowing more sharply than ever. One had to shut his eyes, almost literally, to save the last spark of hope.

The Nikopol *combinat* was being enlarged. Hordes of new construction workers strained our food supplies and housing as never before. One day, in the midst of the inflated hopes for some change for the better, I noticed a contingent of N.K.V.D. soldiers, carrying rifles, around the new building area. It could mean only one thing: that forced labor had been brought in.

I approached the scene. My guess was right. Four or five hundred haggard men and women were working under armed guard. They were as tragic looking a group of human creatures as I had ever seen. Their unsmiling silence was more terrible than their raggedness, filth and physical degradation. They went about their work like people doomed, too apathetic to examine their surroundings or to commune with the free workers near them.

At the end of each day the prisoners were lined up and marched off to special prison barracks a few miles away. I made discreet inquiries and learned that this labor had been "contracted" for by the construction officials in formal negotiations with the N.K.V.D. A flat sum per prisoner, about equal to the amount paid to free workers, was paid to the N.K.V.D. Besides using millions of political prisoners directly—in mining salt or gold, laying rails, felling forests, clearing swamps, building harbors—the N.K.V.D. farmed out its surplus slaves to other Soviet enterprises.

One weekend, that summer, I went down the Dnieper in a motorboat with a friend. We had plenty of food with us, as well as a bottle of wine, and made a picnic of it in a cool wooded spot on shore. Then we took a long walk, following a road along the river edge. Suddenly we heard noises ahead of us. At a bend in the road we came to a flat marshy stretch where some hundreds of men and women were working under military guard.

I felt as if I had intruded on some obscenity. My first impulse was to withdrew, to pretend I had not seen it. But something drew us to the scene. The ragged workers, knee-deep in mud and water, seemed scarcely human. Clouds of swamp mosquitoes hovered over them. The guards had built bonfires to drive off the insects, but the prisoners seemed inured to the pest. My eyes rested on a young woman with cadaverous features; her hands and face were black with mosquitoes but she plied her shovel listlessly, as if unaware that she was being eaten alive.

An officer approached us.

"Why don't you go about your business, citizens?" he said. "This isn't a show."

"I'm a Party man and the head of a plant," I said. "This interests me, purely technically. What are they doing?"

"We're clearing the swamp."

"An N.K.V.D. project?" I asked.

"No, the Nikopol Soviet is doing the job, with 'contracted' N.K.V.D. labor."

We returned to the motorboat in silence, and steered for home. To continue the outing after what we had seen seemed indecent. All morning we had talked of the Constitution and the possibility that its promises might be real. We did not resume the discussion.

4

Between my father and myself a certain restraint had developed in the years since I joined the Party. Somehow, in his presence, I felt impelled to gloss over and explain away the very policies which inwardly I condemned and loathed. In a dim way I was exasperated by his high standards, his nagging humanitarianism, his inability to compromise. Looking back, I know as a fact what I had then only suspected: My father had become for me conscience incarnate. The misunderstanding was not so much with him as with myself. When I should be reconciled with my own conscience, I would be reconciled with him.

During my visits home, father sometimes told me about the arrests and "disappearance" of men we had both known for many years at the Dniepropetrovsk factory. I felt as if he were holding me personally responsible, as a Party member, for every injustice. I told him nothing about similar arrests in Nikopol, about the forced-labor contingent, about the espionage to which I was being subjected.

This irrational impulse to conceal things from my father, of all people, irritated me, made me angry and ashamed. It was as if I were concealing things from myself. . . .

I was not too eager for him to visit me at Nikopol. Somehow I did not want to survey the splendor in which I was living through my father's earnest eyes. Yet I kept urging him to spend a few days with me and finally he agreed to come. As he went through my large house, the flower garden, the orchard, the garage, I became increasingly fidgety and embarrassed.

"You do live like a *pomeschik*, like a squire," was all father said.

When he asked me for passes to the factory, the same unreasonable embarrassment came over me. I was reluctant to have conditions there appraised by my father's harsh righteousness. Yet I dutifully signed a series of passes. In the next few days I saw little of him. He made friends everywhere in the plant. This graceful aging man, his handsome features so lean and cleanly cut, his youthful eyes so stern, was completely at ease among working people anywhere. They accepted him automatically as one of their own. For months after his visit, the men and women at the plant inquired about my father in simple, warm-hearted solicitude.

"Comrade Kravchenko, your father is a fine man, a fine man," old Dubinsky said to me the day he met him. "He makes one proud of being a manual worker. And let me tell you, he understands machinery better than most of our engineers."

"Oh, yes," I agreed, a bit awkwardly, "he was my first teacher in industry."

At the end of that day I was in the office going over a blueprint with several colleagues when I heard a noise in the reception room. My secretary raised her voice.

"I'm asking you, citizen, why you must see Comrade Kravchenko?"

"Is that your business?" my father's voice rose above hers. "Is he a bureaucrat or a comrade, that one must plead for permission? Nothing but passes and permissions!"

"Then I won't allow you to come in, citizen. Rules are rules."

"This for your rules!" he exclaimed and tore open the door to my office.

He was abashed to find other people with me but could not arrest the impetus of his anger.

"What sort of rules are these, Vitya? Why, even in the time of the Romanoffs a man could see his boss. . . . But I beg your pardon, I thought you were alone."

I introduced father to the other men, then dismissed them. Father was apologetic.

"I was a bit rude. Do forgive me. But all this red tape, all this distance between ordinary folk and the officials, gets on my nerves."

When I had reassured him. he asked for a favor. Would I let him see the work records for my sub-plant? Having observed the operations for several days, he wanted to know how much locksmiths, turners, rollers, electricians and other types of workers were earning. He also wanted to know how many had been to the government rest homes and had enjoyed other benefits in the past year. Since none of this information was secret, I rang for the chief bookkeeper and instructed him to make it available to my father.

I remained at the plant several hours longer. When I reached home, father was already there. At supper he seemed preoccupied. We talked at random about commonplaces. I understood that he was saving his ammunition for a "serious" talk later. When he suggested that I give Pasha the evening off, I was certain of it. "No need for strange ears," father said.

I settled on the divan in my study, lit a cigaret and prepared myself to listen.

"All right, father, what's on your mind?"

"For a long time, son, I've wanted to talk to you openly and frankly. You're dear to me, not only as a son but as a human being whom I've watched unfold these thirty years. Yet as time passes it becomes harder for us to be frank with one another. This is sad. It's a symptom of the fears by which we live these days."

"I'm sorry, father. But I do wonder whether you've kept up with history. I mean, whether you're not living in the climate of a past era."

"I admit, Vitya, that you know a lot more than I do about current politics. You're an active Party person and an important official. You have fifteen hundred men under you and produce to the tune of tens of millions of rubles. All the same, I think I know more about the life of ordinary people, workers and peasants, than you do. One drifts away. One begins to see the masses from the wrong end of the telescope. You have lots of money, comforts, cars, servants. . . ."

"Father, I don't think I deserve these reproaches. I haven't stolen anything, have I? The regime gives me these things and in return I work harder than any peasant."

"I don't mean to reproach you. Please try not to misunderstand me. I simply can't help worrying whether you've lost all fellow-feeling for the ordinary people; whether, to put it brutally, you're as content as the rest of the bureaucrats to be one of the bosses over the miserable Russian people."

"I don't quite see what you want me to do. I'm merely a small cog in a big machine. The truth, father, is that I work so hard I haven't the time or the strength to worry about first principles. I'm buried in my job."

"In short, you're becoming an ostrich. You hide your head in the sand and all problems disappear. You say 'The fault is not mine, I'm not my brother's keeper' and that's that. Yes, there were people like that in the old days too. The suffering of your country no longer touches your heart."

"Listen, father, don't get the idea that I don't know what's happening or that I have knuckled under to the system. After all, you don't know what's going on inside my mind—and the minds of a million other Communists. But what can I do? Shall I go into the street and shout 'Help! Murder!'? Besides, there are some positive elements too. New factories, new mines, railroads. . . .''

"Of course, Victor, of course. But revolutions are not made for factories and railroads. They're made for people. The essence of the matter is in personal rights and liberties. Without these, without human dignity, men are slaves no matter how industrialized their prison may be. When you Communists boast of new factories, the implication is that people live better lives. Well, now, do they in our country?"

"As compared with their miserable existence under the Tsars, I suppose they do."

"Vitya, why must you fool yourself? Do you recall your life at grandfather's, and at home when you were a boy? We were not wealthy, but we never lacked for bread and milk and ordinary clothes. You and your brothers even had a nurse. We lived decently. Looking back, our existence seems almost luxurious by contrast with the life of a working-class family today. How many workers nowadays have the kind of homes we lived in at that time? Only a very small minority in the past lived the kind of starved and hopeless lives now lived by the majority.

"I had a reason today in asking for figures on your plant. I happen to remember very well the corresponding figures before the revolution. Locksmiths in Nikopol now get between 145 and 200 rubles a month. Before 1917 they got only 35 to 50 rubles. A skilled roller then earned between 45 and 85 rubles. Today he earns 200 to 350. Taking into consideration also turners, smelters, electric crane operators, wages today average 240 rubles, where they would have averaged about 55 rubles in the old days.

"That sounds good. But what kind of ruble was it then and what kind is it now? Before the revolution a kilo of bread cost 5 kopeks. What does it cost now? Between a ruble and 20 kopeks and 2 rubles. A kilo of meat used to cost 15 or 20 kopeks, now if you can get it at all, you have to pay about twelve rubles—which is sixty times as much! What did you pay for the suit you're wearing?"

"Eight hundred rubles."

"Eight hundred rubles—from three to four months' wages for a skilled smelter! Do you know what it would have cost in the old days? About 15 rubles, 20 at most. So there you see the picture: Money wages have risen three to five times and this is hailed as great economic progress. But the cost of living has risen not fivefold but fifteen times, forty times, fifty times higher. The locksmith who made 50 rubles a month used to be a prosperous workman. Today he earns 200 rubles and he's a miserable pauper."

"But you forget all the privileges he receives nowadays—free vacations, medical care, children's creches. . . .''

"All right, let's look at these benefits. You call them 'free' but you know that a big chunk is taken out of wages to cover these privileges. Including union dues, forced loans and the rest, from 20 to 25 percent of a man's earnings is withheld. For 20 to 25 percent of his wages a worker in the past could have bought himself all the medical help and vacations he needed, without being beholden to the government.

"Why do we need creches? Because so few wives can afford to stay home and take care of their children. On 50 rubles a month a man used to be able to raise a family decently. Now, on 200 rubles, he must send his wife and his grown children to work to make both ends meet. As to the kind of medical service they're getting, the less said the better. When you're sick, Vitya, do you go to the State clinic?"

"No, I send for Dr. Gorkin privately."

"Of course. So does anyone who can afford it. You know as well as I do that the only way to get decent treatment is to pay for it. The medical care, like everything else, is rotten with bureaucracy and apathy. But how about those vacations in rest homes the Communist press is always boasting about? In your plant, Vitya, you have 1500 workers. Do you happen to know how many of them went to rest homes in the past year?"

"No. A few hundred I suppose."

"You're wrong. I checked the figures today. Only 57 in the whole plant. All 1500 paid for the privilege—only 57 collected. The rest homes were full all the time, of course—full of directors, Party officials, top Stakhanovites and other favorites of the State. Sure, I'm for social insurance, medical care and the rest, provided it's given to the people from the profits which the State, as the owner and operator of factories, makes on them—the profits that formerly were made by the capitalists—and not from the earnings of the workers themselves. In that was the gist of the revolution.

"But where are your profits? Your industry and your whole economy work at a loss. And we, the citizens, are forced to cover those losses. What hurts, son, is that you give trifles and boast as if they were mountains. The economic progress, I'm sorry to say, is small when measured against the investments and the sacrifices.

"Only innocent foreigners and young people without any memory of the past believe the fairy tales. To me physical facts are not as important as the political and spiritual facts. But all the emphasis in your propaganda is on material achievement. I'm measuring with your own yardsticks."

"Well, if everything was so lovely, father, why did you go to prison and make a revolution?"

"Don't talk nonsense! You know that I regret nothing and would do it over again. We fought against evils. We risked our lives to overthrow political tyranny and economic oppression. That doesn't mean that we should be proud of the same evils under different names. This business of justifying present injustice by reference to past evils is a low demagogic trick."

"But now everything belongs to the people. There are no capitalists, no exploiters."

As the discussion progressed I became more annoyed, precisely because in my heart I agreed with my father on so many things.

"Don't play the fool, Vitya. The worker who's underfed despite the fact that he and often others in his family are employed doesn't much care who exploits him, a private owner or the State. When he's dragged off to prison or exiled, it's small consolation to him that it's being done in his own name. After all, when the capitalist boss didn't pay me enough or failed to give me decent working conditions, I could change my job. I could propagandize my fellow-workers, call protest meetings, pull strikes, join political parties, publish opposition literature. Try any of it today and you'll end up in prison camp, or worse. Believe me, we had more chance dealing with a hundred thousand capitalist employers than we have now with one employer, the State. Why? Because the State has an army and secret police and unlimited power. All my life I have fought against capitalism, and I'm still its enemy, but that doesn't mean I must shout hurrah for police-socialism."

I was silent. I could only frown.

"At least we could *think* what we pleased. There were many political parties, factions, opinions. Harsh as the absolutism was, it now seems liberal by contrast. Sure, the Tsar's police used to beat and sometimes shot strikers and often shot or exiled revolutionaries. But the whole scale was different. We counted our political prisoners by the thousand, not, as now, by the million. And every injustice evoked protests, demonstrations, mass meetings. Today we have only the silence of a cemetery.

"Take our so-called trade unions. What are they but another instrument for enforcing the government's decisions and pressing more work out of us? There was a time when labor organizations were really spokesmen for the workers. They were political schools in which we learned to demand our rights and to fight for them. Who dares protest against anything today? The press, which poses as a mouthpiece of public opinion, is now the property of the Party and the State. It reflects only *their* opinions.

"Another thing, son. You know that I've never been a believer. But I always valued the right of people to worship God if they wished. How little of that right has remained! What chance would you have of retaining your job and your career if you happened to be a church-goer? None at all!

"Even in the worst Romanoff days, people could leave the country. Now we're all locked in and those who try to cross the border are shot down like dogs. Not only they but their families are punished. Leave the country? Why, you tie workers to their machines and peasants to their land like so many serfs."

"Why do you keep saying 'you,' as if it were all my personal doing?"

"Forgive me, Vitya, but as a Communist you cannot shirk your share of the responsibility."

"Am I the N.K.V.D. or the Politburo? You're a realist on everything else, father, but you don't seem to grasp the fact that even responsible Communists, not only ordinary ones, are as powerless as the rest of the population. Maybe more so."

"I don't want to be unfair, Vitya. I do know how little any man can do. I don't want you to shout 'Help! Murder!' But at least I'd like to feel that my upbringing of you has not been a total failure—that you're at least aware of the truth."

"Yes, I'm aware of it. More so than you suspect. On that score you can set your mind at ease. But I still cling to shreds of hope. I prefer not to be cynical. About the new Constitution, for instance. Perhaps we shall have more freedom after all. . . ."

"I wish I could share your faith. But of what value are words on paper as long as the secret police run things as they please, as long as only one party can exist with its own press, its own god—Stalin—its own courts, and all dissident opinion is treated as a crime? I'm too old to live on illusions. If I see any sign of relaxation of the terror—of the dawn of real freedom—I'll be the first to hail it with real joy. So far I see no such sign. When I read your boasts and your new Constitution, Victor, I cannot help thinking of Voltaire's lines:

> *No other hand so bountiful and kind*
> *In giving men soap bubbles will you find.*

"Don't imagine I find it easy to talk like this. I am not happy that a son of mine is among the new exploiters, even if he is not himself to blame for it. . . . Perhaps the time will come when we shall understand each other better. . . ."

The time did come, sooner than either of us suspected.

CHAPTER XIV

SUPER-PURGE

AFTER A MEETING of the City Committee of the Party, I was driving home with a close friend in the factory administration. He had returned that very morning from Moscow, where he was well connected, and could be expected to have some news. The arrest and impending trial of Zinoviev, Kamenev and other Old Bolsheviks having been announced, I was on the alert, like everyone else, for any scrap of information. Members of Lenin's "General Staff of the Revolution" in prison, threatened with execution! The idea was monstrous, incredible.

The population at large—I judged by the workers of Nikopol—were pretty indifferent to what seemed to them a family quarrel among their new masters. The tragic fate of Lenin's old associates stirred no particular sympathy.

But the Party members, non-Party officials, members of the ruling élite generally, were disturbed to their depths. Until then the Leninist Old Guard had been considered sacrosanct. They might be denounced, banished, smeared with ugly charges, but their lives were held inviolate. Even Leon Trotsky, after his eclipse, had merely been exiled to Alma Ata in Central Asia, then deported to Turkey. But now Gregory Zinoviev, once head of the Communist International, the man whose letter (and possibly forged at that) had been enough to swing an election in England, would be tried publicly on a capital charge! This assuredly was no local storm, but the beginning of a cyclone that would sweep through the entire Party, the entire bureaucracy, the entire country, cutting a savage swath of death and devastation.

"Victor," my companion said in a low voice, conscious of the chauffeur up front, "is your neck pretty strong?"

"What do you mean?"

"I mean that soon a lot of heads will be disconnected from their bodies."

"But what could happen to my head? I am no Oppositionist and never have been. I stick to my job and don't meddle with politics."

"Blessed is he who has faith. Live and learn."

His words were bantering, but his tone was deadly earnest.

"Let's walk the rest of the way. It's such a nice moonlit evening," I suggested, nudging him with an elbow. We dismissed the car. In a land where too many walls have dictaphonic ears and most chauffeurs work also for the secret police, conversation is safest while walking.

"What's up? Speak plainly," I urged.

"Moscow is topsy-turvy, and Leningrad, they say, is no better. Arrests by the thousand. There's no longer any concealment. Communists and non-Party folk alike are taken right out of their offices, in plain sight of everyone. Half a dozen of the key Party people whom I usually look up in Moscow were mysteriously missing. The N.K.V.D. is reaching right up to the top, pulling down big men, commissars, heads of trusts, people inside the Kremlin itself.

"Everyone's gloomy and scared stiff, everyone's paralyzed. Some comrades are convinced that Zinoviev and Kamenev will be killed and that others, lots of others, will follow. It's hard to believe. It makes no sense. But there it is! We'll be treated like kulaks and Whites."

"Who will be next?"

"Your guess is as good as mine. But none of us is likely to be spared. I mean obscurity will not in itself save you and me. Two of our engineers" —he mentioned their names—"were picked up last night. Supposed to be a great secret. Director Brachko was ordered to send them to Moscow on a specific train. At the Zaparozhe station they were removed by N.K.V.D. men and whisked off in a closed motorcar. A friend of mine happened to be at the station and saw it all. Things will move fast now. Just watch!"

They did move fast. No sooner did I reach the plant next morning than one of my assistants confided to me the news of the arrest of the two engineers. Like so many Soviet "secrets," it had spread through the factory. In the course of the morning I received a call from Lensky, second Secretary of the factory Party Committee. He asked me to come over immediately. Though Lensky was mild, soft-spoken and looked like a village schoolteacher, he had a reputation for ruthlessness.

"Comrade Kravchenko, I want to consult you on a very delicate matter," he began. "It's about Arkady Limansky. You've watched his work. He's been to your home, you've been to his. Did he ever talk politics to you? About his political past in Leningrad, for instance?"

"No, we rarely talked anything but shop. His plant and mine have to coordinate work a good deal and that brings us in contact. But I don't recall any political talk."

This was essentially true. Under Soviet conditions few men who work together reach the stage of intimacy where they share opinions on "delicate" matters. Certainly Limansky and I had not reached that stage. Lensky was disappointed and made a mental note, I have no doubt, that I was "shielding" a suspect. There would be a Party Bureau meeting in the evening, he informed me, on the "Limansky case." Meanwhile I must not reveal that I had been consulted on the subject.

Limansky came to the meeting that evening in excellent spirits. He had not the faintest suspicion that the urgent business concerned him. He was a portly fellow of about thirty-five with a flair for good clothes. Having been abroad once, in Germany, on an official purchasing mission, he rather fancied himself a cosmopolite, a bit disdainful of Nikopol provincialism.

The meeting hall was blue with smoke. Lensky presided. Near him sat a stranger—an overfed fellow with a close-shaved bullet head and a scowling mien. Though in civilian attire, he had the brisk, efficient manner that betrayed the seasoned Chekist. From the way he gripped the brief case in his lap, one felt that its contents boded no good for some people.

"Comrades, the meeting of the Party Bureau is called to order," Lensky said. "On the agenda tonight we have only one question: the sub-plant chief and Communist member Arkady Vassilievich Limansky."

"*Me?*" Limansky exclaimed, springing to his feet. There was a fatuous smile on his face. The blow was so sudden it didn't register at once.

"Yes, you! Sit down until you're called on."

Limansky lowered himself slowly in his chair. Every drop of blood seemed suddenly drained from his face. He mopped his forehead with a handkerchief.

"Comrades, has any one of you any comment to make on the subject of inquiry?"

No one replied.

"Very well, in that case stand up, Limansky, and tell us briefly about your activities, especially in Leningrad."

Poor Limansky by this time was trembling as if in violent fever. Normally glib and self-assured, he suddenly found it hard to follow a sequence of events. Stammeringly he zigzagged through his biography, went back to the beginning, and in his confusion brought in irrelevant matters, including a reference to his marriage. The stranger grew impatient.

"We aren't interested in your private life," he said. "We want to hear about your political past."

"Well, comrades, it's no secret. . . . I've explained it a hundred times. . . . I mean about Leningrad. I was then a bit uncertain. . . . I wavered and got mixed up with some Trotskyists. It's no secret and the Party generously forgave me. Yes, it trusted me and I have made a good record. Ask anyone here. Besides, comrades, it was all so long ago. . . ."

"Long ago!" Lensky sneered. "The dirty work of Zinoviev and Trotsky and other wild dogs was also long ago. That alibi will no longer save the enemies of the people. Tell me, Limansky, did you ever speak against the Central Committee and our Beloved Leader, Comrade Stalin?"

"No, of course not."

Lensky motioned to the Chekist who now thundered:

"Citizen Limansky, you're deceiving the Party to its face! Didn't you shoot your mouth off at an activists' meeting in the N—— District in August. . . . ?"

The change from "comrade" to "citizen" was ominous.

"Yes, now I begin to remember," Limansky muttered. He held on to a chair to steady himself.

"Better remember some more. Whom did you know in Leningrad who also 'wavered,' who was also 'a bit uncertain'?"

"It's hard to recall . . . after so many years. But let me see—" He mentioned half a dozen names.

"And where are these worthies now?"

"I have no idea . . . working, I suppose."

"Well, I can tell you. Every one of them is under arrest! By the way, have you signed any Oppositionist document with them?"

"Oh no. . . . I mean I don't think so."

"Then let me refresh your memory. Here's a photostat. Come over and look at it. Do you perhaps recognize this? *Your* signature?"

Limansky looked at the paper, then returned to his place, stumbling like a blind man.

"But you didn't remember, eh? Too busy remembering your wedding day and your trip to Berlin, eh?"

"It was a private paper, in no way political, and so many years ago. . . ."

The cross-examination continued for perhaps half an hour. Limansky, now wholly demoralized, unnecessarily denied unimportant facts and then, confronted with proofs, made admissions. Not one of the items was in itself vital, but taken together, and intoned portentously by the Chekist, then by Lensky, they added up. Some strained discussion from the floor followed. A few people pleaded for the man; a lot more condemned him. Finally the meeting unanimously expelled him from the Party and asked the City Committee to confirm the decision. As we left the room, no one spoke. We avoided looking at each other.

On my way home a little later I saw a light in the window of Limansky's office and, on impulse, went in without knocking. I found him behind his desk, his head buried in his hands, his broad shoulders shaking with stifled tears. Only an hour ago he had been a strong, confident official, not without a touch of bureaucratic arrogance; suddenly he was a pitiful, quaking wreck.

"Victor Andreyevich!" he looked up in astonishment. "Thanks for coming in. This is the end! Expulsion, then arrest, then what? My wife. . . . Oh, God! Maybe I'd better shoot myself."

He would not be consoled, and he was right about it. The City Committee quickly confirmed the expulsion. Limansky was transferred to a minor job in the trust in Kharkov and soon thereafter was arrested. After that no one in Nikopol knew what had become of him.

A week or two later I had some business to take up with Brachko's assistant, a Party man named Alexei Sukhin. I walked briskly into his reception room and was about to go into his office. But his secretary stopped me.

"Please wait, Comrade Kravchenko. Comrade Sukhin is very busy."

"So am I," I replied, annoyed, and barged into the office.

I stopped short on the threshold. Sukhin was at his desk and by his side sat the fat, perspiring Gershgorn, his loose lips twisted into a characteristic sneer. Along the walls, right and left, sat ten or twelve engineers, a few of them Party members. In sheer embarrassment I greeted everyone loudly. Only Sukhin responded. Then I noticed that four uniformed N.K.V.D. men stood guard over the engineers.

I withdrew in confusion and headed for Brachko's office.

"What's wrong, Piotr Petrovich?" I asked.

"I don't understand anything any more. Twelve men in one day! Eight yesterday! If it keeps up. . . . But my head's reeling, Victor Andreyevich."

Brachko seemed to have become an old man overnight. His eyes were unnaturally enlarged, sleep-drunk.

From his office I went to the bookkeeping department, to look for some figures I needed. I remained there about ten minutes. Suddenly one of the clerks, sitting near a window, called out excitedly, "My God! Look at that!" We all rushed to the windows. In front of the building stood one of the grim windowless N.K.V.D. trucks which people called Black Ravens. The engineers and technicians who had been assembled in Sukhin's office were now filing out of the door. One after the other they were being hustled into the wagon by Chekists with drawn revolvers.

As we watched we were at this point startled by a woman's hysterical shriek—then there was silence again. The wife of one of the arrested men, also working in our plant, had gone unsuspectingly to a window, just in time to see her husband thrown into the Black Raven. She had shrieked and fainted away.

When all the engineers were packed in, the truck was locked with a loud bang and drove off. Gershgorn and his colleagues piled into an elegant touring car, which followed the truck. Dozens of people were at the office windows, gazing in a sort of fascination at the tracks in the snow left by the motor vehicles.

Among the workers in my plant was a German Jew, a Communist who had sought refuge in Russia after Hitler came to power, a small man with a lean, sallow face. His name was Zelman. For some reason his Party card had been taken away from him by the Moscow office of the Communist International—foreign Communists were rarely trusted in the home land of Communism; their fidelity to Stalin was always in doubt. He was quiet and self-effacing, as if permanently frightened, this Zelman. He had married a Soviet girl and seemed content with his lot in Nikopol. An exceptionally able foreman, I relied on him a good deal to teach new workers.

One day Zelman was called out by the N.K.V.D. When he returned, several hours later, he was deathly pale and trembling. His habitual timidity was turned into abject terror. In his broken Russian he told me that he had been ordered to leave the country immediately—back to Germany!

"Help me, Comrade Kravchenko. To Germany! Do you realize what it means? I'm not only a Jew but a Communist, not only a Communist but a Jew. Let them send me to Siberia or prison, but not to Germany, not to Germany!"

After that day Zelman did not return to work. I made discreet inquiries. No one knew anything for sure, except that the refugee and his wife had been sent out of Nikopol.

My memory staggers under its burden as I recall those last months of 1936, before we had become inured to the cyclone of repressions. These are only a few episodes drawn at random from the chaos: bits of wreckage in a world that had lost its equilibrium and seemed to be dissolving as we looked on in stark horror.

For some reason the memory of the engineer Stetsevich is sharp on my mind. And I can't think of him without recalling the frail, sweet old woman who was his mother. They were of Polish extraction, as was Stetsevich's pretty wife. Being a non-Party specialist, further handicapped by the fact of his Polish extraction, this engineer avoided politics, worked well and hard, and mixed little with his colleagues.

I became aware that Stetsevich was in trouble when one of Gershgorn's men arrived to interrogate me about his work. In all honesty I could report only favorable facts—another black mark against my record in the N.K.V.D. archives; my refusal to "cooperate" in the campaign against "saboteurs" was to be, at bottom, the main count against me. Soon thereafter the Pole was arrested; his wife and mother were evicted from their apartment.

One evening I was driving to Nikopol in my car. Ahead of us on the road, about three kilometers from town, I noticed a bowed old woman, trudging slowly, a bundle in her hand. As we came abreast I realized that it was Stetsevich's mother. I stopped the car and asked her to step in. I knew how dangerous it was to show kindness to an outlaw, the mother of a "liquidated" man who, moreover, was accused of espionage for Poland, but at the moment I didn't care. I would have picked her up if it had meant certain death.

"Thank you, thank you, Victor Andreyevich," she said. "May God grant that your own mother may not have to suffer as I'm suffering; that you won't have to endure what my poor boy is enduring. I'm going to the N.K.V.D. I'll stand there and wait. Maybe they'll let me send him this parcel. The other women say he'll be in the contingent being shipped to Dniepropetrovsk today."

When we reached the city, she insisted on getting out, to avoid involving me in trouble. My chauffeur turned around.

"Comrade Director," he said, "I may be a son of a bitch who must report everything he sees and hears. Believe me or not, but I swear by my own mother that I will not report this time. My own mother is just a plain woman, not a fine lady like this one. But I love her and, anyhow, thank you, Victor Andreyevich, as one Russian to another."

In my years of ordeal this incident was never brought up, though many less serious "crimes" were thrown up to me. The chauffeur had kept his word.

2

The atmosphere at the Nikopol *combinat* became more oppressive with every day. Kozlov, the Party Secretary, was "transferred" to the city of Krivoi Rog and soon we heard that he was under arrest. One administrative official after another failed to show up for work and their alleged "illness" proved permanent.

The rank-and-file workers at first took the view that these strange doings were no business of theirs. But now men and women close to them, comrades in their shops, workers like themselves, began to disappear. That was a different matter. The alarm became so pervasive that it cut deeply into production totals. The morale of the plant was badly shattered.

When a special session of Nikopol activists was called, we went there with sinking hearts. At the door our credentials were carefully examined, though we knew one another intimately. The old sense of fellowship at such gatherings was no more. A few months earlier there would have been loud greetings. "Hello, Comrade Kravchenko!" "Hey there, you old son of a gun!" There would have been a comradely exchange of gossip, anecdotes, shop talk, Party politics. Now there was only a fidgety solemnity. We moved apart, as if afraid of some dread contagion. *Save yourself, save yourself! Avoid your neighbors!* One could almost hear the unspoken words.

Comrade Brodsky, Secretary of the City Committee, usually so decisive and energetic, now looked as if he had not slept for a long time. His eyes were puffy and his hands shook. His voice sounded hollow, as if he were talking through a megaphone. Few of us suspected that this was his last public appearance; that the powerful, ebullient Brodsky would soon be in some N.K.V.D. cellar along with most of the others now with him on the rostrum of authority.

We had been called together, Brodsky announced, to hear a confidential letter from the Central Committee in Moscow. He read it, slowly, passionately, anxious to attest his full approval, his abject approval. This was a few days before the sentencing and execution of Zinoviev, Kamenev and the rest. The Moscow communication was apparently intended to prepare the Party for the shock and to put fear into any skeptical heart.

Now that it "has been proven," the letter said, that the Trotskyist-Zinovievist monsters had united in their struggle against the Soviet power with foreign spies, provocateurs, kulaks, diversionists, Whites, wreckers, capitalist agents, all Party men must understand the need for extreme vigilance. . . . The proof of a true Bolshevik, it said, will henceforth be his ability to recognize and mercilessly to expose the enemies of the people hiding behind Party cards. . . . There is no room for "rotten liberalism" and "bourgeois sentimentality."

The import of the message was sufficiently clear. A shudder went through the audience. Just as in the past we looked for "enemies" in the general population, we must now look for them especially in our own ranks! Merit hereafter would be gauged by the number of your denunciations of close comrades.

The weaklings, the squeamish ones, who put private friendship above the interests of the Party would suffer the consequences of their "double-dealing."

Brodsky spoke at great length about the importance of the confidential orders. As if his very life depended on the number and extravagance of his adjectives, he eulogized Stalin the Genius, the Sun of our Socialist

Fatherland, the Wise and Infallible Leader. I dug my nails into the palms of my hands until I drew blood.

Others asked for the floor to abuse themselves and the Nikopol Party for "lack of vigilance," for "complacency in the face of danger." There was a stampede of comrades anxious to declare themselves, to debase themselves, to save themselves. In the midst of the muddy flow of obscene oratory, there was a commotion at the door. We all turned around.

Comrade Hatayevich, Secretary of the Regional Committee, member of the All-Union Central Committee, had arrived. He was marching up the aisle to the platform, surrounded by Chekist guards. This was a new touch, perhaps the most terrifying of all: guards and revolvers at a gathering of active Communists! Protecting the leaders against the nation's "best of the best"!

Hatayevich looked weary. His face was pasty and deeply lined and his voice seemed to come from somewhere far away. His speech followed the main lines of the Moscow letter. But he could not conceal his misery. Listening to him, I recalled the scene in the wheat fields during the collectivization drive, when this same Hatayevich had thanked me for fulfilling the plan ahead of schedule—and urged me to understand the need for the "strong" policies; our meetings in the Regional Committee. He had then been so robust, so self-assured. . . .

From this time forward it became a matter of "honor" to denounce and expose "disguised enemies" in the Party. You hesitated to talk to your closest comrades. You disassociated yourself from friends and relatives and colleagues. What if they were infected, germ-bearers of the political epidemic sweeping the land? You forgot that once upon a time there had been such things as integrity, fidelity, friendship.

The fall of any leader or official meant that all his appointees and cronies would be purged. After the arrest of Brodsky, the Black Ravens and the closed N.K.V.D. motorcars picked up his assistants, his friends, the men and women whom he had put into jobs anywhere in Nikopol. The Commandant of the Nikopol Garrison went into the hunters' bag, then the local Prosecutor and all his legal staff; finally the chairman of the Nikopol Soviet himself. The local bank, the newspaper, all commercial institutions were "cleaned." Everywhere new people assumed authority, and often within a week or a month these were, in turn, picked off.

In whispers people told of the arrest of the chairman of the Soviet, the highest civil official in the city. He was a former miner, with a proud civil war record. He was awakened in the middle of the night. His wife and children wept so loud they woke the neighbors.

"I am the representative of the Soviet power in Nikopol," the chairman shouted at the uniformed men. "You have no right to arrest me! Show me your warrant!"

"Step along, you dirty dog! We'll show you who has what rights," the arresting officer growled and shoved him out of the door.

After the chairman's liquidation, most of the high officials of the city government were rounded up, among them the manager of the Communal

Administration, the chief of the Fire Brigade, the head of the Savings Institution, even the chief of Sanitation; some were taken at their homes during the night, others openly in their offices.

A new man, a stranger to our factory, came to take Kozlov's post. His name was Los. He was a dull-witted, fanatic fellow, as strong and raw as home-brewed vodka. The last drops of comradely feeling evaporated in the heat of Los's zealous hunt for culprits. Meeting on the grounds or in corridors, we technical and Party officials looked at one another in surprise. "What! Are you still among the living?" our looks said.

The headquarters of the N.K.V.D. on one of the main streets blazed with lights all night, every night now. That organization was working twenty-four hours a day. Its business was booming. Dorogan, Gershgorn and their associates were in fine fettle; tired but elated—generals in a battle that was going brilliantly. The arrested people were not held long. Nikopol was, after all, only a minor branch office of the business. They were packed off to Dniepropetrovsk, from Dniepropetrovsk to Kharkov, to other centers, to make room for more and still more.

And Nikopol was only one tiny segment in the widening swath being cut by the super-purge. Instructions from our trust, Trubostal, and from the Commissariat in Moscow, were increasingly signed with unfamiliar names, so many of the old officials had been cut down. Hatayevich and a bevy of his colleagues in the Regional Committee were arrested; Hatayevich was important enough to rate a half column of abuse in our local press. Everywhere it was the same story. One could not keep up with the flood of sensations, tragedies, sinister surprises. The most imaginative rumors fell far short of the reality.

The outside world watched the several blood-purge trials staged in the former Hall of Nobles in Moscow. It failed to understand, it does not understand to this day, that the Moscow trials were just a formal facade, a show window, behind which the real horrors were being piled mountain high. The public trials involved a few dozen carefully selected and rehearsed victims. The purge involved hundreds of thousands, ultimately around ten millions who were sorted and disposed of rapidly: these to prison, these into exile, these for the forced labor battalions, these to die.

Crowds of women and children swarmed around the N.K.V.D. building in Nikopol at all hours despite the bitter cold. The N.K.V.D. men would disperse them, but soon they were back again, weeping, screaming, calling the names of fathers, husbands, brothers. Many of these unfortunates were local inhabitants but a lot of others had come from nearby villages, where the *pogrom* was striking down village Soviet chairmen, Party secretaries, Comsomol leaders, presidents of collective farms. This scene outside the N.K.V.D. I shall never be able to expunge from my memory. A great theatrical genius, hoping to convey mass despair, macabre and boundless sorrow, could not have invented anything more terrifying.

And in the midst of the storm, through the howling of the stricken and the grimacing of the suffering, press and radio announced the formal adoption of "the world's most democratic Constitution" in November, 1936.

The hysteria reached a point where jittery Party men went to bed in their clothes, "just in case." Like nearly everyone else, I had a small suitcase packed with the things a man could use in prison: extra underwear, socks, handkerchiefs, a blanket.

"Are you going somewhere?" Pasha inquired innocently when she found the suitcase under my bed.

"Who knows, Pasha, who knows?" I sighed.

Comrade Brachko, having visited Dniepropetrovsk on business, returned laden with dreadful news. In my native city the havoc was, if anything, worse than in Nikopol. At my old factory, he was told, the arrests already exceeded five hundred—and the Black Ravens were still hungry. Many of my Institute classmates—Beretzkoi, Katz, Richter; the list seemed endless—had been snatched from their engineering posts. Every day cattle-cars locked and sealed from the outside hauled their human freight out of Dniepropetrovsk. Four years ago the tragic freight had consisted of peasants; now the quality was better: Communists, government leaders, Army men, technicians, non-Party officials. "What can Stalin and the Politburo have in mind? The whole thing seems unrelieved madness," Brachko said, then regretted having said it, as I could see from his alarmed look.

What can Stalin and the Politburo have in mind? It was precisely the question hammering at my brain. I did a foolish and futile thing. Since I knew one member of the Politburo personally, I decided to ask him what was the meaning of it all. Long into the night, several nights running, I labored over a letter to Commissar Ordzhonikidze.

As calmly as possible—as if I were composing a technical report—I recounted what was happening in Nikopol, Dniepropetrovsk, Krivoi Rog and other places in our province. I named names. I defended the loyalty of the people who had been snatched from their jobs. If such things continued, I warned, there would soon be no one left competent to run industry in our Region. Already production was disorganized, no one dared initiate work, no one dared make decisions.

I sent the letter through private channels and know definitely that it was put into the hands of the Commissar. But I never received a reply. When my own purge began, I was never questioned about this letter and thus I knew, gratefully, that Ordzhonikidze had not turned it over to the police. Any paragraph in my screed would have been enough to guarantee my speedy execution.

3

My turn came in November, 1936.

It came as suddenly as did Limansky's, but I had the psychological advantage of having expected the blow and of having sat through many rehearsals with other comrades in the leading roles. The chief thing, I told myself, was not to lose control of my senses. Through interminable sleepless nights I had tried to imagine what could be charged against me. What would be my "crimes"? Would it be something I had said or done a year ago, five years ago? Would it have reference to the work in my plant?

Other than the doubts in my mind and the heavy sorrow in my heart I was conscious of no crimes against the Soviet state. When the accusations against me were at last unveiled, they had no resemblance to my advance guesses.

We were having a Party meeting in the playhouse of the factory club. It was a brutal, sleety night. The floor was muddy and slippery with the drippings of our boots. Blue clouds of cigaret smoke hung in the air. The hall, the night, the filth will remain with me forever. They became part of a recurrent nightmare. They set the mood for what followed, even as a Wagnerian overture sets the mood for the drama that follows.

Several members had been brought up on charges. Local Communist sections now demonstrated their "initiative" and "Bolshevik vigilance" by acting against their members even before the police got around to it. They were reconnaissance patrols for the N.K.V.D. In three cases the meeting had recommended expulsion. Now the meeting seemed nearly ended.

But suddenly Los rose to speak. I was thinking of something far removed from this ugly gathering when the purport of his words struck me and went through me like an electric shock. *This was the moment!*

"Comrades," Los began, "I suggest that we discuss the case of the director of the pipe-rolling sub-plant, the Communist member Victor Andreyevich Kravchenko. We have reports containing very serious accusations on the past and present activities of this comrade."

"Let the accusers speak up!" someone in the back of the auditorium shouted.

"Quite right," Los said. "Engineer Gregory Makarov may now have the floor."

As Makarov walked to the platform, the comrade sitting at my right got up and walked away, muttering something about "going for a smoke." The man at my left also moved away. I had been turned into a leper. I was surrounded by emptiness.

I knew Makarov from the Institute days. He was one of those incompetent, helpless people who survive by exploiting one's sympathy. I had gotten him his job at Nikopol, had found him an apartment, and had always taken it for granted, naively, that he was grateful to me.

"I've known Kravchenko for many years," he was saying now. "He was a member of the Bureau of the Party Committee at the Metallurgical Institute. Most of his colleagues on that Committee have been arrested; in particular Beretzkoi, who was his friend, also Katz. I wonder whether this is accidental, comrades! This Kravchenko has many friends and 'connections' in Moscow and came to the Institute on the recommendation of Comrade Ordzhonikidze himself. Let me say in passing that some of those Moscow 'connections' of his have been exposed as enemies of the people.

"But that's all by the way, comrades. What I want to say is that in all these years as a Party member Kravchenko has lied to the Party. He has concealed from the Party a most important fact—*the political past of his father!* Why hasn't he admitted to the Party that his father had been an active Menshevik before the revolution and that he has agitated the non-Party workers against the policies of our Beloved Leader ever since?"

"Talk about Kravchenko, not about his father!" someone interjected.

"The apple doesn't roll far from the apple tree," Comrade Los shouted back. "Go ahead, Comrade Makarov."

"That's right," Makarov proceeded, "the apple doesn't roll far from the tree. Kravchenko is no better than his father. He has surrounded himself with 'alien elements.' Is it accidental, do you think, that he has gathered so many non-Party people in his department? Who are his assistants? Who are his foremen? Who is the arrested Menshevik Dubinsky? Who is the arrested German fascist, Zelman? I could mention many others. All non-Party people or actual enemies whose wrecking has been exposed by the N.K.V.D."

In the midst of my distress I thought: *So that's what's biting him; the fact that I did not raise him to full assistant!*

"Comrades, Zelman is a Jew and a German Communist. How can you call him a fascist?" It was a worker interrupting the speaker.

"Very well, you say he is a Jew and a Communist," Makarov argued. "Hasn't Hitler sent thousands of diversionists and spies over here? What better disguise than a Jew and a Communist? What better protection for such filth than under the wing of a Kravchenko with his important connections?"

"Comrade Los," Director Brachko now spoke up, "I suggest the speaker stick to facts and stop messing around in dirt and nonsense."

"I'll give you facts, Comrade Brachko, lots of them. Think back to the time when the new norms were voted in line with our glorious Stakhanovite movement. Wasn't it clear to all of us that Kravchenko opposed the change? Only one worker was so ungrateful as to attack the norms, a man named Kiryushkin. What did Kravchenko do, this big-hearted humanitarian? Why, he rewarded Kiryushkin with a better job! Yes, I accuse him of protecting all the anti-Soviet elements in our midst, and I accuse him, above all, of deluding our glorious Party by hiding his father's Menshevism."

As he left the platform there were cries of "Right! Well done!" and also cries of "Lies! All lies! Absurd!"

"Member of the Party engineer Shaikevich has the floor," Los announced.

Shaikevich was an undersized man, with a shriveled little monkey face and tiny cruel eyes.

"Comrades, I also sent in a denunciation of Comrade Kravchenko," he said in a falsetto voice like drawn wire. "I have watched him from

close up for a long time. It's true that the newspapers and radio have
praised him to the skies. How many times his picture has appeared in
the papers! But what if all these services to the country were just a
smokescreen, behind which such an individual carried on his dastardly
work?"

"Facts, not rhetoric!" Brachko called out.

"Kravchenko is a doubter!" The orator, angered by the interruption,
struck an even shriller note in his falsetto. "At the Institute he criticized
collectivization. Everyone knows that much. And the same in the factory—
always a long face, nothing to his grand taste! Even his mother came
snooping around the grounds and lodging complaints. Why has he such a
high position at all? Because he has friends in Moscow and in Kharkov!
Not ability but connections!"

"That's a lie, comrades!" Brachko again called out. "Kravchenko was
appointed by Comrade Ivanchenko after consultation with me. He's one
of the best engineers in Trubostal and the Commissar himself has often
entrusted him with important special projects."

"But you can't deny, Comrade Brachko, that he's the son of an anti-
Soviet father and has concealed this from us!" the falsetto rang out in
triumph. "He deprived all of Stalin's loyal, devoted Communists in his
sub-plant of promotion. . . ."

And now I recalled. I had been sorry for the frustrated, unhappy little
Shaikevich, and had tried to cover up his blunders. But in the end, after
discussing the problem with Brachko, I had transferred him to a department where less demand would be made on his limited knowledge.

After Shaikevich, Yudavin rose to round out the accusations. His
was the authentic voice of the N.K.V.D. Knowing this Yudavin as a
police agent, I had avoided him. Now he was ready to pay me back with
interest.

"Comrades," he said, "I not only support the conclusions of the other
speakers but I want to come to the most serious point. Kravchenko is a
saboteur!"

The dreaded word exploded like a cannon. The audience froze into
silence. Until then I had retained my composure. Now I broke out in a
sweat. My heart beat so loud and fast I felt it was being heard above
Yudavin's words. What in the world could he be referring to? What were
this hidden Chekist and his master, Gershgorn, cooking up for me?

"Yes, a saboteur! This Kravchenko has deliberately frozen a million
rubles worth of Soviet currency and any amount of foreign *valuta*. How
did he do it? A simple device, much too simple! He has ordered all sorts
of expensive instruments and piled them up in his sub-plant. His department is jammed up with costly machine parts, none of which is ever
used. Some of it has never even been unpacked! I charge that this is
all deliberate and calculated to do harm to the government and the
country!"

Now that the charge was out I felt relieved. The accusation was too
far-fetched, I felt, and therefore might prove self-defeating. Because Los,
like everyone else, was impatient to have the session over and go home,

I was spared more attacks. He called on me to comment. Summoning all my reserves of will power, I mounted the rostrum.

"Comrades, members of the Party," I said, "I want to talk to you frankly, whatever the consequences. I have been in the Party for eight years. My record speaks for itself. I have my human failings, I've made mistakes. Maybe I've promoted men who did not deserve it, or ousted others who did not deserve it. A man in a post of authority must make decisions, and since he is only a man, some of these decisions are bound to be wrong. You all know that Makarov and Shaikevich have personal grudges. What's the point of going into that? It's perfectly obvious to anyone acquainted with this plant.

"I insist I am guilty of nothing! What's more, I'm afraid of nothing! I beg of you only one thing. Give me time to bring the proofs that these charges are malicious inventions. Appoint a commission to look into the charges. Then, if I do not convince the commission, I shall be ready to accept the consequences.

"The whole tempest has been aroused because, so it is said, my father is a Menshevik. Let me make it perfectly clear. I do not renounce my father. I love him and admire him. It was he who implanted in me those proletarian ideals which eventually took me into the Comsomol organization, then into the Party. He is non-Party, but his services to the working class are well known. He is highly esteemed by the workers who know him best, the workers of Dniepropetrovsk.

"The simple fact is that he was never in his life a Menshevik or a member of any other Party. He was merely a good revolutionary who fought the Tsar and the capitalists but did not wear any political label. He used a gun behind the barricades in 1905. He worked with Mensheviks—but also with Bolsheviks—and shared prison cells with every variety of revolutionary fighter. All this I can prove, if you give me the necessary time.

"As for the sabotage talk, it's just too silly. True, I have a great deal of instrument inventory in my sub-plant. But every kopek of it is known to the Commissariat. I have reported it regularly and placed it at the disposal of the trust, which could have drawn on the supply any time. In every case the material was ordered to meet an actual need.

"How does it happen that I have so many expensive instruments and parts, some of them little used? The answer is that I was often entrusted with special jobs, calling for special tools. There was the rush order for pipe for the Baku oil fields, you'll all remember, for example. Then it happened that the quantities at first ordered were curtailed. Sometimes an assignment for which we prepared ourselves was cancelled altogether because of changes in the plans. In this way expensive instruments piled up. We have kept them because they might be needed any time, without warning. But all of this was above board, not underhand as my accusers insist. It all grew out of decisions in Moscow, not in my own head.

"To interpret that as sabotage is too ludicrous, comrades. I can prove by the documents how and when and especially why every item in the inventory was obtained. Everything else that's been said is trivial. I don't want to tax your patience with a detailed answer. I ask you to allow me to prove my innocence, here in this hall—*not somewhere else*. But whatever happens, remember that I am guilty of nothing."

There was a scattering of restrained, inhibited applause as I returned to my seat. There were also cries of "Expel him! Menshevik! Wrecker! Speculating on his 'connections'!"

A workman in his sixties, a Comrade Silinin with whom I was acquainted only casually, rose and was recognized.

"As long as Comrade Kravchenko is still head of the sub-plant, it would be wrong to interrupt his work. There seems to be lots of doubt in this case, so why should we act in haste or in panic? There will be time enough, comrades, for expulsion and administrative measures. Kravchenko's own suggestion is a good one. I propose that we ask the City Committee to designate a commission to investigate and that the comrade put his proofs before the commission."

The proposal was accepted, with Yudavin, Shaikevich and Makarov and some others voting against it. Only Brachko and old Silinin dared approach me as we left the playhouse. From this time until the end of my ordeal, more than eighteen months later, I was an "untouchable," as isolated as any case of Black Plague.

CHAPTER XV

MY ORDEAL BEGINS

I OPENED THE Nikopol newspaper next morning to find myself infamous. As if anxious to live down frequent praise of me in the same columns in the past, the local press now cut me to shreds. The choicest libels of the previous night were filled out with dark hints and the stock phrases of Soviet derogation. "According to trustworthy evidence," one account said, "this character Kravchenko has succeeded through all the years in hiding that his father was a big landowner-exploiter." Another said that I was a White and had long served happily as the "lackey" of enemies of the people; that I had patronized and protected elements hostile to the Party; that I was engaged in "wrecking" activities.

In the recklessness of the misinformation, in the exuberance of the accusations, I sensed the inspiration of outside quarters.

Brodsky's successor in the City Committee was a man named Filline. I was astonished to receive a phone call from him while I was having a hurried breakfast.

"We have a full report of yesterday's meeting and have read the morning papers," he said. "Please don't worry, Comrade Kravchenko. Keep on working and see to it that production schedules are maintained. For the time being, no one will touch you."

I thanked him, greatly relieved. For a while, at least, I was safe. Filline would not have dared to reassure me unless he, and others around him, thought the "case" against me flimsy.

When I reached the plant I found the investigating commission, appointed by Filline, already at work. It included Los, which was hardly encouraging, but also Brachko, which propped up my courage; it also included chief engineer Vishnev. They were all in the supply room, examining the "hoarded" instruments.

"Good morning," Los greeted me icily. He had adopted the manner of a prosecuting attorney. "Let's get down to business. Are you the one who orders instruments here?"

"Yes."

"Then you don't deny ordering all this hoarded material?"

"Of course not."

"And who authorized it at the plant here? Who countersigned the papers?"

"Comrade Vishnev, as chief engineer."

Vishnev was visibly startled.

"Oh, no, I don't think I remember doing that," he said nervously. "Or if I did, it must have been on orders from the center."

"Who made out the preliminary list of instruments to be ordered?"

"The mechanic Kiznamenko, with the authorization of Comrade Vishnev."

Again Vishnev, now more worried than I, put in a flurried denial, insisting he did not remember this.

"Well," Brachko said, "the papers ought to give us the facts."

"I'll try to find them," I promised, "but I can only hope that the copies are on file or that I can get access to originals in Kharkov and Moscow."

The search for those documents would become my main preoccupation for long weeks. Those pieces of paper turned into ghosts, now taunting me, always eluding me. If ever I grasped them and held them fast, I could show that the instruments—particularly a large consignment from America which was never used—had been considered necessary to fulfill specific orders from Moscow; that the quantities were carefully calculated in connection with the quantity of pipe to be manufactured and processed.

I was never to know whether the office copies had been honestly lost or maliciously destroyed. With the permission of both Brachko and Filline I set out the same day for Kharkov, and if necessary Moscow, to search for proofs that the purchase of various costly instruments was not a devilish piece of sabotage.

A grotesque accusation and a grotesque mission—but seen in the distorted mirrors of that feverish day absurdities had a logic all their own. If Trotsky, while organizing the Red Army, had been a "German spy"; if the giants who made the revolution with Lenin had in reality been "wild dogs" in the pay of foreign reaction, why couldn't Kravchenko, down in Nikopol, try to topple over the Soviet regime by buying a million rubles' worth of unnecessary instruments for pipe-making? Only an enemy of the people would make light of such a supposition!

Filline's friendliness was the one cheering fact in my predicament. I told him, before leaving, that I would also stop in Dniepropetrovsk to line up proofs that my father had never belonged to the Mensheviks.

This time I took my family unreservedly into my confidence. The psychological tension between my father and myself seemed broken at last. The gap was in some ways closed. At the heart of my distress thenceforth was the consolation that a long estrangement had been more or less ended. Suddenly I felt as close to my parents as if I were a little boy again. I was no longer a "firm Bolshevik."

My news from Nikopol was matched by events in my native city. The heads of three families, in our own neighborhood, had been cut off by the purge madness during a single night. All of them were non-Party men. They were people we had known for a great many years, people with whom my father and brothers and I had worked at various times.

The first was Zarvin, a factory foreman. One of his sons was a surgeon, another a metallurgical engineer. Neither they nor their mother had any idea why the old man was being arrested. "Hurry up, you louse!" the N.K.V.D. man shouted as he hustled Zarvin, only half dressed and sleep-groggy, into the Black Raven. Those words constituted the only warrant.

the only indictment, the only explanation Zarvin's family would ever know.

The second was a Pole, Kashelski, a sociable and energetic man popular with his neighbors. His son was a Comsomol. I ran into him during this visit.

"But Comrade Kravchenko," he said in pathetic bewilderment, "how could my father be a 'Polish spy'? He's such a simple, open-hearted man. It's just crazy. He and I are very close friends. If anything had been suspicious, how could I have failed to notice?"

The third, and the most tragic, in the one-night haul among our immediate neighbors was Blinov. He had been in my shop when I worked in the Petrovsky-Lenin plant; a tall, good-looking and very able man, respected by his fellow-workers. He and Mrs. Blinov, being childless, had adopted a little famine orphan and were devoting their lives to her.

When the Chekists dragged him off that night, his wife's cries awoke the neighbors. Barefoot, in her nightgown, she ran screaming after the sinister truck through the snow until it was out of sight. Then she returned to her room and hanged herself. The adopted daughter, once orphaned by a man-made famine, was orphaned again by a man-made cyclone.

Living in the midst of such tragedies, multiplied a hundredfold night after night, my family naturally took a gloomy view of my own plight. Father was no longer working, having been retired on a pension to which those who had worked for a certain number of years were entitled. But he remained in friendly contact with his shop-mates and knew the extent of the terror among administrative and technical personnel in his factory. He knew that merely to be accused was, in ninety-nine cases out of a hundred, in itself a proof of guilt. Yet we clung desperately to the hope that by some miracle I would be the hundredth, the exception.

My sleep was fitful and lurid with harrowing dreams. As I shook off a nightmare of pain, I noticed a light in my mother's room and went over, on tiptoe, to see if anything was wrong. I saw mother on her knees before the icon, praying, her eyes closed, her head tilted back. Though her cheeks were tear-streaked, her face was tranquil, suffused with an inner glow. I heard her murmur my name. I tiptoed back to bed and slept soundly, peacefully, for the first time in months.

In the morning I had a long talk with my father. He was boiling over with fury.

"If I have done anything wrong, why don't they arrest me?" he kept repeating. "Why must they take it out on my son? Is a son responsible for his father? The stupidity and the bestiality of it! When I was on the barricades and the police arrested me, I alone suffered. It didn't occur to the Tsar's police to bother my father or my brother or my family. But now—the indecency of it!—fathers and sons and wives are held responsible for each other. The Tsarist Okhrana, believe me, was a philanthropic institution compared to the N.K.V.D.!"

"Being angry won't help any, father. What we must do is round up the evidence that you were not a Menshevik."

"As if being one were a crime," he said. "Some of the most heroic revolutionists belonged to the Mensheviks."

That day father visited several well-known local Communists, men of his own generation, who remembered his activities. Each of them wrote a declaration, officially certified, summing up what he knew about the elder Kravchenko and attesting that he had not been a member of any particular party. Then I went with him to call on the widow of Dr. Karavayev.

She was a tall, thin, gray-haired and intelligent old woman. Her husband had been a member of the Duma and the author of the agrarian reform bill. He had been secretly killed by Tsarist agents in his home. She was living on a Soviet pension and counted many of the key Bolsheviks among her friends. She had known father for over thirty years and greeted him with real joy. All revolutionists who had been part of her revered husband's circle seemed to her haloed with light, men molded from some divine clay.

"How wonderful to see you again!" she exclaimed, embracing him and kissing him on both cheeks. "How wonderful! So this is your Vityenka—a grown man and an engineer!"

For all her friendships in high places, she belonged to a world in eclipse. She seemed insulated from reality. At first she simply would not believe that we needed "proof" that father had not been a Menshevik.

"Utterly ridiculous!" she said. "To be a Menshevik in those days called for the stuff of heroism. It meant risking your life every day. I guess I'm getting too old to understand what's happening to people's minds these days. I must talk to Krupskaya about it next time I'm in Moscow!"

But she sat down and wrote a long letter, addressed to the Nikopol City Committee, recalling my father's revolutionary prowess and attesting that he had always been a "free lance," refusing the harness of party discipline.

Meanwhile my mother was spending many hours at the archives section of the Party in Dniepropetrovsk. She implored officials to find Tsarist police records of her husband's arrests and imprisonments. These would indicate, of course, that he was not connected with any specific group. The officials feared to make the search without a request from the Party. I had to telephone Filline, who in turn called the Dniepropetrovsk Party, before they consented to look for the vital records.

"So the Tsar's gendarmes will help rescue my son from the gendarmes of 'socialism,' " father smiled wryly. There was, indeed, a gloomy humor in the thought.

The several days in my home town deepened that sense of horror—of living in a fantastic and tortured dream world—which would not leave me for years. I visited my old factory, only to find that many of my friends had disappeared. From the way in which people evaded direct answers to my inquiries I had no doubt what had happened to them.

The director of the plant, Stephan Birman, was not arrested. When the Chekists came for him they found him in a bathtubful of blood—he had slit his veins to cheat the purge. Birman, a Hungarian, had been a Minister in the short-lived Bela Kun Communist regime in his home land. Good-looking, intelligent and devoted, he had held a series of important government and industry posts in his adopted fatherland: a brilliant career that led him, leap by leap, to suicide.

Before he cut his wrists, Birman wrote a letter to the Central Committee in which he scathingly denounced the barbarities of Stalin. Thousands, tens of thousands, such letters were written. A few were being circulated secretly and with trembling fingers, as if they were explosive charges about to go off, but not one reached the general population.

Among those "over there," I learned, was Josef Manayenkov. A prominent member of the Ukrainian Soviet, he was loved by the workers for his efforts to improve their living conditions. His wife was an active Communist in her own right. Only a few months earlier Dniepropetrovsk had resounded with the glory of the honor which had come to her: she had been photographed in the Kremlin right at Stalin's side! She, too, was under arrest. So was chief engineer Zhdanov, though he had just been decorated for his services to the Five Year Plans.

The story was the same in every other factory in town. Felenkovsky, Kinzhalov, Sochan, Pustovoitzev—hundreds of names which meant nothing to others. But to me, who had worked with them, studied with them, sat at Party meetings with them, their "liquidation" widened and deepened the void. Not one of the leaders of economic, technical and political life in my native Dniepropetrovsk whom I happened to know personally remained untouched. Many of them were, of course, non-Party people.

Mother saw me off at the station when I left for Kharkov. I hoped she would give way to tears, for I knew what choking them down was doing to her.

"Please, Vitya," she told me on the station platform, "control yourself. Yield where you can yield. After all, they are people, aren't they? They must understand. . . ."

At Trubostal headquarters in Kharkov, confusion and panic were palpable things. Everyone seemed numb with terror. No man knew for sure whether or not this was his last day in the office, his last day of freedom. Various officials, who had watched my work for years, tried earnestly to help, but could find no such documents as I needed. They put in long-distance calls to other offices without effect. One of them phoned Moscow, only to be told that the one man who might help, Commissar Ordzhonikidze himself, was too ill to be approached. In despair, I called Brachko at Nikopol.

"Piotr Petrovich, I haven't found a thing," I reported. "The normal confusion has been worse confounded by the purge. Shall I go on and try my luck in Moscow?"

"No, no! Return immediately," he replied.

"But why? What's happened?"

"I can't discuss it over the phone. Come back as quickly as you can. It's important."

I was back in my plant the following morning.

2

Comrade Brachko's alarm was justified. The zealots and self-seekers and my personal enemies had exploited my absence.

To begin with, the N.K.V.D. had "cleaned" my personnel, arresting Dubinsky, Shpachinsky, engineer Bako, more than a dozen others. The workers seemed stunned. In addition, the secretary of my own Party nucleus, a certain Yasenev, acting of course under higher authority, had put pressure on various workers to "denounce" me. His enterprise went under the neat euphemism of "gathering material."

Several men, old hands in the factory, came to me separately and confessed in shame and sorrow that they had signed statements against me, statements woven of lies and guesses. They had done so, in every case, under threats of "dire consequences." I learned, moreover, that the indefatigable Los had sent emissaries to Dniepropetrovsk to collect "compromising material" about myself and my father. He aimed, in particular, to show that I had been on intimate footing with Katz, Beretzkoi, Perlin, Richter, Borisov and other former Institute students now in the hands of the N.K.V.D. and therefore, by definition, enemies of the people.

Los was pushing his persecution with frantic speed. He must dispose of the Kravchenko affair without any more loss of time. In fact, my disgrace would serve as the peg on which to hang accusations against a series of people in one way or another associated with me. Los and his friends wished to "finish me off" without annoying delays. It was for them a matter of honor as well as political expediency. In a few days they called a special closed meeting of the factory Party Committee to resume consideration of my case. I felt like an animal cornered by baying dogs; the circle grew smaller, more confining; the barking came closer and closer.

The meeting was again held in the club playhouse. The fact that the officials were arrayed on the stage under red banners and portraits of the Party leaders, with the footlights blazing, heightened the illusion that a theatrical performance—a strange Soviet morality play—was about to begin. The atmosphere was chill. For all my resolutions to hold myself firm and dignified, I shuddered and could feel a trembling in all my limbs. People who only a few weeks ago were fawning on me now pretended not to notice me. I greeted no one, for fear of being rebuffed, and sat down in the rear, in solitary wretchedness.

Only two comrades dared to come over to me. They were Silinin and Gushchin, both plain workers and both older men. Apparently their age had protected them against excessive education in "Bolshevik firmness."

"Don't worry, Comrade Kravchenko," Gushchin said, gripping my hand. "Should they act against you here, the City Committee will rehabilitate you, or the Regional Committee, provided, of course. . . ." He hesitated.

"Provided what?" I asked, though I knew the answer.

"Provided you're not arrested first."

This time Los had taken precautions against interference with his fanatic determination to smoke out another "saboteur." Every actor had his lines and his cues. A refreshment buffet had been set up in the lobby and many of the prime actors had already drunk themselves into a belligerent mood. Their roles would be played with greater zest. I caught Brachko's eye. He smiled encouragingly and made a gesture which meant, plainly, "Keep a grip on yourself. There's still hope."

Los provided the overture. His speech was a masterpiece of innuendo and mob appeal. My guilt, he said, had been proven "in great part." That my father was in an "anti-Soviet mood" and an active Menshevik was "beyond doubt." The details of my sabotage would be determined "by other means" and "in other places." But wasn't it a remarkable coincidence that so many of my co-workers and friends, in my plant, in the Institute, in our trust, had been struck down by the naked sword of the revolution, the N.K.V.D.?

"We haven't as yet the detailed data to prove that Kravchenko was their accomplice," he declared. His tone implied that the fact itself was certain, the proof merely a matter of time. "We have received any number of statements, all of which boil down to the fact that Kravchenko is a cleverly masked enemy of the people who sacks Communists and surrounds himself with class enemies. Does anyone wish to speak?"

Many hands went up. This time Makarov, Shaikevich and Yudavin had their stories more carefully organized. Yasenev joined them. The trade-union representative in my sub-plant, Balabin, joined them—he had never forgiven my "sabotage" of his "political education" work and told in harrowing language how I had ripped placards from my walls to protect enemies of Stakhanovism. Their speeches were set off throughout by a Greek chorus of rehearsed voices in the audience: "That's right! Get rid of him! Clean him out!"

"Now does anybody wish to speak *for* Kravchenko?" Los asked. He did not have to add, "You do so at your own risk"; his intonation said it without words.

"I do," Gushchin said, standing up. All eyes were turned on him, in surprise, in anger, in admiration.

"I do," he said, "because the whole accusation against this young and able comrade is the product of somebody's overheated brain. Kravchenko is the son of a worker and an old revolutionary. Everything else about his father is lies and spun water. Besides, he's an adult and responsible for himself.

"But there's something more. I wish to tell you, comrades, that Yasenev called me to his office and demanded that I write a denunciation of Kravchenko. When I refused he threatened and swore. That's how much value you should put on the various denunciations!"

"It's a lie!" Yasenev roared.

"Lies! Such cheek!" Makarov and his clique echoed.

"No, it's the truth, comrades. You know I am too old and have been a Bolshevik too long to invent such a thing. I am a worker and I am

for the Party. But this persecution of one of our best and most honest
directors is a scandal."

Bedlam broke loose. Men and women shrieked their opinions. The
fumes of the buffet bottles had become articulate. From their fly-specked
pictures on the walls, Stalin, Molotov and Kalinin looked down on the
scene in consternation. The morality play had been upset by a perverse
spectator's intrusion on the stage!

When order was restored, Brachko asked for the floor. He defended
me against the sabotage charge. All the instruments ordered by my
section, he insisted, had been needed, though some remained unused because of changes in production plans which were no fault of mine.

"Let's have the facts! Where are the famous documents?" Los interrupted.

"I haven't the documents with me, that's true, but I believe we shall
find them. If Kravchenko was guilty, then I was guilty as his superior;
then Vishnev was guilty as chief engineer; then Trubostal in Kharkov
and the People's Commissariat in Moscow were guilty, being in charge
of our work.

"Comrades, I look at you and I'm ashamed. What is this, a Party
meeting or a mob thirsting for blood? Are we disciples of Lenin or a lot
of sadists? And who allowed the sale of drinks tonight, while a Party
meeting is on? I beg you, comrades, to come to your senses. This is not
an empty show. It's a question of the life and death of a comrade!"

At this point a booming voice exploded at the back of the auditorium.
It drowned out Brachko's impassioned plea and cut through the noises
in the hall. Everyone swung around to see who it was. In the doorway
stood Dorogan, chief of the Nikopol N.K.V.D. A huge, fleshy man with
gross and oversized features, with cold, expressionless eyes, he stood like a
caricature Colossus, his legs wide apart, balancing himself on the balls
of his feet. He stood there rocking gently, like a buoy in the breeze.
His left hand rested on his Mauser, his right held a cigaret to his lips.
Dorogan was smiling his smile without humor. Dorogan was contemptuous.

"Sentimentality, Comrade Brachko!" he said loudly. "A nice time you
pick for such drivel."

His eyes swept slowly through the audience. Brachko wound up his
speech hastily, a bit lamely. And Los began to hurry the show. Like most
others in the hall, he was assuming that Dorogan had come to arrest me
when this "farce" was over.

"Enough! Let's end the comedy and expel this enemy!" a voice—
Makarov's, I thought—cried out.

"No, comrades," Los declared, "Kravchenko is entitled to the last
word if he wishes. He has five minutes."

I walked to the stage. In my mind I had prepared for this moment
but I had not foreseen the possibility that I would have so little time.
In telescoping my arguments I unavoidably weakened them. I felt that
I was not making the best of this chance. As I talked I could not
keep my eyes from Dorogan, still rocking disdainfully in the doorway. I
knew that everyone of my listeners, everyone on the platform, was more

conscious of this fleshy symbol of the police-state than of the words I
was uttering.

"I'm not ashamed of my father, I'm proud of him," I concluded. "I
have no apologies for the so-called 'hoarded' instruments. They may prove
inefficiency—mine or other people's—but not sabotage. If I am guilty,
then the whole trust is guilty, the whole Commissariat is guilty. It is
they who decide what quantities must be produced. But let me say this
finally: It's not a question merely of Kravchenko. The crux of the
matter is that you are destroying innocent people. I declare that I am
not guilty. Give me just ten more days in which to gather more evidence."

I was still walking down the aisle, looking into the eyes of Dorogan,
when the vote was taken. His mere presence was a form of intimidation.
Only half a dozen voted against expulsion. Los disregarded them.

"By unanimous vote," he announced, "this meeting recommends to
the City Committee the expulsion of Victor Andreyevich Kravchenko."

"Well, are you going to appeal?" Dorogan asked as I reached him.

"Yes, certainly," I replied. "I shall telegraph Comrade Ordzhonikidze
and lodge protests in Kharkov and in Moscow, and tomorrow I shall
appeal to the City Committee."

"Kravchenko," he puffed his cigaret and blew out the smoke slowly
before finishing the sentence, "believe me, it would be a pity to bother
so many people. Yes, a pity. . . ."

I went out into the dark. It was a piercingly cold night, but I did not
even button my overcoat. I seemed to have lost the capacity for physical
sensation. I looked around, fully expecting to see an N.K.V.D. car awaiting me. A few others had rushed out to see my arrest. They seemed confused, even disappointed, that nothing happened. I walked towards my
home. Suddenly I observed two men standing near a lamppost. I could not
make out their faces. Perhaps I would be taken into custody after all!
I stopped in my tracks, in a vague astonishment.

"Victor Andreyevich, it's us, your friends," one of the men spoke up.
They were Gushchin and Silinin.

"Thank you. You *are* my friends to wait for me at such a moment."

They accompanied me part of the way, expressing their sympathy
and trying to calm me. At home I walked through the many rooms, as
if somewhere I should find consolation. I wrote a telegram to Ordzhonikidze, then tore it up. After all, I was only one of millions. In what way
was my plight different from theirs? What could I tell a member of
Stalin's Politburo that he did not already know? Then I searched again
through my desk, as I had done a hundred times, in the hope of finding
some scrap of paper which might serve as "documentary proof." Proof
of what? I scarcely knew the answer.

Finally, exhausted, I threw myself on the bed in my clothes. Why
undress when I might soon have to dress again and precede a Chekist
to my fate? I did not fall asleep. Or rather, my body was asleep while
my mind remained awake, feverishly active, examining one thought from
every angle. My mind played with it, almost tenderly, and a kind of

hysterical joy began to overwhelm me. It was the thought of sending a bullet through my skull. To this day I believe that if my body had not been paralyzed by that waking sleep, if it had not possessed a will of its own, as it were, I would have killed myself.

This curious divorce of mind from body, each with a will of its own, almost as if they were locked in an agonizing struggle for supremacy, was new to me. Later I was to become familiar with it. I would come to watch it almost as if I were "myself" an onlooker, a neutral referee, indifferent to the outcome. And now as I lay, fully dressed, on my bed my mind caressed the tempting thought. You pull the trigger and it's over. One little gesture and you destroy Dorogan, the N.K.V.D., the whole Politburo. They are powerless, all their pretensions reduced to a joke with the forefinger of your right hand in the caressing curve of a little piece of metal. . . .

Through this bitter-sweet revery I heard a knock on my window. It was not a loud knock but I heard it instantly because, all the time, I had been expecting it. My body reacted to it, as though it were foiling my mind, getting the better of it in the tense battle for control.

So they've come for me. That's over . . . ! Thoroughly awake, even resolute, I walked to the door and swung it open. Before me stood, not the uniformed Chekist I was expecting, but the worker Kiryushkin! The laconic former peasant and Red Army soldier who had dared not to lift his hand when the new "norms" were being voted.

"Come in, come in, Comrade Kiryushkin," I exclaimed, vastly pleased. "What brings you here in the middle of the night?"

"Maybe I'd better not come in," he said. "I'd soil the carpet. You see, I'm coming from work, and I've walked. It's a nasty night."

"To hell with the carpets. Come in. Give me your overcoat. How about a glass of tea? How did you locate my house?"

"It's not hard to find you, Victor Andreyevich. It's not as if *you* were looking for *me* in the barracks. All right, I'll come in."

"Don't talk like that. When I worked in the mines I lived in barracks worse than yours. Besides, before long I'll probably be moving to an elegant prison cell."

"That's what brought me here, Victor Andreyevich. You see, the news of your trouble got around in the night shift. The workers are all worried. They respect you and are sorry for you. As for me—how shall I put it?—you mean a lot in my life. It's not the better job, please believe me, though I do live a little better now. It's that you made me feel like a human being, just when I was deeply depressed. I'm not an educated man, Victor Andreyevich, but I understand a lot. My head works. Some, times I think of the revolution and the speeches and the rest of it and I'm offended by the hypocrisy of life. Then I think of how you treated me and I feel better. I say to myself it isn't all chaff, there's some wheat in the mess."

I brewed some tea and served it, with sugar and lemon. Kiryushkin sipped slowly.

"You know," he said, "this is the first time I've had tea with lemon in four years. . . . But why did I come? Well, I'm a man of the past and too small to attract any attention. Having nothing to lose, I have little to fear. How do you Communists say it? Nothing to lose but my chains. Sometimes a mouse can do what a lion can't. Anyhow, Victor Andreyevich, it's my turn to help you as best I can, and so here I am.

"I thought to myself, he probably needs a loyal friend now. I'm no hero, but I'm ready to take chances if need be. Maybe you want to hide something or carry documents or a dangerous message to somebody. I don't understand the theories of politics, but I know its practice and I am at your disposal. You can trust me. . . ."

Despite my troubles, I laughed. How much goodness, how much sensitivity, there was in this simple, modest worker! In his simple fashion he supposed I actually might have something to conceal; that perhaps I needed an accomplice. . . .

"Listen, Kiryushkin, and believe me. I'm no saboteur. I have nothing to conceal. Let the Chekists come. There is nothing compromising in my home or on my conscience."

"Did I say you were a saboteur? But just in case. . . ."

"I want you to understand, Kiryushkin, that you have already done a lot for me. I shall remember you all my life. Your visit is the most precious thing I shall carry away from Nikopol."

He wanted to leave but I retained him, talking about his life and about his fellow-workers, for more than an hour. Several times the telephone rang. Without identifying themselves people from the plant wanted to know how I was, whether I was still home. I did not inquire who they were. It was the established way of ascertaining whether someone you cared for had as yet been apprehended. After he left, I thought a great deal about Kiryushkin. There are millions, I thought, tens of millions of Kiryushkins in the Russia I love. They have no more affection for the Dorogans and Gershgorns and the Moscow bosses than I have. They are waiting for their chance to seize the rights which are theirs. They're not fooled, they're not fooled one bit.

The long talk with Kiryushkin, his quaint offer to face some mythical danger in my cause, had refreshed me. I decided to search the house once again, for the last time, for the wretched documents. As if guided by some fresh intuition, I went to a closet where various cast-off articles were piled in disorder. Right on top of the pile lay a brief case. I had used it last many months before, on a trip to the capital, and on my return had emptied it and thrown it aside. Now, casually and only in deference to completeness, I opened the brief case. It was empty. I closed it and was about to throw it back into the closet.

Then I hesitated, for no accountable reason, and opened it again. This time I looked into the side pocket, and there—miracle of miracles!— were the rough copies of the orders for instruments and the carbon copies which I had been seeking. I gazed at the dog-eared, crushed and smudged half-sheets unbelievingly. I knew what the winner of the first prize in a grand lottery feels like.

Among the papers were copies of calculations made by the Chief

Trust of the Oil Industry, based on plans later curtailed. These would prove, to any sober mind, that the quantities of spare parts and special tools ordered were fully justified by the original specifications. The actual orders were countersigned by Vishnev, as I had thought. The whole sorry case against me now seemed shattered.

I could no longer sleep, in my eagerness to tell the good news to Brachko and particularly to Vishnev, whose fate was probably linked with mine. My first stop was at Brachko's office. With make-believe casualness I tossed the papers on his desk.

"Oh well, here they are, Piotr Petrovich," I said.

"What? The documents?!"

"Yes, the God-damned documents."

For a long time the director looked through them. As he proceeded his face brightened and finally broke into a joyous smile.

"Victor Andreyevich, you're the luckiest of men! You must have been born under a lucky star. Poor Vishnev must be told immediately; he's nearly out of his mind. I'm so happy for you, for Vishnev, for myself."

In the shops the workers stared at me in frank astonishment. During the night a rumor of my arrest had spread through the city. Many of them smiled at me in encouragement; several found an excuse for saying a few friendly words as I passed their benches.

I had photostats made of the precious papers and sent a set to Brachko, another to Vishnev. A third I put into the hands of a close friend, together with a carefully worded deposition outlining the charges against me and indicating how these documents canceled them out. If I should be arrested, I instructed him, he was to lay these proofs of my innocence before the Central Committee in Moscow.

I wrote to Commissar Ordzhonikidze, apprising him of my plight. I also informed Ivanchenko, the head of Trubostal, of the trumped-up charges against me. Then I made a formal appeal to the City Committee to reverse the factory Committee's decision. Comrade Filline called a meeting of the Bureau of the City Committee without delay.

The Kravchenko case had by this time acquired a certain notoriety in Nikopol. My prominent position as director of the biggest pipe-rolling unit was only part of the reason. More important, because it was so rare, were the vigor and the spirit with which I was defending myself.

I am inclined to believe that I owe my ultimate escape, even my physical survival, to this notoriety. The persecution having been started in the open, it became increasingly awkward for the police and the Party to finish it in total secrecy. Under the delusion that they had caught me red-handed—with a hidden Menshevik parent, a hoarded treasure in machine parts and instruments, a group of "enemies of the people" under my wing—the authorities planned to destroy me publicly, "legally." It was a strategic mistake which Dorogan, Los and their hoodlums would not hesitate to tell me they regretted deeply.

In any case, the entire Bureau of the City Committee was on hand in the Party building on the main street of Nikopol, on the Dnieper River. Except for Dorogan and Brachko, it consisted of new people. In less than two months the purge had wiped out the highest Party organ of a vital industrial region.

Los presented the case against me, beginning, of course, with my Menshevik father. Filline heard him to the end of this issue, then read the letters and depositions which my father had obtained.

"These are statements made by good Communists who disagree with the elder Kravchenko's politics," he said. "That makes their testimony in his behalf more impressive. But comrades, members of the Bureau, I have also received in today's mail some interesting archive material—copies of Tsarist secret police reports and prison records dealing with the revolutionary work of this comrade's father. Here they are for anyone who wants to examine them. I have studied them carefully. It's perfectly clear that we are dealing with an unaffiliated hero of the revolution, not a Menshevik."

Dorogan frowned and puffed away furiously. What was he thinking and planning? The question never left me throughout the meeting. The whole case against me had certainly not been compounded without the N.K.V.D. Would Dorogan permit himself to be robbed of his prey?

Los then applied himself to the principal accusation. Both Kravchenko and Brachko talked of documents that disprove sabotage, he said, but they can only talk.

"Oh no, Comrade Los," Brachko interrupted him. "We have the proofs. Here they are!"

Dorogan was so startled he sprang to his feet, then thought better of it and sat down again. Los remained open-mouthed but speechless. Brachko spread the carbon copies on the table and briefly showed how completely they destroyed the charges against me and, by implication, also against Vishnev.

Filline did not conceal his satisfaction.

"To me it's obvious that this clears Kravchenko," he said.

The hearing did not wind up for several hours. Los reeled off names of engineers, technicians, officials who had been arrested and who, he insisted, were my friends. His zeal in incriminating me was so intense and so crude that Dorogan, his professional pride touched, muttered, "Why, Los, you're taking the bread out of my mouth. . . ." Everyone laughed, except Los, who turned beet-red. His most ambitious project in super-vigilance seemed in ruins and he was, understandably, unhappy. If he had planned to raise his stock in the Party and in the N.K.V.D. by catching a big fish in the muddy waters of the great purge, he was failing dismally.

The "evidence" having been presented, various members of the Bureau gave their views. Most of them favored my "rehabilitation." The sad truth is that the documentary evidence and the flimsiness of the charges had less to do with their reaction than did the attitude of Filline. He had set the tone, the others cautiously fell into line. Finally I was called upon for a statement.

"Comrades, there is little I can add," I said. "It is true that a great many men working with me and near me have been arrested. But after all, I hire and fire people on the basis of their work. It's not within my competence to check their political past. I depend on the proper instances, Comrade Dorogan, to do what's necessary on matters not related to the men's jobs.

"But I should like to draw the moral from my own case. What if the documents had not been found? What if the Tsarist archives had been destroyed? In that case I would have been punished despite my innocence. May I express the hope that we should be more careful, more restrained, in throwing around such serious accusations against comrades."

Dorogan permitted himself a grimace of disgust.

Brachko made the formal motion that the factory Committee's recommendation of expulsion be rejected. It was carried, with Los and Dorogan not voting. Then someone offered another motion—that Kravchenko be reprimanded. Though the main charges have been dropped, he argued, I had been rude to Party officials and trade-union officials and ought to be "taken down a notch." It was a transparent sop to Dorogan's self-esteem.

To my surprise, even Filline voted for the reprimand. I could only explain it by the deepening frown on Dorogan's gross face. Having taken a stand in my favor, Filline now acted, like a seasoned Communist, to placate the N.K.V.D. I protested against the reprimand but to no avail.

Brachko and I rode home together. We were well pleased with the outcome, but the reprimand rankled. It was a blotch on my record which might not be easy to erase.

"For heaven's sake, Victor, spit on it all," Brachko urged. "You've saved your skin and that's the main point. Allah be praised that you're still free and alive!"

Deep into the night I wrote letters to friends, to my family, to superiors in Kharkov and Moscow, informing them of my "good fortune." But I was by no means reckless in my optimism. It was too much to expect that the N.K.V.D. would leave me in peace.

3

The favorable turn in my own case was the exception. Throughout Russia the purge gathered new fury. The demonstration trial of Radek, Sokolnikov, Piatakov and other Old Bolsheviks was under way in Moscow. For seven days entire pages in the press detailed the nightmarish "confessions" of these men. Then came the inevitable sentences and executions.

In our factory, as in every establishment and institution of the land, a mass meeting was called to hail the destruction of these saboteurs, spies, and "wild dogs." Los presented the prefabricated resolution.

"We workers, employees and engineers of the Metallurgical Factory of Nikopol, greet the decisions of the Soviet court in the case of the enemies of the people," it declared. "The vigilance of the Party and the government has outrooted the spies and diversionists, the agents of capitalism, who threatened the happy life of our people under the Stalin Constitution. Long live our Beloved Leader and Teacher, Comrade Stalin!"

Meekly the thousands of men and women raised their hands. The orchestra struck up the *Internationale*. Red bunting all around the hall proclaimed the glories of the "happy life" to these overworked, underfed and apathetic masses; to these utterly spiritless masses. Some yawned, a few fell asleep as the orators rehashed the morning's editorials, which in turn had been rehashed from the Moscow editorials. Finally, the ritual was completed, the people returned to their homes or their workshops. They were neither convinced nor especially interested.

If anyone in Russia honestly believed in the fantastic "confessions," I for one did not meet him. Not until I went abroad many years later did I discover that foreigners, in particular "liberal" Americans, had swallowed the macabre hoax, hook, line and sinker; that a capitalist motion picture company had actually fabricated a stupid and illiterate film based on the assumption that the N.K.V.D. fairy tales were true!

Among the defendants in the latest of the Moscow trials, the man I knew best was Piatakov, since he had served as first assistant to Ordzhonikidze. I had visited him personally on business many times and had taken part in conferences where he presided. He was a tall, dignified man with a long, straight beard and the high-domed forehead of a thinker. Always his decisions, in private or in group conferences, were stern and honest. Never content with secondhand judgments on technical matters, he would take a slide-rule and compute, check, recheck, in intense concentration before authorizing work or expenditures.

The Piatakov I knew had not the faintest resemblance to the "criminal" depicted in the trial or in the drivel which I later read, in astonishment, in a strange American book of fiction called *Mission to Moscow*. Because of my work and technical contacts I would meet literally hundreds of men intimately connected with the industries and the specific factories where Piatakov's "sabotage" supposedly had been committed. Not one of them believed a word of the charges, of course, though many of them justified the trials on political grounds.

Piatakov's self-confessed "sabotage" was chiefly in the construction industry. The official in direct charge of all construction work under Piatakov was a certain C. Z. Ginsburg, head of the Main Administration of Construction Work for Heavy Industry. Every detail of the work passed through Ginsburg's hands. That sabotage of the magnitude declaimed by Prosecutor Vishinsky could have been carried out, year after year, without the knowledge and active connivance of Ginsburg was physically impossible.

Yet Ginsburg was not arrested. His name was carefully kept out of the trial proceedings, though projects under his personal guidance were discussed in tremendous detail. And after the trial Stalin made him Commissar of Construction Industry. The last time I saw Ginsburg his chest was loaded with medals and stars and decorations. Within our industry it was taken for granted that Ginsburg had played the part of top provocateur and that his outstanding construction job was the manufacture of evidence for the big trials. He was Prosecutor Vishinsky's behind-the-scenes guide.

Another person who figured in the trials and whom I knew personally for many years was Nikolai Golubenko. He was executed in Kharkov without the formality of a trial. To him had been assigned the fictitious role of chieftain of a "terror center" pledged to kill members of the Politburo. Specifically he was supposed to have confessed to plotting to assassinate the Politburo member Kossior and the Secretary of the Ukrainian Communist Party, Postishev. Soon after Golubenko was shot for this "crime," the N.K.V.D. arrested both Kossior and Postishev. Bewildered Party people could only suppose that these two intimate associates of Stalin had collaborated with Golubenko in preparing their own demise.

For a time Golubenko had been director of the Petrovsky-Lenin *combinat* in Dniepropetrovsk. I had seen him and talked to him frequently. He was a courageous and outspoken man and his real crime was that he objected to the continuous blood-letting. The last time I met him—he was then chairman of the Dniepropetrovsk Soviet—he already knew that he was doomed, a living corpse. Only that can explain the candor with which he talked to me.

The *pogrom* on the Communist Party, he said in substance, was merely the last step in liquidating all independent thought and even independent feelings in our country. Stalin, he said, was carrying through a purposeful counter-revolution: the remnants of power still held by the Central Committee of the Party, the remnants of prestige and popular influence still held by the generation that made the revolution, would be eradicated, leaving the Politburo—which is to say Stalin—as the absolute dictator.

Golubenko did not head a "terrorist organization." Had there been such an organization, it would have committed at least one act of terror. But he opposed the counter-revolution and despised the dictator. His official murder therefore was not meaningless or frivolous. It was an act of war by Stalin in his final and bloody conquest of unlimited power.

Golubenko, Piatakov, perhaps Kossior and Postishev, were "guilty" only in the sense that they would not yield meekly to Stalin's absolutism. The nameless millions, Communist and non-Party people, liquidated during the super-purge were not even guilty of that "crime." I was horrified, years later, to learn that abroad the victims were being described by some knaves and fools as a "fifth column." A "fifth column" of nine or ten millions, including 60 to 80 per cent of the top leaders of the Party, the Comsomols, the armed forces, the government, industry, farming and national culture—merely to state the absurdity is to expose its grotesqueness.

At the Piatakov trial, a certain Shestov was accused of plotting to kill the Secretary of the Siberian Party, P. Eiche. Shestov was executed—and soon thereafter his appointed victim, Eiche, was arrested. Prosecutor Vishinsky's energetic assistant, Matulevich, did a ruthless and shrewd job in preparing the defendants for the firing squad. Soon after the trial, Matulevich himself was liquidated. The whole trial had been concocted by Henry Yagoda, the merciless head of the N.K.V.D., but soon enough Yagoda himself, and his main assistants, were in their turn arrested and shot. Most of the men who had drawn up the Stalin Constitution were by now dead or imprisoned. Soon the outstanding Red Army leaders, including the world-famous General Tukhachevsky, were "tried" behind closed doors and shot; before long nearly all his "judges" were shot in their turn. The "fifth column," apparently included everyone but Stalin, Molotov and U. S. Ambassador Davies.

Though myself cleared, except for the reprimand, I was tormented by the horrors all around me; by the unceasing arrests and disappearances in my own shops and offices. I plunged into work, sometimes fourteen, eighteen, twenty hours of it without break, to keep myself from thinking, to safeguard my sanity. I had no personal life, no satisfaction in my work, no hope for my own or the country's future.

Thus the tragic day in February, 1937, arrived. I was at my desk, writing a production report addressed to Ivanchenko in Kharkov and Ordzhonikidze in Moscow, when one of my assistants burst into the office. He was in tears.

"Victor Andreyevich," he blurted out, "Sergo Ordzhonikidze is dead! What a misfortune!"

I sat motionless, speechless, as if paralyzed. The tears rolled down my cheeks. I had lost a friend and a patron.

The very next day I received a telephone call from Gershgorn. What a tragedy, he said, "Your patron in Moscow is dead." Maybe we had better meet soon, have a "little chat" about "this and that"? The dam was down. The stormy waters were churning all around me.

CHAPTER XVI

A SEARCH FOR JUSTICE

I WAS ASKED to speak at the factory mass meeting in honor of Ordzhonikidze's memory. For once, at a Soviet meeting, I was able to talk from the heart. Seven years had passed since Ordzhonikidze picked me for training as one of "our own technical intelligentsia." Through these years he had encouraged me, protected me with an almost paternal solicitude; and I knew, of course, that I was only one of thousands whom he had thus shielded and used in the country's interests.

I must have communicated my own sense of loss to the audience, for dozens of my listeners wept unashamedly. The masses who went glumly, even sullenly, through the ritual approval of blood trials and the bogus Constitution, were capable of honest feeling. The ancient springs of Russian emotion were not yet dried up.

The newspapers published a long laudatory obituary on the Commissar, signed by Stalin and nineteen others of the supreme leaders. The Politburo designated a committee of seven distinguished industry and government people to organize the official funeral. Four eminent physicians certified that the departed had died of "paralysis of the heart." These figures stuck in my mind, where they point up the sinister political arithmetic of this period: before the year was over, only nine of the twenty who signed the obituary were still alive and free. The others had been shot, had committed suicide or were rotting in prisons. Of the seven on the funeral committee, only two remained alive and free; three were executed, one committed suicide and another was buried alive in a penal labor colony. Of the four physicians, only one survived and he lived in constant dread of liquidation.

Why was an elaborate certification of the leader's death necessary? Because the Russian people, and the Party membership especially, no longer believed that men in power die natural deaths. Many had been made cynical by strange events. A case in point was the death, some years earlier, of Stalin's young wife, Nadezhda Alleluyeva.

Prodigious efforts were made at the time to conceal the circumstances of her sudden end. All the same, many of the sensational facts became known and gained circulation, at least in the higher circles of authority.

Alleluyeva was the daughter of a pre-1917 revolutionist and apparently had inherited some of his outmoded humanitarian prejudices against mass terror. The brutal collectivization drive was more than she could tolerate, even from the father of her two children. She did not limit her expressions of horror to the family circle but repeatedly assailed her husband's policies at Party meetings at the Academy in which she was taking technical courses.

Merely to allude to these facts was enough to land one in prison, yet they percolated through the higher bureaucracy, where scandal, sensation and intrigue are as rife as in the old Romanoff court. When, in the midst of her one-woman revolt, Alleluyeva's death was announced, the only element of doubt was whether she had killed herself or had been poisoned at Stalin's behest.

And so now, despite the deposition of the four doctors, doubts about Ordzhonikidze's death were widespread. It happens that I know some of the true circumstances. The time has not yet arrived when I can reveal the sources of my information, since it would mean their torture and death. But, because this Commissar's last years were so closely twined with my own, I feel it my duty to record the facts briefly.

Ordzhonikidze had long suffered from acute asthma and a crippled right kidney. He often joked about his ailments. More than once I saw him exhausted to the point of collapse, after a long day of work despite sharp pain. When the super-purge began in 1936, sweeping up thousands of his closest friends and colleagues in the Party and in Heavy Industry, he protested to Stalin, created stormy scenes at Politburo meetings, fought like a tiger with the N.K.V.D. His health took a turn for the worse. The blow of the arrest of Piatakov, his closest associate, made him desperately ill.

A friend of mine was in his office when someone brought him the news of the arrest of a distinguished engineer, the head of one of the big trusts under Ordzhonikidze's authority. The Commissar grew purple with fury, his eyes bulged, he swore and cursed as only a temperamental Georgian can swear and curse. Yagoda, head of the N.K.V.D. and chief architect of the first purge trials, had by this time been shot. The new chief of the Soviet inquisition was the hated Yezhov. Ordzhonikidze now phoned Yezhov and, in unbridled language, demanded to know why the engineer had been arrested without his permission.

"You little snotnose, you filthy lickspittle," my friend heard the Commissar shout, "how dare you! I demand that you send me the documents in the case, all of them, and right away!"

Then he phoned Stalin, on the direct circuit connecting the principal leaders of the dictatorship. By this time his hands were shaking, his eyes were bloodshot, and he kept pressing the spot on his back where the bad kidney was acting up.

"Koba," my friend heard him yell into the phone—Koba is Stalin's intimate nickname—"why do you let the N.K.V.D. arrest my men without informing me?"

There was a long silence while Stalin talked at the other end. Then Ordzhonikidze interrupted:

"I demand that this authoritarianism cease! I'm still a member of the Politburo! I'm going to raise hell, Koba, if it's the last thing I do before I die!"

Ordzhonikidze slammed down the receiver. He sat at his desk in a daze of futile anger.

Such scenes occurred almost daily. They sapped the Georgian's vitality. He made good on his threat and kicked up scandals at Politburo meetings. Kossior, Rudzutak, Chubar and Antipov usually supported him —all four were later arrested and disappeared in the course of the purge. After a time he was too ill to attend meetings. But even from the confinement of his sick room he kept his many telephones hot with angry demands for the life or the liberty of officials who had worked under him and in whom he had faith.

During this final illness Ordzhonikidze's wife, Zinaida, to whom he was deeply devoted, was not allowed to visit him. N.K.V.D. guards, ostensibly protecting him, barred his friends from his bedside. The only visitors admitted were Mikoyan and Voroshilov, both members of the Politburo. They tried several times to convince the invalid to make peace with Stalin by acknowledging the necessity for the great purge. The visits, however, always ended in heated quarrels.

Though too ill to move around, he was by no means on the point of death. He might have lingered, as an invalid, for many years. From his bed he dictated letters to the Central Committee and the Politburo in which he condemned Stalin and demanded a plenary session of the Central Committee to consider the state of the country and to curb the floods of murder and destruction. His letters were written with passionate conviction. If they have survived, historians in some distant future will have a detailed indictment of the Stalinist counter-revolution from the mouth of the man who carried out the first Five Year Plans.

Two days later, to the complete surprise of his family and his attending physicians, Ordzhonikidze died. There are those who believe that in a moment of despair he took poison. There are others who believe that he was poisoned by Dr. Levin—the same doctor who later confessed to having poisoned Maxim Gorki. That he died by violence, that his end was not "natural," my sources have not the slightest doubt.

If they are right, then the elaborate funeral, the nationwide eulogies, were part of an obscene farce. In the published pictures, the widow—who had been kept from seeing her husband—stood by Stalin's side at the funeral. In the next few years Ordzhonikidze's name was soft-pedalled and after a time it was rarely mentioned. Cities, streets, factories bearing his name have gradually been rechristened. Very young Communists now rarely know who he was.

The new Commissar, succeeding Ordzhonikidze, was Valerian Mezhlauk. I was amazed when he summoned me to Moscow in a personal message. Mezhlauk was apparently taking stock of available technical personnel, sharply reduced by the purge, in taking the reins of the nation's heavy industries into his hands.

He was a solidly built, handsome fellow who had lived abroad. He had both the appearance and the manners of a European. Though a capable administrator, he had little political power or influence. Stalin was taking no chances, it seemed, on another "independent" Commissar in this key post.

"I'm thinking of appointing you to head up one of our largest plants, Comrade Kravchenko," he said. "Your Nikopol record justifies it. How would you feel about it?"

"Permit me to ask you, Comrade Commissar, who recommended me?"

"Why do you want to know?"

"Well, you see, I am in a lot of political difficulties in Nikopol. I have been accused of sabotage and other sins. Perhaps you should know about this before you promote me to more responsible work."

I informed him, in some detail, about my recent troubles.

"Strange, strange that I wasn't told," Mezhlauk shrugged his shoulders. "I know that Ordzhonikidze valued you highly. Maybe you're right. Let's let matters rest as is, for the time being."

Subsequently I had reason to thank that lucky star under which I had been born. Mezhlauk was soon arrested and disappeared as if swallowed by mother earth, soon followed by his brother Ivan. Had he appointed me to an important position, I undoubtedly would have paid dearly for the compliment.

In the first days of March, Stalin delivered a long address at a Central Committee meeting. It was published in full. As usual, droves of Party hacks chewed over his words in endless popular and Party conclaves. Press and radio quoted and applauded by the hour. The racket could not obscure the core of his message: the purge to date, horrible though it had been, was only a beginning; more and worse would come.

"The sabotage and diversionist work," Stalin said, "has reached, to a greater or smaller extent, all or practically all our organizations." He reproached the Party with "having forgotten that Soviet power has conquered only one-sixth of the world and five-sixths of the world are in the hands of capitalist states. . . . As long as our capitalist encirclement remains, we will always have saboteurs, diversionists and spies. . . ."

It was, in scarcely veiled language, his declaration of war on all the country's organizations, on anyone who now, or in the future, might object to his absolutism. Hard work and even brilliant achievements, he warned, must not be accepted as an alibi where a man's faith was incomplete: "The real saboteur must from time to time show evidence of success in his work, for that is the only way in which he can keep his job as a saboteur. . . . We shall have to extirpate those persons, grind them down without stopping, without flagging, for they are the enemies of the working class, they are traitors to our homeland!"

The sadists, the inflamed vigilantes in every community thus had their signal. Ruthlessness had the right of way. We felt the results immediately in our own community. Several days after the release of Stalin's speech, the director of a large farm-implement plant was arrested and with him all his associates. The administration and technical staffs of the Nikopol manganese mines, of every other enterprise in the region, were decimated.

One morning, arriving at the plant, I found Brachko waiting for me. He was in a state of panic.

"Victor Andreyevich," he announced sadly, "the Secretary of the City Committee, Comrade Filline, was arrested during the night."

Later that day Comrade Los called me. He could hardly repress a note of triumph.

"We'll have to put your case before the City Committee again," he informed me gleefully. "You see, you were saved last time by Filline— an enemy of the people. Now we'll take care of you, never fear!"

My purgatory, which I had thought ended, was only beginning.

2

The "little chat" promised by Gershgorn was not too long delayed. When I reached the N.K.V.D. building at eleven at night, as instructed, he had not yet arrived. I waited for him in the crowded reception hall, my brain seething with frenzied theories. What diabolical trap were they setting for me? Would I be allowed to leave this house of horror?

It was nearly one o'clock when Gershgorn finally showed up—his fat cheeks freshly shaved and powdered, his bald peaked dome glowing. He was rested, brisk, ready for "work." I followed him into the large, bare office with which I was already too familiar. A vast polished mahogany desk, a few chairs, a huge safe and divan were all the furnishings it contained. Its bareness and cleanliness somehow suggested a surgeon's office.

"Well, Kravchenko," the head of the Economic Division began with spurious cheerfulness, "I trust you and I will understand each other quickly. So far you've managed to squirm out of it in the Party with those silly pieces of paper. But this hocus-pocus won't go with the N.K.V.D. We'll get to the bottom of that instrument business and your father's Menshevism and your connections with known enemies of the people."

In this first of many nights Gershgorn went over much of the ground already covered publicly. Referring to the *dossier* stuffed with reports by his agents all around me, he revived the memory of accidents at the plant, occasional failures to fulfill orders. In every item, and particularly in my relations with people involved who had since then been arrested or otherwise liquidated, he smelled wrecking and tried cunningly to snare me into contradictions and admissions.

Until four in the morning the interrogation went on. It dealt in large measure with other people in the metallurgical industry. Through me the N.K.V.D. aimed to fortify its cases against other arrested officials, just as, no doubt, they were being pumped for incriminating data or opinions against me.

Had any of those unfortunate people really been engaged in sabotage, I would have seen evidences of it. Their plans, their products, their mistakes and achievements were reflected in my plant. But I had seen no sign of sabotage. There had been plenty of inefficiency and confusion and delays, but these were generic infantile diseases of newly born industries. No matter how hard I tried, I could not twist the facts into proofs of conscious wrecking.

Gershgorn was disgusted with my "stubbornness." As the night wore on he grew more impatient, more wrathful. The mock politeness of the start gave way gradually to an insulting insolence, peppered with ripe

Russian oaths. It seemed to him a personal affront that I should dare to resist his insinuations and puncture his fantastic theories. He acted, indeed, as if he were the victim, as if I were imposing on his good nature by forcing him to sweat and swear on account of my headstrong refusal to "cooperate."

A new day was dawning as I left the N.K.V.D. building. The surface of the Dnieper was soft, ripply silk. One could plunge into it and be shrouded forever in forgetfulness. I was never to leave this grim building without yearning for the comforts of death. *Why don't they let me alone? I want only to work, to give the best that is in me. Why don't they let me alone? Why?* My thoughts, like my body, were staggering. They could not adhere to a straight line. The few people who saw me walking along the street that chill, foggy morning must have been sure that I was intoxicated. . . .

I went to work at the plant that day, after a brief sleep, in a stupor. My temples throbbed with pain. I looked forward to the night as a kind of release. But late that afternoon Gershgorn's office telephoned. . . . I was to come once more, at eleven again, to proceed with our little "chat." I was there as ordered, weary, nervous and bitter. With only a rare break, the interrogation continued for nearly a month. It was the beginning of an ordeal by sleeplessness the horror of which I cannot expect anyone who has not experienced it in his own flesh and nerves to understand.

The wolves of Nikopol—Dorogan, Gershgorn, Los and the rest— howled for my blood. They were impatient to tear me limb from limb. One could almost see the saliva dripping from the corners of their mouths in anticipation of the feast. Why? Why? What could they have against me, who had done them no personal harm?

There were logical answers to these questions. Having liquidated scores of people, in our factory and elsewhere, whose activities meshed closely into mine, sheer consistency called for my head. As long as I was free, the purge picture in their territory seemed askew; a robust doubt of the guilt of those others, it seemed to them, would remain and flourish among the "masses" until this hole in the jigsaw puzzle of their fevered hoax was properly filled. Moreover, having initiated and advertised my case, it would be politically harmful to permit me to writhe out of it. Their "authority would be undermined," as the stock Soviet phrase had it.

But logical answers are only surface answers. The deeper reasons for the seemingly wilful persecution must be looked for in the slimy dregs of human perversity. The business had resolved into an exciting hunt and the huntsmen would not be deprived of their kill. No doubt they had begun without any special sentiments about me, one way or the other, but in the heat of the chase, in the moments of frustration, hate of me was born. They wanted to win, to add my hide to their bloody pile of trophies.

At the same time the hunters seemed minded, again perversely, to stick to the rules of the chase, at least outwardly. Simply to arrest me and shoot me in one of their slippery cellars would have made them look ludicrous in the eyes of Nikopol. Mine had become one of those instances in which the kill must be made in the open, with public exposure and confession.

For several weeks, while I was being kept awake, tormented and insulted in the secret sessions, the public phase of my persecution was also carried out. The procedures of my first expulsion were unreeled again; once more there were investigating commissions, talk-fests at Party meetings, smears in the papers. I went through them in a state of feverish thirst for sleep and rest. Sometimes my body felt as if it were filled with lead, crushing me by its immense weight; then suddenly it would become feather-light, it would seem to float. Waves of heat and chill swept through me alternately.

New charges had been added to the old. The sabotage story was broadened and diffused, since the specific accusation seemed a bit shopworn. The revised accusations put the emphasis less on my personal actions, more on connivance with men already properly identified as saboteurs; if not connivance, at least traitorous tolerance and lack of watchfulness on my part. The more tenuous the charges became, of course, the more difficult it was to refute them.

Actually, as the chase continued, I forgot why I was being pursued. I was merely tired, miserable, dizzy and baffled. In desperation, if only to break the weary monotony of the persecution, if only to evade the night sessions with Gershgorn for a little while, I decided to search for justice elsewhere. I put my plan before Director Brachko.

"Piotr Petrovich," I said, "I'm dead tired. My head is spinning and my nerves are at the breaking point. I can neither work nor eat nor sleep. Somewhere there must be a memory of truth and of simple fairness and I intend to go look for it. I shall go to the Regional Committee, the Central Committee, to individual comrades. I shall tell my sad tale to anyone willing to listen. Perhaps somewhere someone may give me advice or help. After all, I have committed no crime. Why should I be hunted like a criminal? Why, having been exonerated once, should I go through the horror a second time, then a third time? Yes, I'm setting out to look for an answer."

Brachko was worried by my condition and my proposal. He had no inkling of my night interrogations—I was under the strictest written pledges of silence. But he sensed that there was more cause for my despair than was evident on the surface.

"It's a foolish and futile quest," he assured me. "What's more, it's hardly wise for you to leave Nikopol now. They'll make good use of your absence. On the other hand, you look terrible and maybe you ought to get away for a bit. If you insist, I'll arrange to send you on an assignment somewhere."

And so I started out on my heart-breaking search for justice. I was to see scores of people and organizations, none of whom knew the address. . . .

I began at my birthplace, in Dniepropetrovsk. A former classmate of mine, Soshnikov, was now Second Secretary of the Regional Committee and therefore a person of some political weight. Two other comrades from the Institute days were on his staff. One of them was Suvorov. He had been pitifully poor then, and I had often taken him home so that mother might feed him and mend his tattered clothes. The other was Ulassyevich. His head was not fashioned for study, so that, with other friends, I used to tutor him for hours to help push him through the courses.

Now all three sat in this Party building and dispensed wisdom to the "masses." Depositions from such a well-placed trio, giving me a good Party character, might be useful.

Soshnikov had grown fat and soft in the intervening years. He sat behind a big desk in a luxurious, softly carpeted office under a smiling portrait of The Leader. For a full minute he did not raise his eyes from the papers before him: a familiar bureaucratic assertion of self-importance. Finally he looked up and said, coldly:

"So it's you, Comrade Kravchenko. What can I do for you?" He used the formal "you" rather than the familiar "thou."

"Since when have you dropped the 'thou' to old Institute chums? Why in hell must you talk like the Lord's anointed?"

Soshnikov was embarrassed and excused himself on the ground of overwork, heavy responsibilities. I decided to come to the point without preliminaries.

"I'm in trouble," I said.

"So I've heard. . . ."

"Tell me honestly, in the years we were at the Institute together, did you observe any sabotaging on my part?"

"Of course not. What nonsense!"

"Then I'd like you to say so in a statement to the Nikopol Committee—you and Suvorov and Ulassyevich."

He squirmed and readjusted his teeming fat. He mopped new perspiration. He tried to change the subject. Finally he rang for the other two. Apparently they, too, had heard something. Their greetings were friendly but cautious, very cautious. I drew a bitter kind of relish from their threefold discomfiture. After some skirmishing they hit on the idea that I ought to go higher up; that it was not seemly for modest people like themselves to interfere in great matters affecting the life and safety of the nation.

"Thank you for your advice. I trust you realize how dirty and cowardly you are," I said and left without farewells.

This trio no doubt knew how to protect their own skins. Some time later Soshnikov became chief of the N.K.V.D. of Cheliabinsk province; Ulassyevich became Secretary of a City Committee in Western Ukraine; Suvorov, too, was promoted.

In the corridor, while looking for the office of the new Secretary, Comrade Margolin, I suddenly heard my name called.

"Victor Andreyevich, hello there! How are you? How nice to see you again!"

I turned around to face Ivan Zolkin, with whom I had worked at the

Petrovsky-Lenin plant. It was good to see someone from those simpler, younger years, before I had become an engineer and a "responsible worker." He seemed really pleased with the accidental meeting.

"How are things with you, Vitya?" he asked. "Why do you look so pale and drawn? Been sick or something?"

"In a way," I smiled. "The national epidemic. . . . Charges of sabotage and what not."

"Oh my dear Vitya, how dreadful . . . what a nasty business! Well, good-bye . . . must hurry for an appointment. Please excuse me. . . ."

And off he rushed. I was to meet him again exactly three years later in the Kremlin, and I was not surprised; the brief meeting in a Dniepropetrovsk hallway convinced me that Ivan Zolkin would go far in our blessed land. Last I knew he was head of an important Division in the Central Committee of the Party, a position he probably still holds.

Secretary Margolin's huge reception room was guarded by Chekists in uniform and in mufti. They watched the people who came and went. They asked me whether I carried any weapons before they let me in and scanned me with trained eyes for any suspicious bulge. Soviet officials, at least before they are arrested, are well guarded; the killing of Soviet officials is an N.K.V.D. monopoly and the N.K.V.D. brooks no competition.

Waiting there in Hatayevich's former ante-room, I recalled that he, too, had been dramatically protected when I saw him last, at the Nikopol Party meeting. Where was he now? I knew he had been arrested, but was he still alive? I had known most of his office staff but none of them was around now; no doubt they had shared the fate of their boss.

I knew nothing about Hatayevich's successor. I had never seen him before. After the several rebuffs, I was steeled for yet another. But amazingly, Margolin proved human. He not only heard me out to the end but didn't hesitate to express frank sympathy.

"I should like you to help me, Comrade Margolin," I pleaded. "Why should my case be reopened just because Filline is arrested? What have I to do with him? I was vindicated on the basis of documents."

"Be patient, comrade," Margolin spoke in a subdued voice. "What's happening to you, come to think of it, is pretty mild. We're in a critical period of the revolution. It's our duty to help the Party, not to criticize. All the same, I'll send a directive to the City Committee about your case."

"Thank you. If you keep your promise, I'll be most grateful."

"Don't thank me, comrade. None of us know where we'll be tomorrow."

The last words were uttered as a cynical pleasantry. But I looked into his eyes and saw that there was in them no trace of humor. On returning to Nikopol I would learn that Margolin had kept his promise: he had written urging justice and fairness. But by that time he had himself been arrested. His intercession, indeed, would plague me for a long time. It would be treated as another serious "proof" of my intimacy with class enemies!

The second stage in my quest for justice was Kharkov. I had counted heavily on help from Ivanchenko. He was one of the dozen or so outstanding industrial commanders of the country. Severe and incisive, uncompromising in his insistence on good work and in punishing laziness or ignorance, he was, all the same, a sensitive and kindly man. I knew that side of him. I knew that he would not hesitate to champion his subordinates when right was on their side.

But I found an atmosphere of panic in Trubostal. Ivanchenko, hero of the revolution and recipient of every honor and reward within the gift of the Kremlin, long a member of the government, had been called to Moscow, presumably on business. When he got there a reception committee of N.K.V.D. men awaited him and whisked him off to prison. Because he was especially popular in Kharkov, the arrest had been staged in Moscow. At the same time all his main colleagues at Trubostal—Shpelty, Strepetov, Spring and others, all of them non-Party men—were rounded up.

I found few to whom I could talk. New men, with frightened eyes, sat in most of the offices. But I did tell my story to a sympathetic engineer. He listened to me, then shook his head in reproof:

"Look here, Kravchenko, you think *you* have trouble! Have you heard what happened to Constantine Shpelty? Or to old man Spring?"

Both Shpelty and Spring were celebrated engineers. I had read and studied their works. Theirs were magic names to young Soviet industralists. Now I heard the details of their arrests; how they had been dragged from their beds, abused by obscene gendarmes and pressed into the truckloads of fresh prisoners. I left Trubostal as one leaves a cemetery . . . a cemetery in which some of the corpses still moved around, pretending to be alive.

On the way to the Provincial Committee headquarters I passed the Gigant, that beehive of a student dormitory where I had once been an important figure. I decided to look in. I went through its halls, peeped into the room where I had lived. Little trace remained of the cleanliness and order I had worked and agitated for. The place still swarmed with students, not much different from those of seven years ago: the same underfed, shabby but eager boys and girls, faith and ambition shining through in their eyes.

For the first time in years, I thought of Julia, the luscious and clever Julia who had been my sweetheart. Where was she? Was she alive? Did she sometimes recall the young Communist from the Gigant?

As I approached the Provincial Committee headquarters, I heard a familiar voice.

"Vitya! Vitya! Hold on there, where are you going?"

It was Senya Volgin, the same Senya who many years ago had argued with my father after Rakovsky's visit to the factory, who had been my co-editor of our plant newspaper, whom I had once reprimanded in the paper for staging a drinking party in the dormitory.

"Senya! How glad I am to see you after all these years!"

"I'm delighted, Vitya, dear one. Let me kiss you!" And he threw his arms around my neck.

"Be careful, Senya, you may regret the kiss. I'm contagious. Things have gone badly with me. . . ."

"The hell you say! Well, you must tell me all about it. I'm not one of those who run away. Say, remember what he called me, that father of yours? A 'spring chicken' who couldn't teach an old hen like him any politics! And, by God, he was right!"

We sat on a bench in the park—until a few weeks ago it had been called Postishev Park, but now Postishev was under arrest and the park was nameless. Senya was in military uniform and carried an important-looking brief case. He had gone gray at the temples. But the official trappings didn't suit him. He was still small, simple, unpretentious.

We sketched in our respective stories for the years since we had last been together. Senya now held a high post in the Provincial Committee.

"Yes, Vitya, you're sitting with a distinguished proletarian leader . . . 100 per cent Stalinist. Did you ever see carcasses hanging in the butcher shops? On their thighs they have a stamp: 'Tested—edible.' That's me, Vitya, tested and edible. But whether and when the Cheka boys will get around to eating me I don't know."

"Senya," I said, "this is no time for joking, it's a time for crying."

"I've done more than my share of crying. I have no more tears. So another friend is snuffed out, and another. . . . So my own turn is coming soon. . . . I have one advantage over you. I have a dependable source of consolation. It comes in bottles. Yes, it's true, I've been hitting the bottle pretty badly, but believe me, in bloody times like these I'm sorry for you teetotalers."

We compared notes on mutual acquaintances. Most of them were under arrest.

"So what shall we do, Vitya? Cry? No; doesn't do any good. Remember the song: *'What has passed won't come back, just as summer won't come back. . . .'* Red-headed Grisha used to sing it, remember? He used to wash his underwear himself, at the commune, and as it was drying what was there for him to do except sing while he waited? He used to put an overcoat on, sit down on a footstool, strum the guitar and sing. Poor Grisha was arrested a few weeks ago. You and I, we're still waiting, so let's have sense enough to sing."

We parted with fervid pledges to meet again soon. But it was not to be. The N.K.V.D. got Senya about two months later. His family told me that he had been pretty drunk when the N.K.V.D. came for him and sang at the top of his voice in the middle of the night. What did he sing, I wanted to know. An old favorite: *"What has passed won't come back . . ."* they said.

The train for Moscow was not leaving until late that night. I had already bought the tickets. It occurred to me to find out whether Eliena was in town. I telephoned her apartment. Eliena herself answered. To my own complete surprise, her voice did not stir me as I thought it would. My sufferings and inner despair seemed to have deadened softer feelings. I asked myself in some alarm: Have these scoundrels burned out old feelings in me? Have they erased the romantic streak in my make-up?

Eliena met me in my hotel. She was still beautiful, with that curiously rhythmic grace that used to go through me like a knife. But she had aged; the sadness in her eyes was deeper than ever. Her husband, she told me, had been arrested and sent to a concentration camp again and she was living with her mother. She had a modest job in an architectural bureau. I did not ask her whether she was still working for the N.K.V.D.

"Ah, Vitya, things have grown worse, not better," she sighed. "I know about your sufferings. You see, whenever I'm in Dniepropetrovsk, which isn't often, I try to see our mutual friends. You've forgotten me, but they haven't. How wonderful to find people who have remained clean, untouched, through all these dirty years. It's a miracle."

When she saw me off at the railroad station we promised to meet again. Both of us knew well enough that the promise would not be kept.

3

I had come to love Moscow. It's not an elegant or a beautiful city. For all its new "skyscrapers" and widened streets, it remains "the largest village in Russia." The Moskva River, curling through the city, seems to impose its wayward nature on the whole town, with its multitude of narrow, twisting alleys, provincial-looking squares, sudden Byzantine touches. No, it's not beautiful to look upon, except through a Russian heart.

What touched me, what touches any Russian in Moscow, is the curious sense of its age, its permanence. It was there before the Romanoffs and remained after them; it was there before the Communists and will remain long, long after them. It has a quality beyond politics, even beyond planned modernization. Somehow personal grief recedes, becomes smaller, almost negligible, in the presence of this eternal city.

I decided to avoid registering in a hotel. That would be too much like putting myself into a fish-bowl on an N.K.V.D. mantlepiece. Instead I asked Comrade Misha and his wife to let me live with them a few days.

Misha was a famous old revolutionist and was now active in the Society of Former Tsarist Political Prisoners. The government provided him with a comfortable apartment and a pension sufficient to keep the aging couple alive. He had fought on the barricades by my father's side. He had spent more than ten years in chains in the Alexandrovsk prison, until released by the revolution. Comrade Misha and his wife had always treated me like a son and they were now overjoyed to take me in, though alarmed by my pallor and harried looks.

"And how is my dear Andrei? Is he still puttering along?"

"Yes, father is well and as indignant about life and things as always."

"We are durable men, my generation. I wish I could see him again, to talk about old times."

At dinner I told him what had brought me to Moscow. I hid nothing. Comrade Misha had known Lenin, Bukharin, the other giants of the revolution personally. He called the present leaders, from Stalin down, by their first names. Lenin's widow, Krupskaya, often met him. He had been treated—at least until the period of the super-purge—as one of their own by the new masters.

As I told my story, especially about the charges against my father, his comrade of the barricades, old Misha grew furious. He pushed back his chair in wrath and strode to a closet, from which he dragged out a heavy, rusty chain. He raised the clanging metal with both hands above his gray head and shook it in uncontrolled fury.

"I wore these shackles for ten years because I believed in truth, in fairness, in a better life!" he shouted. "And now the ruffians who call themselves revolutionists torture our children! A curse on them! A curse on the sadists who are bleeding our Russia!"

He was a tall, spare and sickly man. Standing there holding the rusty shackles aloft, he was terrible to behold. Misha's wife and I tried to calm him.

"What I don't understand, Comrade Misha," I said later, "is why all this terror is necessary. It can't be that we are all spies and saboteurs— a whole country of spies and saboteurs—all except the Politburo. . . ."

"Nonsense! There are no exceptions. In the Politburo itself, many have been arrested, and more than three-quarters of the membership of the Central Committee has been liquidated. Kossior, Rudzutak, Chubar, Postishev—under arrest. And lots of those close to the Politburo— Antipov, Mezhlauk, Bubnov and many, many others—have been swallowed up. Yakovlev, Stetsky, nearly all the best ones in the Central Committee, too. The *pogrom* is as bloody in high places as down below.

"Stalin and his clique want a Party that doesn't think, a Central Committee that obeys orders blindly, a Politburo that always agrees with him fully. And he's getting it. He's dealing with the problem the way Peter the Great dealt with it—by chopping off heads."

In the course of the evening we got down to discussing whom we might approach to intercede in my behalf. Krupskaya was out of the question. Only the fact that she was Lenin's widow saved her from arrest. Her hatred of Stalin and his methods was notorious and anyone for whom she said a good word would only suffer for it. Other close friends of Comrade Misha were themselves in a precarious position. But suddenly he had an inspiration:

"Yaroslavsky!" he exclaimed. "Yes, if Emilian has not been thoroughly corrupted he must listen to us!"

Yaroslavsky, one of the few Old Bolsheviks still in power, was looked upon as the official theoretician of the Party, Stalin's personal high priest. He was head of the Society of the Godless and wrote elaborate articles explaining and justifying every new Stalinist outrage. I had little hope, therefore, from that direction, but Comrade Misha talked himself into optimistic expectations. Hadn't Yaroslavsky known him for dozens of years? Hadn't they fought together against the Tsar, been in prison together?

Next morning Comrade Misha telephoned and arranged the appointment. That in itself was an achievement. Passes were waiting for us when we arrived at the Central Committee. Yaroslavsky wore a Russian blouse.

He embraced and kissed Comrade Misha and shook hands cordially with me. For a moment hope stirred in my heart. Here was a comrade of the old stamp, a man of my father's idealistic generation.

But no sooner did Comrade Misha begin to explain the purpose of the visit, than Yaroslavsky's face froze into an expression of alarm. He chewed on the straggly ends of his nicotine-stained mustache in growing nervousness.

"Well, Emilian, that's the whole story," Comrade Misha concluded. "If you help us, I'll love you like my own brother. If you don't, I'll know that you, even you, Emilian, are lost. . . ."

"Forgive me, Misha," Yaroslavsky's tone had become official. "When you come to me as an old friend, it's one thing; when you come to me as to a responsible leader of the Party Control, it's another thing. It's my duty to protect the Party and its Leader against enemies. There's no room for friendship and favors. We can't afford to be soft. Do you see?"

"Yes, I see. But why all this rhetoric? I'm not a mass meeting, or a page in the *Bezbozhnik*. Will you help or won't you? Speak plainly."

"Now don't get excited, old friend. Comrade Kravchenko, will you leave us for a few minutes, so I can speak more freely?"

"No, no, he remains here, Emilian!" Comrade Misha exclaimed. "I'll have none of your newfangled secrets and intrigues. Are we comrades or aren't we?"

"All right, have it your way," Yaroslavsky shrugged.

We left his office dejected, broken in spirit. Comrade Misha's eyes were blurred with tears; he had to hold on to my arm for guidance.

"So even Emilian is dead—I mean the frank and courageous Emilian who was once my comrade. Ekh, Vitya, I'm glad I'm old. I shan't have to watch the ugliness much longer."

The only concession to friendship which Yaroslavsky made was to give me the names and telephones of several important functionaries at the Central Committee, and permission to use his name to obtain an audience. In the next few days I saw these people. From the formality of their behavior—friendly, smiling but rigidly formal—I suspected that Yaroslavsky had tipped them off to treat me well and to do nothing. Even men close to Stalin, apparently, could not afford to give aid and comfort to a "saboteur."

I looked through my list of Moscow addresses. Was there anyone I ought to look up? As I read the names, I crossed many of them off: this one dead, that one a suicide, the others arrested. Finally I came to one that gave me pause.

"Lazarev!" I said to myself. "I'll look him up. In a sense it was he who started me off on the journey that led to this dead end. Wasn't it his influence, back in the Donetz Basin coal mines, that led me into the Comsomol organization?"

When I rang his doorbell, two elderly women came to open the door. They stared at me in alarm when I asked for Lazarev, and one of them began to weep.

"My poor boy's gone . . . nearly a year now. . . . Didn't you know?

They said he was an enemy of the people. The infidels! The torturers!"

And thus I learned that my first preceptor in the Communist movement, too, was among the outcasts. He was paying for that part of him reflected in Tolstoy's picture by the side of Lenin and Karl Marx.

Fatigued by the failures and sorrow of these days, I was impelled to visit the family A——. I could always count on old Mrs. A—— and her charming daughter, Tanya, for a pleasant hour or two. Despite many tragedies, they had preserved a little of their natural joy in living. Comrade A—— with his wife and a small son had fled to America after 1905 to escape the Tsarist police. Other children were born to them in the United States, a boy and two girls who grew up as typical American youngsters.

After the revolution, the family came to Russia. Lenin himself welcomed them. A—— took a prominent part in the civil wars. While heading a contingent of Red Partisans against Whites and Japanese in the Far East, he was captured. His body was chopped to bits and burned while other prisoners looked on. With the end of the civil war, the broken family moved to Moscow where Lenin gave them an apartment and a pension in recognition of A——'s heroic services. The elder son grew up to be an engineer—it was through him that I met his family. He was sent to a concentration camp in the purge some years back. The women had remained alone.

Now I came unsuspectingly to their home, in an old house covered with sores. Their door was locked and sealed with wax. I made out the dread initials, N.K.V.D. A neighbor stuck her head out to see who was there.

"Oh, God help us, young man. Citizeness A—— and her daughter have been arrested, sent into exile!"

She shut her door quickly, afraid she had said too much. I left the house thoroughly shaken. I hadn't walked many steps when I realized that I was being followed. One glance at his boots and I had no doubt it was an N.K.V.D. man, despite the civilian overcoat. All I needed to fill my cup of sorrow now, of course, would be a report that I had come to visit a liquidated family!

Fortunately a dilapidated taxi was driving by at that moment. I hopped in and urged the chauffeur to drive quickly to the railroad terminal; I was late for my train. At the terminal I paid him off and found another taxi, which took me to within a few blocks of Comrade Misha's house. When I told my kindly hosts about the incident, Uncle Misha once more lost his temper.

"Oh the scoundrels! It's no better than in the Tsar's time," he exclaimed, pacing the room in agitation. "No, worse—a thousand times worse. In those days we had trials, lawyers, a fighting chance. When we were in political trouble, our friends didn't shun us. On the contrary, they visited us and made a fuss over us. There were protest meetings, appeals to the government, to the press, speeches in the Duma. Now there's only horrible silence and fear and cowardice everywhere.

"Another thing, Vitya. In my time the whole world seemed on our side. The democratic and liberal-minded people of England, France, America spoke up against the tyranny and gave us moral comfort. But today we're caught as in a prison. The outside world doesn't seem to know what's going on here. The very people who should be on our side are so often on the side of the tyrants and torturers and—the irony of it, my son!—they call themselves 'friends of the Soviet Union.' "

"Friends of despotism would be a better name for the fools," I said.

"Vitya, at our special library I sometimes see French and English papers. Only a few selected ones are allowed in, of course. Would you believe it, they write about the 'democracy' and the 'wonderful new life' in Russia! I'm not joking. I once saw an American book about our country. I read a few pages and I couldn't believe my eyes. The idiot author had been in Russia but had seen nothing and understood nothing. He described our bleeding fatherland as if it were some heaven on earth. The dolts! The charlatans!"

"But, Uncle Misha, it can't be that the whole world is really ignorant of what's going on here. It can't be that the whole world has gone crazy."

"Sure, it makes no sense, but if someone outside understands I've as yet to see evidence of the fact. I've been on lots of the official reception committees to delegations of foreign labor, foreign educators, students. It's clear from their fervor and from their naive questions that they know nothing of the horrors being visited on the Russian people. They know nothing of the reaction that's in the saddle here. Vitya, it's frightening. . . ."

He sat down, turned his face from me and began to sob.

My final act in the futile quest for justice was to call at the Commissariat of Heavy Industry. A spirit of boundless misery, which no one made the slightest effort to conceal, filled the whole organization. Few of the people I knew remained. It seemed almost indecent to inflict my troubles on officials who so obviously considered their own tenure among the living uncertain; in a place swarming with the ghosts of liquidated high officials, rank and file workers, Communists and non-Communists.

From the few officials who still dared talk to me I heard more about the magnitude of the N.K.V.D. raids on Soviet industry. The man credited with expanding the Soviet oil resources, M. Barinov, was liquidated together with his staff and assistants. So were Alperovich, head of the tool-bench industry, and his assistant, Stepanov, and many, many others. Nearly all of Ordzhonikidze's main associates—Alexander Gourevich, Rukhimovich, Pavlinovsky, for instance—were no longer among the free. Gourevich had been chief of all the metallurgical industries in the country; subsequently I heard that he went blind in prison and died there. His assistant, Anton Tochinsky, considered one of the leading Russian engineers, was also under arrest. Few high administrators, Commissariat department heads, directors of trusts and institutes, had escaped the storm of terror.

Merely to convey some sense of the extent of the slaughter, I want to list a few of the liquidated with whom I had had personal contacts. Their names can mean nothing to an outsider, but to those of us engaged in Russian industry they meant the cream of our technical brains:

I. Bondarenko, director of the Kharkov engine plant; Constantine Butenko, head of the *combinat* at Kuznetzk; Ganshin, who headed up the oil industry in the East; Gvakharia, director of the Makayev plant in the Donetz Basin; Ossipov-Schmidt, head of the synthetic rubber trust; Mikhailov, assistant director of the famous Dnieprostroi dam; S. Makar, the famous builder of Magnitostroi; the top man in the slate industry, the Old Bolshevik S. Schwartz; Gugel, director of the Azov steel combine in Mariupol; I. Kossior, a brother of the liquidated Politburo member and for a time in charge of all Far Eastern industry; M. Vlassov, chief of the Cheliabinsk ferrous smelting plant; G. Krzheminsky, head of the manganese trust in Nikopol; Nikolai Radin, director of a large Mariupol plant; Fyodr Logiyko, director of the Nizhni-Dnieprovsky plant; Zvaisnc, director of the Lysva plant in the Urals; Isak Rogochevsky, director of the Zaparozhe steel plant; Nikolai Donskov, head of the Chusovaya metallurgical factory; Khazanov, chief of metallurgy of all the Urals; Trachter, head of the Krivoi-Rog Ore Trust.

I choose the names almost at random and could prolong them for pages from memory. And I choose only top-shelf names.

On the train from Moscow I ran into my friend Jacob Vesnik, then director of the metallurgical *combinat* at Krivoi Rog. I paid less heed to his words than they merited, but somehow they remained in my mind, growing bigger, more meaningful as time passed. Vesnik was a great revolutionist and an important builder, an Old Bolshevik who had not yielded to the new totalitarian ways. He had been loaded with the highest decorations in the Red Army and then, when transferred to industrial work, had been close to Ordzhonikidze, Molotov and other Kremlin leaders. Frequently he had represented our country abroad on vital economic missions.

He was pleased by the accidental meeting. It turned out that he, too, had been in the capital in an effort to head off arrest. Vesnik's attractive wife, Eugenia, who was prominent in her own right, had recently been photographed with Stalin in the Kremlin. The publication of this photograph seemed a guarantee of immunity for herself and her husband. But Vesnik had no such illusions.

"I expect to be arrested on my return to Krivoi Rog," he told me. "I, too, found Moscow will give us no help. It all stems from the very top. You will hear us, the Old Guard who fought under Lenin, slandered as plotters of fantastic international frame-ups; you will hear us branded as traitors and enemies of the people. Remember, these vilifications are a screen for something else. Stalin and the Party cannot tell the masses the truth: that there is a conflict within the Party. For then the masses would want to take sides, and Stalin fears that the majority might win."

We talked a good deal. His many journeys abroad were mentioned. He looked into my eyes.

"If ever you get the chance to tell the outside world about the horrors here, Victor Andreyevich, it will be your duty to do so. At this stage a Russian who loves his country and his people can do no greater service. The struggle for the liberation of Russia cannot and must not cease."

His expectations of arrest were justified. His wife, too, was arrested, notwithstanding the brief glory of having shared a photograph with The Leader. In time my friend's words came to sound prophetic in my ears.

4

It was evening when I reached Nikopol after the useless journey. I was feeling low, hopeless. As I approached my cottage, I wondered why it was in darkness. Where was Pasha? I had written her that I was coming and she should have been here. I tried the door. It was locked. I knocked, louder, still louder. No answer. Fingers of fear suddenly clutched my throat.

My voice was so choked up I could barely make myself understood when I went to the next house. My neighbor, a factory official, looked at me in surprise, as if he were seeing a phantom.

"Victor Andreyevich!" he whispered. "Is it really you? Alive? Not arrested? Thank God!"

"What's happened? Where's Pasha? I've merely been to Moscow on business."

"Didn't you know, Victor Andreyevich? You've been removed from your post and ordered evicted from your house. I don't know where your belongings are. A wagon came and took them away. . . ."

I asked for permission to telephone Brachko.

"Oh, I'm glad you're back, Victor," the director said.

"But Piotr Petrovich, what's happened? Why have I been locked out of my house?"

"Don't worry. Keep a grip on yourself. By order of the City Committee I had to relieve you of your position. I'm putting you in charge of the Technical Division of the plant. You understand that I had no alternative, that I'm heartbroken."

"Of course I understand, Piotr Petrovich. Where shall I spend the night?"

"Oh yes, I've reserved a room for you at the plant's hotel in Nikopol. Not much of a room, but the only thing available."

I rode back to town. The hotel manager was expecting me. He was sympathetic. He knew what a come-down it was for me, after my luxurious house with its garage and garden, and so he apologized when he showed me into the room. That cell-like cubicle with its peeling wallpaper would be my "home" for the rest of my stay in Nikopol. My books and other belongings had been dumped in disorder in corners. Aside from the bed, there were a small table, a cupboard, a small mirror, and a faded portrait of Stalin on the wall. There was no washroom, not even a washbasin.

But I was tired, too tired to think or feel. I slept late into the next morning.

CHAPTER XVII

TORTURE AFTER MIDNIGHT

MY HEART sank within me when I recognized Gershgorn's voice on the telephone.

"Well, well, so the little bird's returned from its long journey. . . . I hope you like the new quarters at the hotel. . . . Come to see me at midnight!"

As usual I had to wait for him. It had been the first day in my new post as head of the Technical Division of the factory. I had worked long and late and had been on my feet most of the time. The emotional strain of my degradation, and of the eviction from my house, had taken more out of me than the physical effort. In any case, I was exhausted, despondent, half-dizzy when Gershgorn finally let me into his office.

"Well, Kravchenko," he smiled wryly, "I hope you've had a profitable trip. We don't like having our investigations interrupted in this way."

"I had the necessary permissions," I said.

"I know, I know. And I gather you went to find 'protection'—through people like Ivanchenko and Margolin, eh? Now, alas, both of them are under arrest as enemies of the people!"

"It's true, Comrade Gershgorn, I wanted help from Ivanchenko. And why not? He had been my superior for a number of years and a member of the government. As for Margolin, he happened to be the Party Secretary for the Region at the moment. After all, I wasn't the one who appointed them to these posts."

"Of course you weren't. But an amazing coincidence—all your friends and patrons turn out to be traitors! Filline, Margolin, Ivanchenko, so many others. Tell me, how does it happen that Margolin wrote a favorable letter about you to the City Committee? An old friend of yours, no doubt."

"I saw the man only once in my life, that day in his office."

"I'm not so sure of that. . . . But let that rest for the moment. I'm more interested in the dirty saboteur Ivanchenko. You've known the traitor for a long time——"

"Yes, but I didn't know him as a traitor."

"You never observed any acts of wrecking and sabotage on his part, working so close to him, being so friendly with him?"

"No, never."

"What can you tell me about his work insofar as it touched on the pipe-rolling industry?"

I recounted all I knew, what the whole country knew. Gershgorn's fat, glistening face now wore an angry grimace. His thick sausage-like fingers —I noticed how carefully they were manicured—drummed impatiently on the desk.

"Kravchenko, quit being funny. You know this isn't the information I need."

"It's the only information I have."

"I think we can help you remember a lot more before we're through 'training' you. We've had stubborn customers like you before. Now what do you know about Ivanchenko's relations with Kabakov?"

"Kabakov until his arrest was Party Secretary in the Urals and a member of the Central Committee of the Party. Naturally Ivanchenko had to see him often. But I know of nothing special or unusual."

"In other words, you won't talk."

"I'd gladly talk, but surely you don't expect me to invent information."

The new day was visible through the window, but Gershgorn, louder and more insulting as he grew more tired, was still hammering at me.

"Tell me, Kravchenko," he said suddenly, in the middle of another question, "why are you so afraid of arrest? Why do you chase around looking for help—even from Comrade Yaroslavsky? Maybe because you feel, deep inside, that you're guilty?"

"Please forgive me. It's now 5 A.M. and at eight I must report to work. If I'm not yet under arrest, it's not a very good hour to begin a philosophical discussion."

"Quite right, quite right. . . . We'll have many other nights together to explore the subject. I'm a student of human psychology, in my own way. You, as an engineer, test the resistance of metals, their pliability, their special qualities, yes? I, as a good Chekist, test the resistance of human beings, the political pliability of their minds and so on. Well, good-bye until next time."

I arose. I was so fatigued that I staggered. Wearily, holding on to the edge of the desk, I said:

"Look here, Gershgorn, I've known you for several years and you've known me. Do you really, honestly think I'm a saboteur? Please answer me."

"Sure, I'll answer you. We Chekists start by believing the accusations. Otherwise we'd get nowhere. As far as I'm concerned everyone's guilty unless he can prove his innocence. That's all for tonight. You can go!"

Late that afternoon I was at my desk in the new unfamiliar office. Drugged with sleeplessness, aching in all my muscles, my eyes burning, I tried desperately to focus my mind on the technical reports before me. The telephone rang. It was Brachko, but his voice was so dejected that I barely recognized it.

"Victor Andreyevich! Now it's my turn—the Factory Committee has just ended its meeting. I've been expelled from the Party! Expelled, after more than twenty years!"

"Piotr Petrovich, it can't be. . . ."

"Yes, and tonight a closed meeting of the Party organization in our plant will finish the job. I want to ask you—how shall I put it? But I'm sure you'll understand. I want to ask you not to speak for me. It would only make things worse." He hung up.

After a few uneasy hours of sleep, I went to the meeting. The new Secretary of the City Committee, Kondrashin, had been an engineer in my section. He was a sly, cautious man. He had that talent for avoiding responsibility which was so incalculably valuable under Soviet conditions. He let Comrade Los, the young man so hungry for power, conduct the case against Brachko.

In a long, impassioned and completely jumbled speech Los loads Brachko with all the sins on the super-purge calendar. The bad housing, the high percentage of spoilage, the low wages, the immense number of arrests in all departments of the factory—all of it, by Los's inflamed logic, is Brachko's fault; all of it is proof of purposeful and devilish sabotage!

"Out with him!" someone cries, and others take up the chorus. "It's about time! Down with wreckers!" Among the most vociferous, I notice, are several workmen, barracks people. In the nature of the case they can know nothing of the work or the character of the director of the great *combinat* in which they are insignificant cogs. They are merely expressing their private discontents, taking out their resentments, conveniently, on the highest administrative official. They do not stop to remember that wages as well as prices and appropriations for workers' houses are fixed by the authorities in Moscow.

"Does anyone wish to speak?" Los asks.

One after another Party members demand expulsion. Each adds a few more charges to the mountain of absurdity already piled up. Then a woman worker takes the floor. There is no room for doubting her sincerity.

"Comrades," she declares, "I work in the Nikopol Metallurgical *combinat*. Now, at last, it is clear to me why we live so poorly, why there are no houses for us workers, why we walk around without decent clothes. These Brachkos live in grand style, but the hardships of the proletariat don't touch them. Out with the saboteurs! They have jeered at us long enough!"

Her intenseness evokes stormy applause and cheers.

Finally Brachko speaks. He knows that his case is hopeless, that his words will not touch this excited meeting. These people are famished for vengeance, they need a legitimate scapegoat for their various private discontents. Brachko begins by telling of his twenty years as a loyal Communist. He tells how, before the revolution, as an officer at the front and a secret Bolshevik, he won over the soldiers to the workers' cause. He is interrupted with jeers, with dirty epithets.

"Don't play the demagogue! Enough of this manure! Pitch him out!"

Tears roll down Brachko's sunken cheeks. But the epithets revive his fighting spirit and he raises his voice above the interruptions. An embarrassed silence, a guilty silence, suddenly fills the large hall. He raises clenched fists above his head.

"I, Brachko, with these two hands stormed the Winter Palace of the Russian Tsars! I fought against the Whites and against interventionists! I carry a dozen wounds which I suffered for the revolution. Then, for fifteen years, I worked day and night to build, build, build, despite terrible handicaps.

"And now I stand before you who are ready to tear me to pieces. Why? Where I built you wish to tear down. You blame me for the very conditions against which I struggled with all my strength. I ask you for nothing. I expect nothing. Go ahead and finish the dirty job. It's clear to me that I'm finished no matter what you decide here. But I want you to think of what you're doing. I leave my fate to your conscience. None of your speeches, none of your insults, changes the fact that I'm completely without guilt.

"Believe me or not, comrades, I love the people of this my native land. I have risked my life a thousand times for them, and if now they reward me by destroying that life with their own hands, I take it like a soldier. That's all I have to say."

The vote for expulsion was almost unanimous. I left the meeting and drove to Brachko's house, where the servant girl let me in. After a while he arrived, quiet as a shadow, his shoulders shaking in tearless sobs.

"Somehow I knew you would be waiting for me, Victor Andreyevich," he said. "Thank you from the bottom of my heart. Don't forget, if you ever have the chance—if this madness ever subsides—tell those who will listen that these were insane lies they have told about me."

He would not let me remain for more than a few minutes. If the Chekists found us together, it would be bad for both of us. He had no doubt that he would be arrested. The N.K.V.D. had wanted a "popular" approval in advance in this case; it would make their labors in Nikopol easier.

Brachko did not show up to work next morning. I learned that he had decided to go to Dniepropetrovsk to appeal to the Regional Committee. But he got only as far as Zaparozhe, where he was removed from the train. I never saw him again, and to this day do not know his fate. Two days later his wife, his wife's sister and his secretary were arrested. Only his aged mother and a six-year-old niece who lived with them remained, and they were evicted from the house. The old woman, her mind snapped by the tragedy, wandered through the streets of Nikopol for months asking people whether they had seen her "little Piotr" who was "lost." Then she, too, disappeared.

2

The same week, the City Committee took up the "Kravchenko case" again. It was generally assumed that my number was up. But my lucky star had not lost its magic; it was Brachko, I recalled, who first referred to that mythical star, at the time I discovered the missing documents. That very day a long front-page article appeared in the Nikopol press accusing a group of engineers in our factory of various political sins, especially rudeness to workers. The chief culprits, according to this article, included Makarov and Shaikevich—my principal accusers!

The blow prepared for me was thus miraculously deflected. No doubt Los felt that it would be awkward to drag out his time-stained accusations when his main witnesses were themselves in hot water. The Committee forgot the scheduled subject and devoted itself to the new sensation. Both Makarov and Shaikevich were thrown out of the Party. Subsequently I came to know that the publication and timing of the article which saved me were not accidental; old Silinin and other friends had maneuvered it that way.

Brachko's arrest sent new currents of fear through the factory. Inevitably many of those who had worked close to him, whom he had befriended, would be rounded up. Chief engineer Vishnev was in a mood of black melancholy. I had to see him about some problem in my department. After the first few words I realized that his mind was no longer normal. He sat at his desk, wearing his best clothes, with his Order of Lenin pinned on his coat lapel. He was crying like a child, in breathless gasps.

"You see, Victor Andreyevich," he said, "when they come to arrest me, they will also arrest Lenin. Nobody talks to me any more. They no longer recognize me as the chief engineer. Only Lenin talks to me."

I would hear two years later, through a friend, that Vishnev's mind, already clouded, broke entirely during his torture. The secret police thought his insanity a "trick" to avoid "confession" and continued the torture until they were convinced his madness was genuine.

One night, a few weeks later, I was aroused from sleep. I was wanted on the telephone, in the lobby below. I got dressed and went down. It was Gershgorn. He ordered me to come to the N.K.V.D. at once.

Again I sat in his surgeon-like office. I envied the fresh, healthy flush on his face. If only I had my old physical vitality. . . . Acute insomnia, worry, the hopeless chaos in the factory were draining my strength, leaving me weak and nauseous.

"Well, let's get on with our little chat," Gershgorn exclaimed, flaunting his health, his energy. "And I do hope you will be more sensible, *more cooperative*, this time."

"What do you want from me?"

Gershgorn banged the table. Then he shook his hand in my face.

"Here *we* ask the questions!" he shouted. "All you do is answer them! Do you understand?"

"I understand. . . . Only I'm still not under arrest, I'm still a Party man in good standing . . ."

"That doesn't concern us here. To us you're a saboteur. I ask you again, what do you know of the sabotaging activities of Ivanchenko? You've had time enough to think it over."

"I know nothing."

"Look here, Kravchenko, it will be better for you, and will save me a lot of trouble, if you start talking. We have ways and means to make people talk. We make them soft as silk and yielding as butter. Do you understand?" There was a voluptuous, almost erotic, quality to his voice.

"If you value the shape of your face—you're not a bad looking fellow—you'll be more helpful. . . ."

"I'm speaking honestly. I can't tell you things that I don't know or that aren't so."

"So you don't want to talk?"

At that point the telephone rang. He was wanted by Dorogan, Gershgorn said. Would I please wait for him—in the corridor. We stepped out of the room together and I was turned over to a uniformed Chekist.

"Have this citizen wait for me," he said.

Four or five men were already standing in the corridor, their faces turned to the wall, their hands clasped behind their backs.

"Citizen, go over there, take the same position," the Chekist said, shoving me towards them.

"But I'm not arrested. I'm here just at Comrade Gershgorn's request."

"Shut up! Do what you're told! Face the wall, hands behind your back, and don't dare turn around. And don't rest your head on the wall either."

I took my place near the other men. We could not see each other, in the dim corridor light, nor could we see what was happening behind our backs. In the course of the four hours I was kept standing there, other men joined the line-up. I had heard of this form of torture, one of the mildest in the N.K.V.D. book; now I was suffering it in my own flesh.

No one who has not been forced to stand in one position, facing nothingness, hour after hour, can ever be made to understand what it's like. Your hands, your arms, your feet become heavier, more leaden, by the minute. You begin to feel every part of your body, each finger, each joint of the finger, as a separate weight . . . tons and tons of crushing weariness. You know you can't endure it, yet you endure. . . .

Heart-rending shrieks came from the rooms along the corridor; shrieks and curses, the sound of blows and the dull thud of bodies hitting the floor. People were being questioned, beaten, threatened. I don't know how long I had been standing there when I heard steps and voices at one end of the corridor. Someone began to sing:

> *Full of strength, aromatic and gentle*
> *The apple-tree bloomed in our orchard.* . . .

"Shut your gullet!" a Chekist shouted. "I'll make *you* bloom if you don't shut up."

"No use yelling at him, he's stark mad," another said, as the group went off somewhere.

I broke out in a cold sweat. Tears of humiliation flowed of themselves, without my knowing it, down my face. My whole body itched intolerably. When I uncrossed my hands to scratch myself, the guard ordered me to put them back or he would blow my brains out. As if to illustrate his threat, an unearthly howl, scarcely human, came from somewhere behind me. . . . Daylight began to filter into the corridor. I saw it reflected on the gray wall.

"Well, come along Kravchenko. Sorry to have kept you waiting. There's so much work, so much work. . . ."

It was Gershgorn talking, in a fresh cheerful voice. I turned around. I followed him through a blur. Sitting in his office, I felt no sense of relief. It was as if I were still standing, still pinned down by tons and tons of fatigue. Gershgorn asked questions but I caught only single words. They made no sense to me.

"All right, go home, get some sleep. You'll need it. I'll call you again . . . soon. And by the way, these little talks are nobody's business but yours and mine. Our little secret. If you babble to anyone, you'll regret it."

Back at the hotel, I washed myself with ice-cold water, then lay sleepless on the unmade bed until it was time to go to work. A message from the N.K.V.D. awaited me: I was to be there again at midnight. . . .

That night Gershgorn was unctuously polite, almost cordial at the outset. He even offered me tea and cookies, which I declined. I was not really being kind and considerate of him, he said. I was obliging him to behave like a beast—keeping me waiting in the corridor, for instance— when in fact he was not at all a beast. Did I think his was a pleasant job? Did I think he enjoyed it? But what is a man to do when he was born with a strong sense of duty?

"Tonight you can do us a little favor, Kravchenko," he said. "The N.K.V.D. will appreciate it, the Party will appreciate it. You see, we're not asking much of you."

"What's the favor?"

"Just your signature, your honest freely-given signature as an engineer, a Soviet director and a loyal Party member. You see, it's about a serious matter. A defense matter. Pipes with impurities have been provided by your factory for the chemical defense works. No fault of yours, of course. You didn't make the metal. Quite clearly it was organized sabotage which began way up high, in Moscow, and percolated down to Kharkov, then to the Zaporozhestal where the director was the enemy of the people Rogochevsky, now under arrest, and where the steel for your pipe was smelted."

The idea, I saw at once, was a horrible police fantasy. The steel we received was often of bad quality. I had reported it and protested repeatedly. Sometimes Brachko and Vishnev had been in despair about it. But there were simple, technical causes fully known to Ordzhonikidze, to Piatakov, to Ivanchenko—causes related to honest errors and inexperience at the smelting end.

"In the first place, Comrade Gershgorn, I'm not at all sure that the impurities and the bad quality were due to sabotage," I said. "Secondly, I should like to read the document you want me to sign."

"By all means. Here it is." He handed me a sheaf of some twenty long closely typed sheets.

I read slowly, for almost an hour. Waves of heat and of chill swept through me as I read. It was an extraordinary mixture of half-truths and full lies, carefully, ingeniously, fitted together to make a predetermined melodramatic pattern. The document was peppered with names, some of which I knew, dozens of names: nationally prominent engineers in the chemical and steel industries, plant managers, foremen. Ivanchenko and Brachko were there, officials in half a dozen Commissariats, Piatakov— an amazing "amalgam" of important and obscure people.

There was a certain logic, a certain consistency, to the story—provided one accepted without question the premise that everyone concerned, from leading figures in the Commissariats in Moscow to smelters in Zaparozhe to foremen in Nikopol, was a disciplined, daring and diabolically clever member of a conspiracy.

"I can't sign such a document," I announced when I had completed reading. "I made pipes with the steel sent to me. Sometimes the steel contained impurities. That's all I know and that's all I could possibly sign to."

"Very well. Why then did some of our most eminent professors and industrial managers sign it? Do you set yourself up as a greater expert than all of them?"

The document, in truth, was signed by outstanding Soviet scientists and distinguished engineers. Their collective verdict was "sabotage." I could readily imagine how those signatures had been extracted. But in this place I could merely repeat that I would confirm nothing of which I had no personal knowledge.

"If you wish," I said, "I'll testify that there were impurities in the metal."

"Are you joking with me, Kravchenko? Have you forgotten where you are? Impurities! We don't need your testimony on that. What we need is your confirmation of sabotage. Pipe production was under your direction."

I was silent. Gershgorn argued with me, screamed at me, until dawn. He read passages to me and pointed out how "obvious" the wrecking intentions had been. The only thing obvious to me—even in my trance of fatigue—was that the Nikopol N.K.V.D. had been ordered to obtain what was in effect my indirect confession. It was a missing link in the chain of fantastic hypotheses. Once I consented to provide the link, I would be strangled with the same chain. I was not being heroic in refusing to sign; it was perfectly clear to me that the signature would be tantamount to my own death warrant.

Finally I was dismissed, with a string of curses and a pointed warning to think it over.

Night after night for many months I was summoned to headquarters, interrogated, threatened, cajoled. The ordeal of sleeplessness was calculated to wear me down. All day I worked; I could not afford to relax in my new post, because any error or failure would be construed as additional "evidence" of wrecking. And most of the night I was tormented.

Meanwhile the machinery of Party justice kept grinding. A new investigating commission reported, reluctantly, that the original accusations had been refuted by documents. The decision in my case reached under Filline was sustained under Kondrashin. Though a coward and an opportunist, the new Secretary was not displeased by the outcome; when no one was looking he pressed my arm in congratulation. I was still a Party member, theoretically one of "the best of the best," one of the *élite* rulers of the land.

But the wretched nocturnal affliction went on without reprieve. Every night new accusations were hurled at me. What were my relations with those "wild dogs" Margolin, Brachko, Vishnev, Ivanchenko, Filline, Rosengoltz? Wasn't it a fact that I had consorted with the "Menshevik spy" Dubinsky? Hadn't I given aid and comfort to the "fascist spy" Zelman? Every new name and new subject provided Gershgorn with subject matter for hours of cross-examination and brow-beating. I was dazed and stupefied, aching in every nerve and muscle.

Soldiers on a battlefield know what prolonged sleeplessness is like. I felt like a swimmer carried far from shore by the tide, still flailing weakly, still above water, but his last ounce of strength flowing out of him with every painful stroke.

One night, after I had been kept standing in the corridor, face to wall, for four or five hours, Gershgorn sent me home without questioning. Sorry, he said, but he couldn't spare the time for further "chatting." The following night, however, he sprang a brand-new accusation.

"Kravchenko, you had two Americans living with you, didn't you?"

"Yes. They were helping us operate some American machinery."

"Why did the traitor Brachko put them precisely with you, not with someone else?"

"I suppose because I'm a bachelor. I was living alone in a big house."

"Tell me, did you ever complain about the Soviet regime to these foreigners?"

"No, of course not. They're still in the U.S.S.R. You can check up."

"Don't tell me what I can do. I'm getting tired of your insolence. What were your political connections with these Americans?"

"None at all. I treated them kindly, which was my duty."

"But it was Ivanchenko who ordered that machinery from the United States."

"Yes."

"Sabotaging plans between Ivanchenko and the American firm are therefore quite possible."

"I wouldn't know that."

"You wouldn't? You're an innocent and naive little lambkin. But"— and spoke slowly, ominously, as if about to make a devastating revelation —"but you visited these Americans in Kharkov, didn't you?"

"Yes, I ran into one of them on the street. He pressed me to come with him to the Krasnaya Hotel and I couldn't very well refuse."

"And you met them again in a Moscow hotel?"

"No. I was at the Metropole, eating, quite alone. The Americans were at another table, drinking, with a couple of girls. They yelled my name across the dining room. I had no alternative but to go over and accept a drink. I sat with them only five minutes or so, then left."

"And why did one of your Americans make a sudden air trip to Stockholm? And why did he bring you a present?"

"As far as I knew he went on some personal matter. There was no reason why he should tell me. As for the present, it was a piece of special steel, and certain materials for thermal tests, which we could not produce at home. It was just a favor to me and to our plant."

"But he also brought anti-Soviet directives for Ivanchenko from counter-revolutionary centers in Stockholm, didn't he?"

"I know nothing about that."

Interrogation about the Americans took up several hours. Suddenly the door opened. The hulking Dorogan, savage with anger, stamped in. His fleshy lips were twisted into an ugly grimace. Gershgorn stood up respectfully.

"Gershgorn, how long will you let this wrecker twist you around his little finger? Are you a Chekist or a dirty rag? Too bad we didn't arrest him a year ago instead of letting the City Committee mess with him."

Gershgorn seemed alarmed. Obviously he trembled in the presence of his chief.

"Comrade chief, I've been doing my best. Been working on him every night for a month. If you wish me to use firmer methods——"

Dorogan ignored him. He was towering angrily over me.

"Watch out, Kravchenko, or you'll get badly hurt!"

He went out, slamming the door. When Gershgorn released me, an hour or so later, I decided to talk to Dorogan. I wanted the ordeal wound up, one way or another. Outside his office, I gave my name to the guard. I was allowed to enter.

"Well, what in hell do you want?" Dorogan yelled.

"I wanted to ask what you want of me. I've been tortured so long. . . . Every night new accusations are invented. Comrade Dorogan, you're a member of the Bureau of the City Committee. You know I've been vindicated twice. I ask you as a Communist——"

"As a Communist!" he shouted and rushed at me like an infuriated bull. He slapped me with an open palm, first on one cheek, then on the other. He grabbed me by the throat and began to choke me, at the same time shaking me violently from side to side. He was a powerful man, his hands were shackles of iron being pulled tighter, tighter. Everything began to go black. . . .

"Get out before I kill you!" I heard him yell as he shoved me through his door.

I staggered against the wall and remained there for a few minutes, until the iron ring around my neck relaxed. I hardly know how I managed to get back to the hotel. Painfully I climbed the stairs. I threw myself on the bed and fell into a deep sleep.

3

One afternoon, about one o'clock, my office door opened and Gershgorn walked in, shaking the snow from his military greatcoat. "He's come to get me!" I thought.

"Hello, Kravchenko." The "hello" was reassuring. "Where is engineer Valentin Bichkov, the head of your chemical laboratory?"

"He's in the casting section. They're working with the electrical smelter."

"Call him immediately, immediately I say, but don't tell him why."

I got Bichkov on the telephone and asked him to come over to see me. He explained that he couldn't leave the smelting and pleaded to see the job through.

"I'm sorry, drop everything. It's important." I hung up the receiver.

"May I know why you want Bichkov?" I asked. "After all, he's my subordinate."

"Look here, Kravchenko. Wasn't what Dorogan gave you the other night enough? You *are* difficult to train. Incidentally, report to me at eleven tonight."

"Can't I have a single night of sleep?"

"You sign what needs to be signed, cooperate a little, and you'll sleep all you want."

Bichkov arrived, suspecting nothing. He was in overalls, perspired and grimy.

"Good day, Victor Andreyevich," he said, then, noting my visitor, and still unsuspecting, he added, "Good day, Comrade Gershgorn."

He extended his hand to Gershgorn, who ignored the gesture.

"Don't 'comrade' me, you wrecker!"

"What's wrong, Comrade Gershgorn? Don't you know me?"

"I know you all right. Your name!"

"Bichkov."

"First name and patronymic?"

"Valentin Ivanovich."

"You're under arrest as a wrecker. Come along!"

"But what's happened? I don't understand."

"Step on it! Forward, march!" Gershgorn had drawn his revolver and pointed it at his prisoner.

The bewildered young engineer went out, followed by the N.K.V.D. official.

I locked the door of my office. I had no more strength left. Perhaps I should sign, anything, everything. What was the use? What chance did I have against these power-drunk sadists?

An hour later, Bichkov's young wife came to see me. Their two-year-old daughter was with her. Mrs. Bichkov, a pretty woman, was weeping hysterically. The child, too, was crying. I tried to calm them, to reassure them. . . . And at night, doubly exhausted by the day's events and my own troubles, I went through another long session of questioning that pulled my nerves tighter, tighter. . . .

In three or four days Bichkov's wife called on me again. It appeared that a camera, a stop-watch and other plant property which her husband kept in his office had disappeared. Until they were restored, the financial department refused to pay her the wages due to the arrested man. I called Bichkov's assistant. He swore he knew nothing about this property, but I had a shrewd suspicion that he had stolen it. The plight of the woman and her child obliged me to call Gershgorn.

"Please ask Bichkov where he put the camera, watch and other items,"
I pleaded with him.

"Ask him yourself," Gershgorn replied. "Come over right away and
I'll permit you to talk to him."

I wondered why he seemed anxious to stage this meeting between the
arrested chemical engineer and myself. Within the hour I was in the
N.K.V.D. Gershgorn rang for the guard and ordered him to bring in
the prisoner "from the cellar." Soon two Chekists arrived and between
them, hardly recognizable, was Bichkov.

I shuddered at the sight. His face was bruised and swollen. One eye
was closed. His overalls—the same ones in which he had been arrested—
were torn and bloody. His hands were caked with blood. A foul odor,
the odor of prison and illness, hung around him. I could not believe that
this battered creature was the same handsome young engineer who had
come to my office a few days earlier.

And I knew why Gershgorn had asked me to come. He wanted to
give me a glimpse of what happened to those who wouldn't "cooperate"
with him.

"Valentin Ivanovich," I said, averting my eyes from the depressing
sight, "where did you leave the camera, stop-watch and other plant
property?"

"All those things, Victor Andreyevich," he replied in a tremulous voice,
the voice of a man in agony, "are in the hands of my assistant. He used
them in the laboratory."

"Thank you, that's all I wanted to know."

"Victor Andreyevich . . . my wife and daughter . . . my poor
Mariusa. . . ." He began to cry aloud.

"That's enough, Bichkov," Gershgorn banged the desk with his hairy
fist. "None of your dramas or we'll begin training you all over again.
You didn't cry when you poisoned workers in your department, did you?
Get out of here!"

So that was the charge against Bichkov! Recently we had worked
on stainless steel pipe, which had to be etched in nitrous acid, in improvised wooden troughs. Bichkov had instructed the workers on the
process in line with official instructions prescribed for all plants. Four
men, having disregarded his instructions, were overcome by fumes and
rushed to the hospital. Now, apparently, Bichkov was being accused of
deliberately "poisoning" workers! It was the most fashionable sort of
accusation, since it aimed to line up the workers against the engineers.
The thing was not only far-fetched but insane.

Back at the plant, I summoned Bichkov's assistant, who happened
to be a Party man though Bichkov was not. I threatened to turn him over
to the N.K.V.D. as a thief if I didn't have the missing items on my desk
in ten minutes. They were on my desk in two minutes. When Mrs. Bichkov
arrived to claim the several objects for delivery to the administration
office, I told her I had seen her husband.

"Valentin is well and looks rested," I lied. "Of course he misses you
and asked me to tell you not to worry. He sent you and the child his
love and kisses."

What else could I tell the unfortunate woman? She thanked me and left. I never saw her again, nor do I know what happened to her husband.

During most of the autumn, the N.K.V.D. kept me up nights only intermittently, but towards the end of 1937 the inquisition was resumed on an uninterrupted schedule. There was no dearth of subjects for "chatting"—every new batch of liquidations in the industry offered new complications on which my testimony was considered vital. It was then that I took the step from which I had long shied away in dread of offending the inquisitors.

I wrote to the Control Commission of the Central Committee, at its Dniepropetrovsk headquarters, complaining that I was being hounded with unjustified charges of sabotage. I didn't mention the N.K.V.D., having been warned a hundred times to keep my nocturnal sessions secret, even from the Party. In theory at least, the Control Commission kept an eye on the rights and honor of Party members. Formally I based my request on the reprimand which was still on my record; I asked the Commission to remove that stain.

A few days later an investigator arrived. I had been exonerated by the City Committee, he said, so why was I complaining?

"There is still a reprimand against me," I said. "It ought to be erased. I'd like the Control Commission of the Party to check the accusations against me." I outlined the main charges which were being thrown in my face night after night.

The investigator puttered around for several days, interviewed various people in the Party administration and in the factory, and departed. My nightly questioning proceeded with few interruptions. I had lost weight. My eyes were now chronically inflamed. Friends who had not seen me for a long time had difficulty in recognizing me.

Nikopol at this time was plastered with placards about the first "democratic elections" in Russia under the Soviet Constitution. On December 12, 1937, the peoples of Russia would exercise their proud right to choose members of the Supreme Soviet by "secret ballot." The posters, the press, the radio loud-speakers on Nikopol streets and in the metal factories and manganese mines were blaring forth the glad tidings.

"Rally around the Party! Vote for the happy socialist life! No one should fail to use his privilege of the secret ballot! The most democratic Constitution! Long live our Beloved Leader and Teacher, Comrade Stalin!"

It all seemed a mockery of my own sufferings and the sufferings of millions of others. No one took the "elections" seriously, of course. Like the mass meetings and the resolutions, it was a ritual which men went through, out of fear, in undisguised boredom, while the agitators and the radio horns shouted slogans. At this time new arrests were being made at our *combinat*—the head of our Financial Department, B——; the chief electrician, Romanchenko; and others.

On December 12, I stood in a long queue in the city and finally received the "secret ballot." It contained a single list of names drawn up by the Party. There was not even a space for voting "yes" or "no"; nor a space for writing in other names. If we were opposed to anyone on the list, we had been instructed, we had the right to cross off his name. In the closed booth I folded the slip of paper and threw it into the receptacle. Among the five thousand voters in our factory, probably not one had dared to strike out a single name. The press boasted of this unanimous approval of the "happy life."

Election day was a holiday, a day for meetings and refreshments. Gershgorn celebrated the occasion by keeping me standing in the corridor for several hours and by being exceptionally brutal in his interrogations. From his questions I judged that Ivanchenko was being accused of wrecking in the pipe-rolling industry and that to round out the N.K.V.D. picture it was essential that I "confess" guilty collaboration.

"I cannot honestly tell you more than I know," I kept repeating.

"To hell with your honesty. What I need is facts, not your confounded honesty. What a shame we didn't pull you in at the proper time. You'd be silky and yielding by now all right."

My resistance was cracking. I yearned for an end to the long torment, on almost any terms. Sometimes I found myself drifting off into a drowsy daydream: I signed my name in large bold letters . . . the orchestra struck up the *Internationale* . . . I was conducted in triumph to a big downy bed and tucked in by my mother and grandma Natasha. . . . Whether my tormentors knew it or not, I knew myself that I was in a mood for surrender. Another week or two of this hammering, another beating or two, and I would give in, take the consequences. I was not made of steel, alas.

It was at this juncture that old Silinin came to visit me at my hotel. Had he guessed that I was reaching the end of my endurance, that I might capitulate? Watching me at a distance, had he surmised what was happening and realized that I needed some moral support?

"Why do you look so badly?" the old man began. "Tell me frankly, because I suspect the worst anyhow. You can trust me."

I needed little urging. The yearning to tell someone, to pour out my aching heart, was like a torturing thirst. I told him everything: how for these many months I had been kept awake, how various incriminating papers were being put before me to sign.

"I beg you, comrade, not to sign," Silinin said. "You've held out this long, hold out to the end. Signing won't save you. It will only spring the trap and you'll be lost forever."

"But how long, how long can human flesh and nerves take the punishment?"

"I know, I know, my dear. I have seen a lot in my long years and I have had experience of suffering. But I think the purge is easing off. There are not many more left for purging—about 40 per cent of all Communists in the Nikopol district have been expelled or arrested, and for every Party member purged, at least eight non-Party people have been arrested. I have it from someone at the City Committee—though I can't vouch for it—that there's a new directive; no more arrests of Communists without the consent of the Party. For pity's sake hold out a little longer. Dorogan has raised the question of your arrest at least five times at the City Committee. He's furious. If you yield to the rascals now you'll be letting us all down."

I promised. It was his faith in me, more than his advice or his optimism, which stopped me on the brink of capitulation.

"And now," Silinin said, "let's drink to the New Year."

Until that moment I had not realized that this was New Year's Eve. At the N.K.V.D. that night I stood from eleven till three in the morning in the dim corridor, facing a discolored wall, listening to the cries of the victims and the curses of their torturers. Neither Gershgorn nor Dorogan came for me—no doubt they were celebrating the advent of 1938 with their families and comrades.

Arrests in the plant took a new spurt in the next few days. Every time the *pogrom* seemed to have subsided, the pause merely turned out to be the prelude to a new attack. The brakes had been completely released with the death of Ordzhonikidze. His successor, Kaganovich, had none of Ordzhonikidze's scruples and squeamishness. He "cooperated" and arrests of technical and industrial personnel increased sharply. Among those now removed from our plant was Myron Ragoza, the commercial director of the *combinat*. His wife and adopted daughter were driven out of their apartment.

In the first week of January Gershgorn put a new document before me. It was my "voluntary deposition," in effect a confession. A long and devious statement it was, full of ambiguities and oblique admissions. The crimes of my friends, my superiors, my subordinates were outlined boldly; my own share of responsibility was treated lightly, almost casually. It was there by implication but not stated outright. This was calculated to make my capitulation easier, more tempting.

"Please understand," Gershgorn said as I read page after page of the technical fairy tale, "this is the *absolute minimum* which the N.K.V.D. expects from you. There's no room for bargaining. If you don't agree, you're declaring war on the N.K.V.D. and you won't get away with it. I'm as weary of this drawn-out examination as you are, so be sensible. Will you sign with a pen or a pencil?"

"With neither. The things I know in these assertions are not true . . . the rest I don't know. I have made no such admissions as you put into my mouth here."

"And I say you'll sign, you saboteur! The way Bichkov signed, the way Ivanchenko signed!"

"Do what you wish. I'll not confess to crimes of which I'm innocent."

Gershgorn sprang up in sudden fury and rushed at me, screaming, "Saboteur, wrecker, rascal! Take this—and this!" His huge fists were crashing into my face like a couple of pistons run amok. Blood spurted from my nose. Blood filled my mouth with a warm briny nausea. "Now will you sign?" And again the hailstorm of blows and kicks enveloped me. Blood from a head gash was in my eyes, blinding me.

I heard, rather than saw, Dorogan stride into the room. My nerves had learned to recognize his heavy step. He, too, began to pound me with his fists. I fell to the floor and rolled into a ball, as if crawling deeper into my own skin, while four heavy, cruel booted feet stamped and kicked me.

I moaned with pain. Gershgorn must have rung for the guards, who were picking me up.

"Take the rascal away! Throw him out!" Dorogan bellowed.

As I was dragged through the door I felt his fist crash once more into the back of my neck. The guards led me into a small room, where I was left to nurse my wounds. I sat there for an hour, perhaps two hours. Time was an agony without dimensions. I could not organize any thoughts. I was not even angry.

Then Gershgorn came in.

"Well, have you thought it over or do you want some more persuasion? We have much better arguments than you've tasted tonight."

"No, I won't sign. You may kill me but I won't sign."

"I'm giving you three days to think it over. Now get out!"

And so I left—but my Party card was still in my pocket. . . .

I found myself in the street, stumbling through a bitter snowstorm. The gale lashed my butchered face with a thousand whips. I crawled to the hotel. In the lobby my mind took in, mechanically, the words on a large placard, left over from the elections: "Rally around Stalin for the Happy Socialist Life!"

I lay down on my bed without taking my clothes off. No matter how I turned, I saw the portrait of Stalin against the peeling wallpaper. I did not think of the physical pain, but of the humiliation. "So now, Comrade Stalin," I spoke to the portrait, "our acquaintance is complete. Nothing has remained unsaid. Everything is clear. Greetings, Comrade Stalin."

A profound sadness filled me, an impersonal sadness. I was suffering for the whole human race. I was humiliated for all mankind. *I suffer for my motherland and my people . . . for my poor "Socialist Russia."*

The pain seemed to recede. Pity was healing my body, the pity that flooded my soul and was not self-pity but universal compassion.

Gershgorn, and you too, Dorogan, and your Führer in the Kremlin, you no longer can hurt me. You don't understand that I shall not sign . . . because as long as I hold out, there is hope. You don't understand that the fate of our country, maybe the fate of mankind, depends on my resistance. . . . I'm not silky and yielding. I'm resilient steel. I'll bend but I shan't break. I can strike back and I shall strike back. . . .

For a while I dozed off, carried away on a big soft cloud. Then I awoke again and the pain flooded back into my tortured body. I looked into the cold eyes of Stalin up there on the wall and I hated him and his regime as I had never hated anyone or anything. Now the old recurrent fantasy, the bitter-sweet fantasy of shooting myself, gripped my mind and prodded my body. But my body would not move. I was too tired to go to the suitcase to draw out the revolver, to pull the trigger. My mind was doing those very things, while my body remained inert on the blood-stained bed.

I was falling asleep, under Stalin's watchful eye. But part of my brain was alert for steps in the hall. Tonight they would come to take me. There, I knew it! The steps echoed through my sleep. There was a knock at the door. I opened my eyes, arose painfully and stumbled towards the door. I held the doorknob for a few moments, my last moments of freedom. . . . Then I opened the door.

In the semi-darkness stood a gray-haired little woman, her winter coat covered with snow. She had a suitcase in her hand. At first I didn't understand. I thought it was part of a waking dream. Then I knew.

"Mother, dear mother!" I cried and fell into her arms.

4

Mother washed and dressed my wounds. She didn't cry. She didn't ask questions. Instead she talked about herself. Instinctively she drew my pity away from my troubles to her own. She was a woman of immense will power.

"Forgive me for coming like this, unannounced, Vitya," she said. "I felt there was something wrong. A mother's heart, I suppose. I've walked four miles from the station through this awful storm. I couldn't find a carriage or even a peasant cart. Several motorcars passed, but they didn't see me when I shouted. Four miles in this gale is a long walk, dragging the suitcase. You didn't think your old mother could still do it, did you, Vityenka? But we small women are the hardiest mothers of the lot."

She had brought me woolen socks, a blanket, some warm shirts . . . the things a man might need in prison or in concentration camp. I had told the family nothing about my ordeal. Yet my mother knew. She had no need to ask questions . . . Soon the light of the new day, reflected on the snow piled up on the window sill, came in through the window.

"Yes, Vitya, I'm experienced," mother sighed as she unpacked the suitcase. "I used to prepare these same things for your father when he was taken to prison. . . . The years roll on, but the prisons remain. Here's a pair of fur mittens, may God help us!"

Tears at last were flowing down her cheeks.

In the excitement of the reunion I had forgotten Stalin. But there he was, still looking down on me. A choking fury suddenly filled my heart. When mother left the room for a while, I pulled the Stalin portrait off the wall, slowly, deliberately, as if I were performing a difficult but terribly important rite. With ceremonial earnestness, not with relish but in sorrow, I tore it into shreds, then tore the shreds into still smaller pieces. Then I carried the little pieces of paper carefully, as if they were terribly precious, to the toilet in the hall, threw them into the bowl and pulled the chain.

I listened to the gurgling of the water, and I knew that never, never again would I feel the same about the Party, the Leader, the Cause. The umbilical cord that had so long bound me to these ideas and symbols, despite everything, was finally and forever cut. I would work for the government, I would accept important Party assignments, I would make speeches. But it would all be play-acting, strategy, while waiting patiently for the chance to escape: Escape! I thought of it not as the end of the struggle but as a chance to begin the struggle in earnest.

5

At the plant I parried solicitous inquiries about my swollen eyes and bruises with a tale of accident, but I saw in their eyes that people were not convinced. A notification awaited me from Dniepropetrovsk: the Control Commission would take up my case the day after tomorrow and requested that I be present. The new director of the plant, Comrade Shalakhov, refused to give me a leave of absence. But I decided, in my mind, that I would go without his permission.

That night I saw Mother off at the station, calmed her as best I could, and told her that I would be home for a visit two days later.

Saying nothing to anyone about the scheduled hearing before the Control Commission, I left for Dniepropetrovsk. That night, the three days of grace being up, Comrade Gershgorn would wait for me in vain. The two full nights of sleep had given me new strength and with strength came new hope.

In the reception room of the Control Commission, at Regional Party headquarters, a Chekist was on duty. Beyond the large double door, I thought with a sudden surge of alarm, strangers would be deciding my fate. Eight or ten other men sat on the padded bench around the waiting room. From their morose looks I surmised that each of them had some problem not unlike my own. The Party investigator, the one who had come to Nikopol, came out of the Commission session. He recognized me.

"Oh, I'm glad you've come, Comrade Kravchenko," he said. And he smiled in a way that quieted my nerves a little.

Then another functionary came out and called a name. A tall, distinguished looking bearded man of about forty, flaxen-headed, arose excitedly. The functionary motioned him into the inner chamber. About fifty minutes passed before he came out again, deathly pale, mopping perspiration and obviously jittery. He resumed his place among the waiting men on the padded bench.

Suddenly two uniformed N.K.V.D. men came into the waiting room with cocked revolvers. One of them called the same name we had heard earlier. The man with the beard got up, looking dazed.

"You're under arrest," the N.K.V.D. officer announced. "Come along!"

"But it's impossible. . . . There must be some mistake. . . . The Commission is considering my case. . . ."

"Come along, and come quickly, or we'll carry you out!"

The Chekists and their prisoner left. The rest of us remained in silence, not daring to look at one another.

Finally I was summoned to the Commission. I found myself in a large, brightly lit room. Five men sat behind a long table covered with a red cloth. I was too nervous to take in the scene all at once. My first impression was merely that no one was smiling, an impression of unrelieved grimness.

"Good day, Comrade Kravchenko," the man who was evidently presiding said. "Take a seat. Answer questions briefly and clearly. And don't worry."

As I sat down I scanned the five faces. And suddenly I observed that one of them was smiling, nodding recognition. *Thank God. . . . Gregoriev!* . . . Gregoriev was an Old Bolshevik, of pre-revolutionary vintage. He knew me since childhood. He had worked with my father at the Petrovsky-Lenin plant (now called merely the Lenin plant, Petrovsky having disappeared). A weight was lifted from my spirits. There would be at least one man who would understand, who knew that I was not made of the stuff of saboteurs, who knew that the elder Kravchenko was never a Menshevik. It gave my mind and my heart something to cling to, to steady themselves. I was able to speak out more boldly, more clearly.

For more than an hour I answered questions. One of the questioners, a dark Georgian with a dyspeptic face and a rasping voice, seemed hostile to me. The chairman and the worker Gregoriev seemed sympathetic. I answered questions about my father, about the "hoarded" instruments, about my relations with a long list of "enemies of the people." Having nothing to conceal, I replied without hesitation, always to the point at issue.

At one juncture Gregoriev, dropping the formal prosecutor technique, suddenly said:

"Comrade Kravchenko, I've known you and your family for a long time. Tell us frankly, how do you feel about things?"

"Frankly, comrades," I said, "I feel lousy. I've been tormented for more than a year now. Tormented, do you understand, comrades?" Unconsciously my hand went to my bruised face. "You should know that I came here without permission and that I don't know what awaits me when I return."

"And who is it that torments you?" the dark Georgian asked raspingly.

"I can't tell . . ."

"Never mind, never mind," the chairman interjected hurriedly, "let's get on with the inquiry."

And soon I was in the waiting room again, sitting where the man who had been arrested had sat. I began to smoke. Every time the outer door opened I felt sure that the N.K.V.D. was coming for me. After about fifteen excruciating minutes, I was summoned back before the Commission.

"Comrade Kravchenko," the chairman announced, now smiling broadly, "the Commission has decided to confirm the decision of the Nikopol City Committee and, in addition, to remove the reprimand. You may go back to work. No one will bother you again. But I would suggest that you change your place of work. A new start somewhere else, you know.

Have faith in our Party and our Leader. Good-bye, comrade, and good luck."

At the time, of course, he could not know that two months later both he and Gregoriev would themselves be arrested as "enemies of the people"!

All five men shook hands with me. I walked out. But I was not overwhelmingly happy, as I had been in my first purge at the Institute. I was free, safe, but the faith that had been in me was no more. A stone of hate was in its place.

I slept a deep dreamless sleep that night at the home of my family. In the morning I telephoned to one of my superiors at Glavtrubostal in Moscow. I explained to him that I had been fully vindicated by the Control Commission and that, upon its suggestion, I wished to be transferred to some other city. He understood and agreed to wire the Nikopol director that I was wanted immediately for a conference in the capital.

At Nikopol, Gershgorn did not call me again. Director Shalakhov ignored my breach of discipline in leaving without his authorization; he was intimidated by the message from Moscow. Having attended to some neglected work in my department, I set out for the capital.

Lazar Kaganovich, member of the Politburo and reputedly one of Stalin's very few trusted associates, was now holding the post once held by Ordzhonikidze. The path to his office had been opened for me by Glavtrubostal. Late one night, after the usual hours of waiting in a crowded anteroom, I was admitted to the Commissar's august presence.

I had seen Kaganovich several times earlier in his career. He had then worn a small dark beard and looked almost the typical intellectual. The man I now faced had changed startlingly. The beard was gone, replaced by a Stalinesque mustache. The face had grown heavy, jowly, brutal. It was not merely a physical change; the inner man seemed different; the intellectual had been transformed into the bureaucrat. As we talked, Kaganovich played nervously with a string of amber. This had become the fashion among high officials, a kind of Bolshevik rosary.

Briefly I told him about my troubles in Nikopol which, apparently, had now come to an end.

"The Party and the people are cleansing themselves of enemies," Kaganovich declaimed importantly. "It is unavoidable that sometimes the blows will fall in the wrong places. When the forest is cut down, the chips fly."

"That doesn't make things any easier for me, Lazar Moiseyevich."

"A Bolshevik must be hard, brave and unbending, ready to sacrifice himself for the Party. Yes, ready to sacrifice not only his life but his self-respect and sensitivity. Remember we live surrounded by capitalist sharks. From time to time we must examine our ranks, and purge them of capitalist agents—with fire and sword if necessary."

I did not argue. Ordzhonikidze would have understood my suffering, would have uttered a word of apology or compassion, but not this man Kaganovich with his steely cold eyes and his stale speeches. How tired I was of these harangues, these pious invocations, this sticky verbiage covering human horror!

The Commissar at first suggested that I become chief engineer of the Nikopol *combinat* but in the end I convinced him that I could not give my best efforts in that place filled for me with so many evil memories. Then he said he would leave the problem to Glavtrubostal. As I departed I recalled the phrase he had made notorious in the past two years: "We'll break their skulls in," Kaganovich had said in talking of class enemies and saboteurs.

Before I left Moscow I had been commissioned to the Andreyev metallurgical plant in Taganrog.

Back in Nikopol, I went to the City Committee offices to transfer my formal Party affiliation to Taganrog. Secretary Kondrashin was stickily affable. He informed me, in a whisper, that he had resisted bravely Dorogan's pressure for my arrest. He wanted to make sure of the credit. Who knows? Some day this battered Kravchenko might be in a position to save him in return. In the new Russia one hoards credits against a rainy day, politically speaking.

Outside the Committee headquarters I came face to face with Dorogan.

"So you're running away to Taganrog," he sneered. "Don't crow! You're never beyond our reach. There's no place on earth we can't run you down if we have to!"

"That's your affair," I said.

"What a pity I didn't clap you into prison right away instead of allowing the idiots to start a public expulsion process. . . ."

"But tell me, Dorogan, why do you hate me so? I have never done you any personal harm."

"That's my business," he snarled and walked off angrily.

In the plant I said good-bye to my workers. I was deeply touched by the simplicity and honesty of their affection. Though they did not guess the details, they were aware of the depth of my suffering and felt with me. Silinin embraced me with real feeling. So did Gushchin. Then I caught sight of Kiryushkin, wiping his hands on his apron, and went to him. I grasped his hand and pressed it heartily. We had little need for words between us.

"Farewell, Victor Andreyevich," he said, "may God watch over you. Whatever happens, remember that millions of us Kiryushkins are on your side, always on your side . . . even when we're helpless."

I had come to Nikopol, early in 1935, keyed to hope and eager to make good as an engineer and industrial executive, for the sake of the country and its people. I was leaving it, nearly three years later, shorn of all hope, emptied of ambition, insulted in my very soul. I would gladly have exchanged my higher income and so-called privileges for obscurity in the gray tattered herd of toiling humanity.

What, in the final balance, was my chief accomplishment in these three years? Only this: that I had remained free and alive while millions of others, as guiltless as myself, had been killed, or turned into slave labor for a merciless state, or driven from their positions.

There was a time when the industrialization of my country had been a challenge to stir young blood. I loved engineering. I thrilled to the rhythm of production, intense, ordered, unafraid—raw stuff fed in at one end of the process and finished products poured out at the other end! That creative impulse had been beaten out of me. Bold technical vision had been displaced by fear, caution, suspicion. My special training and technical aptitudes now seemed to be a cruel trap. I was caught forever, condemned to shoulder responsibilities in which there could be only danger but no joy.

CHAPTER XVIII

LABOR: FREE AND SLAVE

TAGANROG, in the Rostov province, lies on the Azov Sea. An immaculate and leisurely town of spacious gardens and orchards, it was now overcrowded by the Five Year Plans. It had become a city of smoke, soot and fishy emanations from the new canneries, a city overflowing for miles with new houses and barracks around aviation, motorcycle, metallurgical and shoe factories.

The Andreyev plant, named for a member of the Politburo, manufactured railroad wheels, sheet metal, pipe and other steel products. The management of the pipe section was to be my special responsibility, of course. I was assigned to a comfortable apartment in the administration compound, where the *élite* residences were located.

Had the planners been intent on dramatizing the contrast between the upper and lower classes in the Soviet world? I doubt it. Yet the contrast was there, it shrieked at you, made you uncomfortable. Beautiful shade trees shut out the sight of the factory structures and barracks. Gravel walks flanked by lilac bushes led to a swimming and boating strip (reserved for officialdom, of course) on a well-combed beach. There were also tennis and croquet courts, billiard rooms, an attractive special dining room.

The only thing lacking in this grandeur, indeed, was a smiling face or a cheerful expression. The worst of the purge hysteria was ended, but its fumes lingered. Nearly half the administrative personnel, Party and non-Party, had been swept out and those who remained were jittery, haunted, feeling almost ashamed to have been spared so long. A new Secretary, Dvinsky, formerly in Stalin's own Secretariat, had come directly from Moscow to rule the Rostov province Committee and a new director, Semion Resnikov, commanded our plant. But the phantoms of the liquidated leaders seemed with us always.

Ordzhonikidze, in giving advice to engineers, used to say often: "Learn technological culture and cleanliness from Boris Kolesnikov." The Taganrog metallurgical plant, of which he was director for a number of years, was Kolesnikov's show-piece. He had lived in the United States and was doing his utmost to introduce American organization and efficiency. He carried his "Americanization" to a point where associates thought him a difficult man. Now this Kolesnikov and his wife had been arrested; rumors insisted that both he and his wife had been shot and that their children were confined in the special Kharkov prison for minors.

Though only a few months had passed since Kolesnikov and most of his staff had been liquidated, at the time I arrived, few traces of his passionate Americanization remained. The work for which he had been loaded with praise and medals lay in ruins. Sloth and confusion were everywhere. Production had broken down. Director Resnikov and I were appalled by the task ahead of us.

On meeting local and regional Party officials, I realized that my reputation had preceded me. The Nikopol Committee and Dorogan had transmitted full "materials" about me; I would not be permitted to start with a clean slate. The local Party bosses made me feel right away that I was on probation and at their mercy. They probed my mind and character, often crudely, looking for soft spots, trying to catch me off guard.

It was not exactly an encouraging start. My state of mind, moreover, was hardly improved by the fact that forced labor was much more in evidence here than it had been in Nikopol. A large contingent of N.K.V.D. slaves did most of the heavy work of loading and unloading at our warehouses. They worked ten to twelve hours a day under armed surveillance. An even larger group toiled on new construction projects at the neighboring Sulinsky Metallurgical plant; and I was always running into gangs of these helots on the auto-highway between Taganrog and Rostov.

The sight of the haggard, scarcely human creatures, in their filthy rags, squelched any stray spark of enthusiasm in my heart. The awareness of these millions of slaves working and suffering, dying like flies, all over Russia was so painful that I kept pushing it into the background. Every direct confrontation with the cruel facts was therefore a new shock. What sharpened its poignancy, always, was the feeling that but for an accident I, too, would be in the legion of these damned; that for all I knew I would be in their midst soon anyhow.

About two weeks after my arrival, when I had barely had time to analyze and organize my job, I was called to the Taganrog headquarters of the N.K.V.D., late one night. The deputy chief of the Economic Division, whose name I no longer recall, received me. He was correct but reserved in his manner. Spread on his desk, I noticed at once, were the "materials" about me prepared by his Nikopol comrades.

"It's my special assignment to keep an eye on your pipe-rolling shop," he announced, "and I thought we might as well get acquainted." He settled back in his chair, like a child preparing to listen to a bedtime story. "Well, tell me about yourself."

"I don't know what to tell you. It seems to me that you know everything already."

"No, no, my dear Kravchenko, everything is never known. Would you tell me, for instance, how long you have known engineer Nikolai M——, and how you happen to know him?"

M—— was assistant chief engineer at the plant. We had worked together at various times and I had a high opinion of him.

"What did he have to do with your appointment here?" the Chekist wanted to know.

"Nothing at all. I did not even know he worked here."

"Why then did M—— talk about you, and in an enthusiastic way, to Resnikov?"

"I haven't the slightest idea. Knowing me, he naturally might mention the fact."

"At the N.K.V.D. we see nothing natural about it. On the contrary, I consider it very strange that you, a Party member, should be treated like a protege by a non-Communist whose loyalty, between ourselves, is a bit uncertain."

His questioning then shifted to the former director Kolesnikov.

"Look here, comrade," I said with some heat, "I have answered these same questions hundreds of times for nearly a year and a half while I was being purged. I answered them at N.K.V.D. inquiries, at the City Committee, before the Control Commission, until I'm sick and tired of them. I've been sent here by Moscow to work. I've been cleared. Can't you let me alone?"

"Now, now, control yourself, Comrade Kravchenko." He looked at me in puzzlement, as if I were some obnoxious specimen in a bottle. "Please remember that it does happen that a man is cleared all along the line and then—bang!—he's arrested on new evidence."

I took the hint. Wearily I reiterated the stale information, the familiar denials, which had been squeezed from my weary mind and memory in the past year. This police official played with me, hour after hour, as a mischievous child plays with a beetle and, as far as I could see, with about as little reasoned purpose. He would drop a line of inquiry only to return to it suddenly—a trick to which I had been subjected too often in the past.

The one thing that he made me understand by his questions was that here, as at Nikopol, every engineer and manager was encircled by spies, both at his work and at his home. It was obvious, too, that the Taganrog N.K.V.D. was intent upon concocting a case against this M——. I surmised that, though free, the poor fellow was being given the same kind of nocturnal "training" which I had myself received.

With only two or three hours of sleep, I was in my shops that morning, making decisions on millions of rubles' worth of production. The cruel irony of it!

2

My stay on the shores of the Azov Sea was to be extremely brief. Without explanation, I was summoned by Glavtrubostal to Moscow. The chief of the organization, Merkulov, in the presence of his assistant, Kozhevnikov, announced that Commissar Kaganovich and the Party were about to pay me a supreme compliment.

"The Novo-Trubni (New-Pipe) plant in the Urals," he said, "has been a hotbed of wrecking and sabotage. Most of the rascals have been cleaned out and others will be taken in hand soon. We are strengthening the administration with able, qualified and politically reliable people."

"That lets me out," I smiled. "I'm a sinner, Comrade Merkulov. I've been purged and exonerated, but I'm besmirched from head to toe with foul charges."

"We know all about it, but we trust you."

"Come, Victor Andreyevich," Kozhevnikov added, "stop feeling offended for what's past."

"In any case," Merkulov continued, "we are appointing you head of our largest pipe-making sub-plant, the largest not only in the U.S.S.R. but in all Europe."

"But I don't want to go to the Urals. I'm tired. What do I want that awful place for?"

The Novo-Trubni plant at Pervouralsk, about forty miles from Sverdlovsk, was notorious in our industry. It had been built in a forelorn area miles from nowhere, in the midst of marshlands, mudflats, pine forests and concentration camps. It had been put into production years too soon, before essential departments were completed, before adequate power was available. Under the circumstances, output had been small and bad. The unfortunates sent to manage the unfinished plant usually paid with their liberty for mistakes made by the planners in Moscow.

"We know that Pervouralsk is a mess and will therefore give you fullest support," Merkulov promised. "Comrade Kaganovich himself will back you up. We'll give you the top salary, a bonus for every percent of improvement, a new automobile and anything else you ask for."

"I ask only to be allowed to remain in Taganrog."

"I'm sorry. I had expected you to show more appreciation of the Party's confidence. Your appointment stands. It has been passed through the Central Committee."

Alone with Kozhevnikov later I could not resist remarking:

"If you think that forced love will bear fruit, and since you threaten me with disciplinary action, I am accepting the appointment and will do my best."

"Well, that's splendid!" he laughed. "Love, you know, is a matter of habit. First comes constraint, then comes habit and finally love. So the matter is settled. Let's get down to work."

I met the newly appointed director of the whole *combinat*, Jacob Osadchi, who would be my only superior at the Urals post, and others just designated to work with us. An entirely new administration was being assembled in Moscow—without a hint, as yet, to the engineers and executives running the *combinat*. I looked forward to the new tasks with bitter misgivings. Novo-Trubni was producing only 35 to 40 per cent of its monthly norm, and was often cited in the press and in official speeches as a horrible example of mismanagement and sabotage. I was inheriting one of the worst headaches in the entire metallurgical field.

The atmosphere in Moscow just then, moreover, was nicely calculated to deepen my pessimism. It was the second week in March, 1938: the week when the third and most sensational of the blood-purge trials took place. The country by now was acclimated to grotesque accusations against the Fathers of the Revolution and even more grotesque "confessions." Yet it stood aghast, incredulous, for the defendants included Bukharin, Rykov, Krestinsky and others whose names were closely linked with Lenin's.

Nikolai Bukharin, brilliant, ascetic, a "Bolshevik saint," had been the special idol of the Communist youth of my generation. I recalled our meeting long ago at Ordzhonikidze's office, and subsequent meetings in his own office. Even after he was expelled from the Politburo and was known to be in disfavor, Bukharin's appearance at a public meeting evoked ovations second only to Stalin's. Alexei Rykov had been Lenin's successor as Chairman of the Council of People's Commissars. He had the head of the fanatic, with a ragged beard and burning eyes; even his notorious weakness for the bottle did not lessen his popularity. Now these men, and others like them, defiled themselves, outraged the worship we had lavished on them. Now they were shot as spies, agents of capitalism and traitors.

I can attest that no one I met in Moscow attached the slightest value to their confessions. These men had consented to serve as puppets in a political morality play not in the least related to truth. Stalin was destroying his personal opponents and had succeeded in forcing them to participate in their own humiliation and extinction. We wondered about the techniques he had used. But even Party people were not expected to believe the trial testimony literally. To do so would have been tantamount, among Communists, to an admission of congenital idiocy. At most we accepted the fantasies in a symbolic, allegorical sense.

Old Comrade Misha, whom I visited on this trip, was badly broken up. He had known the executed leaders intimately before and after the revolution. His explanation of the confessions, though far from satisfactory, was the nearest I would ever come to a logical appraisal of the phenomenon. It was based on information obtained through his many friends in the Kremlin.

"To begin with, Vitya," he said, "a lie remains a lie no matter how many people confess to it. Let's forget rhetoric. Bukharin, Rykov and the others, for all their heroic past, were flesh-and-blood human beings. You told me yourself how near you came to signing a lot of lies under pressure in Nikopol. But what you went through was child's play against the moral and perhaps physical coercions used against these leaders."

"But these same men, Comrade Misha, held out against persecution and threats by the Tsar's police in their day."

"Unfortunately there's no comparison. The secret police of the Tsarist Okhrana were too primitive, not so scientific, not so devilishly clever as the present system. I wonder how many of us old revolutionists would have held out if the Okhrana had subjected us to the scientific sadism of the N.K.V.D.

"And there's another thing, equally important, Vitya. In the old days these men had a deep faith to sustain them. Men will sacrifice themselves and—what is more difficult—their loved ones for a great belief and a passionate hope. What did they have to sustain them under N.K.V.D. torture and solitary confinement? Neither hope nor faith. They were disillusioned men. Their life's work lay around them in ruins, beyond re-

pair. Why play the hero for a dead cause? Why continue to fight when
there is no longer a glimmer of hope? Try to understand that and you'll
begin to understand why yesterday's heroes became soft, pliant and
devoid of all dignity."

"Do you credit the talk about bargains struck between the victims
and the prosecution?"

"I believe it to be a fact and, you must understand, I base the belief
on pretty intimate information. You know that the N.K.V.D. rarely
liquidates a man without also liquidating his family. Do you really suppose
it's an accident that Rykov's daughter, whom he loved above all other
people, remains alive and free? Or that Bukharin's father, Rosengoltz's
wife and other close relatives have not been touched? I take it for granted
that the men besmirched themselves—played their assigned roles in the
tragi-comedy—to save those they loved.

"Let me tell you what I know from comrades close to Yezhov, who's
been in charge of the obscene business since Yagoda's liquidation. The
scenario for the spectacle was prepared by the N.K.V.D. on Stalin's
personal orders. Every actor—prosecutors, defendants, witnesses, judges—
was letter-perfect in his role before the curtain went up. Those of the
accused who wouldn't cooperate were killed off in the dark. The others
were paid off with the lives of their children, wives, parents, close friends.
They were promised in addition that they would have the right of appeal
to higher instances, even to the Politburo. A little hope goes a long way
under such circumstances.

"But in the case of Bukharin, Rykov, Krestinsky and a few others
the bargains were more specific. If they went through with the parts as
written, their death sentences would be commuted and they would merely
be exiled to distant places, they were promised. Stalin even played on
their vanity. How could he permit them to be shot, he said, when their
names had such great historical weight?

"Well, the victims carried out their part of the arrangement. Stalin
didn't. Obviously he never intended to. Within a few hours after the trial,
the executions took place. Bukharin and Rykov died with curses against
Stalin on their lips. And they died standing up—not grovelling on the
cellar floor and weeping for mercy like Zinoviev and Kamenev.

"And here's another piece of inside information. Stalin has created a
commission to write a new history of the Party. History will be revised,
events will be twisted, to conform with the phantasmagoria of these trials.
You and I will laugh at the distortions, or cry over them. But a new
generation is growing up, without memory of the past. Already the
libraries are being cleansed of any and every past book or article which
contradicts the stupid inventions at these trials. The nightmare will take
root as the official truth. The lie will have conquered. Ekh, Vitya, and
for that I spent ten years in chains in damp Tsarist prison cells . . ."

Such was the state of things in Moscow as I left to clean those Augean
stables in the Urals.

3

At the railroad station in Sverdlovsk (formerly Yekaterinburg and famous as the city in which the last Tsar and his family were slaughtered) I was met by an official from the Novo-Trubni plant. Fortunately he was someone with whom I was fairly well acquainted and he could afford to be frank. As we drove the forty miles to Pervouralsk, he brought me up to date on the plant. Though he talked with restraint, my worst forebodings were confirmed.

I would have to bring orderly production out of physical chaos and moral collapse. Some six thousand workers and their families, a total of seventeen or eighteen thousand people, were living under primitive conditions. The only ones who could be counted on not to run away were those born in the district and the forced-labor groups on construction jobs. The technical personnel, or what was left of it after the purges, was demoralized and, of course, shied away from responsibility. Because of the unsavory living and working conditions they felt themselves exiles and hoped only for speedy transfer elsewhere.

About seven or eight miles from Pervouralsk, I suddenly saw the barbed-wire fence of a concentration camp a few hundred meters off the road. We stopped the car so I could take a better look. The camp, acres and acres of bleak barracks in a huge clearing in the woods, seemed deserted, silent as death. It was six-sided and at each of the six corners there was a watchtower, equipped with big searchlights and machine guns.

"Where are the prisoners?" I asked my companion.

"At work this time of the day," he said. "A few of them are in our own factory, the rest in other plants, mines and on construction jobs. Victor Andreyevich, I see you're new to the Urals. You'd better get accustomed to the prisoners everywhere."

We resumed the drive. A pretty introduction to my new life!

Osadchi, the new director, had arrived before me. He was glum. One look at the *combinat* had been enough to extinguish the enthusiasm he had flaunted in Moscow.

"Comrade Kravchenko, we certainly have a job cut out for us," he sighed as we walked through the various buildings and shops. "It will be years before this *combinat* is self-sustaining. We don't have our own electric furnaces for making instruments. There's no thermic section, no satisfactory mechanical shop. The electric power is way below our needs and the gas station is a long way from being finished. There are no facilities for chromium-plating of instruments. In short, this isn't as yet a factory at all. It's only the beginning of one."

My own eyes confirmed his story. The mechanical department was a joke. The galvanic shop was unworthy of the name. The warehouses were not yet finished, so that thousands of tons of steel and other metal lay under the open sky. Metals of all types and qualities were heaped indiscriminately, without the slightest attempt at organization. The piperolling machinery itself was of the most modern American and German makes, representing millions of rubles in *valuta*. But of what avail were they without adequate accessory services? Even the imported machines were crusted with dirt and out of repair. Everywhere, protruding from the muck, I saw heaps of expensive tools and machine parts gathering rust.

An inspection of the workers' quarters completed my sense of despair. The housing I had glimpsed behind the barbed wire, under the muzzles of machine guns, differed very little from these wretched wooden boxes, damp and dirty, in which the free proletarians of our factory swarmed.

I engaged several of the women in conversation. They were sullen. Evidently they looked on us as the people to blame for their troubles, not as comrades in work. There was little farming in this part of the Urals; only the half dozen top officials, with automobiles at our disposal, could hope to obtain sufficient provisions in Sverdlovsk. The workers lived chiefly on bread, a few local vegetables and canned goods. In the brief summer the barracks were hot as ovens, in many barracks the rain came through holes in the roofs and saturated the plank walls. In the long Ural winters they provided no protection against the extreme cold.

After spending an hour in the barracks, I blushed with shame as I surveyed my own four-room apartment in one of the three-story brick houses, set among trees on the other side of the factory grounds. Elsewhere, even in Nikopol or Taganrog, it would have been considered a drab enough residence. But in Pervouralsk it seemed the last word in luxury, with its private bath, carpeted floors, good furniture and good kitchen. Along with the apartment, I inherited Dunia, the slovenly middle-aged peasant woman who did the cooking and cleaning, from my predecessor.

The promised limousine was waiting for me, as well as a small Ford which, in the muddy season, was more serviceable. I also had good horses assigned for my exclusive use. My basic salary was 1500 rubles a month but with bonuses and other incentive pay my average sometimes would be closer to 3,000 rubles. What this meant may be judged from the fact that unskilled laborers earned about 150, skilled mechanics around 250, and qualified engineers around 600.

An engineer would have to spend an entire month's salary for a plain suit of clothes; but this was purely theoretical, since no clothes were available in Pervouralsk and rarely even in Sverdlovsk. Only those of us who could make occasional business trips to Moscow or Leningrad managed to buy shoes and clothes. For the rest, a limited supply was at the disposal of the administration and we distributed this to deserving engineers, foremen or even workers.

I had been at work less than two weeks when the chief bookkeeper brought the semi-monthly payroll for my signature. As I studied the document I noted a curious item: a considerable sum "to the N.K.V.D."

"What's that for?" I asked, puzzled.

"That's under our labor contract, for the 160 penal laborers assigned to your section. Half their wages goes to the N.K.V.D."

"Are they from one of the concentration camps?"

"No, no, Comrade Kravchenko. That's quite another department of the N.K.V.D. The contract laborers live here, like the free workers. But they have barracks of their own. They are men deported here for various crimes."

Subsequently I was told by the directors of other sections that all of them had contingents of this forced labor—250 in one shop, eighty in another, fifty in the third. The free workers did not associate with them, and in any part of the plant one could usually pick them out by their exceptionally pitiful appearance.

Once I talked to one of these forced laborers in my pipe-rolling mill. He was a short, cadaverous looking fellow. I found it hard to draw him out; evidently the wretched creatures were under strict orders to keep their mouths shut. But I learned that he had been a foreman in a Leningrad factory, liquidated three years earlier.

"But what's to stop you from running away?" I asked.

"Running away!" he shook his head sadly. "Where to? Where could we hide and for how long? But I would suggest to you, chief, that this talk isn't healthy for either of us."

We began the appalling task of digging our way out of the confusion. Electric furnaces had been lying around forgotten. We cleaned them up and after weeks of strenuous labor—a fourteen-hour day seemed a holiday—we had one furnace in operation. I installed a large mechanical section and assigned the qualified workers to teach the others how to operate it. I created a thermic shop and arranged for the training of novices to operate it. The chromium-plating section was built and equipped from scratch. Production in the past years had been slowed up by the lack of an internal telephone system and a proper despatchers' station; these too I built under handicaps which only a technician can quite appreciate. We set up indispensable ovens, cranes, work benches.

Besides such minimal technical installations, I put hundreds of men and women to work cleaning, scrubbing, painting, removing accumulated dirt. Without elementary order and cleanliness, I realized, there was no hope of raising output. Sabotage? It seemed to me miraculous that the plant had managed to produce even 35 to 40 per cent of the quotas assigned by headquarters.

Within two months the place was scarcely recognizable. My colleagues had been infected by my own determination and their eagerness to work had percolated down to the humblest bench hands and floor sweepers. By May we had not only raised production to 80 per cent—an achievement that had seemed impossible when I first arrived—but had improved the quality. Impurities in our pipes declined from an average of 12 per cent to an average of 5 or 6 per cent.

Naturally, this colossal effort left me no margin for a personal life. Besides being in charge of production, I was personally responsible for the housing, feeding, technical schooling and medical care of the two thousand workers and their families under my direct control. Though I had ample assistance, some of it competent, the ultimate responsibility was mine and there was rarely a day when my energies were not siphoned off by problems not directly related to production.

To add to my burdens, the purge hysteria was far from ended. Valuable men were snatched from me when I needed them most; those who escaped direct attack lived and worked in an atmosphere of unrelieved apprehension. By this time I had schooled myself to ignore the multitudinous spying and denunciations. I had trained my brain and nerves to focus on the job in hand, without expending nervous energy on futile angers. All the same, I was still shaken and sometimes paralyzed in my work at crucial moments when I discovered that the Economic Division of the local N.K.V.D. knew details of the work, details of technical decisions, even before I did. It made me feel naked, unprotected.

The Special Department of our factory, headed up by Comrades Kolbin and Stoffin, served as the eyes and ears of the Secret Police. Besides receiving copies of all orders and technical reports, these determined men had their agents deployed through every shop and office. That, however, was only the routine of surveillance. The *combinat* in addition heaved and staggered under the weight of endless special commissions of investigation, control brigades and individual inspectors. They came, quietly or with a fanfare of official trumpets, from the Regional Committee, the Central Committee in Moscow, Glavtrubostal in Moscow, the Commissariat of Heavy Industry and a dozen other organizations.

Nor was that all. Orders for pipe, routed through Moscow, always originated in other industries which therefore sent commissions to check on progress and to hurl sabotage threats at our dizzy heads. We produced pipe for tanks, aviation, artillery, ships, oil installations, automotive plants and numerous other purposes. Because the orders were invariably too large for our facilities, and the final products rarely up to exacting specifications, the trusts and industries involved, as well as the armed services, filed protests which in turn generated inspections, investigations, and of course new epidemics of N.K.V.D. "vigilance."

Hardly a week went by without its array of controllers and plenipotentiaries from this or that bureau, armed with awe-inspiring mandates, nostrils aquiver for the spoor of "wreckers." They took up my time, stamped and swore in my office and convoked myriad conferences. Depressed by the dullness of life in this remote place and by the stupidity of their own assignments, many of them ended by washing down their sorrows in vodka or expunging them in card games for high stakes.

In bed at last after a fourteen-to-sixteen-hour day, I could rarely count on uninterrupted sleep. There were long-distance calls from Moscow, again checking, pleading and threatening. There were police calls in connection with the incessant arrests. I had no sooner dozed off than someone on the night shift phoned with tidings of accidents, mislaid tools, spoiled products.

From the talk around me I was able to piece together a picture of the fearful havoc wrought by the purge before my arrival, in the Novo-Trubni plant and in every mine and factory of the vicinity. The story of Semion Magrilov, director of another metallurgical factory, within the town of Pervouralsk itself, remains indelibly impressed on my nerves.

His plant was perhaps the oldest in Russia, having been started, according to local legend, by Peter the Great himself. It was manned by workers whose fathers and grandfathers had worked there before them. They lived in their own clean small homes, cultivated tiny gardens, had some pigs and poultry and in general maintained a standard almost up to the pre-revolutionary level. In sending Magrilov to manage this factory, the Party was in effect awarding him a sinecure. He was a Party member of long standing, well along in years, a close acquaintance of Lenin's widow and of Lenin's sister, Maria Ulianova, and regarded as one of the most influential figures in the region.

But the cyclonic purge madness did not spare him. The local N.K.V.D. hounded him with accusations. He was charged with sabotage and with protecting other saboteurs. After a few months of persecution, he gave up. He locked himself in his own office, pointed a revolver down his throat and pulled the trigger. . . . He left a long letter proclaiming his innocence and inveighing against the terror. The N.K.V.D. confiscated the letter, yet somehow the contents became known to the workers in the factory. Several of Magrilov's closest associates, because they were suspected of having read the suicide epistle, "disappeared" without leaving a trace.

The Magrilov tragedy was exceptional only because of the prominence of the victim. I heard the details of literally hundreds of arrests, torture sessions and suicides. But I could not permit them to affect my work. I learned at last to blot out disturbing knowledge. It's not an easy art to acquire, but only those who master it can survive as industrial executives in the U.S.S.R. Those who cannot keep their compassion under strict control, almost in a special air-tight compartment of their beings, are doomed to heart-break or insanity.

Moscow took cognizance of the remarkable improvement at the Novo-Trubni. A Moscow meeting of activists at the Commissariat, in the presence of Kaganovich, commended my work. According to the report in *For Industrialization*, the plant had been in a bad way, until the arrival of "Kravchenko. active young engineer and Party member," changed the picture.

4

The chief of the Pervouralsk N.K.V.D., Comrade Parshin, whom I had already met at Party conferences, paid me a visit. He was lavish with praise of the "miracles" I had wrought in stepping up production. Always the policeman, he consumed hours of my time with questions about the various orders on which we were then working, and about the "political mood" of various individuals under me. I could scarcely conceal my annoyance at the extent of his detailed knowledge about my work. It gave me conclusive proof that there were many informers around me.

"You're certainly eliminating the results of the sabotage of your predecessors," he finally said. From his mouth that was the highest conceivable praise. "I therefore hate to impose on your time, Victor Andreyevich. But tonight you can do me a favor. I'll call you later and tell you when to come."

The appointment, when it came through, was for two in the morning. The N.K.V.D. was housed in a well-built two-story structure, the most imposing on the muddy main street of Pervouralsk. Despite the hour, there were lights in every window; clearly business was brisk. The chief greeted me cordially and led me into his office.

"Make yourself comfortable," he said. "I'm afraid you may be here quite a while."

"What do you want of me?"

"Well, here's the story: We have an enemy of the people arrested here, an out-and-out wrecker. It's clear to us that he's to blame for much of the disorder you found in your plant. But he's an obstinate customer. My plan tonight is to question him in your presence. With a specialist like you listening in, he won't be able to pull the wool over my eyes."

"Frankly, I don't like the business at all," I said in dismay.

"That's strange. You surprise me. Didn't Lenin himself say that every good Communist must be a Chekist? Well, let's begin." He rang for his secretary, "Tell the guards to bring the prisoner from cell 7."

The chief prepared for the interview by pulling some thick files out of the huge safe—and by placing a revolver demonstratively on his desk. As he waited for his prisoner, he seemed to become tense, a tiger about to spring on his prey. Soon the door opened. Two guards with drawn revolvers entered and between them the remnants of what was once a man. The guards withdrew, leaving the three of us in the room.

"Hello," the prisoner said weakly, looking around as if dazed.

Parshin did not respond. I acknowledged the greeting. The prisoner was little more than a skeleton in rags. His face was of a pasty gray hue and looked like a death mask. A raw gash, purple with congealed blood, zigzagged from one temple almost to his chin. He stood with hands behind his back, his head bowed.

The Chekist began to read the prisoner's indictment, by way of acquainting me with the facts of the case. I learned that he had been under arrest for over thirteen months. Though he looked like a man of sixty, he was only in his early forties. He had been the chief construction engineer at the Novo-Trubni plant up to the time it was put into production. Looking at the man, I could not help thinking, "There, but for the grace of God, stands Victor Kravchenko."

"Comrade Parshin," I said in a low voice, "couldn't you let the prisoner sit down?"

"This is my affair," he replied. "This is the N.K.V.D. It isn't a vacation resort."

Having finished reading, Parshin addressed the prisoner in a stentorian voice:

"I shall question you concerning your wrecking activities in the pipe-rolling plant. Answer precisely, clearly and without mixing things up. You are in the presence of a trained engineer who knows the plant. You can't fool me any more. The first question: Why did you as chief engineer of the Capital Construction Board of the factory build wooden roofs over the furnaces, which could easily have been set afire?"

"According to plan," the prisoner replied with extraordinary precision, considering his physical condition, "the roofs should have been of iron. But a government order came through, passed by Commissar Ordzhonikidze himself, to use wood because of the great deficit of iron at the time. The order applied to our factory and to dozens of others. The Commissariat records should prove that easily. I considered it technically unwise but I had no power to countermand the Commissar's explicit instruction especially when I knew about the lack of metals."

"Your opinion?" the chief turned to me.

"The citizen—" I began.

"He's no citizen but an enemy of the people."

"Well, the prisoner is entirely correct. We had wooden roofs at the Nikopol plant and for the same reason, though by this time they're covered with galvanized iron. I happened to be present at a conference in Comrade Ginsburg's office when he, acting with the consent of Ordzhonikidze, approved wooden roofs for all shops except the smelting and Martens shops."

The Chekist was a little discomfited.

"Please bear in mind," he said, "that you will be held accountable for your testimony!"

"I'm fully aware of that," I said.

"Second question," he declaimed, turning again to the prisoner. "Why did you build a large pipe-making shop without galvanic, thermic and mechanical departments, without a base for repairs and without facilities for making the necessary precision instruments?"

"The project was for a large, modern *combinat*," the prisoner replied. "All of the departments you mention were to be outside the main shops, centralized in special service shops. The State Planning Commission and the Commissariat failed to provide the money, materials and equipment for these supplementary service shops. Thus it happened that the main plant was finished before the others were more than started. Then to our surprise we were ordered to start production, which I considered highly undesirable, and later I was arrested."

Whatever his thirteen months of suffering might have done to this man's mind, it worked well enough on professional questions. *A first-rate engineering brain,* I found myself thinking.

"What do you say to that?" the chief asked me.

"The prisoner is entirely right. The factory was started long ahead of schedule. Even now it is far from complete. If we were to wait until everything is finished according to the original plan, we would not be able to work for another year. Personally I think it was a mistake not to build the service sections in the main plant, but that's a decision made in Moscow. The completion of the main installations before the accessory portions certainly was not sabotage."

"Are you absolutely sure of this?"

"Quite sure. . . . May I give the prisoner a cigaret?"

"All right."

I handed the whole pack to the man, but the chief would not permit it.

"One cigaret is enough," he shouted. "Let him sign and acknowledge his wrecking and he'll smoke all he wants."

When the engineer put his hand out, from behind his back, I saw that it was wrapped in blood-stained rags.

For several hours the questioning went on. In every case I was able, in perfect honesty, to side with the engineer against the police officer. At about five-thirty, in the midst of a harangue by Parshin, the prisoner collapsed. I watched him slide down slowly, as if in a slow-motion film. After he was revived, by dashing cold water over him, the guards brought a chair for him, and the questioning was resumed. It was after six before the unfortunate was led out. I shall never forget the gratitude in his eyes as he looked at me from the doorway.

"I'm going to work on the protocol of this inquiry," Parshin announced, "and it will be brought to you for your signature in a few days. Sorry to have held you this long."

"Since it's too late to go to sleep anyhow," I said, "could you show me through the building?"

He hesitated, puzzled by the unusual request.

"There's nothing interesting to see," he said finally. "But if you wish. . . . It might help impress on you the responsibility you take in giving correct and true answers. . . ."

He combed his hair, put on the flat officer's cap with its red crown and blue top, and stuck the revolver in his hip pocket. We both put on our overcoats. Accompanied by a guard, we made a tour that will remain fresh in my memory for the rest of my life. We entered a yard, an iron door was opened, and we descended a steep stairway to a basement. The stench struck me like a physical blow. A weak bulb glowed in the corridor.

I observed that the guard, who sprang to attention as we entered, had been reading an instalment of the *Party History* then appearing serially in *Pravda*. I remember marvelling that this man, living in the awful stench of Stalinism in practice, should be so resolutely studying its theory. . . .

A commotion began in the rows of cells flanking the corridor. "Important guests!" someone shouted. The guard opened one of the doors and commanded "Rise!" Twenty-odd men rose to their feet. They were unshaven, indescribably pathetic, and most of them carried evidences of beatings. The only "furnishings" in the room were a bucket of water with a tin cup attached to it; another bucket in the far corner for human needs; the rough boards that served as beds; and a kind of wooden shelf loaded with the prisoner's rags and bundles. The cell would have been overcrowded by five, let alone twenty, prisoners.

The other cells were no less horrible. I lost all desire to see the rest. Several of the cells were reserved for women.

"Your ventilation isn't working," the chief said to the young Chekist at the door as we were leaving. "You'll stink yourself into the grave."

"I go to the public bath every day when I finish here," he explained cheerfully, "otherwise my wife won't let me into the house. The ventilators haven't worked for a long time."

When I emerged from the building, I found my chauffeur asleep at the wheel and aroused him.

"Ah, Victor Andreyevich, you were so long I began to wonder. . . . When we drive important people to this place, we never know whether we'll drive them back."

"I'm very tired, Petya. Let's go straight to the factory. No sleep for me tonight."

That afternoon my chief assistant came to see me. Could he stay away for three hours? A little probing disclosed that he had been summoned by the N.K.V.D.

"I can't spare you during working hours," I said. "Phone and say you'll be there after six. And by the way, after you've been there, come and see me again."

Late that night he did come to see me. He could not tell me what had happened, having been warned not to talk. But in the course of conversation I stumbled on the theory that he had been consulted on the very same case.

"Did you know the chief engineer on construction before his arrest?" I asked, as if casually.

"Yes, and Victor Andreyevich, I couldn't recognize him. . . ." He stopped himself, realizing he was giving away the secret.

Two days later Stoffin of the Special Department brought me the promised protocol.

"Just sign it and I'll rush it to Pervouralsk," he said.

"In the first place I don't intend to sign it without a very careful reading. In the second place, I don't propose to interrupt important work. I'll read it after work hours."

"But my orders are not to leave it out of my sight. I can't——"

"Just call your chief and tell him what I said. That will clear you."

Tremulously he phoned the N.K.V.D. Parshin was incensed. Finally, out of sympathy for the scared, brow-beaten Stoffin, I took the receiver from him.

"Kravchenko, you'll show more respect for the N.K.V.D.!" Parshin shrieked. "Especially after our visit to the cellar!"

"And you'll show more respect for the head of this plant!" I replied. "If you don't stop bothering me I'll call Kaganovich directly and tell him who's interfering with output."

The threat did the trick. Suddenly Parshin was apologetic. He was so overworked, he pleaded, and I must not think harshly of him. Of course I could read the deposition, and naturally on my own time.

At the end of the workday, with Stoffin waiting gloomily in the offices of the Special Department, I settled down to read the supposed summation of my night's testimony at the N.K.V.D. My hair stood on end. Everything I had said had been arbitrarily twisted into its opposite. Incriminatory words were put into my mouth. The prisoner's answers and my comments were doctored to support the allegations of deliberate wrecking.

On every page there was a warning, in large letters, that no alterations were permitted. All the same, I dipped my pen into the red ink and laboriously, sentence by sentence, edited the document. In many instances I even rephrased the questions, which had been distorted to falsify the intent of the answers. In a good many cases I needed only to insert the word "not," the meaning had been so completely misrepresented.

When I called Stoffin and handed him the blotched protocol, every page of it more red than black, he was bug-eyed with horror. Nothing so blasphemous had ever before happened in his experience. The blood left his face.

"But it's not allowed, Comrade Director. This is terrible," he wailed.

"Give it to your boss. The responsibility is mine."

I did not hear again about this matter. But a hurt and peeved expression spread over Parshin's long horsy face whenever we met. About three weeks later the news spread through the factory that the old chief construction engineer, after fourteen months in the stinking N.K.V.D. cellars, had been freed. Certainly it was not my intervention that was responsible; many others must have given the same kind of answers. But the stupid and inhuman officials who had humiliated and tortured him for more than a year were not even reprimanded. They continued to rule arrogantly and to arrest at will.

5

The young engineer Panov, in charge of my night shift, was one of my most conscientious colleagues. A man with even features, modest and taciturn, he made a good impression on people. The fact that his shift lagged on the production norm weighed on him and he put in many extra hours in the attempt to speed up the work.

What piqued my curiosity about Panov was the utter wretchedness of his appearance. The pallor of his features spoke of undernourishment. His one suit of clothes was threadbare and in all weather he walked around in canvas slippers. On inquiring I readily saw the cause of his poverty. Of his 550 rubles a month, 150 were taken away in taxes, loans and various dues, leaving him 400. On this he had to support his wife, a baby daughter and an old mother, who lived with him in a two-room apartment in the administration residences.

I saw to it that Panov received shoes and a work-suit from the factory storehouse. Touched by my concern, he screwed up the courage to talk to me about his troubles.

"Victor Andreyevich, may I talk to you frankly?" he asked, sitting in my office.

"But of course."

"Well, I'm here to implore that you help me to leave this hell-hole. I have a few connections and hope for an engineering post in the Army, but I need your cooperation."

"But why are you so dissatisfied here, Panov? You're young. You're getting valuable training under difficult conditions. Do you know what this flight from a difficult job is called in Party terminology?"

"I know, I know . . . opportunism, cowardice, and so on. But look at my side of it. I spent five hungry, cold years at the Institute. My wife, whom I married while I was still a student, looked forward to my life as a full-fledged engineer. But what has she got? More hunger and loneliness and awful poverty. I can see that her love for me is fading out under these blows, and I want to save it. I want to save our little girl, who can't get enough milk. Do you blame me for trying to rescue our family life?"

"As for myself, Panov, I don't. I can understand it."

"Well, in the Army I'll be drawing 750 rubles, besides my uniform, an apartment, free rations. I'll be able to give nearly all my earnings to my family. Besides, I'll be devoting myself to defense, which is also vital."

In the end I agreed to help him obtain his release from the plant. Years later I learned, through the newspapers, that he had distinguished himself in the war. Under the Ural conditions he would have been turned into an embittered, broken man in a short time. It was clear to me that other men, intrinsically good human material, were being spoiled by a senseless emphasis on production which ignored the comfort and the health of the human beings behind the production.

No less destructive than the physical hardships was the constant pressure of insulting doubts about the men's honesty. No matter how hard we toiled, the whole system was geared to the assumption that we were traitors and scoundrels who would wreck our own handiwork if not kept under observation twenty-four hours a day.

There was the time a special commission came to see me in connection with an order for the Defense Industry Administration No. 14. The order called for pipes of extreme precision, for the production of which we were hardly prepared. Several other pipe-rolling mills had refused to undertake it on the ground that they could not fulfill it.

I called a conference of my factory heads and laid the problem before them, in the presence of the Defense representatives. We agreed that while we might tackle the assignment, the chances of failure were enormous. It would require rapid retooling, a search for specialized types of steel, and then work under great pressure.

I accepted the order only after having exacted a written document in which it was acknowledged in advance that results could not be guaranteed. I was given 20,000 rubles to distribute in bonuses if the task were completed on time. Not only my technical staff but the workers, realizing the importance and the challenge of the job, put their hearts and souls into it.

We fulfilled the order in fifteen days. There were times when I remained in the plant three and four days at a time, taking my meals in the office and snatching a few hours of sleep amidst the din of machinery. My assistants worked as hard as I did. Surely there could be no reasonable doubts of the honesty of our effort. Yet the Special Department and Defense investigators shadowed us every day, sniffing for sabotage. Our human dignity and professional pride were outraged. Neither the bonuses nor the deluge of congratulatory telegrams could remove the sour taste left with all of us.

Kolbin, Stoffin, the officials of the Economic Department of the

N.K.V.D. and even the secretary of the City Committee, Dovbenko, were puffed up over their "triumph" on this order. They acted as if their annoying vigilance, rather than the skill and sweat of the workers and engineers, were responsible for the success.

"Why so much suspicion? Why all this joy that no one did any wrecking?" I asked Parshin.

He could scarcely grasp the questions, espionage seemed to him so natural. It seemed to him, indeed, the most vital part of any job!

"Besides, Victor Andreyevich," he took me into his confidence, "our success on this assignment sets a new task before the Economic Division. We must now find out why the other plants refused to accept the order! We've demonstrated that it was possible, why then did those directors refuse to touch it? Maybe they were telling the truth—but maybe they were sabotaging the defense industry. So you see how important our function is. . . ."

Several other special jobs—always in the hectic atmosphere of doubts and threats and pervasive spying—were finished with flying colors. The reputation of our Novo-Trubni plant was rapidly improving. Correspondents from *For Industrialization* and other papers wrote enthusiastic descriptions of how the "leftovers of sabotage" were being "liquidated" in this Ural plant. But output still stood around 85 per cent and Moscow, demonstrating its "Bolshevik firmness," pressed for 100 per cent. That meant grief as a reward for our success.

6

I had reason often enough to recall the advice I had been offered on the day of my arrival: to get used to the pervasive presence of prisoners, concentration camps and forced labor colonies. In Pervouralsk and its environs we were in the center of one of the large slave-labor regions of "socialist" Russia. One could not travel far off the main highway in any direction without running into the horror.

Elsewhere a discreet silence might be thrown around the subject. But here the reality was too big, too close for such reticence. One would say, quite casually, "There's good fishing on the Chusovaya River, a kilometer or so this side of the N.K.V.D. colony," or "You'd better follow that road to the left, past the concentration camp."

Our gas station was fueled with peat provided by the Uralturf trust. When I had occasion to complain about deficiencies in gas deliveries, the trust officials rang up Uralturf, which as a matter of course rang up the proper N.K.V.D. official for an explanation. Thousands of prisoners, women as well as men, cut and pressed the turf in the Sverdlovsk region. Peat constituted one of the fuel sources also for Uralenergo, the trust which supplied us with electric power.

I tried to avoid the sight, because it depressed me for weeks. Always I was sickened by the fear that I might find myself looking into the eyes of someone I had known and loved, so many hundreds of my friends had been swallowed up by the super-purge. Once, while on a day's outing with a colleague, we came across a dismal stretch of marshes where perhaps three hundred prisoners, mostly women, were at work. All of the unfortunates were indescribably dirty and grotesquely clad, and many of them stood up to their knees in muddy water. They worked in absolute silence, with the most primitive tools and seemed utterly indifferent to the two strangers.

It was a scene out of some Dantesque hell which I could not drive out of my memory for months. The very word "peat" made my flesh creep.

Driving to and from Sverdlovsk, I became familiar with the sight of the big camp which I had stopped to see on the day of my arrival here. Its main entrance, in the side of the hexagon facing the road, was topped by an elaborate, rather modernistic wooden cornice, into which was set an oval portrait of Stalin. Often strips of red bunting inscribed with the current slogans were stretched on the cornice. At night small colored electric bulbs lit up the picture and the inscriptions.

A stranger, glimpsing this façade from the road as he motored by, might assume that some noble socialist establishment was housed behind the decorated gateway. Those of us who lived in the district knew that the hexagon of horror cut off 2,500 men from the world of the living. Searchlights in the six watchtowers played on the camp all night, revolving automatically, each in its turn, as in a lighthouse. These pillars of light, sweeping across the night sky, made pretty patterns—for those who did not know what they connoted.

Working in plants, mines and on construction projects in the surrounding area, most of the prisoners walked six or seven miles to and from work every day in all weather. This meant that in addition to working ten or twelve hours a day, they walked about three hours more, and few of them had footwear suitable for these forced marches.

Not far from Pervouralsk is the town of Ryevda, site of another metallurgical factory. Every time I went there, I passed a concentration camp with accommodations for about two thousand prisoners. A large part of this number worked in the factory, where construction was still under way, and most of the others were engaged on road building or were contracted for the nearby copper mines.

Another camp, containing only about a thousand prisoners, stood on the shore of the Chusovaya, a lovely, swift-running stream in a picturesque setting of dense pine forests on a turbulent hilly landscape. During the summer months our engineers and officials sometimes took their families to the banks of the Chusovaya for swimming, fishing and rest. They were careful to stop at a respectable distance from the camp; why spoil the outing with a grim reminder?

Having heard so many people rave about the beauty of this river, I finally decided to explore it. My two companions, both Party members, were also newcomers in the district, so that none of us knew about this particular camp. We were driving along, in my Ford, talking about factory affairs when suddenly we found ourselves on a hillock looking down on the barbed-wire enclosure, in a forest clearing several hundred yards from the river's edge. As usual, there were the four towers at the corners of the quadrangle. Guards with fixed bayonets were in evidence. At the farther end of the enclosure several hundred prisoners, men and women, were working on the construction of a new row of barracks.

Our expedition was ended there and then. All desire to see more of the river left us and we drove back to Pervouralsk in silence. The truth is that even the most faithful and unthinking Communists in their heart of hearts despise and are ashamed of the slave-labor system. In the very heat with which some of the more fanatic comrades defended the system I often sensed an uneasiness. In calling the victims foul names—kulaks, wreckers . . . scum . . . dirt . . . they seemed to be shouting down their inner disgust. Every one of them knew quite well that another turn of the political wheel, another purge or crisis, might easily put them among the outlaws whose toil was fortifying our curious brand of socialism.

CHAPTER XIX

WHILE HISTORY IS EDITED

W HEN I THINK back to my sojourn in the Urals, filled with odious memories, one dismal episode crowds out the rest.

It all added up to a hoax played on Russian public opinion, an extravagant hoax in which big and little officials, in Moscow and in Pervouralsk, worked together to dupe the public. They did it so adroitly, dovetailing their lies so expertly, that to this day the "great victory at the Novo-Trubni plant" is cited as an example of the wonders worked by "socialist enthusiasm."

The affair began with the noisy arrival at our sprawling Urals outpost of a brigade of activists from Moscow under instructions to boost Stakhanovite standards at our pipe-rolling plant. Now that we were producing 85 per cent of the norm, one big Moscow-style heave and shove would push us "over the top" to 100 per cent or more. Where there's a will there's a way. There's no bastion we Bolsheviks can't take. Team work does it. All together, comrades, for our Leader and Teacher. . . .

Before leaving the capital, the heave-and-shove brigadiers had been received by Commissar Lazar Kaganovich, in the presence of the press. They came to Pervouralsk armed with extraordinary powers, and buoyed up by airy ignorance of our problems. The rhythm of production, which I had toiled so hard to attain, was suddenly smashed. The brigade called mass meetings and technical conferences and subjected us all to long agitational harangues. The walls of all our shops and offices, dining rooms and recreation halls broke out in a rash of red slogans. Suddenly no one talked, everyone shouted.

The workers shrugged their shoulders and shut their minds against the uproar. But the engineers and executives were driven to nervous frenzy. Only yesterday we were commended for reaching 85—now outside pressure was being applied to drive us to 100. We smarted under the implied slur. Director Osadchi went around with a long face.

"We've got to do something drastic, Victor Andreyevich," he sighed. "The Moscow press is making a great to-do about this Stakhanovite show and we just can't afford to fail. My head—and yours as well—are at stake."

Osadchi was a type of factory executive all too common in our country. The politician in his make-up always took precedence over the engineer. Official acclaim concerned him more than the actual production; records more than quality. What he lacked in technical knowledge he more than made up in "important contacts" in the proper quarters. He was a bit of a sybarite with a sweet tooth for Sverdlovsk girls.

"But what can we do?" I replied. "You know as well as I do that it's impossible to squeeze more than we're now getting out of the plant. Oratory is no substitute for tools and metals."

But Osadchi was already neck-deep in a brilliant scheme. He asked me to provide him with a detailed inventory of finished pipe accumulated in our warehouses. The quantity, it appeared, was considerable. There were stocks produced without specific orders in the preceding year, for instance. I gave him the figures.

Not until later did I realize why he needed this information and I was horrified. Osadchi, in connivance with the brigade, sent a special agent to Moscow who came to a secret understanding with Kozhevnikov, now the head of Glavtrubostal. Kozhevnikov in turn made arrangements with the Central Administration of Metal Supplies for Industry. Our agent returned to Pervouralsk with a batch of orders for various types of pipe to be produced for stockpiles throughout the country.

By a wonderful coincidence, the orders called for precisely the kind and quantities of pipe which we had in our warehouses. We needed only to clean, oil, pack the stuff—and credit them to current production! Cunning bookkeeping would save the day, or the month to be more precise.

It was a bald-faced fraud. But Osadchi, the City Committee, the Regional Committee, the brigadiers, indeed everyone was delighted. And everyone pretended to be blind to the chicanery. Only the Chekists snickered up their sleeves, knowing that this deception gave them a whip hand over some more of the industrial *élite* in their territory. Victory—not merely 100 per cent but any percentage we wished—was in the bag.

The big month, June, began. From the outset the daily totals were on a brilliant "Stakhanovite level." "Keep up the good work!" messages from Moscow urged me. We did, consistently; but not a word was said about the fact that some days more than 25 per cent of the claimed output was fraudulent, consisting of pipe from the warehouse. The foremen and workers, of course, were not fooled. They read the daily and weekly tallies . . . but they knew the truth.

As the month wore on, the delight of the conspirators took on an edge of anxiety. They were a bit frightened by their handiwork, particularly by the big play their "success" was receiving in the newspapers and on the air. Every one of them realized that some day the trick might be thrown up to them as "fooling the government and the Party." They drew together—the Moscow brigadiers and the local functionaries—in a feeling of common guilt and common danger.

I refused resolutely to be drawn into their circle. I made up my mind that, everything considered, I would be safer if I took no part in this jugglery of figures. I was aware, especially, that the artificially high June totals would set for me an impossible standard for future months. As the end of the great Stakhanovite month approached, I therefore gathered the essential documents and, for the record, wrote a full report exposing the trickery. I addressed it to Commissar Kaganovich, Kozhevnikov at Glavtrubostal, Osadchi and to Comrade Dovbenko, Secretary of the Pervouralsk City Committee, with copies for my private safe as insurance against the future.

Osadchi and Dovbenko were thoroughly scared. They immediately telephoned their confederates in Moscow, at Glavtrubostal, as I learned. Assured of support higher up, they summoned me to the City Committee.

"Are you crazy, Kravchenko?" Dovbenko roared. "Everything is going splendidly, Kaganovich is in raptures about our progress, and you want to throw a monkey-wrench into the works. What if we use a trick or two, when the goal is to raise the morale of the working masses? Have you no sense of duty?"

He was pacing his office in anger. Osadchi was biting his lips to keep down his righteous wrath.

"I'm sorry to disagree with you," I said. "I had no part in the scheme and I won't shoulder any of the responsibility. I warn you that after the noise has died down, we'll be back to the old percentage and we'll be blamed for not matching the June output."

"Damn it, we'll cross that bridge when we reach it!" Dovbenko declared. "You're treading a dangerous path, Kravchenko, putting your opinion ahead of everyone else's. You're discrediting the brigade sent by the Commissar, by a member of the Politburo! That's playing with fire."

"Sometimes super-honesty is super-stupidity," Osadchi put in. "We need a little worldly wisdom."

I refused to withdraw my report.

Soon the great month was ended, with the glorious over-all production total of 114 per cent! Moscow, Sverdlovsk, Pervouralsk rang with the victory. Accounts of the "magnificent triumph at the Novo-Trubni plant" filled the press. On the morning of July first I received a telegram from Moscow:

"Congratulations on your great victory. We share your happiness. We authorize you to give premiums to the individual workers. We trust that now the plan will continue to be regularly overfulfilled."

Reporters flew in from Moscow and motored in from Sverdlovsk to describe the miracle of Stakhanovism in action. Novo-Trubni, which was kept at 35 or 40 per cent by its sabotaging management only a few months ago, now stood proudly at 114 per cent under its loyal new Bolshevik leader, Comrade Kravchenko! Delegations from other Pervouralsk factories came to greet their victorious comrades.

Joy reigned everywhere, but in my own heart there was despair. Unwillingly I had been made part of a fraud and pushed into the position of accepting thanks and cash rewards for my part in perpetrating it. Behind closed doors, with the help of my three assistants and the chief bookkeeper, I computed the actual output for the month. Without the spurious "production" out of stockpiles, the figure stood at 87 per cent, that is to say, a shade better than normal. Half a dozen times I was interrupted during this sad exercise in arithmetic by long-distance calls of congratulation. The telegrams of praise kept piling up; one of them was from Kaganovich himself.

That night I began to work on a careful and very specific report of the fraud addressed to Kaganovich.

Meanwhile a mass meeting of the entire factory was called to celebrate the achievement. A platform, draped in red, was erected on the factory grounds and decorated with huge portraits of the Kremlin leaders. A brass band played incessantly. Thousands of workers and officials—many of them perfectly aware of the fraud—were massed in front of the platform. I thought I detected deliberate irony in the unwonted heat of their applause and in the volume of their hurrahing, as Osadchi, Dovbenko, Regional Party representatives, then brigade leaders orated.

Osadchi read some of the messages of congratulation. The workers, he said, by their wonderful showing this month had confounded the skeptics and critics. They had given a resounding answer to the dirty saboteurs and deviationists. Here he screamed:

"Long live our Party and its dear beloved Leader, Teacher, Father and Comrade, Our Comrade Stalin! Hurrah, comrades!"

"Hurrah!" thousands of throats echoed and the band struck up the *Internationale*.

I stood on the platform and was congratulating myself on having avoided the ordeal of a speech. But Dovbenko evidently meant to commit me publicly to a share in the "victory."

"And now," he announced, "we will hear from the comrade whose leadership was so valuable in attaining the glorious total of 114—Comrade Kravchenko!"

I arose. I made no reference to the June production, speaking instead of the difficult problems ahead of us and the need for steady, organized effort. I thanked the workers for what *they* had done and emphasized that an occasional spurt of energy was not enough, that output must be continuous. I received a huge ovation and left the platform with the feeling that some of my listeners, at least, had understood me.

The meeting wound up with the award of a Red Banner to my subplant, which I accepted from the Regional representative without a smile.

The brigade, on its arrival in Moscow, was received in audience by the Commissar, again under the eyes of the press. It was decorated and stuffed with bonuses. *For Industrialization* devoted a full page to the Novo-Trubni miracle and other papers pronounced their editorial blessings. I was still receiving telegrams of praise when I mailed my report to Lazar Kaganovich.

A few weeks later I made an excuse for going to Moscow, in the hope of bringing Glavtrubostal to my side in what, I feared, might explode in a national scandal. Kozhevnikov did not hide his displeasure with me; as one of the prime movers in the fraud, his own career was at stake.

"Try to understand me," I pleaded. "How can I face the workers and the technical staff when they all know or suspect that the great victory was just a great hoax? You know perfectly well that in the months ahead we shan't be able to live up to this artificial record. The workers will gain nothing from it. What's the sense of the whole thing?"

"Relax, Victor Andreyevich," he replied, acidly. "Your attitude, if I may say so, is very naive. You should take the long view on such things. If the Party finds it necessary to popularize a certain kind of activity—in this case Stakhanovism—it becomes a political necessity, in which the end justifies any means. Your alarm is nonsensical."

"You're wrong," I insisted. "We can't build on the basis of lies. They're sure to boomerang."

Kozhevnikov was losing his patience.

"I'll give you some advice, Comrade Kravchenko. Stop making noise about this business or you'll get hurt in the process."

I then called on the editor of *For Industrialization*. He professed to be horrified when I laid the facts of the fraud before him and urged me to write an article about it before I left Moscow. I did, and I sent a copy to *Pravda*. I never heard again from either of those newspapers, nor did I ever hear from Kaganovich.

On returning to the plant I found the workers, foremen and lower engineering personnel in a state of sullen resentment. There had been much talk of bonuses. These people, however, were paid on a strict piece-work basis of accounting. Since they did not actually produce more than usual their only reward was a share in the noise and the Red Banner. But the administrative staff, including Osadchi and myself, received handsome bonuses: 150 per cent of our basic salaries. That made my June pay more than 4,000 rubles—a handsome reward for a hoax which I was trying unsuccessfully to disclose.

Echoes of my Moscow efforts had reached Pervouralsk, and officialdom was in a state of murderous fury. At the City Committee—significantly, in the presence of Parshin of the N.K.V.D.—I was accused of "undermining their prestige." Why was I trying to make trouble for all of them? Why was I "blowing up a fire that had already died down"?

It took months before these officials and factory colleagues forgot my "betrayal" and smiled at me again; but I did not regret my action. Whatever happened, my record was clear. In sober fact, nothing happened. Too many influential bureaucrats were involved in that piece of charlatanism. The "magnificent victory" became solemn history.

2

The publication in 1938 of a new official *History of the Communist Party* marked the tapering off of the super-purge.

I do not mean that the terror was stopped, that the Black Ravens remained unemployed. "Normal" arrests by the thousand, executions without trial, arbitrary exile of "undesirable elements" whose labor was desirable in forsaken regions, tortures and inquisitions continued. The population of concentration camps and forced labor colonies multiplied as never before. Already, among Communists close to the Kremlin throne, whispered estimates placed the slave labor forces at more than fifteen millions; in the next few years the estimate would be closer to twenty millions.

I mean only that the specific campaign to cleanse the Party and the bureaucracy, planned after the assassination of Kirov, was now almost completed. There was not an office or an enterprise, an economic or cultural body, a government or a Party or military bureau, which was not largely in new hands. Had a foreign conqueror taken over the machinery of Soviet life and put new people in control, the change could hardly have been more thorough or more cruel.

The magnitude of the horror has never been grasped by the outside world. Perhaps it is too vast ever to be grasped. Russia was a battlefield strewn with corpses, blotched with gigantic enclosures where millions of wretched "war prisoners" toiled, suffered and died. But how can the mind's eye take in anything so vast? One can only look into this or that corner, and judge the whole from its parts. I was able, through the Kremlin, to obtain a few official figures. They do not compass the whole reality, they merely hint at its extent and malignity.

In the Council of People's Commissars, only Molotov remained; all the rest were killed, imprisoned or demoted. The Central Committee of the Party, in theory the heart and mind of the ruling group, counts 138 members and alternates; only about a score of them remained in that body when the super-purge had run its course. Of the 757 members of *Tzik,* the Central Executive Committee, sometimes described abroad as Russia's "Parliament," only a few dozen survived the storm.

The ruin was even bloodier in the so-called autonomous "republics" and regions. Without exception the commanding staffs of their governments and their Party organizations were wiped out by orders from Moscow—a sufficient commentary on their supposed autonomy. Industry and technology, the arts and education, the press and the armed forces—all were turned upside down, their leaders and most gifted personalities being shot, imprisoned, exiled or at best, stripped of influence.

The temptation in looking at the piled-up horrors is to concentrate on the famous and important victims, whereas the *pogrom* extended to the whole population. In the ruling Party, 1,800,000 members and candidates were expelled, which was more than half the total in these classifications; and in most cases expulsion meant concentration camp or worse. At least eight million more, Comsomol members and non-Party people, were liquidated—meaning anything from execution to exile or removal from their jobs.

But even these colossal figures don't sum up the tragedy. They're big but they are cold. Their very immensity makes them a bit unreal. One must think of the victims not in such impersonal terms, but as individuals. One must recall that each of these multitudes had relatives, friends, dependents who shared his sufferings; that each of them had hopes, plans, actual achievements which were shattered. To the historian of tomorrow, to the sociologist of today, these are statistics. But to me, who lived through it, the digits have bodies and minds and souls, all of which were hurt, outraged and humiliated.

I know, moreover, that millions who escaped the purge were maimed in their minds and wounded in their spirits by the fears and the brutalities amidst which they lived. For sheer scale, I know of nothing in all human history to compare with this purposeful and merciless persecution in which tens of million Russians suffered directly or indirectly. Genghis Khan was an amateur, a muddler, compared to Stalin. The Kremlin clique had carried through a ruthless war on their own country and people.

It was the wind-up of this long war that was signalized by the appearance of a new history. It proved to be a document probably without precedent. Shamelessly, without so much as an explanation, it revised half a century of Russian history. I don't mean simply that it falsified some facts or gave a new interpretation of events. I mean that it deliberately stood history on its head, expunging events and inventing facts. It twisted the recent past—a past still fresh in millions of memories—into new and bizarre shapes, to conform with the version of affairs presented by the blood-purge trials and the accompanying propaganda.

It was bold, specious, conscienceless fiction. There was a certain magnificence in its unabridged cynicism, its defiance of the common sense of the Russian people. The roles of leading historical figures were perverted or altogether erased. New roles were invented for others. Leon Trotsky, one of the creators of the Red Army, was represented as a fiendish agent of foreign capitalists who had sought to sell out his country, in collusion with Rykov, Bukharin, Zinoviev, Kamenev, Bubnov, Krestinsky, Piatakov and virtually all the other Fathers of the Bolshevik Revolution. Joseph Stalin, of course, emerged as the sole leader inside Russia before the revolution, and as Lenin's one intimate and trusted associate thereafter. All books, articles, documents, museum materials which contradicted this extraordinary fantasy parading as history—and that means nearly all historical and political writings and documentation—disappeared throughout the country!

More than that, living witnesses, as far as possible, were removed. The directing staff of the Institute of Marx, Engels and Lenin in Moscow, repository of ideological truth, were removed and the more important people among them imprisoned or shot. The same thing happened in branches of the Institute in various parts of the country. I happened to be intimately acquainted with the story of one of the outstanding figures in the Institute, Professor Sorin, and it seemed to me to sum up the whole shabby and tragic era of coerced falsehood.

Sorin at one time had been publicly denounced by Stalin because he had dared to write that the "dictatorship of the proletariat" was in Russia identical with a "dictatorship of the Party." Then the culprit duly "confessed his errors" and emerged as one of Stalin's mentors in Marxist theory, fabricating speeches and articles to which Stalin attached his name. He was made assistant director of the Marx-Engels-Lenin Institute, dug diligently for documents and quotations to support any policy Stalin wished to foist on the country, and seemed happily adjusted.

But a point seemed to have been reached at which the meek Sorin balked. He was willing to find and quote texts as required—but he drew the line at *inventing* texts and *falsifying* quotations. And so in the middle of one winter night the N.K.V.D. wagon came to Professor Sorin's fine apartment and took him away. No trace remained of him. His wife and child were evicted from their home and left to shift for themselves. All of the professor's books, documents and notes were carted off to the N.K.V.D.

Other Institute people who knew too much about Communist history and theory to accept the faked version were similarly shut up, among them the chief director, Adoratsky. The head of the Party's propaganda division, Stetsky, was arrested. Thousands of others from the historical, political and literary "fronts" were sent on the one-way road to oblivion. The path was thus cleared for falsification without measure or limit. The new "history" became possible.

To brand the shame more deeply on our minds, "study" of the new version was made obligatory for all responsible Party people. History classes met nearly every night in this period and lecturers from Sverdlovsk came to our town to help hammer home the lies, while most of us fumed inwardly. Whatever human dignity remained in our character was humiliated. But even the most gigantic lie, by dint of infinite repetition, takes root; Stalin knew this before Hitler discovered it. As I looked on I could see terrible falsehoods, at first accepted under pressure, become established as unquestioned "facts," particularly among younger people without personal experience to the contrary to bother them.

What concerns the outside world especially in this falsified history is the directive issued in the introduction to this manual. "Study of the history of the Communist Party," it states, "strengthens the certainty of the final victory of the great task of the Lenin-Stalin Party: the victory of Communism in the whole world." Notwithstanding the new emphasis on Russian nationalism, this directive remains unchanged. Even when the Communist International was supposedly "abolished," the certainty of a Stalinist world revolution was not revised or discarded. The history is still official, not only for Communists in Russia but for Communists in America, England, China and everywhere else.

It fell to me to deliver a "lecture" on one phase of this Party history to responsible Party members of the Pervouralsk district. I went through the painful farce, of course, only because it was an order from the City Committee which I dared not disobey. My specific subject was "The Communist Party in the Struggle for Collectivization of Agriculture." I crammed my mind with the appropriate passages from the official history, read up Stalin's speeches on the subject, then stood in an auditorium filled with people and lied, as I was forced to do, for more than an hour.

Every falsehood tore open the half-healed wounds of my own shattering experiences in the collectivization drive and its aftermath of famine. I felt as if I were mocking the children with bloated bellies among whom I had worked and violating the corpses I had seen piled up in the villages. And all the time, as I spoke, I had no doubt that my listeners, too, knew I was lying. My words and their applause were equally spurious; we were so many actors going through our prescribed parts in a tragic political comedy.

Why did I, why did the audience, submit to the indignity? For the same reason that you hand over your wallet to a footpad who points a gun at you. Let no outsider, secure in his human rights, take a superior attitude towards Russians obliged to "lecture" as I did and obliged to applaud as my audience did.

Along with the "education" of the Party and non-Party people in line with the refurbished history, the official propagandists relied on two effective foreign angles. The first was a one-sided and distorted description of life in the capitalist world, especially the United States and England. The lecturer would show pictures clipped from the foreign press in which strikers were being beaten by police, unemployed rioters were being drenched with fire hose, tear bombs were being hurled at the proletariat. Presented as a complete portrayal of capitalism, this material made a deep impression; it seemed to be authentic, documented, irrefutable.

The second was the citing of attacks on the Soviet Union by hostile foreigners in which there were slighting or insulting remarks about the Russian people. These writings failed to draw a clear line between the Russian people and the Soviet regime. The human self-respect as well as the national pride of the listeners were outraged.

Another result of the big purge deserves mention. Every Communist carries a Party card. It is his personal passport, his political patent. The booklet, besides personal data, has on it the signatures of the local Party officials who issued it. Because most of the leading Party officials had been purged, it transpired that most Communists had their blessed status affirmed by enemies of the people. The Kremlin could not tolerate this ironical touch. With a view to erasing the handwriting and the memory of the dead and the imprisoned, a new registration of Communists was therefore ordered in this fall of 1938. Where cards had been signed by liquidated "enemies of the people," new ones were issued.

The process was turned into a new, though minor, purge. Every Communist again appeared before three-man commissions and submitted himself to elaborate questioning. The new cards, besides, were no longer the simple affair they used to be. They now included a photograph. Besides, a special booklet was now compiled for every Communist, in two copies, containing detailed biographical data, a record of activities, rewards, punishments; one copy was deposited at his City Committee, the other at the Central Committee in Moscow. The whole procedure looked like a police documentation rather than a record of members of a political organization. The last pretense that we were participants in a voluntary association of comrades was dropped.

That there might be no illusions in this respect, a new rule was put into effect: Thereafter a Communist wishing to leave one city or region to settle in another—even if the change were on orders from above—had first to wait for a formal decision by the City Committee authorizing his departure. The ruling Party became, in effect, another prison—fitted out with comforts and a thousand privileges not enjoyed by the inmates of the larger prison called Russia, but still a place of confinement.

One day, as the first breath of a new winter could be felt in the Urals, Secretary Dovbenko informed me that I would have the honor of a leading part in the coming "elections" to the Supreme Soviet. The Central Committee of the Party had selected Comrade Kuzmin as a candidate for election from the Pervouralsk district to the Supreme Soviet and it would be my privilege to "nominate" this man formally at a general meeting of the electorate.

"But why Kuzmin?" I asked. "He's never lived here and no one here knows him. As Vice-Commissar of Heavy Industry he lives and works in Moscow. Besides, I scarcely know him myself."

My objections were brushed aside. My factory having been in the limelight as winner of a Red Banner, I was considered the appropriate man to introduce Kuzmin to the sovereign voters. He would, of course, be the only candidate. The thought that there might be an opposition candidate, to challenge the Party's choice, did not even enter anyone's mind; it was outside the experience of the new generation.

Equipped with a file of information about "my" candidate, I put in several nights preparing the nomination speech. In the ritual phrases of Soviet demagogy I lauded Kuzmin, "a true son of the Party and the people," for his services to the revolution and his loyalty to The Leader. Dovbenko and his colleagues read the manuscript, made various changes, and declared themselves satisfied.

Several days later an echelon of elegant motorcars drew up in front of our factory. "My candidate," of whose existence I had been only vaguely aware until that week, stepped out, surrounded by his Chekist guards and his Party retinue. Kuzmin was a remarkable sight: a rough-hewn fellow, with a day's growth of beard, in shabby clothes. His embroidered Russian blouse was mended at the collar; he wore a workman's cap and Red Army boots. In short, he had come disguised as a proletarian!

I was disgusted by the masquerade and flushed crimson at the thought of my own share in the imposture. At four o'clock the electoral meeting got under way in the main square of Pervouralsk. From all the surrounding factories came delegations, with their banners and bands. Comsomol contingents marched to the scene, their young voices lifted in robust song. The red-draped tribune was adorned with the pictures of Stalin, Molotov, Kalinin, Voroshilov and others. I took my place on the platform, along with Dovbenko, Osadchi, Kuzmin and other dignitaries as an orchestra blared the *Internationale* and other hymns.

In due time I unreeled my speech, praising Kuzmin as "the best of the best." The populace cheered and the bands thundered forth their approval. A few others delivered standardized orations. Finally Kuzmin himself stepped forward to thank the people for their "confidence" and to assure them of his devoted services "if they should elect him."

"Long live the Brain, the Heart, the Strength of the Party and the Soviet Peoples, our Beloved Leader and Teacher, Comrade Stalin!" he concluded and the music once more reinforced the applause.

As we left the platform, headed for the gala dinner awaiting the top officials, Kuzmin took my hand.

"You spoke well, Comrade Kravchenko," he said. "Thank you, thank you. When you come to Moscow come to see me. I'll always be delighted to be of help to you."

I could not avoid noticing, as we shook hands, that his fingernails were beautifully manicured.

Soon thereafter I did go to Moscow and, as it happened, in connection with business in which Kuzmin could be useful if he wished. His offices were large and sumptuously furnished. Rather to my astonishment I had to wait a long time. When I finally entered his private office I faced a man only remotely resembling the proletarian specimen on the Pervouralsk platform. Kuzmin was wearing European clothes, punctuated by a loud necktie. There was no trace of the negligent, common-man manner in this typically puffed-up, well-groomed, overfed politician.

"What is it, comrade?" he said in annoyance, looking at me blankly. "Where are you from?"

It was then that I realized, with a shock, that he had already completely forgotten his sponsor, the man who had presented him to his "constituency." It was the crowning touch to the farce of one-party, one-candidate elections under "the world's most democratic Constitution."

3

I have said little about my private life in the Urals, and before that in Taganrog and Nikopol. I feel the lack myself. I can almost hear the reader ask: Are Soviet industrial managers, then, mere machines, without personal dimensions to their existence?

I would be exaggerating if I answered with a plain affirmative. We Russians are gregarious folk, warm and talkative and quick to kindle in friendship. We wear our hearts on our sleeves. I am no exception in this respect.

The fact is that I made dozens, even hundreds, of friends in those years. Let it be remembered that to thousands of the men and women around me I was a person of consequence, one of the Party elect. I had favors to dispense. Under my roof they found abundance and comfort—things and conditions for which all but a handful of people were tragically starved. My standards of life were modest, even bleak, when compared to those of men in my position in America. But in Nikopol, Taganrog, Pervouralsk or even Moscow they were so far above the average, so remote from the working-class level, that I seemed to live in a world apart. Few of those who envied their well-paid *novi barii,* their new masters, or caught a glimpse of the sorry splendors of our life, realized the weight of fear, lack of personal freedom and professional independence, the torment of uncertain tenure under which we enjoyed our advantages.

Yes, I made friends and now and then even romance ventured through my door. But looking back, the sum total of these things seemed pitiably small. Human relations in this period, for men in my position, were all in a minor key, drowned out by the din of excessive labor and the howls of excessive politics. Sparks of romance could not hold out against the winds of fear. Few of us felt settled, rooted. Our days seemed hurried and transitory—way-stations to another assignment or to sudden extinction. In making friends we had the frustrated sense of passengers meeting briefly on the station platform before taking trains in opposite directions.

But that tells only part of the story. If the years seem so empty, despite their clamorous events, it is because I lived in a spiritual void. Having lost faith in the Great Experiment, I had nothing to cling to—nothing but work and the dim and improbable hope of escape. How was one to retain inner dignity when the whim of some Poo-Bah in Moscow, or the zeal of some local Party or police official, might blot out one's personality without a moment's warning? How nurture self-respect under the myriad eyes of vulgar and too often malicious spies?

There were moments in which I coveted the family life of some colleagues and wondered whether I might not be happier with a wife and children. But the thought of how much more dreadful arrest must be to a husband and a father quickly cured me of envy. In my limited free time I used to go to Sverdlovsk for the opera and theatre. I also did a lot of reading—literature for my own enjoyment and political-economic works as a Party obligation; one could not fall behind in one's knowledge of Lenin, Stalin, Marx, Engels.

The Kolpovskys—Constantine Mikhailovich, who was our chief engineer, his pretty wife Vera and Ninnochka, their seven-year-old daughter—were one family group which touched my nostalgia for a normal home life. They seemed so integrated by a natural, undramatic love that you could hardly think of one of them without implying the others. I used to visit them occasionally and to little Ninnochka I became Uncle Vitya, with the privileges and obligations of affectionate unclehood.

When Kolpovsky went to Moscow on business, towards the end of the summer, he asked me to keep an eye on his family. The evening before his return, Vera and the child were at my home drinking tea and munching *zakuski*. Constantine Mikhailovich had been gone nearly two weeks, and his family could not restrain the joy and excitement of tomorrow's reunion. They could talk of nothing else.

I had invited director Osadchi to drop in and after a while he arrived. He greeted Mrs. Kolpovsky and the little girl in a rather nervous and even resentful manner, as if he were disturbed by their presence. I dismissed his mood as of no importance; probably merely the reflection of some office troubles. But soon he found an excuse for drawing me away to the balcony. It was a mild night, filled with pungent pine odors from the surrounding forests.

"Why didn't you tell me that the Kolpovskys would be here?" he asked in a low, tense voice.

"What a strange question! What difference does it make?"

"You don't understand, Victor Andreyevich. The situation is rather awkward, because Kolbin told me in great secrecy . . ."

"Told you what?"

"Well, you're not to say a word, but maybe you ought to know. Kolbin and several Sverdlovsk N.K.V.D. people will meet the express train from Moscow at Sverdlovsk tomorrow. They have orders to arrest Kolpovsky."

"It can't be! Poor Vera, poor Ninnochka. But why, why?"

"As to why I don't know any more than you do. You know how it is. . . . But we'd better go back or they'll begin to wonder."

In a few minutes Osadchi mumbled some excuse and left us. Vera and Ninnochka remained an hour longer—garrulous, ebullient, impatient for tomorrow, and full of plans for their drive to Sverdlovsk.

"Constantine always pretends that he didn't expect us and that he's overwhelmed by surprise," Vera laughed.

"And do you know, Uncle Vitya, daddy will surely bring me a beautiful doll and picture books and candy and lots of other things," Ninnochka said. She hugged me in her exuberance. "He's the best daddy in the world and I'll have a bouquet of field flowers for him. I'll pick them myself."

Retaining my composure, pretending to join in their happiness, drained all my strength. When at last they left, I sank into a chair exhausted. The thought of what awaited them stabbed at my heart. It would have served no purpose to forewarn them and might only have gotten them, Osadchi and myself into serious trouble.

About midnight my phone rang.

"Victor Andreyevich, this is Kolbin. Could I borrow your Ford tomorrow? I have to go to Sverdlovsk urgently."

"No, I'm sorry, Kolbin, I need it myself," I replied brusquely. I did not relish the use of my car for this dirty business.

"But you have your new car. Please don't make trouble. This call is just a formality—I already have Osadchi's permission anyhow."

The knowledge that my own motorcar had taken one of the arresting officers to the station added to my burden of sorrow the next morning. Even while I was at work, part of my mind saw the gruesome scene. And my imagination was not too far from the reality. The scene was described to me, with undisguised glee, by Kolbin himself.

As the train pulled in, mother and daughter were waiting. They were in their holiday best, smiling and happy, flowers in their hands.

"There he is!" Ninnochka cried, and they rushed towards Kolpovsky as he alighted, carrying two suitcases. He was a handsome, broad-shouldered man with a shock of dark hair. His face lit up with a joyous grin as he watched his "two girls," as he always called them, approach.

But three uniformed N.K.V.D. men, revolvers in hand, stepped in between. They informed the stunned engineer that he was under arrest, took his suitcases and hustled him to a waiting closed car. They did not even give him time to greet or kiss his family. Mrs. Kolpovsky and the child wept hysterically. An N.K.V.D. man went in the car with them—their home would be searched and this was to make sure Vera did not touch anything.

After that nobody dared to associate with Kolpovsky's wife, and Ninnochka's playmates taunted her, with the cruelty of children. "Your daddy's an enemy of the people and we won't play with you ever again," they chanted in chorus. I recalled with a pang the times, long long ago, when little boys in Yekaterinoslav made sport of me because my father was in prison. The Kolpovskys, of course, were evicted from the factory apartment.

The arrest of the chief engineer alarmed the entire technical staff. Rumors of every kind filtered through the shops. Because I had been in close business relations with Kolpovsky, my arrest was generally expected and, indeed, I was surprised that it did not take place. To this day I have no inkling of the charges against him—his work had been both competent and loyal and he seemed all engineer, a Party member but almost indifferent to politics.

I learned later that after a few months in prison Kolpovsky was "rehabilitated" and even restored to Party membership. He made a great career in his profession and in time was even decorated by the government. But the period of suffering had undermined his health. His old vivacity, his old joy in living, were no more.

4

For an outsider the personal history of a Soviet official can have the third dimension of reality only if the background is never blurred or forgotten: The background of half-hungry, shabby, long-suffering and despised masses, denied elementary political and economic freedoms.

There was rarely a day when some worker or his wife didn't come to me with a tale of poverty and disease. I did what I could, which was always pitiably little. Sometimes I succeeded in cutting through red tape to obtain a pair of shoes or a suit of work clothes for someone who needed it badly. Now and then I stirred the hospital service into action where the life of a child was at stake. But the evils were too many and too deep to be mitigated, let alone cured, by the efforts of a few thin-skinned officials here and there. The worst of it, as I look back, is that the sufferings of the people were taken for granted. They were accepted as natural and inevitable, like the mud and the inclemency of our Urals weather.

Despite official measures to tie workers to their jobs, our turnover of labor was shockingly high. In my own shops, from two to three hundred disappeared every month, in a total of some seventeen hundred. What this did to the continuity and efficiency of operations is self-evident.

Only a real improvement in living conditions could have solved the problem. The worker who packed his poor belongings and set out to find work elsewhere was driven by sheer despair. Perhaps he had heard that somewhere else his family might receive bigger wages and rations, a cleaner place to live in. But our new masters preferred to overlook causes and to deal with effects. The government propaganda evolved a lot of insulting names for these citizens seeking a better life. It called them loafers, deserters from the labor front, unstable elements. And it prescribed a larger dose of the one Soviet remedy for all social complaints: force.

The remedy took the form of a new "labor book" for all workers. Though formally put on the statute books on January 15, 1939, the actual distribution of the new document began several weeks earlier. It was hailed in the press as proof of the "growth and success of the working class, its loyalty to the Socialist Fatherland." Though decided upon by the Politburo and inflicted on the masses, who saw it clearly enough as another lock on their prison lives, it was presented as the workers' own weapon in the struggle with "lazy disorganizers of production."

The labor book became for the rank and file workman what the Party card was for the Communist. He could no longer leave his job without a written entry in the book authorizing him to do so. He could obtain no other work unless the book showed his release at the previous place of employment. Moreover, the document carried a permanent record of any reprimands or punishments the holder may have received for lateness, production mistakes or other sins. Thus the worker was condemned to drag the burden of his entire past with him always wherever he might go; he could no longer hope to make a fresh start in some other city or industry.

I talked to dozens of the men and women at the Novo-Trubni plant at the time the new labor books were being issued. Without exception they hated it. The simplest-minded unskilled worker looked on the device as a piece of official trickery. Even those who had no intention of leaving their jobs felt themselves trapped.

"Who wants to leave a factory if life there is half-way decent?" they would tell me. "In what way will we be different now from the people in the concentration camps around here?"

But in the usual Soviet fashion, the victims were forced to accept their new chains not merely "willingly" but "with enthusiasm." It was not enough to suffer the whipping, they had to kiss the strap and shout hurrah. The trade-union officials conducted an "educational campaign" on the beauties of the new "discipline." They staged mass meetings at which selected Party people among the factory hands rhapsodied about the new blessings and at which shrill resolutions of approval, prefabricated in the City Committee in the spirit of the Moscow prescriptions, were adopted unanimously.

A commission of investigation arrived at our factory to make sure that the distribution of the new Stalin labor books had been duly carried out. One of its members, it turned out, was a classmate from my Institute days. At the supper table, in the intimacy of my own apartment, we got around to the question of labor books. Having been at a great many factories, my friend sounded dejected. The general resentment among workers had affected him.

"Yes, I make burning speeches about this new Soviet achievement," he sighed, "but, Vitya, I don't talk from the heart. First police cards for the Party members, now yellow tickets for the workers!"

I heard the same designation, curiously, from another source. One of my assistants came to the office on business.

"Well, Victor Andreyevich," he said with a wry smile, "you can congratulate me. Like a prostitute, I've just received my yellow ticket. . . ."

Having made certain that the proletarians could not run away, the government then took another step towards "socialism": It ordered a nationwide revision of labor norms. The trade unions were again in charge of the excitement, and the revision was in every case, of course, upward. Once more, at public meetings, the employees of our various departments adopted resolutions "voluntarily" enlarging their work quotas which meant, in truth, lowering their own wages. The Pervouralsk newspapers were lyrical in describing the great enthusiasm of the occasion, though no one present had seen anything beyond routine hand raising and routine hand clapping.

Having tied the workers to their machines and exacted more work for the same pay, we were ready for the next and most humiliating proof of the dignity of labor under the dictatorship of the proletariat. First came a loud and lusty propaganda storm on the theme of loafing and lateness. In various cities "demonstration trials" against "loafers" were staged. The proverbial man from Mars, had he descended at this time and place, would have been certain that we Russians were a nation of lazy louts, lolling in our featherbeds until the sun rode high; in our loutishness he would have seen a simple explanation of the pervasive deficiencies.

Then came the Draconian edict on "strengthening socialist labor discipline." Let foreign innocents who profess to see "economic democracy" and a "workers' society" in Russia study this edict. Let them consider whether the oppressed workers in their benighted lands would tolerate such treatment.

The new law provided that anyone late to work by more than twenty minutes must automatically be denounced to the local Prosecutor. He must then be tried and if found guilty, sentenced to prison or to forced labor. For fear that "soft" officials and "rotten bourgeois liberals" in the local courts might be lenient, the decree made arrest and punishment mandatory for executives and others who failed to report or otherwise shielded the "criminals" of lateness! Only serious illness, formally attested by the factory physicians, or the death of some member of the family, was acceptable proof of innocence. Mere oversleeping or transport difficulties could not be offered as excuses.

In my years as an industrial administrator I had seen many blows descend on the hapless heads of the workers. But none of them had been as incredible, as stunning, as this one. At first most people assumed that it was too drastic an edict to be enforced. But we soon understood that Stalin was in earnest. Twenty minutes was the margin between the limited slavery of "free" workers and the total slavery of the forced-labor contingents.

Every morning a list of the latecomers, with the exact number of minutes of their lateness, was placed on my desk. Party and labor-union offices in the plant received copies of this document. I had no alternative but to sign it and turn it over to the director who in turn sent it to the Prosecutor. The "criminals" were quickly summoned to a court hearing. We found it hard to believe that bread-winners would actually be torn away from their families, condemned to a year or more of forced labor, for such frivolous reasons. But we were dismally wrong. Aside from the warning contained in the law itself, the courts had received stringent instructions to be ruthless. They did their duty, though few of the prosecutors and judges could conceal their sense of shame.

In the first three months, throughout Russia, about a million workers and employees were brought to heel for loafing and exceeding the twenty-minute period of grace and most of them were convicted! Fathers and mothers were dragged out of their homes, leaving their infants to starve or to be put into orphanages, for having overslept or because their illness had not been judged serious enough by the official doctors. In my own shops, dozens of workers were condemned every day. A great wail of sorrow and despair rose over the bleak barracks and apartment houses but it was not loud enough to reach the ears of the Politburo. To this day it has not been heard by the idiots who seek to extend the blessings of such "economic democracy" to other nations and peoples.

An old lathe hand came to see me. I knew him as a competent and industrious worker. He was crying. Even before he spoke I knew what it was about. I had seen his name on the daily list of sorrow.

"I was late by thirty minutes," he admitted. "But I am an old man. These hands have labored for forty years. What will happen to my wife and my children? Help me, help me, Comrade director!"

"Why were you late?"

"I have a bad toothache. It kept me up all night. Finally I fell asleep towards morning and didn't wake up in time. I ran to the shop almost without dressing, as if all the devils were chasing me. But I didn't make it!"

"I believe you, comrade, but I have no choice in the matter. If I should take off your name, I'd go to prison myself. I can only send a note to the doctor asking him to help you."

I wrote the note. But evidently the doctor was concerned about his own skin. The old man was sent off to court.

A woman worker pushed my secretaries aside and rushed into the office. She was weeping loudly in peasant fashion.

"Sit down and control yourself," I pleaded.

It appeared that she had been almost an hour late and had already received a court summons. She was a widow, supporting two children, an eleven-year-old daughter and another two years old, with her work in the factory. The elder child, she explained, was very sick. She had sent for a doctor but by the time he came and examined the patient, she found herself late for work.

I promised to talk to the doctor. Unhappily the little girl, in his opinion, was not as ill as a fond mother imagined. He could not honestly testify that the illness justified the lateness. The mother was sentenced to work on a forced-labor basis at our plant.

In another case the workman pleaded that he possessed no clock and had been in the habit of rising by the sun. An exceptionally dark, cloudy morning was responsible for his downfall. The explanation did not save him.

It was obvious to me that the curing of lateness was only one object of the Draconian decree. The other, and perhaps more vital, purpose was to expand the forced-labor population. The courts had specific orders. The machinery of "justice" worked diligently: free workers were stuffed in at one end, by tens and hundreds of thousands, and newly minted forced laborers emerged at the other end.

These bitter disciplinary measures against the common man, destroying the last shreds of his human dignity, coincided with an exceptionally bitter winter. The slaves in the Urals N.K.V.D. colonies worked outdoors despite the brutal cold, frost-bitten, gangrened, deformed. In the neighboring concentration camps, men and women were often frozen to death in the forests and in the unheated barracks and mud huts behind the barbed wire. In our barracks the suffering was intense. All in all, Pervouralsk was not exactly a joyous setting for our vaunted "socialist labor."

Indications from Moscow that I might be transferred to another undertaking were therefore welcome. There was always the illusion that things might be, if not better, at least less distressing, somewhere else.

For many months the metallurgical industry had been agitated by reports of a grandiose pipe-rolling project in Siberia—specifically, in Stalinsk (formerly Kuznetzk) where gigantic new industrial enterprises were already in operation. It would involve construction to the tune of over a hundred million rubles. In the prescribed Soviet fashion, the plans were being ballyhooed well in advance. I had heard the reports and read some of the ballyhoo in an impersonal way—but suddenly it all focussed for me to a sharp and terribly personal point. Without consulting my preferences, the Commissariat and the Central Committee of the Party selected me to direct the entire construction of this new plant at Stalinsk.

CHAPTER XX

SIBERIAN HOAX

"THE PEOPLE's Commissar of Ferrous Metallurgy has named Comrade V. A. Kravchenko director of the metallurgical factory to be built in the city of Stalinsk, Siberia," the Moscow *For Industrialization* announced on February 28, 1939.

The reference was to the great new enterprise in Stalinsk, Siberia, planned to produce 170,000 tons of steel pipe yearly. Molotov himself, in his "thesis" for the coming Eighteenth Congress of the Communist Party, had stressed the importance of the Siberian undertaking. Construction, he said, would start soon and the first sections would be in operation by 1941.

To have my name thus linked with an industrial giant singled out for attention by Molotov—and inferentially therefore by Stalin as well—instantly threw a halo of glory around my head. My appointment was made publicly, as part of the build-up for the Congress. That was more significant than the post itself. It meant that I had "arrived," that I was in the upper brackets of the economic and political aristocracy. Friends and acquaintances who had shunned me during the difficult purge years suddenly recalled that they knew me and hastened to inform me of their pride in my success.

In preparation for the Siberian job I had a lot of work to do in Moscow, where I was given a fine room at the Metropole Hotel, all expenses paid by the government, and plenty of money. I could have what I wanted. Oh, it's no small thing to be a favored son of the Central Committee. The whole business of dictatorship, in fact, looks different, less grim, less tyrannical, when viewed from somewhere near the top.

No doubt this was the thought in my father's mind when he warned me, half in earnest, half ironically, not to lose touch with common folk now that I was among the "high and mighty." "Don't let 'them' buy you off with titles and honors," his letter said. I noticed with satisfaction this proof that time had not softened his attitude towards people in power. I should have been disappointed if he had made an exception for his own son.

The news of my designation, when it appeared in the press of my native city, seemed to my mother a wonderful sign that the ordeal of persecution was finally behind me.

"May God give you health, luck and success, dearest son," she wrote. "Do try to forget past insults. Turn your eyes forward. Work hard for our beloved land and our people, dear one. As for us, we live as always. Forgive me for mentioning it, but should you come home for a visit, bring what you can from Moscow—fats, sugar, tea, fish. . . . Alas, we have nothing here. I would not mention it if conditions were not so terrible."

Father's letter supported her suggestion. Casually, as if merely in passing, he said: "We're told, my son, that we have achieved the 'happy life.' But don't let the slogans stop you if you can find a pair of shoes for your mother. Somehow the 'happy life' has bypassed Dniepropetrovsk."

My new status as a trusted executive, of course, did not exempt me from the routine solicitude of the N.K.V.D. boys. On returning to the hotel I would frequently find the telltale signs that my suitcases and wardrobe drawers had again been painstakingly searched. Now, as always, new acquaintances tried to draw me into dangerous political discussions. Happily I had learned to smell the *provocateur*; a kind of sixth sense, born in those night sessions in Nikopol, warned me to shut my mouth when people seemed too eager to "open their hearts."

I had learned, too, to guard my bachelorhood against the attentions of those denizens of the expensive hotels whom we called "Liubyanka ladies," Liubyanka being the N.K.V.D. headquarters in the capital. These girls were chosen by connoisseurs of female flesh and were decked out in costly elegance, including splendid fur coats, at the expense of the shabby proletariat. Those who had a smattering of foreign tongues specialized in seducing foreigners: diplomats, American and German engineers, newspaper correspondents. The others preyed on lonely bureaucrats important enough to rate rooms in the big hotels.

One night, for instance, I was settled in my room reading a metallurgical journal when the phone rang.

"Piotr Ivanovich," a woman's voice complained, "why haven't you called me so long? I'm lonely for you, dear."

"I'm sorry but there's no such person here," I said brusquely.

"Stop joking, Petya. As if I didn't recognize your voice!"

"I'm not your Petya. Please let me alone."

"So! I suppose you're with some other girl! Well, I'll come over and see for myself!"

In about twenty minutes there was a knock at my door. A tall, slim, striking blonde stood in the doorway. Snowdrops glistened on her coquettish little fur hat. She pretended surprise but smiled sweetly.

"Is Piotr Ivanovich home?"

"Listen, my little pigeon, I live here and there's no Piotr Ivanovich. Please let me be."

"But why so rude, my dear? An interesting-looking man like you should speak more civilly to an attractive woman."

"I'm busy. Forgive me but I must say good-night."

"Ekh, appearances are so deceiving. . . . You seem a real gentleman but don't even offer a lady a chair."

"Good night!" I said firmly. As I closed the door I could not resist adding, "Your technique isn't too good. You need lots more practice."

Because I needed to consult certain metallurgical officials in Dniepropetrovsk, I was able to make my visit home at government expense. I was provided with a separate compartment in the first-class or so-called "international" cars. I was well dressed, travelling in top-category comfort. Any citizen could see in me at a glance another solid, well-placed bureaucrat. The conductor was obsequious. I felt annoyed, to be thus accepted as a very symbol of the inequality which I despised.

The "hard" or third-class cars at the other end of the train, beyond our "international" dining car, were filled with ordinary humanity crowding double tiers of wooden shelves. As I walked through those cars, out of curiosity, I could sense reproof and even hatred in the eyes that examined my respectability. At stations, when I went out to stretch my legs, I thought I detected the same sort of hostility in the tattered peasants hawking a few vegetables, dried fish and milk.

Soon we were in my native Ukraine. The very landscape seemed more friendly than in the northern Russian provinces. But my heart contracted in pain as I looked at the poverty and neglect everywhere in evidence.

As we drew into a station beyond Kharkov, I was in the dining car. I was startled by several little faces peering through the window with sad, hungry, envious eyes. These were *bezprizorni,* homeless boys and girls in motley rags. They were staring at one of their "socialist uncles" at lordly ease under the dictatorship of the proletariat.

This in the Ukraine, which once upon a time provided food not only for all its population but for a large part of Europe! I paid my bill nervously, suddenly depressed, and hurried out of the dining car. What a gulf lay between the Russia of propaganda and official statistics and the Russia of flesh and blood! What a strange machine is the human mind that can shut out reality with walls of paper victories and empty slogans!

At the Sinelnikovo station I went out again for a walk in the invigorating cold. At the door of the first-class waiting room I watched a uniformed Chekist shooing off a peasant family—man, wife and several children, all of them laden with heavy bundles. "You belong over there, citizens, in the third-class waiting room," he said, and they walked off meekly. It would never occur to them, any more than to the gendarme, that people so work-worn might intrude on the first-class precincts in this our "classless society."

Several adolescent girls, provincial and pleasant-looking, their youthful faces framed in colored shawls, had come to meet the train. It was no doubt one of the great thrills of life in a provincial town like Sinelnikovo. In excited eagerness they peered into first-class windows, giggling and nudging one another. Perhaps they dreamed that some important firstclass Prince Charming with a Party card and an Order of Lenin, rich and powerful, would see them, fall in love at once, and carry them off to the never-never land in Moscow.

The Dniepropetrovsk station was clean and orderly. My brother Constantine was waiting for me on the crowded, noisy platform, and with him was his wife. Having been away from home for over a year, I had not yet met this new member of the family. I embraced and kissed them both. They helped me with the huge packages of food and clothes which I had brought from the capital and soon we were on our way home, the luggage in one carriage, the three of us in another. It was good to see again the familiar streets and squares and buildings, huddled in their blankets of snow as I shall always remember them.

"Ekh, Vitya, you look like a real Moscow eagle, a regular little Stalin," Constantine laughed. "Didn't I tell you, Klava, that my brother was a mighty important man?"

I thought I detected a serious note under the jesting. The older my brother grew the more he resembled our father. He had the same lean, clean-cut good looks, the same strain of irony.

"Why do you say that, Kotya?"

"Don't be offended, little brother. But you do loom magnificent in my provincial eyes. How shall I put it? Maybe it's that self-satisfied look that comes to proletarian leaders after a life-time of self-denial. . . ."

"Now stop it, Kotya," his wife broke in. "You wait for Victor Andreyevich as anxiously as if he were your sweetheart, and first thing you do when he arrives is attack him."

"But darling Klava," he explained, "this is the first and probably the last chance I shall have to attack a little Stalin to his face!"

We all laughed. Knowing my brother inside out, I could not dismiss his joke as lightly as his wife did. I knew he loved me deeply. As if reading my thoughts, he pressed my arm affectionately, just as he used to when we were children. His bitter mockery was not aimed at me but at the breed of self-important, comfortable and spiritually callous bureaucrats. It seemed to me that he was echoing the cynicism with which life among the working masses was saturated.

The stalwart Constantine was in many respects a typical Russian intellectual. He had resisted all pressures to draw him into the Party; but he had a profound love for our country and our people. Several years later, when the Germans attacked our fatherland, he would be among the first to go to the front and ultimately, as an officer, to lay down his life in defense of Russia. Whatever the press might say about the valor of such men, I was certain, when the news reached me in Moscow, that it was not for Stalin and his regime that he had fought and died, but for his people and his country.

Could he have had a premonition of his own fate and the fate of millions? In our talks during this visit he said at one point: "Our country is one thing, Vitya, its regime quite another. . . . Let's not confuse the two." At the time I paid little attention to the remark—though it expressed what I felt myself—but later it would recur to me constantly.

2

My parents had both aged visibly since our last meeting. With three sons helping financially, they lived far better than most of their neighbors. Yet existence was hard. Even with money it was impossible to obtain the kind of food they needed in their declining years. Besides, father suffered in his own flesh and nerves every blow struck at the workers—the labor books, the lateness decree, the stepped-up norms, the growth of forced labor. All his life he had identified himself so completely with the plain people that every new humiliation hurt him to the quick, notwithstanding the fact that he was himself safe.

Mother seemed to have become more frail. My heart went out to her. The goodness in her seemed a tangible thing. It lit up her countenance and made it beautiful in a way that words could never convey. I never tired of watching her as she prepared our meals or bustled over her brood of grown-up men. Somehow I was pleased that the lamps still burned under her icons, as I remembered them from babyhood, witnesses that she had an unfailing source of consolation. She was convinced that it was her prayers which saved me in the super-purge, and I did not contradict her.

In the evening my brother Eugene arrived with his wife. It was a memorable reunion. Father, who had never learned to relax completely, to forget the world and its troubles, tried again and again to talk politics but was duly squelched by his three sturdy sons. There was much to talk about. Constantine's wife was an engineer, Eugene's a teacher, and all of us thus close to the tough everyday realities.

The following day my work took me to the Lenin plant. Its administrative staff was entirely new. It would have been foolhardy to mention Birman or Ivanchenko or any of the others who in the past had stood at the head of this great industrial undertaking; even Petrovsky, whose name was once linked with Lenin's in the title of the factory, had become unmentionable. But among the workers in the shops I found men who had known me for ten or fifteen years. They greeted me affectionately and crowded around me.

"You've made a name for yourself, Victor Andreyevich," one of them said, "and I'm happy with all my soul."

"Yes, old Kravchenko's boy will still be a People's Commissar. Just give him time," another laughed.

But before I left two of the older men talked to me in a more earnest vein. They were not only distressed but deeply insulted by the new decrees.

"Now we're bound to our machines, like our grandfathers were bound to the soil under serfdom," old Larin sighed. "Eh, Vitya, life is bitter and every day it gets worse."

"Yes, tell us, now that you're up there, when will we finally begin to live like human beings? We've been waiting twenty-two years now!"

What could I do but reassure them in the stock phrases of the editorials? Fortunately these men really did not expect answers from me. They knew that I was as helpless as the least of them, just another and more expensive cog in the same machine.

When I returned home father was waiting for me. He would not be robbed of the pleasure of a serious ideological talk with the one son out of three who had inherited a little of his political passion. Besides, I suspected that he considered it his sacred paternal duty to guide me on the path of righteousness. His great fear was that I, too, might yield to the temptations of power; that I might betray the class from which I had sprung for the fleshpots of the dictatorship.

I reassured him on that score. We talked for hours. He was, in the final analysis, one of the very few human beings to whom I could uncover my wounded soul without fear of being denounced. His own feeling, as he watched events, was one of disappointment. Mine went far beyond that. My doubts had ripened into a profound hatred of the new rulers, a vast contempt for their socialist verbiage, a dread of their engines of sadistic terror.

"And I'm not the only one who feels that way, papa. Stalin's purges have done him no good. True, a lot of ambitious newcomers have rushed to bring him their fervid oaths of allegiance and to fill the soft places held by those slaughtered and imprisoned. They owe their careers entirely to the purges. But Stalin's enemies are still numerous in the Party. Yes, they're in every office, in every trust, in the Kremlin itself. You simply can't kill and torture so many people without leaving bloody trails of hatred and passionate yearning for vengeance.

"Of course, there's also a new generation of Communists around Stalin who actually believe that all their predecessors were traitors and enemies of the Party. They simply don't know any better and no one dares tell them. These are the people who love and trust him and would go through water and fire for him. They're Stalin's strength and the country's tragedy."

Father reminisced about his revolutionary youth. What has happened to the Russian people, he wanted to know. Were there no longer young men with flaming ideals, with the courage to protest?

"A lot of us would like to speak out, to shout to the world," I said. "But we know it is impossible. Death comes too quickly for those who try it. Only the few who escape abroad can tell the truth. Here the terror is too complete, too all-embracing." I paused and looked into my father's eyes. "If I ever succeeded in leaving the country, papa, and decided to speak out with a full voice, do you realize what might happen to you, and to mama?"

A dream had been growing in my mind and heart: a dream of escape. I ached to throw the yoke off my neck, not only for my own sake, but for the sake of the land and the people I loved. If I could tell the outside world the whole terrible truth, could they fail to listen and to understand? I am not sure that the dream had already taken such definite shape at that juncture. Yet this question I addressed to my father was proof that it was already gestating in my deepest self.

"Don't worry about us," father replied. "We're old people who've lived their lives. Always do what you consider your duty, Vitya. Nothing else counts. To suffer pain yourself is nothing. The knowledge that you're the cause of pain to people you love, that's harder. How well I know it, son. Do you think it was easy for me to go to prison and leave my dear wife and my children to starve?"

When I departed from Dniepropetrovsk, my mother was with me. It required a lot of argument and the help of the whole family to persuade her to come to Moscow. She had never been in the capital and it gave me intense pleasure to be able to show her the city in grand style. Also, I wanted to give her a vacation from housework. Despite my assurances that there would be plenty to eat in the first-class dining car, she packed her suitcase with provisions for the journey.

The luxuries of the "international" car, and of the elegant rooms at the Hotel Moskva which awaited us, left her speechless. During nearly two happy weeks I saw Moscow through her unblurred eyes: performances at the Moscow Art Theatre and the Maly Theatre, opera, ballet, sport spectacles at the Dynamo Stadium, the art galleries, the Park of Culture and Rest. Usually Irina, a woman whose acquaintance I had made several months earlier, was with us.

"Vitya, why did you insist on bringing me to Moscow?" my mother asked me, out of a clear sky, as we sat one evening in the hotel restaurant.

"What a question, mama! It's a kind of present, to show you how much I love you."

"Yes, of course, of course. But maybe"—she looked at me with a mischievous smile—"maybe it was also because you wanted to show me Irina? Now, now, don't blush, Vityenka. I can see you're in love."

"I confess, mama. You're right, though it isn't that I'm terribly in love. I'm tired of loneliness and I admire Irina tremendously."

"All I can say is that you show wonderful taste. Have you registered yet?"

"No, but it's all decided. Irina has work that she can't leave and I'm rather glad of it. I don't want to start my life as a family man in far-off Siberia."

Irina was tall, good-looking, with large blue eyes and light-brown hair. The daughter of a French father and a Russian mother, she made her living translating literary works from German and French for various Moscow organizations. I met her at a crowded house party to which a highly placed friend took me. Something about her—was it the sweetness of her expression, the sound of her voice, her quiet, easy bearing?—made a deep impression on me. I scarcely exchanged a word with her that night, although I was conscious of her presence every minute. And when I asked whether I could escort her home when the party broke up, she was not surprised. It was as if she had expected it all along.

There had been no drama about our meeting, none of the feverish tension, none of the hectic pouring out of confidences which had marked my first meetings with Julia or Eliena many years ago. Yet within a few weeks we knew that our lives would be tied together. Our relations had depth without turbulence. I had watched her first encounter with my mother without anxiety, knowing for a certainty that they would adore each other. Though so different in background and education and mental make-up, Irina seemed to me somehow cut of the same cloth as my mother. What they had in common was a goodness so unconscious, so selfless, that it added a dimension of spiritual beauty to their every word and act.

When Irina joined us after dinner—we were going to hear *Prince Igor* that night—my mother embraced her and kissed her. There was no need for words.

At first my mother was as excited as a young girl by Moscow, but after a while she grew thoughtful and sometimes even melancholy. It seemed to her unjust that we—and others—should be spending hundreds of rubles for hotel rooms and dainty meals and entertainment while others didn't have enough to eat. I had bought the three tickets to *Prince Igor* from a speculator.

"A hundred and twenty rubles!" she exclaimed when I told her. "But that's as much as a conductress on the trolley cars in Dniepropetrovsk earns in a month. It's not right, children, I tell you it's not right. And look at the audience here! I've never seen so many overstuffed and overdressed people in one spot since the revolution. And all the time I thought there'd been a revolution."

"Come now, *mamochka*," Irina chuckled, "forget politics and enjoy the opera."

"But 120 rubles!"

One afternoon I took her to the Agricultural Exposition. She examined everything with intense interest—the farming machines, the blooded horses, the prize cows and swine. She removed the steel-rimmed spectacles from her tiny nose to read the slogans and statistics plastered on every wall.

"Well, how did you like it, mama?" I asked as we drove back to the hotel. "Why are you so quiet?"

"Vitya, call me a foolish old woman if you will, but to me it all seems a masquerade. Whom does it do any good? If there are so many cows in the country, why is there no meat in Dniepropetrovsk? If there is so much new cotton, why can't I buy a shirt for your father? It's a masquerade, Vitya, and those who put it on ought to be ashamed of themselves."

I did not reply.

"If not for the fact that I've met Irina," mother said, "maybe it would be better if I had gone to my grave without seeing Moscow. It's a city with two faces. A few fat hotels, theatres, museums, restaurants, but leave the main streets and there's the same poverty as in the provinces. Yes, two faces! From the towers of the Kremlin you call for world revolution, but a few blocks away people live without rights and in privation."

"Mama, you've grown up politically in two short weeks. . . . Don't tell papa; he'll be shocked. I really think he loves you especially for your old-fashioned political innocence."

3

The territory of West Siberia was vital to the national defense, being so located that it could serve either European or Asiatic Russia should war break out on either flank. In planning the development of the region, the War Commissariat played as large a part as the industrial commissariats. And Stalinsk was considered a crucial bastion in the system of defense. In Western Siberia many strands of the new industrialization—machine-building, automotive, aeronautical, chemical, metallurgical—were being knotted.

In the Russia of our time, where symbols often outweigh substance, it was a circumstance of the highest moment that the old West Siberian town of Kuznetzk, on the river Tom, had been renamed Stalinsk. The name of the almighty Georgian in his Kremlin heaven was never invoked in vain. It meant that the spot was earmarked for glory; and indeed, small accomplishments in Stalinsk sometimes loomed larger in the national propaganda than big achievements elsewhere.

It smacked of sacrilege, therefore, when I insisted on inspecting the site of the planned Stalinsk pipe-rolling factory before undertaking its construction. Comrade Kozhevnikov, who by now headed Glavtrubostal, was outraged and tossed me like a hot potato to Comrade Merkulov, who by this time had become Commissar of Ferrous Metallurgy.

"What's the idea, Victor Andreyevich?" Merkulov said. "I gather you want to make a personal check-up on a decision confirmed by the Commissariat, the State Planning Commission, the Metallurgical Project Institute, the War Commissariat, the Central Committee of the Party and the Politburo. Are you in your right mind?"

Put that way, my proposal did sound preposterous. But experience had taught me the lesson of caution. To assume responsibility blindly was for a Soviet industrial manager the surest short-cut to disaster. In a capitalist society a man merely gambles his money or his job; under Soviet conditions I was staking my life.

"Since I'm to be trusted with a hundred and fifty million rubles' worth of construction," I pleaded, "you should at least enable me to study the site of the project, the availability of labor and materials and construction conditions in general."

"Funds for the factory have been appropriated. The Project Institute in Leningrad has been working on the blueprints for months. But since it can do no harm, I'll authorize the trip. Only bear in mind, Victor Andreyevich, that we can't fool around with a Party decision!"

After four days by train, accompanied by my chief engineer, Gerardov, I reached Stalinsk. The small filthy station scarcely lived up to the city's inflated reputation. Dirt and confusion, in fact, seemed indigenous to this Siberian outpost. For miles around I saw structures in various stages of progress. As usual, work on ambitious industrial enterprises had been started with little if any thought of decent living arrangements for the workers.

Already over 150,000 people crowded into a town that had housed perhaps 30,000 a few years earlier. In addition Stalinsk drew heavily on forced labor, some 8,000 slaves being available in nearby concentration colonies. Some of the newly built administration structures and residences for the upper crust of workers, having been erected mainly by prisoners and at terrific speed, were already sagging and cracking. Every house and every hovel in the old town crawled with humanity. Behind the magnificent new administration colony and the new houses for qualified workers were the odoriferous slums, called "shanghais," and they were, in fact, as filthy and swarming as the worst oriental anthills.

Vast barracks colonies had mushroomed outward from the fringes of the old city. The overflow population, thousands of families, lived in the damp dugouts in the ground we called *zemlyanki*. These crude holes in the ground, covered with hand-made gabled roofs, were pathetically familiar sights around new enterprises in the Soviet Union where housing could not keep pace with new population. They were usually sixteen or eighteen feet long, eight or ten feet wide and six or eight feet deep—about enough to sleep two persons. The gabled roofs were normally made of boards and reinforced with tree branches, straw, baked mud, whatever happened to be at hand. The lucky ones might also have a few planks to prop up the earthen walls and to cover the slimy floor.

In Soviet practice, new factories and administration buildings are erected first, housing for the ordinary workers only later. What a contrast, I thought, as I went through Stalinsk, between these "shanghais," these mud "homes," and the propaganda pictures in our films and magazines! How little there is in common between the official pretense and the unofficial truth!

The Stalinsk city fathers received us cordially, even enthusiastically. They were proud of their "boom" city and pleased to see another great unit added to its industrial expansion. But even at the first interviews I detected a certain uneasiness when the details of my construction picture were under discussion. Gerardov and I soon realized that this embarrassment was fully justified.

Conditions for undertaking the pipe-rolling project here were not merely difficult or unfavorable, they were utterly impossible. The factories already in progress were stymied by shortages of wood, cement, brick, fuel. Despite the prison camps there were neither enough workers nor living space for workers; the authorities had to use strong measures to prevent the directors of various jobs from stealing labor forces from one another. Available power was inadequate for present demands, let alone the new works being planned.

When we saw the site where our factory was to be erected, we were horrified. It was a huge naked stretch of muddy river front a considerable distance from town, without electric or gas lines, without railroad tracks or a trolley line, without so much as a negotiable road. It was more like building a new city in the desert than another factory in a functioning industrial community, so that neither the funds nor the time allotted to us could possibly suffice.

Most serious of all, the terrain was wholly unsuitable for a metallurgical establishment. One did not have to be a construction engineer to observe that the ground would not support big buildings and the heavy machinery called for by pipe-rolling. Gerardov and I looked at one another and shrugged our shoulders in disbelief. How in the world had so many engineers and commissions approved the site and the plans? Who had hoodwinked the Commissariat and the Central Committee? Who had permitted the outlay of millions of rubles in advance planning for an undertaking that was clearly doomed to failure?

We did not know the answers. But we did know that it would be tantamount to suicide for us to undertake the work. Any doubts we might have had were dispelled by a visit to an Institute building a short distance away and on the same type of terrain. We found its cellars flooded, its walls soaking wet, and the whole thing sagging though it was less than two years old.

Equipped with photographs, charts and other materials, we returned to Moscow. It was a heartrending task I faced—to unsell the government on a widely ballyhooed enterprise which had the imprimatur of the highest authorities and involved the reputations, perhaps the freedom, of scores of big and little officials whose bureaucratic indifference or technical illiteracy was at the bottom of the inept project.

My report to Merkulov and his staff, including Kozhevnikov, had the force of an earthquake. Everyone stared in stupefaction. All of them, it was evident to me, thought only how to extricate themselves from what might snowball into a political catastrophe. The picture I drew was too clear, too detailed to be wished away. Besides, it quickly appeared that voices had been raised in warning before, but had been silenced by fear. The responsible officials looked at me with angry, accusing eyes, as if my findings rather than their own ineptitude were responsible for the unpleasant situation.

There followed weeks of stormy conferences, filled with veiled threats that my head would be forfeit if I made too much noise about the business. But I resisted all pressure to undertake the job despite the certainty that it meant wasted millions and wasted energy. In the end a solution was found: a perfectly typical Soviet solution, one, that is, which saved face for officialdom and concealed the gigantic mistake from wider circles.

At Kemerovo, about 160 miles from Stalinsk, also on the Tom, another important industrial center was under development. At the time the project was planned, this place too had been mentioned as a possible site for this pipe-rolling factory. Galvanized by fear, the bureaucratic machine now went into high gear and soon all the enthusiasm pumped up for Stalinsk was being efficiently diverted to Kemerovo.

All along the line, planning bureaus and Academicians, Party functionaries and technical authorities, suddenly discovered that Kemerovo must take precedence over Stalinsk. The "political conjuncture" abroad—by which we meant the tense relations with Japan—and the interests of Siberian industrialization generally, it appeared, demanded that Kemerovo receive preference. Stalinsk could wait—forever, I knew full well, though no one as yet dared to concede that openly.

And thus it transpired, in the confusion which seems inevitable in planning on so large a scale, that my appointment to Stalinsk catapulted me into Kemerovo. Again I demanded an opportunity to examine the ground and this time the Commissariat and Glavtrubostal could not demur.

Fortunately Kemerovo proved entirely satisfactory. It was a town of some 125,000 inhabitants, with wide streets, spacious parks and extensive blocks of new housing and especially beautiful buildings for officials and administrators. There were the usual acres of ugly barracks on the periphery and even some wretched *zemlyanki*, but in general conditions were unusually pleasant. I saw only one slum meriting the label "shanghai." In the public markets, where the *kolkhoz* peasants of the district brought the produce of their private gardens, fresh vegetables, meat, milk, butter, poultry, seemed abundant; the prices were considerably lower than in Moscow. By comparison with the Urals, this seemed a foretaste of heaven.

The site of our proposed factory evidently had been intended for some other project, now abandoned. We found some finished buildings, the completed foundations for a series of buildings, a railroad track, gas and electric conduits, water pipes and other installations which would greatly simplify our work. Moreover, we were almost within the city limits, making the housing and transport problems for our labor that much simpler. Gerardov and I were overjoyed.

Kemerovo officials bent backward to be helpful. Our arrival meant that about 150 million rubles would be added to the city and the local press shrieked its pride in the coming construction. Though it had a coke factory, coal mines and war plants, the principal fame of Kemerovo (aside from a notoriety won through the Moscow blood trials to which I shall revert later) rested on its chemical industry. It was an open secret that the chemical *combinat*, one of the largest in the world, was geared for the production of military essentials.

We were warmly received by Comrade Sifurov, an engineer now serving as Secretary of the City Committee of the Party. Two N.K.V.D. officials, as if accidentally, sat in at our first interview. From their questions it was obvious to me that they had a shrewd understanding of the muted scandal behind the sudden shift of construction from Stalinsk to their city. Whether Merkulov, Kozhevnikov and others knew it or not, the eyes and ears of the Secret Police all around them had been wide open all the time. The Bureau of the Kemerovo City Committee, to whom I made a report, approved the transfer of the project to their city.

I returned to Moscow. Then I spent several weeks in Leningrad, working with the Metallurgical Project Institute, which had dropped the Stalinsk assignment and was hurriedly finishing plans for Kemerovo. Substantial amounts of money were deposited at the Kemerovo Bank to our account and I set out for my new post with my new staff.

Irina saw me off at the Moscow station. The gloom of our separation was lightened by the knowledge that my work would bring me frequently to the capital.

4

Hard work is the opiate of the disappointed. It was thus, at least, in my case. I applied myself to the tough assignment in Kemerovo with an intensity that was in large part desperation. The more ruthlessly I drove my body, the more easily sleep came at night. In drugging my mind with immediate worries about business details, I succeeded in blotting out disturbing thoughts about the larger national picture. The more deeply I hated the whole regime of terror, in fact, the more loyally I focussed my energies on the job in hand.

Though I had been entrusted with an enterprise running, ultimately, into many millions of government funds, I was not trusted to select my own administrative staff. The top officials were appointed directly by the Commissariat and the chief of Glavtrubostal, without so much as asking my opinion. This system aimed to encourage officials to watch each other and tended to create mutual distrust among people brought together for common tasks. It was sheer good luck that Gerardov proved both a competent and a likable chief engineer, but both of us were saddled with some people who were neither able nor tolerable as human beings. Some of the local appointees, it was evident, were merely espionage agents for the Regional Committee at Novosibirsk, the Kemerovo City Committee, the Economic Department of the N.K.V.D., and Glavtrubostal.

From the outset our efforts were snarled in red tape and blocked by bureaucratic stupidity. I had to accumulate materials and tools and arrange for their transport and storage. Thousands of skilled and unskilled workers had to be mobilized, then provided with homes and elementary care. Under normal conditions such problems would not involve insurmountable difficulties. Under our Soviet system every step required formal decisions by endless bureaus, each of them jealous of its rights and in mortal dread of taking initiative. Repeatedly petty difficulties tied us into knots which no one dared untie without instructions from Moscow. We lived and labored in a jungle of questionnaires, paper forms and reports in seven copies.

I shall spare the reader technical dissertations. But a few examples may convey the flavor of business under the planlessness which is euphemistically called planned economy.

We were in critical need of brick. Hundreds of prisoners marched from their distant camps to toil fourteen hours a day to meet construction demands for this material by various Kemerovo administrations. At the same time, however, two large and well-equipped brickyards stood idle. They happened to belong to another commissariat which was "conserving" them for some mythical future purposes. I begged and threatened and sent emissaries to Moscow in an attempt to unfreeze these yards, but bureaucracy triumphed over common sense. The brickyards remained dead throughout the period of my stay in the city.

While we were making frenzied efforts to find homes for our workers, a bloc of new houses stood like a taunt, unfinished and useless, on the outskirts of Kemerovo. The credits made available for this project, it appeared, had been exhausted before the work was finished. I had the necessary money to buy and complete this housing but never succeeded in breaking through the entanglements of red tape. The organization which had started the building was willing to relinquish its interest. Everyone, in fact, seemed willing and authorization for the deal seemed about to come through—only it never did.

A vital tramway line running through our area was nearly completed. Several tens of thousands of rubles would have sufficed to put it into operation, and the funds were on tap. But because of some budgetary snarl the city fathers dared not release them without a decision from higher up. I wrote dozens of urgent letters demanding that the line be opened. There were stormy sessions of the City Committee of the Party and the Kemerovo Soviet on the issue. But month after month passed and nothing happened. Meanwhile thousands of weary men and women spent two and three hours a day trudging to and from work.

Such vexations were endless, piled one on the other. They turned every minor task into a major problem. They pinned down hundreds of useless officials on futile jobs and thus, in a sense, gave them an economic stake in expanding and prolonging the confusions. Every conflict and red-tape blockade, besides, was aggravated by feverish spying, denunciations and investigations.

I could not honestly charge the troubles and delays to malice, though tempers flared and harsh words were exchanged. The true explanation lay in the pervasive fears which paralyzed individual officials and whole organizations.

Kemerovo, it happened, had suffered more than its normal share of the purge terrors and therefore had been slower to recover. Few of its top layer of technicians and executives had as yet thawed out from the fearful impression of the blood-letting. The city had figured sensationally in the Moscow trials. Its chemical works and coal mines had been pictured as among the main targets of sabotage activity; and it was in Kemerovo that a "secret printing press" was supposed to have been installed and used by the Opposition leaders.

The chief "conspirator" in this city had allegedly been Comrade Norkin, who was one of the defendants in the Piatakov trial and duly executed a few hours after the trial. He worked in Kemerovo as representative of the Commissariat of Heavy Industry. For my sins I had to sit now in the very office from which Norkin, if his senseless confession were to be believed, had directed his crimes. I was in daily contact with some of the men who had worked with him and several who had testified against him.

As my acquaintance with these people flourished, it was inevitable that Norkin's name should come up now and then in conversation. Invariably they would be overcome with embarrassment and, it seemed to me, also deep shame. They scarcely needed to tell me—though at least one did— that they had lied under N.K.V.D. pressure to save their own skins. Several times a gnawing conscience got the better of their discretion.

On one occasion, after a serious accident had occurred in the chemical works, I found myself alone with a prominent Communist employed there. Having told me some of the details of the accident, he suddenly exclaimed:

"And this is just the sort of thing for which Comrade Norkin and a lot of others were executed! The 'saboteurs' and 'wreckers' are dead, but the accidents go on. I suppose they're directing it from their unmarked graves. . . ."

"But what about Norkin's own confession, Comrade L——?"

"Don't be naive, Victor Andreyevich. If those engineers had really wished to make trouble they could have blown the whole *combinat* sky-high. Why would they have limited themselves so considerately to minor

damage and petty tie-ups of production? Why would they poison workers?
Confessions. Fairy tales for foreign idiots!"

It was apparent to any engineer that the chemical works, like so many
of the new Soviet industrial projects, operated under great handicaps. Construction was shoddy and in many respects incomplete. Montage was
inept. Workers were inadequately trained. The truth is that inexperience
and honest blunders were at the bottom of the accidents here before the
purge and continued to cause accidents now that the "enemies of the
people" had been destroyed.

"The Commissariat of Heavy Industry files are crammed with reports
about conditions that might lead to accidents," Comrade L—— said.
"Many of these reports were written by the same men who later confessed
sabotage. Does it make sense for engineers to warn against disasters they
were themselves plotting?"

"I suppose not."

"And consider this: what would have been the effect on public opinion
if the government had revealed these reports in court? Ekh, I'd better hold
my tongue. When the heart's full it overflows."

What held true for the chemical enterprises applied also to the coal
mines. One day Secretary Sifurov called me to his office at the Party Committee. That morning one of the mines had been flooded. The news of the
accident was all over town and Sifurov was very much upset.

"Comrade Kravchenko, we must have several hundred pair of rubber
boots for the men pumping the mine," he said. "I'm told you have a stock
of boots and I want your cooperation."

I agreed, of course, to lend him the boots. Then I steered him into a
discussion of the accident. Was it perhaps another piece of sabotage, I
wanted to know.

"No point in rushing to such conclusions," Sifurov said. "Show me a
coal enterprise anywhere, here or abroad, that doesn't suffer an explosion,
collapse or flood now and then. It's in the nature of the job, especially
here, where installations are still pretty primitive."

"All the same," I persisted, "we know from the trials and confessions
that the Kemerovo mines were honeycombed with wreckers."

The Secretary looked at me for a long time, smiled wryly, and changed
the subject.

Some time later, at the local headquarters of the coal trust, I was in
conference with an official with whom I had become friendly. Our negotiations stretched beyond the regular work hours and soon we found ourselves
alone. Suddenly, apropos of nothing in particular, he went to a filing cab-
inet and drew out a manila folder, which he handed to me without a word.
I opened the folder and began to read at random carbon copies of reports
to the Coal Administration in Moscow.

They were reports made long before the explosions and other accidents
subsequently called sabotage had taken place. In urgent and sometimes
desperate language they warned that to avoid loss of life and property
protective measures ought to be taken without delay. The significance of

these warnings was clear enough. Saboteurs would hardly have pleaded so vigorously for action to head off their own calculated crimes. . . .

Norkin's confession about the underground printing set-up had been confirmed at trials in Kemerovo and Novosibirsk by other prisoners and supported by photographs of the press and copies of the anti-Soviet leaflets. It was one of the few confessions seemingly bolstered by documentary evidence. I was intrigued by the story and never missed a chance to get some light on it now that I was on the scene of the crime.

During nearly a year's residence in Kemerovo I was able to piece together the facts, and they proved very unsavory indeed. I dare not reveal how I obtained the information, piecemeal over a long period, since it might endanger the lives of decent people. I am reduced to a bald statement of the shocking truth—a truth so shocking that I could not believe it until I had absolute corroboration:

A secret typographical establishment did exist. Many times I was in the cellar where it had stood; there were still signs of its presence. Leaflets attacking Stalin and calling for mutiny had in fact been printed. But the press had been installed, the leaflets had been composed and printed *by the N.K.V.D. itself.* To make sure that no one would talk, the architects of the ugly hoax used only workers who would be physically unable to talk— prisoners awaiting execution or sentenced to long terms of confinement. The job was done under cover of night. The prisoners were under constant guard, of course, and the technical guidance was provided by Chekists specialized in such things.

"What about the leaflets?" I asked one man who knew these facts. "Thousands of them were supposed to have been distributed here."

"What nonsense!" he replied. "You know well enough that anyone caught with such a leaflet would have been arrested. Yet I don't know of a single arrest on any such charge; neither does anyone else here. No one among the workers seems ever to have seen or even heard about the famous leaflets until the trial. Maybe the conspirators printed them up just to provide themselves with bed-time reading."

In any case, the circumstance that Kemerovo—its coal mines, its chemical works, its building trusts—had been honored with a big role in the plots left a heritage of jittery fears. No one moved without signed and triply sealed evidence of authority from Novosibirsk and Moscow. The incredible part of it, looking back on it all, is that we managed to accomplish as much as we did before the whole undertaking was washed out by another mysterious shift in policy. But in that I am running ahead of my story.

CHAPTER XXI

WHILE EUROPE FIGHTS

THE TREATY of friendship between Adolf Hitler and Josef Stalin which precipitated war in Europe will be forever bound up in my mind with the straggling Siberian city where I worked at the time. It was at Kemerovo that I saw the pact streak meteorlike across our horizon and crash headlong into the minds and consciences of the Party membership. It left us all stunned, bewildered and groggy with disbelief.

The brief and dusty Siberian summer was drawing to a close in a welter of rumors about border clashes with Japan. The flurry of war alarms set off by the Munich settlement of the previous year had not quite died down. Those of us who thought about such questions at all were conscious of threats on both sides. That fascist Germany might make up with the U.S.S.R. and direct its martial energies elsewhere never entered our calculations, we had so long taken it for granted that the Nazis had only one real enemy, the Soviet regime.

I considered the Kremlin capable of any outrage. Its methods by this time seemed to me little better than those of the Nazis, especially in its treatment of its own people and in the forms of organization of power. Reading or listening to anti-Hitler propaganda, I could not help asking myself inwardly, "But how does this differ from our Soviet atrocities?" All the same, I refused to credit the news of a Soviet pact that freed Hitler to make war on Poland and on the rest of Europe. There must be some mistake, I thought, and everyone around me seemed equally incredulous.

After all, hatred of Nazism had been drummed into our minds year after year. We had seen our leading Army Generals, including Tukhachevsky, shot for supposed plotting with Hitler's Reichswehr. The big treason trials, in which Lenin's most intimate associates perished, had rested on the premise that Nazi Germany and its Axis friends, Italy and Japan, were preparing to attack us. Those nations, indeed, were only the spearheads of a world coalition of capitalists sworn to destroy our socialist fatherland. The brutalities of the super-purge had been justified largely on the basis of that imminent Nazi-led assault against us.

The villainy of Hitler had become in our land almost as sacred an article of faith as the virtue of Stalin. Our Soviet children played games of Fascists-and-Communists; the Fascists, always given German names, got the worst of it every time and the triumphant comrades ended by singing the Young Pioneer hymn, *Vsegda gatóv! Always ready!* In the shooting galleries the targets were often cut-outs of brown-shirted Nazis flaunting swastikas.

Only a few weeks before the pact we had listened, at a Party meeting, to a boringly familiar lecture on the world situation. As always, Hitler figured as the arch-criminal, creature and tool of the world plutocracy which was preparing to strike at us. When the orator said that Hitler and his Party were dictators, that the Führer and his clique were deified, that in Nazi Germany there was no freedom of speech or press, that everyone there lived in a state of fear and terror, many of us could not help thinking he was giving an accurate picture of our own regime.

An old anti-Nazi picture, *Professor Mamlock*, was still being shown in the cinema theatre on Kemerovo's main street. It portrayed Hitler's government as a sadistic gang of sub-human plunderers obsessed by hatred of the Soviet Union.

Not until we saw newsreels and newspaper pictures showing a smiling Stalin shaking hands with von Ribbentrop did we begin to credit the incredible. The swastika and the hammer-and-sickle fluttering side by side in Moscow! And soon thereafter Molotov explaining to us that Fascism was, after all, "a matter of taste"! Stalin greeting his fellow-dictator with fervent words about their "friendship sealed in blood"!

To gauge our astonishment one should know the official Communist "line" on the Nazis and Fascism generally up to the moment of the pact. Fascism, we were told, was not different from capitalism in kind but only in degree. It was simply capitalism in its final or death-agony stage, capitalism without its camouflage of "democracy" and "parliamentary trickery." In Italy and Germany, according to our version, capitalism had been forced to drop its "democratic mask" and was openly unleashing against the workers the terror which was being applied in disguised forms in America, England and elsewhere. It was only a matter of time, in fact, before the rest of the capitalist world, driven to the wall by its economic sins, would likewise abandon its spurious democracy and enter upon open fascism.

Hitlerism, we were instructed to believe, was thus merely the iron fist of the whole plutocratic, imperialist world. A war between Nazi Germany and its capitalistic patrons was unthinkable, illogical. Now that just such a war had come, it seemed to us no less insane than the compact of friendship between the U.S.S.R. and Germany—the compact which should be known by the names of Stalin and his Politburo, rather than the U.S.S.R., since neither our Party nor our people were consulted.

But there is no intellectual infamy that a government in absolute control of press, radio, schools and platforms—with police to enforce unanimity of opinion—cannot perpetrate. Once the shock had worn off, the new version of world relations was generally accepted. We now repeated endlessly that French and British imperialists, backed by American big business and Polish landlords, were engaged in a conflict to repress German imperialism and the outcome was of no importance to the one "socialist" nation. Those of us who retained doubts about this picture buried them deep in our hearts, where the teeming informers could not spy on them.

Professor Mamlock vanished from the cinema screens, along with *The*

Family Oppenheim and all other anti-Fascist films. The libraries, similarly, were purged of anti-Fascist literature. Voks, the Society for Cultural Relations with Foreign Countries, instantly discovered the wonders of German *Kultur*. Visiting Moscow on business, I learned that several exhibits of Nazi art, Nazi economic achievements and Nazi military glory were on view or in the process of organization.

The theatres of the capital were developing a great interest in German drama. In fact, everything Germanic was the vogue. A brutal John Bull and an Uncle Sam enthroned on money bags figured in the propaganda, but the Nazis were exempt from such ridicule. Hundreds of German military men and trade officials were in evidence in Moscow hotels and shops. They were busy with the gigantic program of Soviet economic help to Hitler's crusade against the "degenerate democracies."

The Soviet hierarchy does not need impressive arguments to line up Party opinion. An instinct for survival does the trick. To avoid trouble one not merely believes, but believes deeply, fervently, whatever absurdity is prescribed from on high. The great Stalin knows what he's doing—ultimately that was the sum-total of the Party reaction.

We talked about the new turn of events not only at formal discussion meetings of the various Party nuclei, but privately, in our own homes and offices. How can we people in Kemerovo, we said or implied, pretend to understand such grave matters? Our job was to build and run factories, and to govern the people working in the factories, secure in the faith that our Beloved Leader could make no mistakes. Only a recalcitrant few among the Party people, indeed, continued to think about the matter at all. The rest were soon as apathetic as the population at large. After twenty-two years of life under a dictatorship, genuine public opinion had become unthinkable.

All we knew for certain was that our country had extricated itself from a bloody war which was devastating the rest of Europe, and that seemed something to be grateful for. More than that, we were receiving some of the spoils of the war—half of Poland, Bessarabia, later the three Baltic countries—as a bonus on the Kremlin's clever neutrality.

Few of us foresaw that Russia would eventually be pushed into the fire, let alone that it would suffer more losses in life and substance than all the other nations combined. We took it for granted that the fighting countries would in time bleed each other to death, leaving the U.S.S.R. the real master of Europe. While the capitalists fight it out, the political formula had it, we shall strengthen ourselves, accumulate arms and benefit from the war experience of the others. When capitalism and fascism will have weakened each other, then, if need be, we shall throw twenty million men armed to the teeth into the scale of history; by that time the revolutions in many European countries will have passed from the theoretical into the practical stage.

This cynical view our leaders called "Bolshevik realism." It left some of us ashamed and perturbed. The role of vulture, picking the bones of a dead continent, went against our moral grain. We preferred to revive some of the romanticism of the early revolutionary years. At some point in the struggle, many of us consoled themselves, the working masses would rise against their exploiters. Then the imperialist war would be turned into a civil war and an all-European revolution might even restore the revolutionary spirit and idealism of our own country. . . .

Though everyone accepted the new friendship with the Nazis, along with the mounting attacks on other European countries, I can attest that there was nowhere any enthusiasm for these things. The whole business was edged with embarrassment. Our political meetings, at which speakers from the center explained the new situation, seemed constrained and fidgety. This was particularly true after the U.S.S.R. invaded Finland at the end of November. When David fights Goliath, even Goliath's friends have a sneaking sympathy for the doughty little David. How could the simplest-minded worker at our mass meetings believe the fable that tiny Finland, unprovoked, attacked its colossal neighbor? The fact that we paid with hundreds of thousands of dead, wounded, frost-bitten and prisoners for a narrow strip of Karelo-Finnish marshland before that episode was ended added a good measure of humiliation to the unpopularity of the adventure.

In the light of future events, one thing should be made clear. Stalin entered into his compact with Hitler in earnest. Had the Kremlin played with the idea that we must ultimately fight Germany anyhow, some part of the existing hatred of the Nazis would have been preserved; our anti-fascist propaganda would not have been so completely abandoned in favor of "anti-imperialist" (meaning anti-British and anti-American) propaganda. At least the more trusted Party officials in the Kremlin itself, many of whom I knew intimately, would have been apprised of the continuing Nazi danger.

Nothing of the sort happened. On the contrary, any whisper against Germany, any word of sympathy for Hitler's victims, was treated as a new species of counter-revolution. The French, British, Norwegian "war-mongers" were getting their deserts.

The theory that Stalin was merely "playing for time" while feverishly arming against the Nazis was invented much later, to cover up the Kremlin's tragic blunder in trusting Germany. It was such a transparent invention that little was said about it inside Russia during the Russo-German war; only after I emerged into the free world did I hear it seriously advanced and believed. It was a theory that ignored the most significant aspect of the Stalin-Hitler arrangement: the large-scale economic undertakings which drained the U.S.S.R. of the very products and materials and productive capacity necessary for its own defense preparations.

The simple fact is that the Soviet regime did not use the interval to arm itself effectively. I was close enough to the defense industries to know that there was a slackening of military effort after the pact. The general feeling, reflecting the mood in the highest official circles, was that we could afford to feel safe thanks to the statesmanship of Stalin. Not until the fall of France did doubts arise on this score; only then was the tempo of military effort stepped up again.

2

Forty-seven million rubles had been assigned for my work in Kemerovo in 1940. By the end of 1939 the essential preparations had been made and we were ready to start on the main buildings of our projected factory.

In accordance with Soviet procedure, the actual job of construction was farmed out, by contract, to the building trust, Kemerovostroi. With them rested also the responsibility for gathering together the necessary workers. But since I had the biggest stake in the speed and quality of the job, I naturally took part in all the negotiations for labor forces.

And it was thus that I found myself, for the first time, directly involved in the technique of a large-scale deal for slave labor.

Both the Regional Party Secretary at Novosibirsk, Comrade Barkov, and our Kemerovo Secretary, Sifurov, were helping the trust to arrange for adequate labor forces. The Kemerovo Soviet, too, was active in the matter. A substantial number of free workers would be used, but the chief reliance would be on convict labor.

The N.K.V.D., representing its regional bosses, agreed to supply two thousand prisoners to begin with, the number to be enlarged in the spring, when construction on a bigger scale would become feasible. The details were arranged at several sessions in Kemerovostroi offices and at the N.K.V.D. headquarters. There was a lot of cold-blooded bargaining on the qualifications of the slaves to be supplied and the prices to be paid. An outsider intruding midway in the discussion would have assumed that horses or mules, rather than living men and women, were concerned.

At the first meeting I listened and said little. I thought: _So this is socialism in practice in the classless society of the happy life. . . . So this is the new life we are trying to impose by force on Finland at this very moment. . . ._ A shudder went through me and I must have blanched. I felt weak. Sifurov looked at me with a puzzled expression.

"Aren't you well, Victor Andreyevich?"

"No, no, I'm all right . . . just haven't had enough sleep this week."

The N.K.V.D. spokesman explained that there was no dearth of prisoners, including the necessary percentage of skilled workers and foremen. He could provide five thousand, ten thousand, any quantity we wished. There was a ring of professional pride in his voice—a horse-breeder proud of his stables. The only difficulty was where to put them. The several concentration camps in the immediate Kemerovo district now held about fifteen thousand and he doubted whether any more could be crowded in.

Could a new camp be erected and staffed quickly enough to serve our purposes? Perhaps additional barracks might be thrown up in the existing camps? Finally we agreed to inspect one of the largest of the local enclosures before making definite recommendations on this matter.

On a bitterly cold and windy morning we set out in a limousine to see for ourselves. There were four in the party: an N.K.V.D. functionary, a representative of the trust, a Secretary of the City Committee and myself.

It was slow driving through the snow but in about twenty minutes we reached our destination.

The camp stood on an elevation overlooking a stream that branched off from the Tom. It was an almost square enclosure, surrounded by a tall picket fence topped by barbed wire, with look-out towers at the four corners and a sentry box near the entrance, where we now alighted. The wooden barracks were arranged parallel to the sides of the enclosure, forming a big square and leaving a large expanse, like a parade ground, in the center. This open space was in direct range of the machine guns in all the towers, so that a concentrated fire from all directions could be let loose in case of trouble. Near the entrance stood several well-built houses, which contained the administration offices and quarters for the guards.

We were expected and were immediately ushered into the main office, where the chief of the camp met us. He was not only cordial but almost obsequious. He was a short, chunky blond fellow, with rather handsome weather-stained features. It was evident that he stood in awe of the City Committee and the N.K.V.D. official in charge of our party. The reason for this I learned later. It appeared that he was an important Communist who had been exiled from Moscow. Though put at the head of a camp, he was himself an exile, his political loyalty under continuous scrutiny. Therefore the main Party functionary and the Kemerovo N.K.V.D. were keeping an eye on him and reporting regularly on his conduct of the camp.

On several other occasions I had been inside concentration camps, but I was not yet accustomed to the experience. I was still gripped by a morbid curiosity about every detail of camp life. Only a man inspecting the prison where he expected some day to be confined could understand my state of mind.

Looking out of the window, I saw about fifteen women prisoners, grotesquely bundled up against the cold, piling wood near one of the brick buildings. One of them wore a sack on her head. Several others had their hands bound in rags, in lieu of gloves. Soon four other women came into view, carrying huge buckets from which rose clouds of steam.

"What are they doing?" I asked, addressing the chief.

"Feeding the pigs and the poultry," he said and then added, with a certain pride, "We raise our own meat here."

"For all the prisoners?"

"The prisoners!" he laughed, as if I had said something witty. "You don't suppose we feed enemies of the people meat? This isn't exactly a spa or a restaurant, you know. But believe me, the food problem for ourselves and the guards isn't too easy either."

"And who are those three old men over there?"

I pointed to three bearded men in tattered overcoats, their heads wrapped in shawls, who were working on a pile of stones.

"Two priests and a rabbi. They're too weak to walk the eight kilometers to Kemerovo factories, but they're earning their bread doing chores in the camp."

"A curious thing," the representative of the trust commented, "how well priests and rabbis get along together once these counter-revolutionaries are put behind barbed wire. I've noticed that fact in many camps."

"That's quite true and I've thought about it myself," the warden agreed.

Sitting in the office, we discussed our problem. Though the camp, with about three thousand inmates, was already overcrowded, the warden thought it might be possible to accommodate another thousand, though it wouldn't be easy. Some of the barracks, he explained, already did double service, one shift sleeping while the other was out working. Unfortunately it was not always easy to arrange this, so much depended on the kind of work for which the prisoners were farmed out. One possible solution, he thought, might be to build a third tier of "beds."

"True, it would be crowding them a little but the one in the middle tier, at any rate, would be warmer." He laughed again.

In order to make this plan clearer, he invited us to go through some of the barracks. We put on our hats and overcoats and followed him.

Chekists carrying rifles with fixed bayonets were in evidence at regular intervals. The barracks, made of unpainted boards, the interstices plugged with sawdust, were bolted and locked from the outside.

"How many does one of these structures hold?" I asked.

"That depends. Normally between 300 and 350. This one," the warden said, as a guard unlocked the door, "takes care of 310 women."

"Stand!" the guard shouted into the long, dim, low-ceilinged hall.

The prisoners obeyed with alacrity, those on the upper shelves clambering down in panicky haste. Only three or four remained stretched out; apparently they were too sick to move. They were women of all ages and nationalities, young and old, but all equally ragged and exhausted looking. The thick odor of stale sweat and squashed bedbugs made me slightly nauseous. Very little daylight filtered in through the dirty barred windows. Several small electric bulbs hung from the ceiling, but they were not burning now.

The barracks was so cold that our breath was visible, but many of the women were only half dressed. Here and there one of them, surprised by the unexpected visitors, tried to cover her breasts with a garment but most of them seemed indifferent in their sullenness; the last drop of natural modesty had now been drained out of them. Several of the faces were very young, even more were old and wrinkled, but the great majority, it seemed to me, were in their twenties and thirties. Many of them, I could judge by their faces and remnants of their old clothes, were intellectuals; despite the dirt and exhaustion, I could see traces of education and culture in their features.

The "beds" were bare boards, perhaps four feet wide, attached to heavy beams in two tiers—just a series of double shelves, without any sort of bedding. Here the prisoners slept, one on a shelf, in their clothes, some ragged garment rolled up for a pillow under their heads. Near the center of the hall stood a small wood-burning stove, pathetically inadequate for a barracks this size. Except for a few slop buckets for the prisoners' physical needs, near the entrance, there was no furniture, no benches, no tables, literally nothing.

On arriving at a camp, prisoners were deprived of all letters, photographs of relatives and friends and all other reminders of the free world beyond. Bed linen and even such elementary comforts as toothbrushes and scissors were taken away from them. They were provided with metal cups and bowls and a wooden spoon. These possessions they kept on their "beds" or hung on their walls. Books, paper and pencils were strictly prohibited and, it goes without saying, there were no radio receivers. Correspondence with relatives was neither allowed nor physically possible.

Along one of the narrow walls, however, there was a kind of iron trough and over it a water basin with drip-faucets. Our official guide, in pointing this out, referred to it as "their washing accommodations." Then he enlarged on his idea that an additional tier added to every "bed" might make it possible to cram another hundred women into this one hall. He might have been talking about cattle, and with as little consideration for the prisoners who stood silently listening to our conversation. On one of the walls I noticed a frayed strip of red bunting on which I read the slogan, inscribed in white paint: *Work—the Road to Rehabilitation.*

"Are these prisoners all criminals?" I asked as we went out.

"No," the warden said, "these are all politicals—kulaks and other counter-revolutionaries. In the men's barracks we put them together but among the women, we have found, it's best to keep the criminal elements and prostitutes separate from the politicals. The problem of discipline is much harder with women prisoners.

The Chekist let us into another barracks, somewhat smaller. Here the women were all criminals, some of them prostitutes, the camp chief told me. Guessing that I was more interested in the camp than in the negotiations which had brought us here, he seemed quite willing to enlighten me.

Again the prisoners stood at attention. I suppose there is no more horrifying sight for the normal man than a few hundred filthy, diseased looking, shabby women. The deep-rooted romanticism of the male is outraged.

"*Starosta,* come here!" the warden ordered.

The *starosta* or overseer of the barracks stepped forward. She seemed in her middle thirties, in a torn, patched dress which once had been elegant. Her features, too, showed traces of former comeliness. She stood rigidly at attention, her hands behind her back.

"Everything in order here, warden," she reported in a clear but expressionless voice. "One sick. The rest ready to receive food and report for work."

"Good, dismissed!"

My eye caught a placard nailed to the wall near the door where we stood. I read it—a printed list of rules, enjoining cleanliness and strict obedience. At the end, in large black letters, I read the provisions for punishment: first infraction, two days without food; second offense, solitary confinement for not less than a week; third offense, at the discretion of the authorities, prolongation of the prisoner's term of confinement

or "the highest measure of social defense," which is the Soviet formula
for death by shooting.

When we left this barracks I asked our host whether he had been
obliged to impose the death penalty on prisoners.

"Not since the mutiny last year," he replied. Apparently he was
assuming that as a Kemerovo official I would know what he was alluding to.

The men's barracks, to which he now took us, were identical with
those on the women's side. Having become somewhat accustomed to the
sights and smells, I was able to study the prisoners more closely. Though
most of them were Russians, there were also many Uzbeks, Turkomens,
Tartars, Armenians, Jews, Poles, even a few Chinese. Despite the fact
that they were all unshaven and indescribably squalid and emaciated, I
picked out faces which seemed to me intelligent, even distinguished. Perhaps engineers, professors, literary men, disgraced Party leaders, I said
to myself. I observed one tall, broad-shouldered prisoner, standing erect
and looking straight into my eyes. I felt as sure as if he were still in
uniform that he was a military man. But the great majority, of course,
seemed ordinary peasants and workers.

In one of the barracks the overseer was a powerfully built fellow with
a broken nose and tiny, shrewd eyes.

"This is *Shchelkunchik*," the warden explained. The word means "nutcracker."

"Why nutcracker?" I asked.

"Oh, he's a famous safe-cracker and known by this nickname through
half a dozen provinces," he laughed. "Criminals make better overseers
in the barracks than politicals. They're not as soft."

"Most of them look down on the political prisoners," the N.K.V.D.
man added, smiling. "You see, they're not enemies of the people . . . just
scoundrels who've run afoul of the law."

"What's the proportion of criminals to politicals?" one of us wanted to
know.

"Usually not more than 10 to 15 per cent here are criminal elements,
and that includes the prostitutes. But of course we make no distinction in
their treatment."

On the way home I gathered a few more details from the N.K.V.D.
officer. The prisoners, I learned, are not permitted to smoke in the barracks. Only in rare instances do their relatives know where they are
located. People condemned to short terms are usually put into prisons or
labor colonies, so that the camps are filled largely with men and women
serving sentences of five, eight, ten or more years or for life.

The term in truth matters little, since very few are released. They are
not set free automatically at the end of their sentences but only on
special orders from the N.K.V.D. in Moscow, which usually extends the
sentences arbitrarily to keep its forced-labor armies at full strength. Those
released are rarely if ever allowed to return to their original homes.
Instead they are compelled to settle in prescribed regions, usually remote

parts of Siberia, the Far East and the Far North. There are large communities, indeed, composed almost entirely of former prisoners.

The more infamous camps in the Far North and the Far East and in the Siberian taiga count as many as thirty or forty thousand prisoners each. Because the death rate is fearfully high, some of these camps have special brigades of prisoners whose sole duty, twelve and fourteen hours a day, is to bury the dead.

In the camp we had just visited the bread ration for prisoners—and bread is their main food—was from 300 to 800 grams (11 ounces to 30 ounces) a day, depending on the kind of work to which they were assigned, the nature of their crime and the fulfilment of production quotas. In addition they were given a thin hot soup of potatoes and vegetables twice a day, porridge and occasionally some dried fish. Failure to fulfill work norms was punished by reducing these rations. Scurvy, dysentery and other diseases of undernourishment as well as frostbite are commonplace in all camps. Few of the prisoners whom I observed were without running sores, inflamed eyes and other visible evidence of broken health. Under a true slave system, such as existed in the United States before the Civil War, for instance, the slaves represent an economic value and therefore receive at least the kind of care and protection given to work animals. The position of the Soviet slave is infinitely worse. The supply is well-nigh inexhaustible and the slave-holder, the Soviet state, apparently finds it more economical to let them die in droves than to feed and clothe them.

"What was that mutiny he mentioned?" I inquired.

"Oh, that happened at the end of 1938," the Party Secretary volunteered. "Some of the prisoners refused to go out to work . . . something about the food being rotten. The administration of course acted with vigor. Fourteen of the ringleaders, twelve men and two women, were shot. The executions took place in the camp, with all prisoners lined up to see the show. Then details from every barracks helped dig the graves, just outside the barbed-wire fence. Not much chance for another riot as long as the memory of this one remains fresh. Naturally the head of every camp has power of life and death over all prisoners. This is no time for rotten liberalism in dealing with enemies of the people."

The last statement was obviously by way of political insurance. Our N.K.V.D. companion was the Secretary's intimate friend, but why take chances?

Before the housing problem for our two thousand slaves was solved, the whole undertaking was called off—"conserved," in the bureaucratic vernacular.

3

Not suspecting that all my Kemerovo effort was being tossed into the garbage pile, I was pleased with the sudden summons to Moscow at the end of December. It would enable me to celebrate the New Year with Irina. I assumed that nothing more serious was involved than final con-

sultations on our 1940 plans. But I found Comrade Kozhevnikov looking
very grave.

"I have bad news for you, Victor Andreyevich," he said. "There's a
Central Committee and Sovnarkom decision to stop work for the time
being on the Kemerovo pipe-rolling project. The appropriation has been
cut to one million rubles, just enough to conserve the work already done."

I stared in confusion.

"But that's impossible! We've worked so hard. Everything is in such
fine shape. How can it be?"

"Don't ask me, I'm only the head of Glavtrubostal. I wasn't consulted
—I was merely informed. Between ourselves, I'm as upset as you are."

"Millions have been invested in preparations," I went on. "Immense
quantities of building materials are ready. Anyone familiar with Siberian
industry knows that the project is essential. What in the world's behind
it all?"

"I can only assume that it's the new international situation. Now that
we're friends with Germany, there's no rush about defense enterprises.
We have a breathing space."

"But wasn't the Kemerovo project mainly connected with the Far
Eastern dangers? There's still Japan."

"Oh well, these are matters of the higher politics and we'd better keep
our noses clean. With the Soviet-German pact, I take it, the Japanese
danger, too, is no longer considered urgent."

"How about myself, Comrade Kozhevnikov? After all, I'm the responsible director and have spent millions of rubles in preliminary work.
Shouldn't I let the Party know my reaction to the decision?"

My education in the great purge had made me sensitive to danger. I
was aware how easily innocent officials might become the scapegoats for
blunders at the higher levels of power—and the scrapping of Kemerovo
seemed to me a terrible blunder.

"I'd suggest that you keep quiet, Victor Andreyevich. Just wind up
affairs in Kemerovo and come back here. Kemerovostroi has already been
instructed to stop work."

Should I follow his advice about accepting the decision in silence?
I wrestled with this problem for weeks. An expression of opinion on my
part would offend the bureaucrats responsible for the decision. It would
make enemies for me. On the other hand, a passive attitude might in some
future purge be thrown up to me as proof of indifference, of deficient
Bolshevik zeal. After all, the project had important military significance.
I had reason to fear that if the international situation changed, scapegoats
for the abandonment of the work would be sought, new "enemies of the
people" would be punished. Neither the Central Committee nor the
Sovnarkom would be blamed—they are by definition sinless—but innocent
bystanders like myself. Besides, my thinking on the subject was colored
by emotion. I felt frustrated.

Even under the deadly impersonal system of state planning, a man
tends to identify himself with his job. I had thrown myself unsparingly
into the Kemerovo undertaking. Its scale and its importance to the future

of Siberia had interested me deeply. I had worked and schemed and quarreled with all kinds of officials in the interests of those big mills I saw with my mind's eye rising on that site. Now it was not easy for me to acknowledge that the whole thing was wasted.

My doubts about my course of conduct were resolved when I returned to Kemerovo. The city fathers, I found, were dismayed by the turn of events. Both the City Committee and the Regional Committee at Novosibirsk drafted formal reports to Moscow pleading for a reconsideration of the decision. The project, they said, was well advanced and a great many vital factories had counted on this new source of steel pipe. Both reports, moreover, praised the administration of the project and especially myself as its director.

I felt that I had little choice but to support their plea—a mistake that would plague me for a long time. In a statement addressed to the Central Committee of the Party and to Comrade Merkulov, Commissar of Ferrous Metallurgy, I pleaded for a continuation of the Kemerovo construction.

Returning to Moscow, I discovered quickly that my action had plowed up more malevolence against me than I had thought possible. Every Soviet organization is a hotbed of personal feuds, competing cliques, festering jealousies. This is almost inevitable in an atmosphere where political skill and influence are the decisive values. Kozhevnikov was peeved because I had ignored his advice. His assistant, Golovanenko, whom I had crossed on several engineering questions, had apparently long been hostile to me. Now he had a peg on which to hang his resentments.

Commissar Merkulov, indeed, seemed the only one who approved my action. But he was hardly in a position to offer me support. Confidentially he apprised me that the whole ferrous metals industry was under investigation by a special commission of the Central Committee of the Party headed by Malenkov. Ivan Tevosian, an Armenian who stood high in Stalin's favor, was in the commission. It was clear, he hinted, that he, Merkulov, was slated to be made the sacrifice for the cumulative ills of the industry. Soon thereafter, in fact, he was removed, being succeeded by Tevosian.

More than a month passed without a response to my report from the Central Committee. I became uneasy. On the advice of politically alert friends, I sent a copy of my statement to Stalin's personal Secretariat. While this step might protect me against direct punitive action by offended or alarmed officials in the Commissariat, it magnified my offense in their eyes.

They got their revenge, in ample measure and with interest. By concocting a petty and far-fetched court case against me—which I shall deal with later—they managed to embroil me in two years of fantastic litigation. They did not succeed in sending me to prison, and ultimately I was fully exonerated by the highest court. But they did succeed in giving me many anxious months and a too intimate acquaintance with Soviet jurisprudence.

While waiting for a new assignment, I remained on the payroll of

Glavtrubostal. The unaccustomed leisure tasted sweet. Night after night I took Irina to theatres, concerts, the opera, the ballet. Like most Russians, I like Moscow best in its hushed winter mood of brief days and crystalline nights, when its life is muffled in thick blankets of snow.

In those early months of 1940 Moscow was one of the few European capitals not blacked out by war. This fact was emphasized endlessly as proof of the sagacity of the Beloved Leader and Teacher. The war news was confined to small print on the last page of the newspapers, as if it did not really concern us. Yet people read that first and read it avidly. Instinctively they doubted the official assumption that our country could remain forever immune to the spreading holocaust. Perhaps it was this sense of its impermanence that gave the artistic and social life of the city that winter a special tang, a kind of hectic flush.

There seemed to be more house parties than usual. The street lights and the few electric signs seemed to blaze more arrogantly. The presence of German officials and some officers—especially in the larger hotels and restaurants—added a martial touch to the scene.

The war was also manifest in this neutral capital in another fact. The so-called open shops, where the state sold goods to all who could pay un-rationed prices, were suddenly lush with unfamiliar foreign items; with suits, dresses, shoes, cigarets, chocolate, crackers, cheese, canned goods, a hundred other items obviously of non-Soviet origin. This was the overflow of goods from the frontier areas taken over by the Red Army. At the beginning these foreign luxuries came from Polish and Finnish territories; later in the year loot seized in the Baltic countries, then in Bessarabia, began to show up.

According to the propaganda theory, we were "liberating" these territories from capitalist exploitation and poverty. In practice Muscovites were thrilled to be able to buy these wonders of capitalist production, in the "socialist" capital. Thousands of Soviet officials sported looted elegance and amazing stories, sometimes no doubt exaggerated, about the good things to which the Soviet liberators helped themselves in the conquered areas spread through the capital.

Glavtrubostal was considering a suitable post for me. Any Soviet citizen, of course, can be assigned to work anywhere, arbitrarily and without so much as advance notice. In the case of highly responsible work, however, the sensible practice is to make the process as voluntary as possible. The Commissariat offered to put me in full charge of a metallurgical plant in the Transbaikal region of Eastern Siberia. I was also sounded out about a position as chief engineer in a Urals plant. At one point the job of director of a metallurgical plant in the Gorki region was under consideration for me. But not one of these possibilities materialized.

As to my own preferences, I was weary of the years of wandering and yearned with every nerve for a settled home life. I was eager to remain in Moscow. It seemed a paradise by contrast with the rest of the country. It took finesse in maneuvering and also some discreet political influence, in which Politburo member Andreyev was useful, but in the end I was given work in Moscow—in a metallurgical mill in Fili, on the outskirts of the capital. It was a modest post, two rungs below those I had already filled, but because it was in the capital I was content.

The factory was a pre-revolutionary one, enlarged and modernized in recent years, employing about a thousand workers and bearing the same name as the trust, Glavtrubostal. Steel tape and pipe were its principal products. As assistant chief engineer I carried the main responsibility for actual production.

The top administrative officials had worked together in this factory for a long time. They formed a closed and intimate clique. There was the director, Manturov, tall, redheaded, every inch of his face covered with freckles. He was a rough-hewn, self-educated fellow, inclined to conceal his total ignorance of everything technical with confused bluster. He had attained some fame as a partisan fighter in the civil war period and still lived on this political capital. Though he had headed industrial enterprises for many years, their operation remained an enigma to him and sometimes he actually resented the engineers who knew their way about.

His crony and main support was Comrade Yegorov, Party secretary for the factory as well as chief of its Special Department. A short, stocky, middle-aged man with big bushy eyebrows, he was self-important by reason of his connection with the Economic Department of the N.K.V.D. When he stalked through the shops and offices with a possessive air, some of the workers behind his back muttered about "our little Stalin." His fierce eyebrows threw their shadow over my spirits during the year I spent near him. The third member of this inner clique was the head of the trade-union section, Comrade Papashvilli, a swarthy Georgian with a native zest for intrigue. The editor of the factory paper and a few other Communist activists played with the executives, making a cozy family.

Under the new Commissar, Stalin's friend Tevosian, lusty efforts were made to raise output. Fat bonuses were authorized for fulfillment of orders, with additional cash premiums to the administration for every percentage of over-fulfillment. Since the inner clique could not vote themselves rewards without extending the windfalls to the top technical officials, I was amply supplied with money. There were months when my salary and bonuses came to over 4,500 rubles. Irina's work as literary translator netted her about a thousand rubles. Our combined earnings were therefore, in good months, from twenty to twenty-five times higher than those of an average workman.

Despite this wealth, our "apartment" consisted of two small rooms on the top floor of a three-story building in the center of town, at number 5 Rozhdesvenka Street. Once the building had been a hotel. Now a batch of families were deployed along our corridor, with their furnishings, their servants and their assorted problems.

Among my neighbors were an ex-ballerina and her grown daughter; a factory foreman and his wife; the sloppy and soured widow of a former merchant, in the threadbare remnants of her ancient finery; a responsible official of some Commissariat. Some of them had servants. We merely had a houseworker who did not live with us but came in every day.

Though we lived close to this miscellaneous group of Muscovites for several years—so close that we stumbled over and exasperated one another —we did not really learn to know these people. The blight of suspicion was upon us, as it was upon every such group living in enforced and annoying proximity. Those who imagine romantically that common problems draw human beings together have never lived in an overcrowded Moscow communal apartment. Our many households shared two kitchens, one bath room and toilet, the one telephone in our common corridor. We closed our ears to the quarrels, the love-making, the arguments that swirled all round us. When the telephone rang, everyone rushed to answer. There was the pervading suspicion, too, that among our neighbors there might be informers.

In our apartment the N.K.V.D. informer—this I discovered much later, during the war—turned out to be the one person we would not have suspected. It was the merchant's widow, Silina by name. She listened to our telephone conversations, eavesdropped at our doors, and reported regularly. Unquestionably she had been drawn into this service by fear, to avoid being sent far away as a "hostile class element." Sometimes we wondered how she managed to obtain extra food rations; when I discovered her function in our corridor community, the answer was clear.

Aside from this woman, however, we were a neighborly enough group. Like typical Russians, we were ready to forget small disagreements; when misfortune knocked at someone's door, all were ready to help.

Let no one suppose, however, that we were badly off as living conditions in Russian cities go. Irina was lucky to have obtained such an apartment in a choice part of Moscow and I shared her good fortune while begging and conniving for space in one of the new residences going up in the city. We possessed an upright piano, good mahogany furniture, expensive rugs, a few paintings. Less fortunate friends, visiting us, spoke with genuine envy of our good life. . . .

Except for the interval when I served in the Red Army, I was to live in this place for more than three years. It was the nearest I would come in my mature years, to a stable family life. At the Glavtrubostal in Fili I worked long hours—often from seven-thirty in the morning to ten or twelve at night. But on free days and on the occasional evenings when I returned home reasonably early Irina and I felt that we had real home life at last.

Sometimes we entertained. My friends were almost all Party people, Kremlin and Central Committee officials, and technical specialists, whereas Irina's circle of intimates was drawn from the artistic and literary fringes of Moscow life. The two groups did not mix too well and we tried to keep them apart as far as possible. Perhaps this apartness was symbolic of our marriage which never ripened into a deep all-embracing relationship. Two people, I found, can develop true affection and respect for each other without really merging their lives.

My activities in the factory, my Party work, political lectures, meetings, engineering interests were all foreign to Irina's background and interests. Our two worlds touched but rarely overlapped. Besides, Soviet officials as a matter of safety tend to keep their wives ignorant of their outside professional and political affairs. Experience has taught them that the less a man's family knows about his work and problems, the safer they are in the long run. With the threat of purge and arrest always over their heads, the servants of the all-powerful state try to safeguard their loved ones by telling them little or nothing.

In any event, it is a fact that I rarely talked to Irina about my industrial work and never about my political thoughts and doubts, though she was an intelligent and warmly sympathetic woman. Often I ached to share my troubles, to "talk out my heart," but fear of making her a partner to my "dangerous" political state of mind always curbed my tongue.

"Tell me, Vitya dear, what's bothering you," she often pleaded. "Why are you so unhappy? Is it my fault? Isn't there something I can do to help? Tell me, I beg you!"

"No, darling, it has nothing to do with you. It's just that I work too hard, I suppose. Nothing to worry about. . . ."

How is one to hope for a normal domestic life under the mental terrors of a totalitarian existence?

4

One day in June I received a letter from Glavtrubostal asking me to explain certain payments made by my commercial assistant in Kemerovo. I was puzzled but not yet alarmed. I did not grasp at once that this was the neat revenge arranged by Golovanenko and others whom I had unwittingly offended.

Under the Soviet law certain types of responsible workers, when appointed to posts in distant parts of the country, like the Far East and Siberia, were entitled to substantial additional payments, covering transportation and other expenses. The payments are made on the basis of individual formal contracts with the enterprise which employs them. Now it developed that in several instances there were no such contracts to cover payments made by my plant.

My assistant and the chief accountant therefore did not consider it necessary to draw any contracts. The law, backed by Kozhevnikov's signature, seemed to them sufficient. Personally I had neither hired these people nor authorized the payments. Nevertheless, as head of the project I was now held technically responsible for the oversight and charged with unlawful payment of funds, a crime punishable by as much as three years' imprisonment.

The scheme to involve me in this far-fetched accusation apparently had been worked out without Kozhevnikov's knowledge. He seemed surprised and embarrassed when I rushed to him with the letter. The charge was nonsensical, he thought, and ought not to worry me. But he felt that he could not inject himself into the affair without seeming to shield laxness in his own organization.

"Just answer the letter," he suggested, "as best you can and forget about it. I imagine the matter will not be carried any further. It's too silly."

But he was wrong. A month passed. I took it for granted that the "criminal" charges against me had been dropped. But suddenly I was served with a notice that the Commissariat of Ferrous Metallurgy, in the name of Ivan Tevosian himself, had lodged a formal accusation against me in the People's Court. Thus I found myself the defendant in a serious criminal suit, in the ordinary civil courts, in connection with a "crime" with which I had not the remotest conscious connection. The chief book-keeper in the Kemerovo project, Matveyev, was my co-defendant. My commercial assistant, who had made the actual payments, was not among the accused.

I managed to reach various officials in the court in an attempt to have the case quashed. They agreed that it seemed worthless on the face of it, but after all the accusation had come through Tevosian, not only a People's Commissar but, more important, a rising star in the Stalinist heaven. The machinery of "justice" could not be stopped. I would have to go through a trial. Everyone, in fact, took a grave view of the situation. When one citizen was accused by another, he might hope for an objective verdict in a Soviet court. But when a mere individual stood accused by the government, his chances were usually slim. Not abstract justice but "defense of the proletarian dictatorship"—which is to say defense of the regime—was the main purpose and obligation of the Soviet legal system.

First I underwent a number of preliminary examinations in which I was urged to plead guilty.

"Don't be a fool, Comrade Kravchenko," one of the prosecuting officials of the N.K.V.D. said, "avoid a trial and take your medicine. In that way your sentence will be much lighter."

"But how can I plead guilty to a crime about which I did not even know? I don't intend to accept a criminal record because of a stupid technicality! The moneys were paid out with official signed consent from Glavtrubostal."

I would not have believed that the examination in such a case would be conducted by the N.K.V.D. rather than the court magistrate; there were no political issues in the indictment. But where a Party makes the law, and executes the law as well, nothing is surprising.

"In that event you'll have to stand trial."

Four days before the scheduled trial I applied to the Collegium of State Defense Lawyers for an attorney. There is no real private legal practice in our country. You deal with the neighborhood Collegium, accept the lawyer assigned to you and pay the prescribed fees to the Collegium. Of course, since the lawyer is paid a miserable monthly salary, the common procedure is to reward him privately if he is amenable, taking care that no one knows about it.

A bored woman, yawning in my face, listened and perhaps even half-understood my story.

"Petrov," she called across the room to a man buried in papers, "a case under Article 109, trial in four days. Can you take it on?"

"No, I'm too busy," Petrov called back.

"All right, I'll find someone else," she said.

A first acquaintance with the lawyer she finally assigned to me was not exactly calculated to raise my spirits. He was a decent enough little man, with harassed eyes and hollow cheeks. He was meek and apologetic. When he heard that the charges had been preferred by Tevosian his expression changed from worry to despair. A Soviet lawyer, to keep out of trouble, must put the interests of the Party and the State above the interests of his client. My frightened little defender did not relish the role of opposing a People's Commissar. Indeed, he had no intention of playing any such dangerous role. . . .

The People's Court met in a shabby, badly ventilated room on the second floor of what was apparently a former schoolhouse. The lurid yellow paint on the walls was fly-specked where it wasn't peeling. Portraits of Stalin and other leaders, of course, were deployed all around the room. I waited, along with Mateyev and our respective lawyers, among twenty-odd people whose cases were on the day's calendar.

"The court is coming. Rise!" a functionary shouted at the top of his voice.

We stood up as two men and a woman entered through a rear door and took their places behind a red-draped table on a raised dais. For several hours I watched the proceedings in other cases. The presiding judge is a permanent court official and does most of the questioning; the other two are "people's representatives," a kind of equivalent of the jury in Anglo-Saxon countries. In this instance the people's representatives were a young worker, fidgety and self-conscious under the weight of this honor, and an elderly woman who, I thought, was probably an office secretary somewhere. Neither of them opened their mouths.

After questioning by the chief judge, the prosecutor and the defense lawyers made impassioned speeches—passionate oratory is a tradition of Soviet jurisprudence—and the three judges retired. In a few minutes they emerged with the verdict.

The questioning of Mateyev and myself followed the same lines as in the preliminary interrogations. Until then I had refused to believe that I might actually go to prison on such a preposterous pretext. But as my trial unwound my heart sank. My subjective innocence seemed beside the point. Objectively I had "squandered government funds." They had the Commissariat's word for it and the whole case seemed cut and dried.

After the judge was through with me I felt the prison walls closing in. Then the prosecutor took me in hand. He was a stout fellow, with a great mop of black hair. I felt that he resented my well-groomed person, as if it were somehow my fault that he had to support a family on 600 rubles a month.

"How much **did you earn** in Kemerovo?" he asked me at one point.

"I averaged 2,500 rubles a month, sometimes more."

He shook his unkempt head as if he had proven some important point and looked significantly at the judges.

"And what are you earning now?"

"Three, four, even as high as five thousand . . . it depends."

Again the prosecutor nodded knowingly and pursed his lips in ironic accusation. He had clinched some obscure logic which, I guessed, had more to do with his own embittered poverty than with the case under consideration.

"There you see, comrade judges, in what conditions the accused lives!"

"But what has that to do with the charges?" I could no longer restrain myself. "I conduct a big factory and I'm paid according to the law."

"The accused will please not interrupt!" the presiding judge admonished. "We trust the People's Commissariat which brings the charges, as referred to by the Prosecutor, more than we trust you."

The prosecutor's speech was loud and lusty. He gesticulated wildly. He dug into literature and the Leader's speeches for grim colors with which to paint these two "monsters" who had "wasted the people's money." An outsider unfamiliar with the facts would have supposed that poor Matveyev and I had embezzled millions and topped it off with murder. Three and a half years in prison, the orator demanded. Why three and a half, not five, not capital punishment, he failed to explain. The whole thing was so nightmarish that I wondered when I would awaken from the dream.

My defense lawyer, considering his Party membership, really made a heroic effort in my behalf. But one felt that he considered himself defeated before he started, that he was merely going through the forms. He didn't argue my guilt—even to him that seemed pretty clear!—but urged my pure conscience by way of mitigating the punishment.

The judges were gone perhaps ten minutes. They returned with a verdict: Two years' imprisonment, with the right to appeal within seven days. I was a convicted "criminal" because someone somewhere, in the Moscow offices of Glavtrubostal had tangled some red tape! A Commissar had signed a piece of paper laid on his desk by some zealous underling, after which the comedy played itself out almost mechanically. I know that it sounds grotesque, but such, alas, were the essential facts. The presiding judge and the Prosecutor were, first of all, Party members. They were dealing with accusations lodged not merely by a Commissar but by a member of the Central Committee of the Party. What chance did justice have under such conditions?

An appeal was duly filed in my behalf, which postponed my arrest. Several times, at intervals of a few months, I was called for interrogation by a variety of judicial functionaries, and early in the spring of 1941 a hearing was held at the main City Court. Again I refused to plead guilty. The Court took the case under advisement and in about thirty minutes announced its decision. The sentence was reduced to one year's "compulsory labor at my present place of employment."

This is a unique Soviet judicial invention. The convicted citizen continues to live and work in freedom—but 10 or 20 per cent of his earnings are forfeit to the N.K.V.D. In my case it was 10 per cent. Tens of thousands of Russians through this strange device are forced to pay a part of their income as tribute to the secret police under guise of punishment for crime.

Notification of my new status was received by the bookkeeping department at the factory. From then until the case was thrown out as worthless by the Supreme Court, 10 per cent of my wages and bonuses was deducted every month for the N.K.V.D. treasury.

I shall disregard chronology long enough to wind up the story of my career as a "criminal." I appealed to the highest court immediately. By the time it got around to my troubles, however, war had come, Moscow was under Nazi bombardment, and the court had been evacuated to the Urals. In the process the court archives were put in such a sorry condition that no trace of my appeal could be found.

While I was in the Red Army, serving as a captain in an engineering unit and Political Commissar, Irina continued to work on the matter. The 10 per cent was not important. What was important was to erase the stain on my record. Soon after I was released from military service, in the first part of 1942, the Supreme Court reviewed the Kravchenko case. It reversed the decisions of the lower courts, attested my complete innocence and the case against me was dropped.

Had it not been for this exoneration, I probably would never have been allowed to work for the Council of People's Commissars (Sovnarkom) and certainly I would never have been permitted to leave the country. The animosities out of which the "criminal" charges against me were born had long been forgotten; when I ran into Golovanenko at the Glavtrubostal offices he barely remembered that he had once been angry with me. But the malevolence, once unloosed, operated on its own inertia and came close to wrecking my life.

CHAPTER XXII

THE UNEXPECTED WAR

ON THE morning of June 22, 1941, Soviet cities and airdromes were being bombed, Soviet armies were already in panicky retreat before Nazi *Panzer* divisions on a vast front. Germany's sudden invasion of Russia was in the headlines all over the world. Before sunrise that morning, everywhere in our country, the secret police began to sweep up "undesirables" by the tens of thousands.

But I knew nothing about the catastrophe that had spilled over the heads of the two hundred million people of my country. Neither did anyone else at the plant when I reached my office early that morning. Yesterday's war dispatches still reported smugly the exploits of Hitler's armies, the discomfiture of his enemies, the "capitalist jackals" and "plutocratic warmongers."

There had been, in recent months, not the slightest change in the tenor of official propaganda. There had been no careless word of compassion for the nations overrun by the Nazis, no risky expression of blame for the Hitlerite marauders. Though millions of Russians were deeply stirred by pity for the victims of the Nazi onslaught, we could not show our feelings openly. Only a few days before this fateful morning, in the Machine Import Department of the Commissariat of Foreign Trade, I had conferred with German representatives. We ironed out the technical details of German deliveries of electric-welding machinery to the Soviet Union.

On June 20, two days before the invasion, I had addressed a political meeting of workers and employees on the "imperialist war." My talk followed the prescribed line. Germany, I repeated, was eager for peace despite its great victories, but British imperialists, backed up by American finance, insisted on prolonging the war.

Neither I, nor anyone outside the inner Kremlin circle, knew that as early as January the State Department in Washington had warned our Ambassador, Constantine Oumansky, that Hitler was making ready to strike at Russia. The warning was repeated by Mr. Sumner Welles five weeks later and reinforced by similar British advices. They were all dismissed as capitalist tricks intended to break the beautiful friendship guaranteed by the Hitler-Stalin pact.

Cautious warnings had also been conveyed to their superiors by Soviet agents in Germany. They reported ominous movements of troops in our direction on a scale too vast for mere policing. Because I had a large acquaintance among officials of commissariats and factories producing goods for the Nazi war machine, I had been in touch often with trade representatives just returned from Berlin. They were warned about Hitler's intentions. Germans had told them frankly, on occasion, that a clash was inevitable. But all this, too, Stalin and his court brushed aside as inspired mischief-making. They seemed mesmerized by their own propaganda.

As far as the mass of Russians was permitted to know, Soviet-Nazi collaboration was an idyl without blemish. To doubt this would have been to doubt the infallibility of Stalin. The suggestion that a German betrayal of our Leader's confidence was within the bounds of possibility would have seemed a venture in counter-revolution. To express open sympathy for the victims of the Brown Scourge was to court arrest.

And so the historic day got under way without so much as a rumor to disturb its routine. Work at our plant was already in full blast when it was announced that we would pause to hear an important radio address by Commissar Molotov. This procedure was unusual and sent a tremor of apprehension through the plant. We made wild guesses as to the Commissar's subject. No one guessed the awful truth.

Molotov's stammering and tearful words left us all stunned. What could we conclude from his sensational announcement? The *Führer*, crafty and deceitful, base and stupid, had unloosed his familiar *Blitz* on the country which for nearly two years had been depriving itself of sorely needed food, fuel, metals, oil and munitions to help him subdue Europe. We had scrupulously fulfilled our obligations. We had supported the Nazis not only with goods but with worldwide propaganda and diplomatic pressures. Now our reward was perfidy.

In a few hours a Party speaker arrived. We called a lunch-hour meeting of all our workers. I sat on the platform, along with the director, Manturov, and the head of the factory Party Committee, Yegorov. I scanned the tired, frowning faces of our workers as the orator reviled the treachery of the German dictator and extolled the honesty of our own dictator. I saw anger, consternation, as well as weariness, bafflement and sorrow. Some of the women cried.

Both Manturov and Yegorov made speeches in which they repeated, feebly, awkwardly, the new and strange slogans. It was not yet easy for any of us to refer to the "democratic countries" without an ironical inflection or to assail the Germans who only yesterday had been the victims of imperialist warmongering. It seemed fantastic to speak of England and France, so suddenly, as partners in a common cause when we had so long looked on them as the main threats to our national safety.

The workers, stunned by the news, clapped without enthusiasm at the proper pauses, then returned in a daze to their lathes, their desks, their drawing boards. We worked as usual to the end of the day. And yet it is likely that the coming of war shook many minds out of their years-long lethargy. There was Sergei Golovlyov, an electrical engineer and a Party member, for instance. He approached me after the meeting.

"So now it's our turn," he said. "It's a tough life we've been leading all these years, Victor Andreyevich. War, revolution, destruction, Five Year Plans, hunger and purges—and now we're back to war! When at last are we going to begin living like other people?"

"We must work and work, Comrade Golovlyov," I replied. "There is no other way."

"That's right. We must work and fight. But one can't help thinking. . . ."

"You had better go back to work." I assumed an official tone, just to play safe. "We'll talk about it some other time."

In my office, that afternoon, I was informed that the shift superintendent, Vadim Alexandrovich Smolyaninov, had not reported for work and that it seemed impossible to reach him by phone. I picked up the receiver and called his number.

"Is this the Smolyaninov apartment?" I asked.

"The *former* Smolyaninov apartment," I was told tartly.

"Please call Vadim Alexandrovich to the phone."

"Who are you?"

"The assistant chief engineer of his plant is speaking."

"He isn't here and won't be any more."

"Who is this? I'm speaking officially."

"I'm also speaking officially. This is an official of the N.K.V.D."

I dropped the receiver. So my friend Smolyaninov had been arrested! What a tragic end to a revolutionary career! A competent engineer and an educated man, Smolyaninov had been active in the revolution and had become personal secretary to Lenin. Later he served as head of the Office of the Council of People's Commissars, Chief of Construction at Magnitostroi, President of a Soviet Trade Delegation to the United States, director of Gipromez, a vital metallurgical Institute. In short, he had been an important figure in the Soviet regime.

In the big purge, however, he was expelled from the Party and reduced to assistant foreman in our plant. In time this former secretary of Lenin became foreman and finally shift superintendent. Recently he had been reinstated in the Party. His only son, a sergeant in the Red Army, was at the frontier. Now Smolyaninov was under arrest.

He was only the first of the victims of the merciless wartime terror to come to my attention. Dozens of others around me disappeared in the following days. A long time before, an N.K.V.D. friend had told me that in case of war all "dangerous elements" would be stamped out. In every village, town and city long blacklists were ready: hundreds of thousands would be taken into custody. He had not exaggerated. The liquidation of "internal enemies" was, in sober fact, the only part of the war effort that worked quickly and efficiently in the first terrible phase of the struggle. It was a purge of the rear in accordance with an elaborate advance plan, as ordered by Stalin himself.

Several years later, in America, I was to hear the amazing nonsense— apparently accepted even by intelligent Americans—that "there was no fifth column in Russia" because the blood purges had wisely eradicated all "traitors" in advance. I read this obscene absurdity in a strange, half-literate book by former Ambassador Joseph Davies, in the frivolous writings of others who pass as experts on the subject despite a profound ignorance of the nature of Stalin's policies and regime. I could only marvel at the success of this childish propaganda evidently exported by Moscow.

I say "exported" because inside Russia the government took the very opposite tack. It insisted that our nation was rotten with fifth columnists. From the first day the press, radio and speechmakers howled for the lives of teeming internal enemies, spies, disorganizers, rumormongers, saboteurs, fascist agents. And the N.K.V.D. followed up the howling with mass arrests and executions. In the initial period, at least, we had the distinct impression that the Kremlin was no less frightened of its own subjects than of the invaders.

We had no fifth column in the sense of pro-Germans or traitors—this *despite* the blood purges. But we did have millions of patriots who hated the Stalinist despotism and all its evil works. To that extent the fright of the ruling clique was justified.

The savagery of collectivization, the man-made famine of 1931–33, the gargantuan cruelties of the purge years had all left deep scars. There was hardly a family that had not suffered casualties in the regime's offensive against the masses. Stalin and his associates were not worried about our loyalty to Russia; they were worried, and with good reason, about our loyalty *to themselves*. Perhaps, in their nightmares, they saw twenty million slaves suddenly crashing through prison walls and barbed-wire enclosures in a multitudinous stampede of hatred and vengeance, in a flood-tide of destruction. . . .

In any case, ruthless suppression of potential opposition took first place in the government's plans. It took precedence over measures of military defense. Soviet citizens of German origin, no matter how remote the taint, were arrested almost to the last man. The whole population of the Volga German Republic, nearly half a million men, women and children, was driven out of the region it had inhabited since the time of Catherine the Great and dispersed through Siberia and the Far East. Next came the turn of Poles, Balts and many other nationals who had not been bothered before the war. The isolators and forced-labor stockades bulged with additional millions. Our rulers behaved like a frightened wolf-pack.

Several days after the outbreak of the war, "military tribunals" were set up in Moscow, headed by the former President of the City Court, Comrade Vasnev. Branch offices of this new agency of terror mushroomed throughout the capital and its suburbs. The same was true in every other city. All the pores of Soviet life were blanketed by this organization, vested with extraordinary powers to arrest, to try in secret, to mete out death. There were special railway tribunals, river transport tribunals, Army tribunals—a nationwide army of witch-hunters under N.K.V.D. specialists, charged with the noble task of squelching discontent. Clearly the regime was in a state of panic.

The tasks of the new agencies, expanding but not supplanting the available instruments of surveillance and suppression, were summed up by Stalin himself twelve days after the invasion began:

"We must organize a ruthless struggle with all disorganizers of the rear, deserters, panic-mongers, cowards, disseminators of rumors. . . . It is necessary immediately to turn over to the courts of the military tribunals all those who by their panic-mongering and cowardice interfere with the defense of the country, irrespective of who they are."

Why this febrile fear of "disorganizers of the rear" in a country so recently "unified" by purge inquisitions, so often certified "monolithic"? Was not this vision of a whole nation corrupt with disloyalty and cowardice evoked by Stalin's threats in itself "panic-mongering" on a grand scale? Evidently the home-front enemies were too numerous to be handled by the hundreds of thousands of N.K.V.D. police, so that new tribunals had to be established. How could this happen in a country intoning hymns to the "happy life" under the "sun of the Stalin Constitution"?

Perhaps the Davieses and Durantys can answer these riddles. But listening to Stalin's throaty warnings, uttered slowly in his Georgian accent, I knew only that they did not fit into the picture of a nation cleansed of traitors in oceans of blood. And the deeds which they touched off belied that picture even more than Stalin's words.

In Moscow alone thousands of citizens were shot under martial law in the first six months. One word of doubt or fear or distress was frequently reason enough for hauling the culprit before the military tribunals. Thousands of spies kept their ears and eyes open in the bread and kerosene queues, in markets, shops, theatres, streetcars, railroad stations for any mutterings of despair, doubt or criticism. Every house committee reported on its tenants, every servant on her employers. It got so that people were afraid to mention that they were hungry, lest they be accused of reflecting on Stalin's wisdom or ignoring wartime difficulties.

It became widely known in Moscow Communist circles that as the enemy rolled closer to Moscow thousands of men and women who had been in prisons or labor camps for many years were summarily shot. They were the more prominent political prisoners of the Left—Socialists, Bukharinists, Social Revolutionaries, Anarchists, ex-Communists. They were the people whom the Kremlin dreaded most because, in case of a revolution, they might offer leadership to inchoate masses. Again that nightmare of the twenty million slaves bursting their chains. . . .

It was no secret that the machinery of military mobilization, too, was used to destroy those of little faith in the Soviet regime. N.K.V.D. *dossiers* were turned inside out. Lists of suspects—border cases where arrest seemed unnecessary—were in the hands of every neighborhood draft commission. Those told off for speedy extermination were promptly inducted and rushed with little or no preparation to the most dangerous sectors of the fighting fronts. It was a kind of left-handed purge.

The magnitude of the terror inside Russia cannot be overstated. It amounted to a war within the war. That was one expression of the Kremlin's jittery distrust of the Russian people. The other expression was an almost overnight scrapping of most of the "socialist" catch-phrases under which we had lived and suffered for twenty-four years. After a quarter of a century of Communist indoctrination, the government in its hour of peril reverted to the traditional appeals of national patriotism, race loyalties, love of soil, later even religion. We were not exhorted to defend the land of "socialism" but the Russian land, the Slav heritage, the Orthodox God.

A more complete repudiation of the values we had lived by—coerced and temporary though it was—is hard to imagine. Socialism? Collectivization? The classless society? World revolution? The more territory the Germans overran, the less was said about these ideas for which the country had been tormented. Not until much later, when the tide of invasion was stemmed, were the familiar Soviet slogans revived. No doubt there were millions of ordinary Russians who retained faith in the Soviet type of society and thought. That faith, it seemed, was not shared by their masters in the Kremlin.

2

But let me return to the first day of the war.

In the director's office that evening I found Manturov himself, Yegorov and the director of a sub-plant, Larionov. We discussed the war. The radio was open, because we were eager for news. Suddenly a voice crashed through the martial music. In pure Russian it boomed:

"Citizens of Russia! Russian people! Listen! Listen! This is the headquarters of the German Army."

We looked at one another uneasily.

"Hadn't we better turn the scoundrel off?" Manturov said.

"To hell with him! Let's hear what the bastard has to say!" Yegorov decided.

"For twenty-four years you have been living in hunger and fear. You were promised a free life and got slavery. You were promised bread and got famine. You are slaves without any human rights. Thousands of you die every day in concentration camps and in the frozen wastes of Siberia. You are not masters of your own country or your own lives. Your master is Stalin. You are driven worse than galley slaves. Millions of you are at this moment in prison cells and forced labor camps. Your rulers have destroyed your Orthodox faith and replaced it with worship of Stalin. What has become of your freedom of speech and press? Death to the parasites of the Russian people! Overthrow your tyrants!" Then followed curses, anti-Semitic slogans, and the other vulgarities characteristic of German propaganda.

"Choke him off!" Yegorov cried.

Manturov hastily turned the knob. The ensuing silence was oppressive. We dared not look into each other's eyes. Soon we parted in clammy embarrassment.

About an hour later I returned to Manturov's office. I wanted to consult him about a substitute for the arrested Smolyaninov. As usual, I entered without knocking. To my surprise I found both Manturov and Yegorov again listening to an enemy broadcast. I understood their curiosity perfectly. For the first time in a score of years it was possible to hear the Soviet regime denounced aloud, instead of hearing the regime denounce others.

"Come to us with these leaflets in hand," the radio voice was saying as I entered. "They will be your pass. Why fight for slavery and terror when the Germans bring you a free life?"

Manturov cursed as he turned the knob. Yegorov, no less disconcerted by my arrival, stalked out of the office. I talked about the Smolyaninov matter and other pressing items of business. Manturov interrupted me in the middle of a sentence:

"By the way, Comrade Kravchenko, it's best not to mention that we heard German propaganda on the radio. You know, just in case. The Lord protects those who protect themselves."

"I'll bet half of Moscow was listening," I said.

"They won't tomorrow. I've just had a telephone call: tomorrow all radio sets will be requisitioned."

"Requisitioned? What for?"

"For safekeeping, I suppose."

That was precisely what happened, in Moscow and the rest of the country the following day. All citizens, under threat of punishment, surrendered their radios to the local police. Subsequently I saw mountains of radio sets piled like so much cordwood into trucks being carted to storage places. For the duration of the war Russians were allowed only loud-speakers connected with the official radio stations. Elsewhere, in Germany and German-conquered countries for instance, listening to enemy broadcasts was forbidden and punished. In Russia the people were not trusted that far; they were simply stripped of their radios.

This was the first step in a blackout on information that was well-nigh total. The censorship of mail was not limited to letters to or from the fronts but embraced ordinary civilian correspondence. The war communiques in the first weeks proved so misleading, that few Russians believed them at any time thereafter. Little wonder that the authorities were plagued by disseminators of rumors and panic-mongers. Those things merely reflected the popular assumption that their government was lying.

At our factory we worked under growing strains. The mobilization decimated our labor forces. Dislocation of transport left us without essential materials. In theory our country had enjoyed twenty-two months of peace during which it could prepare for the cataclysm. In practice nothing was prepared. Disorder reigned in every department of our lives.

We could not believe the whispered reports that the German tide of conquest was rolling eastward at terrific speed. What of the colossal Red Army about which we had boasted? What about the strategic defenses presumably gained when we pushed our frontiers deep into Poland, Rumania, Finland, the three Baltic countries? What about the advantages supposedly derived from our long period of neutrality?

The communiques told us less than nothing, adding a dimension of confusion to the flood of rumors. Police cordons were keeping refugees out of the capital, to safeguard its morale. But enough of them trickled through to give us a sense of the growing disaster. The communiques avoided frank admission of defeats. They even implied successes. But the name places were sufficient proof that the fighting was coming closer.

"During the past night," a communique at the beginning of July declared, "battles were fought in the Murmansk, Dvinsk, Minsk and Lutsk direction. . . . At Murmansk our troops offered stubborn resistance to the enemy, inflicting great losses upon him. . . . At Dvinsk and Minsk battles developed that exterminated the foremost tank units of the enemy. . . ."

But on July 3 Stalin came to the microphone for the first time. A horrified nation heard the truth about the holocaust spreading quickly towards the capital.

"The Hitlerite troops," Stalin said, "have managed to seize Lithuania, a considerable part of White Russia, a part of Western Ukraine. A grave danger hangs over our fatherland."

We could scarcely credit our ears.

"The aim of this war against the Fascist oppressor is to help all the peoples of Europe who are groaning under the heel of German Fascism," Stalin continued. "In this war we shall have faithful allies in the peoples of Europe and America. . . . Our war for the freedom of our fatherland will merge with the struggle of the peoples of Europe and America for their independence, for democratic freedom. . . ."

For the first time we thus heard Stalin himself using words like freedom and democracy in the old-fashioned sense, without satirical quotation marks. It all seemed topsy-turvy: the survival of our Bolshevik regime suddenly linked with the victory of the "degenerate democracies" . . . the leading capitalist countries promising to give all possible aid to the Soviet Union. An almost forgotten dream of liberty stirred again in many a Russian heart. Though it took a terrible war to accomplish the miracle, our isolation from the free world seemed about to be broken.

"Brothers and sisters, I address myself to you, my friends!" Stalin had exclaimed. In sixteen years of his reign we had not been thus addressed by him. A friend in my plant, made bold by the excitement of the moment, remarked to me in a low voice: "The Boss must be in a hell of a pickle to call us brothers and sisters."

We could not comprehend the reasons for our defeats. For two decades we had been starved and tortured and driven in the name of military preparedness. Our leaders had boasted of Soviet superiority in trained manpower and armament. Now the humiliating rout of our armies was being explained by lack of guns, planes, munitions. Three successive Five Year Plans, each of them sacrificing food, clothes, household goods for war industries, had been carried out "successfully." Yet at the first test of strength our country of two hundred million was trying to stop the tank *Panzer* divisions with bottles of gasolene! Tens of thousands of Russians were being hurled under the wheels of German tanks because, after twenty years devoted almost exclusively to military production, we did not possess any anti-tank rifles. It's all well enough to give up butter for guns—but in this case we had neither guns nor butter.

There were no reasonable explanations for the Soviet failures, nothing to assuage our humiliation. Poland had been surprised, then stabbed in the back by its eastern neighbor. France had been smaller, weaker than the assailant. But why should prodigious Russia, two years after the outbreak of war, with every advantage of numbers, time, military concentration, behave like a backward little country caught off guard? Had we been no bigger than France, we would have been crushed four times over in the first four months.

Only the boundless Russian spaces, the inexhaustible Russian manpower, the unsurpassed heroism and sacrifice of the Russian people in the rear as well as at the fronts, development of new and existing industries in the rear, installation of evacuated plants saved my country from extermination. These were the things that made a deep and costly retreat possible, while resources for a counteroffensive were gathered. The regime was able to arouse and use the deep national spirit and patriotism of our people. Later, after Stalingrad, the flow of American weapons and supplies began.

Mobilization was carried out in fevered haste and confusion. Reservists were rushed to the fronts without a chance to say good-bye to their families. Workers were driven almost directly from their shops to the battlefields. All this despite the fact that we had one of the world's largest standing armies, tempered by invasions of neighboring countries and by a full-parade war on Finland. The government was caught so pathetically unawares that it did not even have enough uniforms. In those first months even officers went to their death in makeshift garments and without adequate training. Millions of new soldiers trudged through the mud in canvas boots and the early winter caught them in summer uniforms. I saw recruits training with broomsticks instead of rifles.

The draft commissions worked from morning until late at night, inducting men from seventeen to fifty. They were guided, as I learned later, not by the existing law but by secret instructions of the State Defense Committee, drawn up after the war had started. Certain categories of essential workers, of course, had to be exempted; at the outset men with two or more dependents incapable of work were also let off. Beyond that, the mobilization was crude and heartless. The medical examinations took two or three minutes per draftee. I saw men with one eye, men who limped, consumptives, men suffering heart ailments and stomach ulcers, bearded fifty-year-olds so work-worn that they could barely drag their own weight, adjudged fit for the fronts. Only between one and two per cent were rejected on physical grounds. This, the press boasted, proved the high level of health attained under the Soviets. In fact it proved only a total contempt for human life.

The conflict had been in progress only a few weeks when the Party called for the formation of a Citizens' Volunteer Army. It seemed to many of us a startling confession of the same lack of preparedness. We recalled the words of War Commissar Voroshilov in September, 1939, at the time the war in Europe was already under way:

"The experience of the Tsarist Army has amply demonstrated that the so-called Citizens' Volunteer Army was very weak and utterly untrained; it showed that hasty preparation in time of war was not very effective. Completely untrained people were sent to the front and all of you know how it all ended."

Now we were doing the very same thing. Worse, we were resorting to a volunteer system at the very beginning of the conflict, whereas the Tsar's regime had done so much later. "I deem it pertinent to remark," Voroshilov had said on the same occasion, "that the numerical growth of the Red Army and of the Navy is in complete consonance with the international situation, which our government, the Central Committee of our Party and Comrade Stalin are always studying attentively and closely." What was the quality of that study when within a few weeks after the German invasion "our government, the Central Committee of our Party and Comrade Stalin," without shame or pity, were sending hordes of untrained civilians to certain slaughter?

One July morning I was called to the Party Committee office in our factory, where Yegorov instructed me to conduct a meeting to enroll volunteers. I urged that he do it himself, as our Party leader.

"No, no, Victor Andreyevich. This has to come from the masses rather than the Party. You're very popular with the workers. It will be easier for you than for me."

The mass meeting started. I saw before me the grimy faces of my fellow-workers. I talked to them as one Russian to another, carefully avoiding the very words Communist and socialist. Like all of them I loved my country. I knew that it was something distinct from the gang who ruled and terrorized us. I was able honestly to put my heart into a plea for the people's militia. The fact that I could muster a sincere enthusiasm for victory, a passionate hatred for the invader, though I detested the Soviet regime, is the key to the mystery why the Russians fought and in the end conquered. They did not fight *for* Stalin but *despite* Stalin. No one knew this better than the Kremlin clique itself, as their every summons to a Patriotic War revealed.

To set an example, I was the first to register as a volunteer. Dozens of our factory workers, office people and technical staff followed suit. But not one of the uppermost crust of administrators volunteered. They squirmed under the questioning eyes of the workers but made no move to sign up.

Later that day I went to see Manturov. I pretended to take for granted that he would volunteer.

"Well, Viacheslav Ivanovich," I said breezily, "when are you signing up?"

His face turned the color of his flaming red hair. He shifted his weight uneasily. His little eyes darted all around the room and he cleared his throat.

"What I will do in the great war is a question to be decided by the Party District Committee. I have responsibilities. The factory will soon have to be evacuated . . ."

"You ought to enlist anyway," I urged. "The workers are talking.

If the Party wants to keep you here, it will do so. Meanwhile, why not enlist?"

But Manturov was taking no chances. Neither was Yegorov. They both ended the war with high-sounding titles and Orders of Honor by keeping carefully out of range of enemy fire. They should not be blamed personally, however. They were simply following out a policy made manifest by the Kremlin. Stalin was determined to conserve his *apparat*, the bureaucracy upon which the Soviet regime, in the final analysis, rested. Even in the most trying months, "indispensable" officials—and that included the Special N.K.V.D. Troops, the dictator's Praetorian Guard—were for the most part saved for the final showdown with the people of Russia. It was a showdown that never came.

My enlistment was canceled by order of the District Committee. Manturov and Yegorov would have been delighted to see me sent to the front without delay. They never forgave my attempt to sign them up, since it became known throughout the factory. But for the time being it saved face for them that Kravchenko and other volunteers among the top personnel were not permitted to leave.

3

The marshy strip of Finnish wilderness for which Russia in 1940 paid with hundreds of thousands of lives reverted to the enemy almost immediately. The Stalinist adventure in aggression thus achieved exactly nothing—except to drive our Finnish neighbors a little faster into the arms of Germany. Neither did the Soviet rape of Poland, nor the grab of the Baltic countries delay the invaders by more than a short time. "Strategic security" as an excuse for seizing frontier territory makes little sense in the epoch of mechanized warfare and long-range aircraft.

But among all the myths grown in the Communist hothouses of propaganda the most debased, because it is the most false, is the myth that Stalin used the twenty-two months of peace won by his appeasement of the Nazis to prepare against them. It is a lie. It is an insult to millions of Russians who suffered and died precisely because the interval was squandered. The war, when it came, found us with all our defenses down, and without so much as sensible plans for saving the people and the valuable war properties directly in the conquerors' path.

Those who doubt this need only read the proceedings of the Eighteenth Congress of our Party, held in February, 1941, only four months before the German invasion. Speech after speech drew a picture of industrial difficulties and failures, particularly in branches of economy related to war needs. I had a thousand proofs, in the course of my own work in the war years, that they had not overdrawn the picture.

Within a week after war started Moscow, the best supplied city in our land, was without bread. Queues blocks long waited for tiny rations, those far back in the lines never sure there would be enough bread, kerosene and other essentials for everyone. The capital of the Soviet Union was not even provided with decent bomb shelters. Not a single important war plant in western and southern Russia was evacuated, or made ready for evacuation, *before* the onslaught. In accordance with the Kremlin's theories, we had prepared only for an offensive war and therefore failed to evacuate in proper time immense areas which immediately became battlefields. Millions of tons of raw materials and war equipment, grain, fuel, and most important, tens of millions of men, remained in the most vulnerable western sections, where they fell quickly into German hands.

I was in daily official touch with commissariats responsible for factories and stockpiles and workers in the area under attack. It soon became apparent to us that no one in the Kremlin had bothered, in the twenty-two months of grace, to formulate a program for the evacuation of people and property. The initiative, of course, could have come only from the very top. For anyone else to raise the question would have opened him to charges of "defeatism" and "demoralizing rumors." The suggestion that the glorious Red Army might have to retreat, even temporarily, would have been treated as sacrilege of the most reprehensible sort.

In the years of work in administrative positions in industry, I was often present and participating when secret mobilization plans were worked out. We took into consideration all sorts of needs—nonferrous metals, oil, coal, machinery, manpower—and the problems of their storage and transport. It was in conformity with these long-range plans that the government accumulated immense reserves of war and strategic materials. But the planning was concerned expressly and solely with offensive operations. They were tied to the assumption, often repeated by Stalin and therefore beyond challenge, that the war would be fought on foreign soil.

Faced with a defensive war of immense weight, we were helpless. We had to improvise everything from scratch—evacuation, mobilization, guerilla resistance in the enemy's rear. The Hitler gang had succeeded so well in putting Stalin to sleep that every British and American effort to waken him to the realities failed. Had he acted on the first warning proffered by the American State Department in January, he would have had five months in which to evacuate millions of people, scores of industrial establishments and tremendous quantities of reserve provisions and materials.

Because the Kremlin frittered away the period of grace, it left to Hitler as a prize of war a large part of what the Soviet people had created in blood, sweat and tears during fifteen years of industrialization. Factories, machine tractor stations, hydroelectric installations, mountains of supplies, not to mention tens of millions of work hands were abandoned to the bestial Nazis in the Ukraine and White Russia.

The habit of fear was so deeply rooted in the bureaucracy, after the super-purge, that few dared to take action even after the Nazis struck. Panic-stricken local officials and industrial trusts drew up plans for evacuating valuable machinery or supplies, as well as people. Not daring to act even in the most preliminary fashion, they wrote reports, filed them for decision by the "highest instances," then waited helplessly. In most cases they were still waiting when the Germans arrived.

Before Hitler, and especially after his ascent to power, the Kremlin had spent millions of dollars on intelligence and counter-espionage work in Germany. It had gathered data on that country's political and war organizations. But during the super-purge, up to 1939, the great majority of the men in the intelligence services and in the General Staff of the Red Army were arrested, imprisoned, executed; many of them fled beyond our frontiers. The result of their years of effort was cancelled out as "counter-revolutionary and wrecking activities." The new intelligence services, it now became quickly and tragically clear, were weak and ineffective. We were paying the price of those years of ruthlessness.

A new supreme body had been set up to meet the crisis: the State Defense Committee. It became the chief repository for State and Party power, the brain and the force in all defense activities throughout the country and at the fighting fronts, the policy-making body on national and international affairs alike. This Committee in effect displaced the Supreme Soviet where power theoretically resided. The Council of People's Commissars became simply an executive organ, carrying out the orders of the new Committee and watching over the various Commissariats. In every province the representatives of the Committee enjoyed unlimited authority. The State Defense Committee was the most dynamic, flexible and ruthless body that ever existed in Soviet Russia. All its members were drawn from among the powerful members and alternates of the Politburo.

The military forces, beheaded in the blood purges, had not yet developed new leadership. Voroshilov, Budenny, and the other famous incompetents put in command of various fronts at the outset were worse than useless. Not until October were most of them removed and new men given the reins. That, too, was a measure of Stalin's failure to prepare for the ordeal.

The Germans, having helped to build and equip most of the vital industrial objects in Ukraine, knew the location and significance of every screw and bolt in these factories. They were able to drop their bombs with satanic precision on electric-power centers, water towers, transport points to halt production and to prevent last-minute evacuation.

A lot of to-do would subsequently be made in the Soviet propaganda about the factories evacuated to Siberia from White Russia and the Ukraine. In truth only a minor part was removed. Nothing would be said of the hundreds of plants left as a present to Hitler. Virtually every factory I had worked in or been connected with—in Dniepropetrovsk, Krivoi Rog, Zaparozhe, Taganrog—fell to the enemy almost intact. The same was more or less true of Kiev, Odessa, Kharkov, Mariupol, Stalino, Lugansk. Stalin's mistake in trusting Hitler was responsible for the fact that we abandoned to the enemy industry with a capacity of about ten million tons of steel a year, plus about two million tons in finished steel. It was all returned to us in time in the form of death-dealing tanks, guns, shells and bombs. The story was no less tragic for other industries.

During the period of the pact, Stalin helped Hitler conquer Europe by providing him with metal, ores, oil, grain, meat, butter, and every conceivable type of material, in accordance with their economic pact. After the invasion, Stalin helped him by leaving him immense riches in military goods and productive capacity and—most shameful of all—tens of millions of people.

Failure to prepare will be held against the Stalin regime by history despite the ultimate victory. It was to blame for millions of unnecessary casualties, for human wretchedness beyond calculation. Why was not the population of Leningrad evacuated? This "oversight" is ignored by the hallelujah-shouters, though up to May 1, 1943, more than 1,300,000 died of hunger and cold, and the rest will carry the marks of their suffering to the grave, in three successive winters of terrifying siege. It was an exposed city. The preparations for saving its inhabitants should have been made long in advance, but they were not undertaken even after the war started. Responsibility for the gruesome sufferings of Leningrad rests directly on two members of the Politburo—Voroshilov, as the then commander of the Leningrad front and Zhdanov, the supreme master of the Leningrad region.

The same can be said for the unfortunate people trapped in Kiev, Odessa, Sebastopol, a hundred other population centers, including my own native city. My mother and father were caught in Dniepropetrovsk, together with Klava, my brother Constantine's wife, and her infant child. Only her iron will, fortified by religious faith, saw my frail mother through her frightful experience. She was chased from place to place by the Germans and finally confined in one of their filthy concentration camps. Both she and Klava survived; whether my father did I do not know.

There are millions of such fathers and mothers and children in Russia who paid in life and incalculable pain for the Kremlin's criminal "oversights." When finally evacuation got under way, the new Soviet system of class privilege made itself manifest in the crudest way. First priority in departing, and in using transport facilities, was reserved for the "indispensables," which is to say the leading bureaucrats, Party politicians, trade union functionaries, police officials making up the regime's "apparatus." Ordinary mortals were allowed to take only two suitcases, abandoning everything else, but top-priority aristocrats carried off even their bulkiest furniture. Skilled workers and others essential for the evacuated plants were evacuated but often had to leave their families behind, in going off with transferred machines. The favored officials, however, took along their real and imaginary relatives unto the tenth generation.

I repeat, the great alibi for the deal with the Nazis—the gaining of time—is a base myth, a fairy tale, a cynical propaganda lie.

4

It took months of direct experience with German brutality to overcome *the moral disarmament* of the Russian people. They had to learn again to detest the Nazis, after two years in which Hitler had been played up as a friend of Russia and a friend of peace. Let it not be forgotten that in the early weeks entire Red Army divisions fell prisoners to the enemy almost without a struggle.

Had the invaders proved to be human beings and displayed good

political sense they would have avoided a lot of the fierce guerilla resistance that plagued them day and night. Instead the Germans, in their
fantastic racial obsessions, proceeded to kill, torture, burn, rape and
enslave. Upon the collectivization which most peasants abhorred the
conquerors now imposed an insufferable German efficiency. In place of
the dreaded N.K.V.D., the Germans brought their dreadful Gestapo. Thus
the Germans did a magnificent job for Stalin. They turned the overwhelming majority of the people, whether in captured territory or in the rear,
and all of the armed forces against themselves. They gave the Kremlin
the materials for arousing a burning national hatred against the invaders.

Refugees and escaped prisoners disseminated the bloody tidings of
German atrocities and high-handed stupidity. The Nazi barbarians, we
learned, treated all Slavs as a sub-human species. I know from my own
emotions that indignation against the Germans drove out resentments
against our own regime. Hitler's hordes succeeded in inflaming Russian
patriotism more effectively than all the new war cries of race and nation
launched from the Kremlin.

Had we been at war with a democratic country, humane and en-
lightened, bringing us a gift of freedom and sovereign independence
within a family of free nations, the whole story would have been different.
But the Russians were merely given a choice between their familiar tyranny
and an imported brand. The fact that they preferred the native chains
is scarcely an item in which the Soviet dictators should take excessive
pride.

In its propaganda to the armed forces and the population at large the
Kremlin insisted that the invaders were intent on restoring landlords and
capitalists. This was an effective morale builder and, indeed, offered the
most solid common ground on which the regime and the people could
meet. Except for a negligible minority, it should be understood, the
Russians categorically did not desire such a restoration, under any disguise, no matter how sincerely they might detest the political and economic
despotism of the Soviet system. Anti-capitalist education and indoctrination during a quarter of a century had sunk deep roots in the Russian
mind.

But millions who fought courageously against the Nazis, on battle-
fronts and in guerilla actions, did dream that a new Russia, freed from
a dictatorship of one party or one person, blessed with democratic freedoms, would rise from the ashes of the holocaust. The government nur-
tured this illusion, especially in the territories overrun by the enemy, as
long as the war was going against us. The texts of the Atlantic Charter
and Mr. Roosevelt's Four Freedoms were published in our press, quietly
and without comment; even that thrilled us with new hope. In the propaganda beamed to the conquered areas, these documents were exploited to
the limit, to give the partisans an implied assurance that they were
fighting for a new Russia, not for the one that had betrayed them by its
terror and one-party tyranny. In their suffering and despair people were
eager to accept the smoke of agitation for the incense of freedom.

The regime and the people both strove to save the country—but their hopes and purposes were as far apart as the poles. The dominant purpose of the regime was to save itself and its system for the further development of its Communist adventures at home and abroad; the people were moved by unadulterated love of their fatherland and the hope of achieving elementary political and economic freedoms.

The guerilla movement and the "scorched earth" tactics have been depicted by some romantic writers as spontaneous phenomena. Actually they were carefully planned and at all times controlled from Moscow. In his radio speech of July 3 Stalin said:

"In the regions occupied by the enemy it is necessary to create partisan detachments, both mounted and unmounted; to organize diversionist groups for struggle against the units of the enemy army, for spreading the partisan war everywhere, for blowing up bridges, roads, damaging telephone and telegraph communications, setting fire to forests, storehouses and caravans. In the regions seized it is necessary to create unendurable conditions for the enemy and all of his helpers, to pursue and destroy them at every step, to undermine all of their undertakings."

He also proclaimed that in the retreat all valuable property which could not be taken along must be "unconditionally destroyed." By this time it is no secret that many peasants and city dwellers resisted this policy, fiercely and sometimes bloodily. The scorching was done, in the main, not by civilians but by the military forces.

The staff of the partisan resistance was organized in the capital. The Secretary of the White Russian Central Committee of the Party, Comrade Ponomarenko, was in charge of guerilla warfare in White Russia. Ukrainian resistance activities were commanded by Demyan Korotchenko, Secretary of the Ukrainian Central Committee. In the Baltic countries the same role was played by a Comrade Latsis. These were Party leaders of long standing, though later the propaganda played up unknown people who arose from the fires of actual underground conflict.

In accordance with plans, certain large Red Army units remained in the German rear, to become the centers of guerilla movements. Soldiers who had strayed from their outfits and found themselves cut off naturally joined the partisan battalions. Many thousands of non-Party Soviet officials, Party activists and the like, trapped behind the lines, knowing that their fate in Nazi hands would be torture and death, swelled the ranks of the resistance. The Germans themselves, by their policy of unrelieved *Schrecklichkeit*, did the rest.

Another aspect of the planned resistance is never mentioned anywhere. I refer to the N.K.V.D. agencies deliberately left behind in every area abandoned to the enemies, primarily to observe the behavior of Soviet citizens in the German rear. Tens of thousands of Soviet men and women later were executed, hundreds of thousands condemned to slave labor, on the basis of these observations. N.K.V.D. agents also joined in the partisan movement, so that the familiar system of Soviet espionage among its own people prospered even under German occupation. The families of those left in the German rear on special assignments were evacuated to the Soviet area and served as hostages to guarantee the loyalty of the agents.

Nor should it be taken for granted that the populations in occupied areas were all uniformly friendly to the partisans. In the Baltic regions, naturally, a large part of the inhabitants—often a majority—received the Germans as liberators from an unwelcome Soviet yoke and the guerillas were harrassed by civilians as well as German military force. But even in Russia proper—particularly in the Don and Kuban regions, where collectivization and famine had taken the cruelest toll—the partisan movement remained small and often faced popular opposition.

In the Ukraine, too, old grudges against the Stalin set-up frequently found murderous vent. The Ukrainian situation, however, was so complex that it would require a long chapter merely to summarize it. There was an out-and-out pro-German movement headed up by *émigrés* long trained for their role. There was a tremendous honest native movement that was equally hostile to the Nazis and the Soviets. A great many of the celebrated guerilla deeds in this vast area were inspired by detestation of Stalin no less than of Hitler. Even those who cooperated loyally with Moscow, taking orders from Korotchenko, were fed with calculated illusions about real autonomy—a new deal for Ukraine—once the invader should be driven out. In addition, of course, there were guerillas with a clean-cut separatist program, looking to the ultimate establishment of a completely independent and sovereign Ukraine.

The underground resistance will deservedly be glorified in Russian annals. It demonstrated the courage and tenacity of our people, a deep-rooted love of their own soil, their fortitude in the hour of disaster. But to twist all this into spurious evidence of the popularity of the Stalinist despotism, as so many naive outsiders were encouraged to do, is as pernicious as it is silly. For the sake of truth it must be recorded that a considerable job in the enemy's rear was done by special forces of the N.K.V.D. army, trained and equipped for diversionist guerilla warfare. Troops prepared for special sabotage undertakings were constantly being parachuted behind the German lines.

On September 18 the government decreed universal military training for all men between sixteen and fifty who had not yet been drafted. Actually men up to fifty-six were being taken for active military service and up to fifty-eight for non-combat services. In practice every man, whatever his age or physical condition, well enough to work was obliged to report for training at the end of his working day, which in most cases was twelve hours long. In the squares and on the boulevards of Moscow, weary, bleary-eyed men, half starved and inadequately dressed, drilled with sticks. With one or two rifles to a platoon, they received instruction in the art of shooting. Neither rain nor deep mud exempted them. Indeed, part of the training consisted of advancing through mud, crawling close to the ground through mud or snow.

Let the romanticists cite these drills as further proof of war fervor. The truth is less edifying. The training was obligatory. Abstention was punished as desertion, through the revolutionary tribunals of the N.K.V.D. Even as regards to the military forces, there would be less heroic drivel written on the subject if the world knew the nature of the discipline enforced in the Red Army, especially the extent to which capital punishment was imposed for slight infractions without trial. It is true that Russian soldiers did heroic deeds, holding their posts in the face of hopeless odds, giving their lives to save their country, their people and their comrades. Stalin's subjects fought against Hitler as valorously as the feudal serfs under Alexander I fought against Napoleon. But those who make of our native grit, our capacity to fight and die, a special virtue reflecting glory on the totalitarian Soviet regime are either fooling themselves or fooling others.

It is not known abroad—and truth demands that it be recorded—that behind the Red Army at the fronts there were special "retreat-blocking" detachments. They were composed "Government Security" troops of the N.K.V.D. and cooperated with the political administration of the Army. Their task was to intercept fleeing soldiers, to prevent unauthorized retreats. They had the right to shoot anyone who left the ranks without permission for whatever cause and did not hesitate to use it; normally, however, they turned the apprehended soldiers over to the military tribunals.

We became familiar with the sight of truckloads of deserters, guarded by Chekists, coming out of prisons. Presumably they were being taken to some quiet spot for mass execution. Their heads were close-cropped, their faces earthy gray; skinny, miserable creatures shivering in ragged military uniforms. I know from intimate sources that the proportion of desertions was strikingly high.

The fact that millions of men unfit for fighting by any civilized standards were mobilized pell-mell and sent to face fire without sufficient preparation helps explain this phenomenon. So does sheer animal fear. Our simple peasants could face dangers they understood, but modern tanks, flame-throwers, air bombardment left many of them paralyzed with horror before they got accustomed to them. Lacking weapons to match the enemy's weapons, forced to use "Molotov cocktails" in place of anti-tank guns, droves of new recruits cracked under the strain. The government conveniently designated as cowardice the results of its own inexcusable failures. Contemptuous of life, it was perfectly content to match Russian flesh against German metal, Russian blood against German gasolene.

The terrifying size of Soviet casualties has been cited a million times as proof of our heroism—it should be cited, at least this once, as proof of the Kremlin's blundering brutality.

5

The evacuation of Moscow began in August and continued far into 1942, until the danger to the capital was definitely averted. For about a month, until I was taken into the Red Army, I busied myself with the task of disassembling our factory and preparing its machinery for shipment to the Urals.

As Nazi aerial bombardment intensified, part of the population began to leave of its own accord. Optimists and hotheads shouted about cowardice and desertion. Soon enough, however, as the railroads and highways around the capital became clogged, we grieved because the authorities themselves had not organized this cowardice and desertion at the very start.

It was grueling labor for our half-starved men and women to take equipment off their foundations and to remove massive machinery. Even harder was the awareness that we were uprooting and destroying something for which we had paid with unbounded sacrifice, something which had become dear to us as the symbol of much-postponed industrial prosperity. We toiled in utter gloom. Not even the wildest detractor of the Soviet regime would have supposed that only six weeks after the outbreak of hostilities it would be necessary to begin to evacuate the nation's capital.

The normal hustle and bustle of our plant subsided. Life ebbed and seemed about to expire. Our workers, naturally so friendly, now plodded through their days in depressing silence. We all hoped against hope that the danger was being exaggerated. Once that hope seemed to have come true—we received an order from our commissariat to hold up the dismantling of equipment. But in the midst of our enthusiasm the order was reversed and we were urged to speed up the evacuations.

While a certain number of specialized workers were selected to go east with the machines, the rest were laid off in great masses, with two weeks' pay. The same was happening in all other Moscow enterprises. To the horrors of air attacks, food shortages, cold, disrupted electric and water supplies, was now added the horror of joblessness.

Though the Nazis were not to reach the suburbs of Moscow for another month, the atmosphere in the capital by the end of August was already that of a city doomed. The higher officials were packing their families and possessions off to Sverdlovsk and other Ural cities in automobiles, railway trains, airplanes. Hundreds of our leaders camped in their offices, suitcases and government cars in readiness for instantaneous flight. We worked all day, drilled all evening and fought the effects of bombings all night.

All responsible personnel in our plant, as in all of the capital's industrial establishments, were declared to be on "military footing." For weeks I did not go home, eating and sleeping where I worked. I shall never forget the scenes of horror—and of heroism—when we remained at our machines and posts while bombs and shells fell all around, while German airplanes howled overhead, while some women and youngsters in some of our shops cried hysterically. It was a test of nerves in which the Russian people around me showed amazing strength.

It was with a sense of relief, of taking my rightful place in the fighting ranks, that I entered the Red Army. Early in September my local draft commission notified me to appear for examination. A decent interval having elapsed since my voluntary enlistment was canceled, Yegorov and Manturov crossed me off their select list of "indispensables." My physical examination required all of two minutes.

I was assigned to Bolshevo, about 20 miles from Moscow, in the War Engineering College, retaining the rank of captain which I already enjoyed. I was enrolled in a special division in which officers were prepared for higher posts. Along with hundreds of other engineers of every kind, I undertook intensive courses in military engineering, as well as straight combat training.

Because Bolshevo was so close to the capital, Irina and I did not as yet have any sense of separation.

CHAPTER XXIII

PANIC IN MOSCOW

IN BOLSHEVO I was appointed Party organizer, which made me top political commissar among my officer schoolmates. In all military matters, of course, I took orders from Colonel Varvarkin and his assistants. The mounting tragedy of our country's sorrows drew us all together. There was a contingent of boys in their late 'teens taking the courses, but my division consisted of mature men, tempered by long and tough experience in Soviet industry and politics, men immune to illusions. I did all I could to make the lot of my comrades easier.

In my heart I was a confirmed enemy of the regime. I loathed its brutalities. Evidences of its incompetence now piling up all around us deepened that loathing. Stalin's bargain with Hitler—the "realism" that backfired—was in retrospect so shameful that even Stalinist fanatics smarted under the memory. But I loved my native land and was moved by the deepest sympathy for my people. I knew many others who were in a similar state of mind. Without exception we kept our resentments under control. Without exception we were prepared to die for Russian victory.

The training being dispensed at Bolshevo was unworthy of a third-rate nation, let alone a Great Power after two decades of all-out industrialization. The tools we were given for building bridges, pillboxes, airdromes were so primitive that they practically came down to an axe and a shovel. Where, we wondered, was the high technique that had filled Communist oratory? I listened to a lot of ironic comment and plain swearing on this subject.

"This equipment for dynamiting," one of the officer-instructors told me with a straight face, "must be respected as a national heirloom. It has come down from the dim past."

"Aren't the Germans going to shoot us down like partridges while we put up such a cumbersome pontoon bridge?" I asked privately after a lecture.

"Unfortunately that's true, Comrade Kravchenko," the lecturer sighed, "but it's the only equipment we have."

With few exceptions, unhappily, the instructors were as primitive as the equipment with which they worked. The lieutenant colonel who lectured on road building might have taken lessons with profit from any foreman on a road-building job. But he was a trusted Communist and devoted nearly all his time to reminiscing about his exploits in the civil war period. Besides, as officers we devoted a lot of time to reading and discussing the selected works of Lenin and Stalin. Obviously we could not be expected to lay mines and build bridges without a decent knowledge of Stalinist falsifications of Leninism.

Despite handicaps and annoyances, we studied hard and devotedly. All of us were deeply aware of the importance of our training. In due time, we knew, we would be responsible for the lives of soldiers under our command and for the solution of critical military problems.

By reason of my position as Party organizer I was in constant touch with affairs not only in our engineering unit but in the capital. I attended all meetings of our school Party Committee, along with the commanding officers. We heard confidential reports, consistently pessimistic, so that we were more dejected and for better cause than the non-Party officers.

I was in Moscow proper quite often and therefore subject to its deepening mood of despair. As the evacuation expanded and the Germans came nearer, confusion and alarm increased. As alarm grew, police repressions were intensified. It was a vicious circle which made the final climax of panic and looting—so carefully concealed from the outside world—inevitable.

By the end of September fear and disorder were spiraling upward toward explosion. Favoritism in evacuation made ordinary Muscovites fume with rage. For the first time in twenty years, in fact, I heard open cursing of officialdom. Every bureau and administrative office drew up lists of persons entitled to use trains to Kuibishev, Sverdlovsk and other places of refuge. In theory the sole test was "indispensability"; actually nepotism and political drag were the final arbiters.

The parasites of political power took up space for their furniture, their wardrobes, their mistresses, their relatives, while thousands of wretched families camped amidst their bundles and suitcases at the railroad stations in the vague hope of a place or even a foothold on some train going anywhere eastward. These were the lucky ones, Muscovites with official permits to depart. Thousands of others fled on foot.

The evacuees around the stations grew more numerous, more frightened, more noisy with every day. Their jitters infected the rest of the city. I sat in on conferences to discuss the problem. Had we been dealing with cattle we would at least have worried about fodder for the long journey. As it was, it occurred to no one to raise the question of food for the evacuees, how they would get to the designated points and how they would keep alive after they got there.

When the crowds at the stations became too large to control, cattle cars, open coal cars, even subway cars, would finally be rounded up. Without cleaning or disinfecting, these vehicles would be crammed tight with Soviet citizens and sent on their slow and hideous journeys. The process was marked by tears and hysteria. Children were lost, families were separated, people were forced to abandon cherished possessions. Often the pathos of these evacuations was raised to a pitch of delirium by air raids, stations being among the favorite Nazi targets.

Meanwhile, as if to taunt the miserable mobs, comfortable caravans of official motorcars streamed out of Moscow, loaded with the families and household goods of the *élite*. The abyss between classes seemed deeper and uglier against the frenzy of war and danger.

In the first week of October the capital seemed to have lost its hold on life. A city, like an individual, can suffer a nervous breakdown. Trams and autobusses worked in fits and starts. The shops were mostly empty, but hungry people queued up anyhow. Although Irina had better connections and more money than most people, she was often in dire need of food. Homes and offices were unheated; water and electric service was intermittent and uncertain.

Day and night smoke belched from the chimneys of the N.K.V.D., the Supreme Court, the Commissariat of Foreign Affairs, various other institutions and Party headquarters. Our leaders were hastily destroying records, wiping out the clues to their decades of official crimes. The government, evidently under orders from the top, was covering up its traces. The first snows of October were sooty with burnt paper.

One night, in strictest secrecy, the casket in which the embalmed body of Lenin lies in his mausoleum on Red Square was loaded by Chekists on a truck. It was taken in a special car to the city of Tyumen in Siberia where it was to remain until the end of the war nearly four years later. The most valuable items in the Kremlin and museums, too, were removed to the interior. The bombing of Moscow became with every day more frequent and more frightening, though not nearly as destructive as we had expected.

On October 12 the Germans showered our Bolshevo area with leaflets. I led a company of trusted Communist officers which picked up these German messages. We were, of course, forbidden to read them—anyone found with a leaflet in his possession was subject to immediate arrest. But we did try to read them surreptitiously as we worked. They left us unimpressed, even contemptuous of the enemy. The German propaganda seemed to me signally stupid. Its arrogance was repellent and it made the mistake of confounding love of country with love of Stalin.

The same night we were aroused by an alarm. Within half an hour three battalions of our young, half-trained officers in full battle array were driven to the western outskirts of Moscow. Forty-eight hours later about one-third of them straggled back, bloody, frozen, hungry and dispirited; the rest never returned. Most of these youngsters were fanatical Comsomols. They had gone into battle shouting: "For Stalin! For the Party!"

Beginning with October 13, all of us lay in the snow in the Bolshevo forests guarding a segment of the approaches to the capital from our side, where it was supposed that German paratroops would descend. I was wearing summer underwear, light canvas boots, a summer cap, a frayed army overcoat in temperatures already far below zero. My equipment consisted of a training rifle and exactly three cartridges. Though all of us were officers, only a few were any better protected against the cold, only the lucky ones had as many as five cartridges. The munitions which we had been promised by headquarters had failed to arrive. Many of us, of course, had warm civilian clothes with us; personally, for example, I had a fine pair of boots, woolen underwear and other things. But we were rigidly forbidden to use any but regulation clothes. And so we froze and suffered for the glory of military stupidity.

Those days and nights in the snow, from which many of my comrades emerged frost-bitten and feverish, will remain forever engrained on my mind. More depressing than our lack of proper clothes and equipment and munitions, in that unpleasant memory, was the sight of automobiles filled with the parasites and their property, running away from Moscow. An officer crouching beside me in the snow-filled ditch exclaimed:

"If I see another car with bureaucrats I'm going to shoot the bastards full of holes."

"Better save your three bullets for the Germans," I said.

Marching back from Bolshevo after a night in the open, weary, starved, frozen, we sang one of the prescribed songs:

> *To battle for native land!*
> *To battle for Stalin!*
> *Battle honor is dear to us.*
> *Our good horses beat their hoofs*
> *As we rush against Stalin's foes. . . .*

I had little love for Stalin at such moments. Not horses' hoofs but my slippery canvas shoes were beating the wintry ground. But I sang with the others. The words in our martial songs and the emotions in our hearts did not always jibe.

On the evening of the fifteenth two companies of qualified engineers were dispatched to Moscow on a confidential mission. In my capacity of Party organizer I became aware of the nature of their assignment, confided to me as a top secret. They were to be joined by other groups, from the special N.K.V.D. engineering units. Their job was the mining of Moscow. Explosives were deposited under the Moscow subway, the main Kremlin buildings, the electric power station, the waterworks, railroad stations, museums, theatres, the principal government structures, communications and fortifications. Everything was in readiness to "scorch" the capital. A heavy toll of German life, and a heavier toll of Russian life, would have been taken. The mines were not removed until the summer of 1942.

On the morning of the sixteenth, Colonel Varvarkin sent me to Moscow. I found the city in the grip of a full-blown panic. The most hysterical rumors spread everywhere. It was said that a *coup d'etat* had occurred in the Kremlin, that Stalin was under arrest, that the Germans were already in Fili on the edge of the city. Distraught people were sure they had seen German parachutists land in Red Square. They told one another that Germans were among us in Red Army uniforms. Crowds surged from street to street, then back again in sudden waves of panic.

Already rioting and looting had begun. Stores and warehouses were being emptied by frenzied mobs. The impression spread that there was no more government; that millions of Muscovites had been abandoned to their fate without food, fuel or weapons. Order was collapsing.

In the Savoy, Metropole, and several other fashionable hotels and restaurants panicky women and ordinary prostitutes were assisting in dissipated carousing with high officials who had not yet left town. Wine and vodka flowed freely. Perhaps these parties were less orgiastic than the reports insisted, but the indignant stories were themselves symptomatic of the breakdown.

That some of the reports, at least, were true I learned subsequently in great detail. At Sovnarkom headquarters on the Sadovaya-Karetnaya Boulevard, for instance, high officials rounded up the younger women employes for a drunken debauch that went on for hours. In hundreds of other government offices and private apartments people behaved as if the end of the world had come. Aerial bombardment and rumors whipped the panic to frenzy.

I managed to return to Bolshevo by nightfall. There I found a disorderly, shouting mob milling through our buildings. The looting had begun soon after my departure and had been under way for hours. Local inhabitants had been rapidly reinforced by peasants from nearby villages. Our commanding officers had disappeared. Once the military stores were broken into, many of the officers had joined the marauding crowds to salvage some warm clothes. The locust swarm devoured blankets, sheets, uniforms, shoes, food supplies, everything that was not tied down. The premises looked like a shambles, the snow all around was trampled and strewn with discarded articles.

I succeeded quickly in locating Colonel Varvarkin. Evidently he was swamped with reports and helpless. He listened to the information in annoyance. No doubt he was reflecting the panic in the capital. Colonel Varvarkin assumed that Bolshevo would be evacuated anyhow. Better, perhaps, that our own people loot the supplies than to leave them for Nazi looters. . . . By midnight he and other officers returned, the looters had left and a semblance of discipline was restored. Soon we were again crouching in the forest snow, only too well aware that we had neither the force nor the faith to stop any Germans who might come our way.

Meanwhile in Moscow distracted men, women and children churned through the streets and beleaguered the rail stations. On the seventeenth, raging mobs in quest of food again broke into warehouses, markets and shops. The police seemed inactive. The Mikoyan meat combine was stripped of every last pound of meat, sausage and canned goods. Hungry people, left to their fate by the government, stormed the candy factory near Mayakovsky Square, distributing among themselves tons of confections, as well as sugar, butter and other raw materials. Dozens of other establishments were looted.

The disorders continued all day and well into October eighteenth. Thousands of Communists, believing that they were trapped in a doomed city, destroyed their Party cards, political literature and portraits of Stalin and other leaders. I can assert a terrible truth which was confirmed to me hundreds of times thereafter by people in a position to know.

The Germans could have taken Moscow during those days virtually without a struggle. Two or three parachute divisions dropping from the sky would have had the city at its mercy.

The hastily organized workers' battalions deployed on the fringes were untrained and ineffectively armed, and inside the capital the authorities were paralyzed. The first German tanks to reach Himki met with negligible resistance. Why they turned back is a mystery only the Germans themselves can solve for history. Presumably they overestimated Moscow's defenses and decided to wait for Spring and reinforcements. It is even conceivable that they interpreted the suspiciously weak defenses as a Russian trick to lure them into some hellish trap. The only thing certain is that they did not suspect the truth that the capital was practically defenseless and that psychologically it had already surrendered.

Beginning with the nineteenth the situation improved. The first seasoned Siberian and Far Eastern forces began to arrive. The police and the N.K.V.D. shook off their lethargy. That day Stalin over his own signature issued a decree which was conveyed to officialdom and put into effect immediately, though it was not published until two days later. The very tone of the document echoed the knowledge that Moscow was in a turmoil of unorganized revolt.

"For the purposes of securing the defense of Moscow in the rear, in order to reinforce the rear of the troops and also for the purpose of terminating the undermining activities of spies, diversionists and other agents of German Fascism," the decree began. It then prescribed extreme and summary punishments for all sorts of people: "Provocateurs, spies and other agents of the enemy, apprehended for disturbing law and order, must be shot on the spot."

The orders were addressed to General Sinilov, Moscow Commandant but, they specified: "At his disposal are to be the troops of Internal Defense of the N.K.V.D., the Militia and volunteer workers' detachments," the last named being a euphemism for Communists. Stalin preferred not to entrust the task to the Red Army, fearing, in the light of experience a quarter of a century earlier, that the regular soldiers might refuse to shoot their own people. He counted instead on the animal fear inspired by the very name N.K.V.D., just as the Tsar's advisers under similar circumstances had staked their safety on the dreaded Cossacks and gendarmerie.

The military tribunals worked around the clock. Though many thousands were arrested and shot, it was not terror which squelched the panic. It was the news, confirmed by fleeing peasants and soldiers from the most advanced lines, that the Germans were withdrawing under blows from the newly arrived Siberian and Far Eastern troops and apparently consolidating for a winter siege.

In Bolshevo meanwhile we received orders to evacuate. By order of the High Command we burned political books, military cards and archives. No sooner had we made ready to depart than the orders were countermanded. A few days later, however, the command for withdrawal eastward was renewed, this time in earnest.

My personal troubles were complicated by a gnawing toothache. At the military hospital a half-baked dentist filled a cavity in one of the molars with soaked cotton and sealed it with cement. That should hold me, he thought, until I reached my undisclosed destination. My experience in the next month, which included a horrible seventeen-day trip in a cold and overcrowded freight car, followed by a six-day trek on foot in rubber-soled canvas boots, transpired in a haze of torment that sometimes shot up to peaks of agony. My cheek kept swelling and pain sent its lightning through every nerve of my body.

2

Far East troops, hardened in border struggle with the Japanese, and Siberian forces inured to winter warfare were rushing westward across a continent to hold the invaders. At the same time other, much smaller, contingents from the west moved slowly in the opposite direction, across the Volga and beyond the Urals, for training and tempering. Most of them were fresh recruits; but among them were also troops salvaged from the smashing defeats on all fronts, hardened by disaster. All of them would be trained anew, equipped anew. The real preparation for resistance was just beginning!

The tragic delay in preparation which this picture revealed would enable Hitler to overrun more Russian territory than Napoleon or any other conqueror out of the West in Russian history. Literally millions would be slaughtered, millions more maimed. We would pay a horribly exorbitant price for the blundering complacency of our masters. But in the end the reorganized forces would turn the tide of the war—and the blunderers, by an irony of history, would receive all the credit. . . .

My engineering unit became part of the detachments crawling eastward, away from the danger zones, toward the retraining centers. The daily and almost hourly sight of long troop trains heading westward would be reassuring, but also distressing, since most of us smarted under an unreasonable sense of guilt. It would seem to us somehow shameful to be moving away from the fire, though we were under military orders. I had asked to be sent to the front; most of my comrades had done the same.

A battalion of officers despatched to the railroad station to prepare our train for evacuation found that fifty assorted freight cars had been assigned to us and that almost all of them were crammed to the roof with huge rolls of newsprint. A lot of qualified engineers sporting impressive military titles therefore spent the whole night, far into the next morning, heaving paper into the snow. Then we deployed into parties to seize stoves, lanterns, boards, anything we could find to make our journey more tolerable. Some of us were set to drilling holes in the roofs of the cars for smoke vents while others helped load equipment into the cars designated for the purpose.

In the evening wives, mothers, children, friends arrived to bid us farewell. There were the trite but ever heart-rending scenes. Irina was so concerned for my swollen cheek and unseasonable clothes that she forgot to weep.

Normally, Soviet cars according to the wartime schedule accommodated twenty-four persons. Our cars were loaded with fifty or more, so that we could not all sit, let alone stretch out, at the same time. We had no bunks, no benches, no provisions for washing or answering calls of nature. We slept by turns.

In my own car a small stove gave feeble warmth in its immediate environs. We took turns in thawing out. There was not a single flashlight among us and the candle quickly gave out in the one lantern someone had commandeered from a Bolshevo cottage. Within a few days half our men were suffering with acute colds, digestive troubles and other illnesses; my own jaw kept getting worse.

That was how we traveled for seventeen days, to cover a distance made in twenty-four hours by ordinary passenger trains. Several times a day we were shunted on sidetracks to allow the passage of troops and heavy equipment hurrying to the front, or de luxe civilian trains filled with officials rushing to refuge cities on the Volga and beyond.

Only several of the top officers and commissars knew our destination. I was among them. I knew that we were headed for the small town of Menzelinsk in the Tartar Republic, of which the ancient city of Kazan is the capital. Menzelinsk lies on the river Kama, an eastern tributary of the Volga.

Twice, sometimes three times, daily we were fed at the larger stations. Though our train was always stopping for long periods at tiny way stations and even between stations, we were strictly forbidden to step out without express permission from the car commander. Permission was rarely given. This stupid and even insulting rule caused suffering and generated bitterness. We failed to grasp why officers bound for the interior of the country should be so rigidly guarded, and tempers grew shorter as the journey grew longer.

At one of the minor stops my friend Captain Numidov asked to leave the car for a minute and was refused. "This isn't a train for Soviet officers but a prison!" he muttered in stifled fury. The car commander did not hear him but a few others did. Some scoundrel among us—I suspected it was a Communist who coveted my job as political commissar—must have informed the higher authorities without, however, disclosing the identity of the "culprit." No doubt the denunciation was directed against me as Party organizer rather than against Numidov. In any event, at the next station I was hailed before the Senior Commissar L.

"There has been a counter-revolutionary demonstration in your car," he shouted at me. "Why haven't you reported it? As Party organizer that was your duty."

"I'm not aware of any demonstration," I said.

"Others are aware of it. You must denounce the class enemy who said we're traveling like convicts."

"I don't know who said it. Besides, we're only human. One says things in heat without meaning any harm."

"You're much too tender-hearted, Kravchenko. This is war, and the sooner you learn it the better. Come along to the car and we'll smoke out the rascal."

Comrade L. strode to my car with the air of an avenging angel. He made an angry speech demanding that the "German agent" be exposed instantly. I glanced at Numidov as the commissar fumed and threatened and saw that he was white as a sheet and that his face muscles were twitching. I was frightened that he might give himself up. I happened to know Numidov's story. His family, a wife and two children whom he worshipped, had fallen into German hands. He hated the invaders with a murderous hate. Yet he was in peril of being shot as a "class enemy" and "German agent" because he dared resent a senseless rule. Fortunately no one gave him away.

The following day the episode was repeated but with more serious consequences. A young lieutenant in our car, who had already been under fire at the front, lost his temper when refused permission to step off for a minute.

"This is outrageous!" he exclaimed aloud. "Out there I was trusted to lead a company against the Germans but in this car I'm not trusted to go out for my needs!"

At the very next station Lieutenant Colonel Sergeyev, to whom this "insubordination" had been duly reported, arrived to chastise the criminal. The young officer, a slim, good-looking boy with hair the color of straw, was placed under arrest, his insignia of rank and officer's belt were removed, and he was sentenced to stand under guard on an open platform for ten days. Anger surged through our echelon.

From five in the morning until midnight the "culprit" was forced to stand in an open car moving through the fierce Central Russian winter. His guards were changed at every station. When he returned to our car for the brief night respite, we showed our sympathy by massaging his frozen limbs, giving him food and pressing our warmest garments on him. In addition, we managed to warn the guards that if they valued their own skins they had better let the prisoner smoke and take shelter under the tarpaulin between stations, when the commanding officers could not observe.

After the second day of this inhuman spectacle I could no longer hold my tongue. I sought out Comrade L. and begged him to intercede.

"We all appreciate the need for strict discipline," I argued, "but shouldn't we also use a little common sense? We'll be expected one day to command troops in action. We'll need a feeling of authority and self-respect. Does it make sense to guard us so closely, as if we were looking for a chance to desert? Tomorrow is November seventh, the anniversary of the revolution. I'm sure everyone in our unit would consider it a holiday present if the lieutenant were released."

Under my urging Comrade L. finally consented to see Sergeyev. He returned to announce that the sentence had been postponed until we reached our destination.

"But please don't drag me into any such affairs again," he said. "This is war, not a picnic."

It was our commander's theory that to keep us from going soft on this long trip we must do calisthenics every morning, when the train stopped, preferably before sunrise, stripped to the waist despite the Arctic temperature. At the first morning stop we would therefore be roused by a bugle and would pile out, shivering with cold and groggy with sleep, to do exercises. The sick were not exempted. Even on days when strong winds turned the sleet into myriad whirling needles, the calisthenics routine was not called off. Clearly our notions of discipline were inherited from medieval Tsars.

Those of us who had some money in our pockets tried to buy things from local peasant hucksters at the stations where we were fed. We found, alas, that the prices, already inflated, had skyrocketed in the few months of war. The cheapest tobacco cost forty rubles a glass, which is the peasant measure; a pint of milk cost fifty rubles; a chicken, 1200 rubles or almost the equivalent of two months' pay for an officer. The ordinary private, whose pay ranged from eight to twelve rubles a month, would have to serve nine years to pay for one chicken at open prices in November, 1941.

At one of the junctions, before we reached Kazan, while our train was sidetracked to permit the passage of a long line of troop cars, we were allowed to stretch our legs. With several fellow-officers I wandered off toward a forest close by where we could see trees being felled. On approaching we surmised that the men and women at work there, a pathetic lot, were not Russians. Though most of them wore peasant *lapti*, the Russian bast shoes, the rest of their clothes had a foreign look despite the fact that they were already caked with dirt and ragged in the best Soviet manner. Evidently these people were not accustomed to this sort of grueling winter labor.

From an armed N.K.V.D. guard we drew the information that they were, indeed, foreigners—Letts, Lithuanians, Estonians, Poles, Jews, just a sampling of perhaps two million "class enemies" and assorted "undesirables" deported for hard labor from the areas seized by the Soviet Union under the shield of the Moscow-Berlin pact. We returned to the train in depressed silence; every reminder of that bargain with Nazism was a painful reproach to the *amour-propre* of Russians.

A group of *bezprizorni*, the homeless waifs, meanwhile had gathered around our freight cars. The unwashed, ragged, half-frozen children, with prematurely old eyes in their haggard little faces, were begging bread in their sorry singsong. They seemed tamer, sadder, less arrogant than previous generations of *bezprizorni*, perhaps because they were still so new to the rootless life. A group of the unhappy war orphans had gathered also around the embers of an idle locomotive. They were singing the song of the homeless children so familiar during the civil war days twenty years earlier, and now revived by the war orphans:

> *Oh, I'll die, I'll die—*
> *I'll be buried*
> *And no one will know*
> *Where my grave is.*

We gave the unfortunates what little we could spare. Luckily we had plenty of bread. Even when these roving groups, having no other alternative, turned mischievous or thieving, no Russian had it in his heart to be harsh with them. They were a living reproof to the inhumanity of the grown-up world.

Our destination, in the first stage of the journey, was a station named Agriz, where we arrived on the seventeenth day. We camped overnight on the grimy floors of an abandoned and unheated schoolhouse. In the morning we were instructed to report in Menzelinsk within six days. How best to get there? That was our own problem. In six days we should do it on foot; if lucky we would be helped with rides by friendly peasants. We broke up into groups, each of them under a Party commissar.

Our commanders, who went ahead in motorcars, evidently saw no contradiction in leaving us thus on our own in bleak, snowbound Tataria after guarding us like prisoners on the train.

3

Twelve of us set off, walking briskly to keep warm. Our equipment and six days' rations made a burden that grew bigger, heavier, by the minute. My canvas boots with their slippery rubber soles were hardly intended for trudging in snow and across ice, so that soon every step echoed boomingly in my sore jaw. But someone started singing a plaintive folk tune, profoundly Russian in its sorrowful nostalgia, and it soaked up a little of the fatigue and pain.

We were amazed to see great fields of wheat, unharvested, under the snow and now and then even sheaves of harvested grain. Later a peasant gave us the explanation: With all able-bodied men taken for the army and horses commandeered for the fronts, "only women, children and cows" remained to do the harvesting and immense quantities of produce could not be carried off.

After a time we were overtaken by a couple of peasant sleighs. Only ten of us could be squeezed in, and as Party commissar I insisted on remaining on foot. Dmitri, a man in his early thirties whom I had befriended in Bolshevo, volunteered to keep me company. It was a gray, cheerless day and the landscape, though varied, was covered in the same white shroud of snow. Only rarely a distant plume of smoke or the far-off bark of a dog broke our sense of isolation from the inhabited world.

Staggering wearily through the deepening dusk, towards evening, we talked of the war. Already in Bolshevo I had surmised that Dmitri was as disaffected politically as I was.

"I tell myself every day, Victor Andreyevich, that I'm in this war for Russia—for the good, simple, warm-hearted Russian people—not for Stalin. Otherwise I swear I could not endure it. Unless they're perfect idiots up there, in the Kremlin, they must understand this about all of us. Tell me, do they really suppose our boys are ready to die for Stalin and Beria and the rest of the N.K.V.D. sadists?"

"This is no time for nursing grudges," I said. "Whether we like it or not, the Party, the N.K.V.D. and our country are all mixed up together. Until the Nazis are driven out there's no way of separating one from the other. Have you read Tolstoy's *War and Peace*, Dmitri?"

"Of course."

"Well, do you suppose our feudal serfs, facing Napoleon's cannon, had much reason to love their Little Father in Petersburg? Yet they fought and died and conquered. We in our day don't have to love our Little Father in the Kremlin to fight, to die and to conquer."

"But Stalin doesn't care a kopek for Russian lives—"

"Yes, it would be ironical if history gave Stalin credit for another Russian victory."

After nightfall we reached a silent, huddled village. Too tired to care, we knocked at the first house on our path. A bearded peasant opened the door. In great distress, evidently fearful we might think him inhospitable, he explained that his children were laid up sick. He directed us to a cottage up the road where, he assured us, we would be both welcome and comfortable and would find good food.

He had not exaggerated. The two-room house was warm and cozy, with colorful curtains at the windows and potted flowers on the sills. A gaunt, cleanly-dressed peasant and his gray-haired wife received us as warmly as if they had long awaited our arrival. The rest of the family consisted of a son of twenty-two, another of perhaps fifteen and a shy ten-year-old daughter in pigtails. They all hastened to take care of the strangers. When the older boy removed his jacket we saw that his left arm was missing.

"Vanya got his near Kiev," his father sighed.

The younger children helped pull off our ice-caked boots while their parents heated up water and brought in a big wooden trough. We had our first bath in three weeks. As we soaped one another we saw through the partly open door how the woman was laying out fresh linen and her son's clean clothes for us; the little girl was setting the table for supper.

"This is what I mean," Dmitri whispered. "These are the people for whom I'm willing to die fighting the Germans."

The cabbage soup, though without meat, tasted like nectar after our long march, and the corn cakes with honey were ambrosia. But the bread was cut thin and small, always a sure symptom of hard times in a peasant household. Dmitri and I brought out a black loaf, as well as smoked fish, tea and sugar. Our hostess matched this with cucumbers and peppers and her spouse, not to be outdone, dug up a pint bottle of vodka to warm us. It was a feast to be long relished in memory.

"Here's hoping the plague gets Hitler, God forbid," our hostess said, lifting her goblet.

"But why 'God forbid,' mother?" I asked.

"Oh, I say that out of habit."

"No, mother, you let the son of a bitch off too easy with a plague," the old man said. "I'd take him alive and put him in a cage and show him around through the world. Let people look at that Herod." He hitched his chair closer to the table and addressed his guests. "What interests me is this: what do you good Russian officers think we're really fighting for?"

"For our country, for Russia, of course," Dmitri replied.

"Our country, Russia, of course. . . . I'd send my one-armed son to the front again and I'd go myself for that. But for *what* Russia? The one that took our land away and starved our children—or a new one?"

"I don't understand, daddy," I said, encouraging him to say more.

"What is there to understand? I was at the front myself in the first war against Germany. I fought, I was wounded, I was eaten alive by lice. Then the revolution began. Freedom, they said. Land to the peasants, they said. Everybody hollered his head off and told us we were the salt of the earth, because we had rifles in our hands. Twenty-two years pass but there's no freedom, no land—only another war. Now again they're talking softly and flattering us. . . ."

"But this time it's our own power," Vanya put in, "not Tsarism."

His father withered him with a look. There was no mistaking who ruled this household.

"Don't interrupt me with empty phrases, Vanya. I've kept silent for many years. *Our* power! Who was it, then, that took the bread away from us with all sorts of schemes and plain robbery? *Our* power! Who was it, then, liquidated every fifth family in our village and packed them off to Siberia during collectivization? What I want to know is simply this: Are we human beings or aren't we? I want to live as I like, not as they tell me!"

"All right, dad, you have just grievances," I said. "But how did you live *before* the revolution?"

"A thousand times better," he shot back at me. "What's true is true. I had six *desyatins* of land, a good horse, a filly, a cow, a calf, pigs, geese. I kept bees. We were poor peasants, mind you, but we always had enough to eat and to wear. So I ask you, for which Russia did Vanya lose his arm? For which Russia are you two fine, intelligent men going to kill and be killed, the Lord forbid? If it's for the same old Russia of these recent years, there's not much good in it. I'm an old man and I blab too much, but it's good to sink one's teeth into the truth for a change."

The one-armed son, who had listened attentively, now said:

"You talk of the past, father, as if you wanted the landlords to return and exploit us peasants again."

"That's not it at all, Vanya. You're a Comsomol. You know nothing about the past life. I don't want the landlords to come back, but I don't want to work for a pittance for the *kolkhozes* either. Why should we have new masters on our necks? Those *kolkhozes* that work well should remain, but no one should be forced to join. It's not right."

We talked back and forth. All he wanted, our host repeated over and over again, was "to live like a man." He was sick and tired of being pushed around. Our hostess, who had kept her peace as befitted a good wife, finally could no longer hold out.

"Why were the churches taken away from us by force and turned into storehouses?" she exclaimed.

"I don't know, mother," Dmitri said, "but it will not happen again, I believe."

"If I were sure of it I'd pray for Stalin six times a day. Tell me, why does he want to convert everybody to *his* religion?"

We all burst out laughing, especially her elder son.

"Pipe down, Vanya," his father reproved him severely. "Your mother's wisdom is deeper than yours. If she hadn't prayed for you every day you wouldn't have lost your arm but your head. I suppose your Comsomols would have prayed for you."

"But dad," Dmitri put in, "the past is past. We can't turn back the clock."

"I don't give a damn about the past, boys. I don't need the Tsar. But I don't want new Tsars either. I want to live like a free person, to work my own land and worship my own God. Your Soviet god sits too far inside the Kremlin for me, behind too many locks and guards."

We slept cleanly and soundly that night, as if in our own beds. I dreamed, indeed, that I was back in Alexandrovsk, floating on the Dnieper, listening to grandfather's tall tales of the Turks and Kurds. In the morning a hot breakfast was waiting for us. The old woman, we discovered, had been up all night washing, cleaning and mending our clothes. Our shirts and handkerchiefs were washed and ironed and even my socks were darned. I was touched almost to tears by this solicitude. I embraced the woman, stroked her gray hair and kissed her on both cheeks.

"Thank you, dear mother," I said, "may you live long and happily."

Dmitri was no less grateful. Our host, climbing down from the top of the oven, called out in mock anger:

"Hey, there, you rascals, don't get too frisky with my old woman!"

We tried hard to give our hosts some money, but they would not hear of it. They did accept a cake of soap and a spool of thread. The whole family came out to see us off. It was like leaving your own home.

"I shouldn't be sorry to die at the front for people like you," Dmitri said with feeling as he kissed each of our new friends in turn. "You're a piece of what is called Russia, and it's good, very good."

We took our places in the sleigh which Vanya had prepared and were off to an early start. The old woman was still making the sign of the cross over us with her right hand and wiping tears with the left when a turn in the road shut her out of sight. About ten kilometers from the village we induced Vanya to go back. We gave him the key-and-hammer insignia of the army engineers, which he had eyed since our arrival, and enjoined him to thank his old folks again for us.

Late in the evening of the third day we reached the small town of Krasny Bor on the river Kama. Before the revolution the place had been known as Piany Bor, "drunken forest," the fishermen family with whom we stopped for the night explained; now it was Krasny Bor, 'red forest,' but drunk or red, life was no sweeter. Dmitri was coming through the ordeal in fairly good condition, but I was in extremely bad shape. My toes were frozen, my feet blistered and my whole body ached intolerably. The pain in my infected jaw was excruciating.

I did not sleep a wink. In the morning I walked through a cutting snowstorm to the district dispensary, about three miles from Krasny Bor.

Despite its high-sounding title it turned out to be a forlorn-looking set of wooden houses, presided over by a middle-aged woman doctor. Herself a Muscovite—I assumed she had been exiled to this region—she was over-joyed to see someone from the capital and eager for every morsel of news. At the same time she was distressed because there was little she could do for me.

"You have inflammation of the bone structure," she announced after a careful scrutiny. "The infection from the tooth has seeped through your whole system. You should get to Menzelinsk as soon as possible and go into the hospital right away for treatment. Here I'm helpless."

"But you will draw the infected tooth," I said.

"No, I have no anaesthetics. The ampules I found here are at least ten years old and, I'm sure, perfectly useless. Besides, I have no fresh hypo-dermic needles."

I pleaded with her, all the same, to draw out the tooth. She did, cutting into the inflamed tissue and working with a crude ancient forceps. I have no words to describe those fifteen minutes of boundless agony. Then I rested on a couch for an hour and, reinforced by a slug of alcohol, walked back to Krasny Bor. With the offending molar out, the pressure on my nerves seemed a little less cruel. Dmitri made me rest that day and another night at the fishermen's house, and the following day, the fifth since we left the train, we crossed the frozen Kama. We ran into several other groups from our unit and on the sixth day reached Menzelinsk.

It was a typical Tartar town, with its maze of narrow streets and its distinctive Oriental odor. We were housed in an old school, where there was neither light nor water. Several iron stoves were commandeered but they did little to relieve the cold. Practically all our men had frozen, blis-tered and in some cases bleeding feet. I was too exhausted to move, but Dmitri somehow dug up a straw mattress and a straw-filled pillow for me. My body, wracked by pain, seemed to me to have swelled to mountainous proportions. Dimly, through the haze of agony, I heard the men around me swearing at their food, their quarters, their sorry fate. The prospect of life in Menzelinsk made them all sulky and despondent. The commanding officers, for once, were too sensible to make arrests for complaints, and kept discreetly out of sight.

Two days I lay in torture on my straw pallet. On the third day I was transferred to the Menzelinsk military hospital. I had a high fever. Then the tide of pain ebbed and I was able to take in my surroundings. A woman doctor, with good features and kind eyes, was taking my temperature.

"You'll be all right, Comrade Kravchenko," she smiled at me reassur-ingly. "As soon as you're strong enough to travel, you must go back to Moscow for treatment. Meanwhile we'll make you as comfortable as we can."

I gained strength slowly. Dmitri, Numidov and others brought me good things to eat. The hospital itself provided the patients with only a chunk of black, sticky bread, tea without sugar, soup and gruel twice a day. We slept on straw mattresses under stiff army blankets. But the doctor in charge of my ward, Eugenia Vladimirovna, made up with her kindness and understanding for most of the distressing physical conditions. We were an oddly assorted group in my ward—an old peasant soldier, a political commissar with the rank of Colonel, several privates—and we killed time by arguing every conceivable subject. But we all agreed in our devotion to the doctor

We were all in terribly low spirits—it was the December when the fate of Moscow seemed to hang on a hair. There were no newspapers and no radio in the hospital. But the commissar and I learned the news from friends who visited us; our ward became a kind of information center for the whole hospital.

Shortly before twelve one night, after I had been in the hospital some weeks, a servant brought a lighted lamp into our ward. A few minutes later the doctor came in. She was not only in civilian attire but dressed with a touch of elegance. Her dark hair, usually pulled in a tight knot at the nape of her neck, was now piled high on her head in a fashionable coiffure. The patients rose on their elbows and stared in astonishment. I even detected a whiff of perfume as she laid out platters of meat cakes and a bowl of fruit compote for us.

"Happy New Year! Happy New Year!" she exclaimed. Then, noting our surprise she added, a little embarrassed, "It occurred to me that for once you might like to see a woman dressed as a woman should be dressed! I mean, this being New Year's Eve . . . it might remind you of home."

"And it's a wonderful New Year's present for my eyes," the commissar said in a low voice, with deep feeling.

"My old woman back in the village never dressed like that," the old peasant soldier added, "but thank you, Eugenia Vladimirovna, and a happy New Year to you!"

Having greeted us each individually and distributed the food to those well enough to eat it, our doctor went to the next ward. The vision of this Russian woman carrying the gift of her womanliness to the homesick soldiers in the various rooms on this dawn of 1942, in a shabby, ill-equipped, understaffed hospital in Tataria will remain with me forever.

By the end of January a commission of the Military Hospital Service ordered my return to Moscow for further treatment. In the capital, I was not assigned to a hospital but merely reported daily to a clinic. While this process continued I took my meals at the Central Red Army Officers Home. Under Irina's affectionate care I grew well rapidly. My jaw healed and my body cleared. Discharged by the clinic with recommendation that I should rest to regain strength, I called on the proper commission for further orders. Here I was given a perfunctory two-minute examination and pronounced fit for service. My new papers indicated that I would be sent to the front.

I bade Irina farewell, fully expecting not to see her again for a long time, if ever. But when I reported at the Military Commissariat, I was informed that a new order had just been issued. Men with higher technical education would be exempted for pressing industrial work on the home front. It was a sensible order, yet I felt cheated of the chance to risk my life—for Eugenia Vladimirovna, for the peasants, the fishermen, the workmen, my fellow-engineers of these last months. They were my people, my country, in a sense transcending politics and ideologies.

4

This was Moscow's worst winter since Napoleon had looked down on its charred bones one hundred and thirty years earlier. The invaders had failed to take the city. Caught on the frozen Russian steppes like flies on fly-paper, they were suffering and dying in great masses. Even in the backward, impoverished Balkans the Germans could live on the country to some extent, but in the scorched Russia there was miserably little the conquerors could plunder. The troubles of the besiegers, however, were small consolation to the besieged.

The blacked-out capital to which I returned was hungry, frostbitten, pockmarked by enemy bombs. It seemed broken in spirit and almost too weary to despair. Its people huddled amidst the sorry marbled splendors of the subway, in cellars and improvised air-raid shelters until the all-clear signals sounded. They dragged themselves from frozen homes to labor long hours in underheated plants and offices. The city's industries were partially evacuated. What remained was worked day and night at top speed. The loss of the richest Ukrainian and West Russian industrial areas and the overloading of the transport system meant difficulties in obtaining raw materials for normal operation. Yet the capital had been transformed into a mighty arsenal working heroically for the needs of the front.

The official rations were barely enough to sustain life but the shops could rarely meet these pitiful food requirements. Hunger and cold became more of a threat than the Luftwaffe. The war had been under way only eight or nine months, but already the citizens of the capital city of a great country were eating bread made in part of potato flour; they were killing and eating their dogs and cats, and such crows as they could snare. What a devastating commentary on its war preparations!

Just as in the worst days of the revolutionary period, Muscovites broke up furniture and tore down wooden fences in the desperate search for a little warmth. The death rate in the city kept rising and at the same time the military tribunals and the N.K.V.D. added to the toll by their panicky shootings of real and imaginary panic-mongers and traitors.

Irina had lost weight. Since she obtained one skimpy meal at the bureau where she worked, she had been sharing her rations with less fortunate friends. Our apartment was unheated; we wore heavy coats, woolen shawls and even gloves indoors. A large part of the time there was no electric light and often the water supply gave out. Sometimes, for days at a time, the pipes in the one toilet were frozen.

Life was difficult and joyless. Moscow was paying the price of a quarter of a century of bureaucratic confusion and political despotism.

Half the equipment of the Glavtrubostal factory had been evacuated; the other half worked day and night on mines and bombs. But the place was overstaffed. Neither Manturov nor Yegorov encouraged my return to its payroll. I reported to the District Committee of the Party and through its intercession was assigned to the post of chief engineer of Promtrest, a trust controlling nine different factories, most of them working on supplies for the front.

I was overjoyed with the designation, though the physical conditions of work were unappetizing, because it gave me a feeling of direct participation in the war. No less important, as a responsible worker I now had the privilege of eating in the special restaurant reserved for members of the District Committee of the Party. Some of the plants under my technical supervision manufactured hand grenades, mines and several other types of munitions. Several of them specialized in the repair of engineering equipment. I was constantly pushing through urgent war orders, without sparing myself or my staff. I actually felt and tried to imbue those around me with the feeling that we were "under fire."

Our workers were gaunt with hunger and haunted by the knowledge that their families were suffering. Nevertheless, they toiled grimly and devotedly from ten to sixteen hours a day. Frequently, when a rush order was involved, they remained in their factories for many days without a break, snatching some sleep on the premises. I marveled at the fortitude of these simple men, women and children—boys and girls from twelve to fifteen years of age were everywhere doing grown-up jobs—as I watched them working in one shop when the shop next-door had been turned into a blazing hell by a direct bomb hit. I know that these plain people were the real heroes and the real strength of the Russian war. They had no need for morale-building slogans. They were struggling to give all possible support to their sons and brothers and fathers at the fighting fronts. The outside world, in its blindness, might give all the credit to the Soviet dictatorship, but the job was being done by the victims of that dictatorship, and frequently despite its stupidities.

My new assignment brought me into intimate and almost daily contact with high military and government dignitaries concerned with the problems of war supplies. I had occasion now and then to deal directly with ranking officials in the Sovnarkom—the Council of People's Commissars—which, deriving its authority from the Supreme Soviet, was in theory the chief executive and control organ of the State Defense Committee. For the first time in my career I now attended several urgent production conferences within the crenelated Kremlin walls.

One day I found a message on my desk asking me to call a certain number without delay. I phoned and announced myself.

"Oh, yes, Comrade Kravchenko, please be at the Sovnarkom of the R.S.F.S.R. at twelve sharp. A pass will be waiting for you."

The R.S.F.S.R.—Russian Soviet Federated Socialist Republic—is the largest of the constituent "republics," larger, indeed, than all the rest put together. At best the autonomy of the so-called republics is a flimsy fiction; they have far less independent authority than the states in the United States. In essence they are administrative divisions to facilitate the government of a nation as gigantic as Russia, but totally controlled from the center.

In the case of the R.S.F.S.R. even the fiction scarcely exists. Its Sovnarkom is little more than an extension of the All-Union Sovnarkom. Its capital is Moscow, its activities are tied closely into the activities of the whole regime. It does not have an N.K.V.D. of its own as other Soviet republics have, or a Central Committee of the Party of its own. The R.S.F.S.R. is thus in practice though not in theory co-extensive with the U.S.S.R. It is the dominant political unit, where the strength of the regime is concentrated. The ordinary Soviet citizen makes no distinction between the main Sovnarkom and its subsidiary Sovnarkom of the R.S.F.S.R. and I was to learn that, in practice, the popular assumption was correct.

I had been in the building on business a number of times and was familiar with the extraordinary precautions taken to protect its officials. Having produced my passport and obtained a pass, I was relayed from guard to guard and finally found myself in a wide, hushed, heavily carpeted corridor, flanked by heavy oak doors. N.K.V.D. men of officer rank stood outside some of these imposing doors. Little did I guess at this moment that soon one of these offices would be mine and that I, too, would be among the precious ones elaborately guarded against vague dangers.

After a short wait in the reception room, a woman secretary admitted me to the vast office of Comrade Andrei Ivanovich Utkin, vice-chairman of the Sovnarkom of the R.S.F.S.R. Though he was a man above middle height, compactly built, with a protruding stomach and a self-important presence, he seemed dwarfed by the huge chair in which he sat, the field-like expanse of his desk and the immense oil portrait of Stalin on the wall behind him.

He motioned me to be seated.

"Well, Comrade Kravchenko, how are affairs with you?"

"I don't know quite what to say since I haven't any idea why you called me."

"I mean in general. How's your work, how are you helping the Party and the country in the war?"

I told him about the activities of my trust and outlined some of the production problems faced by the nine plants under my care. As I talked I recognized, among the papers in front of him, a questionnaire with my photograph attached which I had filled out on becoming chief engineer of the trust.

"You're talking to *the government*," Comrade Utkin interjected at one point. "There can be no falsehoods, no holding back of facts and thoughts."

"Of course, of course."

He asked questions and I made a series of speeches. Under the Soviet procedure we all became inured to orating about ourselves. I talked almost impersonally, as if I were describing an acquaintance in whose affairs I had merely a friendly interest. At the end of about three hours, Utkin cocked his dark head, looked at me hard through narrowed, cunning eyes and asked the climactic question:

"How would you like to work for the Sovnarkom?"

"That would depend on the work."

"Well, we need an engineer, a Party member, to head the Department of War Engineering Armament. I think you can fill the post. This doesn't mean that the question will be decided today. I merely need your consent before taking the proper preliminary steps."

"I'm not at all sure that I can handle such an important job," I said.

"And I think, on the contrary, that you'll do very well. You have the necessary experience and we've watched your work at the trust."

"If that's your opinion, I should, of course, accept."

"In that case, good-bye for the present. Please report at the Personnel Department on the floor below."

I filled out a series of forms. In a few days I was instructed to report to Utkin's superior, the chairman of the Sovnarkom of the R.S.F.S.R. and one of the most powerful figures around Stalin: Constantine Pamfilov. His tremendous office, his throne of authority, his oil painting of Stalin were all a few degrees larger than Utkin's. The furniture and fittings were a few degrees more luxurious.

Pamfilov was a tall man in his middle forties, broad-boned and impressive. His head and face were clean-shaven and shone like a billiard ball. He wore foreign clothes. He stood behind his enormous desk, one foot on the chair, leaning his weight on his elbow. I was to learn in the following months that this was his natural working stance, even when he was alone. Comrade Utkin, looking even smaller in his chief's presence, was with Pamfilov when I entered.

Again I answered questions. My questionnaires and special reports about me were on his desk.

"Comrade Kravchenko," the chairman of the Sovnarkom finally said, "you have held responsible posts. But working in the government is quite another matter. We are the servants of the Party, and work in the government is, above all, Party work. It is the Party that rules the country."

I assured him meekly that I understood this.

"Comrade Utkin"—Pamfilov turned to his assistant—"has there been an answer?"

"Not yet, Comrade Pamfilov."

Pamfilov lifted one of the receivers in the forest of telephones on a little table behind him and dialed a number.

"Pamfilov speaking. How about the Kravchenko matter?"

He waited two or three minutes. The silence in the room was oppressive. Evidently something was being checked at the other end.

"Yes . . . yes. . . ." Pamfilov finally said. "There are no objections? Very good!"

He dropped the receiver. I had no doubt that he had called the Seventh Department of the N.K.V.D., without whose specific consent no important government positions are assigned. Subsequently I saw the proof that I had guessed right. By accident I came across the formal N.K.V.D. document attesting its approval of my entering the service of the Sovnarkom. Though the Party directs the country and its government, no important appointment for work in the Party or the government is ever completed without investigation and approval by the Seventh Department of the secret police.

"All right, Comrade Kravchenko," Pamfilov announced. "Now you can go. As soon as everything is ready you'll be notified."

Soon I was confirmed in my new position by the Central Committee of the Party. In a few days I was installed in an office next to Utkin's, after I had given the Special Department of the Sovnarkom a written pledge never under any circumstances to disclose anything about the work of the organization. The Stalin looking down on me behind my back was, of course, smaller than in the adjoining office. A special N.K.V.D. officer guarded the portals to my newly consecrated presence in the hushed corridor and two obsequious secretaries presided in my reception room. I was a member of the government in the technical sense of the word. I carried the special red card with gold lettering—a magic booklet, symbol of power.

This was at the end of May, 1942, just as the new German offensive was beginning to roll forward. It would swallow what remained of my native Ukraine, push deep into the Caucasus and reach the Volga River at a place called Stalingrad.

CHAPTER XXIV

THE KREMLIN IN WARTIME

THE RUSSIANS have a word for it. *Vlast*—"the power." It means the government, the supreme authority. But it means a lot more: Stalin, the Politburo, the secret police, Stalin's favorites, whether in official positions or courtiers without titles. In the mouth of the average citizen, moreover, the word has overtones of awe and undertones of resentment, implying "our masters" and suggesting the immeasurable distances separating them from common folk.

In the Sovnarkom I sat near the pinnacle of the *vlast*. For the first time I could look down on the world below from this privileged angle. Now I could observe (though I could not share) the feeling of the uppermost rulers that they were made of finer stuffs, moved in a different dimension of human existence and were, indeed, exempt from ordinary morals and sentiments, which they dismissed as "bourgeois prejudices" and "rotten liberalism."

Now I could understand the complacency with which these people used human life—shifting it, shuffling it, liquidating it—like so much inert raw material for their plans, experiments and blunders. Suddenly I found myself among men who could eat ample and dainty food in full view of starving people not only with a clear conscience but with a feeling of righteousness, as if they were performing a duty to history.

At the head of our Sovnarkom stood Constantine Pamfilov, a man so close to the inner court that when he died, within a year after I entered his service, his ashes were buried in the Kremlin wall on Red Square. Under his chief assistant, Andrei Utkin, there were five powerful departments, one of which I headed. Thus I was only two steps removed from the top. My department was subdivided into an array of specialized functions directed by my assistants.

In recording the fact of my brief eminence, of course, I am not bragging. I had been lifted by someone's whim. I could be pushed off with one polished finger by those above me who, in their turn, could be hurled to the depths without warning by their superiors. Again and again I would see Pamfilov or Utkin tremble in the presence of some Politburo chief or some court favorite of The Boss. I would hear them abused in gutter words like menials in disgrace. In a dictatorship the equilibrium is provided by a nice balance between unlimited power and unbounded fear.

The few of us who represented *vlast* in our Sovnarkom, perhaps thirty men in all, were set off from the middle layers of officials and the mass of employees below in a lot of ways. We had our own floor, as hushed as a church, policed by N.K.V.D. men of officer rank. Our spacious offices, beyond the reception rooms, were insulated by double sets of doors to prevent eavesdropping. We were served good breakfasts and suppers at our desks, free of charge, and had our own dining room for other meals at ludicrously low prices. The Sovnarkom barbers came to the offices of Pamfilov, Utkin and others of their exalted rank, to shave and anoint them for the day ahead. We lesser executives went to the barbers, they didn't come to us. Those immediately below us had no right to the services of the official barbers at all. These subtle gradations mirrored the hierarchy of power. Most valuable of all privileges was represented by a little red booklet which gave me the right to attention at the Kremlin Hospital and to buy medicaments in the Kremlin pharmacy, at a time when doctors and medicines were almost unavailable to the large public.

We even had our own toilet, its exclusiveness watched over by the officers in the corridor. There was, likewise, a special toilet for the less important officials, not quite as comfortable or elegant as ours.

Once the Sovnarkom rang with a scandal. It appeared that a new functionary, not yet familiar with the class distinctions in this particular domain, found himself on our floor and under sudden necessity. As someone left the marbled chamber, he slipped in unnoticed by the guard. When he emerged, the negligent N.K.V.D. man seized the culprit in great alarm, examined his documents and, of course, reported the sacrilege to his superiors. A few secret agents, the "unsheathed sword of the revolution," searched the toilet for time-bombs or other mischief. Then charwomen came with pails and brushes and scrubbed the sanctum until all traces of the infidel intrusion were washed out.

In private life I might be negligible, but at my post in the Soviet *apparat* I was protected like a great national treasure. No outsider could visit me without my express permission. I would write out a pass for the caller, affixing my personal seal, and before it was issued the gate control would phone me for a second confirmation. To make sure that it was not some impostor at the phone, I had to identify myself with a password known only to the N.K.V.D. and myself. My password was "Lena number 17." Having received the pass, the visitor was obliged to run the gantlet of four inspections of his identity before reaching my reception room. Sometimes I was ashamed of this system of super-control introduced by the N.K.V.D., especially when the caller was an old and dear friend.

The same procedure, of course, applied to all strangers entering our portals. No one below my rank had the right to issue passes, no matter how urgent the business. Should one of my assistants require the presence of some outsider, he had to explain the problem to me and if I considered the visit essential I made the necessary arrangements.

And that wasn't all. In our organization, as in the Kremlin, the Central Committee of the Party and a few other places, a system known as *shakhmatki*—"chess board"—was in vogue. Its purpose was to checkmate any plot by treacherous guards to smuggle an assassin, spy or diversionist into the premises. This is how it worked: At irregular intervals, sometimes ten minutes, sometimes longer apart, the N.K.V.D. guards were shifted like pawns on a chessboard. They were moved without warning and according to an intricate pattern by signal from a central control point. No guard could therefore know precisely where he would be stationed at a given time. In that way the collusion of four or five guards to pass an unauthorized visitor was made impossible.

As an additional precaution, only the automobiles of the chiefs of the Sovnarkom could drive through its gates, regardless of how important its occupants. Even People's Commissars had to park their cars outside the gates. The danger that someone might blow up our holy of holies by planting a time-bomb in a motorcar was thus obviated.

The real sign and symbol of my new dignity, however, was neither in this vigilance nor in my password. It was in a piece of furniture, outwardly commonplace but invested with peculiar significance in the life of Soviet dignitaries. It was a safe to which I alone had the combination. Well, not quite I alone—the secret was shared by the N.K.V.D. The point of this symbol of power was that none of my superiors could violate its privacy, thus enabling me to conceal things even from them. Only people high enough in the hierarchy to be entitled to secrets from their immediate bosses had such safes; and only one such safe in the country—namely, Stalin's—had a combination not known to the N.K.V.D.

My safe stood conspicuously, portentously, among my elegant furnishings. Even Utkin and Pamfilov, when they deigned to visit me instead of summoning me to their offices, eyed it curiously. They wondered what notes about their orders and verbal instructions I might have recorded and locked in the safe.

But precisely because it was barred to the rest of the world, the safe was the favorite hunting ground of the Secret and Special Departments. Their right to examine my papers during my absence was so matter of course that they did not bother to cover up their traces after an inspection of my safe or desk drawers. The most effective way to denounce one's betters, in fact, without risking a direct report to the police, was to write out the facts "for yourself" and to "hide" them in your private safe. . . .

Most vital was the fact that I now had the power to act in the name of the government. Within the sphere of my department's responsibilities, I directed the activities of local authorities and of commissariats throughout the R.S.F.S.R. I could request People's Commissars and their assistants to give me full reports on their work; I could order them and even reprimand them in connection with my assignments. I could summon them to appear at my office any time of the day or night, whereas they could not summon me.

It was mine to decide whether to cooperate with or to ignore a particular commissar. I knew from inside what the government thought of various officials—who would be rewarded, who would be "beheaded." Before long I had the feel of the government and the Party "kitchens" and "what was cooking." Often People's Commissars whose regalia shone resplendently in the eyes of common people seemed drab and even pitiful in the eyes of insiders who knew the truth.

I shall never forget my first day at the new post. I arrived at ten in the morning. My secretaries and assistants were already in their places. Documents requiring my attention were neatly stacked on my desk. I paused in the doorway to survey the large, elegant room; the portraits of leaders on its walls; the big painting of Stalin directly above my chair of authority. In a flash I relived the scene in a dingy Nikopol hotel, when I flushed the torn bits of a Stalin lithograph down a toilet drain. No sooner had I seated myself under this bigger and more artistic Stalin than the phone rang. It was an officer of the N.K.V.D. asking, so politely, so respectfully, whether I could receive him for a few minutes. For the first time in my life a representative of the dread organization was asking me for *permission* to pay a visit. . . . I invited him to come in.

"I want to give you this personal seal," he explained, handing me a rubber stamp, "for use on visitor passes and other documents. Please keep it always under lock and key. Now I'll take the liberty of acquainting you with other regulations, since you're new here."

"Please do. I'm listening."

He began by explaining the rules on callers, informed me about my password and warned me to keep it secret. For instance, I must never utter it within the hearing of another person, no matter how important he might be. He then solved the mysteries of the many telephones on my desk. One of them was on the special government circuit, connecting the Kremlin, the Central Committee and the main commissariats. Official business could be discussed only on this exclusive circuit, never on the ordinary phones.

"Also, every piece of paper in the Sovnarkom is a state secret," he went on. "You will be held strictly accountable if you leave any letter, document or carbon copy unprotected. Should you want to discard a document or even a carbon copy, don't simply destroy it. Write your instructions across its face and turn it over to the Special Department for burning."

Having finished the lesson in deportment, he had me sign a paper attesting that I was familiar with the regulations. Then he stood up, saluted, and marched out. He closed the door behind him quietly, considerately, not at all the way Gershgorn used to close the door on me.

At about eleven my secretary, an intelligent, pleasant-looking woman, knocked.

"Victor Andreyevich, will you have breakfast?" she asked.

"Yes, please. How about you? Have you breakfasted?"

"I'm entitled only to a glass of tea and a piece of sugar," she sighed. "I bring bread with me from home. War . . . what's one to do. . . ."

Soon a waitress arrived, carrying a trayful of food. She was a woman in her middle thirties, neatly dressed, wearing a starched white cap. She went about her job silently and efficiently, spreading a white napkin on a little table, laying out the meal: two eggs, some stewed meat, white bread, butter, a glass of hot tea, several lumps of sugar, a few cookies. Everything except the eggs and the tea was clearly of American lend-lease lineage. Though the woman's hands were work-worn, they were clean.

"I see that you keep manicured," I said with a smile.

"But of course. I serve *big men,*" she said. "Well, eat in good health, Victor Andreyevich."

There was something in her pinched features which led me to curb my appetite. I left one egg, a little meat, some slices of bread and a piece of sugar, as if it were more than I could eat. When I rang, my secretary came, stacked the leftovers on the tray and carried it out. A little later, in bringing me some paper to sign, she fidgeted at the desk for a moment.

"I'm ashamed to talk, Victor Andreyevich," she said, "but you're an intelligent man and will understand. I took the liberty of eating what remained of your breakfast. Please forgive me . . . it's so hard to keep alive."

"That's perfectly all right. In fact, I'm glad you did. But frankly, I was thinking that the waitress . . ."

"But Lisa and I have an understanding," she interrupted. "One day I take the leftovers, the next day it's her turn. . . . Hunger is a terrible thing, Victor Andreyevich. It's stronger than shame."

And thus throughout my months at the Sovnarkom I ate only half a breakfast, leaving the other half for Lisa and my secretary. Lisa, I learned, took her share home for her two small children; her husband was at the front. Both these women subsisted on the office workers' rations: 400 grams (15 ounces) of sugar, 500 grams (18 ounces) of cereals and 400 grams of fats per month, and 400 grams of bread daily. What I left uneaten of my first breakfast, if translated into non-rationed market prices, was worth at least 100 rubles—an egg, for instance, cost 40 rubles—and Lisa earned 150 rubles a month. . . .

About noon I had another official guest—the man in charge of the Secret-Special Department, eyes and ears of the N.K.V.D. in every Soviet organization. He was a young man, every inch the police agent even in civilian dress. He was businesslike and a bit officious, behaving as though he were the real master in my office.

"Greetings, Comrade Kravchenko," he said. "I'm pleased to make your acquaintance. We'll be seeing a good deal of each other. You're new here and should learn some rules from the start. We're at war. The enemy is everywhere and we can't be too careful."

"Of course, of course."

"Well, here are the regulations for the protection of state secrets. Please read them slowly and carefully and ask me questions if anything is unclear."

He handed me a sheaf of ten or twelve closely mimeographed sheets. In the familiar Soviet mixture of orders and threats, these pages instructed me how to handle State, Party and military secret documents, how to guard my desk, my safe and the office against strange eyes, how to prevent even my private secretary from seeing certain types of official papers. I learned that there were two stenographic staffs in the Sovnarkom, ordinary and secret. Routine letters could be dictated to the ordinary variety but secret dictation must be given only to the secret stenographers, who must be summoned through the Special Department. Every order from my superiors, the rules emphasized, must be on record in writing.

"But what if Comrade Utkin or Comrade Pamfilov or someone in the Kremlin gives me *verbal* instructions?" I asked at this point.

"In that case, you must immediately enter their words in your personal diary. The same applies to the contents of important telephone conversations. Write things down without delay—that's your best protection in case of repercussions later. Comrade Stalin has taught us to trust people but at the same time to check and recheck."

After I had finished reading, my visitor enlarged on the theme. The essence of his lecture was that I must believe no one and assume that others do not believe me. There must be written proofs, detailed minutes, of every meeting or conversation. Mutual distrust was not merely a fact in the Soviet *apparat*, it was the recognized, obligatory way of life, the only chance of survival. Again I signed a paper declaring that I was familiar with the system and cognizant of the penalties for its violation.

Finally he asked me to read and ponder a thoroughly secret document bearing the signatures of Stalin and Molotov. It turned out to be a Politburo decision outlining the rights and duties of the Sovnarkom. It went into the most minute details and left no doubt that the government, as embodied in the Sovnarkom, was a blind servant and instrument of the Politburo. I signed the usual form about keeping my mouth shut. This subordination of the government to the Party was known to every intelligent Soviet citizen, yet it was treated as a secret.

"Well, good-bye, Comrade Kravchenko. As I said, we're sure to see a lot of each other."

2

Those layers of officialdom to which I belonged were in many respects the least fortunate in the Soviet heirarchy. On the whole we had more responsibility than authority. We did the toughest work and generally our chiefs appropriated the credit. We were too highly placed to relax, as minor officials and ordinary employees could, yet not high enough in the pyramid of power to shift work and blame on other people's shoulders.

Of all the crosses we bore, however, the heaviest was sleeplessness. The week when I averaged more than five hours of rest per day was the exception. The great mass of our office people and specialists worked from nine to five, though now and then I might keep some of them longer or instruct a few of my subordinates to report back in the evening. But my own workday ran from ten or eleven to three or four the following morning, often later. Only rarely I stole a few evening hours at home with my wife. Occasionally I risked an hour or two of uneasy sleep on the divan in my office, with the door locked and the telephone at my ear to avoid being caught in the act.

The schedule of the higher officialdom in Moscow is an extraordinary one, being geared to the peculiar work habits of one man. Stalin normally begins his day around eleven in the morning, working steadily until four or five. He then usually knocks off until ten or eleven in the evening, remaining at work until three, four or even later in the morning. Of these two sessions, the night instalment is by all odds the more important.

There were various theories about the dictator's strange hours. One had it that this schedule allowed him to keep in personal touch with his officials in all parts of the huge country despite four hours' difference in time between its most western and most eastern zones. Another theory was that he intentionally kept his top subordinates out of mischief by breaking their life into inconvenient day and night shifts; it did in fact reduce their opportunities and temptations for a private social existence.

Whatever the reasons, officialdom in the capital regulated its existence by the eccentric Stalin clock. As if on signal, the bureaucracy at its highest levels tensed for action when The Boss (as all of us called him in informal conversation) reached his office and relaxed again only when he went home. The rest of the country, being in continuous telephone contact with headquarters and sensitive to its moods, also reflected this schedule. In effect, therefore, the ebb and flow of official life in all of Russia were governed by the comings and goings of one stoutish, pockmarked Georgian. One organization, of course, worked 24 hours a day—the N.K.V.D. It had no need to conform to any schedule because it never slept.

Beginning about ten in the morning on working days the big bullet-proof Packards with their greenish windows roar down the suburban Mozhaisk Road, through the long Arbat Boulevard and thence to the various citadels of "the power." From the sound of the sirens, from the way in which excited policemen stop traffic to give these noisy speeders the right of way, Muscovites know at once that The Boss, Molotov, Beria, Malenkov, Mikoyan, Kaganovich and other such leaders are being convoyed through their capital. Each of the limousines is preceded by a car (usually a Lincoln) and followed by another, both manned by heavily armed N.K.V.D. guards in civilian clothes. The leaders, of course, always travel separately, not in a group, to reduce the dangers to their safety.

The routes are charted by the special branch of the secret police responsible for the safety of the highest officials. Every inch of the way is expertly policed. The inhabitants of every house on the route are known to the authorities and doubtful people are quickly removed. Thousands of men in civilian clothes and in uniform are posted at key points, their right hands on their revolvers ready for the draw; they know that their own lives will be forfeit if anything should happen to the Beloved Leaders behind the bullet-proof glass. Muscovites never stop to look as Stalin and his closest associates are whisked by. Sensible citizens get out of the way, make themselves scarce and inconspicuous, when their rulers pass.

Officials a cut or two lower—men like Pamfilov and Utkin in our Sovnarkom, for instance—made certain to be at their posts before Stalin reached his, and they remained there until he left. As for myself, I aimed to be at work before my immediate chiefs arrived, just as my assistants were always on hand when I got to the Sovnarkom. I never left without specific permission until my superiors finished their night shift, so that my day was usually seventeen or eighteen hours long. Utkin and Pamfilov took it for granted that I would be at the other end of the telephone when they called me, just as Stalin or Molotov took it for granted that Pamfilov would be on the job when they phoned him. Probably the official routine of no great nation has ever before been so completely adjusted to the whims of a single man.

Our Sovnarkom was the executive and "control organ" for the all-powerful State Defense Committtee. Its chief function for the duration was to direct and check the carrying out of all orders for war supplies in the R.S.F.S.R. With the Germans in occupation of White Russia, the Ukraine and part of the Caucasus, our territory embraced nearly all the remaining productive facilities and population of the nation, so that in effect we were responsible for the largest portion of all war output at that time. A part of this colossal task was concentrated in the department I now commanded. "War engineering armament" was a term that covered supervision and control of output of supplies ranging from tanks, artillery, aviation and communications equipment, landing and camouflage equipment to items like gas masks, compasses, field telephones and even simple picks, shovels and lanterns produced by R.S.F.S.R. industry.

Literally hundreds of orders, decisions, complaints and threats signed by Stalin and his closest associates, by Beria and Molotov and Mikoyan, Vosnessensky, Malishev and Kasygin, came to my desk. I was in continuous touch by telephone with every commissariat, with factories, special industrial bureaus and regional offices throughout the country. In the course of a single hour I might check on production progress in Gorki and Sverdlovsk, in Novosibirsk and Cheliabinsk.

My life became a hectic struggle to find materials, fuel, labor; to push through output in specified periods of time: to stir commissariats and organizations everywhere from Moscow to Siberia into action. I was barked at and cursed by my chiefs and desperate executives of the State Defense Committee. There is probably more obscene swearing at the upper levels of the Soviet government than in the rest of the world put together. A lush, ripe obscenity is the most striking and sometimes the only reminder of the "proletarian" origins of our regime. The master in this domain was Kaganovich; we said that he cussed "like a corkscrew," spiraling up to magnificent heights of bad language. But Molotov, Voroshilov, Andreyev and others were close behind in this art and Stalin himself was no slouch. I can attest, however, that the great majority of the leaders with whom I came in contact were able men who knew their business; dynamic men deeply devoted to the work in hand.

There were weeks of my life embittered by efforts to arrange production of such simple equipment as barbed wire cutters, shovels for digging foxholes, lanterns as a makeshift for flashlights. I shall always remember the night when a Red Army General sat in my office begging, with tears in his eyes, for the barbed-wire cutters. Thousands of our soldiers, he explained, were being needlessly impaled and butchered for lack of this simple piece of equipment. In his presence I called commissars in Moscow and factory directors out of town. But what was the use of my storming and threatening when the factories did not have the necessary steel or tools or machines?

I was in continual contact with Marshal Novikov, Marshal Vorobiov, General Seleznev, General Volkov, Admiral Galler, dozens of other military leaders at the procurement end of the great war effort. Too often, alas, we could do little more than combine our lamentations over the shortages in every direction.

Shall I ever forget the time when we commandeered thousands of the primitive school compasses and apportioned them sparingly to the various fronts? The order, over Stalin's signature, had called for fifty thousand military field compasses, but the proper magnetic steel simply was not available.

Shall I ever forget the conferences, the frantic telephoning, the piled-up threats and the heartbreaks that we invested during the summer in a search for horseshoes? Thousands of animals, and often the cavalrymen as well, perished for lack of this item but their manufacture, it turned out, was blocked by lack of metal and the limited capacity of the two Urals plants making horseshoes. The demand for the horseshoes came from Marshal Budenny and thus, incidentally, gave me the answer to the mystery of the whereabouts of this revolutionary hero. He had been removed from a high post of command originally entrusted to him and since then his name had disappeared; there were even rumors that he had been liquidated. Now I became aware that he had been shunted to a bureau dealing with cavalry supplies.

Day after day I had the direct and tragic proofs of my country's failure to prepare for this life-and-death crisis. I knew as a matter of simple fact that tens of thousands of our bravest fighters were slaughtered for lack of the simplest supplies. Neither Stalin's terse commands nor Beria's "strong measures" could squeeze adequate equipment from factories lacking raw materials and operated by workers on a starvation diet.

I came to know more intimately even than the ranking generals and admirals how valuable American lend-lease weapons, materials and machinery were in achieving victory. Americans may still have some doubts about this, but not the Soviet leaders. For them it is a fact. God knows we paid back in full—in Russian lives—for Allied help, but that does not alter the fact itself. Without the great influx of American airplanes, American motor transport, telephones, a thousand other things we lacked, what would have been the fate of Soviet resistance? Russian production, Russian heroism and sacrifice take first place in any estimate of the factors which made for Russian victory; the Stalingrad triumph was clinched before the great flow of lend-lease got started. But American and Allied help belongs immediately thereafter in the estimate.

The orders reaching me from above were often hysterical in tone. A demand for some essential tank part or vital aviation equipment, signed by Stalin and countersigned by one or another of his secretaries, was invariably barbed with a warning of ruthless punishment:

"Notify the People's Commissars that fulfilment of this decision is a military-political task of the highest importance. Obligate the Prosecutor of the U.S.S.R. to control this order personally and to call those guilty of non-fulfilment strictly to account regardless who they may be."

Or it might read:

"Control on fulfilment of this order is imposed upon the People's Commissar of State Control, Comrade Popov. Everyone guilty of breaking this assignment, regardless who he may be, to be held strictly responsible and to be reported to me."

Strict responsibility meant removal from one's post and trial before a military tribunal. Decisions carrying the signature of Beria, who spoke with the awesome voice of the secret police, might conclude thus:

"Obligate the People's Commissars to fulfil this order regardless of objective conditions. The guilty to be brought to my own attention. . . ."

This was the routine Stalinist style, aped by every bureaucrat in his relations with those below him. It was the language of fear and intimidation, crude, undisguised, frankly intended to remind us of concentration camps and firing squads. Though addressing powerful leaders, men whose very names sent chills down Russian spines, Stalin and his closest collaborators never failed to invoke the dread of arrest and disgrace.

Never before had I worked so hard, so long or under such an overwhelming sense of frustration. Soon enough I had the gray-green complexion, the bloodshot eyes, the edge of fever that come with chronic fatigue. Nearly all the men and women around me drove themselves as hard as I did. Without doubt some others among them hated the Soviet despotism as deeply as I did, but our political views did not interfere with our devotion to the cause of victory. Our country was in danger—nothing else counted against this supreme fact.

If we succeeded in saving a day, even an hour, in supplying the front with some sorely needed piece of equipment, we might be saving the lives of thousands of our people. None of us needed any other spur to action; the threats were wasted on us. The feeling that our efforts were tied directly into the life-and-death struggle of our people was always with us, though we said little about it. We dealt with concrete tasks, with materials, tools, machines, under difficult conditions that left us little margin for indulging our emotions.

The whole organization, from Pamfilov down to the humblest file clerk, was caught in the mighty surge of patriotism that came from the profoundest depths of Russian history and the Russian soul. The little publicity agents of the Stalinist machine, at home and abroad, who try to explain it all as a Bolshevik phenomenon do our Russia an ugly injustice. They are trying to explain an elemental, timeless force in terms of petty partisan ideas. It was not a Soviet but a Russian miracle. When I think of myself, toiling honestly and unsparingly under leaders I despised and distrusted, I see a kind of symbol of Russia at war.

My many months at the Sovnarkom coincided with the most harrowing phases of the war. They covered the soul-searing summer of 1942 when the Germans made their largest gains and their deepest thrusts. They covered the advance to the Volga and the climactic struggle which made Stalingrad a word to rank forever with Marathon and Waterloo in human history. At the core of a nation there is a hard, eternal and unconquerable element—it was this that was bared in Stalingrad, that survived blood-letting and disaster on a horrifying scale. It had nothing to do with Karl Marx and Stalin.

THE KREMLIN IN WARTIME

Official communiques continued to minimize the magnitude of our defeats. The starkest reverses were dressed up to sound like strategic maneuvers. The Russian masses knew less about the actual course of the prolonged duel in the Stalingrad region than the rest of the world. But at our level in the government *apparat* we could not afford self-deceptions. The appeals from the front for supplies and planes, for munitions and manpower, echoed panic and sometimes utter despair. We could not help knowing about the colossal outpouring of blood.

On one wall in Utkin's office there was a big map of Russia. Every morning the pins marking the German advances were moved deeper into our country's flesh and a thread the color of blood marked the extent of our losses. I found Utkin gazing at this map, his round, handsome face puckered with worry.

"I have some urgent business, Andrei Ivanovich," I said, placing some documents on his desk.

"The papers won't fly away. Come here, look what the German sons-of-bitches are doing."

The red line was only about a hundred miles west of Moscow, just beyond Mozhaisk. It cut off virtually all of the Ukraine and lay frighteningly close to the Volga in the direction of Stalingrad.

"What will we do if they grab our oil, Victor Andreyevich? We'll be lost!"

"The picture is awful," I conceded, "awful! All that any of us can do is to work and work and work. It's a good thing lend-lease should begin to flow faster now. . . ."

"Lend-lease!" Utkin exclaimed irritably. "A second front is what's needed! But the capitalist bastards keep dawdling. A lot they care how much Russian blood is spilled! We're paying plenty for their lend-lease. . . ."

Mobilization had long been in force on a total scale unmatched in any other belligerent country. Manpower in industry and on the farms was depleted just when the need for output was greatest. I sat at the precise point in the government where this calamitous picture was most clearly visible. Our fighting men ranged from sixteen to fifty-six. The last pretenses of genuine medical examinations and exemptions because of helpless dependents were dropped, by an order from Stalin himself which was never made public. Tens of thousands of veterans were rushed back to the front lines before their wounds were half-healed. Boys and girls of school age, the mothers of small children, even women from farms already stripped of their men, were rounded up for work in factories.

In this tightening manpower crisis, the compulsory labor of millions of prisoners was a vital, and often the most vital, factor in rescuing Soviet military economy. This truth must be faced, whatever its unpleasant implications. There was an ever-increasing output of war supplies by the evacuated factories, enlarged Siberian and Urals plants, newly built industrial units. But few of them were without decisive *cadres* of compulsory labor. Those people abroad who talk excitedly of the ultimate Russian victory as proof of "the success of the Soviet system" would be closer to the truth if they glorified the success of large-scale state peonage.

With free labor drained by the armed services, our industry became more and more dependent upon the vast armies of prisoners, their ranks now swelled to unprecedented size by war arrests. In official circles twenty millions became the accepted estimate of this labor reservoir. The estimate did not include the boys and girls from 14 to 16 forcibly torn away from their parents and assigned to regions and industries in which manpower shortages were sharpest.

The war industries of the U.S.S.R., like those of Germany, rested primarily on slave labor. The main difference was in the fact that Berchtesgaden enslaved conquered foreigners whereas the Kremlin enslaved its own people. At a time when hunger stalked the land, the horrible conditions under which the prisoners lived and labored can readily be imagined. They were "expendables" and the N.K.V.D. did not have to account for casualties.

With the outbreak of war, the Armaments and Munitions Commissariats had been placed under control of Beria, Commissar of the N.K.V.D., who was also Assistant Chairman of the Sovnarkom and a member of the State Defense Committee. This amounted to putting them under control of the secret police. The nominal Commissars, Oustinov and Vannikov, knew what it meant; so did everyone else, down to the lowliest official. They would have preferred a quick death to the righteous anger of Beria and his organization. Everyone in the plants and offices and institutions directly or indirectly connected with armaments and munitions was gripped by dread fear.

Beria was no engineer. He was placed in control for the precise purpose of inspiring deadly fear. I often asked myself—as others assuredly did in their secret hearts—why Stalin had decided to take this step. I could find only one plausible answer. It was that he lacked faith in the patriotism and national honor of the Russian people and was therefore compelled to rely primarily on the whip. Beria was his whip.

That same lack of faith was manifest in most other industries. Their civilian leaders were superseded by military leaders, or at least persons clothed with military titles and authority. Railroad transport, for instance, was put under the direction of General Khrouliov, Stalin's deputy in the Commissariat of Defense. Acting in concert with the Transport Administration of the N.K.V.D., Khrouliov introduced complete military discipline, substituting unabridged fear for patriotic cooperation throughout the transport system.

In the same way Malishev, an Assistant Chairman of the Sovnarkom and an engineer by profession, was raised to the rank of General and put in command of the tank industry, over the head of the civilian commissar. Military titles were bestowed also on factory directors and other crucial figures in this industry, so that a military regime quickly displaced the normal administration.

The commissariats under Beria's direction, of course, absorbed the largest share of the available slave-labor forces. But there was enough to spare for all departments of national economy. I know from extensive personal observation that few industrial enterprises were without slave contingents and that in dozens of them coerced labor was the principal or the sole reliance.

While in the Sovnarkom I heard a good deal about the special problems posed by the concentration camps and prisons in evacuating territory as the Germans gained ground. It was even more important to remove this slave population than the free citizens. Their labor power was an economic value worth saving, but more important, these prisoners could hardly be trusted to love the Soviet regime and might prove helpful to the Germans. Another consideration, without doubt, was purely political—the apprehension that through the prisoners the outside world might learn some of the monstrous secrets of the extent and nature of the Soviet slave system.

Some of us in the Sovnarkom knew of episodes in which prisoners were killed on a mass scale when it became clear that they could not be evacuated. This happened in Minsk, Smolensk, Kiev, Kharkov, in my native Dniepropetrovsk, in Zaparozhe. One such episode has remained with me in detail. In the tiny Kabardino-Balkar Soviet "autonomous republic" in the Caucasus, near the city of Nalchik, there were a molybdenum *combinat* of the N.K.V.D. operated with convict labor. When the Red Army retreated from this area, several hundred prisoners, for technical transport reasons, could not be evacuated in time. The director of the *combinat,* by order of the Commissar of the Kabardino-Balkar N.K.V.D., Comrade Anokhov, machine-gunned the unfortunates to the last man and woman. After the area was liberated from the Germans, Anokhov received his reward, becoming President of its Council of People's Commissars, the highest office in the autonomous region.

In pressing commissariats for speedy output, I was continually balked by manpower shortages at critical points. People's Commissars knew the situation better than I did; they frequently asked Pamfilov for additional manpower from the N.K.V.D. reserves and he in turn made demands on the N.K.V.D. for working hands to supply this or that key factory; sometimes he put the problems up directly to Vosnessensky, Molotov, Beria. The Central Administration of forced labor camps—known as GULAG—was headed by the N.K.V.D. General Nedosekin, one of Beria's assistants. Nedosekin received orders for slave contingents from the State Defense Committee over the signatures of Molotov, Stalin, Beria and other members and acted accordingly.

I recall vividly an interview which I arranged on Utkin's orders with one of the top administrators of GULAG. He was to supply a certain commissariat some hundreds of prisoners for a rush assignment. We were under terrific pressure from Pamfilov, who was, in turn, of course, being pushed from higher up and I had summoned the GULAG official for a showdown on this manpower.

"But Comrade Kravchenko, be reasonable," he interrupted my speech. "After all, your Sovnarkom is not the only one howling for workers. The State Defense Committee needs them, Comrade Mikoyan makes life miserable for us, Malenkov and Vosnessensky need workers, Voroshilov is calling for road builders. Naturally everyone thinks his own job is the most important. What are we to do? The fact is *we haven't as yet fulfilled our plans for imprisonments.* Demand is greater than supply."

Plans for imprisonments! The fantastic, cold-blooded cynicism of the phrase still makes me shudder. What made it more uncanny was the fact that this official was entirely unconscious of the frightfulness of his remark —the seizure and enslavement of human beings had become a routine affair in his life. Of course, he did not mean that arrests were actually planned to meet labor demands. He was merely complaining, in Soviet lingo, about the fact that the multi-million armies of forced labor were not enough to meet all requests.

The magnitude of child labor in Russia has for some reason remained entirely unknown outside the country. Even within our frontiers it was surrounded with a good deal of secrecy and, of course, disguised in hypocritical slogans. The essence of the system, stripped of verbal camouflage, is compulsion. Millions of children are taken from their homes against their own or their parents' will and impressed into industries on a "mobilization" basis without consulting their preferences. It would be wrong to credit the development wholly to the war, since it was initiated in 1940 and, as is evident from dispatches, has even been intensified since the end of the conflict.

The first decree for the mobilization of children was issued in October, 1940. It provided for the immediate enlistment of from 800,000 to one million city and village children from fourteen to seventeen for industrial training. Besides the compulsory mobilization, volunteer enlistments were permitted. The fourteen- and fifteen-year-olds were mostly told off for more qualified jobs, requiring two years' training. Six months was the term for less skilled trades, for which children sixteen and seventeen were earmarked.

Having completed these terms, according to the decree, the young people would be assigned to plants, mines, building projects, other undertakings at the discretion of the Administration of Labor Reserves for a period of four years. Though surrounded with fine slogans, the procedure amounted to a conscription of child labor. Children were torn from the arms of their mothers and fathers, "for their own good," of course.

By 1943 the child labor contingents were raised to two million a year. The cruel scenes of separation, with youngsters sobbing and struggling, with relatives wailing and lamenting, became more and more familiar in the stricken land. The conscripts were put into uniforms, housed in government barracks and subjected to rigid discipline and a virtually military regimen. Their time was apportioned for work, study and physical training along lines calculated to turn them not merely into obedient but into fanatic servants of the Soviet superstate. Political indoctrination was naturally the important consideration in their training.

Even before the war, when I was still working at the Glavtrubostal plant in Moscow, I saw in various factories large groups of the children who had been forcibly wrenched from their homes. I came to know the whole system at close range. The young conscripts were awakened by bugle call or drums at five-thirty for military drill. Then they had breakfast and by seven were at their work benches, girls as well as boys, in accordance with the spartan principles prevailing in their education as robots of the state.

A touch of macabre irony was added to this regimentation by placing the head of the All-Soviet trade unions, Nikolai Shvernik, a member of the Politburo, in political control of the undertaking. The chief of the Labor Reserve Administration, which was in charge of training the young conscripts and which assigned them to posts in various parts of the country in accordance with the needs of the state, was Maskatov, one of the secretaries of Shvernik's trade unions.

Five times in the course of the war the government made new mobilizations, bringing the aggregate of these uniformed boys and girls to nine millions. In addition, hundreds of thousands of boys, some of them as young as twelve and thirteen, were herded into newly established military schools, to be trained as career officers for the Army, in the same way that the others were being molded for proletarian careers.

The military trainees were largely volunteers, but hordes of war orphans, partly drawn from children's homes and partly from the *bezprizorni* or homeless waifs, were used to fill quotas. In addition, parents unable to feed their children are tempted to send the boys to the military schools: in effect an enlistment for life. Higher education as well as the three senior classes in high school are now open only to those who can pay the tuition fees; the decision imposing tuitions was made, if the Kremlin is to be believed, "in view of the heightened level of the national well-being of the toilers. . . ." Many families, unable to pay the fees, see the military career as the best chance for their sons to escape from the exploited ranks of the working class.

If the system of child industrial conscription continues, and there is every indication that it will, the Soviet state by 1960 should have at its disposal from thirty to forty million workers trained on this regimented basis. It will be a new kind of "proletariat." Home influences reminiscent of a freer past and intellectual influences beyond those prescribed by the authorities will have been reduced to a minimum. Fully indoctrinated with Communist tenets and the Stalinist theories of world revolution, they will be people without a memory of personal freedom, willing or unwilling, of the state. These morally and politically maimed Russians will represent a formidable force in the hands of the regime, whether for use at home or in foreign adventures.

This carefully conditioned body of citizens will be supplemented by perhaps twenty million N.K.V.D. forced-labor prisoners, and by a huge standing army of career soldiers and officers, trained from childhood on the basis of Stalinism solely for defense of the Soviet set-up, over and above the ordinary conscript forces and military reserves. Nor should it be forgotten that tens of millions of other children meanwhile will have been indoctrinated in the ordinary Soviet schools, where devotion to the regime and its methods holds first place in the curriculum.

The mental picture of this mobilized humanity, nightmarish in scale, was constantly before me as I negotiated for manpower at the behest of various commissariats, in the effort to fulfill urgent production plans. It seemed to me the closest approach in human terms to the anthill or the beehive. The fact that it was embellished with hypocrisies about the dignity of labor and service to the "socialist" collective, and administered by "working-class leaders" like the slave-master Shvernik, made the picture even more monstrous in my eyes. My "rotten liberalism," clearly, was too deep to be cured.

3

I became conscious of our tragic deficiencies in war supplies almost at the outset. A conference in the Kremlin called by one of Stalin's most powerful assistants, Alexei Kasygin, underlined the facts for me. Because the agenda covered many items centered in my department, Utkin wanted me at his elbow, under instructions not to speak in that august gathering unless I was spoken to.

Kasygin represented the Politburo in the control of five commissariats and was also in charge of the problems of Military Engineering Armament. Long before one in the morning, when the conference was scheduled, the five People's Commissars are on hand in the large reception room. We are somewhat relaxed, the official masks dropped for the moment. These people know each other intimately, even too intimately; the *vlast*, after all, is a closely-knit world. There are pleasantries, some leg-pulling, an exchange of gossip.

Comrade Ginsburg, Commissar for Construction, a fat little man with a bald head and thick eyeglasses, sits in a corner, quietly drinking tea and chewing cookies. A tall man wearing a colored Russian blouse under his jacket is munching an apple; this is Akimov, Commissar for Textiles. I follow his example and dig into the large fruit bowl. Commissar Lukin, head of Light Industry, winks at me. He is famous as a wit and practical joker.

"How long will you torture us here?" Lukin addresses one of Kasygin's men. "I want to eat—bacon and eggs, for instance. And a glass of vodka to wash it down wouldn't hurt either."

"Yes, you'll need strength tonight," the other replies, laughing. "You'll get hell. Better prepare yourself."

Everyone joins in the laughter, except Comrade Sosnin, Commissar of Building Materials, a tall man with a gaunt and gloomy face. The gloom is understandable: his is a thankless job, his commissariat "gets hell" from the bosses as a matter of course at every conference. The contrast to Sosnin's chronic dejection is provided by the cheerful Okopov, Commissar of Machine Construction. Only a little while ago he had been merely the director of a factory in the Urals. Now he is a People's Commissar and reputed to be a court favorite of Mikoyan. His rapid rise in the official firmament is generally credited to his success in producing a new rocket gun, known as a *katusha* and still wrapped in great secrecy.

Okopov is an undersized Armenian with graying hair, a cunning little face and fine eyes.

Then Marshal Vorobiov arrives, accompanied by General Kaliagin. Vorobiov is Stalin's assistant on combat engineering troops and supplies. Since his problems also clear through my Sovnarkom department, we are already acquainted and he greets me warmly. We need one another and both he and Kaliagin are aware how earnestly I'm working to meet the needs of the front. In the midst of the chatter and the tea drinking, our minds are on the big oak doors leading into Alexei Kasygin's chambers. At last these doors are opened.

"Alexei Nikolayevich invites you to the conference," a secretary announces.

A hush descends. Smiles fade out. Everyone assumes his most official mask. In Kasygin's presence we are only one short step removed from the Beloved Leader himself. The room is vast and high-ceilinged, a perfect oval in shape. Portraits of the entire Politburo are evenly spaced around the cream-colored walls. A large radio receiver of foreign make attracts my attention; ordinary mortals are not allowed to possess radios during the war. The conference table, covered with green baize, is large enough to accommodate thirty people.

Kasygin, at the head of the table, wears foreign-made clothes. His expression is grim and his features are as eloquent of sleeplessness and fatigue as my own. He answers the greetings of the Commissars and the Generals with curt nods.

"Be seated," he commands. "The head of GVIUK will report."

GVIUK is the abbreviation of the department under Marshal Vorobiov, who stands up to speak. The fact that he has not been addressed by his name and his title is not lost on any of us, least of all on the Marshal. It's a gruff indication that Kasygin is in a bad mood. We can expect fireworks.

Marshal Vorobiov talks for about fifteen minutes, from a sheaf of notes. He cites figures, more figures. It's a black picture he draws of deficit supplies. There are no motorboats for river crossings, he says, and this is costing us thousands of lives. There are no prefabricated bridges, no mines to slow up the enemy advance, no motorized repair shops, no telephone wire and instruments, no plain stoves for trenches; there are even no axes and shovels for the infantry.

Kasygin's eyes are on the pad before him and he doodles in impatience and irritation. The muscles of his face twitch nervously. *Why is there nothing to counter a satanically efficient and mechanized enemy?* my mind keeps repeating. *Why did we squander those two years of peace?* As he proceeds with the statistics, the Marshal's feelings break through the military crust. There is a catch in his throat as he exclaims:

"People are dying by the thousand at the front this very minute! Why can't we provide them with ordinary shovels and axes, with cutters for barbed wire? Our boys make bridges of their bleeding bodies because they haven't the tools to cut the wire! Comrades, it's shameful, shameful! We have no lanterns—never mind flashlights, just simple kerosene lanterns.

Eight times in the last few months Comrade Stalin has personally ordered these lanterns, but the front still hasn't got them. We are without camouflage equipment. I plead with you comrades who stand at the head of industry, in the name of the simple soldier at the front."

"It's all very clear," Kasygin says in a tense voice, as the Marshal sits down. "What kind of lanterns do you refer to?"

A colonel sitting beside the Marshal lifts a primitive round lantern, a metal frame with glass windows.

"And we can't manufacture this trifle?" Kasygin exclaims angrily.

It happens that I am acquainted with this very problem. With Utkin's permission I speak up.

"Permit me to explain, Alexei Nikolayevich. Production of lanterns is slowed up because we have no sheet metal, no stamping machines, no glass of the proper size and quality. The big sheet-metal plant evacuated from Novomoskovsk is not yet in working order. The glass we can get only from Krasnoyarsk. Perhaps Comrade Sosnin can tell us why it isn't forthcoming."

"The lanterns will be made!" Kasygin suddenly shouts and pounds the table. "I tell you all this criminal inertia must be ended! If I have to rip the lazy hides off the back of scoundrels, war supplies will come through as Comrade Stalin demands! Sosnin—report!"

The lugubrious Sosnin seems crushed. He talks in a hopeless monotone. The machines in Krasnoyarsk are in bad shape, the power station doesn't work, there is no qualified manpower. . . .

Kasygin calls on Akimov and others. Hour after hour the conference grinds on. Every report deepens the prevailing despair. The "bottlenecks" in materials, machines, means of transport seem to grow more numerous— an impenetrable forest of "bottlenecks." Kasygin no longer talks, no longer ask questions. He shrieks, orders, fixes quotas and dates without consulting anyone—and all the People's Commissars, the Generals, fidget guiltily, like a lot of schoolboys being dressed down by a wrathful headmaster. We avoid looking at one another. We all know, and Kasygin knows, that the deficiencies are real, that none of us can perform miracles.

At one point, in the midst of a furious outburst against Commissar Ginsburg, a telephone rings. Obviously Kasygin recognizes the signal. His tone, his facial expression, his very posture change abruptly, become soft, obsequious. "Yes, Josef Vissarionovich. . . . Of course, Josef Vissariono- vich. . . . It will be done! . . . Yes, I'll take immediate measures . . ." he says. Stalin! A tremor of awe and respect sweeps through the men around the table. We all sit as if frozen into statues. Kasygin replaces the receiver quietly, carefully, as if it were made of spun glass. It takes him fully five minutes to swing back into his angry mood of command and abuse.

It's four-thirty in the morning before we are released. Every one of us has been loaded with instructions: half a million camouflage uniforms, a million shovels, a hundred thousand field telephone reels—staggering numbers, dozens of them. We all know that the assignments are impos- sible; if they can be met only by 75 per cent, there will be rejoicing and bonuses and Orders of Merit. We all know, too, that they are deliberately set higher in order to squeeze the last drop of effort from industry and that the needs are far greater than the plans.

At home, I climb the dark staircase to the top floor, feel my way in the dark corridor to our door. Irina stirs. Why am I so late, she asks sleepily; anything wrong? No, no, go to sleep . . . just another conference. The dawn is breaking. . . .

I would attend dozens such Kremlin conferences called by Stalin's deputies: Vosnessensky, Saburov, others. The procedure and the temper of the gatherings were almost exactly as in this Kasygin meeting. Stalin's orders, directives, demands, defying difficulties and insisting on results, dominated all of them.

CHAPTER XXV

THE TWO TRUTHS

As DEPARTMENT head in the Sovnarkom I did not earn half as much as I used to earn in industry, and I received none of the windfall bonuses which factory administrations awarded themselves. But money was meaningless in a time of fearful shortages. What mattered was the size of your rations and the shops in which you were permitted to buy.

And in these respects I was now in the highest, fattest category. I had access to the special stores ("closed distributories" in the pompous official lingo) as well as the shoemaking and tailoring establishments reserved for the *vlast*. In these places I met the *élite* of the Party, the government, the police, the Kremlin; sometimes their wives, chauffeurs and domestics.

Not one Russian in a thousand suspected that such abundant shops existed and, indeed, the authorities operated them discreetly, as far as possible out of sight of the masses. There was usually a line-up of elegant motorcars outside our "closed" food store, for instance, but few passersby knew what they were there for. No ordinary Muscovite got a glimpse, let alone a taste, of the lend-lease and home-made luxury piled up in that shop.

Our purchases, of course, were limited to rationed quotas. But these were far above the average and included items the very memory of which had almost faded out in the general population. I belonged to the category of families exempted from the pressures of *golod* and *kholod,* hunger and cold, which held our people in their merciless grip. The country suffered as cruelly as in the worst civil war years—this after a quarter of a century of "socialist construction" and several successful Five Year Plans.

My monthly *payok* or rations included bacon, canned goods, butter, sugar, flour, salt pork—all brought in from the United States—as well as Soviet fish, fowl, smoked fish, vegetables, vodka, wine, cigarets. Fifteen thousand rubles couldn't buy in the black markets what I carried off in my automobile for about 150 rubles from the "closed" shop, its entrance guarded by a militiaman. If, despite that, there were many days in which my wife went hungry, what was the plight of the average person? Special tailors, working exclusively for the highest officialdom, made suits to order for us out of American and British lend-lease cloth at a time when a second-hand garment fetched thousands of rubles in the open market.

Now and then Moscow clothes shops of the "open" variety—unrationed and therefore dizzily high-priced—had brief flurries of prosperity. The news that consignments of dresses, suits, children's garments had arrived spread like wildfire. Long queues formed instantly, despite the fact that the simplest cotton housedress might cost 500 to 1000 rubles, a pair of socks 50 to 75 rubles, a quite ordinary suit or overcoat 2500 rubles and more. Provided with big bundles of the worn, ragged and often filthy banknotes, people stood for hours, praying that the stocks would hold out until their turn came.

Everyday goods like thread, soap, matches, electric bulbs, table- and kitchenware had virtually disappeared. A pint of kerosene cost 200 rubles in the open market. Even in the center of Moscow electric current was available in residential houses only two or three hours a night; those who couldn't afford kerosene—and that meant the vast majority of people— sat in total darkness behind their blacked-out windows.

In this winter of 1942–43 people burned their furniture, their books, their cherished music scores, anything that might yield a few minutes of warmth. They tore boards from their floors and beams from their roofs to keep their children from freezing to death. People knocked at the doors of starving neighbors of a morning to ask in weak voices: "Vanya—or Maria—are you still alive?"

Irina and I installed a good iron stove in our place, and through the Sovnarkom I obtained some wood. Now and then we spared a bit for our neighbors, though this was a breach of the rules.

Sometimes I wondered whether the evidences of my comparative affluence were not hard on the nerves and tempers of these neighbors. Irina did her cooking on a kerosene stove in the privacy of our own apartment. Though we shared the largesse with friends, we consumed our *payok* with a certain embarrassment. This, after all, was a time when the sight of men and women falling dead of starvation on Moscow streets became too commonplace to attract crowds.

But the dead were buried, the half-dead groaned in their cold homes and the living struggled on. In line of duty I visited a great many factories where output was lagging. Invariably I found that food shortage was one of the main reasons. Where the administration was able to provide at least one fairly nourishing meal, the difference showed up in the tempo of production. "Give us more food and we'll give you more goods," the executives always pleaded. "Our people haven't the strength to meet your deadlines."

Once Pamfilov sent me by automobile to the town of Solnechogorsk, not far from Moscow, to inspect two factories. The milling of plain flour was being held up by the lack of sieves, requiring extra-fine wire which might be manufactured in those factories. I was accompanied by a young stranger, introduced to me as an engineer but obviously an agent of the Economic Department of the N.K.V.D.—not an insulting lack of faith in my honesty but a routine procedure.

The drive took us across an area held for some time by the Germans and devastated by bombs and artillery fire. On both sides of the road we saw smashed German tanks and cars. We passed through villages and hamlets where not a single house was intact. Ghostlike women and children, tattered, vacant-eyed, crawled out of the ruins, and stretched out trembling hands. We had taken along a food package prepared by the Sovnarkom kitchen; but we gave away all of it long before we reached our destination. At many points we encountered large gangs of prisoners under heavy guard working on road repairs.

Solnechogorsk itself had escaped undamaged. I was expected by the factory managers, who proved eager to cooperate. They agreed that their machinery could be converted to make the required wire, but all of them told me the same grim story of acute hunger.

"Our people are willing to work," one of them said. "As you see, we have only very old men, very young children and women who have no factory experience. But they're willing. They remain at their jobs for days at a time if necessary, sleeping in the factory here. But unless they get at least the ordinary bread rations, as in other cities, they won't have the strength to continue."

"Why don't they get the same rations?" I asked in astonishment.

"Because we're located in a farm district. Theoretically, we should rustle our supplies in the countryside. But that's theory. In fact, the peasants themselves are starving. Probably you've seen them along the roads."

My young companion was as disturbed by the picture of misery in those factories as I was. He agreed with me, as we drove back, that any proposal for extracting production from Solnechogorsk was worthless without solving the food problem.

The bosses were away for their evening siesta when I got to my office. By the time they returned, I had a detailed project of a government decision for the immediate conversion and exploitation of the factories drafted. Toward midnight Pamfilov received me. In the presence of Utkin he read my draft. "Good . . . good . . . excellent," he nodded his glistening head. But suddenly his face clouded.

"What is this? 'Five hundred grams of bread a day for the workers and their families. . . . ' "

"Yes," I said eagerly. "That's basic. Those people are plain hungry."

"Strike out this point in the project," Pamfilov ordered.

"But Constantine Gavrilovich, I beg you to leave that in the draft. I admit that a few of the workers may have their own gardens, or relatives among the peasants, but that doesn't help. Those people are doing work and should get the workers' rations."

"I'm as sorry for them as you are, Comrade Kravchenko, but the point must be crossed out."

Before the revised project was sent to Molotov for action, I made another plea to Pamfilov that we emphasize the need of bread to guarantee the operations of the Solnechogorsk factories. The head of the Sovnarkom looked at me with unconcealed irritation.

"Kravchenko, look here. Are you a social worker or a Bolshevik? Humanitarianism is a bad guide in making state decisions. Learn from Comrade Stalin—love the people but sacrifice their needs when essential!"

The fact that the two plants, though provided with sufficient raw materials, did not produce half the fine wire scheduled did not surprise me.

Another journey remains even more sharply etched on my memory. Only a modern Dante in a pessimistic moment could evoke in words that picture of the secret underground factory of the Commissariat of Munitions, operated chiefly with slave labor.

Beyond Podolsk, deep in the Moscow province, only people with special permits were allowed on the train that took us through a thickly forested region. N.K.V.D. officers examined our credentials several times. The train moved slowly, and repeatedly we saw from the windows large numbers of prisoners—there is no mistaking the identity of these unfortunates—cutting and piling up trees and dragging them to the railway lines. Finally we stopped at a dead end of this new rail spur and alighted.

On a clearing stood a munitions plant. In the woods beyond it, invisible, the narrow entrances to their subterranean chambers elaborately camouflaged, were the vast underground shops where thousands of prisoners and free laborers filled grenades, bombs, mines and other munitions with explosives. The entire area embracing this subterranean world was cut off with barbed wire and policed by armed N.K.V.D. guards, some of them accompanied by fierce dogs especially trained for this job.

I had arrived, with a companion, to adjust a conflict between this secret factory and another which supplied some of its materials. After an evening conference with the officials, I was given a room for the night in the plant hotel. Wishing to catch a glimpse of the prisoners going to their work, I arose early. A chilly rain was falling. A little after six I saw a contingent of about four hundred men and women, ten abreast, marching under heavy guard towards the secret workshops.

Through the years I had seen these wretched slaves under all kinds of conditions. I did not suppose I was fated to look on creatures even more tragic than those I had observed in the Urals and in Siberia. Here the horror seemed to have been raised to a more satanic dimension. These faces—of a sickening yellowish color and drained of blood—were shocking death masks. These were walking corpses, hopelessly poisoned by the chemicals with which they worked in a foul purgatory.

Among them were men and women who might have been fifty or more but also young people in their early twenties. They walked in silent dejection, like automatons, looking neither to right nor left. And they were fantastically clad. Many of them wore rubber galoshes, tied to their feet with string; others had bound their feet in rags. Some were in peasant clothes; a few women wore torn astrakhan coats; here and there I noted what remained of good foreign suits. As the grim parade passed the building from which I watched, a woman suddenly collapsed in her tracks. Two guards dragged her off; none of the prisoners paid the slightest attention. They were beyond sympathy, beyond human reactions.

Other such contingents were marching to the underground hell from other directions, from the N.K.V.D. colonies concealed deep in those forests, probably miles away. In the evening I saw a column about twice as long trudging through the rain and mud for the night shift.

I was not allowed to go underground and, indeed, had no stomach for the sight. But from the officials with whom I dealt in the two days there I gathered a sufficiently sharp impression of the piled-up misery and the contempt for human life. The subterranean factory was badly ventilated, having been constructed in panicky haste and with total disregard of the health of its workers. A few weeks in its fumes and stinks were enough to poison the human organism forever. The death rate was high; human beings were shoveled in almost as continually as raw chemicals.

The director of the enterprise was a dour-faced Communist who wore an Order and a row of other decorations on his tunic. When I began to ask questions about his workers he looked at me queerly, as if I were inquiring about the health and comfort of a lot of condemned mules.

"Unfortunately there are not many skilled workers among these creatures," he said, "and I have a lot of trouble with them. You ask me what kind of people the prisoners are, politicals or criminals. That doesn't interest me; it's the business of the N.K.V.D. which provides me with work-hands. All I know is that they're enemies of the people."

For months I could not drive the impression from my consciousness. It colored my feelings even when my mind and my hands were busy with other things. And in the years to come, in a distant country, the memory sometimes would obtrude itself suddenly, persistently, when I heard Americans declaim about the wonders of Soviet communism. I could not help thinking to myself: *If only I could put you fools in that underground factory for two days, no more than two days, you'd be singing another tune!*

2

The one branch of national defense on which the Kremlin had lavished its best men, energies and rhetoric for a dozen years was aviation. Yet our backwardness in this domain became sufficiently clear to me from documents signed by Stalin and Molotov which passed through my department.

Mountains of steel, copper and aluminum had been turned over to Hitler under the economic agreement that accompanied the humiliating pact of "friendship." A large part of what remained had been captured by the invading armies. Aeronautical factories in Kharkov, Kiev, Zaparozhe, Taganrog and other cities had been only partly evacuated; the rest had fallen to the enemy. The result was that our aviators in some cases were flying in aircraft made of plywood. A few incendiary bullets sufficed to finish them off. The casualties in the Russian air forces were higher, I learned, than in those of any other belligerent nation. To make up for the shortage of planes, our pilots flew more missions per day than those of any other nation. The pressure on them was relieved, of course, with the arrival of lend-lease aircraft.

In the autumn of 1942 Stalin issued an urgent secret command for the immediate manufacture of a fire-retarding substance to be used to coat all planes. It was a resinous mixture, based on vinyl chloride, suggested by the Institute of Aviation Materials. Stalin attached the greatest importance to this undertaking which, at its productive end, was concentrated in my department.

There followed weeks of conferences with the heads of the chemical industries and with various aviation bureaus. The suggested formula, it turned out, was highly tentative and incomplete. Ultimately the leaders of the Institute were publicly rewarded for their achievement, but if the truth were known the rewards should have been given to humble chemical engineers and ordinary workers who toiled day and night developing the process. The whole effort, unfortunately, was largely lost motion.

"Assuming that we do succeed in covering the planes with this stuff," I once asked an aviation general in my own office, "will it really help?"

He looked around, as if to make sure there were no strange ears, leaned closer and whispered:

"About as much as ice-cream for a dead man. . . . If hit by the newest German incendiary bullets, the plane will burn like down. Between ourselves, the whole thing is psychological. It may step up morale, for a while at least, among our fliers. They're heroes, every one of them, but they're only human; the use of reconverted civilian aircraft and planes with wooden parts for military purposes is hardly good for their nerves."

Dozens of kinds of instruments, special apparatus and materials had to be manufactured at a forced tempo and under the most unfavorable conditions to bring our aviation into fighting readiness for the impending winter campaigns. The magnitude of our losses made me heartsick.

"All our aviation will be paralyzed this winter unless these special apparatus and instruments are produced, quickly and in the right amounts," Marshal Novikov wrote to Molotov in a secret report that came into my hands.

When I was in charge of plants in the Ukraine, the Urals, Siberia, I used to be exasperated by the incessant calls and telegrams from Moscow and other centers urging speed and more speed. Now, by a turn of the wheel, I was at the sending end. I was continually phoning, telegraphing, begging and demanding. I knew too intimately how annoying this was and often how futile. Yet I persevered. Time was of the essence, and I was myself under relentless pressure from superiors.

Was production held up by lack of some vital material, equipment or manpower? I roused the commissariats which produced the material or equipment, the organizations which controlled manpower—if necessary I put the State Defense Committee, the Party organs, the proper Kremlin officials on the job—and somehow what was needed was provided.

The extraordinary part of it is that the apparatus for which Marshal Novikov pleaded did come through, in the quantity and of the quality prescribed in Stalin's order on the subject. Control of airplane manufacture was concentrated in Molotov's hands, but most of the orders were signed by Stalin himself. To speed up output I drafted plans for supplying workers in certain plants with bread and hot meals, and they were put into effect when Stalin signed them. We rushed oxygen balloons from Gorki to Moscow by automobile. We flew calcium carbide across the front lines from Erivan to Moscow. And in the end the necessary apparatus was produced. Soon, under Kremlin instructions, I was drafting the project of a decree on rewards for those who had contributed most effectively to the fulfilment of the task. The decree, essentially as I had composed it, was published in the press. In a few days Marshal Novikov called me up.

"Comrade Kravchenko," he said in a voice vibrant with feeling, "I want to thank you in the name of our aviators. I have told a lot of them about your devoted work and I want you to know we are all grateful."

The problem of reels for field telephones, too, was a chronic headache. The responsibility for the supply of means of communication at the fronts was centered in Comrade Saburov, one of Stalin's deputies, and my contacts were therefore largely with his office. Specific directives, however, were signed by Stalin personally. At a long night session in the Kremlin, presided over by Saburov and attended by an array of commissars, production plans were discussed and checked. Because there was no sheet metal, it was decided, after long arguments, to make the reels of wood, despite the heated objections of the military spokesmen.

About a month later, representatives of all the commissariats involved and the appropriate military officials, sat in my office. One after another they reported on results. Only one man, an assistant commissar, seemed cheerful.

"Our plans for means of communication," he announced, "have been over-fulfilled—105 per cent!"

That there was something askew with the picture I knew immediately. His commissariat had delivered only a negligible quantity of finished products and instruments. In perplexity not unmixed with anger I insisted that he explain the miraculous figure. He did. It appeared quickly that some parts of the apparatus had been produced up to 270 per cent of requirements, while other elements were available only to the extent of 30 per cent. His proud announcement referred to an *average*. It represented a typical bureaucratic statistical achievement. Actually, of course, the lowest figure determined the number of full sets assembled. His commissariat at best had done only 30 per cent of its job.

Everyone laughed at the man's discomfiture. But it was no laughing matter. As the generals present explained, inadequate telephonic supplies were costing us thousands of lives and sometimes losing battles. The "bottleneck," it appeared, was in the manufacture of those reels. The factories were far behind schedule even with the wooden substitutes decided upon in the Kremlin.

It was in this connection that I visited a wood-products plant on the outskirts of Moscow to check personally why the spools were not being delivered. The director explained that he did not have enough skilled labor; only a few people, I saw, were working on this order.

"And what's going on in here?" I asked, walking into another shop, where production seemed in full blast.

What I saw made me livid with rage. About a hundred and fifty men were engaged in making elegant furniture: divans, desks, mirrored dressers, capacious armchairs, mostly of the best mahogany.

"No skilled workers you say! But here you're wasting them on fancy furniture. Divans—while men are dying in the field! It's a crime and I warn you I'll make a scandal!"

The director did not seem alarmed. He shrugged his shoulders and I thought I detected a suppressed smile at the corners of his mouth.

"I don't blame you for getting mad," he said. "In fact, I'm pretty mad myself. But I'm only a little man. What can I do except obey *big* men? Come to my office, I'll show you."

In his office he produced the records. The furniture had been ordered by top Party, government and Red Army officials, among them, I recall, Vassili Pronin, chairman of the Moscow city Soviet; General Moukhin and Shcherbakov, Secretary of the Central Committee.

I rushed back to the Sovnarkom, still in a temper, and barged into Utkin's office. I began to lay the facts before him. He could hardly credit his ears.

"Making fancy armchairs instead of war supplies ordered by Comrade Stalin!" he exclaimed. "It's outrageous! Those responsible should be put into prison!"

"Agreed—and I'm happy you feel as I do, Andrei Ivanovich! But the director showed me he's making these civilian goods for Comrade Pronin, Shcherbakov, General Moukhin——"

Utkin's expression changed instantly. The brief fury faded out of his eyes.

"So? For Shcherbakov . . . I see," he muttered, squirming. "Yes . . . hmm . . . quite a problem. I suppose the comfort of our leaders is also a war priority. . . . Let me think it over."

He thought it over for a long time, while the factory continued to work on furniture, and the Red Army pleaded for telephone reels, butt ends for rifles, etc. Several times, not without a touch of malice, I admit, I revived the question, but without results. I did not dare to go over Utkin's head to Saburov, and Utkin obviously had no wish to make political enemies.

In the War Engineering Department it was inevitable that I should be initiated into one of the best-guarded and most distressing secrets of Russia at war. It was a secret that weighed heavily on all who shared it. Only the victorious end of the war makes it possible to speak of it.

The fraction of the Russian population equipped with gas masks was small. Even in Moscow only about every fourth person had one; in the rest of the country the situation was far worse; the great majority of villages and smaller towns had none at all. But that was only half the tragedy. The horrifying secret was that few of these masks, whether in the soldiers' kits or in the possession of civilians, were any good. The official estimate was that at least 65 per cent of the masks produced during the war were utterly useless. The principal reason was that, lacking rubber, we were obliged to use a rubberized canvas which failed to seal the wearer's face hermetically. There was also a serious lack of sheet iron, glass and other items entering into mask manufacture.

If the Germans had known this, it is not unlikely that they would have unloosed chemical warfare on a terrifying scale. If they did know it, then we must assume that the warnings of ruthless poison-gas reprisals issued by Roosevelt and Churchill saved millions of my people, on the battlefields and in the population centers.

Once, facing a high military official in the chemical warfare section, I asked him point blank why he accepted these masks.

"But what is the alternative?" he replied, shrugging his shoulders in a gesture of despair. "No masks at all! In this way we have at least the psychological or morale value."

Late one night I happened to be with Utkin as he was preparing to go home. I saw him go to the safe and take out several new, well-made gas masks. Apparently my face mirrored my thoughts.

"Don't look so accusingly," he smiled. "These are for my wife and children. Who knows when it will come. . . . There's no reason for panic, but common sense requires vigilance."

"But Andrei Ivanovich, why don't you use the masks being issued to the public?"

"Are you crazy?" he exclaimed, and then, placatingly, "I'll see about a couple for you and your wife."

With respect to gas shelters the situation for the general population was even worse. The few built could, in case of a gas assault, have accommodated only a tiny fraction of the people in the big cities and most of them were badly constructed, not hermetically sealed. The smaller towns and villages, of course, possessed no shelters at all.

In Moscow the Kirovskaya station of the subway had been converted into a gas retreat for high officials; and there were shelters in the various commissariats. In our Sovnarkom we had one complete with carpets, a buffet, a library. But this was not much consolation for the ordinary citizen. The picture was no brighter in the matter of anti-chemical war defenses, despite the fact that this phase of the struggle had been assigned by the Politburo to the Special Chemical Troops of the N.K.V.D.

But if we had difficulties with gas masks, field telephones, tank parts, mobile weapons, airplanes, we made up for it in at least one respect. One night, while I was working on a stack of reports, Utkin asked me to come into his office. There I found him engrossed in what at first looked like a strange game. Laid out on his desk, on chairs, all around, were strips of board covered with cloth of gold and silver.

"Shoulder straps!" he explained happily.

Scattered around the room, also, were artistic sketches of uniforms in all the services, from Marshals down to lieutenants, showing these items in their proper settings. The fact that the shoulder decorations, once hated as a symbol of Tsarist militarism, would be restored had not yet been made public. The decision had been made by the Politburo and in due time would be "confirmed" by the Supreme Soviet. But production of the item was already under way and these were a selection of samples.

"I'm taking them to the Kremlin," Utkin said. "Comrade Stalin personally will pass on them. Aren't they beautiful?"

He was in a playful mood. What would I like to be, he wanted to know—a Marshal? an admiral? He picked the proper epaulettes and put them on my shoulders.

"No, no, these don't quite fit," he said with mock gravity. "Maybe you'll settle for these—a mere colonelcy, but pretty."

"Andrei Ivanovich," I said, "will not this revival of shoulder straps and the new uniforms be accepted by many as a return to Russian imperialism?"

He laughed.

"What a silly notion! Who cares what some idiots at home or abroad think? The hearts under the gilded shoulders will be true Soviet hearts, beating in unison, just as our men are fighting in unison for Comrade Stalin's ideas." He paused and added slowly, for emphasis, "Besides, if some people do assume it marks a return to imperialism, even that may be politically useful. It will make friends for our country in certain circles."

3

The Party Committee in every Soviet organization, large or small, is the heart of the dictatorial power, just as the Special Department, representing the N.K.V.D., is its strong right arm. The Committee acts for the Party members (normally a tiny minority in any Soviet organization) and supervises their ideological purity; it controls the political activities of the organization and guides the political thought of all the employees. But its authority is also in large measure temporal, so to speak. The secretary of the Committee, though he may remain in the background, is the real master. In the final analysis the head of a trust or a factory takes his orders on all political issues from the highest Party functionary.

In the Sovnarkom, too, we had a Party Committee and carried on a great number of purely Party activities. But there was this difference: Since the Sovnarkom is itself the government, deriving its authority from the Politburo and the Central Committee, it was not subordinated to the Party Committee. At the head of our Party Committee stood a veteran Communist, Mironov. He ruled supreme in all matters of "faith," as it were—political morals, analysis of events and the like. But in the actual work of the organization he could not interfere with Pamfilov, Utkin and others who were the temporal chiefs.

Thus it happened that our Party meetings were conducted on a somewhat higher plane than in most places. We rarely touched on specific Sovnarkom problems, applying ourselves to discussion of larger policies and articles of faith. All the responsible posts, of course, were held by Communists and the proportion of Party members even on the lower levels was unusually high. The Party gatherings were therefore very nearly mass meetings of the whole apparatus.

Foreigners who try to understand Stalin's policies or "the Soviet mind" by studying the Soviet press and the Kremlin's public actions usually come up with a truckload of gibberish. Not one in a thousand among them has grasped the Bolshevik idea of "two truths"—one for the masses, for the world at large, and another for the Party faithful, the initiated, the insiders. At a time when a certain line of propaganda or action is being conducted publicly, Party people might be instructed to disregard it or even instructed to believe the exact opposite.

At this critical stage in the war, a "retreat from Leninism"—in form, not in substance—was considered necessary. "Backward elements" at home and in Eastern Europe had to be pacified with a seeming restoration of religion. The morale values of old-fashioned national patriotism had to be exploited to the limit. Ultimately, though somewhat later, capitalist allies would be placated by "disbanding" the Communist International.

The outside world, and the majority of our own people, accepted all this eagerly as proofs of a change of heart by the Soviet leaders. I was to see articles and books in which this "retreat" was hailed as marking the Kremlin's break with the idea of world revolution. There were even "experts" who announced stupidly that the Soviet Union was edging away from dictatorship and closer to capitalism. They professed to see the democratic and the Soviet totalitarian ways of life moving towards a common ground somewhere in the middle.

Had any one of these experts sat in on our "closed" weekly Party sessions for the higher personnel, he would have been shocked. For us, the "retreat from Leninism" was simply *a temporary tactical maneuver*. The compromise with religion was a humiliating but indispensable concession. Precisely because our Party and regime, in this moment of travail, were forced to compromise, we were exhorted to fortify our devotion to Communism and our inner faith that these tactical retreats were moves in a strategy of Stalinist advance and ultimate victory.

No properly indoctrinated Communist felt that the Party was "lying" in professing one set of policies in public and its very opposite in private. He had no more conscience about it than a general in the field who misleads and disorients the enemy. Until the whole earth has been transformed into a single Soviet Union under the sun of Stalinism, the General Staff of the Revolution—meaning our leaders in the Kremlin—would have to maneuver, now attacking, now lying low, sometimes retreating to consolidate positions, always exploiting the contradictions among capitalist nations. Bourgeois moralizers who prate about double-dealing and perfidy are, to the Bolshevik "realist," just ludicrous leftovers from a dead past and hypocrites to boot.

In the Party work there was no trace of the "profound changes" that had supposedly taken place in the Soviet regime. Except for the fact that the war and its tasks were talked about, a meeting of Party activists was no different now in its political essence, its tone and obsessions, than before the war.

At ten in the evening we foregather for our weekly meeting. Comrade Mironov presides under a huge picture of Lenin; other important comrades are with him on the rostrum. Comrade Yudin, head of government publishing agencies but now representing the Agitation-Propaganda section of the Central Committee of the Party, is our guest tonight. Because we know that he is one of Stalin's foremost theoreticians, we are keyed up to listen attentively. His theme is world affairs. But what he says will not be merely "opinions," in the Western sense. It will represent prescribed beliefs and attitudes from which we dare not deviate—from which, in fact, it would not occur to a faithful Communist to deviate. Yudin will speak with the voice of Stalin, the voice of the Party and the Soviet dictatorship.

But before he begins, another comrade gives us a sketch of the military position. He does not deny the extent of our losses or the magnitude of the danger. Stalingrad is the test. We dare not and we shall not fail. Should Stalingrad fall, should the Germans cross the Volga, we would be cut off from oil; the whole war effort might be paralyzed. But that isn't all:

"Comrades, we must all understand that Stalingrad is not just another city. It is the city named for Stalin, the *vozhd* of world Communism. At Stalingrad two ways of life meet in a death grapple: capitalism in its fascist form and Communism. The armies of Hitler—and the force of the Stalinist idea. As Lenin put it: *kto kovo?* who will conquer whom? The city of Stalin cannot and shall not be given up, whatever the cost. We shall cling to every stone, every brick. Vast reserves of men and materiel are being prepared for this historical duel. The Germans will be drowned in their own blood. The world will know what the beloved name Stalin means. Stalingrad will stand through the centuries as a glorious monument to the genius of our Beloved Leader."

When the applause subsides, Comrade Yudin takes the floor. We listen with every pore of our bodies. Though a Marxist theoretician, he leavens his address with satire. It is his strong suit and he gives us plenty of it, at the expense not only of the Hitler clique, but of the whole rotten, degenerate capitalist world.

In England and America, Yudin tells us, a mighty tide of faith in the Soviet system is rising among the masses. He quotes from Priestley, Laski and others. Neither the Churchills, the Roosevelts nor their socialist and "labor" lackeys can stop it. In England the social fascist Clement Attlee is often the guest of the fascist Lady Astor. Make your own deductions, comrades!

"The English bourgeoisie understands that the war is revolutionizing the masses. It's more important to them to head off that horror than to beat the Germans. But how to do it? The so-called 'Labor Party' must divert the armed masses to keep them from taking power under the leadership of the British Communist Party and the Communist International."

The seeming struggle between Churchill and the Labor opposition, according to Yudin, is therefore just shadow boxing. Both groups are working together to hold down the proletariat and both are ready to sing *God Save the King*.

"As for their attitude to Russia," he declares, "the Laborite leaders love us about as much as we love Hitler."

The quip draws laughter and scattered applause. A thrust at Laborites and other such spurious "democrats" is always good showmanship at a Party session. Turkey and Japan then come in for instalments of Yudin's vitriol. We know, he shouts, that Matsuoko—the man whom Comrade Stalin honored by seeing him off at the railroad station—urged his Mikado to make war on Russia when the Germans were pressing for Moscow, before Pearl Harbor. Japan and its Matsuokos will get what's coming to them after we've disposed of the Hitler gang!

"In Turkey, General Erkilet and a gang of yelping journalists—with the tacit approval of the government, of course—unloose a wild anti-Soviet campaign. A day of reckoning with these good, sweet neighbors of ours will come, we may be sure. . . .

"I come now to America, comrades. There the Roosevelt policy of playing along with the Soviets as long as it's useful has evoked a strong opposition, as is only natural in the greatest stronghold of capitalism. The opposition is led by former President Herbert Hoover and certain reactionary Senators and other people in the pay of Morgan, Rockefeller and duPont, supported by the fascist and semi-fascist press of Hearst, McCormick and the rest and a large band of mercenary journalists.

"Comical as it may sound to us, these people think that Roosevelt has sold out to the U.S.S.R. and to Communism. They don't understand that Roosevelt, like Attlee, represents the last outpost against inevitable Communism. They don't understand that his war alliance with the U.S.S.R. is just a marriage of convenience. We hate capitalism as much as they hate us. We will never, never retreat from the tasks set before us and before history by Lenin and Stalin!"

Loud hand-clapping confirms that if Americans don't understand it, at least we do.

"Comrades," Yudin resumes, "our war partnership with the capitalist nations must not breed illusions. We must hold fast to fundamentals. There are two worlds. Now and then it is possible to throw a bridge across the gulf that divides them, as we have done in this war. But we know that the bridge must collapse sooner or later. The two worlds of capitalism and Communism cannot forever exist side by side. *Kto kovo?*— who will conquer whom?—remains the great question, now as always. It represents the chief problem of the future.

"As long as we live in a capitalist encirclement we are in danger, comrades. Never forget that. Don't fall into errors of thinking on the basis of lend-lease. It's a bargain, in which we are paying dearly with our sacrifices of Soviet blood and Soviet soil. Do not exaggerate the new and unnatural 'friendship.' Remember always that we Party members are the soldiers of Lenin and Stalin and know how to judge the substance of capitalism."

When Yudin finishes, we all stand up and sing the *Internationale*. Whatever recondite meanings others may read into the "retreats" from Communist doctrine, we on the higher levels of the Communist faith know that they are temporary concessions only. They are changes in the forms of the international Communist movement, not in essence—only fools think they mean a repudiation of the movement.

Ideologically refreshed, we return to our various offices. But the "big boys"—Yudin, Pamfilov and a few others—betake themselves to the buffet for a little physical refreshment. With great relish they devour American lend-lease luxuries while, continuing to discuss the theme of the meeting, they enjoy in anticipation the downfall of the capitalist world.

On a subsequent occasion the lecturer was Vladimir Potiomkin, the well-known Soviet diplomat. His views, of necessity, dovetailed into Yudin's—no one in Soviet Russia, of course, has personal opinions; everyone embellishes or reiterates the prescribed "line." But Potiomkin, as a

specialist in foreign affairs, was more explicit about the future of various
European countries. His "opinions," and those of all Central Committee
speakers, reflected the theory of the Party.

Where we must retreat to rear positions ideologically, they emphasized,
it is only to build new bases for new advances. They regarded it as certain
that Communists would enter into the governments of defeated and
liberated countries when victory was achieved. For that purpose the
reserves of revolutionary force and personnel must be safeguarded and
expanded. Capitalism would be attacked from above, through its own
governments, and from below, through mass action.

The most galling of the compromises made necessary by war was in
relation to religion. The clergy had been permitted to write and enabled
to publish a book called *The Truth About Religion in the U.S.S.R.* in
which they signalized reconciliation with the Soviet system. Though few
people among us attached too much significance to the book, we heard
that it created a sensation abroad. With a view to directing our thinking
on this whole embarrassing subject, Mironov called the Party activists
to his office.

"Comrades," he explained, "we have had to make some concessions
to believers, especially as so many of the Red Army soldiers are drawn
from backward villages where religion still has a considerable hold. Also,
the enemy is making use of our anti-religious attitudes for propaganda
purposes, and the improved relations with the Russian Church cuts the
ground from under them. Then there is another important consideration:
our armies soon will be moving into Slav countries which have not had
the benefit of Communist education. Of what value will the Pan-Slav
Committee in Moscow be if we continue the old policy with regard to
the church?

"Our new religious policy will be valuable in smashing the anti-
Soviet propaganda of the Roman Catholic, Lutheran and other religious
groups. Therefore do not underestimate the wisdom of our Party's action.
We must, in the next period, take a broad view of the problem. We have
the chance to draw the Orthodox Church in other countries closer to
Russia and make Moscow the Third Rome."

"But Comrade Mironov," one of the men present spoke up, "isn't there
a danger that the new generation, which will one day take our place, may
be spoiled by religious superstition?"

"Don't worry on that score," he replied, smiling. "There is neither
soil nor sap on which religion can feed in the U.S.S.R. After all, the press,
theatre, radio, schools, literature, all the forces of the mind are in the
Party's sole control. It's clear to everyone that a young man with religious
inclinations cannot possibly make a career. If he is not on our side
spiritually and politically, there is no place for him. This is our supreme
advantage.

"Remember, the Church is separated from the state—and the schools
are in the hands of the state. The Comsomols, you may be sure, will be a
stronger force than the priests. Are we such idiots that we will turn over
the new generation to the priests?"

It was all clear to us—another stratagem for temporary tactical purposes, at home and abroad. It was also clear to us that in discussing the subject with "the masses," we must present the turn in policy as genuine and permanent.

"Even the less developed Party members," Mironov cautioned us, "are not able to understand all that's involved. Great care must be exercised in talking to them about the subject."

When the Communist International was ostensibly abolished, in May, 1943, I was no longer working in the Sovnarkom. But the explanations at closed meetings of important Communists were consistent with what men like Yudin and Potiomkin had told us. Only in the *formal* sense had the worldwide organization been ended, we were given to understand. In fact, the apparatus and personnel and integration of the International must be strengthened now that it would have to operate underground. "Throughout the world, comrades, the forces of our revolution are preparing for struggle—and for victory."

In the fanfare around the supposed dissolution of the International, it was quite forgotten that Stalin's book, *Problems of Leninism,* remained the supreme guide in Communist doctrinal matters. And in that book Stalin leaves no doubt of his belief that the "victorious proletariat"— meaning the U.S.S.R.—has not only a right but a sacred obligation to use force to achieve revolution in other countries when the opportunity presents itself. The established revolutionary regime, Stalin declares, must provide help to the rest of the world, *"acting when necessary even with military power against exploiting classes and their states."*

And the official Stalinist *History of the Party* likewise remained in force and is in circulation today wherever Stalin's followers and fellow-travelers exist. It is explicit enough. "The All-Union Communist Party," the preamble to that book declares, "took and is now taking as its guide the revolutionary teaching of Marxism-Leninism. . . . Studies of the history of the Party strengthen the belief in the ultimate victory of the great task of Lenin and Stalin, *the victory of Communism in the whole world."*

Since these opinions have never been withdrawn, one is prompted to speculate, with a shudder, as to what might have happened if Stalin's state—rather than the United States—had been the first to develop the atomic bomb!

This is not a far-fetched speculation. Russian scientists and intellectuals generally, regardless of their political attitudes, worked loyally and ably to help achieve victory. They helped overcome shortages by producing new strategic materials and gave their country the advantage of surprise in a series of new weapons. It was an open secret that atomic research was being pushed hard under Stalin's own direction.

Toward the end of 1942 we heard the rumor that Stalin had received the head of the Academy of Science, Professor Komarov, and the director of the Physics Institute, Academician Kapitza, in a special conference devoted to atomic energy. Soviet Military Intelligence was exerting itself mightily to obtain secrets of the atomic problem in other countries. At the session of the Academy held in December, 1942, in Sverdlovsk, a lot was said about progress in mining rare metals, including uranium. In

Communist circles it was boasted that Kapitza was achieving amazing results in his work on splitting the atom.

If the Kremlin had possessed the atomic bomb before the world's leading democracy did, would Stalin have used it to promote revolutions of the variety he favored? My answer is only a personal opinion. But it is based on a life-long knowledge of the Bolshevik mind, its boldness, its amoralism when duty to the cause is involved. That answer is *Yes*.

At the very time when the supposed dissolution of the Communist International was announced, bringing joy to the hearts of more naive capitalist allies, I happened to visit the cellar storehouse of "International Book," an organization publishing foreign-language propaganda. There I saw great stacks of freshly printed Party-line literature for distribution in the countries which the Red Army was about to enter. In theory the International was dead; in fact the Central Committee of the Party was hastily preparing for the ideological conquest of Europe along with the military conquest. The personnel of the "abolished" International was being feverishly reorganized for the immense jobs ahead in Germany, France, Poland, Hungary, Italy and all other countries.

The hoped-for conquest of Europe would be achieved by a potent mixture of faith and force. In an array of red buildings in the heart of Moscow, not far from the Kuznetzky Most, selected Chekists were being trained intensively for work abroad, in the liberated Soviet areas and non-Soviet countries as well. These men were all of officer rank and Communists. They were the cream of the police *élite*. They were being prepared for the historical task of "purging" the populations which had been under German occupation and influence—and in the N.K.V.D. lexicon "purge" is a word of terrifying import.

These newly-trained police contingents accompanied the Red Army and the N.K.V.D. troops in the triumphant drive westward. Usually they concealed their police identity by wearing regular army insignia instead of the crimson N.K.V.D. label. In particular they were primed for the arduous and bloody business of disposing of Soviet citizens, millions of them, who might be considered "undesirable" after their temporary vacation from Soviet control. The "loyalty" of countless millions who had already suffered under the Nazi heel had to be measured with the brutal yardsticks of Soviet policedom. Chiefly under the charge of collaboration with the Germans, thousands would be shot, hundreds of thousands exiled, in a fearsome reign of terror. Unspeakable horrors would be inflicted by these *élite* killers on the populations of Voronezh, Rostov, Smolensk, Northern Caucasus, every other region, as the Germans retreated.

Men, women and children who had worked under Germans simply to earn their bread, often under compulsion, were rounded up and put to death without a pretense of investigation, let alone trial. Vast armies of wretched Soviet citizens were herded into cattle cars and shipped to the rear, for slave labor in concentration camps and colonies. The total of these deportees to swell the forced-labor contingents without doubt reached many millions by the time the war was ended. The same sort of "cleansing" took place, of course, in the non-Soviet lands which the Red Army penetrated.

Certainly there were real collaborators, real traitors, who merited punishment. But to assume that treachery had reached the gigantic scale implied by the N.K.V.D. repressions in liberated regions would be a cruel insult to the Russian peoples. With its characteristic disregard of human life, the police-state extended its definition of collaboration and treason to cover anyone who had uttered one imprudent word against the Stalinist dictatorship, expressed one doubt of the "socialism" imposed by the Kremlin.

Truth demands that we acknowledge the grim fact: millions of my people exchanged German enslavement for Soviet enslavement.

4

I became thoroughly acquainted with the system and organization of our government; with the mechanism of administration as it functioned in fact, which had little relation to the mechanism prescribed on paper, in Constitutions. This reality is hidden as in a deep pit, not only from foreigners but from our own people. Nothing short of a treatise on the Soviet power would suffice to convey that reality. Here I must content myself by stating the bold fact that the governing of the U.S.S.R., Soviet in form, is a Party affair in substance. Neither the Council of People's Commissars nor the Supreme Soviet is more than an extension of the Central Committee of the Party and of the Politburo.

Because my post was now so close to the pinnacle I heard plenty of what might be described as the higher inside information. Where the press is completely controlled, there is a ready market for word-of-mouth news. In Moscow, rumors spread faster probably than anywhere else in the world, if only because there was no machinery for overtaking and refuting them. Denials only served to fortify them. Unusual information, particularly if it was touched with piquancy and slightly illicit, was highly prized and shared only with one's most deserving friends.

A quarrel between top leaders, the rise of one official and the disgrace of another, the doings in Stalin's Secretariat, a piquant remark by The Boss himself—these were the raw stuffs of eager confidences. I came to know that Kaganovich and Andreyev, both in the Politburo, hated each other and intrigued continually for primacy in Stalin's favor; that Mikoyan and Molotov competed for preferred position in The Leader's affections; that the rising star, Vosnessensky, and the old star Kaganovich, were constantly at odds—Vosnessensky had treated Kaganovich with contempt at an official session; that Mekhlis, head of the Political Department of the Red Army, had been quietly removed from his influential post because, as a Jew, he had become an effective target of Nazi propaganda among our more backward soldiers; that Stalin's favorite son, Vassili, was in continuous trouble through drink, girls and reckless driving.

Just before leaving for his post as Ambassador to Mexico, the late

Constantine Oumansky, previously our Ambassador in Washington, suffered a shocking personal tragedy. His young daughter had been keeping company with the equally young son of Shakhurin, Commissar of the Aviation Industry. One night there was a jealous quarrel between them and the boy killed the Oumansky girl with his father's revolver. The higher official levels rang with the crime for days but not a word percolated to the Moscow press.

The most stimulating subject of off-record chatter, however, was Stalin himself. His every remark was chewed over and analyzed. His likes and dislikes, the state of his health, his habits and foibles excited more interest among his courtiers than the progress of the war or the fate of the world revolution. I learned that Stalin's hobbies were chess and billiards and that he played both games well enough to enjoy contests with the best chess masters and billiard champions. The favorite wines of The Boss, I was informed in tones worthy of such state secrets, were Kakhetinsky and Kagor, both Caucasian brands.

We were all aware that Stalin had a weakness for proverbs, both Russian and Georgian, and often employed them to cut discussions short. Having concluded his pact with Hitler, he was reported to have sat silently while its implications were being discussed in the Politburo. Finally he summed up the situation with one of his favorite sayings: "I don't guarantee the taste of the dish, but it will be hot!" Sometimes, when people talked too long, he would suggest softly, "Turn the goose over or it'll be over-roasted!" Or, when the speaker failed to come to the point, he might say: "You low like a cow in labor, but where's the calf?"

At a Central Committee meeting Stalin, addressing himself to the self-important dignitaries of his regime, declared: "If your work doesn't improve immediately, we'll spank you"—and after a pause for the threat to sink in—"not literally, but we'll spank you. That's all."

Stalin is reputed to like music but his tastes, alas, are not especially elevated and his understanding of it limited. This, of course, does not deter him from solving musical problems and judging musical creations. The story of how he pushed young Shostakovich into the outer darkness for a period is well known. Less known is the episode involving the young composer Tikhon Khrennikov. His opera *In the Tempest* was hailed enthusiastically by Moscow critics. Then The Boss saw the production and said he didn't like it. Instantly the critics reversed themselves. The opera was removed and hasn't been heard since.

There is one story about Stalin which I never quite believed but which is generally credited among his intimates. It is to the effect that when facing great decisions, he likes to "consult" the dead Lenin in the granite mausoleum on Red Square. According to this story he has been known to spend hours alone in the tomb with his thoughts. A high-ranking Chekist told me at one time:

"I don't dabble in spiritualism, but this is true: When the Germans were at the doors of Moscow, just before Lenin's body was secretly removed beyond the Urals, Stalin remained alone with the corpse for a few hours."

In those uppermost circles it was firmly believed that Stalin is deeply superstitious and has been known to alter plans because the "signs" were unfavorable. Perhaps uniquely among dictators and successful politicians, he is essentially a lone wolf, jealous of his privacy and given to locking himself away for long periods of solitary thinking. He goes into large gatherings rarely and unwillingly, only when political exigencies require it, and at such times he has a talent for behaving like "one of the boys."

I was told in great detail, by a colleague who was present, about a party which Stalin gave for flyers and others who had distinguished themselves in the fighting. When these men returned to the fronts they were able to report that the Vozhd—Russian equivalent for Führer—was a simple and unpretentious fellow. He had joined in their games, their drinking, their jokes and singing, besides loading them with presents.

Those who knew him long and closely, when they talked about The Boss, agreed that he was a "tough" man, trusting only force, and wile, which he regards as a type of force. He is extremely vengeful and has never been known to forgive or forget an offense. When he seemingly yields, in the course of a conflict, it is only to improve his position for a new attack from the rear. And he has tended to surround himself with men of the same tough stamp—forceful, unforgiving, devoid of scruples.

At bottom, of course, Stalin is a lonely man and knows it. In the course of the years he has felt impelled to kill nearly all of his closest friends and comrades—even men like Abel Yenukidze, with whom he had grown up and whom he had long counted as his most intimate friend. The murder of Kirov and the death of his fellow-Georgian Ordzhonikidze left great voids in his private life. His most intimate friends in recent years have been Mikoyan, Voroshilov, Beria and Molotov.

Stalin's distrust of those around him, however, is pathological and makes no exceptions even for the people in his good graces at any given moment. There is little doubt that he believes every one of them, if not now scheming against him, is potentially a schemer.

Such was the trend of the inside information. Stalin was perhaps the only one of the Kremlin leaders whose name was seldom touched by scandal. Tales involving ballerinas, actresses, drunken parties and the like were constantly being retailed about other leaders, but never about The Boss. His attempt to keep his fingers on every important phase of national life presumably leaves him no time for such indulgences. His reading is serious—Clausewitz, Chekhov, Saltykov—and his fund of information on economic and political affairs amazes people who come in contact with him.

Stalin's penchant for solitude and his aversion to public appearances, most of us believed, were not necessarily connected with his unprepossessing appearance. The court painters, and even photographers who have made millions of images of the man, have concealed the fact that he is short, squat and paunchy; that his complexion is darker, more Asiatic, than most people know; that his face is pockmarked, his left arm partly warped, his teeth uneven and half-rotted. If his physical shortcomings have given him an inferiority complex, it may explain why he swallows Byzantine flattery that would turn a normal stomach.

It may also help explain the fantastic fashion in which the facts of his early life, before the revolution, have been doctored to make them more glamorous. For instance, the Tsarist police archives list him often as a bookkeeper; I have personally seen such documents. To this day he has a remarkable professional competence with figures and statistical balance sheets. Yet this humble and in no way discreditable fact has never been permitted to see print.

A good deal of bitter truth could be heard about Stalin's supposed preference for Caucasians, that is to say Georgians and Armenians, over Russians. It was said that he trusted them and understood them better than Russians with whom, after all, he has nothing in common by race or early training. Caucasians are only a negligible fraction of the total Soviet population, yet they are ubiquitous in the regime. Beria, until recently at the head of the police system; Mikoyan the boss of all foreign and domestic trade, Pogosian and Kavtaradze as Molotov's chief assistants, Commissars Okopov and Tevosian, Deputy Commissars Dadyan and Aroutiunov, a hundred others—all Georgians or Armenians.

As November 7 approached, all minds in the organization turned to the holiday. The anniversary of the revolution would be celebrated in a generous spirit despite the disasters at the front, in defiance of the disasters. As usual it was expected that a big-hearted government would issue special rations to mark the occasion, and this year the prospect of something to eat naturally blotted out most other interests.

Offices were decorated, floors were polished, the prescribed slogans for the holiday were posted everywhere. A holiday spirit pervaded our building. Pamfilov toned down his abuse of his subordinates and each of us, in turn, toned down his abuse of those under him. On November 6 the lower employes, including charwomen, floor-polishers and errand boys, came to work equipped with shopping bags made of meshed string. Such bags were standard equipment for the Soviet citizen; one could put them easily into a back pocket in readiness for any windfall of edibles.

Finally the great news was disclosed. On the anniversary occasion, as tokens of Stalin's deep affection for his subjects, every employee in the Sovnarkom would receive one kilo (2 1/5 pounds) of white bread, five kilos of potatoes and three pounds of honey! Excitement ran so high that it was impossible to do any work. The munificence of the presents, of course, was an indication of the influence wielded by Pamfilov. The potatoes would mean a good meal for a whole family; and the honey was better than gold to people long starved for sugar.

"Ekh, you dear little potato, my darling . . ." the skinny, gray-haired Ivanov, floor polisher, sang all morning.

He seemed scarcely the same self-effacing little man whom we saw skating on the wooden blocks on our fine parquet floors. Upon him had been imposed the honor of weighing out the potatoes and he had blossomed forth under the great responsibility. Another man—bold, understanding but not weak, just yet human—had been hidden under the unassuming surface of the emaciated Ivanov. Now that inner man had

emerged and was presiding over the distribution of potatoes, weighing
out five kilos without fear or favor. On such a day, what was Pamfilov
compared with Ivanov, the god of potatoes?

"Andrusha, dear one," an elderly typist pleaded with him, "I have
three mouths to feed at home. I don't ask more than five kilos. But at least
not so many *frozen* potatoes. . . ."

But the new Ivanov was proof against bourgeois sentimentality. For
this once he was an iron Bolshevik.

"Share and share alike," he replied. "Everyone gets some of the
frozen, some of the good ones . . . if there are any good ones. Now move
along, citizeness. Next!"

Poor Ivanov's one-day glory, alas, ended in tears and scandal. The
victims said that the idiot ought to stick to caressing floors instead of
weighing out precious food. Ivanov himself insisted that there simply
had not been enough to go round at the five-kilo rate. However that may
be, it is a fact that the supply of potatoes, frozen and otherwise, gave
out abruptly while twenty-odd employees were still in line to collect their
present. . . .

Officialdom fared much better. We received fat food packages, graded
according to one's rung on the ladder of prestige. Besides, we were provided
with special coupons which, when exchanged at a specified "closed"
pharmacy produced two bottles of port wine and a bottle of vodka.

In the Kremlin Stalin's annual party was under way. Only the most
important and influential people were invited, of course. To be asked to
attend was higher distinction than being knighted by a king. The list
was studied by the N.K.V.D. and every guest was investigated for weeks
before the event. I observed the process in the Sovnarkom. I saw the
profound care with which Pamfilov drew up his list of People's Commissars
and Assistant Commissars who "rated" the supreme compliment. I saw
how, having selected the deserving, he sent the names to the N.K.V.D.
for study and confirmation.

But in the Sovnarkom, too, we had a party. There was no lack of
pomp, flowers, slogans on streamers, music. Tables were set out in the
large auditorium for the upper shifts of officials. Because food and drink
were plenteous, we were reconciled to the inevitable holiday address by
a Party stalwart; one must take the sour with the sweet. At every mention
of The Boss's name, we all stood up and shouted hurrah, which broke up
the speech nicely and made it a little less tedious.

When the ritual oration was ended, we all fell to. Heaping plattersful
were quickly swept clean by the storm of holiday appetites. Then came
the toasts: first to the Beloved Leader, of course, then to the beloved
sub-leaders, Molotov, Mikoyan, etc., each in turn, down to Pamfilov. Comrade Mironov struck up a tune and we all joined in singing a familiar ditty:

> *Let's sing a song, comrades,*
> *About the greatest of men,*
> *About the greatest and most loved—*
> *About Stalin let's sing a song.*

5

For some time I had been pulling strings to obtain the most envied award at the disposal of an omnipotent government: a separate apartment. At last I succeeded.

The wide, straight Mozhaisk Road is the best-asphalted and best-kept highway in all of Russia, for it is the road that leads to Stalin's country villa and to the suburban summer places of many Politburo members working in the capital. Naturally it is under incessant surveillance and inspection, to protect the life of the Beloved Leader. Smart-looking N.K.V.D. men in leather jackets come and go on motorcycles.

A number of fine modern buildings had been erected along this road where it cuts into the fringes of the city. In one of these, through the intercession of the Sovnarkom, I was finally assigned an apartment: two rooms and a kitchen—which was incalculable opulence under Moscow housing conditions. It had a bath of its own, central heating, modern lighting fixtures and other glories. Its windows looked into the back yard rather than into the famous road, but that was a minor defect.

Armed with an order for occupancy, my Sovnarkom credentials, Party card and personal passport, I presented myself at the office of the house chairman. The house chairman (an important functionary in the life of every Soviet citizen) was a pleasant fellow, accustomed to dealing with people of consequence. In the statistics these were "workers' homes" but in fact only bureaucrats swinging sufficient political weight could use them, and that only as long as they were in the good graces of the higher powers.

"Victor Andreyevich," the house chairman said, "it all seems in good order. Now you must report to the assistant chief of the N.K.V.D. of the district, then come back here. It's a formality."

"But what has the N.K.V.D. to do with it? These papers would seem clear enough."

"They're good enough for me personally, but this is a government road. Politburo members pass here every day! This gives the residences along the road a special character, so to speak."

I saw the point. Even though my windows did not face the road, I would not be permitted to live on the Mozhaisk highway until the secret police ruled that my presence did not constitute a danger to Stalin's safety! I called on the appropriate N.K.V.D. official, submitted to a familiar line of questions, and was given the required approval.

But I was destined never to occupy this apartment. It was a new structure and not yet ready for occupancy. The problem of furnishing the rooms also ate up time. Meanwhile the chance of an assignment abroad had arisen—the blessed chance on which I had dared to gaze only in optimistic daydreams mixed with pain. Until that question would be definitely decided, there was no point in moving.

The expanding lend-lease operations made it necessary to send hundreds of people specialized in all branches of economy to England, Canada and especially the United States. More Russians were being enabled to get a taste of the outside world than ever before in Soviet history. As a metallurgical engineer with versatile experience, I qualified for such a post. My political record, formally at least, was flawless, despite my long ordeal during the purges. Yet it would have been bad strategy, and in fact almost impossible, to take the initiative in the matter. The more anxious you were to go abroad, the more carefully you concealed the yearning, lest it be misunderstood—or understood—by the monitors of our Soviet allegiances.

One night I was discussing the lend-lease situation with an official of some standing in our foreign trade set-up with whom I was on most friendly terms. Carefully, skillfully, I guided the conversation. I did not dare suggest that here, before him, sat a man competent to help abroad; but I managed to coax that bright thought into being in his mind. It seemed to him a spontaneous inspiration.

"Victor Andreyevich, how would you like to go to America?" he said suddenly. "I know that we need more men there."

"Well, I'd never thought of the idea. Besides, I'm doing very responsible work here at the Sovnarkom, as you know. Still, if I could be useful to the war effort. . . ."

My friend was no simpleton. He was not fooled by my coyness.

"I'll see about it," he told me. "You can count on me to make the suggestion in the proper quarters."

I thanked him, never supposing that he would really keep his word, never daring to believe that his suggestion would prosper. This was at the end of December. About a fortnight later, Pamfilov summoned me for a private talk. For a moment I thought, with a flush of excitement, that it might have some reference to the American dream. But I was wrong.

Pamfilov said he wished to consult me about a problem that had been dumped in his lap. There was a group of metallurgical factories of various types working under an organization called Glavmetal. These plants were scattered—in Chaliabinsk, Novosibirsk, Molotov, Northern Caucasus and other places—but were administered as a unit from a Moscow headquarters. Their work was in dismal shape, Pamfilov explained, and a strong hand was needed to set them right.

"I need someone in charge whom I know and trust," he said. "I think you're the man. I want you to understand that it is in no sense a demotion. When you've brought some order out of the chaos I'll bring you back into the Sovnarkom. What do you say?"

I made my acceptance sound casual, even a little disappointed. Actually I was pleased. It was unlikely that a responsible department head in the Sovnarkom would be considered dispensable for service abroad. But as an official of Glavmetal my chances of being released would be immensely improved. . . .

Glavmetal had its offices in the long low building making one wall of Red Square, directly opposite the Kremlin: the flat-faced structure familiar to anyone who has ever seen a newsreel shot of the square. Here I was installed in an office and provided with a staff. In continuous personal and telephonic contact with the directors of factories in many parts of Russia, I conducted the affairs of the organization.

My hours were no longer quite as murderous as before. I began to catch up on lost sleep. I could see more of the life of Moscow and more of the friends whom I had neglected under the harrowing Sovnarkom regimen. Perhaps it was a premonition that I had little time left to savor things Russian and people close to me; but somehow I was anxious to crowd a lot into every passing week.

I had an intense impulse, too, to explore the minds of the people around me. What was the war doing to them? And what I found fortified my affection for my own people. I marveled at their amazing fortitude under the hammer blows of adversity. I marveled at their instinctive sense of the political realities. Simple Russians were rendering unto Stalin what was Stalin's and unto Russia what was primordially Russian.

The war was taking a more favorable turn, of that there was no doubt. In the long-drawn contest in the Stalingrad region the slaughter was fantastic, the suffering beyond calculation. But a conviction of victory gradually filled our hearts. The fact that the struggle was so prolonged was in itself an omen of victory. In a war of attrition the advantages were all with us.

The Germans were far from their supply bases and in the unaccustomed winter conditions found reinforcement virtually impossible. They were condemned to fight with such men and supplies as they had accumulated on the terrain—vast amounts of both, yet exhaustible. The Russians, on the contrary, were able to pour blood and metal into the area almost endlessly. Hitler's armies would have had to kill off half of Russia before the Kremlin would acknowledge defeat at Stalingrad. In preparation for the battle a new railroad line had been built along the Volga. It functioned smoothly throughout the contest, serving as a funnel through which new strength was fed incessantly into the mutilated and bleeding city. Supplies and reinforcements also flowed across the Volga.

The inevitable victory was achieved. The Germans had indeed been drowned in blood—their own and Russian. Besides halting the German advance, the triumph had another value which has been generally overlooked or underestimated. The Red Army in that campaign captured enough German armaments to equip thirty to forty divisions. It was a German military theorist, Clausewitz, who counseled generals to fight with the weapons of their opponents. This is precisely what Soviet generals were able to do after Stalingrad. The war materiel captured from the Germans must be ranked with lend-lease in explaining the success of the Soviet counter-offensive. From November, 1942, to November, 1944, my country's trophies of victory included over four thousand airplanes, seventeen thousand tanks, fifty-five thousand artillery pieces, 118 thousand machine guns, 1,500,000 rifles. Much of it, of course, required repair. Hitler's weapons were turned against him, literally.

I was watching the battle of Stalingrad with a deep longing for victory, like every other Soviet citizen, irrespective of his feelings about the regime. At the same time—such is the distortion of mortal perspective —I was watching the outcome of the investigations which would determine whether I would leave the U.S.S.R.

CHAPTER XXVI

PRELUDE TO AMERICA

THE IDEA of my going to the United States began to take shape in January, 1943, and a passport for the journey was actually issued in July. During those six months I felt like a rare beetle on a pin in a huge laboratory where legions of entomologists, zoologists, chemists and other scientists studied the specimen from every possible angle. I was prodded and tapped for hidden flaws. All the energies of an omnipotent state seemed centered on the one job of exploring my humble person and its extensions in time and space through kinsmen by blood, kinsmen by marriage and associates of every degree.

The inquisitive state was cynical in its infinite distrust. Week after week, with trained fingers, it probed my mind and nerves for the combination that would unlock my innermost soul. And amazingly, its vast searching came to naught. My tremulous secret—the decision to escape the U.S.S.R.—remained locked away, undetected.

The great exploration of Victor Kravchenko, son of the Russian masses, Communist Party member and Soviet engineer, began in the office of the Personnel Department of the Commissariat of Foreign Trade. Comrade Shtoob, a nondescript little bureaucrat in thick spectacles, was politely impersonal. To him one beetle was like another; his job was merely to catalogue the insects. The subtler differences would be defined and examined later by more specialized entomologists.

Comrade Shtoob ran through my personal history from birth to the current hour, then fanned out to take in the histories of my parents, grandparents, brothers and relatives in secondary branchings of the family tree. With blood relations put in their proper place, connubial connections were traced minutely and finally the pattern of my humble but shockingly extensive existence was filled out with questions about friends and professional associates through the years.

I had been through this autobiographical maze dozens of times in the past. Every fact had been put on record endlessly by the Party, the armed services, various commissariats, not to mention ordinary and extraordinary purges. Besides, what circumstance in my past was so utterly negligible that it could have failed to find a place in the fat files of the N.K.V.D.?

But the ritual could not be curtailed, let alone skipped. Comrade Shtoob proceeded on the premise that this was a first acquaintance between the government and one of its subjects. He did not even take my name, patronymic and age for granted. This periodical stripping of the Soviet citizen to ultimate nakedness, this unveiling of his most intimate life, this turning inside out of his political thoughts, had acquired through the years a symbolic importance. It was the ceremonial humbling of the individual for the greater glory of the collective. It was man the meek and submissive, cringing and degraded in his nudity before the panoplied state. To retain a secret, to reach for a fig-leaf, was sacrilege.

And it was a rite bristling with dangers. The answers had to be consistent within themselves and consistent with answers given in previous interrogations, questionnaires, forms and reviews. The police-state brooked no evasions and confusions. A slip of the memory, a minor contradiction, and all its suspicious wrath was aroused. Many a Soviet citizen has wrecked his career on a mix-up in dates or some absent-minded confusion of relatives.

Having satisfied himself that my sister-in-law's aunt Vera, whom I did not know in person, was not a menace to the Union of Soviet Socialist Republics, the near-sighted Shtoob took the next step. He provided me with a series of printed questionnaires to carry home and fill out by tomorrow. I must make no changes, erasures or crossings of words, he warned. Fumbling was presumptive evidence of a guilty conscience. The entomologists insisted on neatness and decorum.

I followed orders without deviation. I deposited the papers in the specified number of copies at the specified window. In a few days I received a message: "Continue on your present job. Should the need to send you abroad arise, you will be notified." In Soviet double-talk this signified that I was being thoroughly investigated and, if found worthy, would be investigated some more.

Nearly three months passed. I had all but relinquished hope. Somewhere, I thought dejectedly, an indelible stain had been found on my own or my family's escutcheon. But one slushy April night, arriving home after fourteen grueling hours at Glavmetal, numbed with fatigue, I found a mysterious message awaiting me: I must call a certain telephone number. The touch of mystery, too, was part of the ritual. It guaranteed a few palpitant minutes of fear alternating with hope, since it might mean anything from police trouble to a dizzy promotion.

It turned out to be merely a high official of the Commissariat of Foreign Trade. What was accomplished by the enigmatic anonymity of the message I shall never know. Despite the hour, I was ordered to come over at once. A pass would be waiting for me at a certain window. I rushed to the Commissariat, weariness erased by the new tide of hope. After long and nervous waiting, I found myself in another office under interrogation by a more shrewd and more important exemplar of the Shtoob breed.

For three hours we wandered through the jungles of my past, pausing now and then to rummage in the undergrowth of my political moods and opinions. Now he led me, now he chased me. He put trick questions to trip me up, he threw out false leads, he suddenly retraced his steps to take me unawares. My companion was a practised old cat but this time he was playing with a wary and experienced old mouse. The night courses of training under Professors Gershgorn, Dorogan and others were paying dividends By two in the morning both cat and mouse were too tired to go on. I was instructed to return in a few days to fill out some super-special forms.

A few days later I was composing answers to questions in the longest and craftiest questionnaire I had as yet faced. It was a document so cynical in its assumptions, so acute in its cross-examination, that it made all other questionnaires seem innocent and amateur by comparison. It was a document starting from the assumption that every citizen was a liar and proceeding in a spirit of contempt for everything human. By the time I signed my name and Party number I was soaked in perspiration and utterly humiliated.

When I turned in the questionnaire, I was ordered to take the next step in the ceremonial, which was to collect letters of reference and estimates of my political and business activities from Party organizations in which I had been active and industrial enterprises where I had recently been employed. True, there was nothing any of these offices could say which was not already on record in the N.K.V.D. in great detail through formal reports and informal espionage sources. But the sacramental documents could not be skipped. This provided a good many officials and organizations whose paths had crossed mine with a chance to destroy me if they were so minded.

I addressed myself first to Comrade Mironov, chief of the Party Committee of the Council of People's Commissars of the R.S.F.S.R. I made the appointment by telephone and at the specified hour presented myself at the entrance. My Party documents and internal passport were examined and a pass was duly issued. Thus armed I crossed a courtyard to the building which housed the Party Committee. Here my pass was examined and my face was carefully matched against the photographs on the documents. On the floor where the Committee was situated an unsmiling N.K.V.D. guard studied my papers and features in even greater detail and finally I was told to go to room 503.

Only a few months ago I had held an important post in this very institution. These guards had seen me hundreds of times. But there could be no relaxation in the prescribed vigilance; I might have changed political color since then. In the corridors I ran into men and women who had worked with me and under me. A few were cordial but most of them met me with pointed reserve. I was no longer in the Sovnarkom, they did not know why I had left, and they could not risk a cordial greeting.

Comrade Mironov was courteous but stiffly formal. As a concession to our former intimacy he did ask why I was looking so haggard. To be frank, I said, I wasn't getting enough to eat since I left the Sovnarkom. He smiled in a pleased way at this indirect recognition that "his" Sovnarkom was a privileged place for deserving leaders. Yes, he agreed, these war hardships, but let's get down to business.

While we were down to business a little woman wearing a starched cap and a maid's apron came in, carrying a big lunch tray. It was loaded with crisp white bread, bacon and eggs, canned meat, butter, tea with sugar.

"All American," he said proudly as he dug into the feast. "Lend-lease, you know."

But he did not invite me to partake, on a lend-lease or any other basis. Between mouthfuls he continued to question me. Was I happy where I was now working? How was the Party nucleus at Glavmetal functioning? Crudely, even stupidly, he was going through the formality of testing my loyalty to the government and our Beloved Leader. Not that he cared, not that he thought me a lunatic who would confess some doubts, but simply in deference to ceremonial procedure.

"And so you want a letter of recommendation?" he said. "Well, I'll talk it over with Comrade Utkin. One must think it over. Come in tomorrow about noon."

The next day I went through the same routine of multiple checking of documents and after the usual wait in the anteroom was admitted into Mironov's official presence. I was handed a letter, a good letter, attesting my political and business talents. The fates were on my side. In the following weeks I obtained similar letters also from the head of Glavmetal and the Secretary of its Party organization. My documents were read and re-read, my features were scrutinized, my political probity was tested, a hundred times over. And all this, I knew, was only the surface, below which the real work of digging into my life and mind was being done by the appropriate departments of the N.K.V.D.

At last, however, I had the proof that all was going well. I received orders to report to the medical clinic of the Commissariat of Foreign Trade for a physical examination and to the Commissariat's staff photographer for an official record of my face. Two days later I was notified to report to Comrade Lebedev, Assistant Commissar and one of the right-hand men to Commissar Mikoyan himself.

2

Lebedev was flanked by two assistants, who made notes and handed him various papers during our first interview. He sat at an ornate desk which, for some reason, was planted in the very center of the huge room, amidst the billowing colors of oriental rugs. Stalin, Molotov, Mikoyan and other leaders looked down from their frames on the walls. A thick file, evidently containing copies of my multitudinous questionnaires and special reports from mysterious places, lay ostentatiously before him.

After a formal greeting Comrade Lebedev began to question me from the very beginning: my name, my birthplace, when I joined the Party. He could not conceivably propound a query which I had not answered dozens of times already but even Assistant Commissars must adhere to the sacramental rites. I replied eagerly, with enthusiasm, as if thrilled by the novelty of the questions and amazed by the shrewdness of their formulation. Then I waited while he leafed through the file, tasting a passage here and there, now smiling, now frowning. The two aides sat in dignified noncommittal silence. From time to time he dictated a few suggestions for what would evidently be his report to the Commissar.

Lebedev had a stocky, broad-shouldered figure and a thick double-fold neck. His face was pleasant, even handsome, and had a human quality which did not accord with his deadly official words and manner. He was not a clever man, I decided; how did he ever ascend so high? Then my eyes rested on his hands, their plump stubby fingers covered with a thick black fur. It occurred to me that these were cruel hands, capable of violence.

"Comrade Kravchenko," he finally said, solemnly, "do you appreciate the seriousness of an assignment abroad?"

"Oh yes, I have given it a lot of thought."

"You must justify the confidence the Party is placing in you."

"I shall try, Comrade Lebedev," I said humbly, eagerly.

"You will be informed of further developments. I hope we shall meet again soon."

Five days thereafter I learned confidentially, through a friend in the Commissariat, that Anastas Ivanovich Mikoyan, member of the Politburo, Vice-Chairman of the Council of People's Commissars, member of the State Defense Committee, People's Commissar for Foreign Trade, with his own hands had signed a recommendation to the Central Committee of the Party that I be sent to the United States of America. I continued to manage my affairs at Glavmetal, but my thoughts were now far away. Before long a message was conveyed to me by the Secret Department of the Head Office of our trust. I was to call a certain number. Once more the mystery seemed quite superfluous, since it was merely a woman functionary at the Commissariat requesting me to report at eleven-thirty next morning.

"Have your Party card, passport, trade-union book and army documents with you," she said. "At precisely twelve you will be received at another place."

I followed the prescription to the letter. Having been passed by three or four guards and interviewed by an official of the N.K.V.D., I was directed to the offices of the Central Committee of the All-Union Communist Party. That was the "other place" whose dignity required the extra touches of mystery and red tape. Provided with the necessary pass, I walked to the Party building. Here my documents were re-examined and soon I was walking up a broad marble staircase.

On the landing stood a marble Stalin on his marble pedestal, his Napoleonic mien rather comical in this loneliness. On the second landing another Stalin, no less lonely and ludicrous, looked into my eyes. On this floor I waited for a while and ultimately was ushered into a carpeted office where a third Stalin, this time on the wall, kept me company until the proper official arrived. Clearly Soviet sculptors and painters have no dearth of subjects. The official sat down behind his big desk, scrutinized me a full minute, then said:

"Tell me about yourself. Please don't repeat what I already know from your questionnaires. I'm interested in your outlook, your political state of mind."

I talked almost at random. I racked my brain for some facts or thoughts which had not been worked to death in the previous interrogations and written forms. He interrupted. He got down to the point.

"Did you ever have any doubts about the wisdom of any Party policies?"

"Never," I said promptly. There was no point in going into nuances unless I had to.

"Not even during collectivization, and during the purges, when you yourself suffered some? Not even then did you have any doubts of the Party's general line?"

"No, not of the general line."

"But you had a rather unpleasant time of it in Nikopol in 1936 and '37. You were being checked, investigated, and all that. What was your attitude?"

"Well, of course, I was bewildered, even a little indignant. After all, I knew myself to be innocent. I felt hurt in a way."

"That's understandable. One can't hold that against you. There were excesses at the time; the enemies of the people responsible have been rooted out. But now, Comrade Kravchenko, is there anything left of that hurt, that indignation?"

"Oh, no, of course not." I smiled at such a preposterous question. Naturally I was grateful to all the Gershgorns and Dorogans who had beaten and humiliated me.

The dismal comedy ground on for perhaps two hours. This was presumably the heart-to-heart talk on basic political attitudes prescribed by the ritual. As if there were room for candor in our Soviet lives! As if any two comrades, meeting for the first time, would venture beyond the limits of the anointed hypocrisies and wretched pretenses! As the "chat" progressed I grew more certain of myself, I reeled off more cliches. I derived a certain perverse satisfaction from topping his every slogan, and all the time my mind was gloating over the scene: *I shall escape! Soon I shall be free of this monstrous make-believe, this boring horror! I shall be able to talk, to fight!*

My interrogator was apparently well impressed with me. My mind, he probably decided, had the proper configuration, no untidy doubts, no protruding thoughts. Probably he set me down as a man of few ideas but respectable ones, not too bright but dependable. I felt approval in the pressure of his clammy hand.

"Well, good-bye. You're likely to know the decision of the Central Committee in four or five days."

It was a favorable decision. Within a week Glavmetal was ordered to release me to the Commissariat of Foreign Trade. The following day I reported to the All-Union Raw Materials Import Administration of the Commissariat of Foreign Trade. Here I was given thick confidential volumes of reports and instructions to read and ponder by way of familiarizing myself with the Lend-Lease process, conditions in American industry, details about metallurgical firms with which I would have to deal over there.

Then I was summoned once more to the Central Committee head-

quarters. This time I was presented with two confidential pamphlets. I
was told to read them carefully right there, then return them and sign
a form attesting that I was familiar with their contents. The pamphlets
outlined rules of conduct for Party members abroad and, more particularly, the penalties for their violation. The gist of what I read will
remain with me forever, as a commentary on the grotesque Soviet version
of the non-Soviet world.

After enjoining strict obedience to superiors, the pamphlets warned
against the temptations, pitfalls and seductions of life in capitalist countries. They evoked a picture, at once frightening and alluring, of a
strange, hostile, utterly depraved and lascivious world devoted to the one
purpose of ensnaring Soviet citizens and extracting their state secrets.
The principal business of foreign governments, I gathered, was to undermine the loyalties of visiting Communists.

Those about to plunge into the maelstrom of political vice, grafting
businessmen and perfumed harlots were forbidden to talk with infidels
unnecessarily on any theme, but under no circumstances to discuss politics.
If approached with proposals to sell us "documents" or other secrets, we
must steer the hucksters to the nearest Soviet Consulate. If questioned
about life inside the Soviet Union we must assume that the prying ones
are agents of counter-espionage.

The rules were especially forceful in warning against contacts with
ex-Russians and with publications "unfriendly" to our country. We must
eschew the printed matter put out abroad by counter-revolutionary emigres.
The anti-Soviet devils were ubiquitous: there would be "unfriendly"
harangues on the air, anti-Soviet pictures on the screen. These, of course,
we must flee or be damned.

The rules implied that though capitalism was rotten at its core it was
bright and seductive on the outside, so that our Communist virtue would
be under unceasing assault. We must close our senses to the appeal of
bourgeois fleshpots. The best capitalist hotels were but thinly disguised
brothels where Mata Haras lurked in wait for innocent Soviet men.
While traveling abroad, we must abandon the danger zone instantly
should a comely female be assigned to our cabins or coupes. Should a
woman, especially a Russian-speaking woman, attempt to engage us in
conversation, we must flee forthwith.

Alcohol was described as only second to sex as a lure to Soviet innocents abroad. Never, unless it be for a specific business purpose duly
authorized from above, must we venture into bars, night clubs or other
dens of iniquity where tongue-loosening alcoholic beverages are on tap.
Should duty require attendance at a private or public party, the good
Soviet emissary must hold himself firmly in hand lest he betray some
secret.

What, precisely, were those awful secrets we must guard and which
the outside world would be conniving to squeeze out of us? The rules did
not say. But the answer seemed to me evident enough. What the Kremlin
feared so much was that we might bear testimony to the truth of the
"anti-Soviet propaganda" being spread by "unfriendly" writers, speakers

and publications. The "secrets" to which it had reference were the facts about concentration camps, slave labor, pervasive oppression and human degradation in the U.S.S.R., anything which might spoil the picture of the regime painted by propaganda. The two pamphlets were in effect witnesses to the Soviet regime's bad conscience.

They ascribed to foreign governments every dirty trick which the N.K.V.D. and other Soviet agencies had ever played on foreigners. They warned that in America our baggage would be searched, our passports would be stolen for counter-espionage purposes, our telephones would be tapped, seductive women would be foisted on us. In America, the rules implied, we would be living on enemy soil, despite immediate diplomatic pretenses to the contrary; if we did not watch our steps we would be sucked in by the capitalist quagmires of greed, luxury and hatred of the Socialist Fatherland.

After I had guaranteed my understanding of these cautions and returned the pamphlets, I was delivered to the oratorical mercies of another Central Committee functionary in another ample office. His tone was severe.

"Comrade Kravchenko, you are about to undertake a foreign mission. You will conduct trade in a foreign environment, among the capitalists whom we rightly despise and distrust. We count on you not to have your head turned by the sight of consumer goods and the temptations of a society in the final stages of rotten degeneration. Never forget your historic mission as the representative of the new Soviet civilization.

"True, America is helping us now. But we must not lose sight of the fact that the help is given grudgingly, out of dire necessity. True, some of our war aims at the moment coincide with theirs, but the two worlds remain irreconcilable. Hold fast to the knowledge that as a Communist you are the sworn enemy of the capitalist society whose world center today is America. Communism and capitalism can never be reconciled!"

I composed my features in the serious expression suited to the occasion. It was silly of him to preach such an elementary sermon to a seasoned Party man. But that, too, was part of the ritual. It was what he was paid to do and no doubt had made the identical speech to others like me that very day.

"After you reach America, you will continue to take an active part in the work of our Party. But remember that so far as the American authorities are concerned you are not and never have been a Party member. You must insist that you're not even interested in politics. In America, the organization of the Communist Party of the U.S.S.R. functions on an underground basis. You will not take your Party card with you, but the fact of your membership will be known to the proper people. Outwardly you will be an engineer and nothing more. Is that clear?"

"Yes, I understand."

Next day I returned to Party headquarters. It was now the end of June. I was being "washed and rewashed," as the Soviet phrase has it. Another official, a grade more imposing, awaited me. Two other men—one of them obviously a police agent—were present. The Party official was a heavy-set fellow in dandified foreign attire. A foreign watch on his wrist and a foreign fountain-pen protruding from his top vest pocket proclaimed that he had recently returned from the capitalist deserts, perhaps from London or Washington.

"Comrade Kravchenko, the Central Committee has confirmed your assignment to the United States," he scowled. "Do you realize the full meaning of the confidence placed in you?"

"Yes," I answered.

"Have you read the instructions? Do you understand the consequences of mistakes or misconduct?"

"Yes. I shall remember."

"Your best insurance against error is Bolshevik vigilance and whole-hearted devotion to our beloved Party."

"Yes, of course. I can see that."

"You are going to the country of the most highly developed and rapacious capitalism. The counter-espionage of the F.B.I. is subtle and inescapable. You may receive offers to betray your country. The native capitalists and the emigres will leave no stone unturned to compromise you. The counter-revolutionary and capitalist press, especially of Hearst and McCormick, will try to destroy your faith.

"Don't trust those who pretend to be friends of our country. Many of them are more dangerous than out-and-out enemies. Recently it has become the fashion among certain emigres, not only on the Left but among actual monarchists, to lick our boots. Don't trust them. Once a turncoat always a turncoat. The same applies to bankers, manufacturers and other capitalists who follow the new fashion of admiring the U.S.S.R. Their admiration isn't worth a damn. It can turn overnight to treachery."

I interjected monosyllables of understanding and approval. When would this farce be over, I kept thinking. But the sermon had not yet reached its peak. Having disposed of the government spies and emigre turncoats and two-faced capitalists, he came to the danger that interested him most. In a strangely passionate voice he went on to warn me about the capitalist pitfalls, bright lights, night clubs, ladies of easy virtue.

"These things are symptoms of the disintegration of bourgeois life, Comrade Kravchenko, but they are tempting all the same. I know"—his eyes sparkled and his tone grew lustful—"I know that the agents of capitalism will try to reach you by any and all means."

Released, I merely landed in the armchair of a third preacher. Evidently his department was more technical, concerned with my obligations and opportunities as an engineer rather than my risks as a male. One of my main duties, he said, would be to gather any and all information of an economic, and if possible military character that came my way. I must school myself to note technical details, the planning of factories in any city I visited, methods of production, innovations in machinery, new technical processes, anything not known to us.

"You will become the eyes and the ears of our country in America. Upon arriving in Washington, report to Comrade Serov. Give him the stub you will receive when you surrender your Party card. He knows all about you. Is that clear?"

"Quite clear."

"One more thing: Don't spread the news that you are going abroad. You may tell only friends whom you consider politically reliable."

Why the sending of another purchasing representative should be treated as a secret I did not know. But, of course, I asked no naive questions. Before I left the building I received a stub in return for my Party card. I felt strange, almost naked, without the card. The right to possess the card had once seemed a noble dream. Now I surrendered it without any twinge of regret—I had become immune to political symbolism. At the Commissariat of War my military credentials were taken up and I was formally released from all military obligations. The Foreign Trade Commissariat provided me with a substantial sum in Soviet money and special coupons for the purchase of clothes suitable for emergence into the degenerate capitalist world. I was also given some American currency to see me through to Washington.

All these preliminaries attended to, I presented myself once more to Comrade Lebedev. Several others scheduled to go to America, all Party members, were also there. Now that we had taken the many hurdles and soaked up the graded sermons, Lebedev was smiling and cordial.

"Well, comrades, I'll be brief," he said. "You are all politically literate people. Let me tell you a little parable."

At great length and with evident relish he proceeded to recount the tale of a Soviet emissary to the United States who, alas, was not as circumspect as he hoped we would be. That unfortunate, it seemed, had allowed himself to be framed by American agents. Luckily the Russian had sense enough to take the Consulate into his confidence, and he was saved in the nick of time.

We all nodded our heads understandingly. We would guard ourselves against the wiles of the American secret police.

"Another word of caution and I'm through, comrades. Some of you are going out without your wives. In America there will be plenty to eat and drink. It's a false war prosperity, you know, and will soon be followed by another depression. Anyhow, you know how it is with a racehorse after he fills up with oats." Here he winked slyly and we laughed in obsequious appreciation, though many of us understood the cynicism of his words. "That's right. He begins to neigh. . . . Beware of the legs of American girls." He shook a warning finger. "Well, if you get mixed up with capitalist women, just remember that I warned you."

Then he dropped the bantering tone and applied himself to severe threats. America, he declared, was only a temporary ally. Our watchwords must be prudence and vigilance. One day the bogus friendship would be ended, dialectic realities would reassert themselves. "Learn all you can, observe everything—give nothing in return."

When I went home I carried the little red book, the foreign Soviet passport, in my breast pocket. Circumstances made it the most coveted piece of paper imaginable. I kept touching it to reassure myself that it was no mirage. At home, Irina was expecting me. She saw instantly from my expression that everything was in order. I knew that she was struggling to suppress her tears. She had no inkling of my great secret. Her best protection, the one kindness I could offer in return for her affection, was to keep her totally ignorant of my intentions.

"It's a short-term assignment," I said, with a catch in my throat. "I'll be gone only a few months, a year at most."

3

Knowing in my heart that I might never again see my country and its people I gazed at them in the days before my departure with a sort of premonitory homesickness. I tried to fix their images indelibly on the retina of my mind.

There were, of course, dozens of friends whom I should have liked to see before leaving. The absurd secrecy thrown around my journey made it awkward. Nevertheless I risked a farewell call on Comrade Misha and other people close to me. I tried to make the good-byes casual, so that they might not guess my decision. When I flashed my passport, they stared in bewilderment. To leave the country, to shake oneself loose from Stalin's "happy life" even for a brief period, is the most difficult and therefore the most envied accomplishment.

One of those intimate friends whom I visited, and to whom I exhibited my little red miracle, was a chemical specialist who now held a high post in the government. He was one of those who had been persecuted in the super-purge, then "rehabilitated." Despite his "confession" of complicity in sabotage projects aired in the Moscow blood trials, he rose rapidly in the hierarchy after his release from prison. Now decorations for distinguished war services shone on his breast.

He shook my hand warmly, enviously I thought, and held it long in his strong grip.

"Congratulations, Vitya! You're one in a hundred thousand! If it weren't for my wife and children I'd find an excuse for a trip abroad myself. . . . Ekh, you'll see the strange outside world. How little we're allowed to know about it!"

He paused for a minute and his brows wrinkled, as if he were trying to make up his mind about something. Then he said impulsively:

"Let's drive over to my apartment. We'll have a farewell drink and . . . well, I feel the urge to talk. . . ."

He did talk. Was he made bold by my imminent departure to a distant land? Could he no longer hold his festering thoughts to himself? Whatever the reason, he told me that afternoon things which no sane Russian utters aloud in my country.

"Vitya, the fools imagine they've bought me off with these shiny badges. But they're mistaken. I'm pulling hard for victory against the Germans. I'm a Russian through and through. But I have neither forgotten nor forgiven the year of torture. Sure, I'm on my way up. They need competent people; even I, the ex-prisoner, stand out as a person of ability. Maybe I'll be a People's Commissar one of these days. It's not at all impossible.

"But I've forgotten nothing, nothing! I remember every minute of anguish, every insult, and I cherish them like great treasures against the day of revenge. I was tortured months on end before I signed that foul and lying confession. There were long stretches of solitary confinement in dark wet cellars which I shared with big rats. Do you know, my friend, what it means to be tortured? Let me tell you—"

"Don't, Gregory, don't!" I pleaded. "I've heard enough from others. What's the use of opening your old wounds?"

"They've never been closed, Vitya. I've kept them fresh. I haven't let them heal. Every day I get up with a curse on my lips and every night I go to sleep with that curse. Listen, I have never told this to anyone, but I can no longer keep the horror to myself.

"You've heard about the torture by light, but I've been through it. You sit in the middle of a room with glaring electric bulbs shining in your eyes and you are not allowed to go to sleep. If you begin to nod or to close your eyes, the guards rouse you with blows. Once I sat that way for seventy-two hours, without sleep, without food, without drink. My body retched, my eyeballs burned like hot coals. And at the end of this torture I was questioned again by a fresh, robust sadist.

"Oh, they're clever, these 'socialist' monsters. They know how to squeeze 'voluntary' confessions out of you. I'm sure Hitler's Gestapo couldn't teach us a thing. Hunger, thirst, heat, cold—they play wonderful variations on these themes, our Paderewskis of the torture chambers. In our prison there was one official who prepared his victims for cross-examination in his own way: He had them fed salty foods, like herring, then denied them water. By the time he was ready for them, they were half insane with thirst. As he questioned them he helped himself to long cool draughts of water, or even beer, while the tortured prisoner looked on.

"I know of confessions drawn out of men after they had been hung by their wrists for twenty-four hours. I know of instances when a prisoner's hair was torn up by the roots, along with patches of his scalp. Yes, they're clever, our torture masters. They know when to inflict pain and when to resort to slow, nerve-racking varieties of torture.

"Yes, they beat me too, not once but a hundred times. Finally came the supreme horror. That's the part I have never before told anyone except my wife. She had to know. One night I was being whipped in the torture chamber, with long wet towels. There were three of them with me. First they stripped me mother naked, then they lashed me across my face, across my kidneys. Then I was thrown on the table. Two of the butchers held me down and the third swung the wet towels with all his strength across my thighs . . . across my genitals.

"Think of the worst agony you can imagine, multiply it a million times, and you may approach what I went through. Those brutes were sick men, perverted monsters."

"Don't, Gregory, please don't," I whispered.

"I didn't recover consciousness for many days. When I came to I was in the prison hospital. Nothing seemed to matter to me any longer. I wondered why and how I had held out against them so long. I called myself harsh names for having been an idiotic idealist. I signed whatever was put before me, without reading, without caring. When they released me I was no good to my wife. . . .

"And the fools think they've paid me off with titles and badges. They actually imagine I have forgotten! The higher I rise in their service, the closer I get to the throne in the Kremlin, the more I hate them and curse them and thirst for revenge."

In America, in the next months, I would be obliged to listen to drivel about the "new civilization" in Soviet Russia, about our "socialism" and "economic democracy." Listening, I would sometimes think of what was done to Gregory. A kind of nausea would then begin to creep up on me, so that I hastily thought of something else, something pleasant, to avoid being sick.

Another curious encounter in those final days in Moscow remains sharply etched on my memory. Unfortunately I dare not mention his name. Suffice that he ranks among the most influential Communists and has connections in the upper ruling crust. Suffice that I had once risked my own freedom to save his and that he had not forgotten. I thought it best not to say good-bye to him, but apparently he knew of my scheduled departure and took the initiative. We agreed to meet, as if by accident, in the little park opposite the Bolshoi Theatre on Teatralny Square.

"So everything's in order and you're actually going?" he said when we were seated on a park bench. "Congratulations! Congratulations!"

"I thought it better not to make a farewell call on you," I said. "I knew you'd understand."

"But I felt I must talk to you, Victor Andreyevich. I know how you feel about things. You've never really told me, yet I know. That's why I wanted to see you and to warn you. Here we hold our tongues. But abroad you will be in constant danger of revealing your feelings. Freedom is intoxicating. You'll begin to feel yourself safe and one fine day you may spill over. Then you'll suddenly be summoned home, on some perfectly legitimate pretext, just for consultation perhaps, and when you get back —the end!

"Please don't let the new environment give you a false sense of safety. Bear in mind that you're surrounded by more spies, more informers, even than here at home. If you hold tight to that one fact, you'll come through all right. Our whole regime rests firmly on espionage and provocation. The system is not only carried over but intensified outside the country. It is constantly refined, perfected. Our masters know that we hide our real souls deep inside our shells, like spiritual snails. They want to penetrate this innermost retreat. . . .

"Here at home, I'd estimate, every fifth person in any office is a spy, working for one or another of the seeming control organizations. Where you're going, the ratio is closer to one in every three. And not only Russians. We have plenty of Americans on our payrolls, besides those who don't have to be paid, who do it for the cause. You will be asked innocent questions, you will be provoked to speak out, to complain. Agents will comment on things they've read in the papers or heard on the radio, just to draw you out."

"I think I know this system, my friend, and I shall be careful. I'm grateful all the same. . . ."

"You will be under constant scrutiny from all sides, Victor Andreyevich. Many will be afraid of you, wondering whether you too are an agent. That's the diabolic wisdom of our system—that no man knows his brother. I know how tired you are of all this. If you want to survive it's not enough that you understand my warning. You must *feel* it in the very marrow of your bones. . . ."

We parted. Later, when I thought of him, I always saw with my mind's eye that strange scene on a park bench. I saw how carefully he pulled down the visor of his cap, how he sank his head deeper into his collar, to avoid being recognized. I think of this friend as a miracle—a profoundly decent, warm-hearted Russian who has not only survived the purges but sits smiling and efficient amidst the mighty ones.

Only Irina came to see me off at the Kazan Station. I consoled her, tried to keep up her spirits. Inside of me I wept, knowing what she did not even guess—that this was our last meeting. The knowledge made me wretched. But what could I tell her? Nothing. It was far better to leave her in total ignorance. There was no joy in the departure for America— only a sharp ache, a pervasive and inexpressible sorrow. It was not my fault that I was leaving my country. It was the fault of a corrupt and inhuman regime. The only thing left that I could do for my suffering people was to escape, then try to tell the world all I knew as best I could. Such was the dictate of my Russian heritage. Such was the logic of my whole life.

4

A gray-haired, soft-spoken man with an intelligent face and kindly eyes shared my two-bed compartment. Furtively, in the suspicious Soviet way, we became acquainted. We pooled our food, we discussed the war. I was going to Vladivostok, I said in answer to his friendly inquiry. His response to the same question was even more vague—"beyond the Urals," he said with a deprecating gesture.

During the night there was a knock at our door. A smartly turned out N.K.V.D. officer entered. My heart pounded in sudden apprehension. Though in my mind I was convinced that I was actually leaving the U.S.S.R., my nerves remained on the alert, unbelieving.

"Documents, please!" the officer said politely.

From my upper berth I handed over my passport. He examined it carefully, compared the photograph with the original, and returned the little red book with a snappy salute. To my astonishment my new acquaintance produced an identical foreign passport. Both of us were going abroad, both of us had lied—now both of us felt foolish.

"Tell me, Victor Andreyevich," he said when the officer had left, "why must we lie to one another? Why must we fear each other? We're fellow-Russians, we know many of the same people and places, yet we fear one another. Politics don't interest me. I'm on my way to Outer Mongolia to raise cattle for our country and arrange for meat imports, nothing more mysterious than that. How sad that I should have lied!"

"And I'm going to America," I said, "to help select metal products for our country under lend-lease. Forgive me for lying to you! I feel ashamed."

"There's nothing to forgive; we're in the same boat. Ekh, this everlasting distrust . . . this childish secrecy. . . ."

The stock-breeder alighted beyond the Urals for a change in trains. His place was soon taken by a large man in a leather overcoat, with a thick brief case under his arm. He was loud, fussy and self-important, a man accustomed to attentions and instant obedience. Behind him came a younger man in military attire though without insignia of rank, a revolver at his belt. He was carrying the large man's baggage and busied himself to make his superior comfortable. It was a familiar picture: a high government official and his lackey extraordinary.

I recognized the newcomer at once as Comrade Borodin, former chairman of the Stalingrad Regional Executive Committee. He took off his overcoat, revealing the badge of a member of the Supreme Soviet and an Order of Lenin pinned on his chest. He was pot-bellied and his tiny eyes looked slyly out of a cold flat face. His fleshy hands were meticulously manicured. Demonstratively Comrade Borodin took a Browning revolver out of his pocket, demonstratively he placed it under his pillow. There would be no mistaking his power and importance. Then he deigned to scrutinize his new traveling companion.

"Haven't I seen you somewhere?" he asked.

"Yes, Comrade Borodin, at the Sovnarkom. I've sat in at a number of conferences where you were present. My name's Kravchenko, Victor Andreyevich Kravchenko."

"Splendid, splendid. Where are you bound for?"

"America, Washington."

"You don't say! Most interesting. Smart and strong devils, the Yankees. We must get to know them inside out. Good thing their industry is helping *us*."

Borodin was on his way to the Altai Territory on an official mission. He had started out by plane but had been forced down by "a cough and a sneeze in the motor," as he explained, and here he was crawling along by rail. Fortunately he had brought a lot of food along, and in addition he would see what the train restaurant could scare up. Oh, we'd have a fine trip, never doubt. Did I play cards? Did I like a little drink?

The uniformed orderly, whom Borodin treated like a serf, opened a knapsack crammed with good victuals and laid out a magnificent meal. I yielded to my companion's garrulous invitation to share the luxury, but insisted on contributing my rations. In addition, the cringing dining-car manager, awed by Borodin's ample presence, set up supper feasts for us and a number of other important passengers, including a General and an Admiral, every night after his dining car was closed to ordinary mortals.

Between meals we foregathered in one or another compartment, where some played cards and all reveled in disjointed discussion of the war, the scenery, the relative virtues of various Caucasian wines and other such problems. When we sat down to supper Borodin invariably offered a solemn toast to our Beloved Teacher and Leader.

Only the occasional sight of hungry, half-naked homeless children at stations spoiled our journey. At one station Borodin tossed some well-gnawed chicken bones out of the window. Instantly hungry children pounced on these treasures, fighting furiously for every scrap. Borodin scowled, his eyes narrowed to slits and he muttered something about the terrible war. The pot-bellied "proletarian" leader was annoyed. Nevertheless, he commanded his lackey to give the *bezprizorni* some bread. Then he pulled down the shades and finished his job on the cold chicken.

Our train, we learned, was carrying important foreign guests—a British trade-union delegation headed by Walter Citrine. They traveled in a special car with several Soviet officials and translators, served by their own kitchen and otherwise protected against direct contact with Soviet realities. There was no way, however, in which the famished *bezprizorni* and the ill-clad, starved looking people at some stations could be shut out of view. I could only hope that Sir Walter and his fellow-Britons drew some intimations of the bitter truth from those tragic sights.

There was a continuous flow of trainloads of equipment and armament westward, toward the fighting fronts. "Lend-lease!" Borodin frequently exclaimed as another train rumbled by our windows. "Wonderful American invention!" the General agreed. The closer we got to Vladivostok, the more impressive became this tide of American goods.

Before long Comrade Borodin got off the train, his meek orderly bringing up the rear, staggering under the luggage. The dining-car manager breathed an audible sigh of relief; I couldn't hear what he mumbled under his breath but I'm quite sure I guessed right. The vacated place in my coupe was taken by another member of the Soviet nobility, just as well fed and self-satisfied as his predecessor, though a lot more subdued. He turned out to be the chief of the Regional Department of Art and was on a "cultural mission" to Ulan-Ude in the Mongolian People's Republic.

I was in a highly nervous state throughout the trip. Every inspection of documents—and they were examined frequently—set my heart pounding with illogical apprehension. I slept badly and when finally I dozed off I dreamed that N.K.V.D. ruffians were dragging me off the train. In one such nightmare someone hissed in my ear, "So you thought we didn't know. . . . So you thought we'd let you escape. . . ." I looked around, recognized Gershgorn, and awoke in a cold sweat.

In Vladivostok I stopped at the Intourist Hotel. An orchestra continuously played loud dance tunes, wine and beer were plentiful, and women agents of the N.K.V.D. plied their trade. I visited the free city market, where food and clothes were on sale, at fantastic black-market prices, in greater profusion than I had seen anywhere in the U.S.S.R. Much of this merchandise was clearly American, no doubt stolen from lend-lease consignments or brought in by Russian sailors. I saw a simple pair of women's shoes fetch three thousand rubles in this market. I saw a kilo of bacon sold for 1200 rubles. Small cans bearing colorful American labels brought two hundred rubles and more.

Vladivostok was very much alive. Uniformed sailors and civilian seamen were everywhere in evidence and the docks groaned under mountains of American supplies and equipment. The city was flushed with wartime activity.

Then came the morning when I was taken by automobile, along with others going across the Pacific, to the customs house in the port. We were admitted, one by one, into a closed, businesslike room, along with our luggage. Three Chekists, one in civilian clothes, the others in uniform, went methodically through every suitcase and package, digging into pockets, probing linings and in some cases shaking out shirts and other garments. Then they searched my person no less thoroughly. Every pocket was turned inside out. Every inch of the linings and lapels of my jacket was ruffled with practised fingers. The contents of my wallet were investigated, one of the uniformed men making notes of names and telephone numbers.

An envelope containing snapshots of various members of my family for some reason made the sleuths bristle with curiosity. I was asked about the identity of every person in every photograph.

"And who is this officer?" the civilian customs official pointed to one of the pictures.

"My brother Constantine."

"Where is he?"

"He was killed on the Caucasus front."

"Why are you taking so many photographs with you?"

"They're my folks. After all, I'll be alone, away from them all."

"But you're coming back to the Soviet Union?"

My heart skipped a bit. I swallowed hard before I could find my tongue. But apparently his remark was a shot in the dark, for I was duly passed and certified. Soon I was actually on board the lumber freighter *Komiles*, destination Vancouver, Canada. There were perhaps a score of passengers, men and women, all of us assigned to work in the United States.

Installed in a tiny but comfortable cabin in the officer's wing, I took stock of my thoughts. From the deck I watched the Russian soil recede. It was my last view of my suffering country, where unhappy millions groaned under the oppression of a regime with few precedents in history for systematized and ruthless despotism. To the indignities of an all-embracing serfdom were now added the horrors of war. Nowhere in the world was there such a fearsome concentration of wretched suffering and political despotism, nowhere else was misery so cynically disguised with "advanced" slogans. I could not remain long on deck. Gloomy thoughts and emotions overwhelmed me. Inwardly I was bidding a sorrowful farewell to my friends, my family, my past. Utterly depressed, I went to my cabin to be alone with my thoughts.

The decision to leave, to find the freedom in which to tell the bitter truth about Russia's privations and political slavery, in which to struggle for the liberation of my people, had matured so slowly in the depths of my being that I did not myself know when it took full shape. But for years now it had been a conscious plan, awaiting only a propitious moment. Yet now that the moment had arrived, I was steeped in sorrow. I was poignantly aware of a separation as deep as death, and I felt as if I were being conveyed to my own funeral. At this moment I loved my country and my people with a fierce focussing of emotion that was almost unbearable.

I recalled scenes from my childhood, my youth, my mature life; moments of happiness no less painful, in this hour of total separation, than the scenes of suffering and humiliation. I thought of my experiences in the first famine, in collectivization, in the second and man-made famine, the purges, the hunger, the cold, the nights of torture in Nikopol. I thought of the concentration camps strewn through the length and breadth of the land and of dozens, yes, hundreds, of my closest friends languishing in prisons and forced labor enclosures.

Where was my gentle, high-spirited mother? Where was my incorruptible father, so dour and upright in his loyalty to a vision of freedom? Would they emerge alive from their German captivity? Would they be forced to suffer for my decision? And Irina, would she be punished for my actions? Would she forgive me for having kept her in absolute ignorance of my plans? What would my brother Eugene, a man entirely unconcerned with politics, think of my flight?

My friends, my loved ones, the living and the dead, will you understand why I was constrained to abandon you? Will you understand that I must leave you only in order to be closer to you, in order to attempt to speak of you and for you to a world made dizzy by propaganda and blinded by wishful thinking?

Sailing under the Soviet flag I was still, technically, on Soviet soil. The unreasonable unease still nagged at my waking hours and invaded my sleep. A radiogram, an unguarded word in the presence of the spies who, without doubt, were among us even on this small freighter, would suffice to wreck my passionate hopes and plans.

We passed the shores of Japan. Apprehensively we watched two Japanese destroyers in our wake and, the following day, a Japanese war plane circling us. Several days later we saw land on the horizon and were informed that it was an island where we might see Americans. This first glimpse of American-held territory stirred great excitement among crew and passengers alike. Coming close to the island I saw an American flag fluttering above a group of new houses.

A motorboat chugged alongside. Two American naval officers came up the gangplank and retired into the captain's quarters. Three sailors remained in the boat and we all crowded to the rail for our first close-up of those capitalist "class enemies" against whose wiles we had been so elaborately forewarned. They did not measure up to the role of capitalist menace, these tall, bronzed, smiling youngsters. Several of the girls in our party were English translators and we immediately plunged into conversation.

These American boys, blessedly unaware of their villainous role in Soviet eyes, asked not a single political question. It was plain enough that they were interested only in the Russian girls and that in a decidedly non-political fashion. Someone turned on a gramophone in his cabin and played Russian records for the three sailors down in the boat. One of them asked us to sing *Ochi Chorniye,* but, alas, there were no singers among us.

After the motorboat had departed, we discussed our first sampling of Americans. Everyone was lyrically enthusiastic—the boys' looks, their friendliness, their humor touched our hearts. Then a fanatic Communist (there is at least one in any Soviet group) dashed cold water on our ardor.

"Hadn't we better moderate our admiration, comrades?" he said in a firm, authoritative voice. "Remember that these 'nice' and 'sweet' boys are the children and lackeys of a hostile capitalist world!"

His words recalled us to reality. Some of us looked positively shame-faced, to have been caught off guard so quickly by the temptations against which we had been explicitly warned.

On the nineteenth day we were within sight of Canada. A Canadian inspector climbed aboard, greeting us in dubious Russian but with an undubious smile. Soon we were in the harbor of Vancouver. In less than twenty minutes, without any shouting or confusion, we were docked. The Canadian customs inspectors came aboard, two civilians and one naval officer. We lined up, presented our passports, which were checked in the most cursory fashion and handed back to us. Nobody examined our suit-cases, nobody turned our pockets inside out or searched our coat linings for hidden documents. Most incredible of all, no one questioned us about anything. There was, in short, none of the fear of Soviet citizens we had been led to anticipate, nothing to justify the "vigilance" to which we were committed.

In less than an hour after docking, we were free to go ashore! Even the most bigoted Communists in the group, including the comrade who had dampened our admiration for the American sailors, were amazed and, at bottom, disappointed—they felt like people laden with umbrellas, rub-bers and raincoats on a sunny day. Where was the capitalist sense of class hostility? Why was there so little alarm in their friendly curiosity? Were these people naive or—distressing thought!—contemptuous of the germ-bearers of revolution? It seemed to us unreal, incredible, almost indecent to be turned loose so casually on Canadian soil, and this in time of war.

The Soviet Consul from San Francisco, a Comrade Lomakin, assembled us in the salon and, in a bored, unconvincing way, ran through another lecture on the perils of the capitalist jungle. The poor fellow was just doing his duty. Then we were on our own. Only two guards stood at the gangplank, one Russian, the other Canadian.

I paused for a few seconds before stepping off into Vancouver. I had a deep, earnest awareness of the significance of the moment. For the first time in all my thirty-eight years I was outside the bounds of my native Russian world. For the first time in my mature years I was, it seemed to me at least, beyond the reach of Stalin and his secret police.

CHAPTER XXVII

STALIN'S SUBJECTS ABROAD

VANCOUVER. My head was in a whirl. My thoughts were playing leapfrog. I was free! Who was it once said that only those who have been slaves can understand freedom? It seemed to me, walking through the main streets with a group of my shipmates, that I had never before seen so many relaxed, unafraid, happy people in one place at one time.

What excited us most was the shop windows. This lush abundance of things to wear, to eat, to use! We were like children at a circus, gaping and exclaiming over wonders that to grown-ups were commonplaces. *But this is as if the dream of socialist abundance had come true,* I kept repeating inwardly. *This is what we have been promised for the dim future after an endless chain of Five Year Plans!* There was also a tinge of resentment in my thoughts: These people, our allies, seemed so remote from the horrors and sacrifices of war which had inundated my unfortunate country.

We entered shops to make what was for most of us our first capitalist purchases. Could we really buy all the bread, all the shirts, all the chocolate, everything else we pleased? It bordered on the magical. And the prices seemed ludicrously low. The girls in our party talked in ecstatic whispers about a dress in the window. In Moscow or Vladivostok, if they could have found in war-time, anything so elegant and exquisite, they would have been glad to pay two or three thousand rubles, eight or ten months' wages, several years' savings. In Vancouver it was marked $14.98. . . .

We decided to go into a shoe shop. We were met with smiles and ushered courteously into comfortable seats. "The son-of-a-bitch knows we're foreigners," a misanthropist in our midst growled, "and he's acting up." But we were not convinced, since we noted that Canadians, too, were being treated with the same courtly respect. The clerk, who was dressed as fashionably as the capitalist villain in a Soviet propaganda film, brought many pairs of shoes, different cuts, different materials, a whole museum of shoes. He seemed astonished by our astonishment and perplexed by the delight of the Russian girls.

My sociological interest came to the fore.

"Are you the proprietor of this establishment?" I asked, through an interpreter.

"Oh no, I'm just a salesman here," he laughed.

"Would you mind if we asked how much you earn a month?"

"Not at all. It depends on commissions. About 150 dollars, I'd say."

455

"A hundred and fifty dollars!" the misanthropist forgot himself long enough to exclaim in Russian. Like the rest of us, he was translating the sum into pairs of shoes at the prices we had just been quoted. "Why the son-of-a-bitch could buy thirty pairs of shoes with his monthly salary."

Next we decided to sample a haberdashery. Shirts, ties, kerchiefs, sweaters, topcoats, piles of everything at moderate prices. It seemed to us remarkable that the shop wasn't being stormed by frantic buyers, cleaned out in a twinkling.

These fantastic capitalists not only gave you all your heart's desire but packed it up for you and thanked you for taking it away! Carrying our bundles, we entered a restaurant. To the best of our knowledge no one was trailing us. Unless we informed on each other, not a soul needed to know where we had been, what we had done, what we had said. The food put in front of us completed the picture of abundance.

Intrigued by the excited group of jabbering Russians, an elderly man, immaculately dressed and smoking a long cigar, approached and introduced himself. He was the owner of the restaurant.

"You fellows are sure giving the Germans the licking of their lives!" he declared, shaking hands with every one of us in turn. "I tell you Russia is winning the war and your allies should be damned grateful."

"Yes, it is essential to destroy Hitler's dictatorship," someone in the group rose to the occasion.

"Right you are!" the proprietor said. "I admire all Russians from the bottom of my heart, though of course I'm opposed to Communism. After all, Mr. Stalin also runs a dictatorship."

A breath of frost passed over us. The misanthropist looked at me slowly and meaningfully. "There you are!" he said in Russian. "A fascist pretending to be friendly and under it all he hates our country."

I was about to defend our host's remarks but stopped myself short. I was still among Soviet citizens, there were still strings on my freedom.

Back on the ship, we compared impressions and purchases. We talked late into the night about the marvels of this rich, outspoken world, so far from the realities of war. We told each other, by way of political insurance, that this was merely the beguiling surface, under which were the horrors, the exploitation, the degeneracy and the future crises vouched for by our Stalinist view of the world. Maybe, we thought, those warnings we had received against capitalist fleshpots were not overdrawn after all.

In a few days we were transferred to a train. I walked through the length of the train, to observe people. Even in the day coaches, the passengers seemed to my Soviet eyes to be well dressed. I looked at men and women who evidently were merely farmers, clerks or working people, but they all wore stout leather shoes and good sturdy clothes. Such affluence still seemed to me unreal, a bit extravagant.

Next day an American in uniform, accompanied by another in mufti, came to our car. He looked at our passports, checked them casually, without a trace of decent suspicion, and returned them to us with a smile. Informed that the civilian was a customs inspector, we had all pulled out our suitcases and opened them wide. He glanced negligently at one or two, as a matter of form, then said, "All right, fine, close 'em up."

We felt actually embarrassed by such absurd inefficiency and wondered where was the catch. Personal freedom is one thing, but didn't such lack of vigilance smack of anarchy, chaos? The two men lingered a few minutes, pleased to meet Russians. Then they wished us good luck and departed smiling. Somehow I had imagined that entering the United States would be a long elaborate process, requiring extensive inspections and perhaps interrogations behind closed doors.

We had a short stop-over in a city called Buffalo and used it, of course, to see the sights. I remembered the word Buffalo from having seen it on machinery in Russian factories and was fascinated by the tall buildings, the cleanliness and rectangularity of the place. A number of Buffalo Americans stopped to talk to us but not one, to our amazement, asked a political or economic question. It would take us a long time to become accustomed to people so indifferent to politics and ideology.

The journey to Washington was replete with excitement for me. I was feverishly curious about the new land and gazed in wonder at every new town, at the broad asphalted highways visible through the windows, at the American farmers in their fields, so different from our peasants. I was touched by the easy, open way in which men and women started conversations, asking and answering questions with a childlike frankness and naivete. From the novels by Dreiser and Steinbeck which I had read I was prepared for abject poverty and a deep bitterness of which, as yet, I saw no trace. I would come to know, in due time, that America had its share of misery and injustice. But a Russian fresh from the "socialist" land could hardly share Steinbeck's indignation; his Joads were, on the whole, no worse off than most of our peasants.

On August 19, 1943, I arrived in the capital of the United States, and was met at Union Station by a representative of the Soviet Purchasing Commission. A room had been rented for me with an American family. It was clean, sunny, comfortable, with a private bath, and my hosts seemed truly pleased to have a foreigner—one of those "wonderful Russians"— under their roof. They did not ask me for "documents" and apparently did not have to report me to any house committee. To a regimented conscience this laxness did appear rather disorderly, if not outright sinful. In time this family and I would develop a language of our own, composed of signs and garbled words, sufficient for our meagre social contacts. They accepted me, wholly on faith, as an expert on the war and on all things foreign, let alone Russian, and behaved as if every Soviet military achievement were my own handiwork.

The following morning I reported for work. The interior of our Washington headquarters on Sixteenth Street looked and even smelled remarkably Soviet. It seemed hermetically sealed against the American spirit. Though there was a scattering of native employes in the lowest jobs— typists, stenographers, porters, messengers—the place had an authentically Soviet atmosphere; one sensed something furtive, harried, almost conspiratorial that was uniquely ours.

Comrade Serov was a good-looking and impressive man, tall, dark, robustly built, and filled his new American clothes creditably. He received me coldly, a bit suspiciously, as becomes a vigilant bureaucrat. I handed him the coupon indicating that I was a Party member.

"Number?" he snapped.

I recited it glibly—2486475. For a Communist to forget his membership serial is a species of lese majesty, symptom of faltering faith. A few other questions satisfied him that I was, indeed, the specific Kravchenko assigned to his care, which allowed him to smile, to inquire about my trip and to make small talk about Moscow. But all the time he was studying me with a narrowed, piercing look.

As direct plenipotentiary of the Party's Central Committee, Serov was the ranking Communist emissary in the United States. He had no direct contact with Americans. He took little part in Soviet-American negotiations. As far as the official records went, he was simply another assistant in the Commission. But in fact he was the most potent agent of the Soviet state in America. His word was law for everyone from the most menial Soviet employe to the most important Soviet military, economic and other representatives. Serov spoke with the voice of the Party, which is the real government of the U.S.S.R., whereas even the Ambassador spoke only with the voice of the Commissariat of Foreign Affairs. As far as all Soviet subjects residing here were concerned, he was the Stalin of America.

He unreeled for me the boringly familiar lecture on the dangers and duties ahead of me and the magnitude of the faith lodged in me by the Party. Somehow the stale stuff annoyed me less than formerly. Now I could afford to be amused inwardly: the secret knowledge that soon I would shake off the totalitarian yoke made me immune to the insults implicit in patronizing instructions behind which lurked threats. I even had the boldness to refuse, on the plea that I was too tired, when he asked me to report on conditions in the home land to a staff meeting that night. What could I bring them, in this setting, except the official falsehoods?

My immediate superior, Comrade Serov informed me, would be Alexander Rastarchuk; I would be one of about ten metallurgical specialists in the Metals Division of which he was chief. Tens of millions of dollars in metal goods were being shipped to the Soviet Union under the lend-lease arrangement and it would be my duty to inspect much of this material, to certify its fitness for our purposes, to draw up specifications for myriad items, to select and reject materials of immense value. I would be held strictly accountable for all materials passing through my hands.

2

Our Commission was, to all intents and purposes, a chunk of pure totalitarianism torn loose from the banks of the Moscow River and deposited intact on the shores of the Potomac.

In Washington, D. C., right in the heart of the world's greatest democracy, hundreds of us, men and women, lived the rigidly controlled lives of citizens of the world's greatest dictatorship. Though we resided and worked among free people, we remained the terrorized subjects of a police-state. We did not share the free speech, free press, freedom of conscience and freedom from fear of our American neighbors, except secretly and at the risk of dire punishment.

What we thought, what we read, whom we dared to meet was as completely prescribed and supervised as if we were still inside the Soviet Union. Our every word and act was subject to an elaborate technique of spying. We had a Party Committee, Party nuclei, a Special or Secret Department—the complete equipment of political intimidation and N.K.V.D. surveillance under which we had writhed at home. Here, too, mysterious safes bulged with information and malicious misinformation about every one of us. But what had seemed natural, almost inevitable, in the U.S.S.R. often loomed grotesque and ugly against the American background.

At purely business and technical conferences it was General Belayev—later his successor, General Rudenko—who presided. But at meetings of the Party Bureau of the Commission, where the really vital policies were discussed, Comrade Serov sat in the driver's seat. Occasionally a session attended only by Communists might begin under the General's command and then, when the business phase was finished, he would relinquish his seat at the head of the table to Serov. The doors at that point would invariably be locked so that the Party meeting could get under way.

The same dual system of authority prevailed in every division of the organization. Comrade Rastarchuk conducted technical conferences of our Metals Division, but the nucleus secretary, Markov, took over and Rastarchuk became just one of the rank and file when Party affairs were on the agenda. No one who fails to visualize this picture of a one-party dictatorship pulling the strings behind the facade of government has begun to comprehend the nature of modern totalitarianism.

My basic salary was around three hundred dollars a month. Since I traveled a large part of the time, on an ample expense account, and was provided with extra funds for entertainment when business strategy required it, my real income actually was larger. The most galling restriction, from the outset, was the one imposed on our contacts with Americans.

The people among whom I now lived fascinated me. They seemed to me utterly different from the Russians, and for that matter from Europeans—not only a different race, but almost a different species. But we were strictly forbidden to cultivate their friendship, except for specific business purposes. Having made an American acquaintance, we were obliged to file a detailed report about him, covering not only the routine data of his identity but our impression of his political mood, his feelings about the Soviets. Whether the acquaintance was permitted to prosper depended on the higher officials. It was for them to decide whether the contact was "desirable" or not.

Unavoidably, however, I did come to know dozens of people, in the Washington agencies connected with the vast lend-lease enterprise, and among the handful who were employed by the Commission. I was endlessly embarrassed by their cordiality, their readiness to show me every-thing, their uninhibited talk. To a Soviet official long steeped in intrigue and saturated with fears, the American candor and lack of suspicion seemed almost childlike.

The risks of meeting Americans were vastly multiplied when they happened to be of Russian origin or descent. In that case there was always the fear that they might be supporters of some anti-Stalin faction. At the same time the temptation of making acquaintances among ex-Russians was greatest, if only because of the common language.

The tidal wave of pro-Russian sentiment sweeping the United States after the triumphs of the Red Army was a constant source of danger to Soviet citizens here. Americans were eager to show their good will and appreciation. They pressed us to come to their homes and their clubs, to join them at some bar for a drink. Evading their well-meant hospitality was not always easy. If we did yield to an insistent invitation, we were in line for trouble. We always protected ourselves by reporting the facts.

An elderly American lady holding a very modest post in the Commission asked me several times to pay her a visit. Knowing that I was without a family, her motherly heart was touched. On one pretext or another I avoided accepting her kindness. One evening, as hard luck would have it, I ran into her on the street. It appeared that we were quite near her home and that several friends would be dropping in. I felt that I could not refuse to come up for a cup of coffee without offending her. I remained at her house only an hour. Other guests arrived and we made small talk.

For weeks thereafter I remained in a state of painful alarm. My heart sank every time I was called into the Party Secretary's chambers. What if someone had seen me and "told"? What if the lady herself innocently blurted out the awful truth to the wrong people? Our American co-workers were for the most part ignorant of the pressures under which the Russians worked.

The taboo against mixing with Americans did not apply, of course, to those whom we wished to cultivate for business or political reasons. In that case, on the contrary, we were provided with special funds for lavish entertainment and encouraged to do things in a generous and even showy style. We had to demonstrate that we were "men of the world" represent-ing a rich, powerful and open-handed country.

I have been told of valuable gifts, including expensive furs, pre-sented to Americans whose good will we considered useful. The recipient may have thought it a personal and spontaneous gesture, but in every case it was the end-product of an official discussion and decision. This control of our relations with Americans was carried so far that even New Year's cards were sent to American officials and business acquaintances only with the consent of the proper authorities. We were each instructed to draw up a list of people to whom, in accordance with American usage, we wished to send cards, together with the text of the greetings. The lists and the texts were examined, edited and returned to us with formal permission to prepare the cards. To make sure, however, that we did not depart from the prescribed forms, the actual mailing was done by the Commission.

We were not above using sex appeal to obtain information or the inside track on some deal. Once I was called in by a top-shelf official of the Commission. He explained a "problem" with which he was wrestling. It was important to expedite a certain matter in the War Production Board and the key person in the particular bureau involved was a young woman.

"I want you to meet this woman, Victor Andreyevich," he said, "and get friendly. Take her to night clubs, buy her presents and turn on the charm. The rest will be easy, I'm sure."

He was shocked when I refused categorically to act as the Lothario in the plot. I pleaded a lack of talent in that direction and the difficulty of my inadequate English and in the end escaped the unsavory chore.

Back at my desk after a week or two on the road, chiefly in the company of American technical and business men, the life of the Commission always seemed to me doubly oppressive. I felt as if I were back in a prison compound after a furlough. I had to re-focus my attention on the onerous prison rules under which so many decent Russians suffered in the Commission. Even as in the U.S.S.R., we totalitarian subjects abroad had to keep our thoughts to ourselves, exposing a corner of our true minds and hearts only rarely to a few whom we trusted. Under such trust, at best, there was a palpitant uncertainty. We pretended that we were blind to the liberties enjoyed by Americans. To express admiration or even tolerance for the American way of life would be courting political suicide.

I know that it is not easy to make our attitudes credible to Americans. How could they quite believe my amusing, yet terribly tragic, experience with Mitya? He, too, was a Soviet citizen abroad—working for Amtorg, the Soviet trading organization. One day, while in New York on business, I dropped in unannounced at Mitya's hotel room. I caught him red-handed in the midst of a fearful crime; he was reading a radical Russian-language magazine, a "counter-revolutionary" publication we were forbidden to taste.

"So this is what you read!" I exclaimed, pretending to be shocked.

My friend turned pale. Tears came to his eyes. He knew that his fate was now in my hands. If I should report his blasphemy, his recall to Russia would be almost certain, and after that expulsion from the Party, disgrace, perhaps not only for himself but for his whole family. He tried to defend himself, he groped for words. In a panic of fear he implored me to spare him.

"Believe me, Victor Andreyevich, on my word of honor as a Communist, that I merely wanted to know what these scoundrels are writing about us. I beg you to forget my offense. We've known each other for many years. If you report me, you'll be wrecking my life."

Watching his discomfiture, I began to feel contrite. I assured him that I had no intention of reporting him and that, moreover, I read that magazine myself.

"What slaves we are, Mitya," I sighed. "How scared we are of each other and even of our own thoughts. What do they want to make of us? Spies, liars, stooges incapable of genuine faith and friendship. Why do our bosses fear to let us read what we please? Are they afraid we'll learn some unpleasant truths? It's hard enough to be a slave in Moscow—here in America it's a thousand times harder."

But even this outburst of frankness did not assuage his alarm. On the contrary, it set him wondering whether I was trying to trap him, to draw him into making dangerous statements. He was not entirely quieted until I took him to my room at the Pennsylvania Hotel, opened my brief case and showed him that I had the same periodical in my possession.

Only then he opened up and I learned in the course of a long night session of spirited talk that he despised the Soviet regime as thoroughly as I did. Only the fact that he had a large family in Russia, he said, kept him from breaking loose and declaring his independence. I resisted the temptation of telling him of my own intentions, because I did not wish to burden him with such guilty knowledge.

Though we were not explicitly prohibited to read the New York *Times* or the Washington papers, it was not discreet to do so. Hearst and Scripps-Howard publications were looked on as contraband. The only way to play safe was to read the *Daily Worker,* the Russian-language paper *Russky Golos,* the New York tabloid *PM,* and pro-Soviet weeklies like *The Nation* and *The New Republic. Life,* too, was regarded then as ideologically acceptable—especially after it published a Russian issue which contained far more Soviet propaganda than truth; this favored status, I believe, it squandered later at one fell swoop with an article by ex-Ambassador William C. Bullitt on Soviet policies in Europe.

En route to Washington, in a Pullman car, I was leafing through a copy of the *Saturday Evening Post* when a colleague from the Commission walked in. He sat down and we talked shop for a while. Then I said something about the magazine, its illustrations and advertisements. I was especially interested in an article which, I judged, was critical of the government.

"These Americans," I said, "certainly don't hesitate to say what they think of their officials, from President Roosevelt down."

It was a casual, unthinking remark, which I forgot as soon as I had made it. Several days thereafter the secretary of my Party unit, Markov, called me into his office.

"What kind of a trip did you have?" he asked.

"Oh pretty good."

"You ran into Comrade B——, didn't you?"

"Yes, that's right, I did."

"What was the nature of your argument with him?"

"Argument?" I was perplexed. "I don't recall any."

"I'm afraid, Comrade Kravchenko, we're getting off to a bad start today. You're not being frank with me. Would you like me to remind you? Surely you haven't forgotten that you criticized the Soviet press and complained because we don't attack Comrade Stalin?"

"It's a lie!" I shouted. "I insist that you summon Comrade B——. I'll make him take his lie back."

Comrade B——. in my presence. did not have the courage to stand by the report he had submitted about my "counter-revolutionary remarks." The nucleus secretary decided to drop the issue. But I remained more convinced than ever of the need to curb my tongue.

Another minor episode: Once I fell ill and was confined to bed for a few days. Several of the American employes sent me friendly notes, expressing hope of my speedy recovery. It was a human gesture which gave me a warm feeling of comradeship. When I returned to work I had good reason to regret their kindliness. My English having been unequal to the job of reading the letters in detail, I had brought them to the office and asked someone to translate them for me.

I forgot the whole matter until I was suddenly summoned by the same Comrade Markov. He proceeded to cross-examine me sternly about my relations with each of the Americans who had written me. What is at the bottom of this extraordinary fraternization of a responsible Party man with the "class enemies" around him? He ended with a solemn reprimand and an injunction to beware the pitfalls of our capitalist environment. I counted myself lucky to get off so lightly.

Correspondence was responsible for another crisis in my Washington career. A postcard addressed to me by a corporal in the American Army stationed in Florida was seen, by accident, by a high official of the Commission. I was promptly haled before the Party authorities on charges of unauthorized "communications with the American armed forces." It took a lot of explaining to convince them that the corporal was the son of the good people with whom I lived.

"It was just a friendly human sort of thing and without any political significance," I pleaded. "Besides, I abstained from answering the boy."

The last statement was a lie. Actually I had replied to his greetings. To do less might have made him think that all Russians were boors. A little white lie, however, is small enough price to pay for escape when a totalitarian subject finds himself on such a hot spot.

In the Commission building there is a library. One evening I asked the librarian on duty for two books: the novel *I Love* by Avdeyenko and a historical volume by a writer named Virt in which General Tukhachevsky was mentioned. Neither of the books was available. I borrowed several others and forgot the matter.

But soon thereafter I was called on the carpet by my Party superiors. It appeared that I had committed a whole array of mistakes ranging from simple sins to possible crimes. My presumed interest in the work of General Tukhachevsky, who had been executed as a traitor, was obviously alarming; and was I not aware that this Virt book was no longer read in the U.S.S.R.? My ignorance was no excuse—a good Communist knows who are the "enemies of the people." As for the novel, which once enjoyed great popularity in Russia, it seemed to have been banned for some reason and was now on the literary blacklist. Why had I wished to read that "counter-revolutionary" story at this particular time? In short, I stood deeply compromised in the eyes of the guardians of my Party purity.

The library, in point of fact, was one of the important instruments for supervising our thoughts. Cut off from contact with Americans, most of us unfamiliar with the English language, we were forced to do a lot of reading in Russian. The kind of books and periodicals we picked was carefully noted by the librarian-spies. Even the books we browsed through were reported. These were all useful indications of our state of mind and therefore duly entered in our personal *dossiers*.

The library carried a lot of light reading along with the heavy tomes on Party history and other respectably ideological subjects. To help balance the record of my more frivolous reading, I often borrowed the more respectable books without the slightest intention of reading them. The obsessive fear of our monitors was that we were yielding to the soft bourgeois environment. Our problem, therefore, was to demonstrate continually that our faith remained firm and unspoiled. At Serov's suggestion, we studied again the *History of the Party,* Stalin's *Problems of Leninism,* etc. At closed Party meetings we spurred each other to exhibitions of faith in the Party and The Boss.

The margin of privacy was even narrower than it had been at home. The only address known to our friends in Russia was care of the Commission, where every letter was read before being turned over to us, notwithstanding the fact that it had already been stamped by the Soviet censors. Mail to anyone in Russia, if sent through someone going to the U.S.S.R., had to be delivered *open* for forwarding by the Commission.

We were forbidden to visit night clubs, to see "counter-revolutionary" films or plays, to listen to radio commentators considered "unfriendly" to the Soviet cause. We would sooner have been caught in the act of murder than reading an anti-Soviet book. Being human, we did many of these things—the temptations to political sinning are overwhelming in a democratic country—but always in fear and trembling; many paid with their careers for such transgressions.

The size and complexity of the espionage to which the Soviet official abroad is subjected are truly staggering. Every one of us was expected, as a loyal Party man and also in sheer self-protection, to report suspicious words and acts of the others. That much is taken for granted, whether in Moscow or Vladivostok, in Washington or Chicago.

But in addition the Party had an array of special agents scattered throughout the Commission, seemingly attending to divers technical jobs but in truth devoted to spying on the people around them. Beyond that and most frightening was the network of agents of the N.K.V.D., not known to us, of course, who spied on a more professional basis. Even the General at the head of the Commission and Comrade Serov himself were not exempt from this over-all police control.

Since we did not know who were the spies—normally the agent himself was ignorant of the identity of his fellow-informers—the only safety was in assuming that everyone but one's most intimate friends was an actual or potential tale-bearer. The remarkable thing, indeed, is that despite this demoralizing system many of us did become friendly and did under pledges of secrecy share our thoughts, discontents and despairs. Comrade Serov did not suspect how many of his subordinates had come from Russia in a state of complete disillusionment and how many more had been infected by the democratic contagion in America. Most of these totalitarians abroad were decent human beings, hating the humiliations in which they were involved by a regime based on mutual distrust.

When a colleague showed unusual signs of friendliness, common sense demanded that we consider the possibility that he or she was trying to win our confidence for a purpose. We knew only too well that conversations on "dangerous" themes were often provoked by zealous comrades or professional agents to test our immunity to the sinful American surroundings.

Because of my long years in the Soviet *apparat,* and particularly the period spent in the Sovnarkom, I was personally acquainted with a good many influential Soviet officials and leaders. A few of them I found, to my surprise, occupying strangely modest posts in Washington. I had no doubt that their ostensible jobs were not necessarily their real occupations in the United States. Under the Soviet-American arrangement only a limited number of Soviet officials can come in under ordinary diplomatic passports. Additional intelligence personnel are therefore imported under the guise of economic functionaries and specialists.

On one occasion, in the elevator of the Commission building, I found myself face to face with a fairly important official from Moscow. My mind flashed back to the time when I had seen him at the opening of the play *The Front* in the company of two N.K.V.D. generals. He now pretended not to recognize me. Later, however, he looked me up and warned me not to let on that I knew him and not to reveal his identity, since he was here on a special business assignment. To the American government, presumably, he was just a minor official of the lend-lease set-up, though in reality he was an important official of the Moscow Committee of the Party.

Whatever the specific work of a Soviet economic representative, a major part of his obligation is also to obtain all possible data about American business firms, technology, military affairs, scientific processes and the like. These were part of the explicit instructions which I received before leaving the U.S.S.R. and they were constantly reiterated by Commission officials. In the closed Party meetings we made no secret about the fact that accumulation of economic data and all other useful information must be paramount in our minds when visiting American factories and offices.

The exigencies of war had made us allies with England and America, I was constantly warned, but we must not trust any American. The plutocratic democracies would use the first chance to undermine our system. In our very first interview Comrade Serov had said:

"You should have no misconceptions about our relations with the United States. Today we regard our relations with capitalist America as diplomatically and militarily useful. This does not mean that our interests can ever coincide. In the war itself, and in the future peace period, our roads and aims are quite different. If you bear that in mind, you will understand why we must remain vigilant, suspicious and aloof."

One day the Communists in the organization, who made up about 90 per cent of our responsible officials, were called to a special meeting. When the doors were locked, Comrade Serov announced that he had some important news. He looked solemn. The news was in the form of a very long document, which he read to us, slowly, impressively; then we all initialed it to attest that we were familiar with its contents.

The document was signed by Mikoyan, Commissar of Foreign Trade, but it was clearly the work of the N.K.V.D. in conjunction with Military Intelligence. In effect it was a detailed set of instructions on the kind of information about the United States we must look for, how to gather it, how to cover our traces, how to transmit it to the U.S.S.R. Although in general it merely repeated instructions already given us in the past, it was obviously intended as a refresher course and as a reminder that the highest authorities were depending on us to do our duty in this matter under the cover of lend-lease activities.

3

Everywhere I went in America I received more than my due share of the universal and unbounded admiration for "our brave Russian allies." The extravagance of the adulation sometimes made me wince. All the same, it was good to know that the sacrifices of my people were being appreciated.

But this adulation also became the source of my most irritating and sometimes mortifying experiences here, for it took a curious, even a grotesque turn. By a distortion of logic that had in it a touch of hysteria, not only the recent Russian victories but the shattering defeats that preceded were generally accepted in the United States as proof of the rightness of the Soviet regime. Hitler's offensive proved only that the beast was mighty, but Stalin's counter-offensive somehow confirmed the validity of Bolshevism.

The performance of the Russian people was magnificent. This I knew better than any American enthusiasts, because I was aware, as they were not, that my people were handicapped by a blundering, bureaucratized and despotic government. Yet I could not ignore the fact that we were fighting on our own terrain, with the advantages of almost inexhaustible manpower, full exploitation of our industries, and American technological support. Why Russia's tragically costly victories should be credited to the genius of Bolshevism was beyond me. As a Soviet official under almost constant surveillance I could not speak up, could not defend my countrymen against this monstrous perversion of the facts. A thousand times I had to listen in frustrated silence while the Soviet dictatorship was being given full credit for the achievements of the Russian people.

Inside Russia we had been so ashamed of the Hitler-Stalin pact that we rarely mentioned it at all. Official writings and oratory slurred over that period. But in America the pact was subtly transformed into one more proof of Stalin's wisdom. In one breath people booed the appeasement of Hitler in Munich and cheered his appeasement in Moscow. Somehow it was considered disreputable for the allies to gain time by directing Nazi energies eastward against Poland and Russia, but glorious statesmanship for the Kremlin to divert Germany into a war in the west against France and England.

Americans seemed intent on explaining everything *in Stalin's favor*, to the discredit of the democracies. The Kremlin's every diplomatic blunder, its groveling bargains with the Nazis, its ineptitude in not preparing for the war, its every fumble—paid for with oceans of Russian blood—emerged in the American prints and American conversation as special, almost mystical virtues.

I had expected, naively no doubt, that the sacrifices of my people would make the outside world sensitive to their sufferings. I had expected to hear democratic citizens say: "The least these heroic Russians deserve is a measure of freedom and democracy." I found, on the contrary, a remarkable callousness to the tragedy of the Russian people. It was based in large part on ignorance, which was excusable, but also in part on indifference, which was plainly insulting. The democratic aspirations of Koreans or Hungarians found ready understanding and encouragement here, but the democratic aspirations of the Russians were outlawed and treated as a kind of treachery.

Even in the first weeks after my arrival I could see that someone somewhere had manipulated the surge of fellow-feeling for Russians for Stalin's benefit. What should have been a portent of Russian freedom had been twisted into a justification of Soviet despotism. Stalin's grip on the American mind, I realized with a shock, was almost as firm as his grip on the Russian mind.

"But the British, too, are allies," I recall saying quietly to a new American friend, "yet I've heard you criticize them bitterly. The other day you said that the English masses must revolt against the Tories and imperialists. Why not the same frankness in criticizing the Soviet regime?"

"Oh, that's different."

"You mean the Russians are the only ones in the world not entitled to a revolution?"

"Now you're pulling my leg, Victor."

I wasn't. But I tried another tack.

"We Russians," I said, "fought courageously and died by the million in the first great war against Germany. Did you Americans at that time turn into fanatical admirers of the Tsar and his tyranny? Did you say it was final proof that the Russian masses were devoted to their chains and their prison wardens?"

"Oh that was different."

His obsession was not susceptible to treatment by reason or analogy. Under it, of course, was that tinselly picture of a happy and successful "socialist" nation imposed upon the mind of the outside world by the best propaganda machine in all history. The slightest effort to scrape off a little of the tinsel, to expose the squalor and moral ugliness underneath, was resented by most Americans almost as if their deepest religious convictions were at stake.

An incredible thing seemed to have happened in the American mind: the Soviet dictatorship was fully identified with the Russian people. What the Communists had not yet succeeded in doing in their own country—as the purges and the millions of political prisoners indicate—they had succeeded in doing in America! Freedom of speech and press were not curbed with respect to criticism of other allies—Britain, Poland, Czechoslovakia, China—and were even given full rein with respect to the American government and its conduct of the war. But a sort of moratorium on these freedoms was being maintained, by moral pressure, in relation to the Soviet dictator's interests and prestige. I saw men and women who themselves called President Roosevelt a dictator, grow furious when Stalin was called a dictator.

In the Soviet Union the war made little change in the anti-capitalist propaganda. Criticism of British and American war policies was continuous and often vitriolic. But in America, I found, there was a powerful taboo on any and all doubts of the Kremlin's conduct at home or abroad. A "liberal" publisher actually called for the removal from the bookshelves of all books distasteful to Moscow! I was informed that other publishers, whether on their own or at the behest of the authorities, were refusing to publish certain books solely because they might hurt Stalin's feelings. Only a few periodicals had the courage to print what Americans call "anti-Soviet" articles.

The "news" reaching the American press from its Moscow correspondents seemed to me worse than useless. At home we had learned through the years to discount, to interpret, to read between the lines in the Soviet newspapers. American journalists in Moscow in effect simply transmitted excerpts from the Moscow press; no other sources of information were open to them. But their readers at home were not equipped to see through such material. They accepted it literally, uncritically. Every Kremlin lie or diplomatic twist thus reached American minds with the seeming authority of an American by-line and found readier credence here than at home. How was one to make people raised in a democratic tradition understand that censored, controlled "news" was often worse than none?

The prevailing American notions about the wonders of Sovietism in practice were truly extraordinary. Great chunks of the Communist reality —like slave labor, police dictatorship, the massive periodic purges, the fantastically low standards of living, the great famine of 1932–33, the horrors of collectivization, the state-organized child labor—seemed to have completely escaped American attention. These were things of which everyone inside Russia was deeply conscious. Some of us might explain them as necessary or unavoidable or even noble, but it would not occur to us to *deny* them. Yet when I ventured to mention such things (at times when candid conversation was possible), Americans looked at me incredulously and some even hastened to enter cocksure denials.

The greatest Soviet triumph, it was borne in upon me, was in the domain of foreign propaganda. After a while my conviction on this score shook down into a kind of formula: *If the Soviet Union within twenty years should be half as good as its American admirers think it is already, then it would be the greatest social achievement in history. . . .*

Among those who did know some of the unappetizing truth about life under the Soviets, I found a curious wishful-thinking eagerness to blame it all on Stalin. That enabled them to accept the horrors tolerantly as a kind of interlude before paradise is ushered in. After Stalin—and he's a mortal man, isn't he?—"socialist democracy" would begin to flourish. In Russia, too, I had met this tendency to blame all the piled-up evils on one man, but there was vastly more of this self-delusion in the U.S.A. Unfortunately these evils are inherent in the whole Soviet system, and the system assuredly will not die with Stalin. Some other dictator or dictatorial clique will carry on.

Once I found myself, in a small American industrial town, in the company of some thoroughly conservative anti-labor capitalists. In fairness, they said, they should tell me that they were opposed to the Soviet system, indeed that they hated it and feared its influence on American thought. What was their mental picture of this system they hated? I began to draw them out. To my amazement I discovered that they thought Russia a country in which "the workers ruled," in which the farmers "lived in a cooperative society," in which "everyone was equal"! Because another Soviet official was present, I was in the excruciating position of being unable to explain to these confused men that there is more workers' control, more trade-union influence, more truly cooperative farming, more personal freedom in America than Soviet Russians dare dream of.

In the Commission library I found several speeches of Henry A. Wallace. An interpreter read for me the marked portions about Russia. I could not believe my ears—the Vice-President of a democratic government was praising what he called "economic democracy" in Stalin's police-state! Our Secret and Special Departments in every Soviet factory, state-controlled trade unions, lack of true collective bargaining, the death penalty for strike agitations, the Stakhanovite and piecework systems, labor passports, laws punishing more than twenty minutes' lateness by starvation, and forced-labor colonies—didn't Mr. Wallace know these commonplace facts or did he, by some trick of rationalization, really look on them as aspects of "economic democracy"?

I struggled through Wendell Willkie's book *One World*. I had been working at the Sovnarkom during his visit and I knew, at the time, that no propagandist stunt was overlooked in the plans to impress him. Nothing just happened—everything was arranged. Now I was astounded and horrified by the success of our plans. How could any man, I marveled, be so elaborately deceived in such a short time? Reading his Russian chapters I had the sense that he was referring to a country which I had never visited, a country somewhere on the other side of the moon. The book was a signal triumph of totalitarian propaganda.

Mr. Willkie recounted how he had gathered a congenial group of Soviet journalists in a Moscow hotel for a frank, off-record talk. They locked the door and "took their hair down," in the American expression. If I were writing a play lampooning the gullibility of American innocents abroad, I would incorporate that scene without changes. Did Mr. Willkie and his American monitors really believe that they would get honest opinions by locking the door and excluding "officials"? Did they really fail to understand that every Soviet journalist—or engineer or tourist guide—is an "official" living under continuous duress? The very idea of "off-record" hair-down discussion with a Soviet subject within earshot of another Soviet subject or a possible dictagraph reveals total ignorance of totalitarian realities. Every one of those journalists, of course, reported that session, with special emphasis on his own loyalty in defending the regime and filling Mr. Willkie with prescribed "opinions."

He had no alternative. Every journalist, high industrialist or other Soviet citizen whose work brings him in contact with foreigners is formally and officially "secretized"—that is, pledged in writing to report instantly to the N.K.V.D. all meetings with foreigners and full details on what was said and done. The "frank" exchange of views of which Mr. Willkie was so proud became known immediately and in extreme detail to the Foreign Department of the N.K.V.D., to the Press Department of the Commissariat of Foreign Affairs, the Foreign Department of the Central Committee of the Party and all other interested organizations. No better-recorded off-the-record conference, we may be sure, has ever taken place.

Perhaps my most harrowing evening in America was spent in a Washington motion-picture theatre. I was grateful for the dark, which covered up the distress that, I am sure, was written on my face. The other Soviet official who was with me, also a Party member, squirmed in his seat; I had no doubt he was as shaken as I was. It was the evening when I watched the unfoldment of a film called *Mission to Moscow,* based on a book of the same name by the former Ambassador to Moscow, Joseph E. Davies. What I saw was a brutal, heavy-handed insult to the Russian nation—a caricature of its revolution and a mockery of its long anguish.

The book was more absurd than evil, a hash of ignorance and double-talk and in large part plain silly; but it was mitigated here and there by a streak of truth. The film carefully steered around those streaks and added nightmarish inventions not in the book. Wherever the Hollywood "historians" faced a choice between fact and fiction, between reality and nonsense, they carefully chose fiction and nonsense. It happened that I was thoroughly acquainted with the Siberian factory that figured in one of the purge trials; a more ludicrous cartoon than the Hollywood version could scarcely be contrived. No Soviet propaganda picture would have dared twist facts so recklessly out of their sockets. The American propagandists evidently relied on the ignorance of their audience to "get away with" their fantasy. In that sense, incidentally, the picture was as much an insult to Americans as to Russians. Small wonder that the Moscow *Pravda* lavished praise on Mr. Davies and his book, quoting him to the effect that Soviet justice was flawless, that a fifth column had been wiped out by the purge, that the annihilation of the founders of the Bolshevik Revolution was fully justified. What strange reading it made for intelligent Russians!

Stalin killed off the founders of the Soviet state. This crime was only a small part of the larger blood-letting in which hundreds of thousands of innocent men and women perished. But in the Davies-Warner Brothers film all this horror was reduced to a petty *opera-bouffe* conspiracy by a few comic Old Bolsheviks and foreign agents presented as a "fifth column." A political event which makes the St. Bartholomew's Eve Massacre and the French Terror and the Armenian atrocities look like street-corner brawls was here trimmed down to the dimensions of a parlor farce.

I had been through the purge. Though one of the least among the victims, I had suffered its indignities in my own flesh and spirit. Now in a Washington theatre I saw my own ordeal and that of my country being mocked in terms of caricature and falsification. I watched the macabre scene as Hollywood kicked the corpses around and *heiled* the murderers.

When I emerged from the hours of purgatory that evening I saw that I had drawn blood in my palms with my fingernails. My companion and I looked at one another—one look was enough, there was no call for words. I tossed all night in bed without falling asleep.

Another picture reflecting the American myth about Russia, which drove me to helpless despair, was called *North Star*. It was set in a comic-opera village in a never-never land where well-fed, picturesque and deliriously happy peasants live gaily and amply, singing, dancing and loving from dawn to dawn. It was a magic village, with all the fairy-tale trappings, where the roads were scrubbed by pixies and even the horses and cows were housebroken—at any rate there were no evidences to the contrary in this hygienic village. But we were not in the Land of Oz. It turned out, amazingly, that we were in a collectivized village in the land of Stalin!

This Hollywood view of collectivization had about as much relevance to the truth as the Hollywood history in *Mission to Moscow*. And there were plenty of other pictures, books, articles with the same other-side-of-the-moon quality. American propaganda was not content to present the unpleasant facts about Russia and to explain them away. It took the simpler course of denying the facts and building up a Russia that existed only in their ardent imaginations.

Why, why, I kept asking myself, did these Americans insist on fabricating a paradise and locating it in my tortured country? Why must they whitewash every Stalinist evil and explain away every Bolshevik horror?

There was apparently a group of men and women—Duranty, Hindus, Anna Louise Strong, Ella Winter, Albert Rhys Williams, to mention a few—who had built careers on this inexplicable American sweet tooth for Soviet propaganda confections; reading them was almost like reading the Moscow press. There was another somewhat larger and on the whole more honest group, actual Communists, for whom lying about Russia was a method of class warfare: their shortcut to power. But why did the great mass of Americans swallow it?

What struck me most was the profound ignorance among alleged "experts on Soviet Russia" about the nature and organization of power in the U.S.S.R., the mechanisms of administration of the country. But their propaganda has sunk deep roots in America. Once, in the library of an American university, I had occasion to consult the catalogue. I was amazed to find that the most *shop-worn* cards were those listing the works of Lenin and Stalin. Obviously some people studied them seriously, as guides to a better world. . . . I was not astonished to discover, after this, that some American, Hindu and Chinese students in that university were devoted to the hope of transforming their own countries along the lines of the Soviet pattern. I could only hope that they might not be doomed to pass through the same bitter experience that I had suffered.

In many cases, I came in time to understand, Americans were accepting the myth as a substitute for reality. They were upset by the inequities of life in their own country and needed consolations, in the way that a child in pain is consoled by a shiny, noisy toy. They were not so much deceiving others as deceiving themselves. I was most conscious of this element of anxious self-delusion in the work of so-called liberal writers, in *The Nation, The New Republic, PM* and other such publications. Their attitude seemed to me a fearful waste of noble intentions.

If only such people could attain the intellectual clarity and the moral balance to realize that injustice in America must not be made an excuse for supporting injustice elsewhere! Shouting hurrah for bloody liquidations in Russia may give them temporary spiritual relief, but it hardly promotes the larger purposes of justice everywhere, including the United States of America.

Browsing in American libraries, I discovered eloquent books by Americans who, in the time of Tsarist terror, had dared to reveal the facts. There was, for instance, George Kennan's volume on Siberia. I know, also, that there were scores of Russian exiles, of whom Peter Kropotkin was typical, who escaped beyond the reach of the Tsar's Okhrana to expose and denounce those who kept their people in chains. I wondered whether, as a reward for their daring, they had been called "anti-Russian" by American liberals. Or did more logical, less frenzied, less propagandized generations realize that those men were *pro*-Russian, crying out their pity for the victims?

In America today, I was to learn slowly and incredulously, those who venture to tell some truth about the Stalin tyranny, who speak up *for* the Russian people and against their oppressors, are discounted and dismissed and sometimes pilloried as "anti-Russian." I became aware that my resolve to escape into the free world and to use the freedom to defend my people would not be as simple as it had seemed at a distance. I realized that I must expect to be denounced and ridiculed by precisely those warm-hearted and high-minded foreigners on whose understanding and support I had counted.

The Stalinist propaganda in the outside world had been more successful than any of us in Russia suspected. The myth of a happy "socialist" land is treated as a grim piece of totalitarian ballyhoo inside Russia; it is accepted literally, solemnly, in an almost religious transport of faith by a large part of those men and women who create public opinion in the outside democratic world.

CHAPTER XXVIII

FUGITIVE FROM INJUSTICE

THE NEWSPAPER reports of my break with the Soviet regime said that, having tasted American democracy, I became disillusioned with Stalin's Communism. It was my direct experience of American freedom, they said or implied, which led me to abandon the Soviet Purchasing Commission.

That made it a more dramatic story, as well as a pretty compliment to the U.S.A. But it wasn't true. The truth is that I had made up my mind long before to throw off the totalitarian straitjacket at the first chance, wherever and whenever it might present itself. Had I been assigned to China or Patagonia rather than the United States, I would have made the self-same attempt to achieve freedom for the task I had set myself.

It was a task I had assumed consciously, although I do not know the precise point in my inner existence when I had assumed it. It was the result of feelings that had matured within me, slowly but inevitably. I was under the compulsion of everything I had been and thought. I was moved by a childhood pervaded by the robust idealism of my father, the profound religious faith of my mother. Their goodness, their love of humanity, were different in kind, but somehow identical at the core. And it was this core, no doubt, that remained also in me.

I was moved, too, by the spirit of a nation which had produced rebels in its darkest ages, under the most despotic and ruthless rulers. This I know: had I believed it possible to fight for freedom within the Soviet frontiers, I would have remained there. . . . Had there been a real hope of change for the better—of the introduction of political and economic democratic freedoms, of the abandonment of their international Communist program by the leaders of the regime—I would have remained there. Unhappily the regime, with every year, was moving not *toward* the human ideals implicit in the revolution, but *away from* those ideals.

The hope for our Russia was always dimmer, the economic freedoms and the democratic guarantees were always more remote; even their memory seemed to be fast fading out. The depredations of arbitrary power were growing in magnitude and in recklessness. There was a moment, during the war, when some of us thought that the principles of the Atlantic Charter and the promises of the Four Freedoms would apply also to our country. But that illusion was quickly dissipated. As far as our country and people were concerned, we realized, these documents were merely scraps of paper.

Why did I continue to wear the straitjacket for seven months after I arrived in the United States? The answer is that I needed time to survey the terrain, to assess my psychological resources, before making the terrifying jump. In the same way a convict, having resolved to try to escape, gives himself time to learn the habits of the guards and the geography of the neighborhood.

The Russian raised under the Soviet tutelage, emerging into the non-Soviet world for the first time, is a bewildered and almost helpless creature. The simplest adjustments to life become problems. He discovers that he thinks differently, feels differently, than those around him. He needs time to peel off layer after layer of his totalitarian conditioning; the process is a complicated one.

In America I was a stranger, without a single non-Soviet friend, without a language, without the means of economic survival. Had I possessed as many open and concealed friends in America as the Soviet dictatorship has, my problems would have been solved easily enough. . . . Ultimately, I trust, my engineering training and experience will enable me to make a living. But at the moment of cutting loose from the Commission I would be penniless, friendless, helpless against the awful machinery of calumny and vengeance at the disposal of my offended jailors. Seven months was actually a brief period to acclimate myself to America, to acquire a little vocabulary and a few human contacts.

For at least a month in advance I knew that I would take the irrevocable step at the end of March, 1944. I spent most of that month in travel: two trips to Lancaster, Pennsylvania, and one to Chicago. My main preoccupation was to safeguard my friends and colleagues in the Commission as well as in Russia. I did not betray my plans to any of them, by word or gesture, though I needed confederates and naturally ached to confide in someone. I knew too intimately what it would mean to any Soviet citizen if there were so much as a shadow of guilt on his record, once the N.K.V.D. applied itself to my "case."

A secondary preoccupation was to give the Commission no excuse for making wild charges against my character. My record in the vital lend-lease work entrusted to me had been flawless; I was eager that it should remain so to the very end. Insofar as possible, therefore, I wound up the work assigned to me, leaving everything in such organized shape that another metals specialist could pick up where I left off. On my last morning in the headquarters on Sixteenth Street, I carefully straightened out my finances. Thirty dollars were still owing to me when I departed and I was pleased by this, though every dollar at the moment looked like a thousand.

I have told about the actual breakaway in the opening pages of this book. I had turned myself into a man without a country. I had made myself a target for the malice of American Communists and, what was a lot more terrifying, of their self-righteous fellow-travelers. I had made myself a target of the murderous hatred of the world's strongest and most implacable government.

My prospects were dark and disquieting. Deliberately, in full knowledge of the frightening consequences, I had chosen a precarious freedom as against a comfortable enslavement. Only the seasoned subject of a modern dictatorial police-state can quite comprehend the fear that its power and ubiquity and amoralism can inspire in a man's heart.

At the time I left Washington I was aware that there was a formal decision of the Commission, ratified by Moscow, designating me to a permanent place on its staff. It amounted to a substantial promotion for me. I was to enter upon this new work a few days later, on April 3, with Moscow's blessings. Later I might have returned home with my foreign commercial experience, as a faithful son of Stalin who had weathered the storms of bourgeois temptations. There was no limit to the heights I might then have scaled in the bureaucracy.

But on those heights I would have remained, no less, a slave of the *vlast*, helpless to serve my people, in league with their oppressors. Deliberately I chose to remain abroad. I needed freedom for the fight against despotism, and to attain that freedom I was accepting a multitude of discomforts, economic risks, physical dangers. From now on, Victor Kravchenko was no more. His identity was blotted out. Now he was Italian, Yugoslav, Portuguese, anything but Russian. What names I've had!

In an obscure and depressing uptown hotel in Manhattan I prepared the statement, part of which appeared in the New York *Times* and other papers on April 4, 1944. Reading it now, when the war has been victoriously concluded, there is nothing in the statement I would amend. On the contrary, time, it seems to me, has confirmed my fears and my warnings.

I charged then that the Kremlin, while supposedly allied with Britain and America, was "pursuing aims incompatible with such collaboration." Ostensibly having dissolved the Communist International, I wrote, Moscow continued to direct Communist movements everywhere. Touching on Stalin's policies for Poland, the Balkans, Czechoslovakia, Hungary, Austria and other countries, I sought to show that his objectives were purely Soviet and undemocratic. Then I added:

"While professing to seek the establishment of democracy in countries liberated from fascism, the Soviet Government at home has failed to take a single serious step toward granting elementary liberties to the Russian people.

"The Russian people are subjected, as before, to unspeakable oppressions and cruelties, while the N.K.V.D., acting through its thousands of spies, continues to wield its unbridled domination over the peoples of Russia. In the territories cleared of the Nazi invaders, the Soviet Government is re-establishing its political regime of lawlessness and violence, while prisons and concentration camps continue to function, as before.

"The hopes of political and social reforms cherished by the Russian people at the beginning of the war have proved to be empty illusions.

". . . I maintain that more than any other people the Russian people require that they be granted elementary political rights—genuine freedom of press and speech, freedom from want and freedom from fear. What the Russian people have had from their Government has been only lip service to these freedoms. For years they have lived in constant dread and want. The Russian people have earned a new deal by their immeasurable sacrifices, which have saved the country as well as the existing regime itself, and through which they have dealt such decisive blows to fascism and have determined the course of the war."

Nothing has happened since I wrote those words to alter the picture. The Stalinist dictatorship remains ruthlessly supreme and centralized, its methods of terror unrelieved. I cannot expect the average citizen of a democratic nation to understand the true character of a totalitarian tyranny. Those who drafted the indictment of Nazi war criminals came close to that understanding when they described the Nazi regime. Reading their document I could not help exclaiming: *Here, at last, is an adequate summary of the Soviet regime! We need only change a few names, substitute Soviet for Nazi, and we have a picture of the Kremlin set-up.*

That indictment of the Nazis shows the *Führerprinzip,* the leadership principle, as central in the fascist doctrine and practice. It is the Kremlin principle no less. The indictment declares: "The conspirators caused all political parties except the Nazi party to be prohibited . . . reduced the Reichstag to a body of their own nominees and curtailed the freedom of popular elections . . . established and extended a system of terror against opponents and supposed suspected opponents of the regime. . . ." Except for the identity of the conspirators and the victims, I was reading an indictment of the Soviet dictatorship and of all modern totalitarian police-states.

Yet some of the very people who condemn the Hitlerite conspirators find no words with which to condemn the Soviet conspirators against the liberties of the Russian people. The task of arousing the world's conscience on the Russian horrors still remains to be accomplished.

2

The forebodings with which I began my new life were quickly justified by events.

The Soviet Purchasing Commission, when the news of my action appeared in the press, at first pretended that it did not know me. Obviously it was waiting for instructions from Moscow. Then it acknowledged my existence and proceeded to issue the inevitable statements smearing my character.

Its most significant claim, and one that I had not foreseen, was that I was still a captain in the Red Army. Thus it sought to convert my political escape into a military desertion, setting up a legal basis for demanding my extradition to face Stalin's firing squad. Actually, my brief military career had ended in a hospital more than two years earlier. Thereafter I had been a purely civilian official. Before the Commissariat of Foreign Trade could or would send me abroad, I had been given a formal and total release from all military obligations.

The Communist and crypto-Communist press threw itself lustily into the battle. The *Daily Worker* attack on April 5, signed by one Starobin, was headed: *The Case of a Petty Deserter: Hitler Calls on His Last Reserves Here.* It was composed in the standard style of Party vituperation. But running through it was a note which the uninitiated might not detect but which rang loud in my trained ears.

It was the note of direct threat. Comrade Starobin reported a "disgusting bit of treachery from someone who calls himself an official of a Soviet trading commission." Such traitors, from Trotsky down to nobodies like this Kravchenko, he wrote, "deceive many people for a while." But— and then came the warnings:

"The vigilant and avenging hand of forward-looking humanity catches up with them and finally erases them."

Reading these words, I recalled that in Trotsky's case the avenging hand had gripped a pickaxe, with which it pierced his skull in Mexico City. After a few more paragraphs of abuse, Comrade Starobin returned to his theme song. "Kravchenko evidently has been living on borrowed time," he declared. Then, referring to the fact that I had invoked the protection of American public opinion, he concluded as follows:

"Our country is not a no-man's land for enemies of our allies and our own war effort. . . . It would be a sad day if the United States became a hothouse for lizards of this kind, an asylum for characters who are not man enough to say to the people of the Soviet Union directly what they weep over their beers to the New York *Times*."

The *Daily Worker* thus gave the more stupid of its readers to understand that anyone who is "man enough" can talk to the people of the Soviet Union directly! This after conceding that I had been "living on borrowed time" because the Soviet thought-police had remained unaware of my views! I would be "erased"—not by the secret agents of Comrade Starobin's spiritual fatherland, of course, but by "forward-moving humanity."

I had no trouble in deciphering the message. Unless I sank back into silence, the "vigilant and avenging hand" would do its noble work; there was no dearth of pickaxes. Others might dismiss such warnings as mere rhetoric; unfortunately I knew too much about the methods and the agents of the regime which I had denounced.

Despite my elaborate precautions, Soviet intelligence in New York apparently had no difficulty in tracing my whereabouts. Its agents, unmistakably, were soon loitering on the sidewalk opposite my hotel. Several times I changed hotels and pseudonyms. Now and then I consoled myself that I had eluded them. But quickly enough the same men were keeping their vigil outside my temporary residences. Repeatedly I dived into hallways and grabbed taxis on the fly to evade men who were trailing me.

To free myself for a while from these nerve-racking attentions, I accepted an invitation to spend some time with new friends in the suburbs of a Midwestern city. These friends were Americans who had sought me out after an article of mine appeared in the *Cosmopolitan*. I told no one of my departure and supposed that I had succeeded cleverly in boarding the train without being observed. I was wrong. My friends, awaiting me on the station platform, were thoroughly alarmed. They pointed out three men who had been watching them closely, without disguising their interest, for the past fifteen minutes.

There was no doubt that the trio was waiting for me. One of them, I observed, kept his right hand in his pocket, never withdrew it and never took his eyes off me. When we piled into our car, the strangers hastily piled into another and followed us without effort at concealment. We drove at random through the city in a futile effort to shake them off. Only when we pulled up at a police station did the other automobile pass us and disappear. We succeeded in taking down its license number— subsequent investigations disclosed that it was a stolen license plate.

Several times in the following days the same sinister car patrolled the suburban house where I was living. In addition, there were long-distance telephone calls from New York in which mysterious voices warned me "as friends" that my life was in danger and that I must go into hiding. Evidently the scheme was to intimidate my hosts into driving me out of their home, and then to maneuver me into some obscure hiding place where I could be "erased" more conveniently. I felt as if I were again in the U.S.S.R. rather than in the free United States. Would I ever again, I wondered, be able to live and work without fear for my life?

My friends stood up courageously under these pressures and I shall be eternally grateful to them. My host went to bed night after night with a sharp axe close at hand—the only weapon in the house—for the expected emergency. Other Americans—and some Russians—in other parts of the country proved themselves immune to Soviet intimidation and willing to take a chance to safeguard my life while I was working on this book.

Now the book has been completed. I have told my story. The killers who profess to serve "forward-moving humanity" may in time succeed in "erasing" me. The borrowed time may be used up. But they cannot erase this record, dedicated to the long-suffering Russian people from whom I have sprung. I dare to hope that one day they may enjoy real freedom and real economic democracy.

When that day comes to pass, we shall in truth be close to the ideal of one world. As long as one-sixth of the world's surface, now greatly expanded by aggrandizement and the betrayal of small nations, remains under totalitarian slavery in an intellectual blackout, peace can be at best a precarious thing.

The next step toward world security lies not in a world organization— though that must come—but in the liberation of the Russian masses from their tyrants. One need only suppose that, by some miracle, Russia were suddenly democratized to realize that most of the tensions now threatening humanity's peace would be automatically relaxed and that genuine world cooperation would become possible. The liberation of Russia from its totalitarian yoke, I may be told, is a matter that concerns only the Russians. Those who think so are profoundly wrong. In many ways the safety of all civilization and the chance for enduring peace depend on that liberation.

I am not sanguine enough to expect the miracle in our generation. But this I know for a certainty: an understanding of the Russian reality by the democratic world is the pre-condition for my country's liberation from within. The weight of world opinion, the leverage of its spiritual support, now serving to fortify the Kremlin's despotism, must be diverted to quicken and aid the Russian aspirations for freedom.

This book, in terms of the life story of one typical Russian whose sense of liberty has not been destroyed, is my appeal to the democratic conscience of America and of the world.

POSTSCRIPT

I BEGAN TO WORK on this book immediately after my escape from the Soviet Purchasing Commission and worked on it month after month under harrowing conditions of persecution and threats against my life. I was obliged to wander from city to city, continually changing hotels and private residences, living under assumed names and assumed nationalities, finding safe "hide-outs" in the homes of Americans or my own countrymen. To all of those who showed me kindnesses and gave me moral support I want hereby to express my deep gratitude.

Had the Soviet agents caught up with me during this period, I might have been "erased"; or worse, I might have been spirited to the Soviet Union for a "reckoning." Fortunately, this did not happen, so that today, for the first time in my life, I feel free to speak for my country, for my people, for myself.

When I left the Commission, war was still under way. The urgency of military cooperation between the Western democracies and the Totalitarian Soviet Union imposed great restraints upon me. I accepted those willingly; the need for a common victory took precedence over everything else. But now, with the war victoriously concluded, I consider it not only possible but my imperative duty to speak out fully, candidly, as effectively as I can. Hence this book.

Another compelling reason for speaking my mind is in the fact that since the end of the war many peoples and nations—some of their own free will and others under external compulsion—have been "swinging left." This trend seems to me healthy and inevitable—provided that it does not present the first stage, or as in some cases, a finished model of Totalitarian Kremlin Communism. Unhappily that seems to be the case in large areas of the civilized world where Soviet force and Soviet doctrines have the right of way.

The people of my country are in the clutches of the police-state; they cannot possibly make their views and their hopes and their distress known to the world. In the measure that I can reveal the true physiognomy of the Kremlin dictatorship to the peoples and governments of democratic countries, I feel that I am helping in a small way to warn the world against self-delusions. For the building of a more decent world we need greater mutual understanding and deeper friendship *between the peoples of this globe,* and not only between the governments.

The Communist dictatorship in the U.S.S.R. is not a problem for the Russian people only, or for the democracies only. It is the problem of all humankind. The world dare not continue indefinitely to turn its back on the martyrdom of a great segment of the human race inhabiting one-sixth of the earth's surface. This segment is ruled by a deified group of leaders resting on the Party apparatus of the Politburo and a gigantic police force. The hundreds of millions of people in the U.S.S.R. have no voice in shaping their own destinies and are completely cut off from the peoples and the streams of thought in all other countries.

Though the Kremlin leaders have denied their own subjects the rudiments of economic and political liberty, they and their fellow-travellers abroad seek to make the rest of the world believe that the Soviet system is a species of freedom—that it is *real* democracy as contrasted with the "old-fashioned" variety.

Naturally, I wrote this book in my native tongue, Russian, so that it had to be translated, the English text edited from an American vantage point before publication in English. This was done under the stipulation that all facts, incidents, personal experiences, political events, pictures and individual characteristics, down to the minutest detail, follow faithfully my original Russian manuscript. Moreover, when the English text was completed, I personally checked and edited the final version.

I tried to hold this book to the personal, autobiographical pattern. It was, therefore, necessary to leave out a vast amount of material dealing with the complex political, administrative and police forms, and other problems of the Soviet State. These and other related material I plan to publish later.

In some instances, in order to protect innocent people from the pitiless vengeance of the Soviet State, I was obliged to change some names, disguise some places, alter some circumstances. Where such changes have been essential, the episodes themselves have remained wholly truthful and their significance in the narrative unimpaired.

I dedicate this book to the people of Russia, of whom I am one. I dedicate it to the memory of those millions who have died in the struggle against Soviet absolutism; to the millions of innocents languishing in the Kremlin's numberless prisons and forced-labor camps; to the memory of millions of my fellow-countrymen who died in defense of our beloved fatherland dreaming of a better future for our people. I dedicate this book to the progressive and socially-minded people everywhere who help in the struggle *for a free democratic Russia,* without which there can be no enduring peace on earth.

Victor Kravchenko

New York, February 11th, 1946.

INDEX

INDEX

Nikopol, 197; accusations of, 216–217, 220, 227; purge of, 260

Malenkov, deputy member Politburo, 343, 399, 405

Malishev, General, 400, 404

Manayenkov, Josef, and wife, arrest of, 225

Manturov, Viacheslav Ivanovich, director of Glavtrubostal metallurgical mill, 345, 353, 357, 361–362, 370, 388

Margolin, Secretary of Dniepropetrovsk Regional Committee, 246, 256, 264

Markov, of Soviet Purchasing Commission, 459, 462, 463

Marx, books of, 37, 61, 144, 309, 402, 426

Marx-Engels-Lenin Institute in Moscow, 304–305

Matsuoko, 423

Matulevich, Prosecutor Vishinsky's assistant, liquidation of, 236

Matveyev, chief bookkeeper at Kemerovo, 348, 349, 350

Maxim, Father, at Alexandrovsk, 13, 15

McCormick press, 424, 444

Mekhlis, head of Political Department of Red Army, 428

Mensheviks, 20, 21, 193, 224; Party accusations against father as one of, 217, 223, 224, 242

Menzelinsk, town of, 379, 382; in military hospital in, 386–387

Merkulov, chief of Glavtrubostal in Moscow, 280–281; as Commissar of Ferrous Metallurgy, 324, 326, 327, 343

Metallurgical Project Institute in Leningrad, 324, 327

Mezhlauk, Valerian, Commissar of Heavy Industry, interview with, 240–241; arrest of, 250

Mikhailovna, Julia, 68–73, 74, 247

Mikoyan, Anastas Ivanovich, Commissar for Foreign Trade, 240, 399, 400, 405, 408, 428, 430, 431, 439, 440, 466

Military schools, 407

Military service, 43, 44–49; in hospital, 49

Military tribunals, 355–356, 377, 388, 402

Mines. *See* Coal mines

Mironov, head of Party Committee of Sovnarkom, 421, 422, 425–426, 432, 438–439

Misha, Comrade, in Moscow, 249–251, 252–253, 282–283, 446

Mission to Moscow, by ex-Ambassador Davies, 235, 354; film based on book, 470–471

Mobilization, for World War II, 360, 403

Molotov, Commissar, 254, 316, 399, 400, 405, 414, 428, 430; and collectivization, 86–87; and the Great Purge, 237, 303; and German Pact, 333; and outbreak of war on Russia, 353; control of airplane manufacture by, 416, 417

"Molotov cocktails," 369

Moscow, 428: visits to, 82–87, 249–255, 275–276, 280–281, 316–317, 322–323, 326, 327; 1938 blood-purge trials in, 281–283; contrasts in, 323; life in, 344; wartime conditions in, 362, 374, 375, 388, 412–413; evacuation of, 369–370, 373; mining of, 375; panic in, 375–376; return to, 387; departure from, 449

Moscow-Berlin pact, 332–335, 342, 364, 372, 381, 466

Mother. *See* Kravchenko, Mrs.

Moukhin, General, 419

Munich settlement, 332

Mussolini, Benito, in Italy, 109

Nabat. See Commune on Ilyin estate

Nation, The, magazine, 462, 472

Nazi *Panzer* divisions, 352, 359

Nazism. *See* Fascism

Nedosekin, General, in administration of forced labor camps, 405

New Economic Policy (NEP), 43

New Republic, The, magazine, 462, 472

New York City, escape to, 3–4, 475

New York *Times,* 462; quoted on resignation, 4, 475

Nicolayev, assassination of Kirov by, 167, 168

Nikopol Metallurgical Combinat, 108, 441; investigation of, 78–81; report to Ordzhonikidze on, 83, 84–85; appointed engineer at, 173; conditions at, 174, 178–179; officials at, 175; N. K. V. D. at, 176–177, 180–183, 184–186, 192, 193; "Stakhanovite" shift at, 188; speed-up in, 189–190; difficulties in, 192–195; enlargement of, 198; purge at, 208–222, 226–235, 242–244, 255–271

N. K. V. D., 111, 181, 227, 304–305, 413, 432, 433, 436, 438, 439, 440, 443, 451, 470, 474, 475; at Nikopol, 176–177, 180, 183, 184–186; difficulties with, 192–195, 196, 197; and forced labor, 198–199, 279, 285–286, 405; and the Great Purge, 207, 209, 210, 211, 212–214, 216, 217, 218, 222, 239, 253, 267, 273, 283, 288; and Tsarist Okhrana compared, 223, 282; persecution of Kravchenko by, 226–230, 233–234, 237,